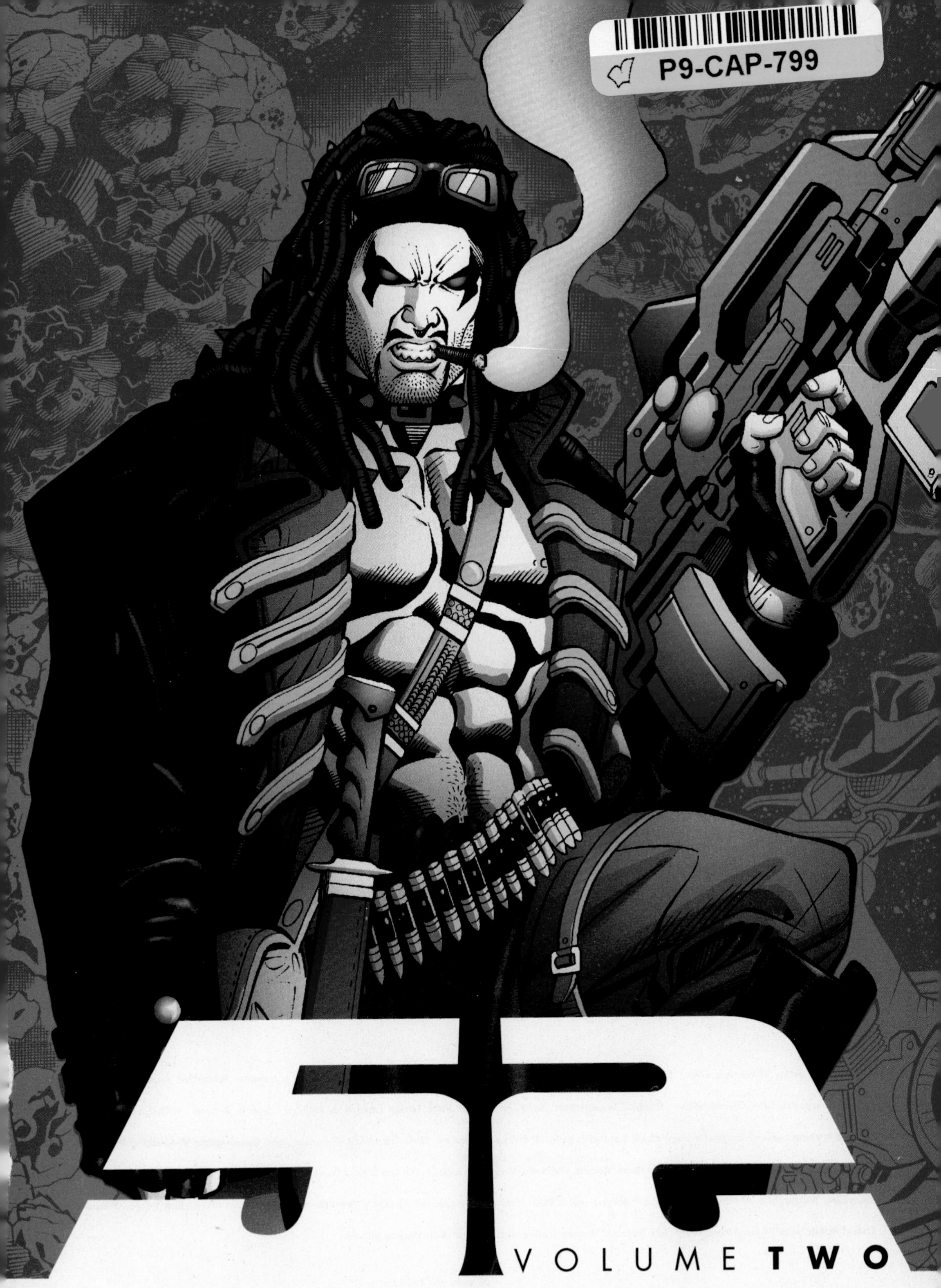

52

VOLUME TWO

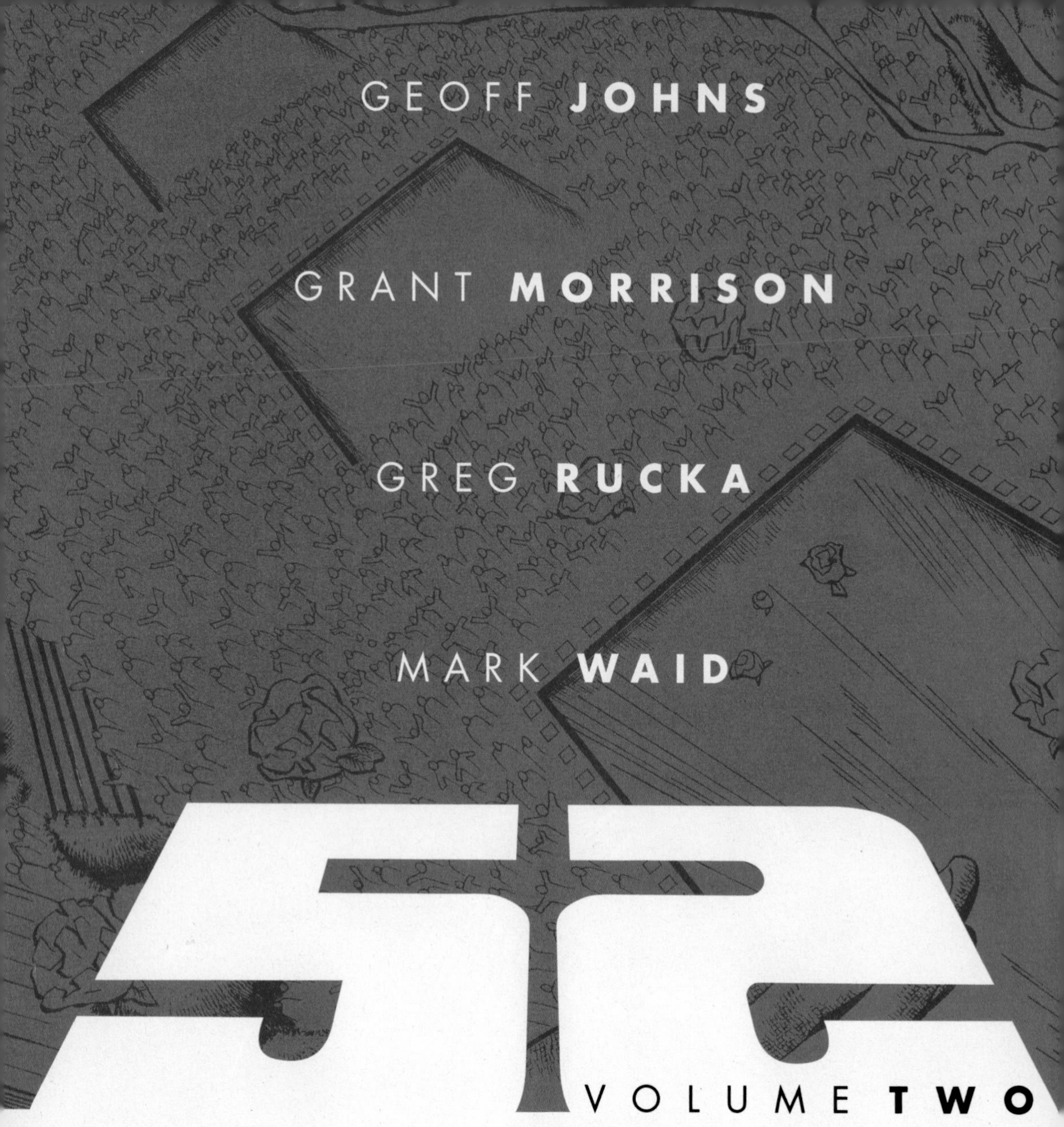

GEOFF JOHNS

GRANT MORRISON

GREG RUCKA

MARK WAID

52

VOLUME TWO

Dan DiDio Senior VP-Executive Editor **Stephen Wacker** Editor-original series **Jann Jones** **Harvey Richards** **Jeanine Schaeffer** Assistant Editors-original series

Anton Kawasaki Editor-collected edition **Robbin Brosterman** Senior Art Director **Paul Levitz** President & Publisher **Georg Brewer** VP-Design & DC Direct Creative

Richard Bruning Senior VP-Creative Director **Patrick Caldon** Executive VP-Finance & Operations **Chris Caramalis** VP-Finance **John Cunningham** VP-Marketing **Terri Cunningham**

VP-Managing Editor **Alison Gill** VP-Manufacturing **Hank Kanalz** VP-General Manager, WildStorm **Jim Lee** Editorial Director-WildStorm **Paula Lowitt** Senior VP-Business & Legal Affairs

MaryEllen McLaughlin VP-Advertising & Custom Publishing **John Nee** VP-Business Development **Gregory Noveck** Senior VP-Creative Affairs **Sue Pohja** VP-Book Trade Sales

Cheryl Rubin Senior VP-Brand Management **Jeff Trojan** VP-Business Development, DC Direct **Bob Wayne** VP-Sales

Cover by J.G. Jones with Alex Sinclair
Publication design by Robbie Biederman

52: VOLUME TWO

Published by DC Comics. Cover, introduction, text, and compilation copyright © 2007 DC Comics. All rights reserved.
Originally published in single magazine form in 52 #14-26. Copyright © 2006 DC Comics. All Rights Reserved. All characters, their distinctive
likenesses and related elements featured in this publication are trademarks of DC Comics. The stories, characters and incidents featured in this
publication are entirely fictional. DC Comics does not read or accept unsolicited submissions of ideas, stories or artwork.

DC Comics, 1700 Broadway, New York, NY 10019. A Warner Bros. Entertainment Company. Printed in Canada. First Printing.
ISBN: 1-4012-1364-2 ISBN 13: 978-1-4012-1364-0

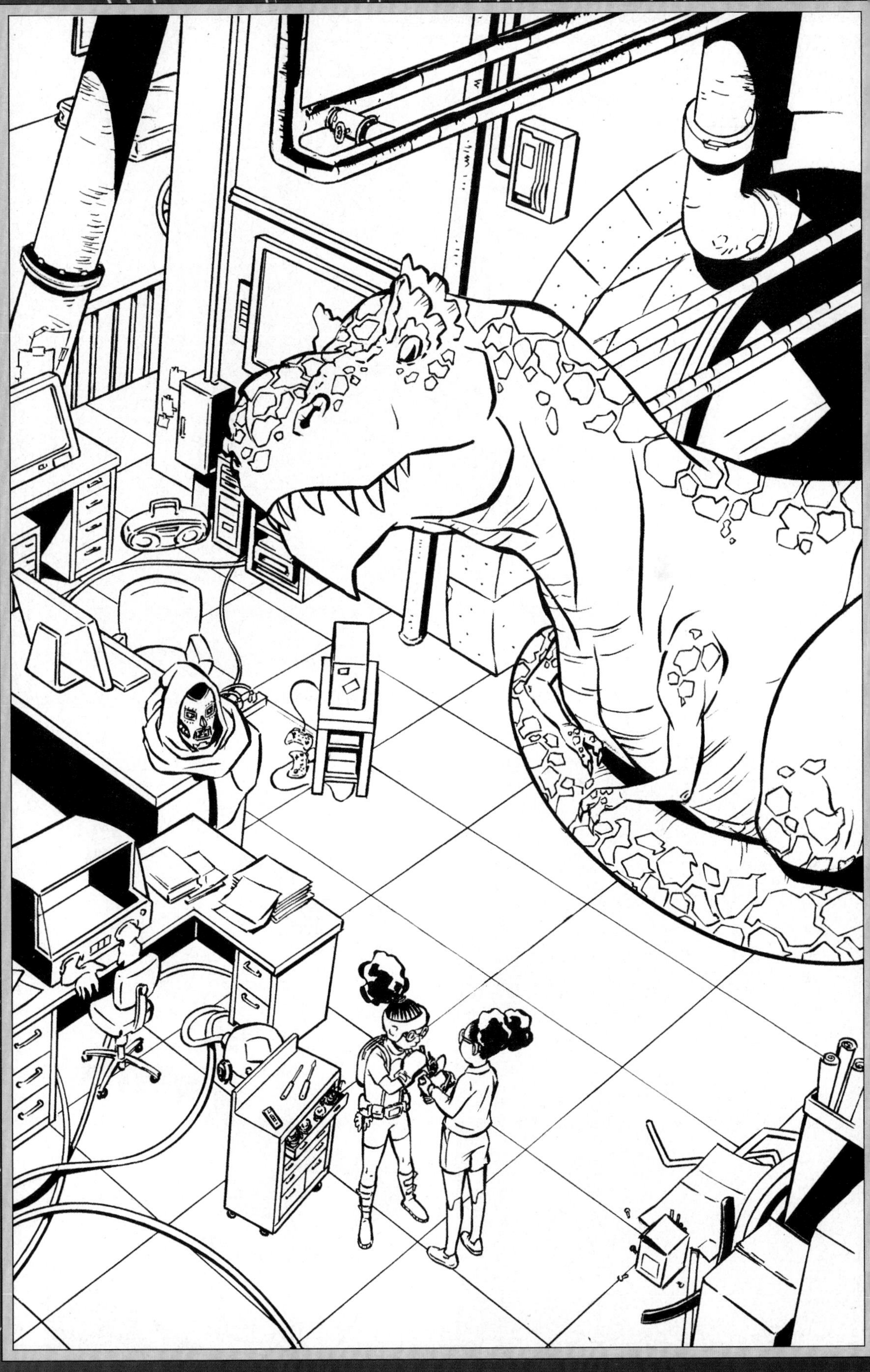

#44. Page 1 ART BY ALITHA E. MARTINEZ

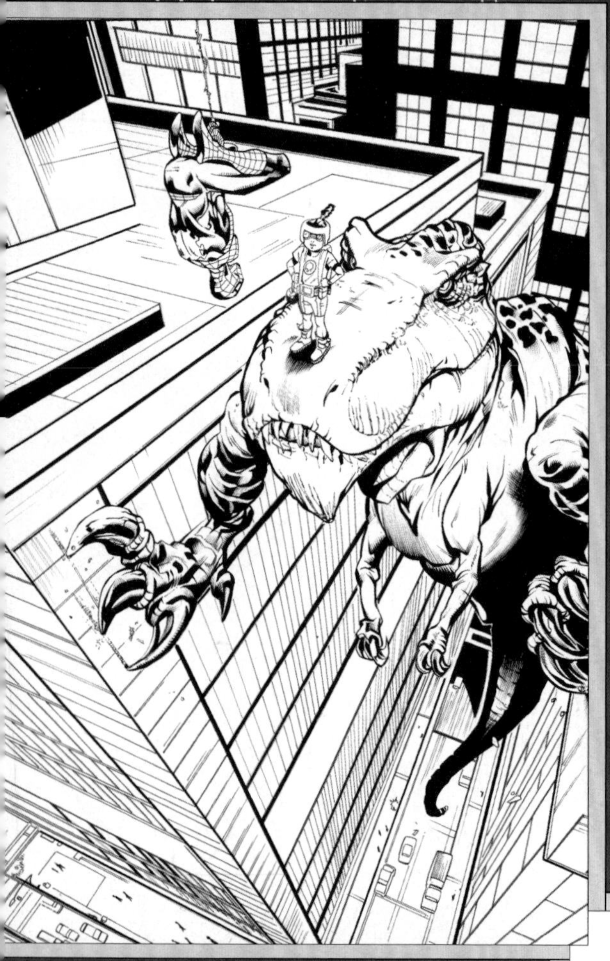

#42. Page 2 ART BY RAY-ANTHONY HEIGHT & Le Beau UNDERWOOD

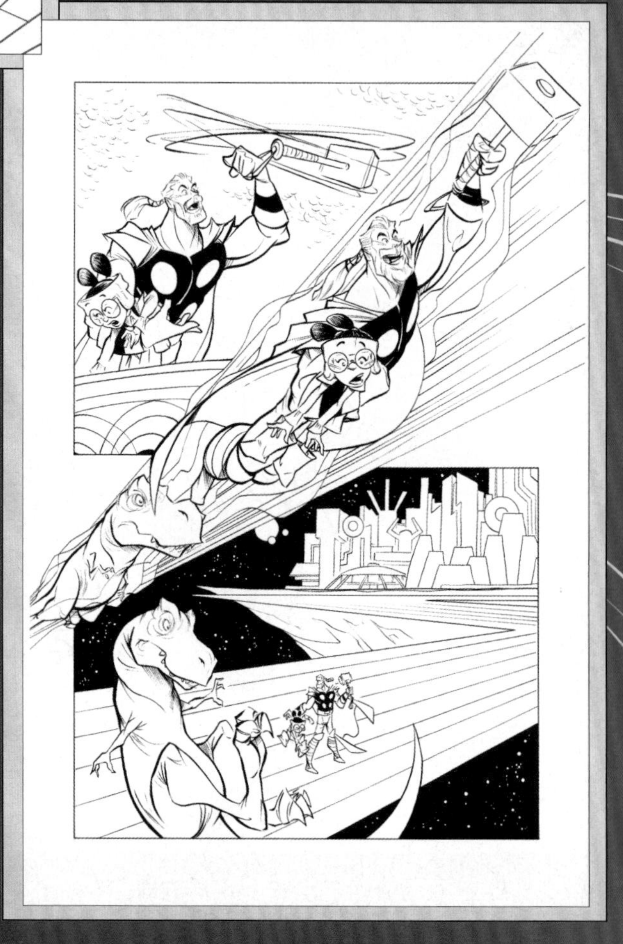

#43. Page 3 ART BY GUSTAVO DUARTE

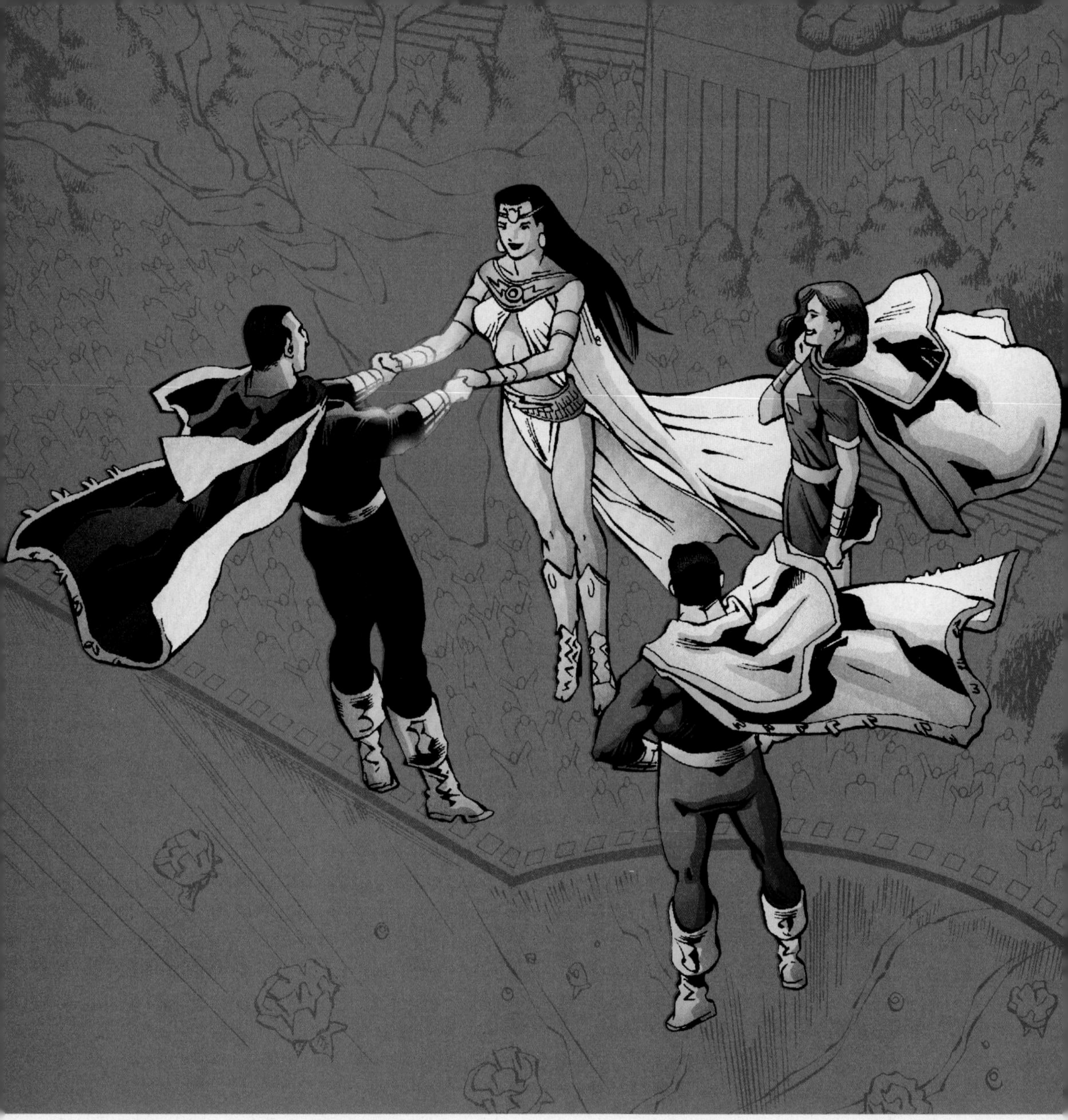

art breakdowns **KEITH GIFFEN** pencils **EDDY BARROWS, CHRIS BATISTA JOE BENNETT, DALE EAGLESHAM, PHIL JIMENEZ, DREW JOHNSON, SHAWN MOLL, PATRICK OLLIFFE** inks **DREW GERACI, JACK JADSON, RUY JOSE, ANDY LANNING, TOM NGUYEN, ROB STULL, RAY SNYDER, ART THIBERT** colors **DAVID BARON, ALEX SINCLAIR, PETE PANTAZIS** letters **PHIL BALSMAN, PAT BROSSEAU, JARED K. FLETCHER, TRAVIS LANHAM, KEN LOPEZ, NICK J. NAPOLITANO** original covers **J.G. JONES** with **ALEX SINCLAIR**

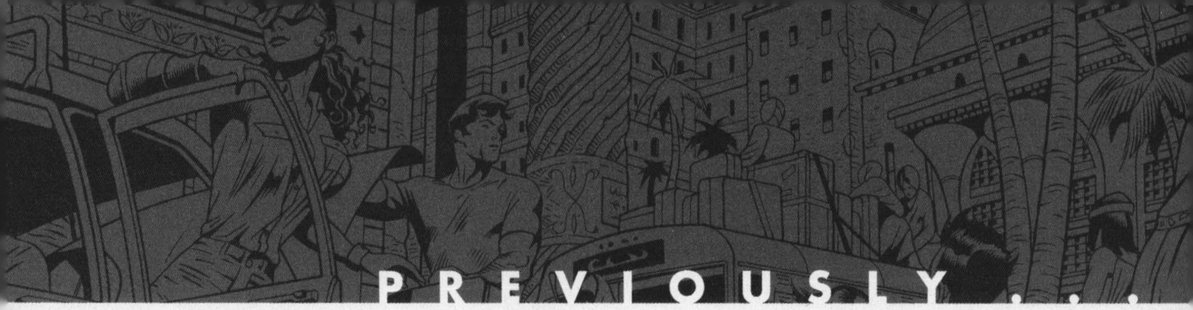

P R E V I O U S L Y . . .

In the wake of the INFINITE CRISIS, the DC Universe is left without its three biggest icons — Superman, Batman and Wonder Woman.

But it is *not* a world without heroes...

In Metropolis, fame-seeking Booster Gold takes advantage of Superman's absence — using his robot sidekick Skeets's knowledge of the future to help prevent crimes and catastrophes. But Skeets's information proves to be inaccurate, forcing Booster to visit time master Rip Hunter for an explanation of why the future isn't playing out the way it's supposed to. Booster comes across an empty headquarters where Hunter is nowhere to be found — and the only things remaining are mysterious notes that read "Time is Broken" and "It's All His Fault" (pointing to a picture of Booster with Skeets).

Meanwhile, a new, mysterious hero has been seen in the Metropolis skyline. The fully masked Supernova has been saving the day a countless number of times, leaving Booster infuriated by the sudden competition.

Elsewhere in Metropolis, Lex Luthor announces a program that gives ordinary people super-powers. Dubbed the Everyman Program, this metagene therapy soon becomes sought after by thousands who are willing to risk whatever side effects may occur to have powers of their own.

John Henry Irons, the armor-clad hero known as Steel, is trying to teach his niece Natasha that she needs to *earn* her right to play super-hero. Frustrated and impatient with her uncle, Nathasha feels she's ready now, and becomes one of the first people to enroll in Luthor's Everyman Program. But soon after, John discovers that he himself is being trans-formed into literal steel — all a part of Luthor's devious plan.

Ralph Dibny, the former hero known as Elongated Man, finds a message on the tomb-stone of his dead wife Sue, which leads him to the discovery of a cult that believes that Superboy (a casualty of the INFINITE CRISIS) can be resurrected. Thinking that his wife Sue might have a chance to live again, Ralph enlists some fellow heroes to help him see if it's possible. The attempt fails, but now Ralph seems more determined than ever to bring Sue back to the living...

Black Adam, leader of Kahndaq, forges a coalition with several other countries in an effort to quell the growing superhuman supremacy of the U.S. A woman named Adrianna Tomaz opposes Adam's actions, admonishing him that his great power is being misused. Adam is struck by Adrianna's words and imparts a portion of his powers to her, transforming her into the mighty Isis! Isis promises Adam that she'll join him on his crusade to change the world for the better...as soon as they find her missing brother.

In Gotham City, former police officer Renee Montoya is trying to wash away her recent, troubled past with too many drinks. Just as she reaches her lowest point, the enigmatic Vic Sage — a.k.a. The Question — enlists Renee's help on assignments that lead to the discovery that Gotham is being targeted by Intergang. Elsewhere in Gotham, the absence of Batman brings forth a new hero — Kathy Kane, a.k.a. The Batwoman! Soon after, we learn that Renee and Kathy have a personal history together.

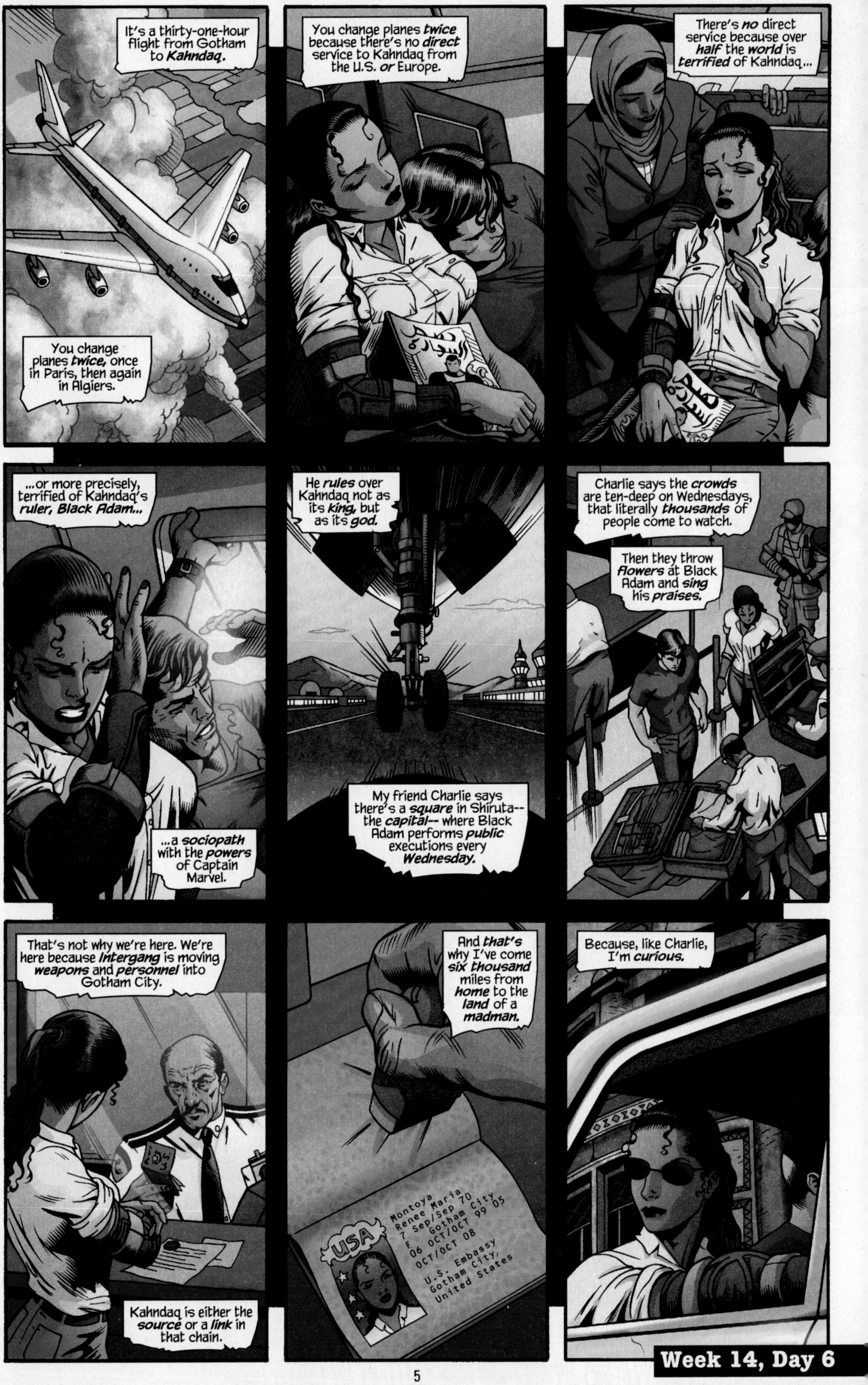

It's a thirty-one-hour flight from Gotham to Kahndaq.
You change planes twice, once in Paris, then again in Algiers.
You change planes twice because there's no direct service to Kahndaq from the U.S. or Europe.
There's no direct service because over half the world is terrified of Kahndaq...
...or more precisely, terrified of Kahndaq's ruler, Black Adam...
...a sociopath with the powers of Captain Marvel.
He rules over Kahndaq not as its king, but as its god.
My friend Charlie says there's a square in Shiruta-- the capital-- where Black Adam performs public executions every Wednesday.
Charlie says the crowds are ten-deep on Wednesdays, that literally thousands of people come to watch.
Then they throw flowers at Black Adam and sing his praises.
That's not why we're here. We're here because Intergang is moving weapons and personnel into Gotham City.
Kahndaq is either the source or a link in that chain.
And that's why I've come six thousand miles from home to the land of a madman.
USA
Montoya
Renee Maria
7 Sep/Sep 70
F Gotham City
06 OCT/OCT 99 05
OCT/OCT 08
U.S. Embassy
Gotham City,
United States
Because, like Charlie, I'm curious.
Week 14, Day 6

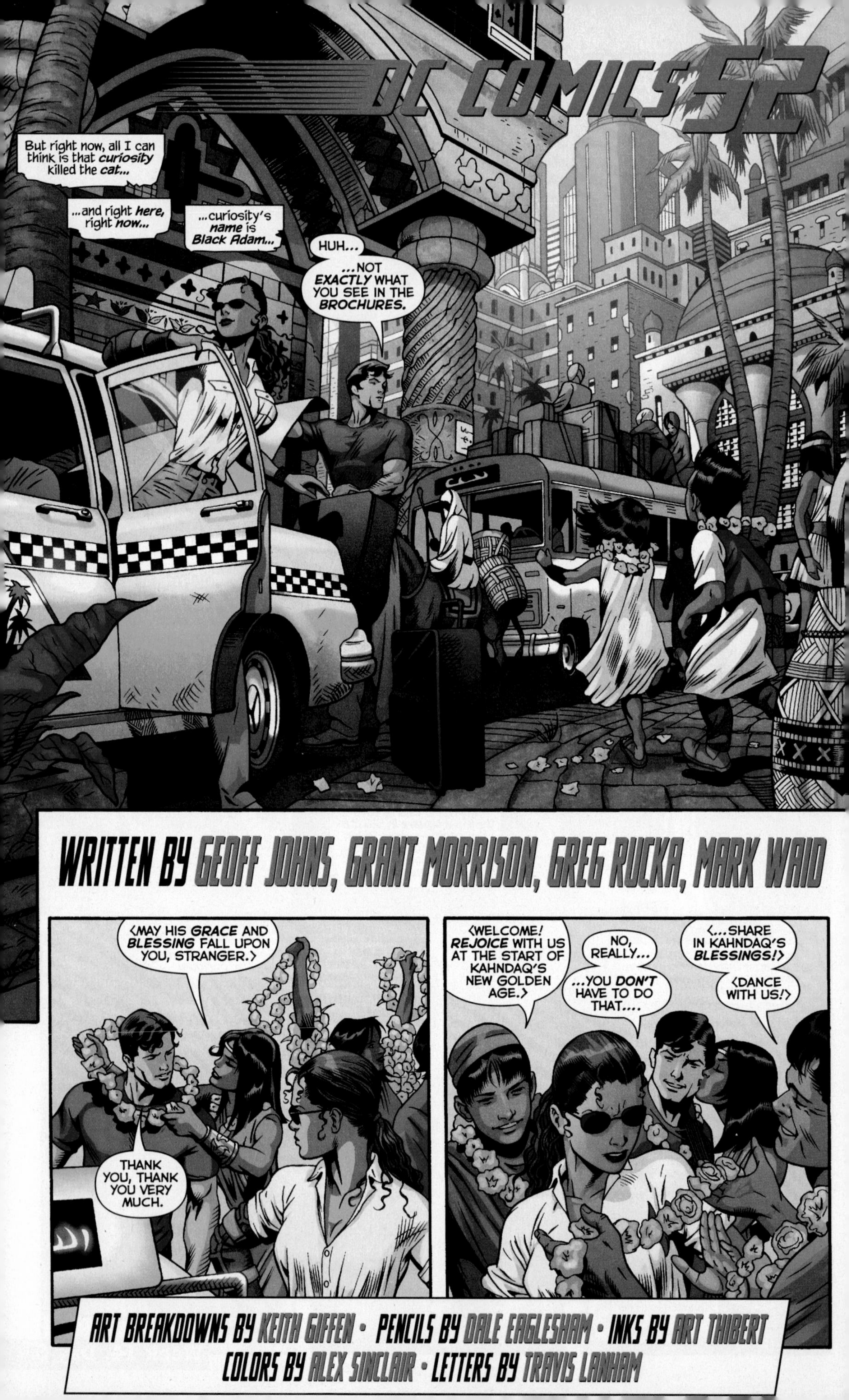
DC COMICS 52
But right now, all I can think is that curiosity killed the cat...
...and right here, right now...
...curiosity's name is Black Adam...
HUH... ...NOT EXACTLY WHAT YOU SEE IN THE BROCHURES.
WRITTEN BY GEOFF JOHNS, GRANT MORRISON, GREG RUCKA, MARK WAID
<MAY HIS GRACE AND BLESSING FALL UPON YOU, STRANGER.>
THANK YOU, THANK YOU VERY MUCH.
<WELCOME! REJOICE WITH US AT THE START OF KAHNDAQ'S NEW GOLDEN AGE.>
NO, REALLY...
...YOU DON'T HAVE TO DO THAT....
<...SHARE IN KAHNDAQ'S BLESSINGS!>
<DANCE WITH US!>
ART BREAKDOWNS BY KEITH GIFFEN • PENCILS BY DALE EAGLESHAM • INKS BY ART THIBERT
COLORS BY ALEX SINCLAIR • LETTERS BY TRAVIS LANHAM

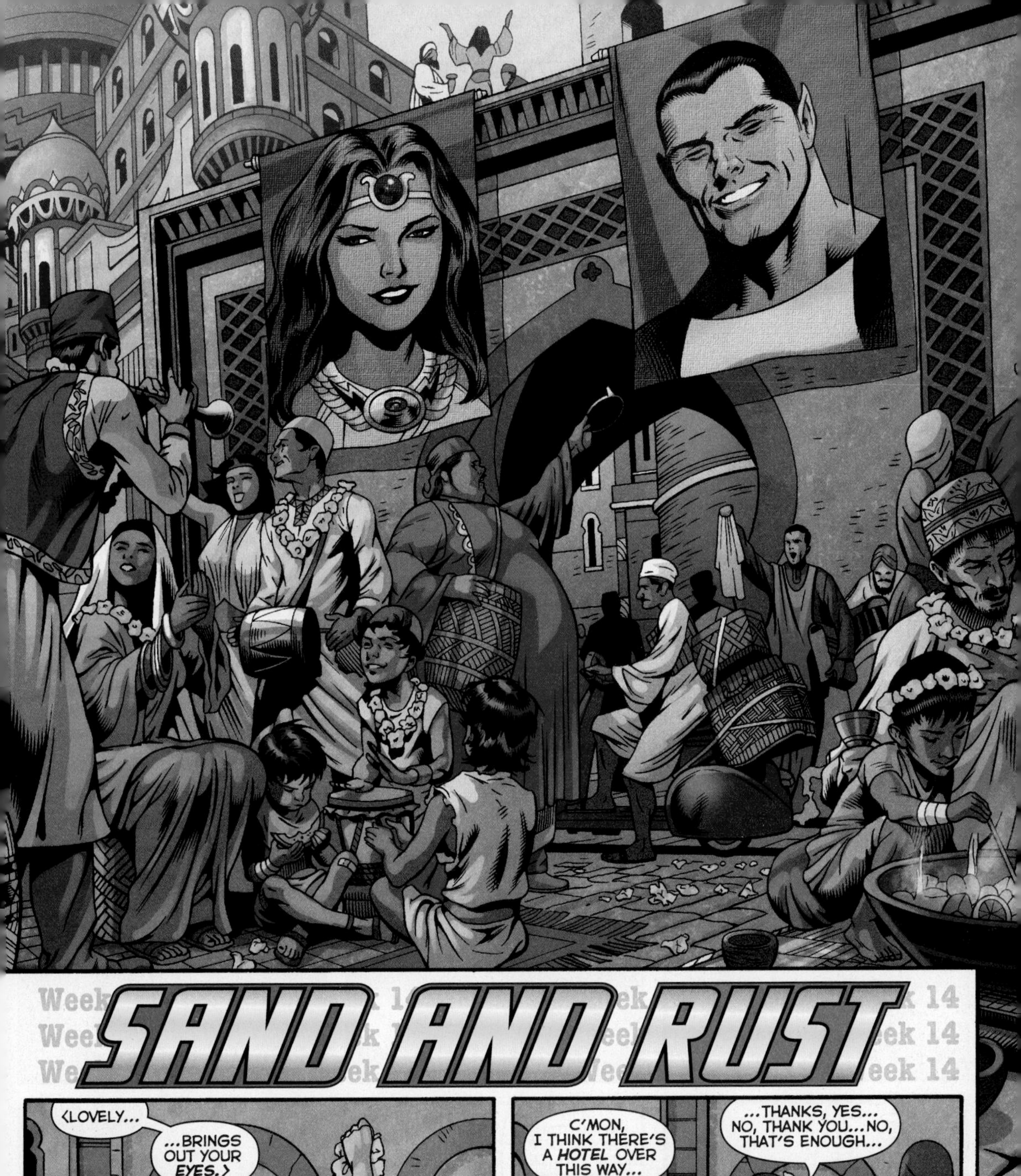

Week 14

SAND AND RUST

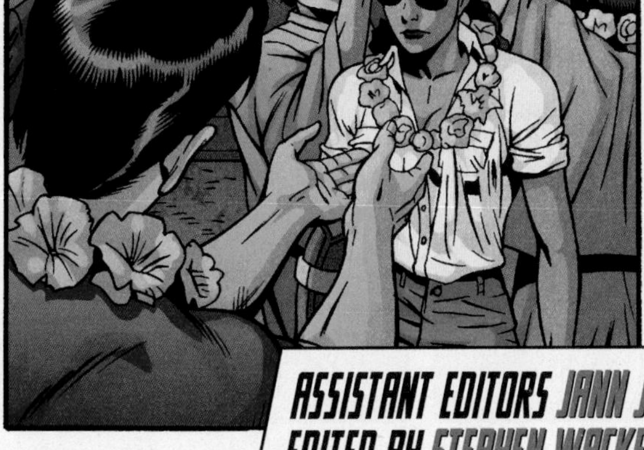
<LOVELY...
...BRINGS OUT YOUR EYES.>

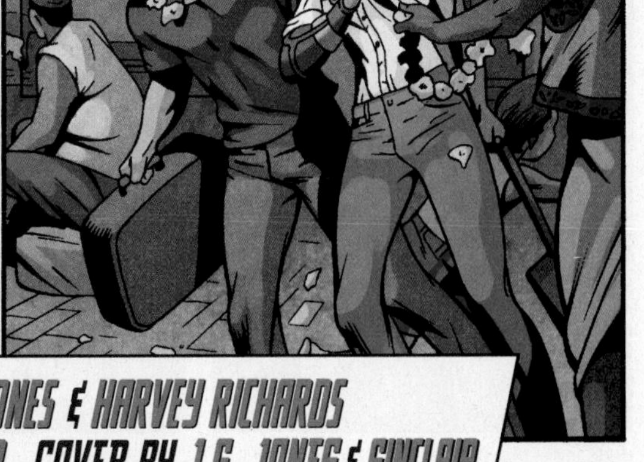
C'MON, I THINK THERE'S A HOTEL OVER THIS WAY...
...THANKS, YES... NO, THANK YOU...NO, THAT'S ENOUGH...

ASSISTANT EDITORS JANN JONES & HARVEY RICHARDS
EDITED BY STEPHEN WACKER COVER BY J.G. JONES & SINCLAIR

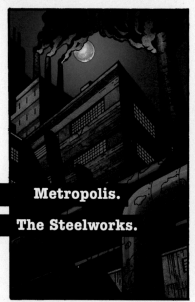

Metropolis.

The Steelworks.

JOHN? JOHN HENRY? IT'S DOCTOR AVASTI, IT'S KALA....

...JOHN, PLEASE ANSWER THE DOOR, I *KNOW* YOU'RE HOME.

NO ONE'S HEARD FROM YOU IN A MONTH.

KNOK KNOK KNOK

I *DON'T* KNOW WHAT YOU'RE *GOING* THROUGH, I ADMIT THAT.

I *DON'T* UNDERSTAND WHAT'S *HAPPENED* TO YOUR *BODY*, WHAT LUTHOR HAS *DONE* TO YOU...

BUT THERE IS A *CURE*, JOHN, AND WE *CAN* FIND IT. BUT YOU HAVE TO *HELP* ME HERE, YOU CAN'T JUST *HIDE* FROM THE PROBLEM...

...I SAW *NATASHA* ON TELEVISION, DID YOU *SEE* HER?

SHE AND A *BUNCH* OF LUTHOR'S *TRADEMARKED* HEROES DID A Q&A ON '*METROPOLIS THIS MORNING.*'

MEDIA'S CALLING THEM LUTHOR'S OWN J.L.A.

TALKED ABOUT HOW *EAGER* THEY WERE TO *FILL* THE SHOES OF SUPERMAN AND WONDER WOMAN, LIKE THAT.

YOU *CAN'T* BLAME YOURSELF FOR *HER* MISTAKES, JOHN.

YOU UNDERSTAND ME? YOU *CAN'T* HOLD YOURSELF *RESPONSIBLE* FOR WHAT *SHE* DOES WITH HER *LIFE*--

WAAM

KLIK

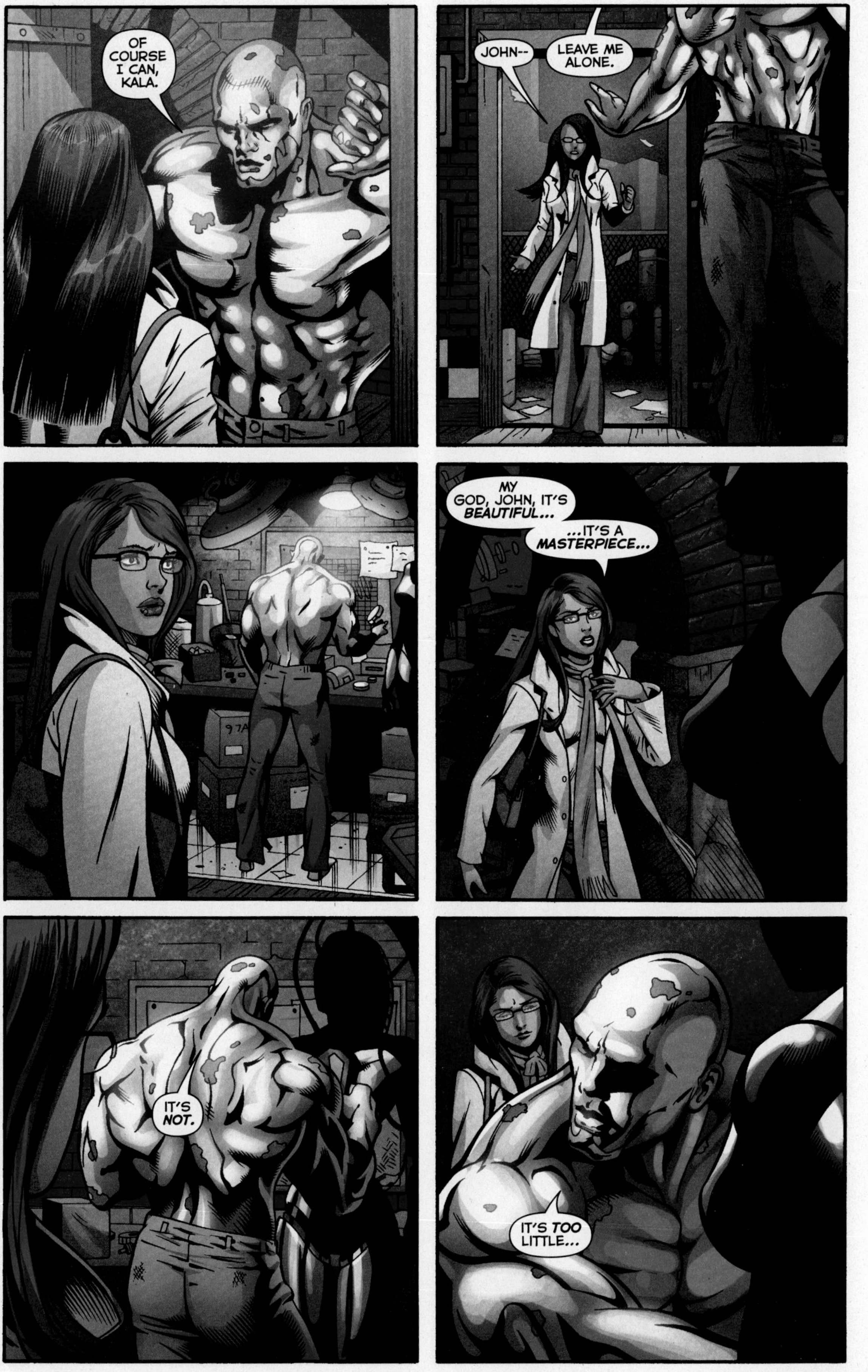
OF COURSE I CAN, KALA.
JOHN--
LEAVE ME ALONE.
MY GOD, JOHN, IT'S *BEAUTIFUL*...
...IT'S A *MASTERPIECE*...
IT'S *NOT*.
IT'S *TOO* LITTLE...

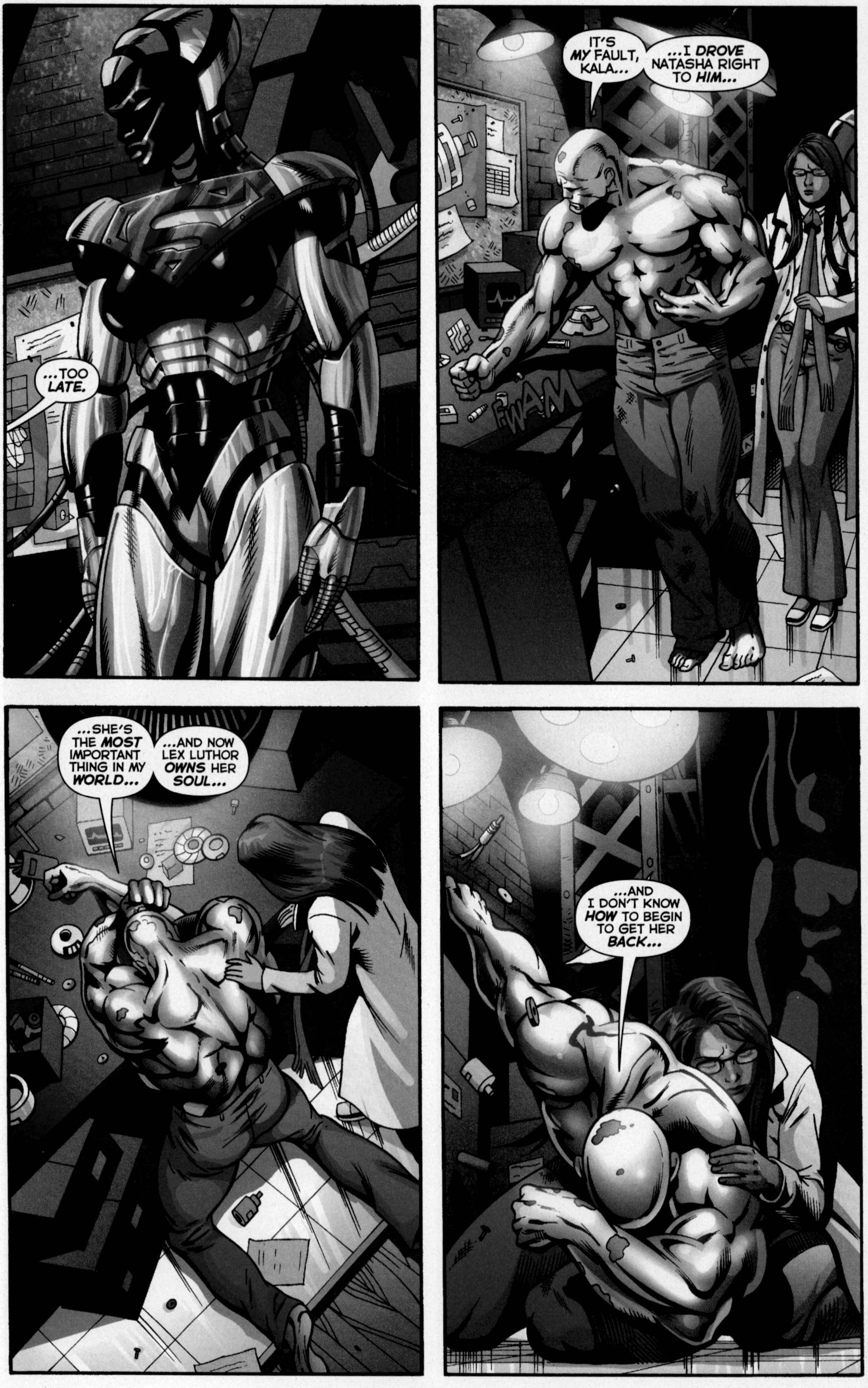
...TOO LATE.
IT'S MY FAULT, KALA...
...I DROVE NATASHA RIGHT TO HIM...
FWAM
...SHE'S THE MOST IMPORTANT THING IN MY WORLD...
...AND NOW LEX LUTHOR OWNS HER SOUL...
...AND I DON'T KNOW HOW TO BEGIN TO GET HER BACK...

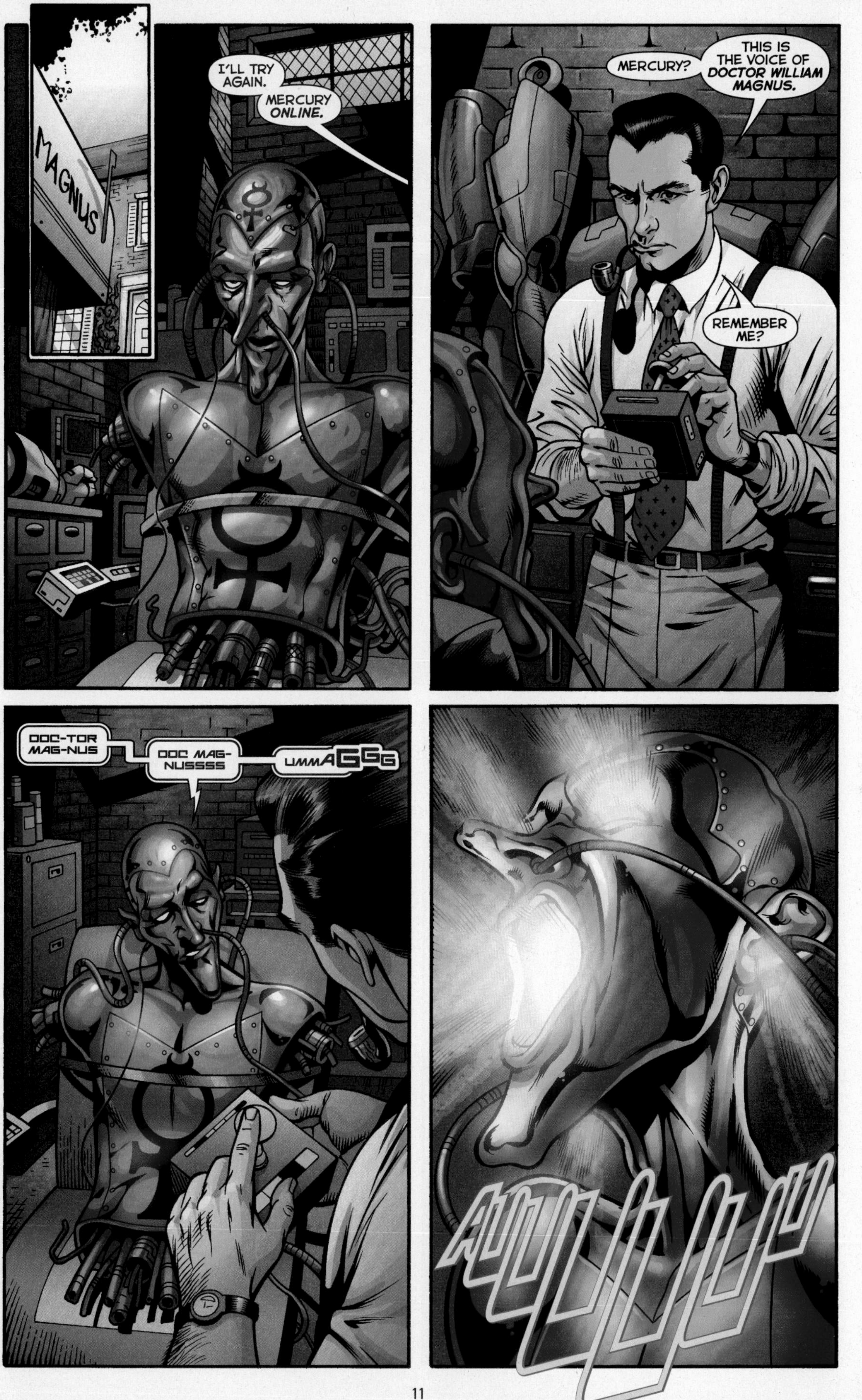
MAGNUS
I'LL TRY AGAIN.
MERCURY ONLINE.
MERCURY?
THIS IS THE VOICE OF DOCTOR WILLIAM MAGNUS.
REMEMBER ME?
DOC-TOR MAG-NUS
DOC MAG-NUSSSS
UMMAGGG

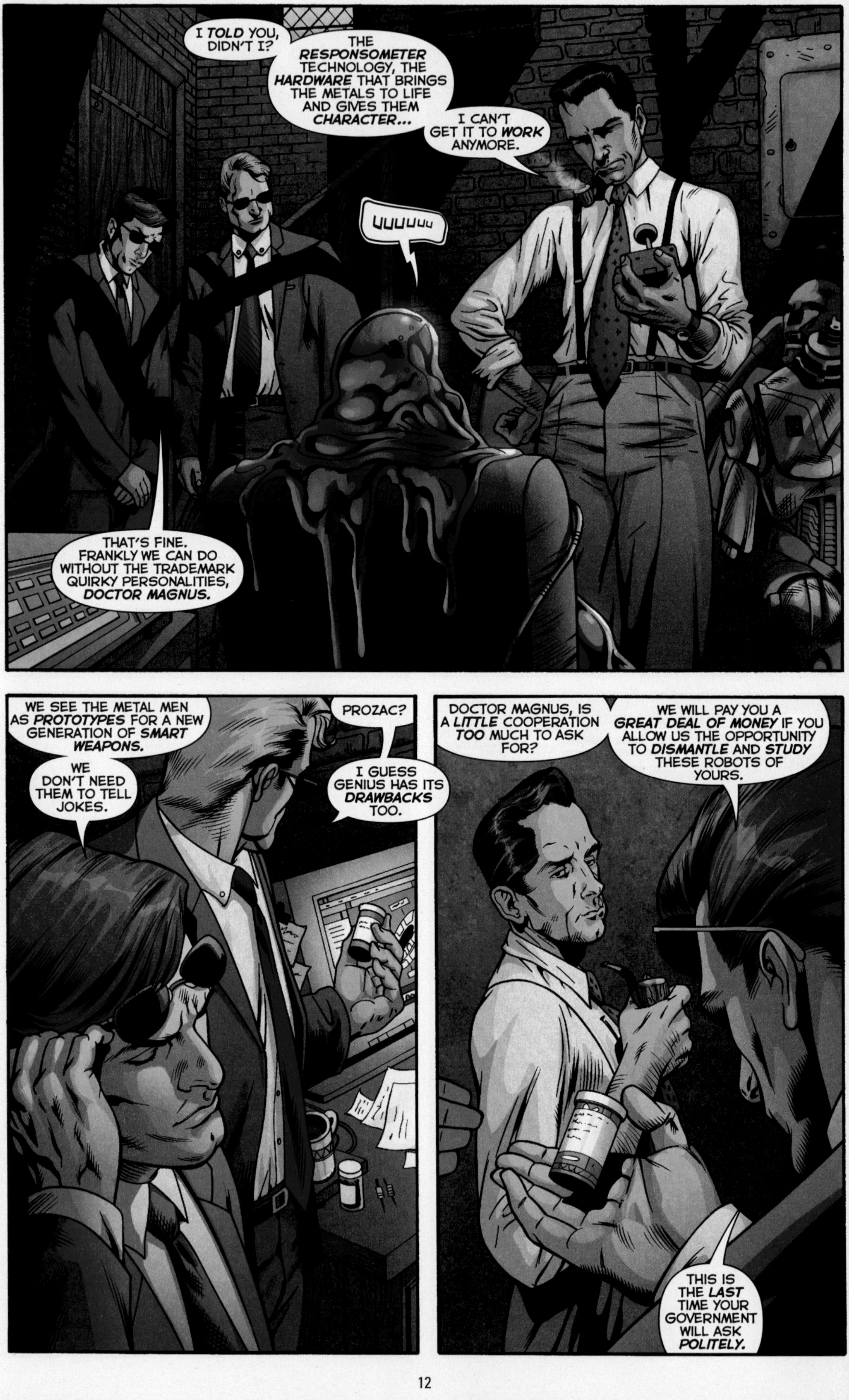
I TOLD YOU, DIDN'T I?
THE RESPONSOMETER TECHNOLOGY, THE HARDWARE THAT BRINGS THE METALS TO LIFE AND GIVES THEM CHARACTER...
I CAN'T GET IT TO WORK ANYMORE.
UUUUUU
THAT'S FINE. FRANKLY WE CAN DO WITHOUT THE TRADEMARK QUIRKY PERSONALITIES, DOCTOR MAGNUS.
WE SEE THE METAL MEN AS PROTOTYPES FOR A NEW GENERATION OF SMART WEAPONS.
WE DON'T NEED THEM TO TELL JOKES.
PROZAC?
I GUESS GENIUS HAS ITS DRAWBACKS TOO.
DOCTOR MAGNUS, IS A LITTLE COOPERATION TOO MUCH TO ASK FOR?
WE WILL PAY YOU A GREAT DEAL OF MONEY IF YOU ALLOW US THE OPPORTUNITY TO DISMANTLE AND STUDY THESE ROBOTS OF YOURS.
THIS IS THE LAST TIME YOUR GOVERNMENT WILL ASK POLITELY.

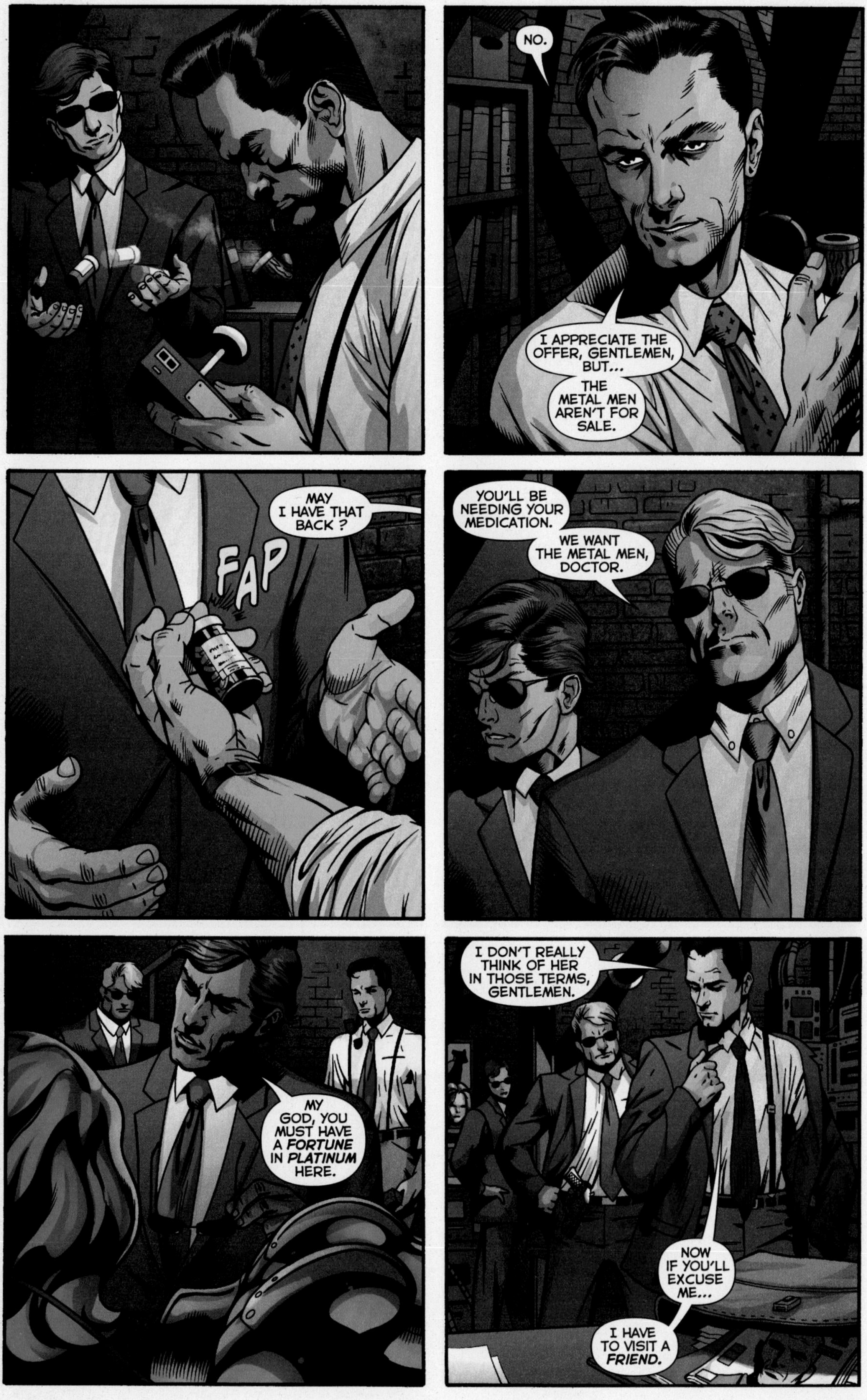
NO.
I APPRECIATE THE OFFER, GENTLEMEN, BUT...
THE METAL MEN AREN'T FOR SALE.
MAY I HAVE THAT BACK ?
FAP
YOU'LL BE NEEDING YOUR MEDICATION.
WE WANT THE METAL MEN, DOCTOR.
MY GOD, YOU MUST HAVE A *FORTUNE* IN *PLATINUM* HERE.
I DON'T REALLY THINK OF HER IN THOSE TERMS, GENTLEMEN.
NOW IF YOU'LL EXCUSE ME...
I HAVE TO VISIT A *FRIEND.*

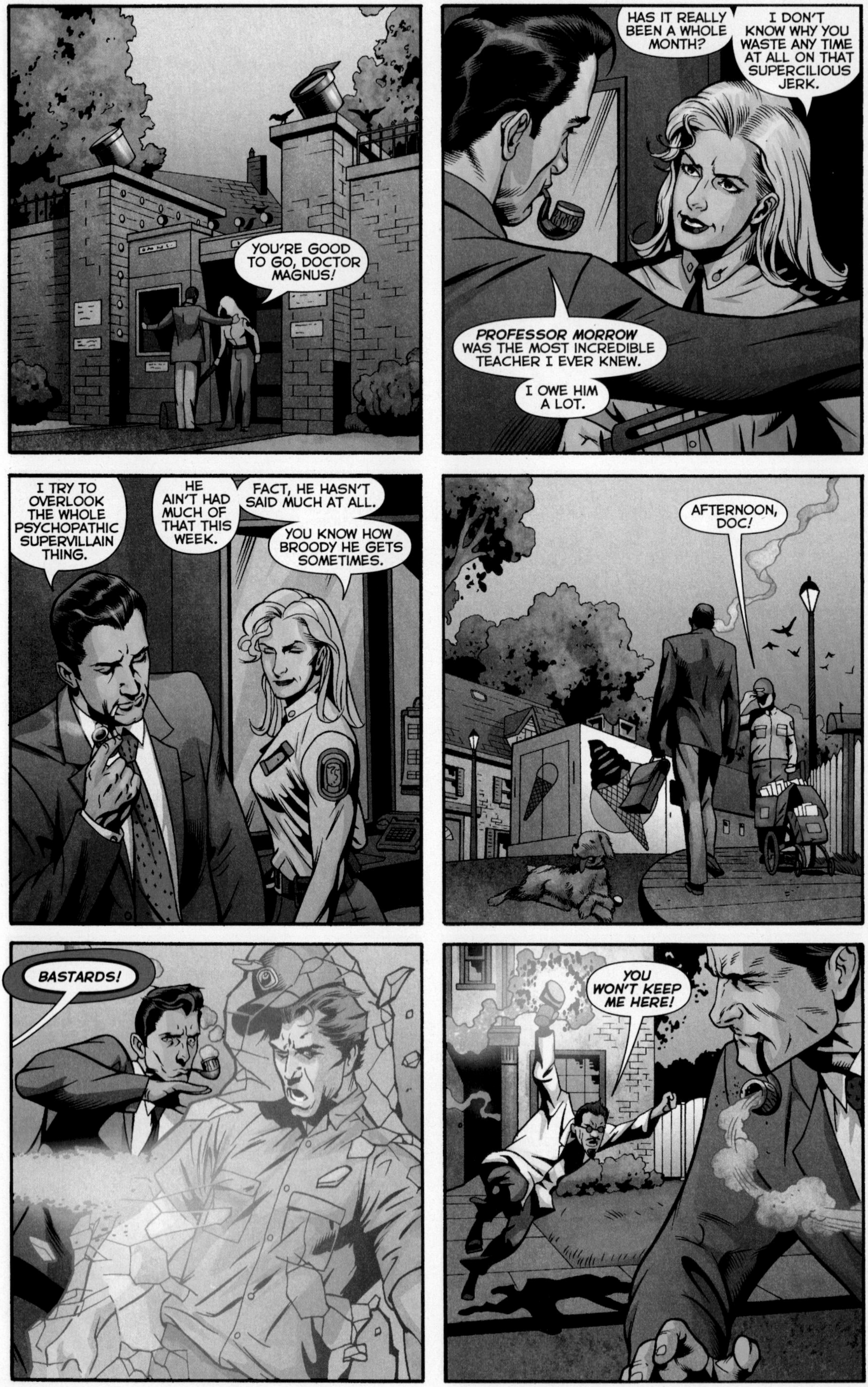
YOU'RE GOOD TO GO, DOCTOR MAGNUS!
HAS IT REALLY BEEN A WHOLE MONTH?
I DON'T KNOW WHY YOU WASTE ANY TIME AT ALL ON THAT SUPERCILIOUS JERK.
PROFESSOR MORROW WAS THE MOST INCREDIBLE TEACHER I EVER KNEW.
I OWE HIM A LOT.
I TRY TO OVERLOOK THE WHOLE PSYCHOPATHIC SUPERVILLAIN THING.
HE AIN'T HAD MUCH OF THAT THIS WEEK.
FACT, HE HASN'T SAID MUCH AT ALL.
YOU KNOW HOW BROODY HE GETS SOMETIMES.
AFTERNOON, DOC!
BASTARDS!
YOU WON'T KEEP ME HERE!

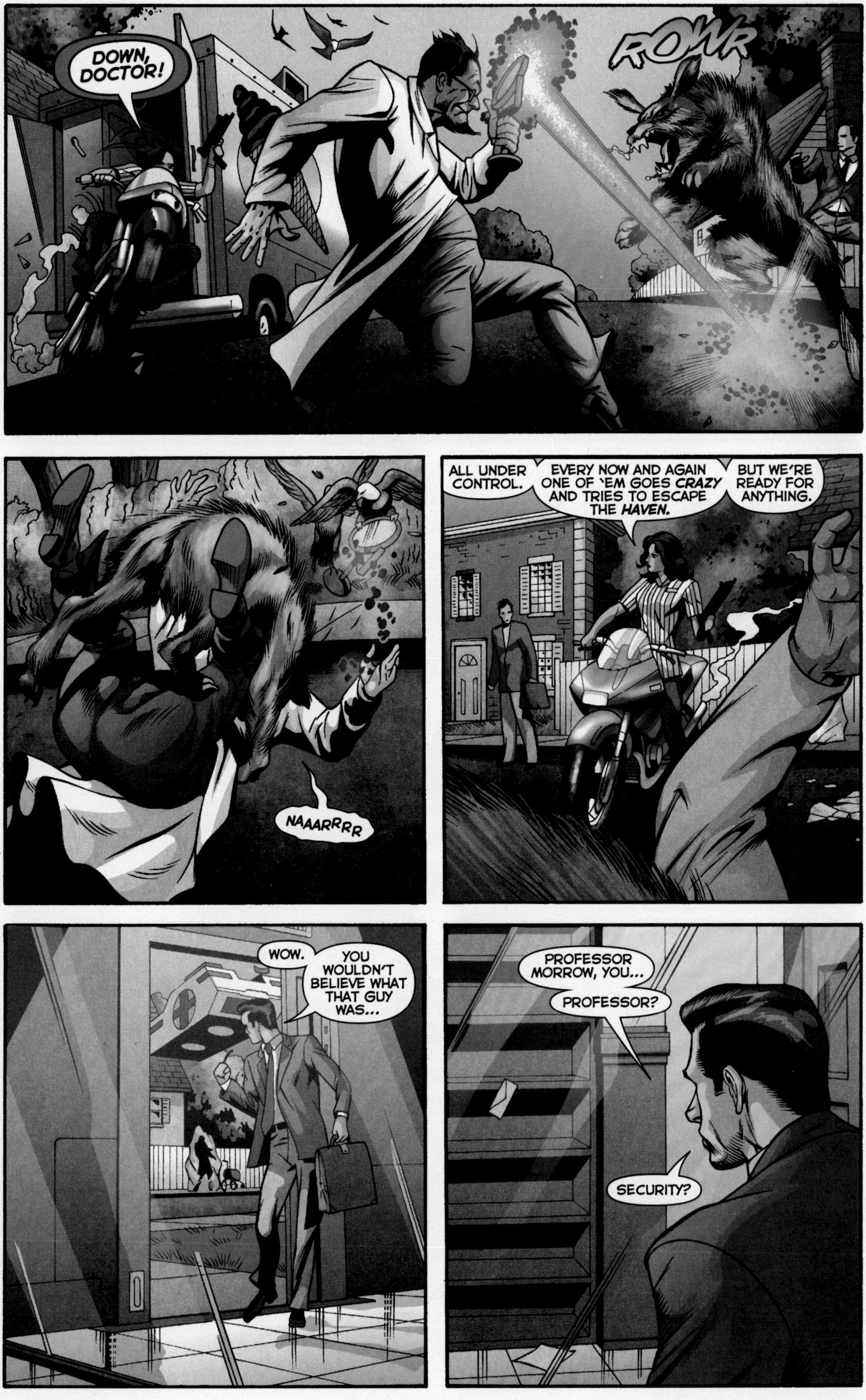
DOWN, DOCTOR!
ROWR
NAAARRRR
ALL UNDER CONTROL.
EVERY NOW AND AGAIN ONE OF 'EM GOES CRAZY AND TRIES TO ESCAPE THE HAVEN.
BUT WE'RE READY FOR ANYTHING.
WOW.
YOU WOULDN'T BELIEVE WHAT THAT GUY WAS...
PROFESSOR MORROW, YOU...
PROFESSOR?
SECURITY?

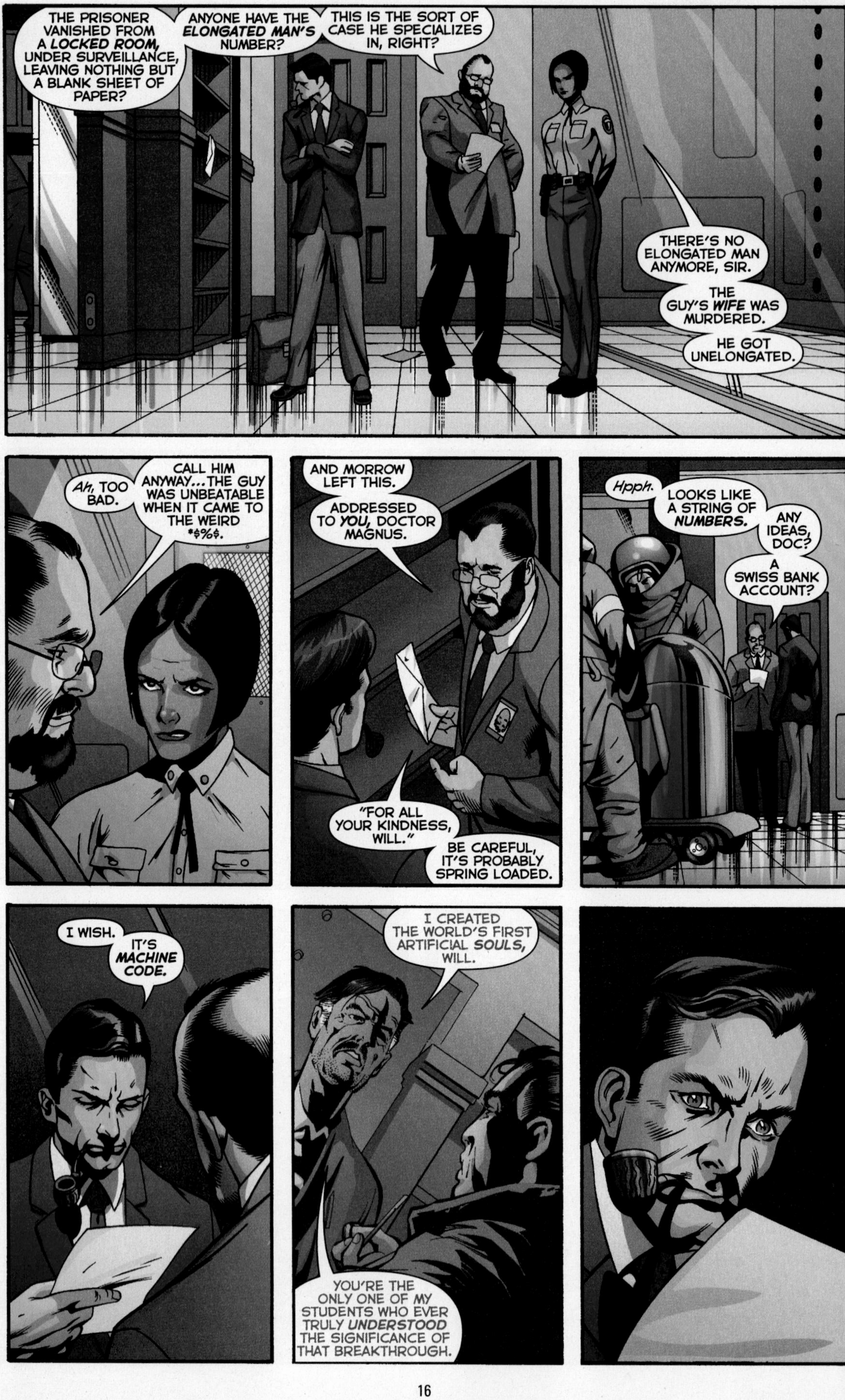
THE PRISONER VANISHED FROM A LOCKED ROOM, UNDER SURVEILLANCE, LEAVING NOTHING BUT A BLANK SHEET OF PAPER?
ANYONE HAVE THE ELONGATED MAN'S NUMBER?
THIS IS THE SORT OF CASE HE SPECIALIZES IN, RIGHT?
THERE'S NO ELONGATED MAN ANYMORE, SIR.
THE GUY'S WIFE WAS MURDERED.
HE GOT UNELONGATED.
Ah, TOO BAD.
CALL HIM ANYWAY... THE GUY WAS UNBEATABLE WHEN IT CAME TO THE WEIRD *$%$.
AND MORROW LEFT THIS.
ADDRESSED TO YOU, DOCTOR MAGNUS.
"FOR ALL YOUR KINDNESS, WILL."
BE CAREFUL, IT'S PROBABLY SPRING LOADED.
Hpph.
LOOKS LIKE A STRING OF NUMBERS.
ANY IDEAS, DOC?
A SWISS BANK ACCOUNT?
I WISH.
IT'S MACHINE CODE.
I CREATED THE WORLD'S FIRST ARTIFICIAL SOULS, WILL.
YOU'RE THE ONLY ONE OF MY STUDENTS WHO EVER TRULY UNDERSTOOD THE SIGNIFICANCE OF THAT BREAKTHROUGH.

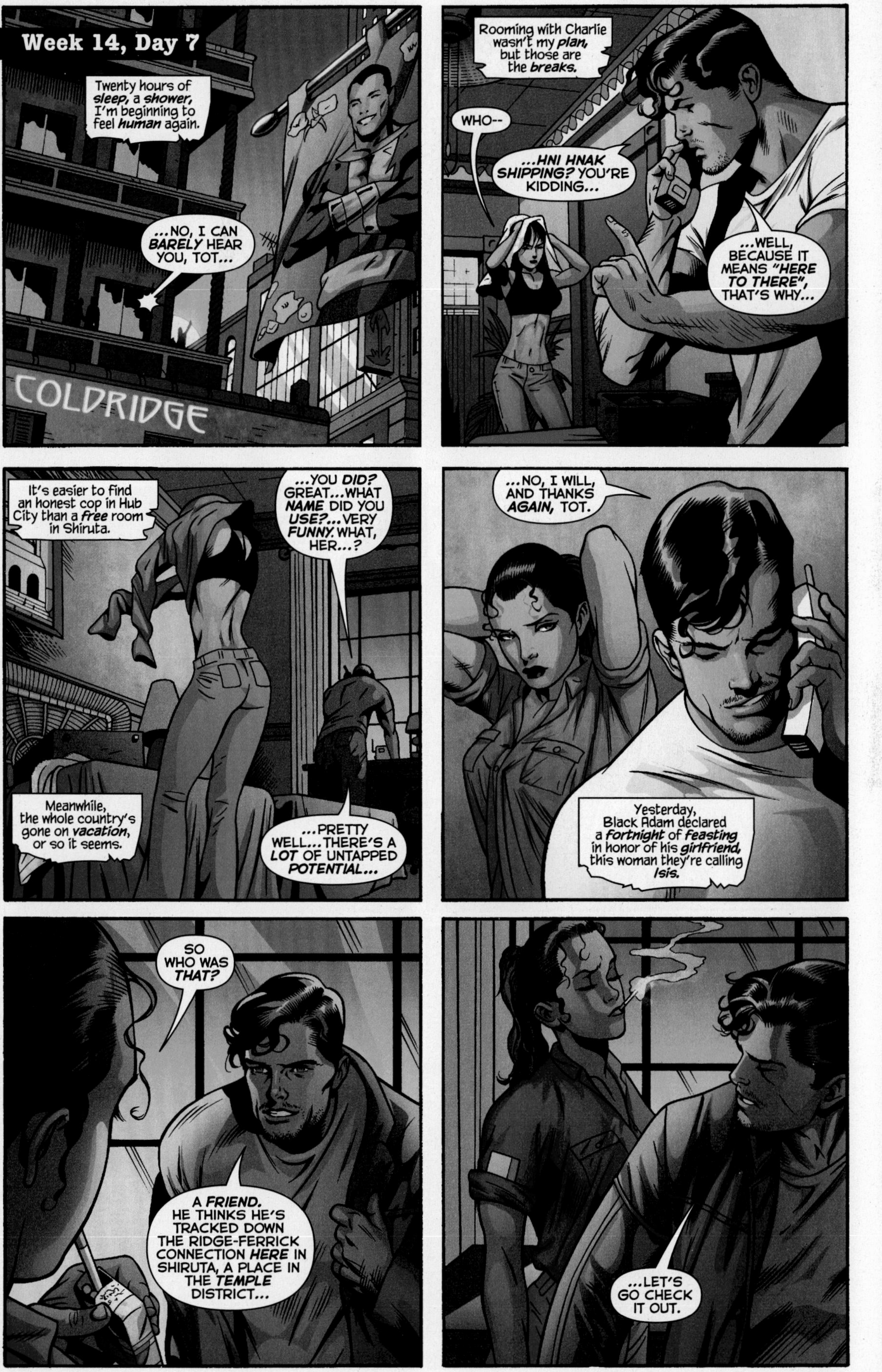
Week 14, Day 7
Twenty hours of sleep, a shower, I'm beginning to feel human again.
...NO, I CAN BARELY HEAR YOU, TOT...
COLDRIDGE
Rooming with Charlie wasn't my plan, but those are the breaks.
WHO--
...HNI HNAK SHIPPING? YOU'RE KIDDING...
...WELL, BECAUSE IT MEANS "HERE TO THERE", THAT'S WHY...
It's easier to find an honest cop in Hub City than a free room in Shiruta.
...YOU DID? GREAT...WHAT NAME DID YOU USE?...VERY FUNNY. WHAT, HER...?
Meanwhile, the whole country's gone on vacation, or so it seems.
...PRETTY WELL...THERE'S A LOT OF UNTAPPED POTENTIAL...
...NO, I WILL, AND THANKS AGAIN, TOT.
Yesterday, Black Adam declared a fortnight of feasting in honor of his girlfriend, this woman they're calling Isis.
SO WHO WAS THAT?
A FRIEND. HE THINKS HE'S TRACKED DOWN THE RIDGE-FERRICK CONNECTION HERE IN SHIRUTA, A PLACE IN THE TEMPLE DISTRICT...
...LET'S GO CHECK IT OUT.

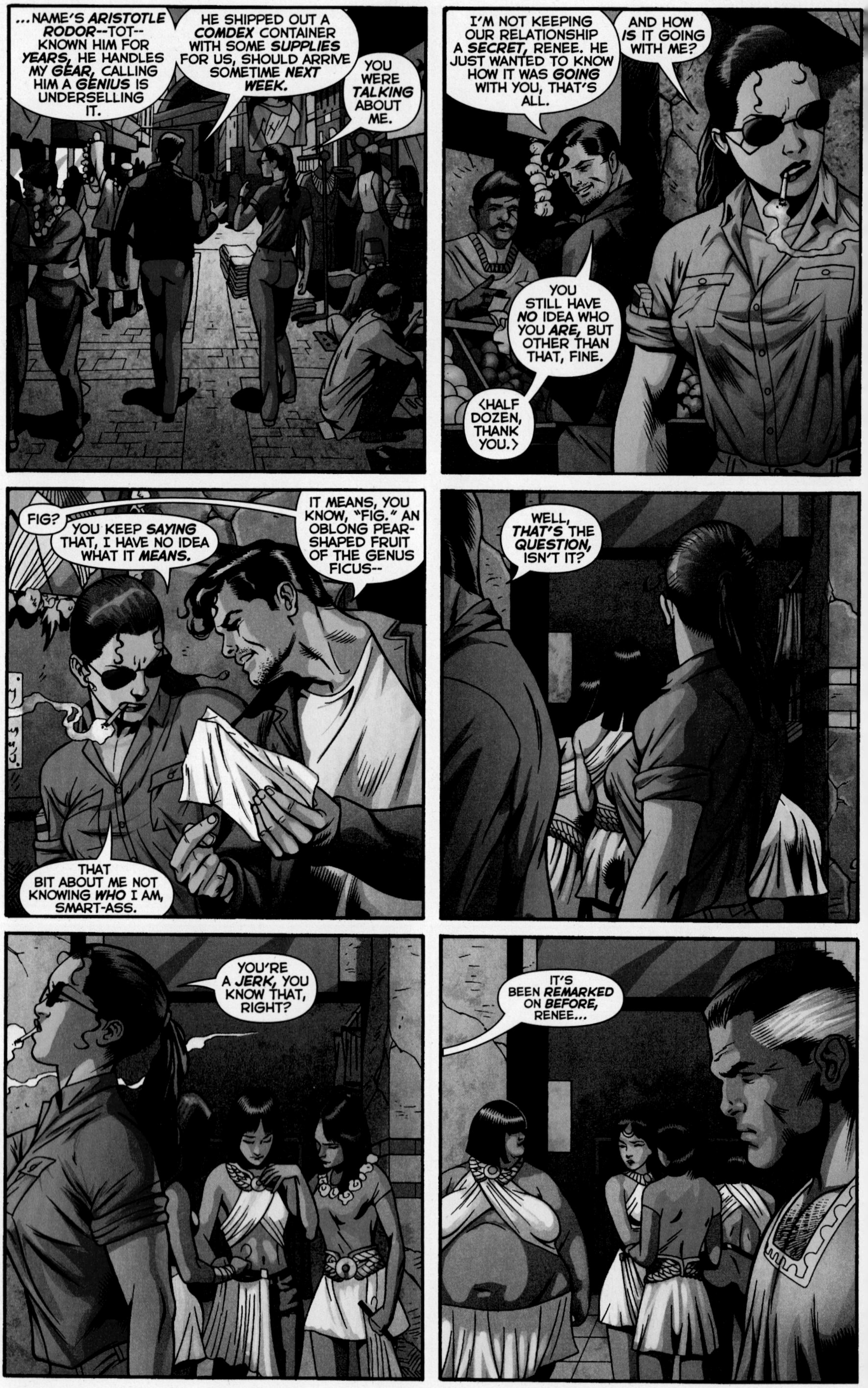
...NAME'S ARISTOTLE RODOR--TOT--KNOWN HIM FOR YEARS, HE HANDLES MY GEAR, CALLING HIM A GENIUS IS UNDERSELLING IT.
HE SHIPPED OUT A COMDEX CONTAINER WITH SOME SUPPLIES FOR US, SHOULD ARRIVE SOMETIME NEXT WEEK.
YOU WERE TALKING ABOUT ME.
I'M NOT KEEPING OUR RELATIONSHIP A SECRET, RENEE. HE JUST WANTED TO KNOW HOW IT WAS GOING WITH YOU, THAT'S ALL.
AND HOW IS IT GOING WITH ME?
YOU STILL HAVE NO IDEA WHO YOU ARE, BUT OTHER THAN THAT, FINE.
<HALF DOZEN, THANK YOU.>
FIG?
YOU KEEP SAYING THAT, I HAVE NO IDEA WHAT IT MEANS.
IT MEANS, YOU KNOW, "FIG." AN OBLONG PEAR-SHAPED FRUIT OF THE GENUS FICUS--
THAT BIT ABOUT ME NOT KNOWING WHO I AM, SMART-ASS.
WELL, THAT'S THE QUESTION, ISN'T IT?
YOU'RE A JERK, YOU KNOW THAT, RIGHT?
IT'S BEEN REMARKED ON BEFORE, RENEE...

I'm *imagining* things.

OKAY, *THAT* WAS THE OLD QUARTER WE JUST LEFT, SO THE TEMPLE DISTRICT SHOULD BE...

...Uh... *THIS* WAY, I THINK...

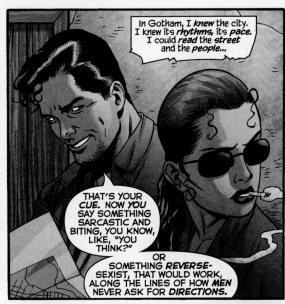

In Gotham, I *knew* the city. I knew its *rhythms,* its *pace.* I could *read* the *street* and the *people*...

THAT'S YOUR *CUE.* NOW *YOU* SAY SOMETHING SARCASTIC AND BITING, YOU KNOW, LIKE, "YOU THINK?"

OR SOMETHING *REVERSE-SEXIST,* THAT WOULD WORK, ALONG THE LINES OF HOW *MEN* NEVER ASK FOR *DIRECTIONS.*

...but *here,* I'm *out* of my *element.*

YOU *LAUGH* AT ME AND I'LL *KILL* YOU, CHARLIE...

WHAT?

...BUT I *THINK* WE'RE BEING *FOLLOWED.*

OH, THAT.

YEAH, HE'S BEEN *ON* US SINCE WE LEFT THE *HOTEL.*

C'MON, IT'S *THIS* WAY...

I swear before this is over I'm gonna hold his dead body in my hands.

...AT LEAST, I *THINK* IT'S THIS WAY...

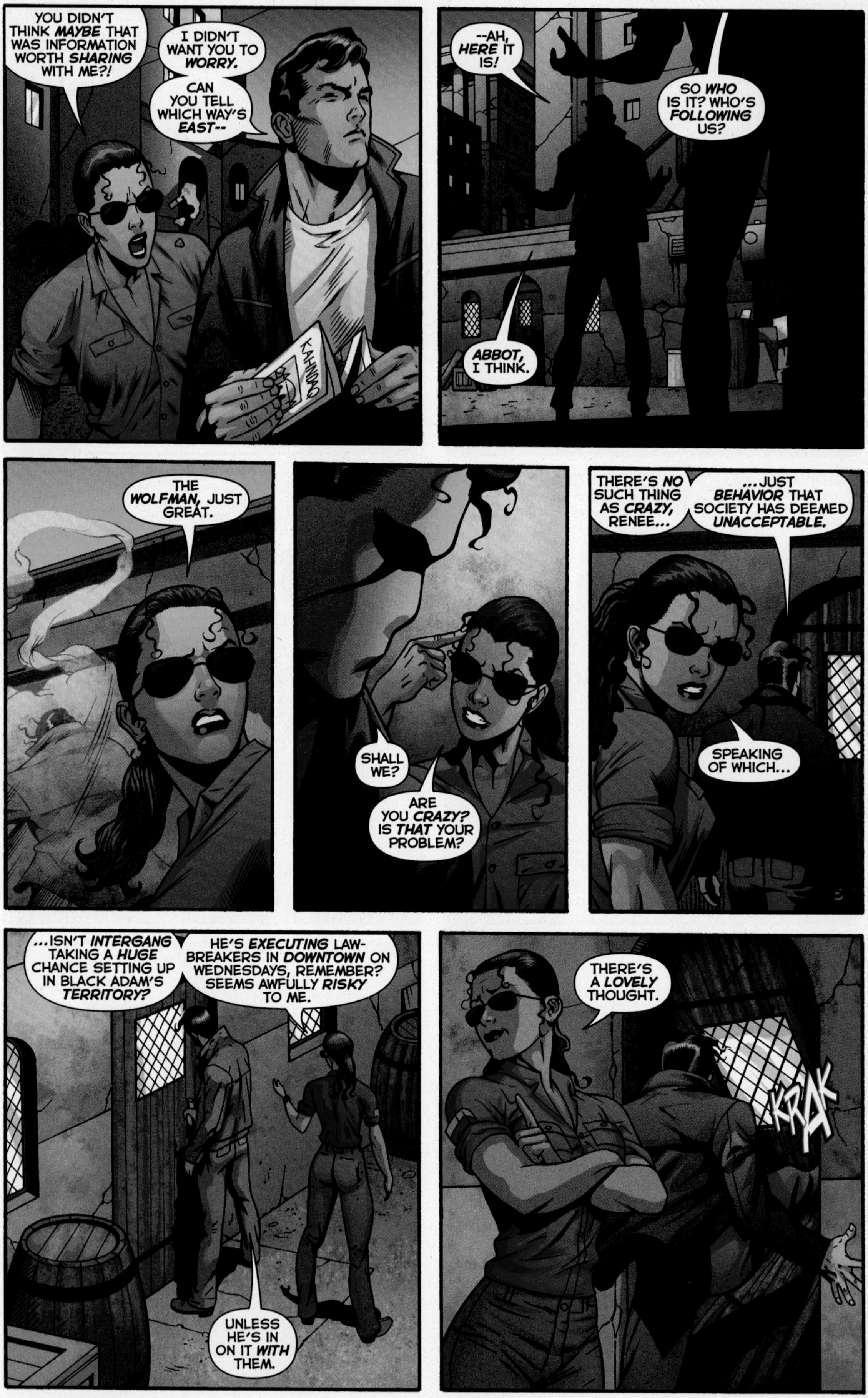

YOU DIDN'T THINK MAYBE THAT WAS INFORMATION WORTH SHARING WITH ME?!
I DIDN'T WANT YOU TO WORRY.
CAN YOU TELL WHICH WAY'S EAST--
KAHNDAQ
--AH, HERE IT IS!
SO WHO IS IT? WHO'S FOLLOWING US?
ABBOT, I THINK.
THE WOLFMAN, JUST GREAT.
SHALL WE?
ARE YOU CRAZY? IS THAT YOUR PROBLEM?
THERE'S NO SUCH THING AS CRAZY, RENEE...
...JUST BEHAVIOR THAT SOCIETY HAS DEEMED UNACCEPTABLE.
SPEAKING OF WHICH...
...ISN'T INTERGANG TAKING A HUGE CHANCE SETTING UP IN BLACK ADAM'S TERRITORY?
HE'S EXECUTING LAW-BREAKERS IN DOWNTOWN ON WEDNESDAYS, REMEMBER? SEEMS AWFULLY RISKY TO ME.
UNLESS HE'S IN ON IT WITH THEM.
THERE'S A LOVELY THOUGHT.
KRAK

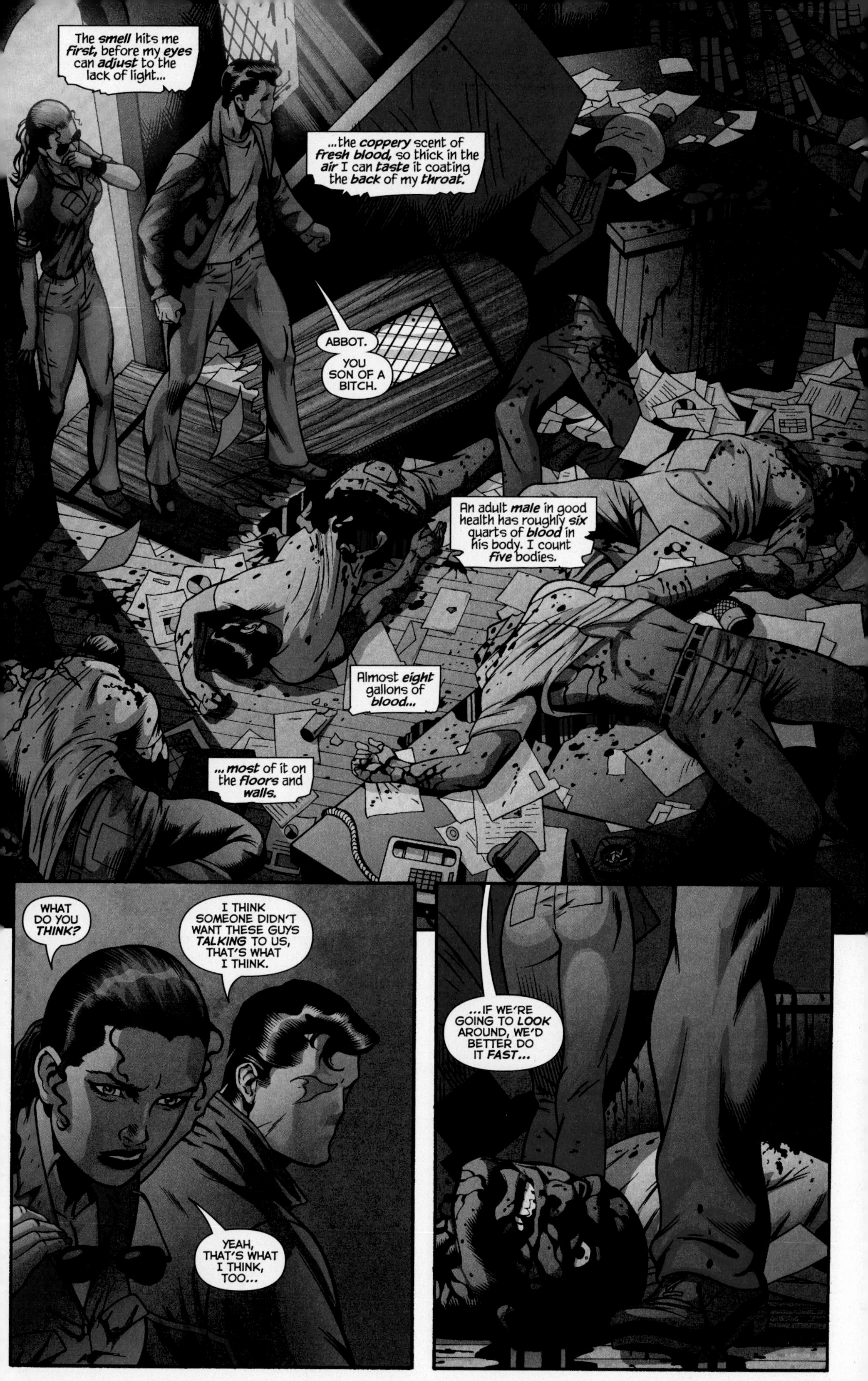
The smell hits me first, before my eyes can adjust to the lack of light...
...the coppery scent of fresh blood, so thick in the air I can taste it coating the back of my throat.
ABBOT.
YOU SON OF A BITCH.
An adult male in good health has roughly six quarts of blood in his body. I count five bodies.
Almost eight gallons of blood...
...most of it on the floors and walls.
WHAT DO YOU THINK?
I THINK SOMEONE DIDN'T WANT THESE GUYS TALKING TO US, THAT'S WHAT I THINK.
YEAH, THAT'S WHAT I THINK, TOO...
...IF WE'RE GOING TO LOOK AROUND, WE'D BETTER DO IT FAST...

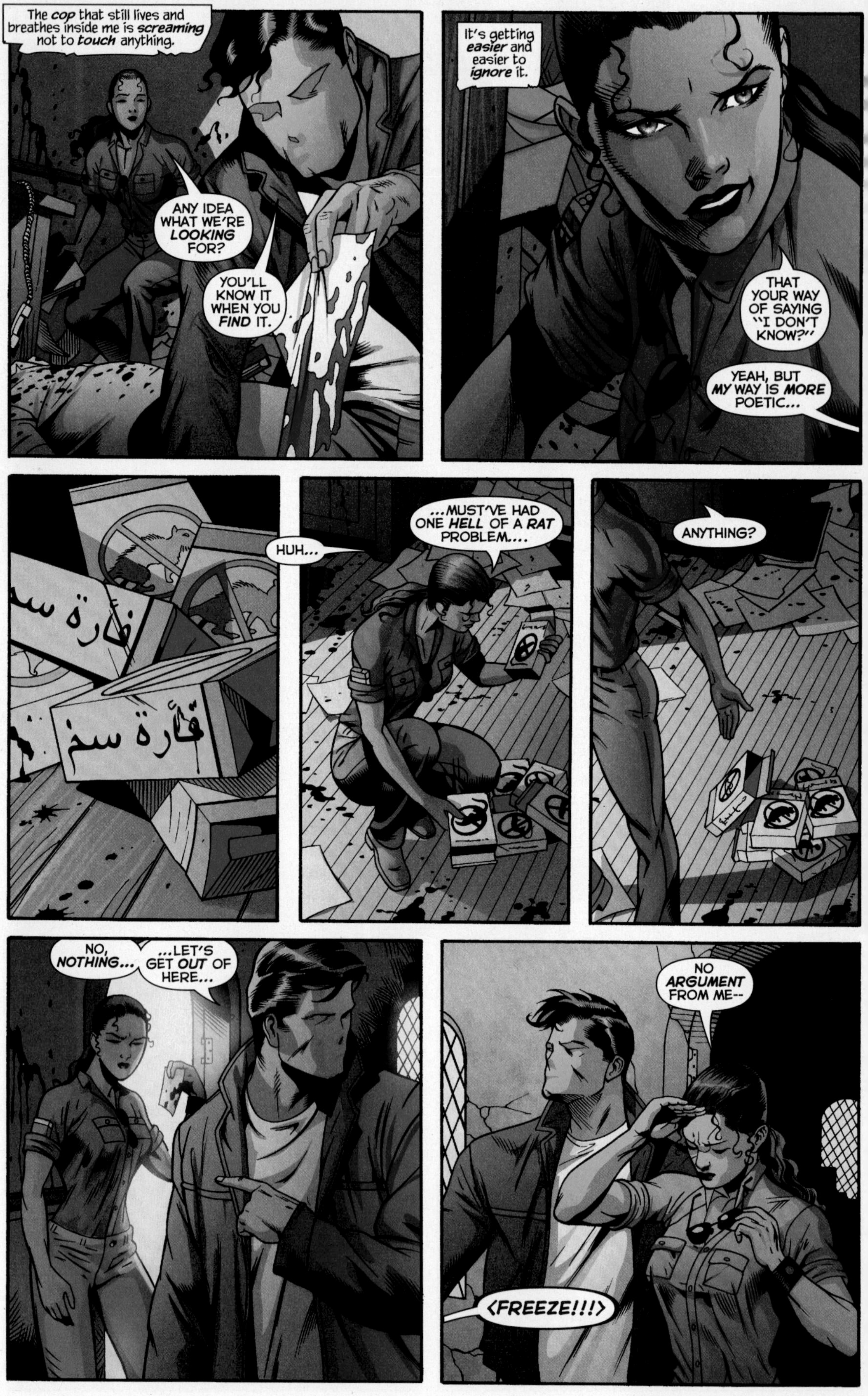
The cop that still lives and breathes inside me is screaming not to touch anything.
ANY IDEA WHAT WE'RE LOOKING FOR?
YOU'LL KNOW IT WHEN YOU FIND IT.
It's getting easier and easier to ignore it.
THAT YOUR WAY OF SAYING "I DON'T KNOW?"
YEAH, BUT MY WAY IS MORE POETIC...
HUH...
...MUST'VE HAD ONE HELL OF A RAT PROBLEM....
ANYTHING?
NO, NOTHING...
...LET'S GET OUT OF HERE...
NO ARGUMENT FROM ME--
<FREEZE!!!>

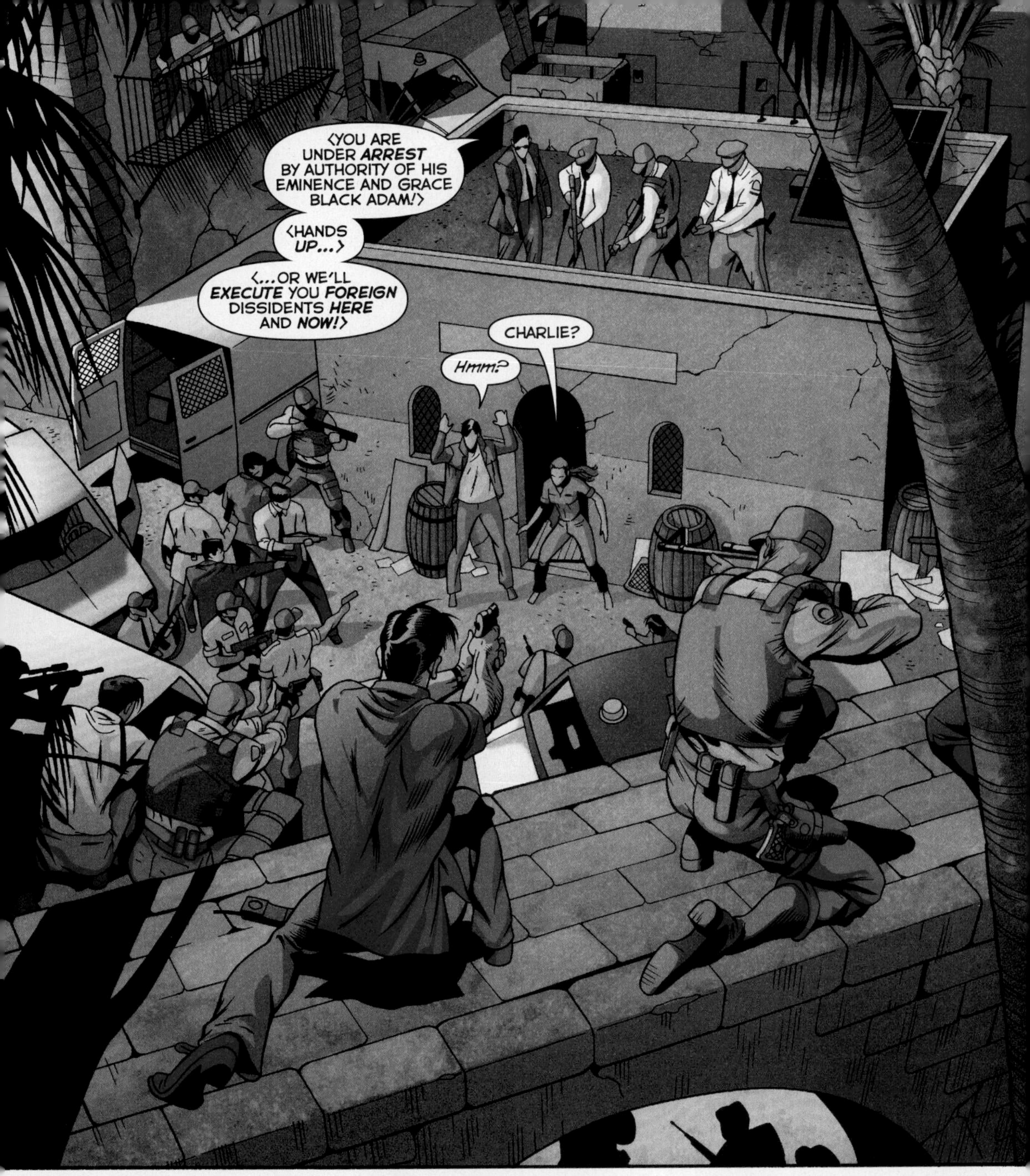
<YOU ARE UNDER ARREST BY AUTHORITY OF HIS EMINENCE AND GRACE BLACK ADAM!>
<HANDS UP...>
<...OR WE'LL EXECUTE YOU FOREIGN DISSIDENTS HERE AND NOW!>
CHARLIE?
Hmm?

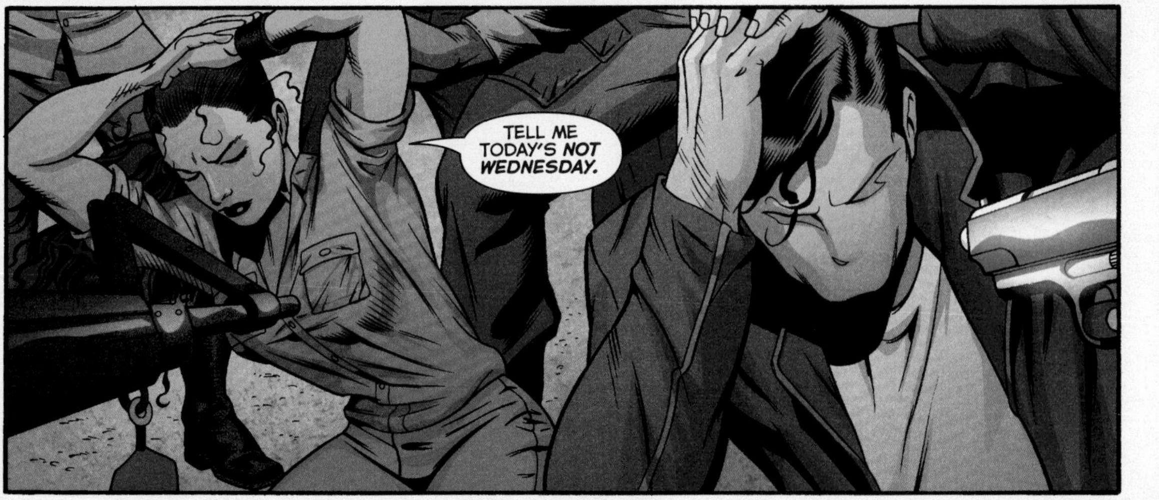
TELL ME TODAY'S NOT WEDNESDAY.

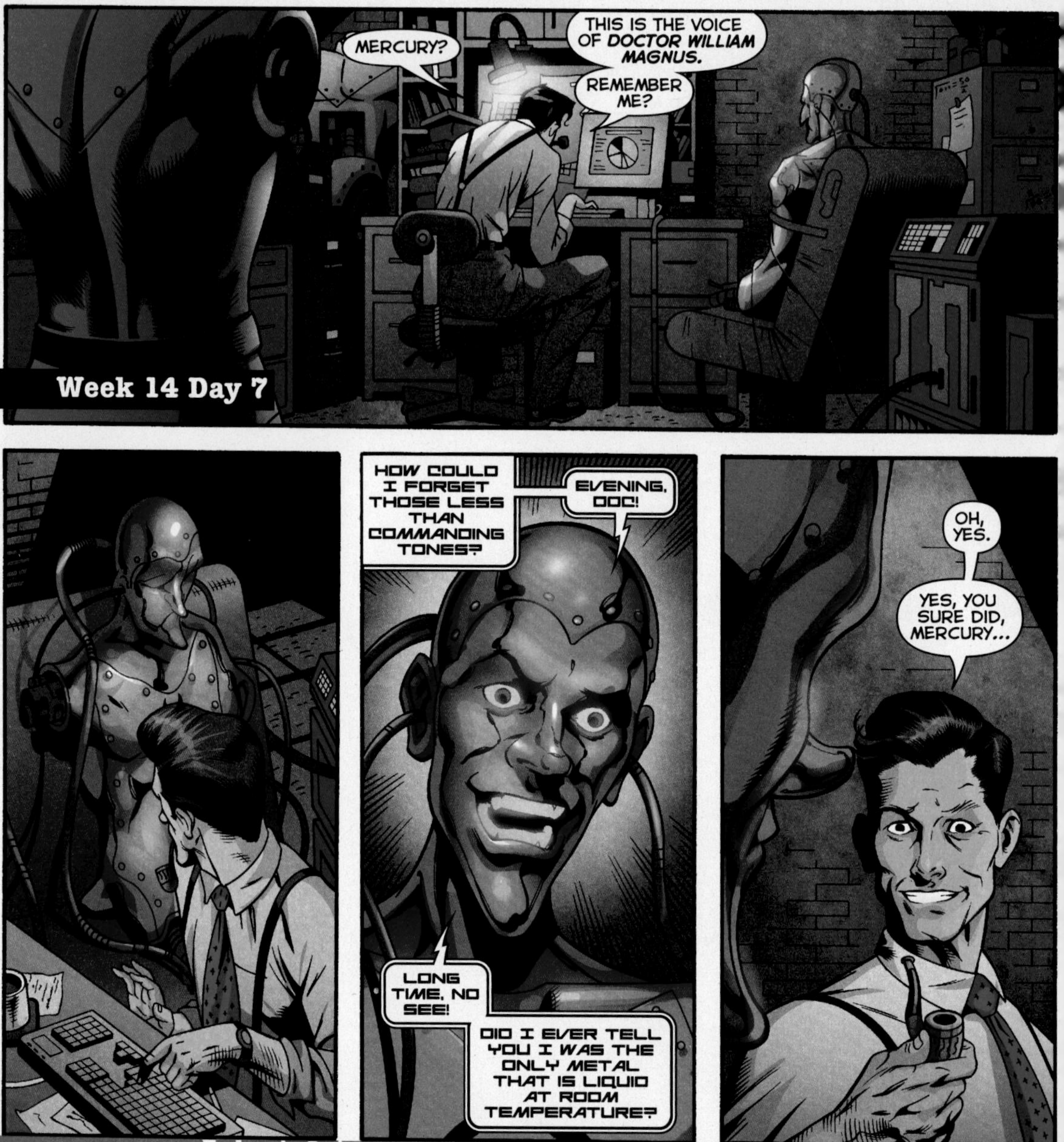
Week 14 Day 7
MERCURY?
THIS IS THE VOICE OF *DOCTOR WILLIAM MAGNUS.*
REMEMBER ME?
HOW COULD I FORGET THOSE LESS THAN COMMANDING TONES?
EVENING, DOC!
LONG TIME, NO SEE!
DID I EVER TELL YOU I *WAS* THE ONLY *METAL* THAT IS LIQUID AT ROOM TEMPERATURE?
OH, YES.
YES, YOU SURE DID, MERCURY...

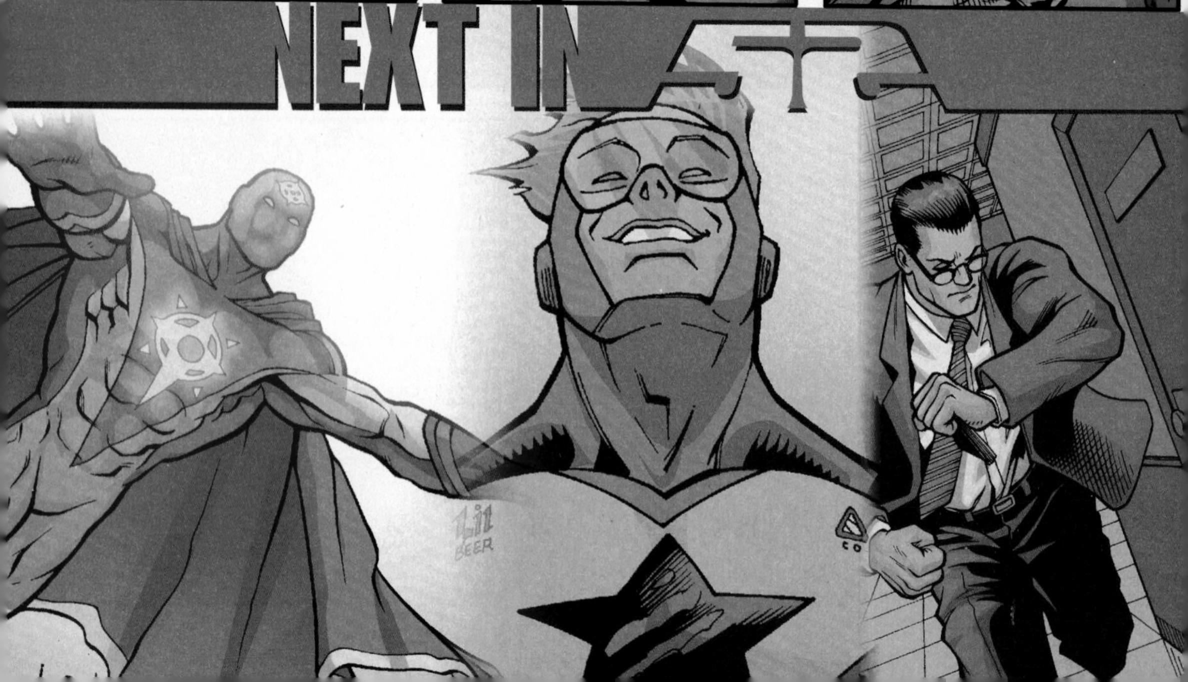
NEXT IN 52

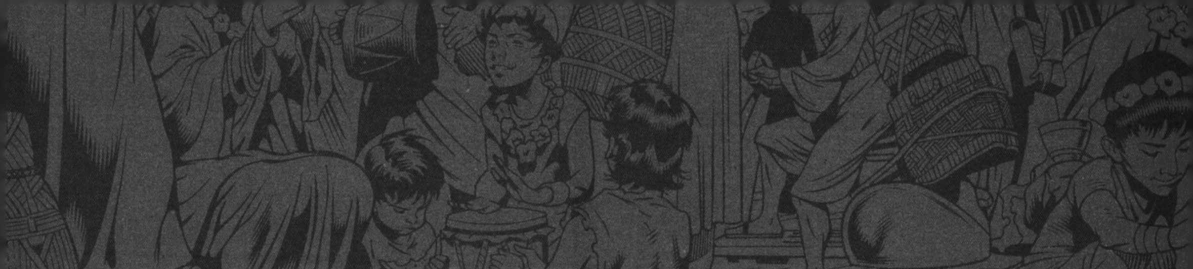

WEEK FOURTEEN NOTES

GREG RUCKA

Ah, yes, the beginning of the Great Kahndaq Mistake. I'll explain that in detail come Week 16, as I don't want to give spoilers here.

The cover for this issue [shown on page 300], incidentally, was love at first sight for Steve Wacker, and you can see why; the pathos J.G. captured in the painting is truly heart-breaking, and I love the possibly (though knowing JG, doubtfully) unintentional Hamlet reference. Not to go too damn high-brow, but all through 52 we return, in one way or another, to questions of identity and determinism — most overtly in the Renee/Charlie storyline ("Who are you?" "Damned if I know."), but seen over and over throughout the Black Adam, Steel/Natasha, Will Magnus, and Ralph arcs.

Steel, in Week 14, is a man in transition, pretty much at his lowest point since the start of the series; the act of building for Natasha a new set of armor, of trying to recapture what has been lost — and perhaps trying to recapture her in the process — is as potentially desperate and pathetic as it is hopeful and loving. Where can he go from here but up?

About Kahndaq — again, I'll elaborate further on this come Week 16 — but one of the things we wanted to show was the impact that Isis has had on Black Adam, and thus on the country. The contrast between Renee's rather dour and pessimistic narrative on the first page of the issue and the double-page spread following it, showing Shiruta in celebration, was obviously intentional, but served a grander purpose, as well — it wasn't that many weeks ago that Black Adam publicly executed a man for all the world to see. And while Isis is inadvertently dictating fashion, much like Jackie O or Princess Di, as we see at the end of the issue — and see even more clearly in Week 15 — just because things in Kahndaq are looking up does not, by any stretch, mean that they've gotten better across the board.

Minor things to add here. I'm not certain who it was who came up with Haven (might've been Grant, might've been Keith, might've been a coalition of *Prisoner* fans — check the reference yourself), but the "locked room mystery" of Morrow's disappearance was one of those things that would come back to haunt; in particular, it would come back to haunt Mark, who, I was learning, *loathes* loose ends.

As a side note, I love that the birds in Haven are trained to attack as the dogs are.

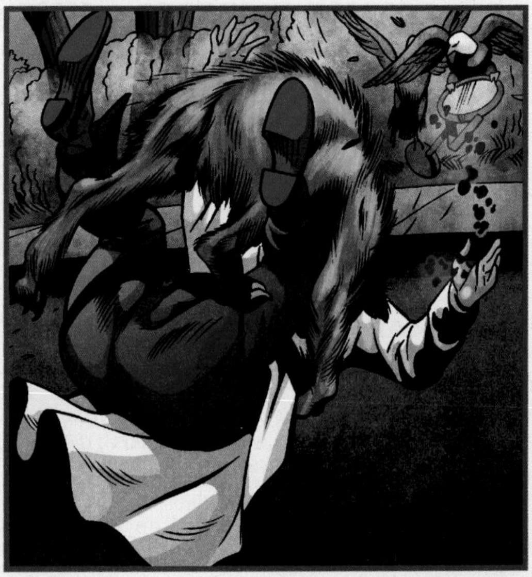

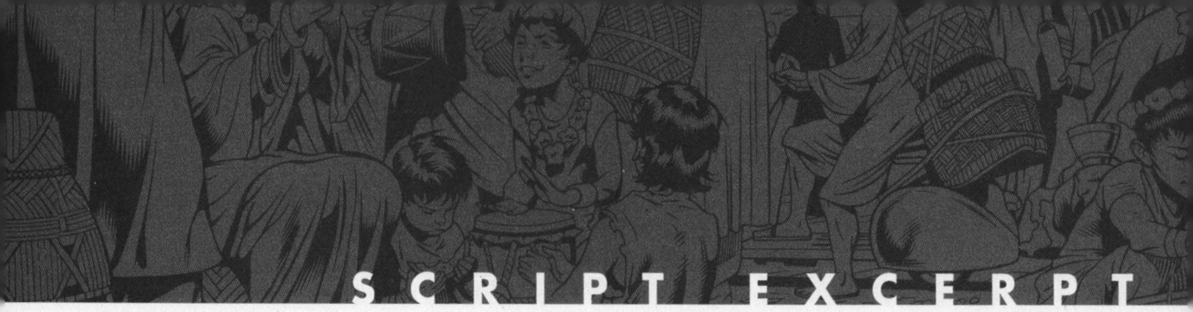

SCRIPT EXCERPT

(COMPARE WITH PAGE 21 OF THIS COLLECTION)

52 WEEK FOURTEEN — PAGE SEVENTEEN

PANEL ONE
Interior angle, wide shot, of the Hni Hnak offices. Dusty, sunlight filtering through the windows. Places feels old, like out of a '40s film.

The place has been thoroughly tossed. PAPERS are scattered everywhere, on the FLOORS, spilling out of FILING CABINETS and DESKS. FURNITURE has been overturned, some of it BROKEN. THERE was a lot of violence committed in this office space.

STREWN about the room are the BODIES of FIVE MEN, all of them Kahndaqi. MOST of them lie in PUDDLES of their own BLOOD, spilling out in rivers across the floor, soaking the PAPERS. MOST of these guys had their insides torn out by Abbot; one or two were lucky and got away with broken necks.

VIC has stepped into the room, MONTOYA visible just past him, removing her SUNGLASSES. Both are reacting to the sight. MONTOYA's look is hard — she's seen the Joker's handiwork up close, remember — she's not squeamish.

> **CAPTION/MONTOYA:** The SMELL hits me FIRST, before my EYES can ADJUST to the lack of light...
>
> **CAPTION/MONTOYA:** ...the COPPERY scent of FRESH BLOOD, so thick in the AIR I can TASTE it coating the BACK of my THROAT.
>
> **CAPTION/MONTOYA:** An adult MALE in good health has roughly SIX quarts of BLOOD in his body. I count FIVE bodies. Almost EIGHT gallons of blood...
>
> **VIC (small):** Abbot. You son of a bitch.
>
> **CAPTION/MONTOYA:** ...MOST of it on the FLOORS and WALLS.

PANEL TWO
Closer on VIC and MONTOYA, taking in the crime scene, affected by its savagery and violence.

> **MONTOYA:** What do you THINK?
>
> **VIC:** I think someone didn't want these guys TALKING to us, that's what I think.
>
> **MONTOYA:** Yeah, that's what I think too...

PANEL THREE
Angle, VIC's feet carefully picking their way amidst the PUDDLES of BLOOD, MONTOYA's feet moving off in their own direction. One of the BODIES in the foreground, his face frozen in terrified rigor.

> **MONTOYA:** ...if we're going to LOOK around, we'd better do it FAST...

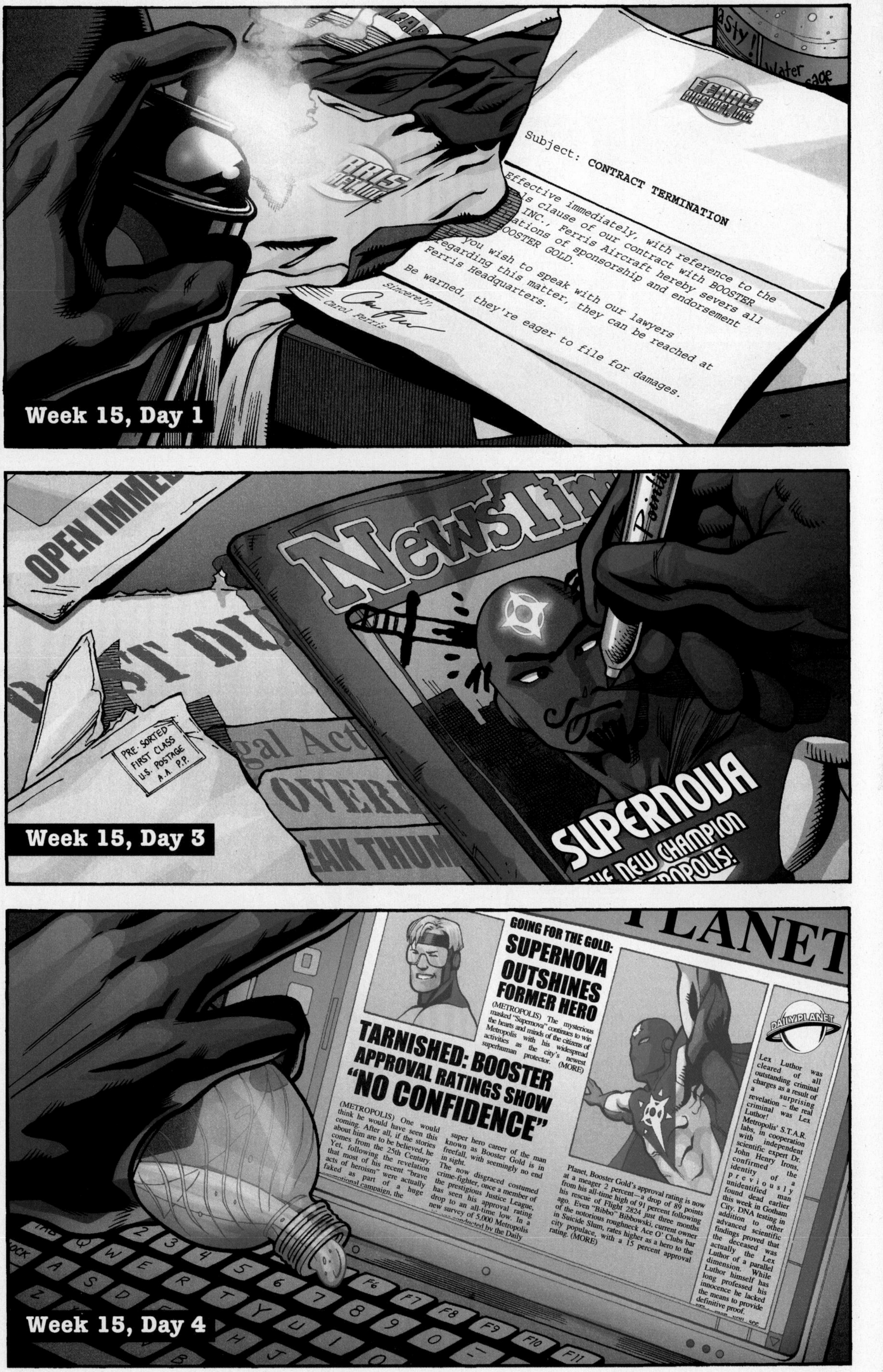
Subject: CONTRACT TERMINATION
Effective immediately, with reference to the
clause of our contract with BOOSTER
INC., Ferris Aircraft hereby severs all
ations of sponsorship and endorsement
BOOSTER GOLD.
you wish to speak with our lawyers
regarding this matter, they can be reached at
Ferris Headquarters.
Be warned, they're eager to file for damages.
Sincerely,
Carol Ferris
Week 15, Day 1
OPEN IMME
PRE-SORTED FIRST CLASS U.S. POSTAGE A.A. P.P.
SUPERNOVA
Week 15, Day 3
PLANET
GOING FOR THE GOLD:
SUPERNOVA OUTSHINES FORMER HERO
(METROPOLIS) The mysterious masked "Supernova" continues to win the hearts and minds of the citizens of Metropolis with his widespread activities as the city's newest superhuman protector. (MORE)
TARNISHED: BOOSTER APPROVAL RATINGS SHOW "NO CONFIDENCE"
(METROPOLIS) One would think he would have seen this coming. After all, if the stories about him are to be believed, he comes from the 25th Century. Yet, following the revelation that most of his recent "brave acts of heroism" were actually faked as part of a huge promotional campaign, the
super hero career of the man known as Booster Gold is in freefall, with seemingly no end in sight.
The now disgraced costumed crime-fighter, once a member of the prestigious Justice League, has seen his approval rating drop to an all-time low. In a new survey of 5,000 Metropolis conducted by the Daily
Planet, Booster Gold's approval rating is now at a meager 2 percent—a drop of 89 points from his all-time high of 91 percent following his rescue of Flight 2824 just three months ago. Even "Bibbo" Bibbowski, current owner of the notorious roughneck Ace O' Clubs bar in Suicide Slum, rates higher as a hero to the city populace, with a 15 percent approval rating. (MORE)
DAILY PLANET
Lex Luthor was cleared of all outstanding criminal charges as a result of a surprising revelation – the real criminal was Lex Luthor!
Metropolis' S.T.A.R. labs, in cooperation with independent scientific expert Dr. John Henry Irons, confirmed the identity of a previously unidentified man found dead earlier this week in Gotham City. DNA testing in addition to other advanced scientific findings proved that the deceased was actually the Lex Luthor of a parallel dimension. While Luthor himself has long professed his innocence he lacked the means to provide definitive proof.
Week 15, Day 4

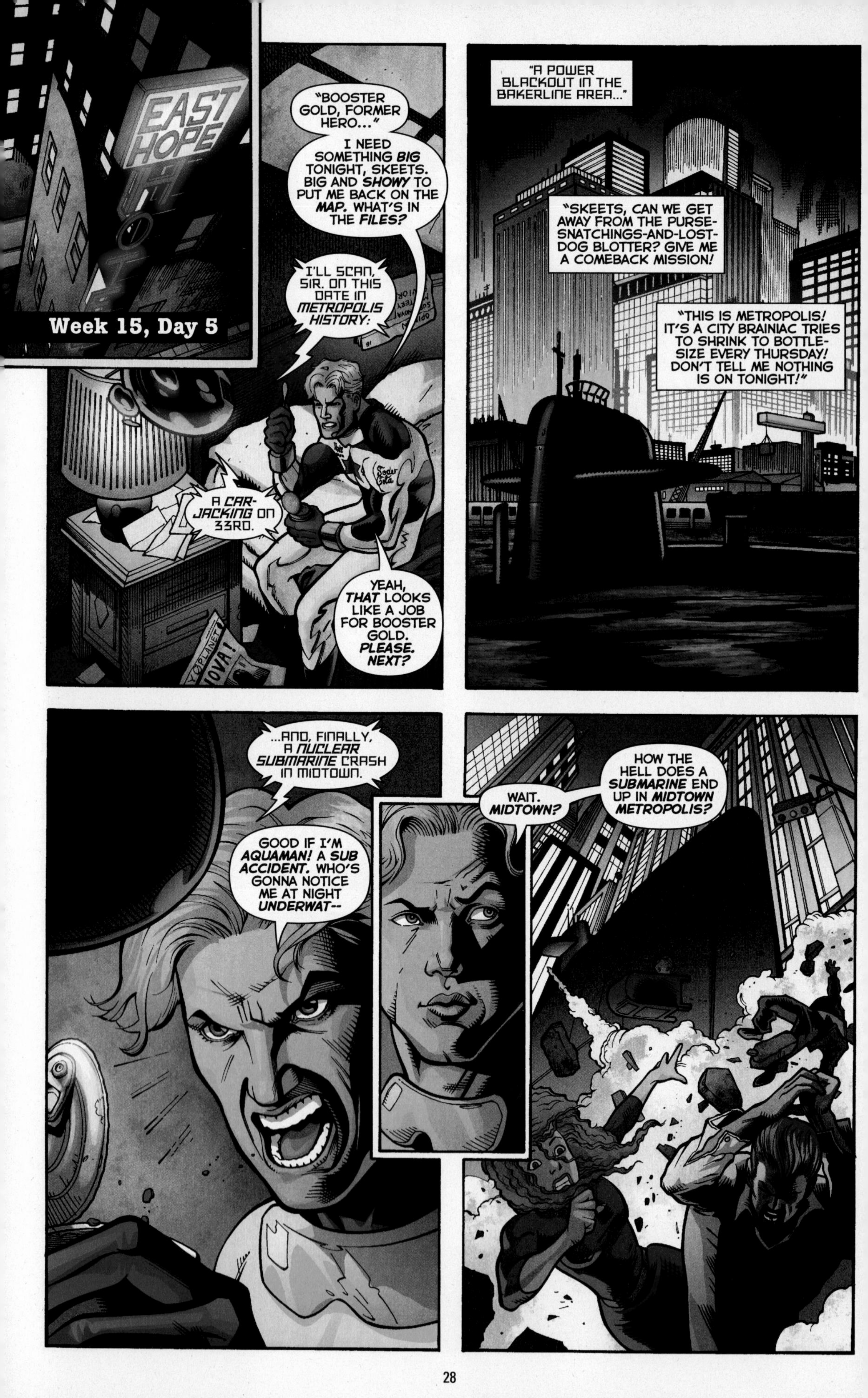
EAST HOPE
Week 15, Day 5
"BOOSTER GOLD, FORMER HERO..."
I NEED SOMETHING BIG TONIGHT, SKEETS. BIG AND SHOWY TO PUT ME BACK ON THE MAP. WHAT'S IN THE FILES?
I'LL SCAN, SIR. ON THIS DATE IN METROPOLIS HISTORY:
A CAR-JACKING ON 33RD.
YEAH, THAT LOOKS LIKE A JOB FOR BOOSTER GOLD. PLEASE. NEXT?
"A POWER BLACKOUT IN THE BAKERLINE AREA..."
"SKEETS, CAN WE GET AWAY FROM THE PURSE-SNATCHINGS-AND-LOST-DOG BLOTTER? GIVE ME A COMEBACK MISSION!
"THIS IS METROPOLIS! IT'S A CITY BRAINIAC TRIES TO SHRINK TO BOTTLE-SIZE EVERY THURSDAY! DON'T TELL ME NOTHING IS ON TONIGHT!"
...AND, FINALLY, A NUCLEAR SUBMARINE CRASH IN MIDTOWN.
GOOD IF I'M AQUAMAN! A SUB ACCIDENT. WHO'S GONNA NOTICE ME AT NIGHT UNDERWAT--
WAIT. MIDTOWN?
HOW THE HELL DOES A SUBMARINE END UP IN MIDTOWN METROPOLIS?

DC COMICS 52
OUTSHINED
Week 15 Week 15 Week 15 Week 15 Week 15 Week 15 Week 15 Week 15 Week 15 Week 15 Week
Week 15 Week 15 Week 15 Week 15 Week 15 Week 15 Week 15 Week 15 Week 15 Week 15 Week
Week 15 Week 15 Week 15 Week 15 Week 15 Week 15 Week 15 Week 15 Week 15 Week 15 Week
Week 15 Week 15 Week 15 Week 15 Week 15 Week 15 Week 15 Week 15 Week 15 Week 15 Week

WRITTEN BY GEOFF JOHNS, GRANT MORRISON, GREG RUCKA, MARK WAID

ART BREAKDOWNS BY KEITH GIFFEN • **PENCILS BY** SHAWN MOLL • **INKS BY** TOM NGUYEN
COLORS BY ALEX SINCLAIR • **LETTERING BY** JARED K. FLETCHER

ASSISTANT EDITORS JANN JONES & HARVEY RICHARDS
EDITED BY STEPHEN WACKER • **COVER BY** J.G. JONES & ALEX SINCLAIR

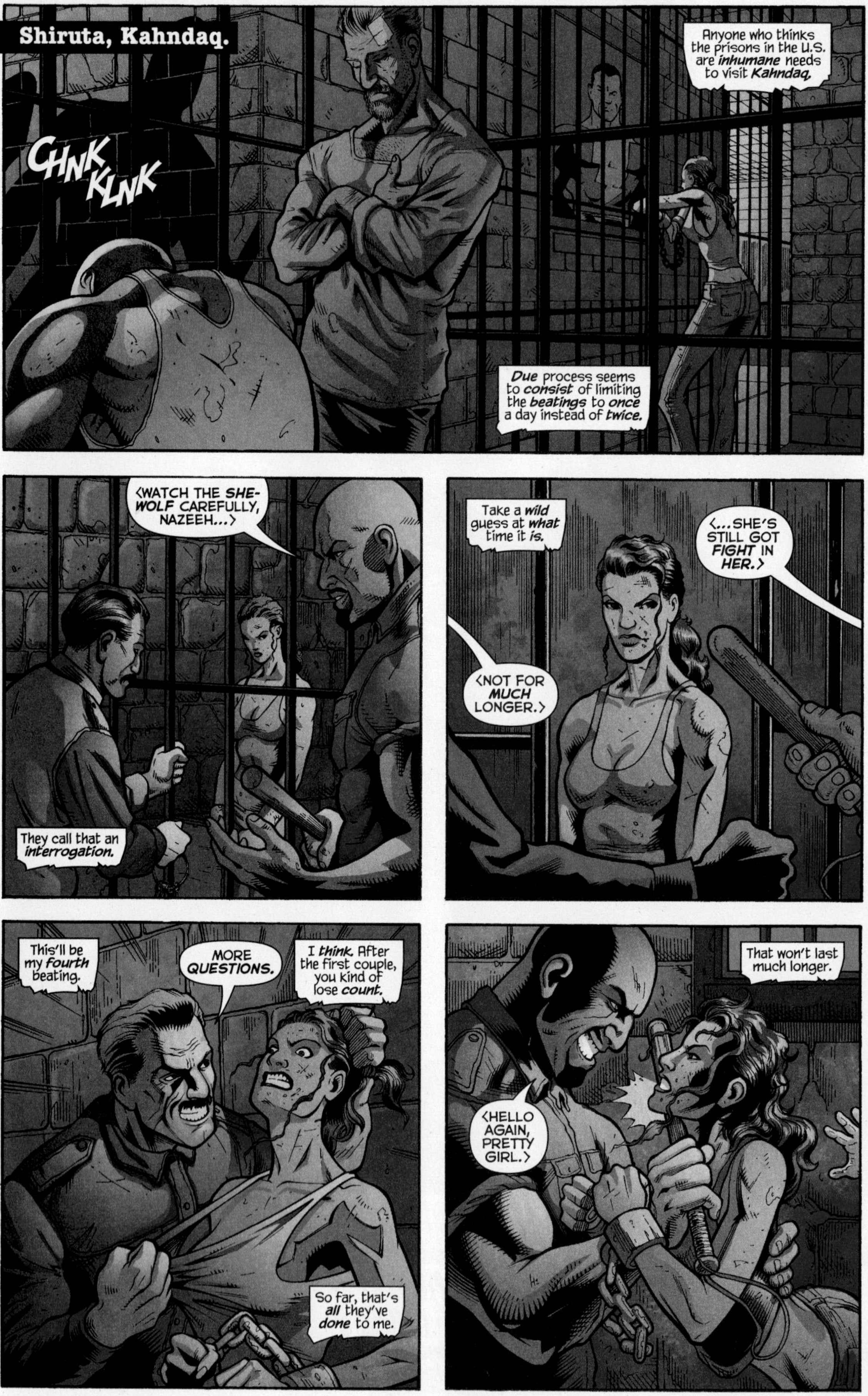
Shiruta, Kahndaq.
Anyone who thinks the prisons in the U.S. are *inhumane* needs to visit *Kahndaq.*
CHNK KLNK
Due process seems to *consist* of limiting the *beatings* to *once* a day instead of *twice.*
<WATCH THE *SHE-WOLF* CAREFULLY, NAZEEH...>
They call that an *interrogation.*
Take a *wild* guess at *what* time it *is.*
<...SHE'S STILL GOT *FIGHT* IN *HER.*>
<NOT FOR *MUCH* LONGER.>
This'll be my *fourth* beating.
MORE *QUESTIONS.*
I *think.* After the first couple, you kind of lose *count.*
So far, that's *all* they've *done* to me.
That won't last much longer.
<HELLO AGAIN, PRETTY GIRL.>

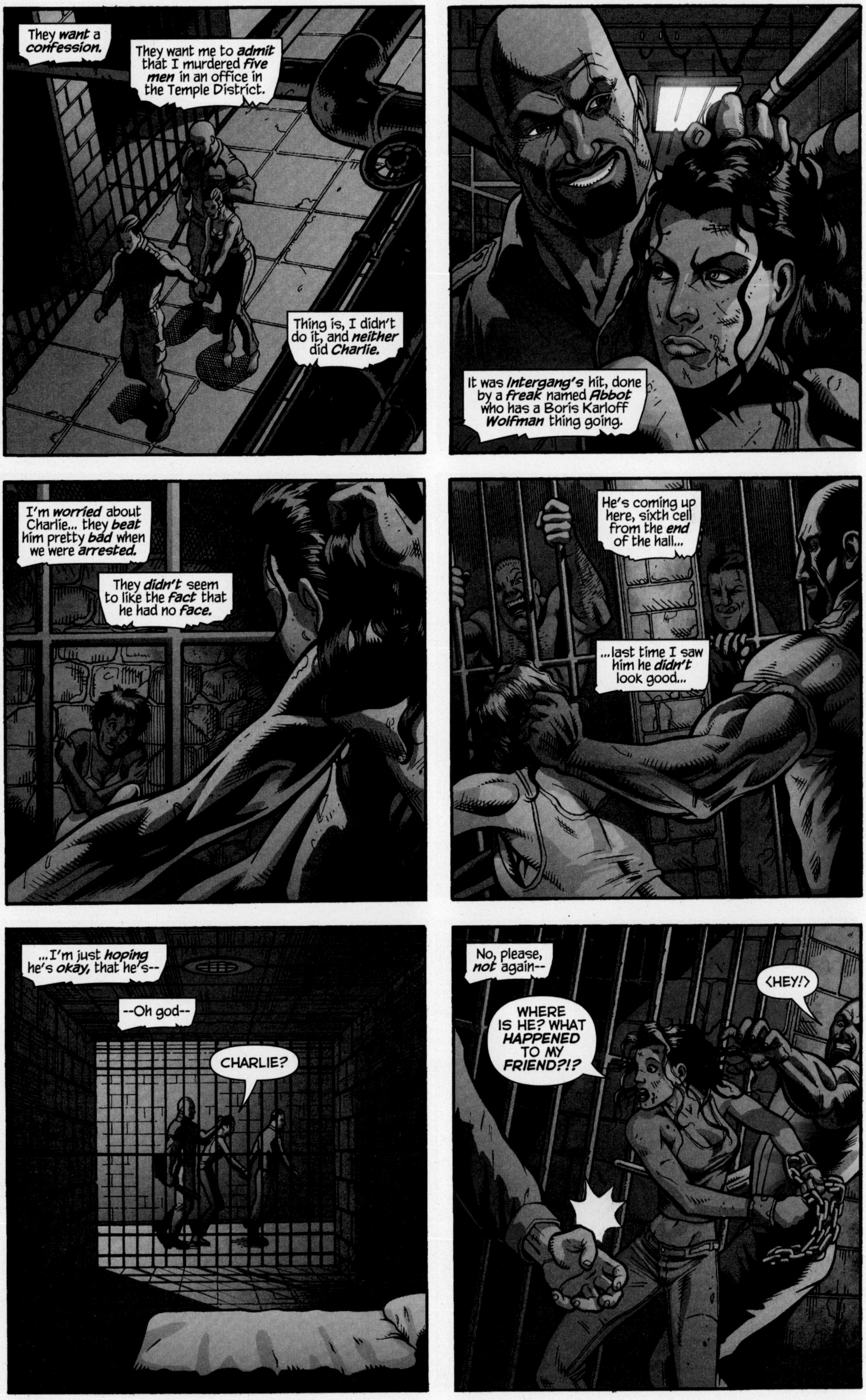
They want a confession.
They want me to admit that I murdered five men in an office in the Temple District.
Thing is, I didn't do it, and neither did Charlie.
It was Intergang's hit, done by a freak named Abbot who has a Boris Karloff Wolfman thing going.
I'm worried about Charlie... they beat him pretty bad when we were arrested.
They didn't seem to like the fact that he had no face.
He's coming up here, sixth cell from the end of the hall...
...last time I saw him he didn't look good...
...I'm just hoping he's okay, that he's--
--Oh god--
CHARLIE?
No, please, not again--
WHERE IS HE? WHAT HAPPENED TO MY FRIEND?!?
<HEY!>

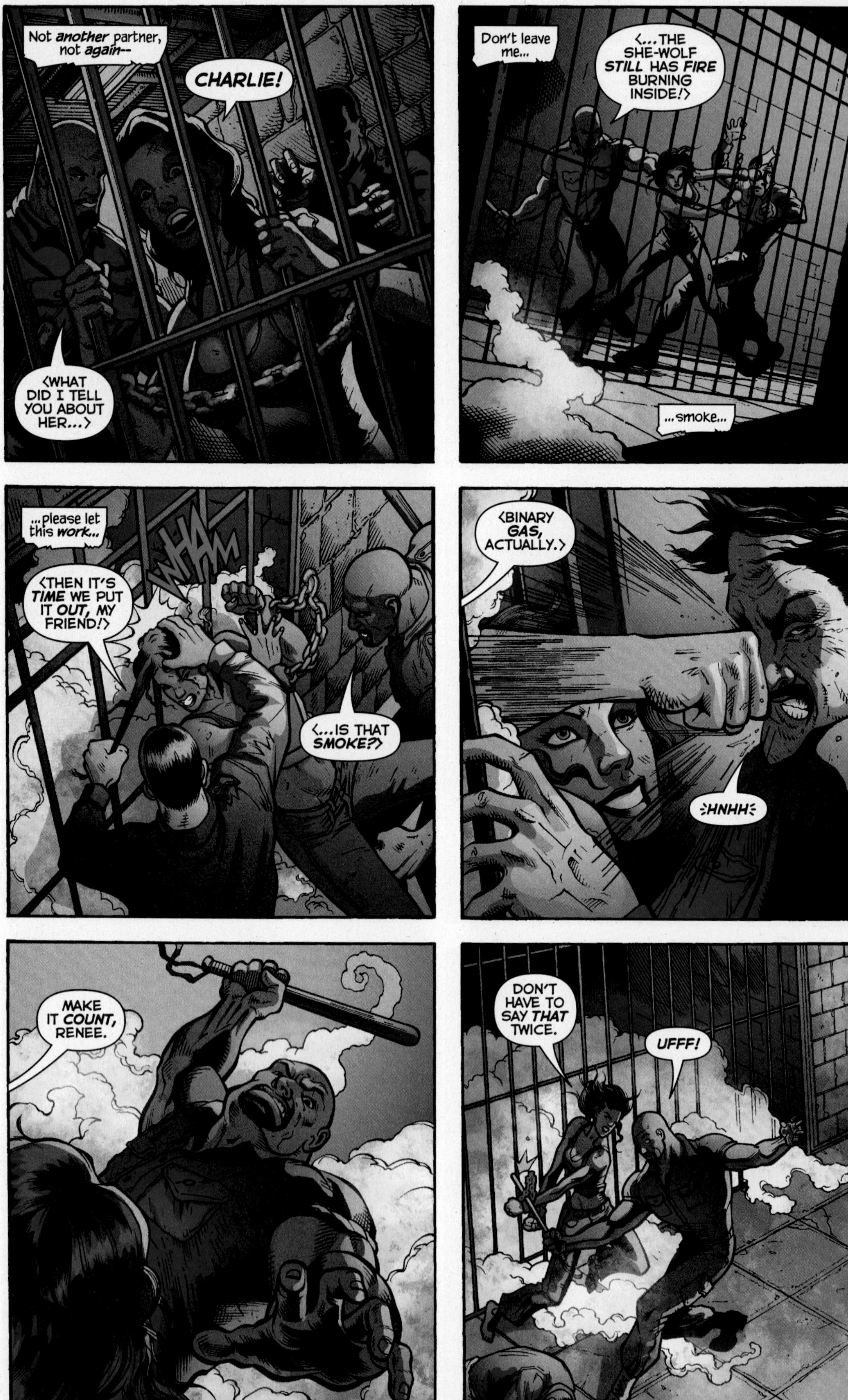
Not another partner, not again--
CHARLIE!
<WHAT DID I TELL YOU ABOUT HER...>
Don't leave me...
<...THE SHE-WOLF STILL HAS FIRE BURNING INSIDE!>
...smoke...
...please let this work...
WHAM
<THEN IT'S TIME WE PUT IT OUT, MY FRIEND!>
<...IS THAT SMOKE?>
<BINARY GAS, ACTUALLY.>
HNHH
MAKE IT COUNT, RENEE.
DON'T HAVE TO SAY THAT TWICE.
UFFF!

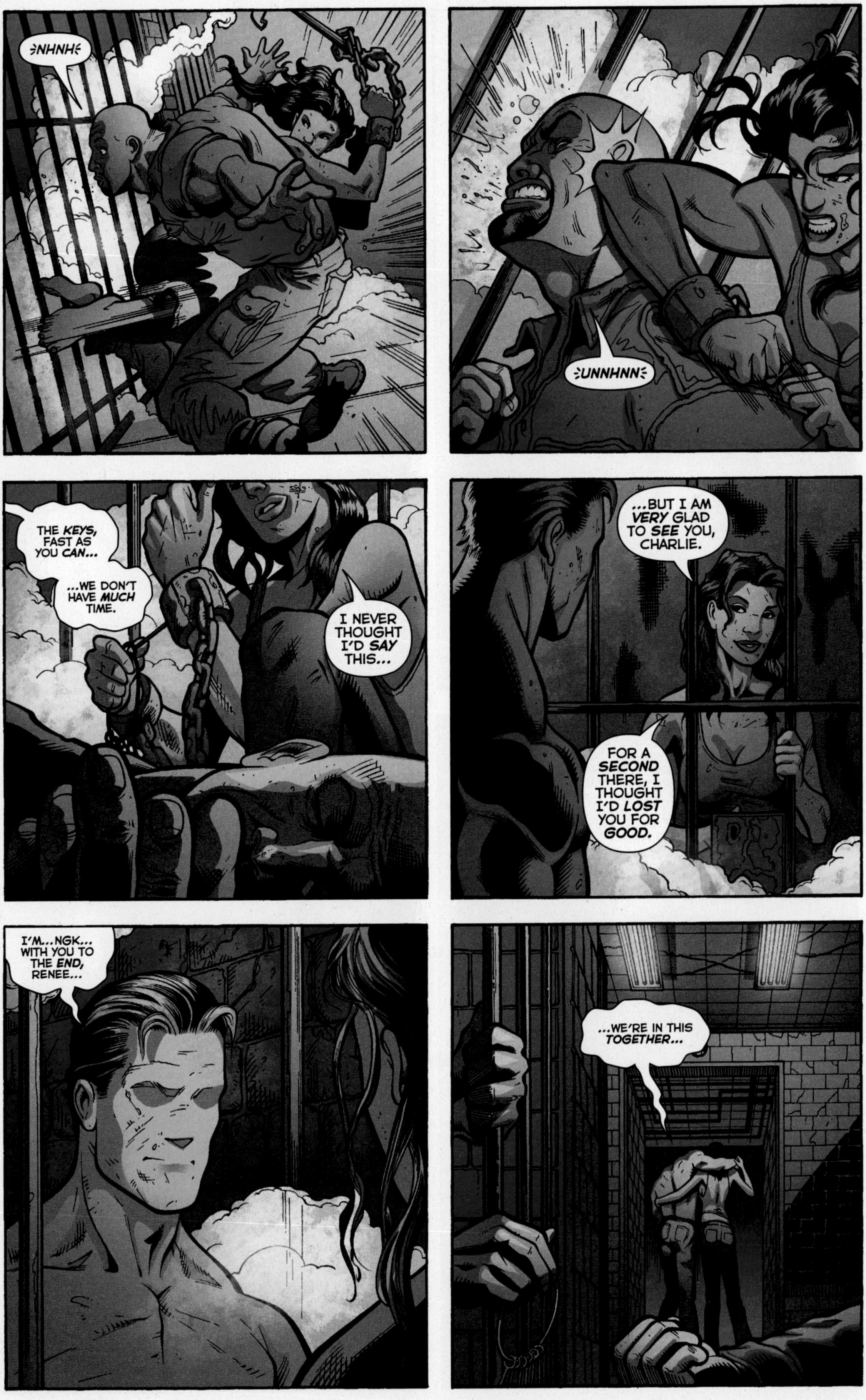
NHNH
UNNHNN
THE KEYS, FAST AS YOU CAN...
...WE DON'T HAVE MUCH TIME.
I NEVER THOUGHT I'D SAY THIS...
...BUT I AM VERY GLAD TO SEE YOU, CHARLIE.
FOR A SECOND THERE, I THOUGHT I'D LOST YOU FOR GOOD.
I'M...NGK... WITH YOU TO THE END, RENEE...
...WE'RE IN THIS TOGETHER...

THIS LOOKS LIKE A JOB FOR *SUPERNOVA*.

Metropolis.

THE *SUB* WAS A *NUCLEAR CLASS SSBN* THAT WAS ATTACKED IN THE *MID-ATLANTIC*, MR. KENT-- BUT WHAT IS THAT *FRIGLY THING CARRYING* IT?

I'M COUNTING ON YOU TO TELL *ME*, SANJAY! TRY CROSS-REFERENCING *ATLANTIS* AND *AQUAMAN!*

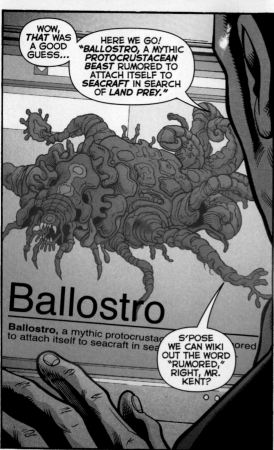

WOW, *THAT WAS A GOOD GUESS...*

HERE WE GO! *"BALLOSTRO, A MYTHIC PROTOCRUSTACEAN BEAST* RUMORED TO ATTACH ITSELF TO *SEACRAFT* IN SEARCH OF *LAND PREY."*

Ballostro

Ballostro, a mythic protocrustac~~~
to attach itself to seacraft in sea~~~

S'POSE WE CAN WIKI OUT THE WORD *"RUMORED,"* RIGHT, MR. KENT?

MR. KENT?

AH, STORE ROOM, MY OLD FRIEND... I MISS YOU ALREADY...

Store Room

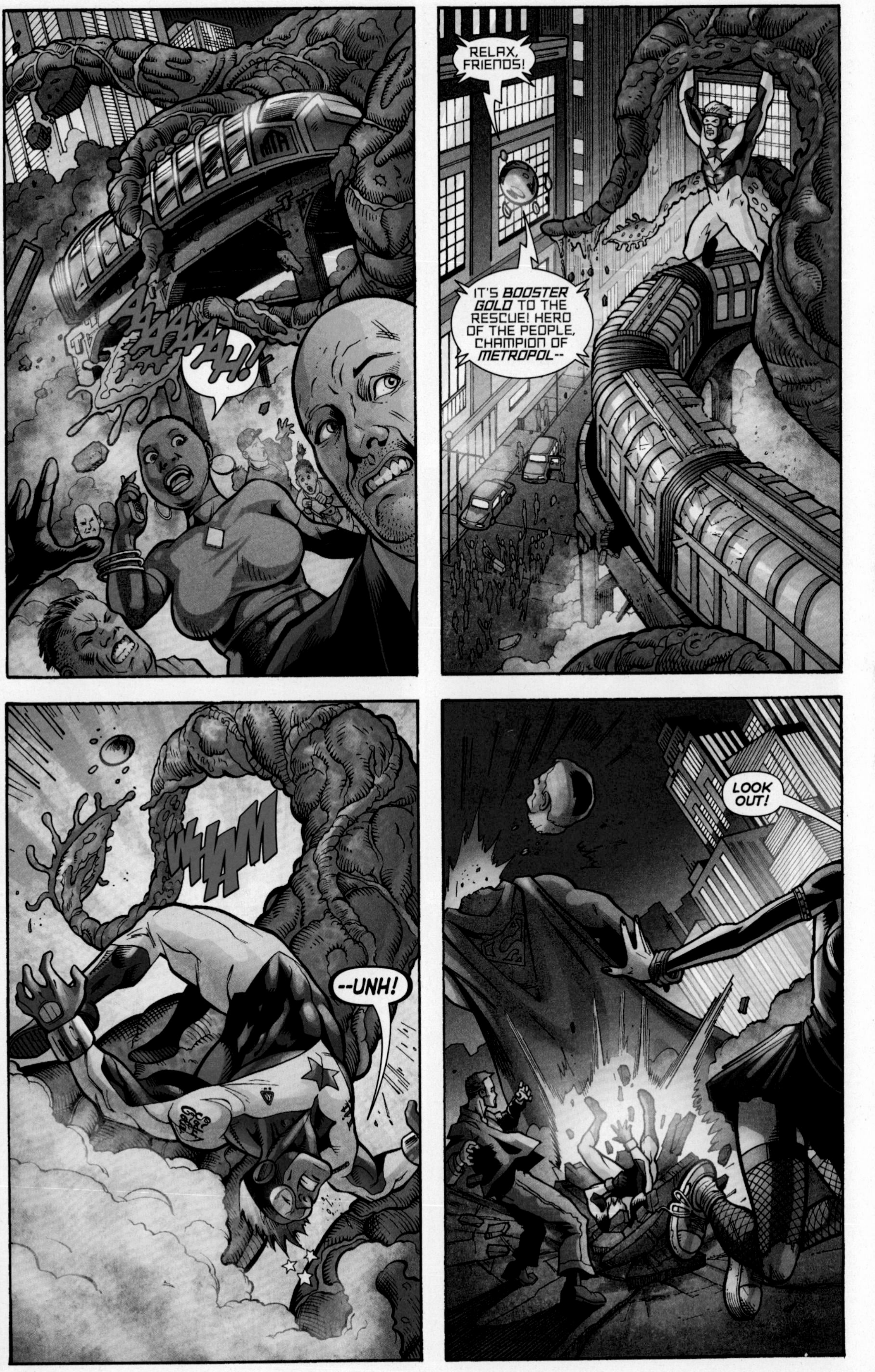
AAAAAAH!
RELAX, FRIENDS!
IT'S *BOOSTER GOLD* TO THE RESCUE! HERO OF THE PEOPLE, CHAMPION OF *METROPOL*--
WHAM
--UNH!
LOOK OUT!

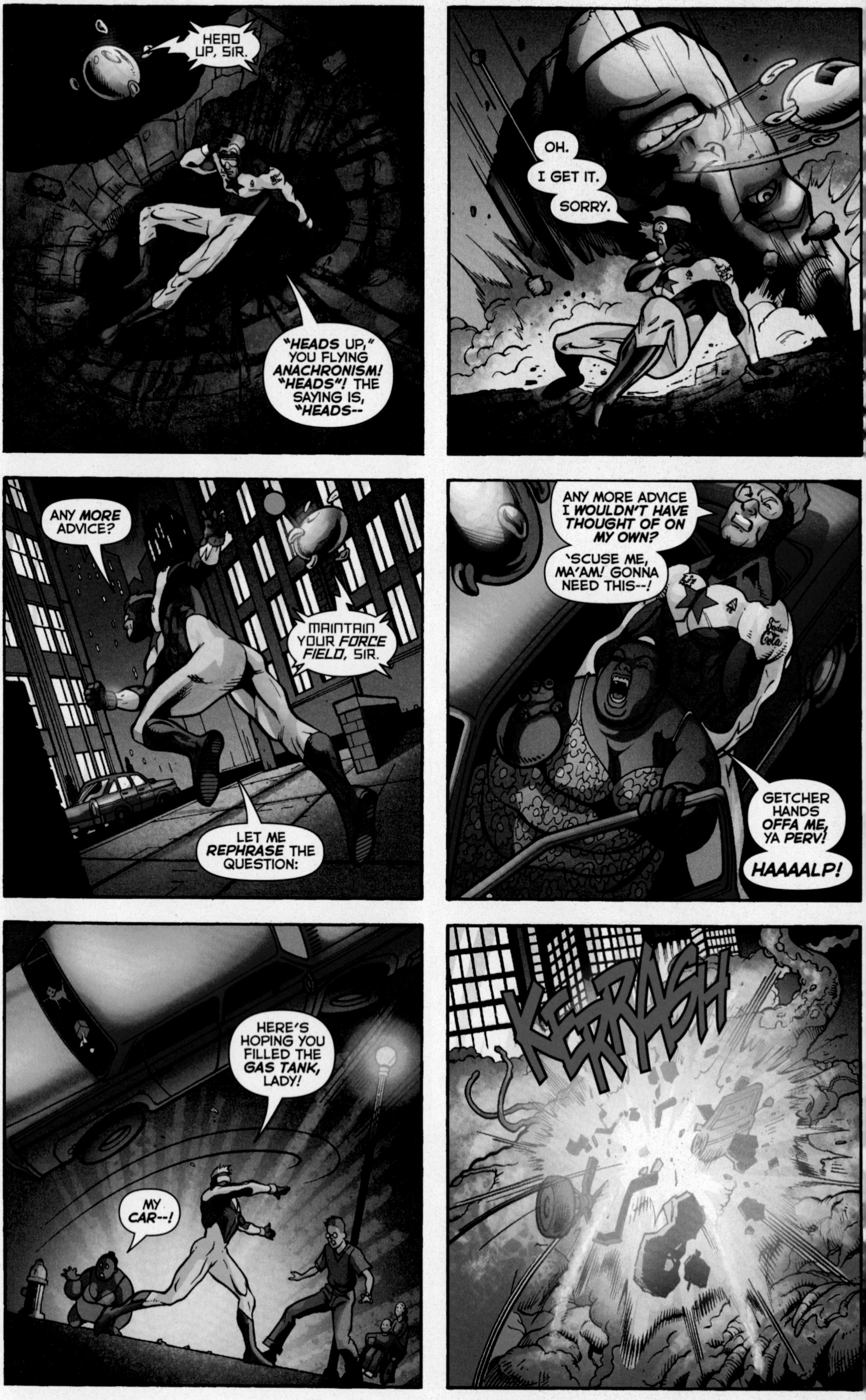
HEAD UP, SIR.
"HEADS UP," YOU FLYING ANACHRONISM! "HEADS"! THE SAYING IS, "HEADS--
OH.
I GET IT.
SORRY.
ANY MORE ADVICE?
MAINTAIN YOUR FORCE FIELD, SIR.
LET ME REPHRASE THE QUESTION:
ANY MORE ADVICE I WOULDN'T HAVE THOUGHT OF ON MY OWN?
'SCUSE ME, MA'AM! GONNA NEED THIS--!
GETCHER HANDS OFFA ME, YA PERV!
HAAAALP!
HERE'S HOPING YOU FILLED THE GAS TANK, LADY!
MY CAR--!
KERASH

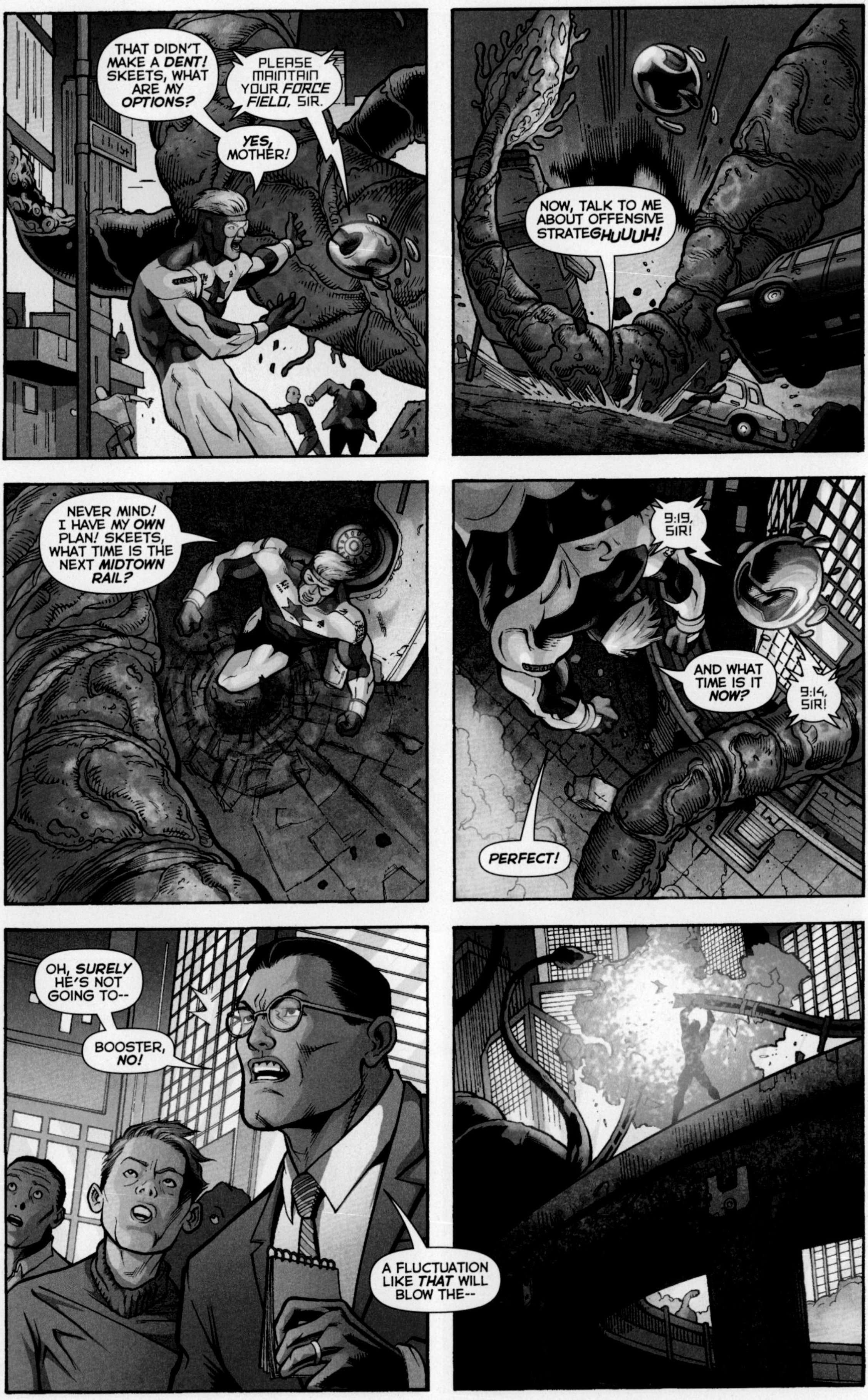
THAT DIDN'T MAKE A DENT! SKEETS, WHAT ARE MY OPTIONS?
PLEASE MAINTAIN YOUR FORCE FIELD, SIR.
YES, MOTHER!
NOW, TALK TO ME ABOUT OFFENSIVE STRATEGHUUUH!
NEVER MIND! I HAVE MY OWN PLAN! SKEETS, WHAT TIME IS THE NEXT MIDTOWN RAIL?
9:19, SIR!
AND WHAT TIME IS IT NOW?
9:14, SIR!
PERFECT!
OH, SURELY HE'S NOT GOING TO--
BOOSTER, NO!
A FLUCTUATION LIKE THAT WILL BLOW THE--

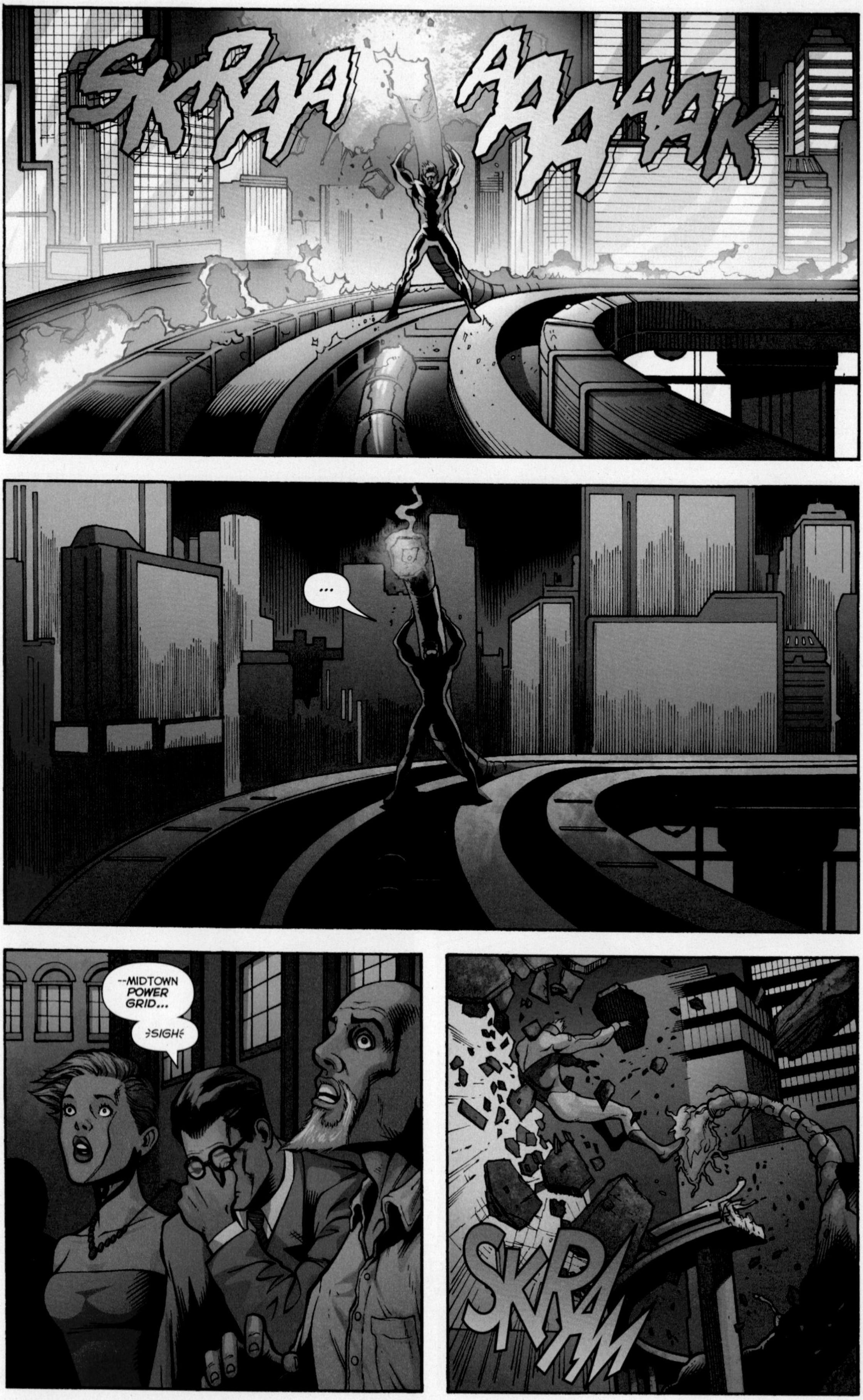
SKRAAAAAAK
...
--MIDTOWN POWER GRID...
SIGH
SKRAM

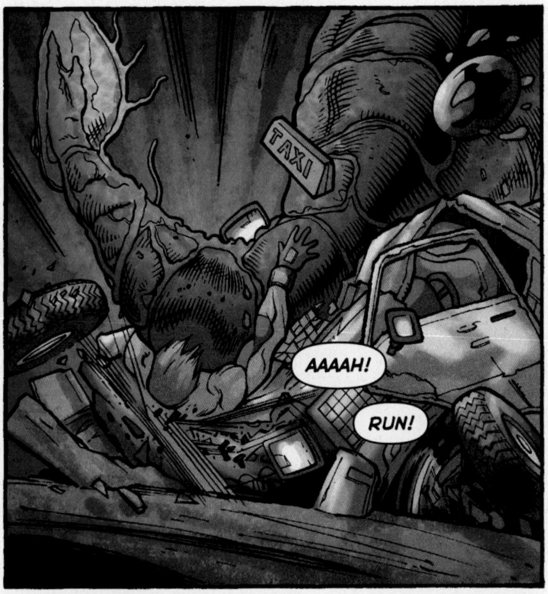
TAXI
AAAAH!
RUN!

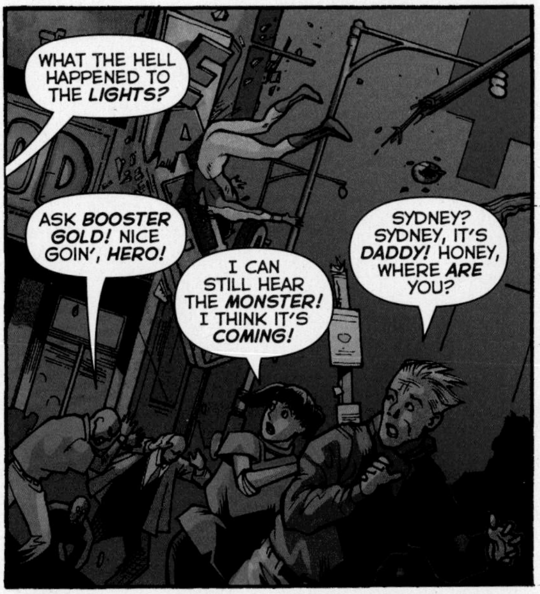
WHAT THE HELL HAPPENED TO THE LIGHTS?
ASK BOOSTER GOLD! NICE GOIN', HERO!
I CAN STILL HEAR THE MONSTER! I THINK IT'S COMING!
SYDNEY? SYDNEY, IT'S DADDY! HONEY, WHERE ARE YOU?

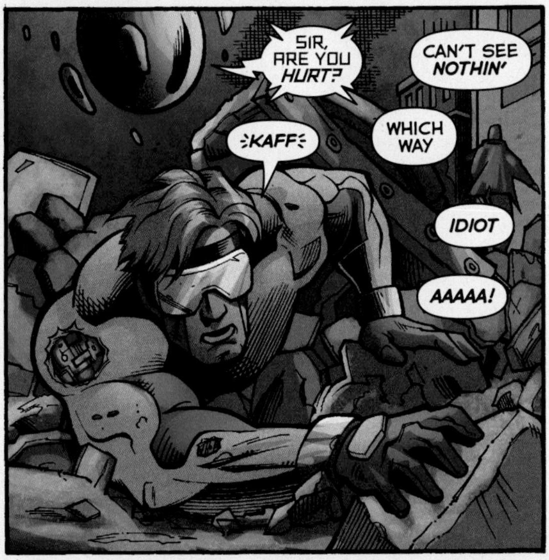
SIR, ARE YOU HURT?
CAN'T SEE NOTHIN'
KAFF
WHICH WAY
IDIOT
AAAAA!

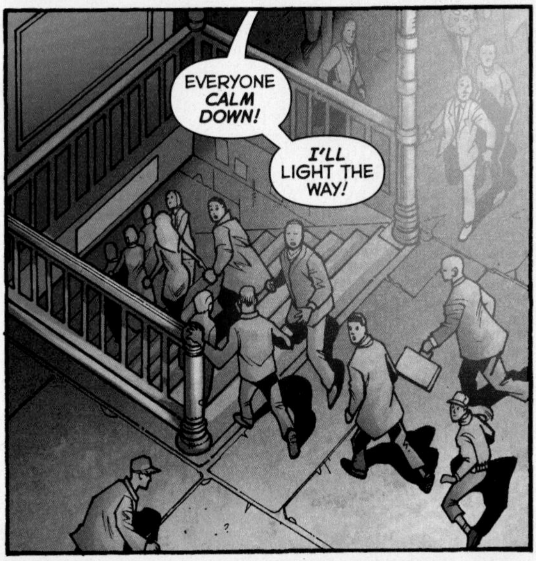
EVERYONE CALM DOWN!
I'LL LIGHT THE WAY!

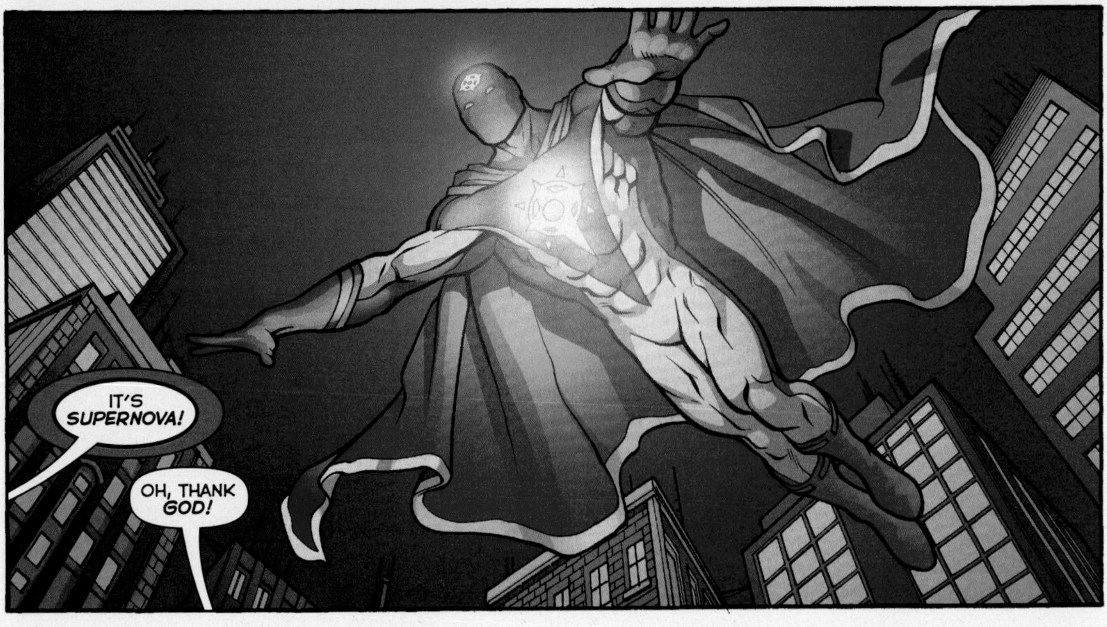
IT'S SUPERNOVA!
OH, THANK GOD!

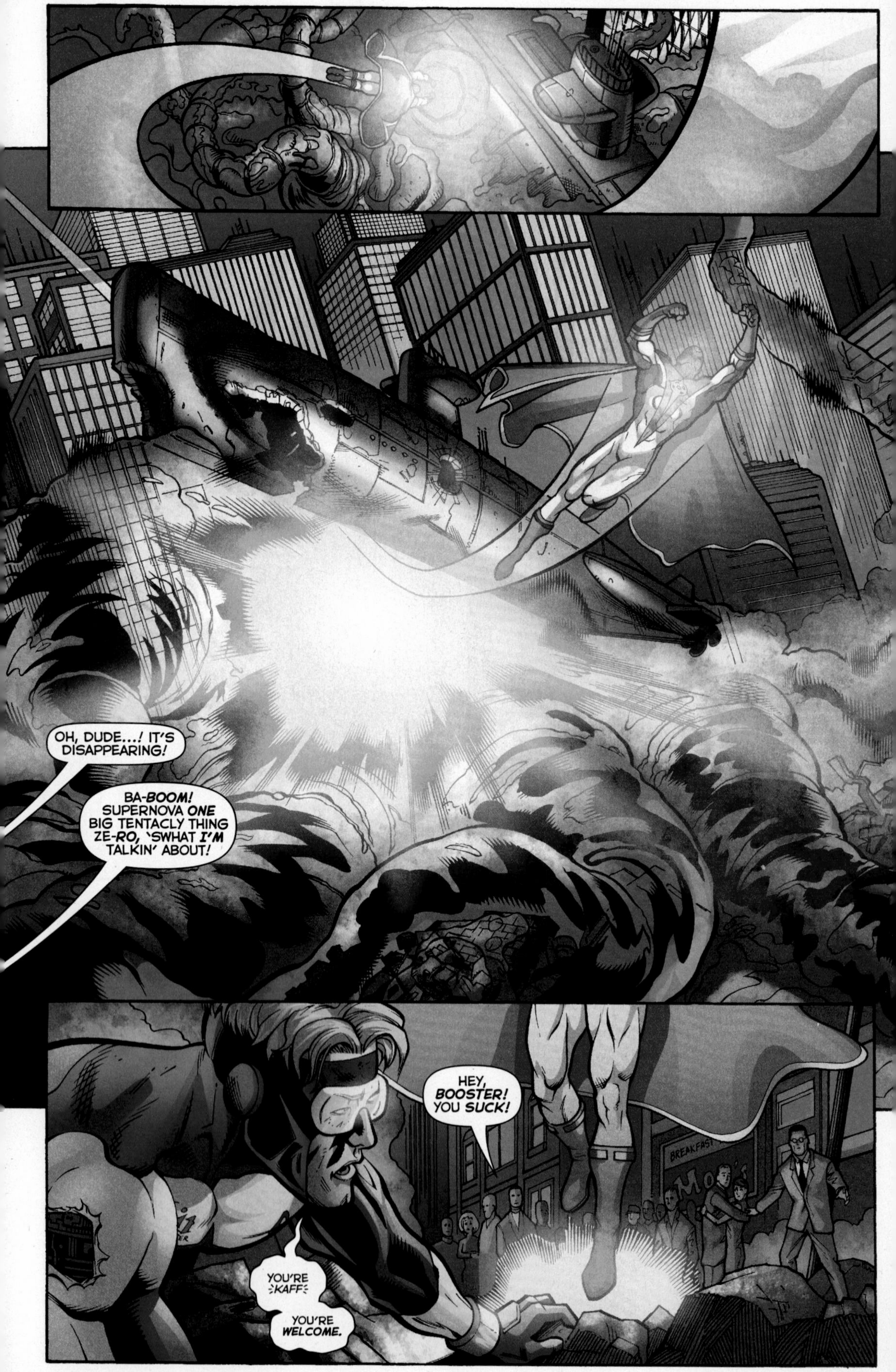
OH, DUDE...! IT'S DISAPPEARING!
BA-BOOM! SUPERNOVA ONE BIG TENTACLY THING ZE-RO, 'SWHAT I'M TALKIN' ABOUT!
HEY, BOOSTER! YOU SUCK!
YOU'RE KAFF
YOU'RE WELCOME.

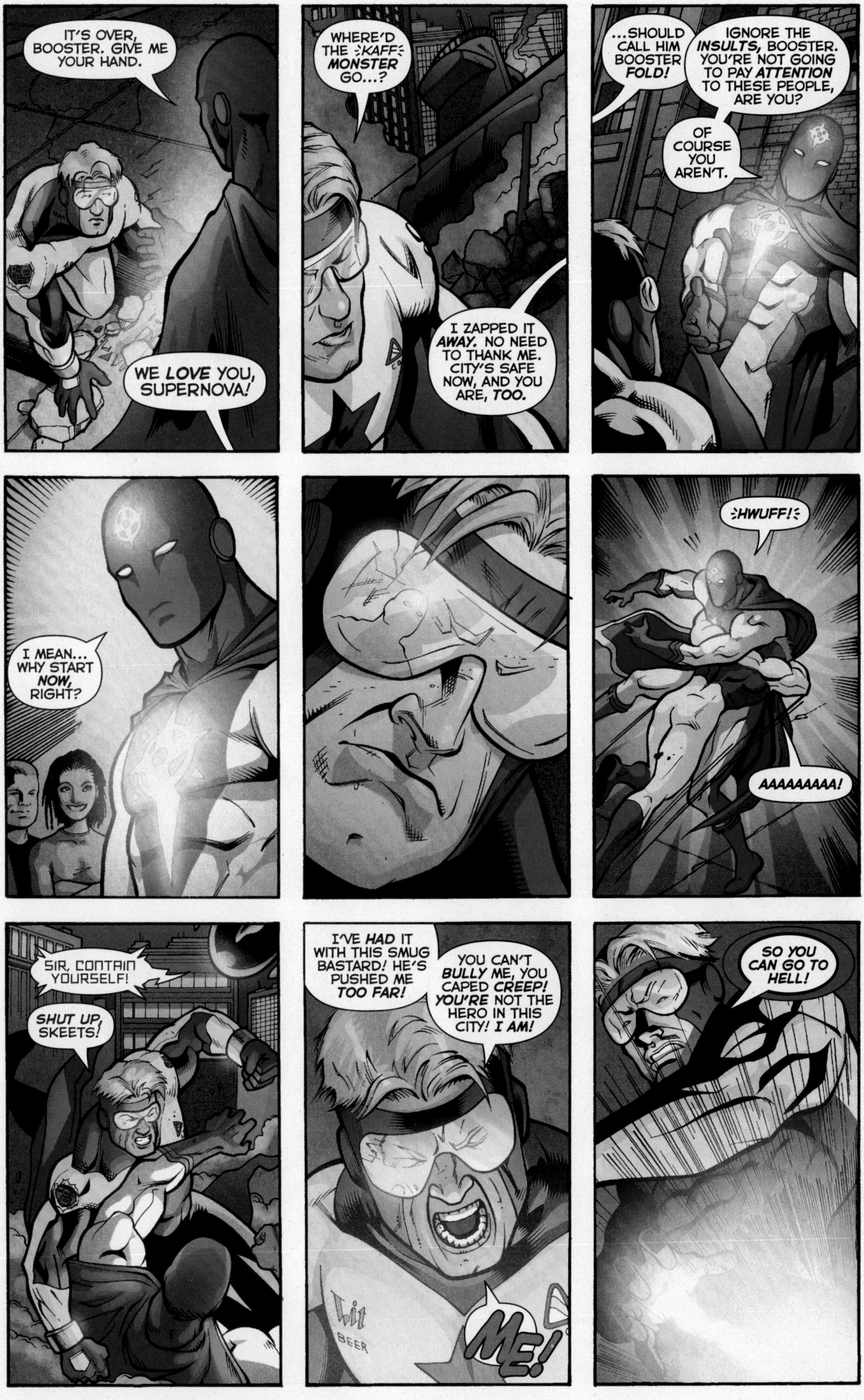
IT'S OVER, BOOSTER. GIVE ME YOUR HAND.
WE LOVE YOU, SUPERNOVA!
WHERE'D THE KAFF MONSTER GO...?
I ZAPPED IT AWAY. NO NEED TO THANK ME. CITY'S SAFE NOW, AND YOU ARE, TOO.
...SHOULD CALL HIM BOOSTER FOLD!
IGNORE THE INSULTS, BOOSTER. YOU'RE NOT GOING TO PAY ATTENTION TO THESE PEOPLE, ARE YOU?
OF COURSE YOU AREN'T.
I MEAN... WHY START NOW, RIGHT?
HWUFF!
AAAAAAAAA!
SIR, CONTAIN YOURSELF!
SHUT UP, SKEETS!
I'VE HAD IT WITH THIS SMUG BASTARD! HE'S PUSHED ME TOO FAR!
YOU CAN'T BULLY ME, YOU CAPED CREEP! YOU'RE NOT THE HERO IN THIS CITY! I AM!
ME!
SO YOU CAN GO TO HELL!

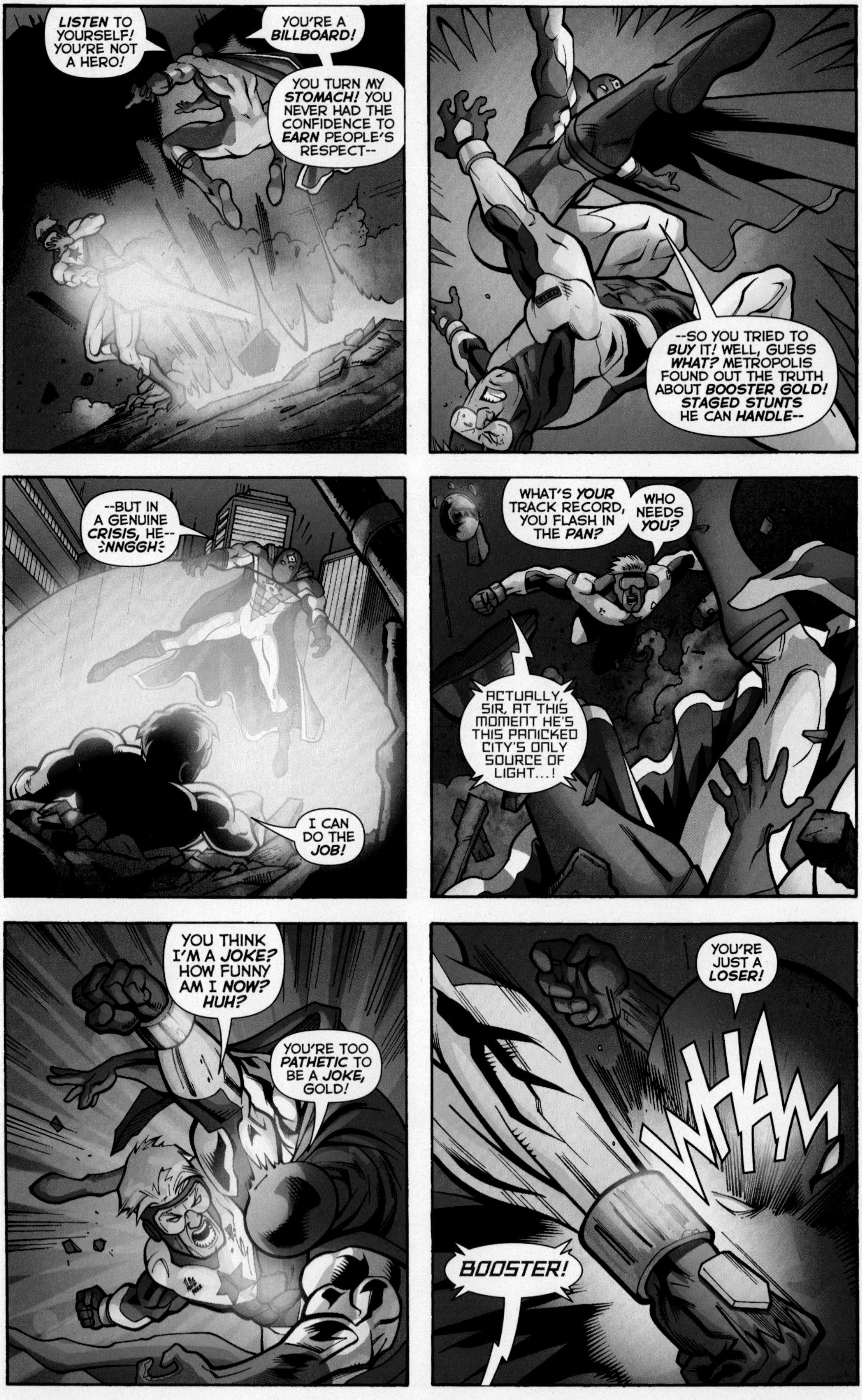
LISTEN TO YOURSELF! YOU'RE NOT A HERO!
YOU'RE A BILLBOARD!
YOU TURN MY STOMACH! YOU NEVER HAD THE CONFIDENCE TO EARN PEOPLE'S RESPECT--
--SO YOU TRIED TO BUY IT! WELL, GUESS WHAT? METROPOLIS FOUND OUT THE TRUTH ABOUT BOOSTER GOLD! STAGED STUNTS HE CAN HANDLE--
--BUT IN A GENUINE CRISIS, HE-- NNGGH
I CAN DO THE JOB!
WHAT'S YOUR TRACK RECORD, YOU FLASH IN THE PAN?
WHO NEEDS YOU?
ACTUALLY, SIR, AT THIS MOMENT HE'S THIS PANICKED CITY'S ONLY SOURCE OF LIGHT...!
YOU THINK I'M A JOKE? HOW FUNNY AM I NOW? HUH?
YOU'RE TOO PATHETIC TO BE A JOKE, GOLD!
YOU'RE JUST A LOSER!
WHAM
BOOSTER!

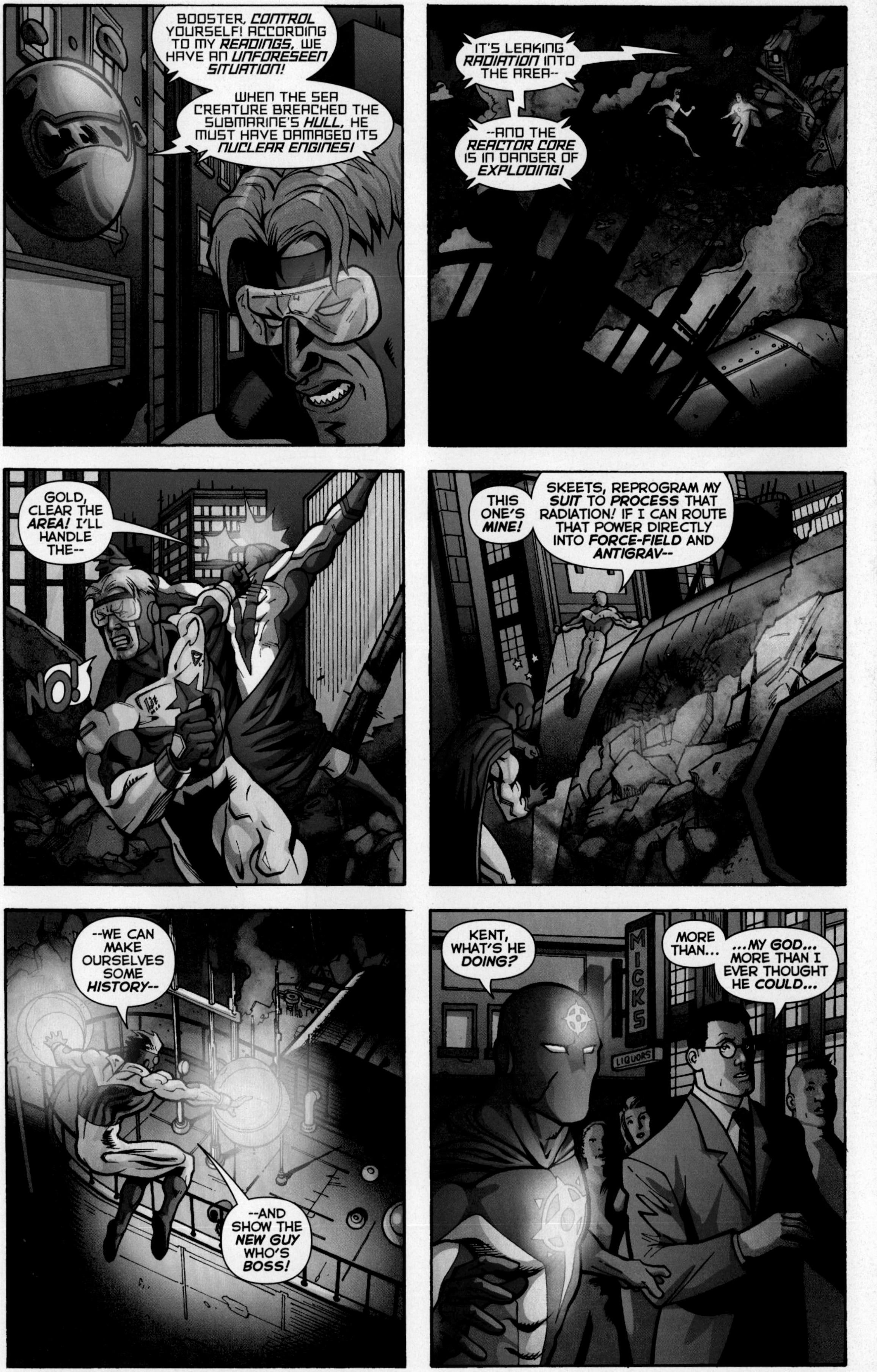
BOOSTER, CONTROL YOURSELF! ACCORDING TO MY READINGS, WE HAVE AN UNFORESEEN SITUATION!
WHEN THE SEA CREATURE BREACHED THE SUBMARINE'S HULL, HE MUST HAVE DAMAGED ITS NUCLEAR ENGINES!
IT'S LEAKING RADIATION INTO THE AREA--
--AND THE REACTOR CORE IS IN DANGER OF EXPLODING!
GOLD, CLEAR THE AREA! I'LL HANDLE THE--
NO!
THIS ONE'S MINE!
SKEETS, REPROGRAM MY SUIT TO PROCESS THAT RADIATION! IF I CAN ROUTE THAT POWER DIRECTLY INTO FORCE-FIELD AND ANTIGRAV--
--WE CAN MAKE OURSELVES SOME HISTORY--
--AND SHOW THE NEW GUY WHO'S BOSS!
KENT, WHAT'S HE DOING?
MICKS
LIQUORS
MORE THAN...
...MY GOD... MORE THAN I EVER THOUGHT HE COULD...

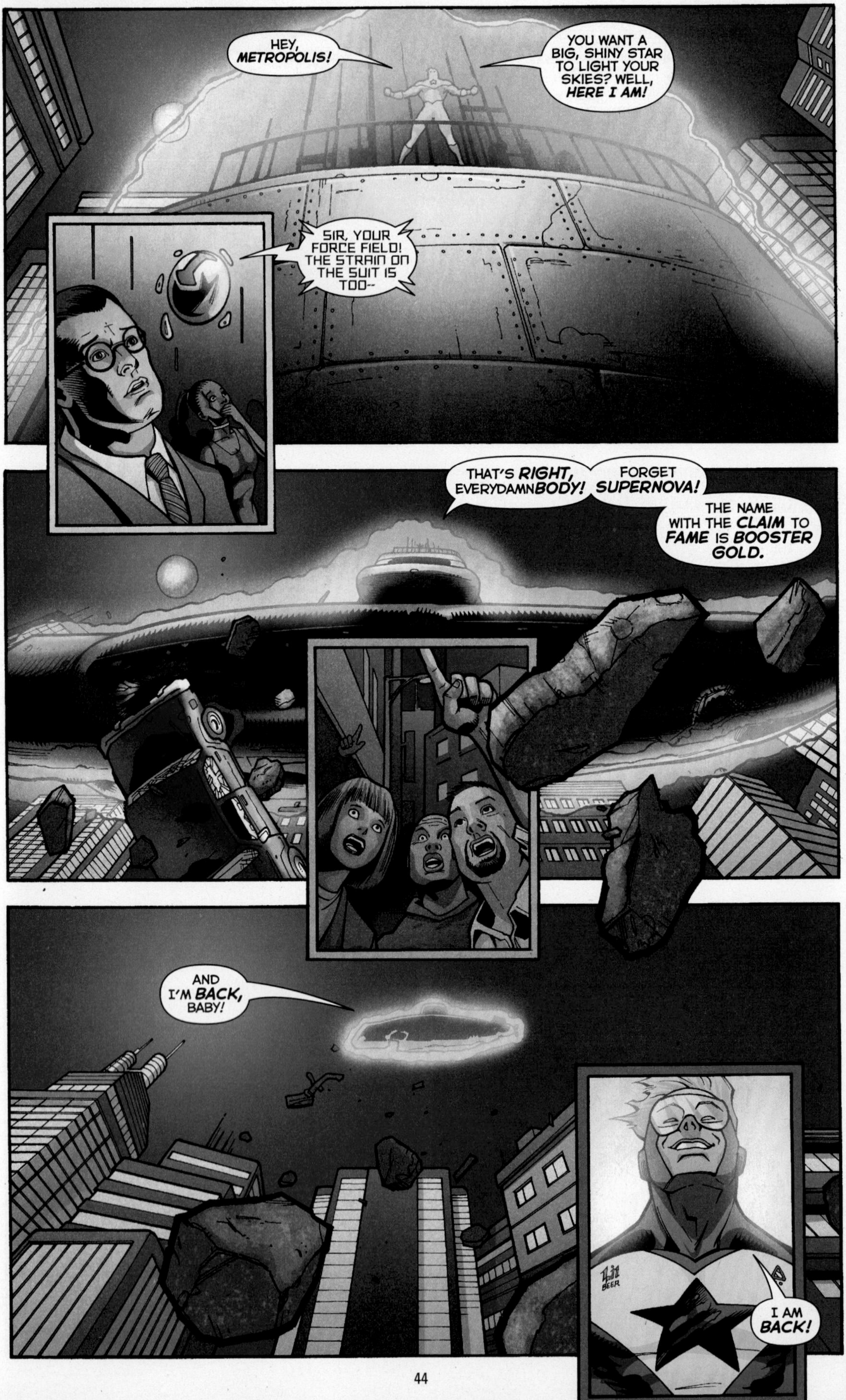
HEY, METROPOLIS!
YOU WANT A BIG, SHINY STAR TO LIGHT YOUR SKIES? WELL, HERE I AM!
SIR, YOUR FORCE FIELD! THE STRAIN ON THE SUIT IS TOO--
THAT'S RIGHT, EVERYDAMNBODY!
FORGET SUPERNOVA!
THE NAME WITH THE CLAIM TO FAME IS BOOSTER GOLD.
AND I'M BACK, BABY!
I AM BACK!

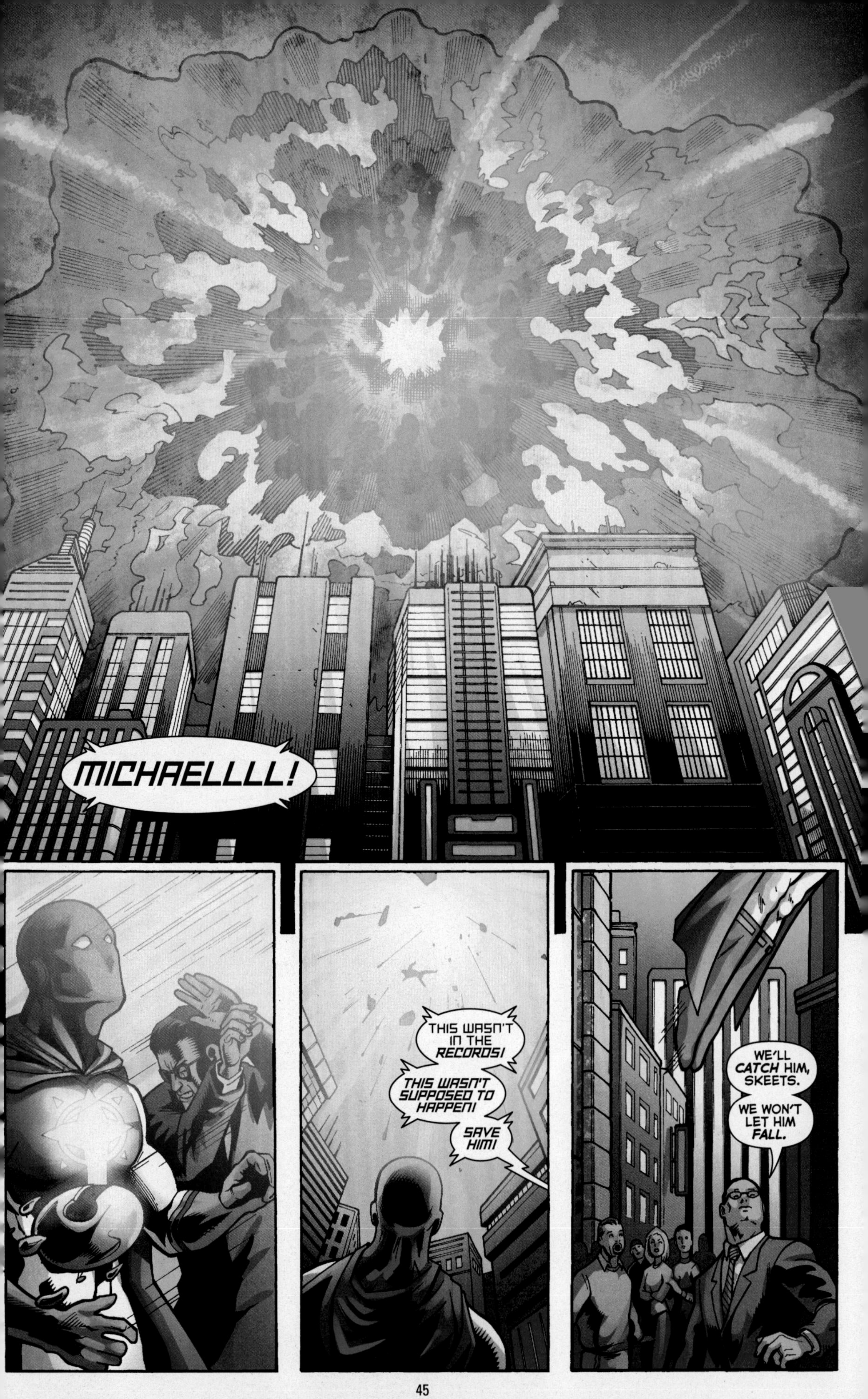
MICHAELLLL!
THIS WASN'T IN THE RECORDS!
THIS WASN'T SUPPOSED TO HAPPEN!
SAVE HIM!
WE'LL CATCH HIM, SKEETS.
WE WON'T LET HIM FALL.

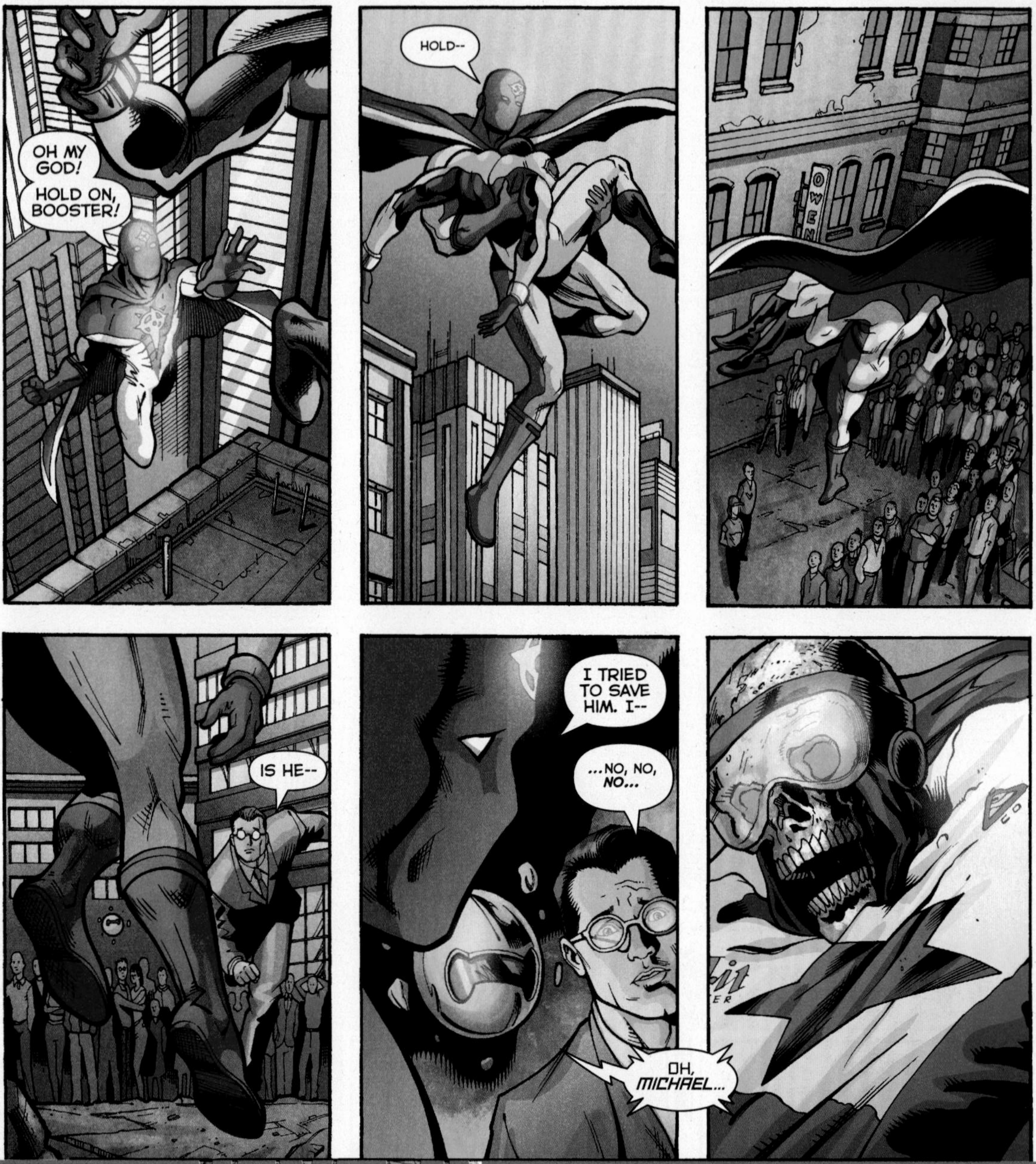
OH MY GOD!
HOLD ON, BOOSTER!
HOLD--
OWEN
IS HE--
I TRIED TO SAVE HIM. I--
...NO, NO, NO...
OH, MICHAEL...

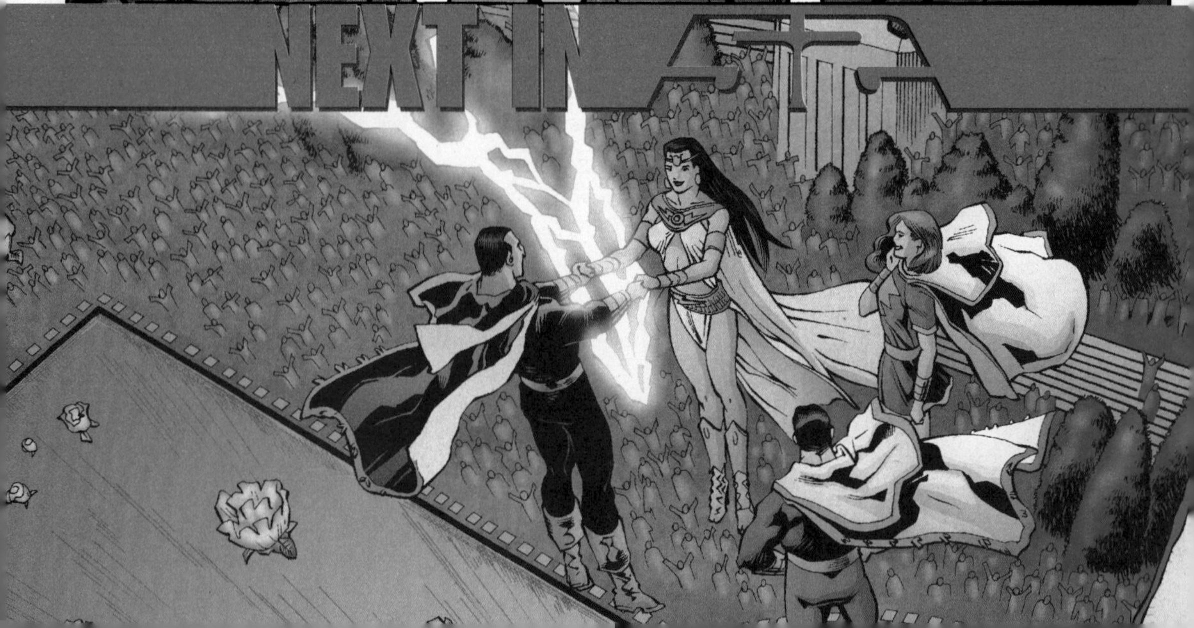
NEXT IN

MARK WAID

The notion of Booster and Supernova battling hammer and tong was Geoff's, but more important, so were the vicious taunts with which Supernova bludgeons Booster — which, once you read this story a second time and already know the secret of Supernova, (a) are especially disturbing and (b) may be clues to Geoff's own inner psyche that we needn't explore too deeply. (Everyone thinks that Rucka is the dark one. Dream on.)

We wrote at least six full drafts of the last four pages of this issue. If, at any point during the week of March 13, 2006, you had asked me what I did for a living, I would have told you, "I write 52 Week 15, pages seventeen through twenty."

That's because Comic Book Heaven has a revolving door. Characters return from the "dead" with such frequency that, by now, it's almost impossible to convince readers that we're serious when we pull the trigger. In at least three drafts, we showed Booster turned to dust by the nuclear blast — but with no actual body, no corpse, it came across as a trick. Keith suggested we show him literally bisected, with his torso landing on an awning and then his lower half splatting, a beat later, on a nearby fruit cart. As we quickly learned, there is no way to draw this that isn't laugh-out-loud funny. Eventually, and I want to remember it as Keith's idea, we ended up with Booster's desiccated skeleton. And yet, for some reason, impossibly, we still weren't certain readers would buy that Booster was really dead. Why? Aaaaugh. What was missing?

The voice of authority. As initially plotted, Supernova was the only other character on-site, but because his identity and motives were still secret, readers subconsciously wouldn't trust him when he said Booster was dead. Clark Kent, on the other hand, is an unimpeachable witness. Adding him to the scene closed the sale.

Until the very last rewrite, Booster's farewell speech in the end was radically, radically different. But I can't tell you why that was until we get around to discussing Week 37, so don't let me forget.

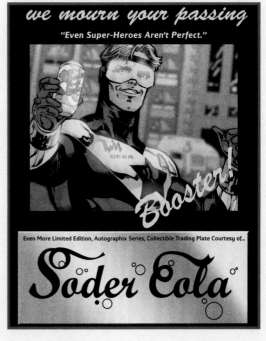

we mourn your passing

"Even Super-Heroes Aren't Perfect."

Booster!

Even More Limited Edition, Autographix Series, Collectible Trading Plate Courtesy of...

Soder Cola

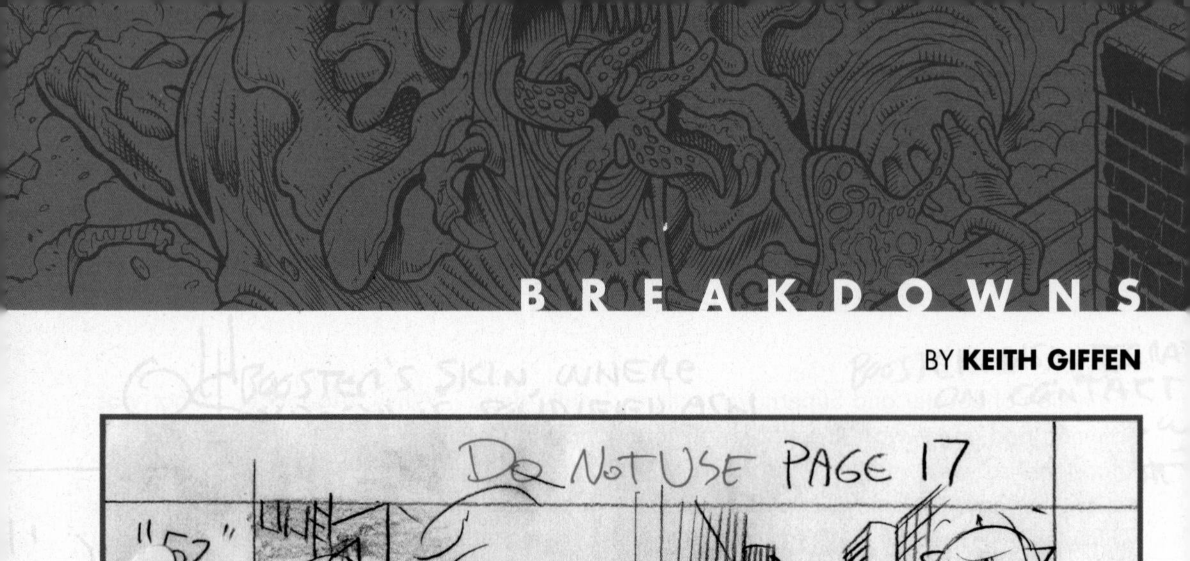

BREAKDOWNS

BY **KEITH GIFFEN**

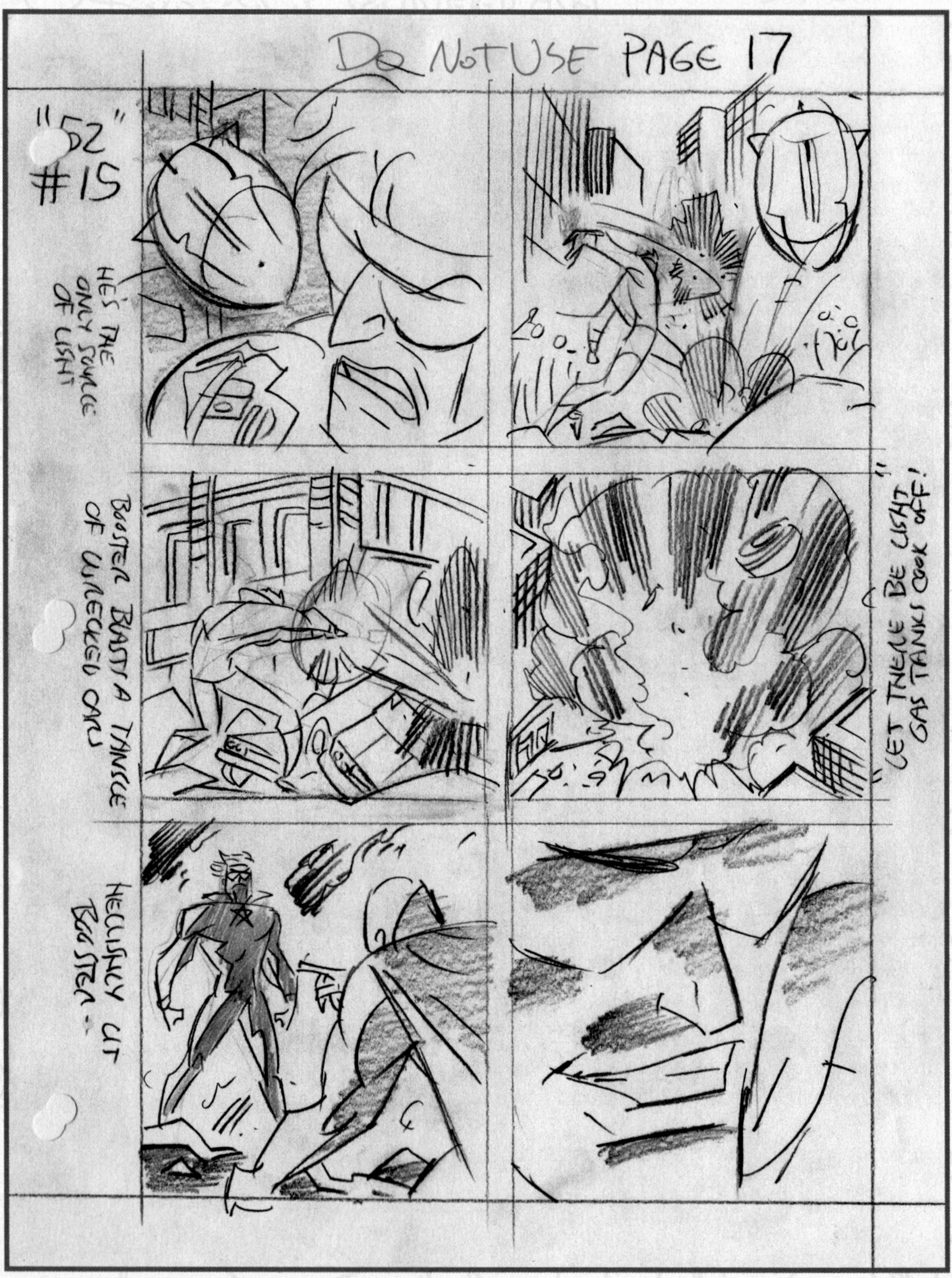
DO NOT USE PAGE 17
"52" #15
HE'S THE ONLY SOURCE OF LIGHT
BOOSTER BLASTS A TANGLE OF WRECKED CARS
"LET THERE BE LIGHT" GAS TANKS COOK OFF!
HELLISHLY LIT BOOSTER -

The original breakdowns for Week 15 show a very different ending. Compare with the printed version, starting on page 43.

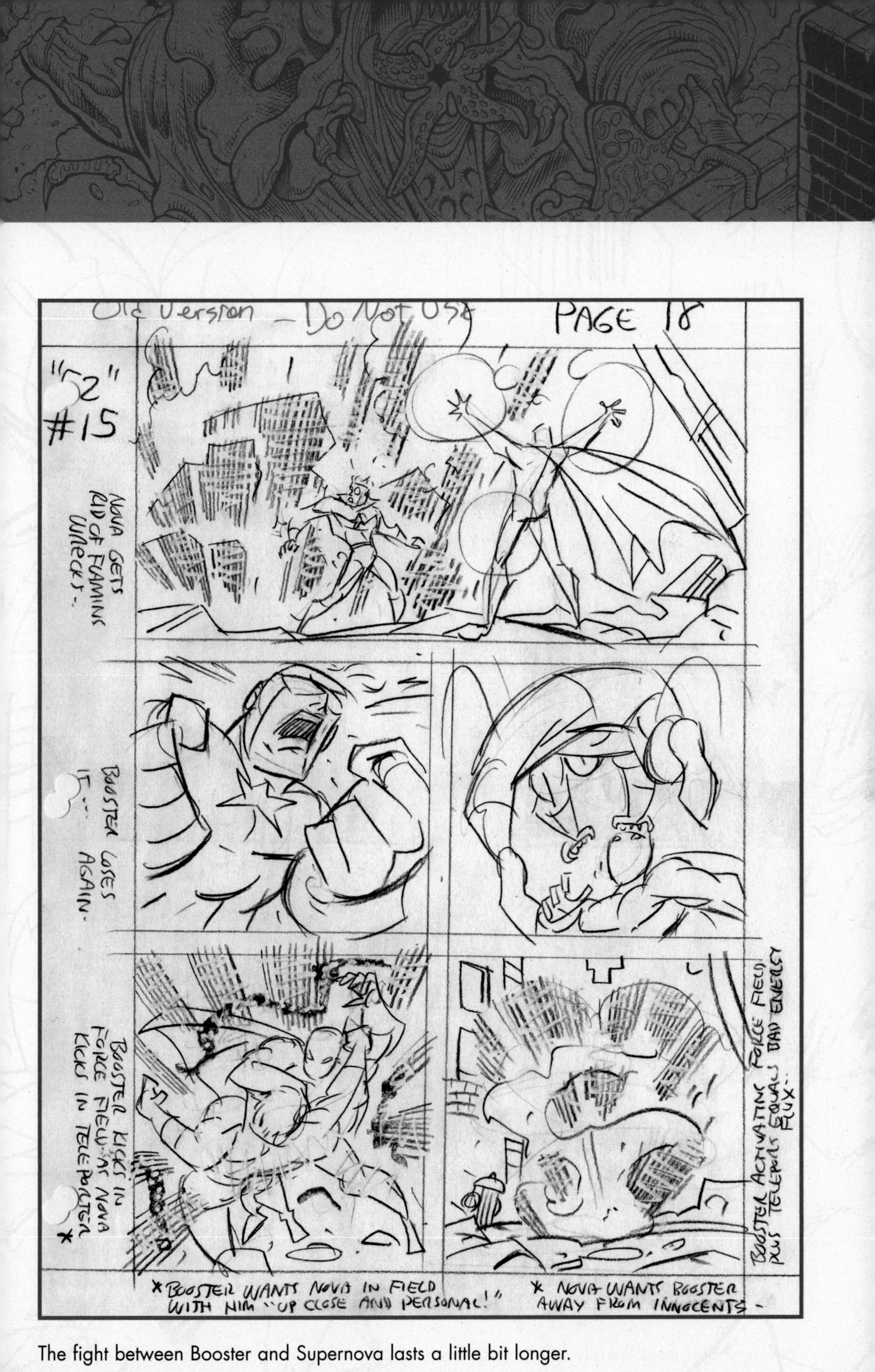
Old Version _ Do Not Use
PAGE 18
"52" #15
NOVA GETS RID OF FLAMING WRECKS.
BOOSTER LOSES IT... AGAIN.
BOOSTER KICKS IN FORCE FIELD AS NOVA KICKS IN TELEPORTER *
BOOSTER ACTIVATING FORCE FIELD PLUS TELEPORTS EQUALS BAD ENERGY FLUX.
* BOOSTER WANTS NOVA IN FIELD WITH HIM "UP CLOSE AND PERSONAL!"
* NOVA WANTS BOOSTER AWAY FROM INNOCENTS.

The fight between Booster and Supernova lasts a little bit longer.

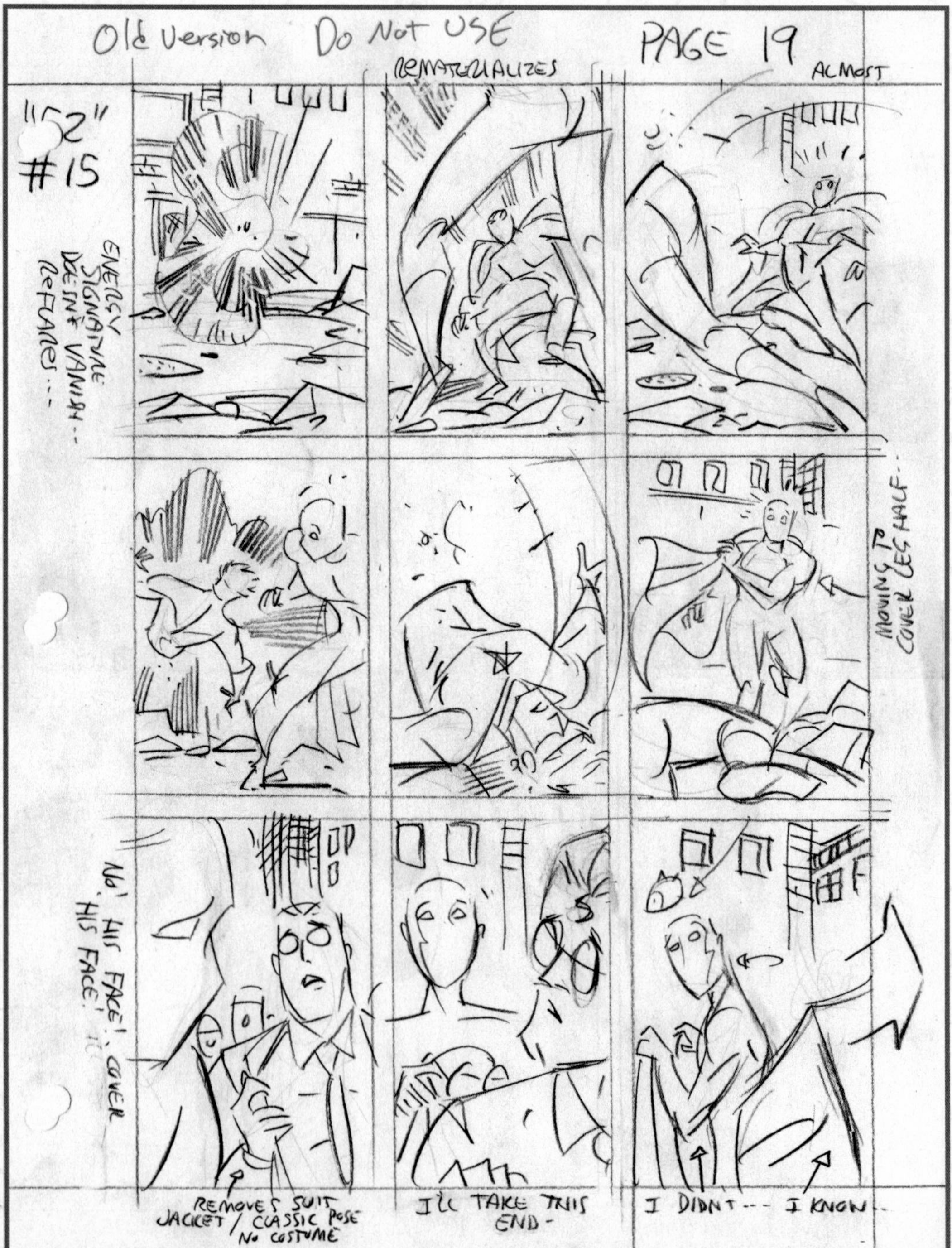

Old Version Do Not USE
PAGE 19
"52"
#15
REMATERIALIZES
ALMOST
MOVING TO COVER LEG HALF...
NO! HIS FACE! COVER HIS FACE!
REMOVES SUIT JACKET / CLASSIC POSE NO COSTUME
I'LL TAKE THIS END-
I DIDNT--- I KNOW-

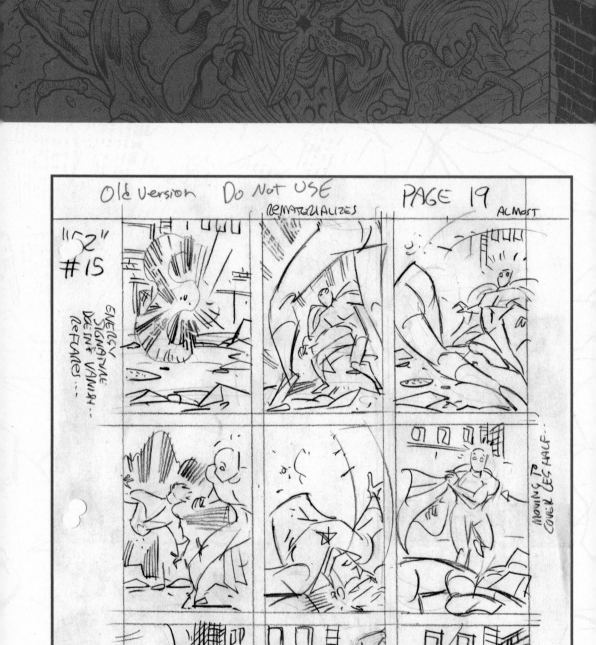

Whoops! Booster is literally split in two.

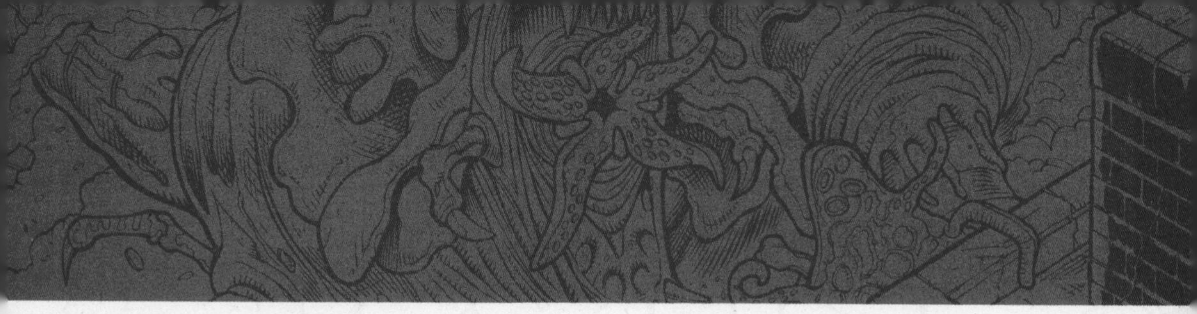

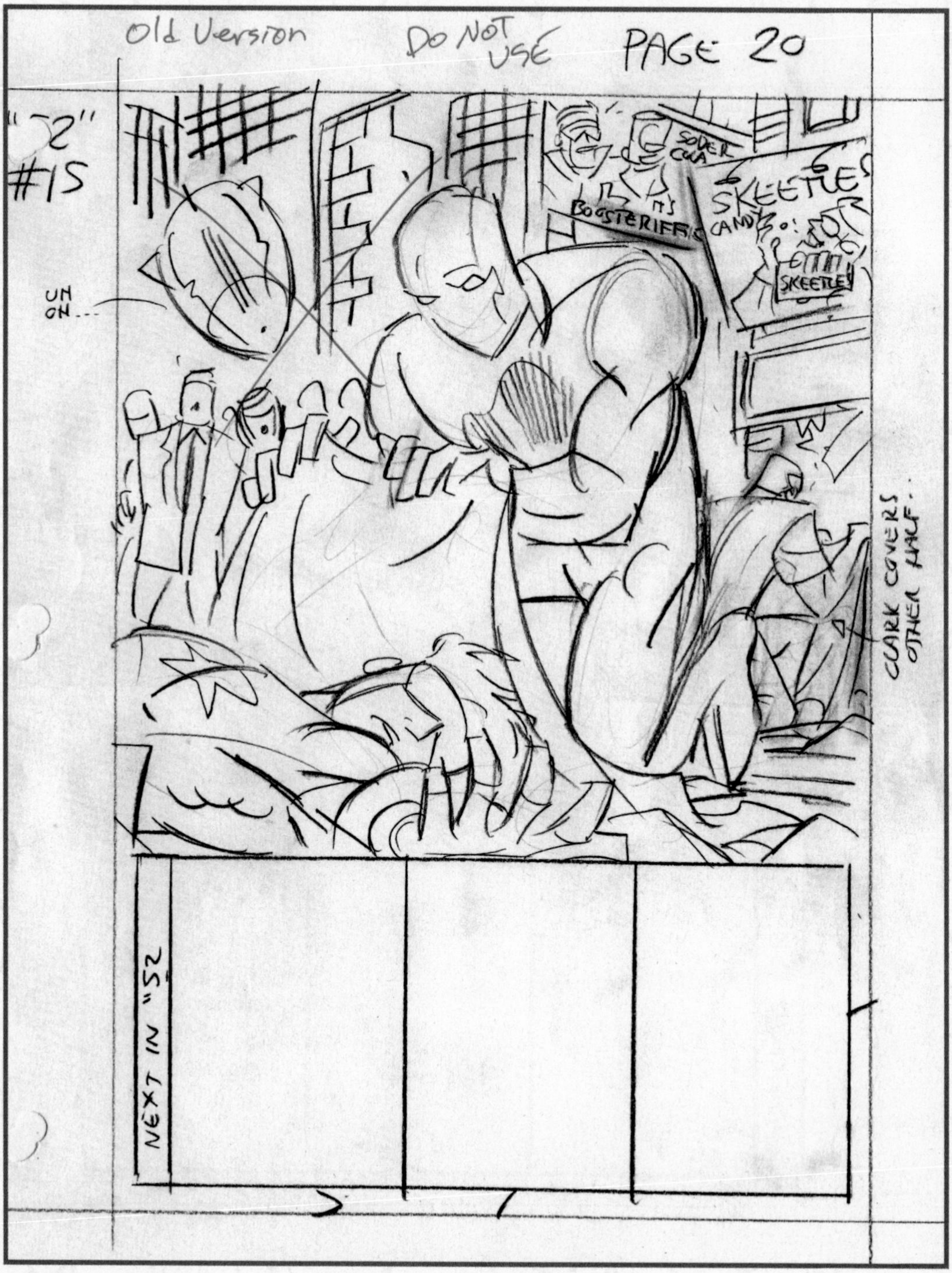

Old Version
DO NOT USE
PAGE 20
"52" #15
UH OH...
IT'S BOOSTERIFFIC
SKEETLES CANDY
SKEETLES
CLARK COVERS OTHER HALF.
NEXT IN "52

Superman and Clark Kent respectfully cover Booster's remains.

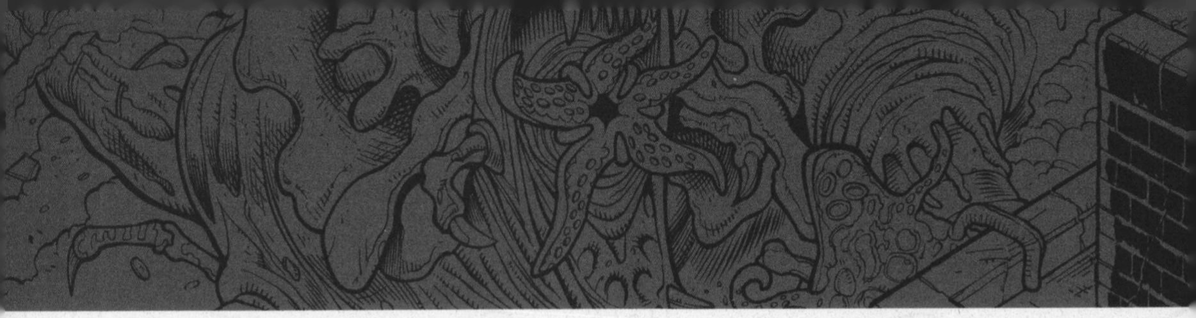

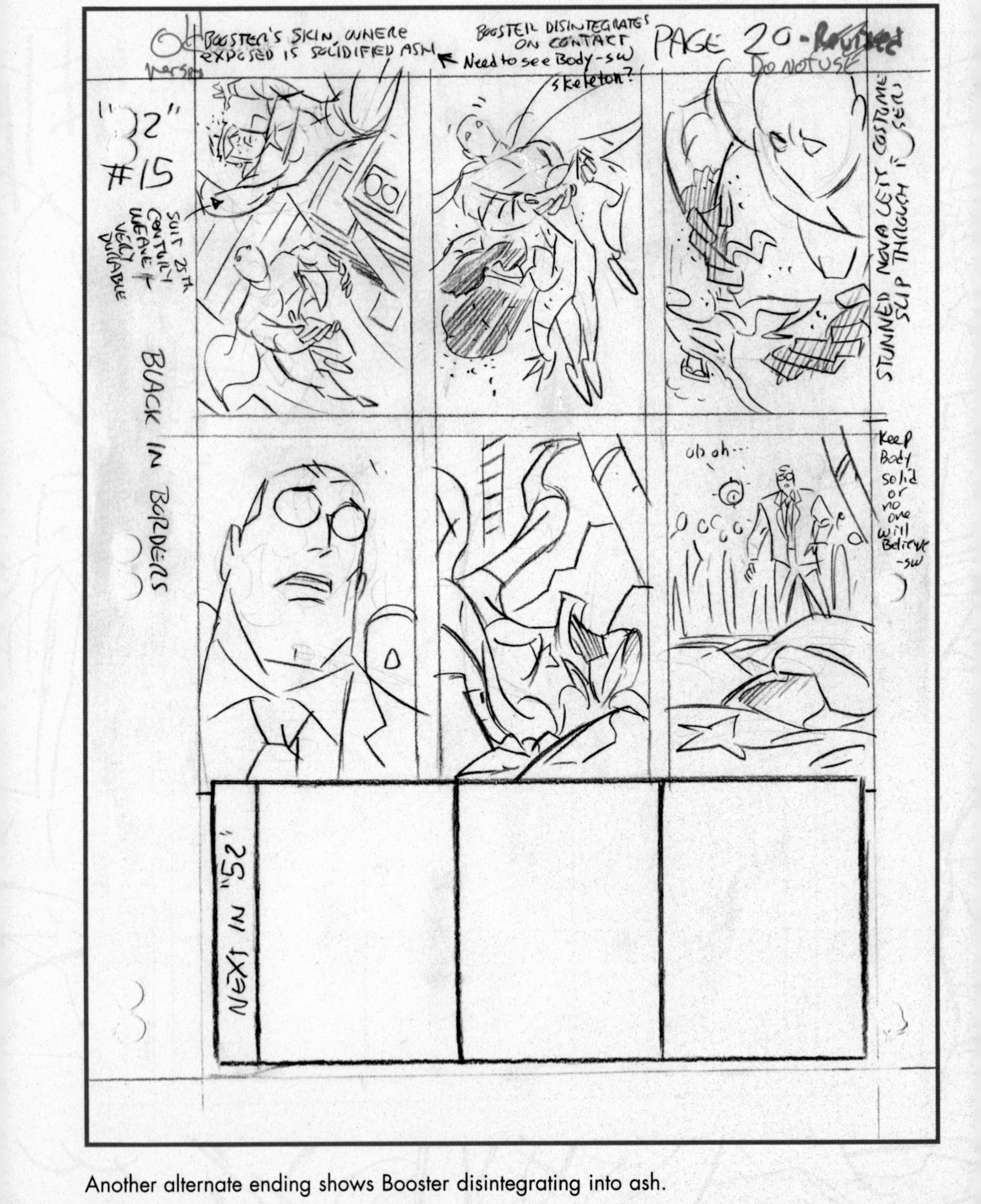

BOOSTER'S SKIN, WHERE EXPOSED IS SOLIDIFIED ASH
BOOSTER DISINTEGRATES ON CONTACT
Need to see Body-sw
skeleton?
PAGE 20
Do NOT USE
"52" #15
SUIT 25th CENTURY WEAVE — VERY DURABLE
BLACK IN BORDERS
STUNNED NOVA LET COSTUME SLIP THROUGH (SEEN)
Keep Body solid or no one will Believe -sw
oh oh…
NEXT IN "52"

Another alternate ending shows Booster disintegrating into ash.

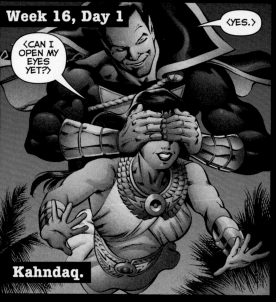

⟨CAN I OPEN MY EYES YET?⟩

⟨YES.⟩

Kahndaq.

⟨IT'S *BEAUTIFUL.* WHAT IS THIS?⟩

⟨THE CHILDREN PLANTED IT. FOR *YOU.*⟩

⟨FOR GIVING THEM THEIR *LIVES* BACK.⟩

⟨YOU AND I DID THAT TOGETHER, ADAM.⟩

⟨BUT I WOULD NOT HAVE DONE ANY OF THIS WITHOUT YOU, *ISIS.*⟩

⟨*EVERYTHING* WOULD BE DIFFERENT WITHOUT YOU.⟩

⟨DID YOU SAVE THAT PART FOR ME, CHILDERN? WHAT WOULD YOU LIKE ME TO GROW THERE? JASMINE AND LYCHNIS, PERHAPS?⟩

⟨NO, ISIS! THIS LAND IS TO REMAIN UNTOUCHED!⟩

⟨THE GREAT BLACK ADAM HAS TOLD US ABOUT YOUR BROTHER-- *AMON.* HE IS LIKE US, BUT HE IS STILL NOT FREE.⟩

⟨WHEN HE COMES HOME, THAT LAND WILL BE PLANTED AND THE GREAT GARDENS WILL BE COMPLETE.⟩

⟨WE PRAY FOR HIS RETURN, OH SWEET ISIS.⟩

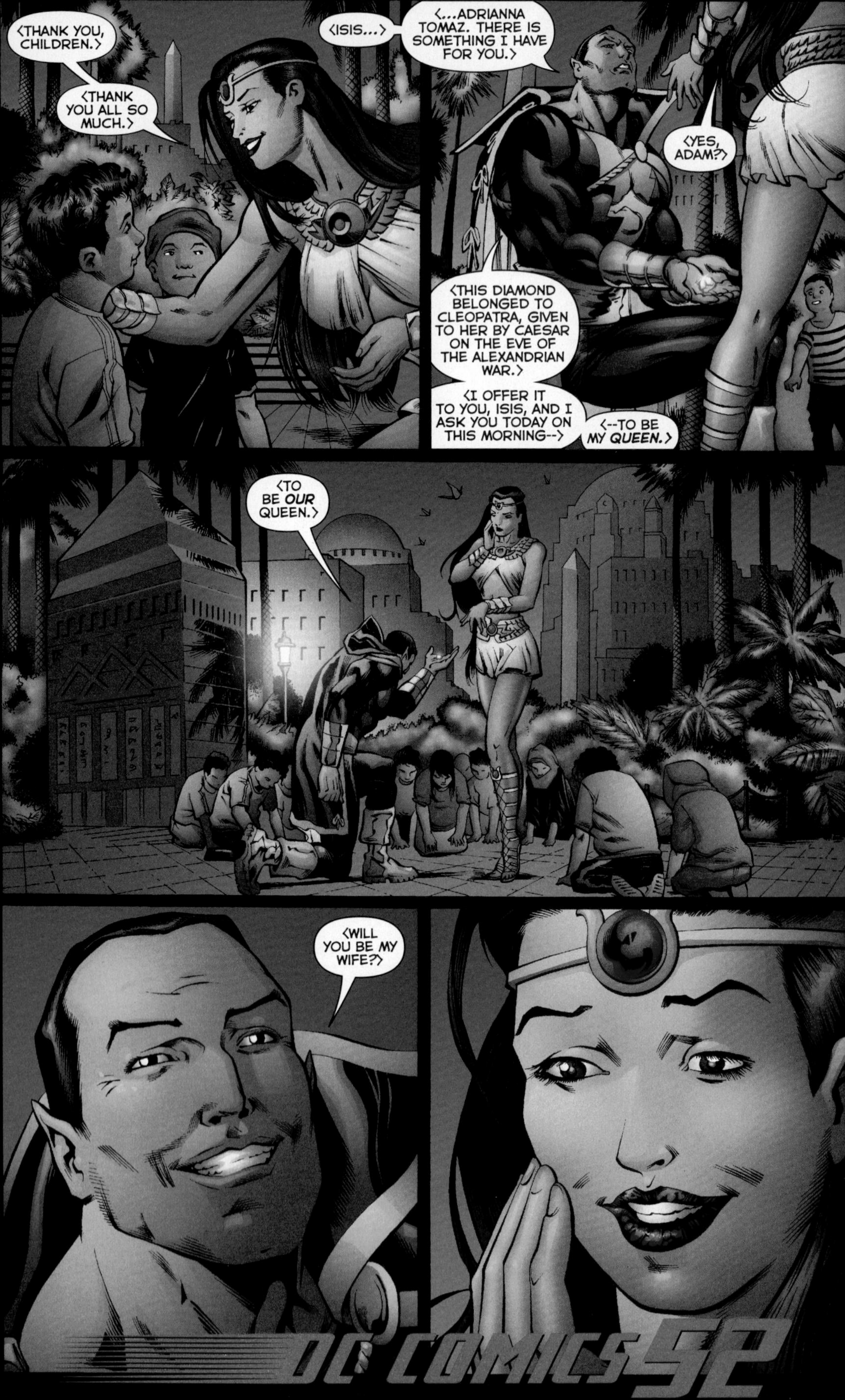
<THANK YOU, CHILDREN.>
<THANK YOU ALL SO MUCH.>
<ISIS...>
<...ADRIANNA TOMAZ. THERE IS SOMETHING I HAVE FOR YOU.>
<YES, ADAM?>
<THIS DIAMOND BELONGED TO CLEOPATRA, GIVEN TO HER BY CAESAR ON THE EVE OF THE ALEXANDRIAN WAR.>
<I OFFER IT TO YOU, ISIS, AND I ASK YOU TODAY ON THIS MORNING-->
<--TO BE MY QUEEN.>
<TO BE OUR QUEEN.>
<WILL YOU BE MY WIFE?>
DC COMICS 52

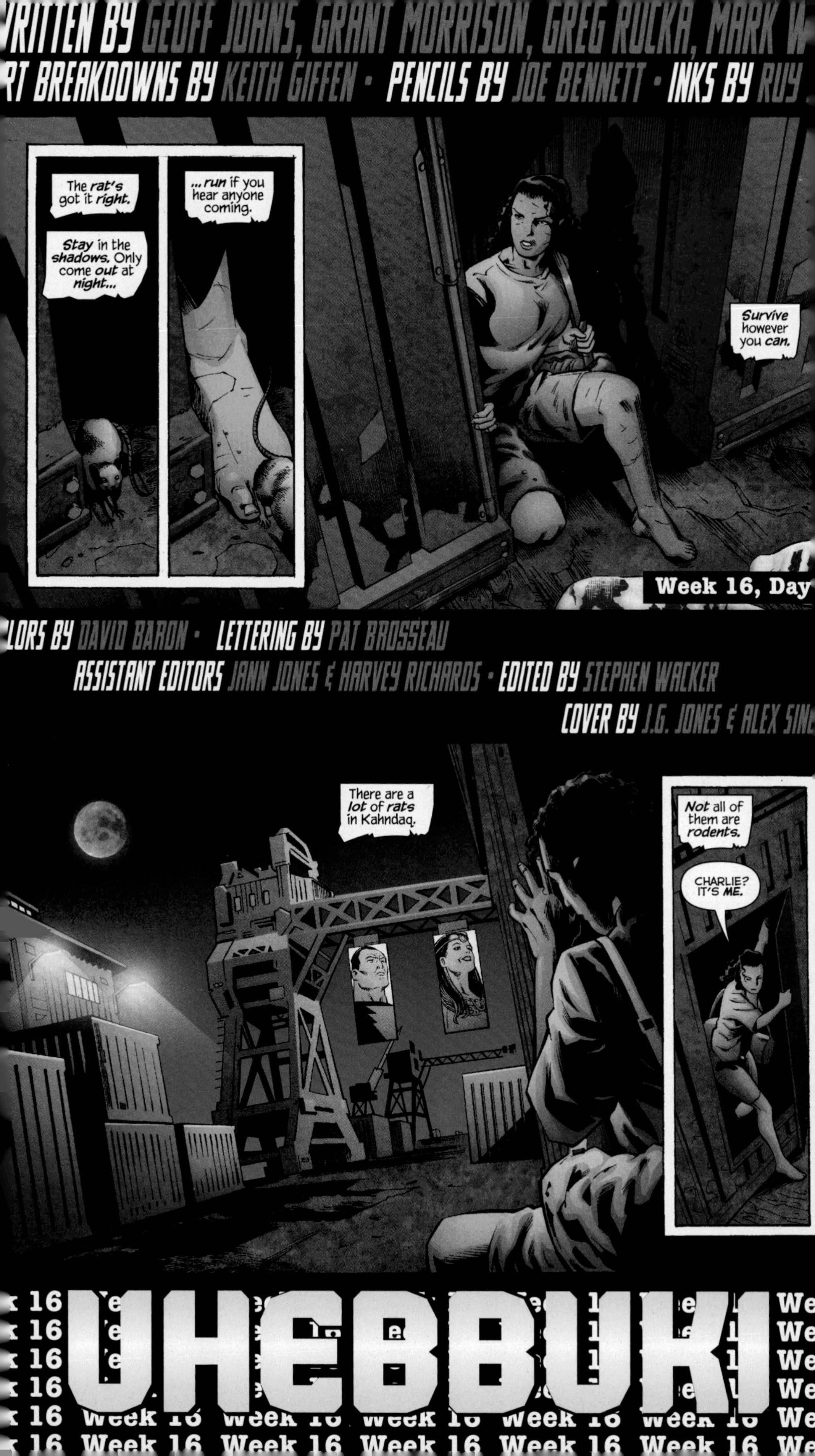

WRITTEN BY GEOFF JOHNS, GRANT MORRISON, GREG RUCKA, MARK W
RT BREAKDOWNS BY KEITH GIFFEN · PENCILS BY JOE BENNETT · INKS BY RUY
The rat's got it right.
Stay in the shadows. Only come out at night...
...run if you hear anyone coming.
Survive however you can.
Week 16, Day
LORS BY DAVID BARON · LETTERING BY PAT BROSSEAU
ASSISTANT EDITORS JANN JONES & HARVEY RICHARDS · EDITED BY STEPHEN WACKER
COVER BY J.G. JONES & ALEX SIN
There are a lot of rats in Kahndaq.
Not all of them are rodents.
CHARLIE? IT'S ME.
Week 16

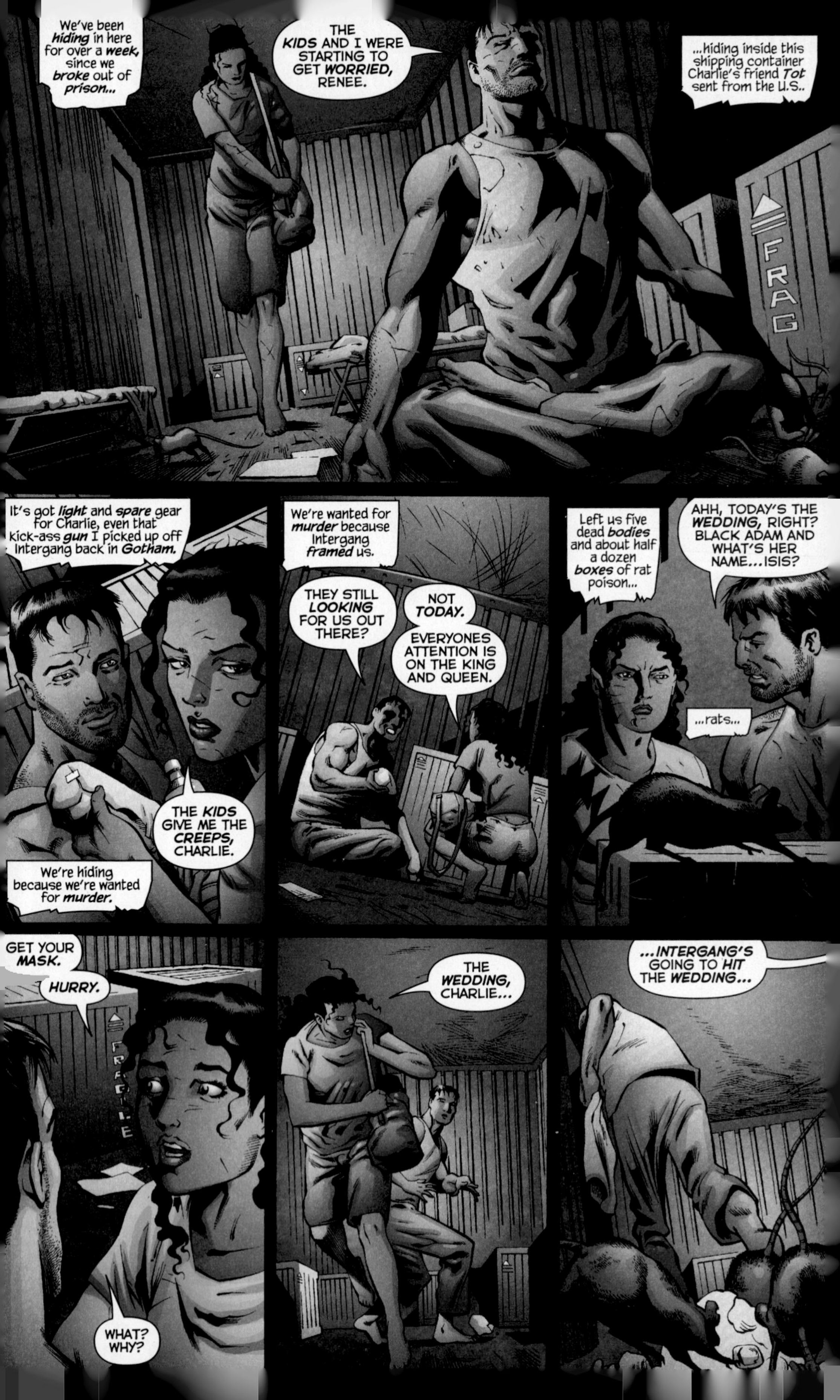
We've been hiding in here for over a week, since we broke out of prison...
THE KIDS AND I WERE STARTING TO GET WORRIED, RENEE.
...hiding inside this shipping container Charlie's friend Tot sent from the U.S..
FRAG
It's got light and spare gear for Charlie, even that kick-ass gun I picked up off Intergang back in Gotham.
THE KIDS GIVE ME THE CREEPS, CHARLIE.
We're hiding because we're wanted for murder.
We're wanted for murder because Intergang framed us.
THEY STILL LOOKING FOR US OUT THERE?
NOT TODAY.
EVERYONES ATTENTION IS ON THE KING AND QUEEN.
Left us five dead bodies and about half a dozen boxes of rat poison...
AHH, TODAY'S THE WEDDING, RIGHT? BLACK ADAM AND WHAT'S HER NAME...ISIS?
...rats...
GET YOUR MASK.
HURRY.
FRAGILE
WHAT? WHY?
THE WEDDING, CHARLIE...
...INTERGANG'S GOING TO HIT THE WEDDING...

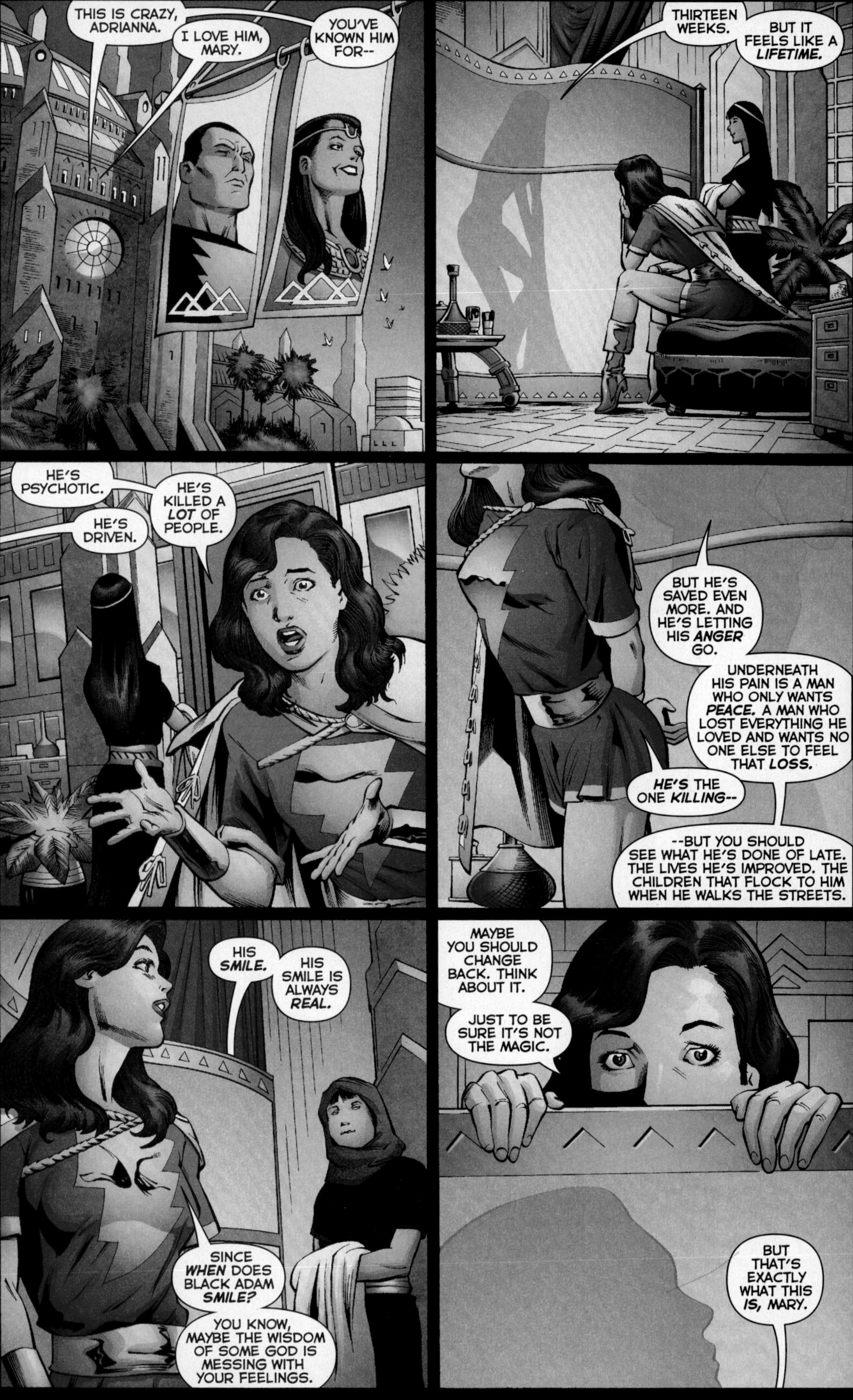
THIS IS CRAZY, ADRIANNA.
I LOVE HIM, MARY.
YOU'VE KNOWN HIM FOR--
THIRTEEN WEEKS.
BUT IT FEELS LIKE A *LIFETIME.*
HE'S PSYCHOTIC.
HE'S DRIVEN.
HE'S KILLED A *LOT* OF PEOPLE.
BUT HE'S SAVED EVEN MORE. AND HE'S LETTING HIS *ANGER* GO.
UNDERNEATH HIS PAIN IS A MAN WHO ONLY WANTS *PEACE.* A MAN WHO LOST EVERYTHING HE LOVED AND WANTS NO ONE ELSE TO FEEL THAT *LOSS.*
HE'S THE ONE *KILLING*--
--BUT YOU SHOULD SEE WHAT HE'S DONE OF LATE. THE LIVES HE'S IMPROVED. THE CHILDREN THAT FLOCK TO HIM WHEN HE WALKS THE STREETS.
HIS *SMILE.*
HIS SMILE IS ALWAYS *REAL.*
SINCE *WHEN* DOES BLACK ADAM *SMILE?*
YOU KNOW, MAYBE THE WISDOM OF SOME GOD IS MESSING WITH YOUR FEELINGS.
MAYBE YOU SHOULD CHANGE BACK. THINK ABOUT IT.
JUST TO BE SURE IT'S NOT THE MAGIC.
BUT THAT'S EXACTLY WHAT THIS *IS,* MARY.

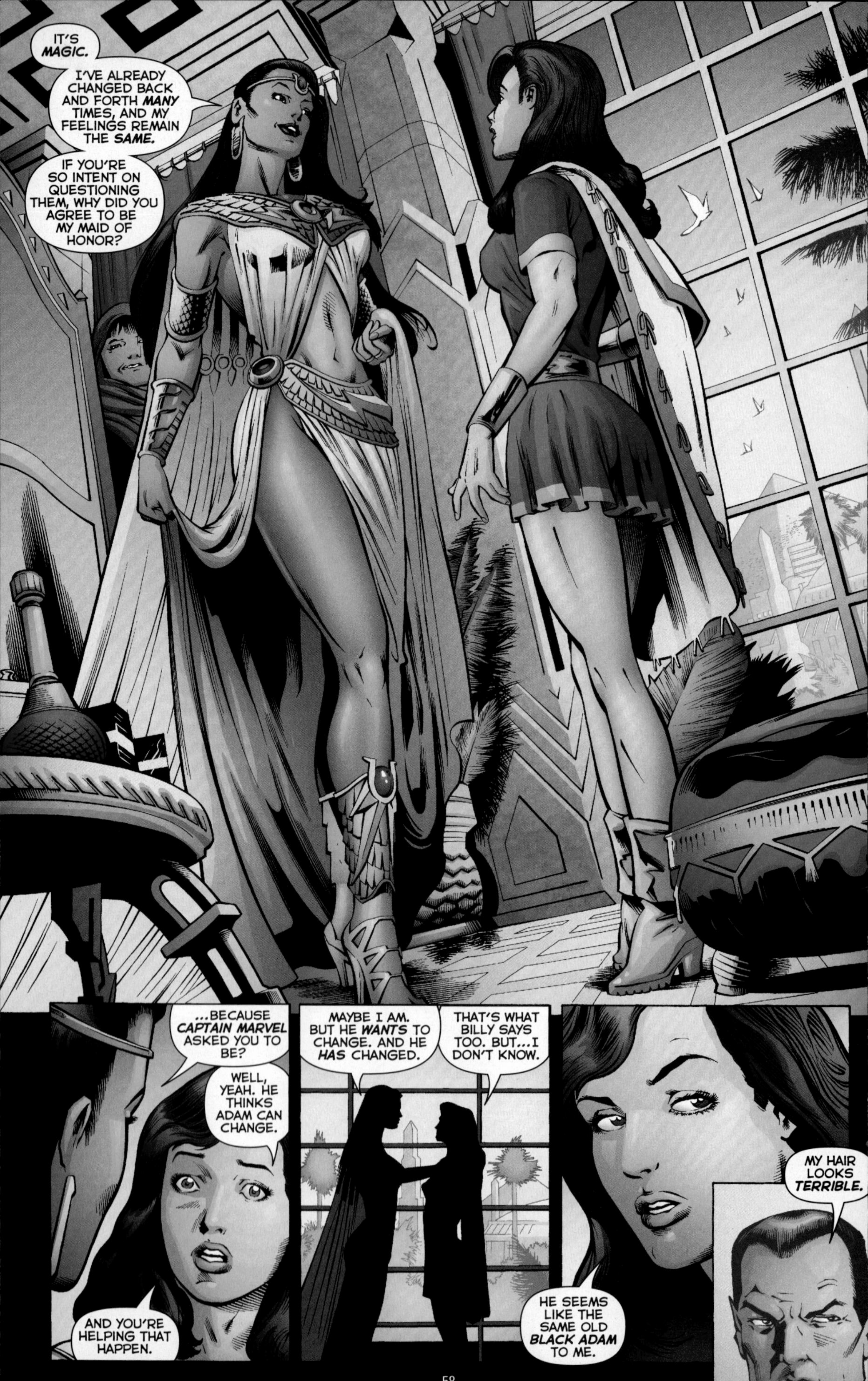
IT'S MAGIC.
I'VE ALREADY CHANGED BACK AND FORTH MANY TIMES, AND MY FEELINGS REMAIN THE SAME.
IF YOU'RE SO INTENT ON QUESTIONING THEM, WHY DID YOU AGREE TO BE MY MAID OF HONOR?
...BECAUSE CAPTAIN MARVEL ASKED YOU TO BE?
WELL, YEAH. HE THINKS ADAM CAN CHANGE.
AND YOU'RE HELPING THAT HAPPEN.
MAYBE I AM. BUT HE WANTS TO CHANGE. AND HE HAS CHANGED.
THAT'S WHAT BILLY SAYS TOO. BUT...I DON'T KNOW.
HE SEEMS LIKE THE SAME OLD BLACK ADAM TO ME.
MY HAIR LOOKS TERRIBLE.

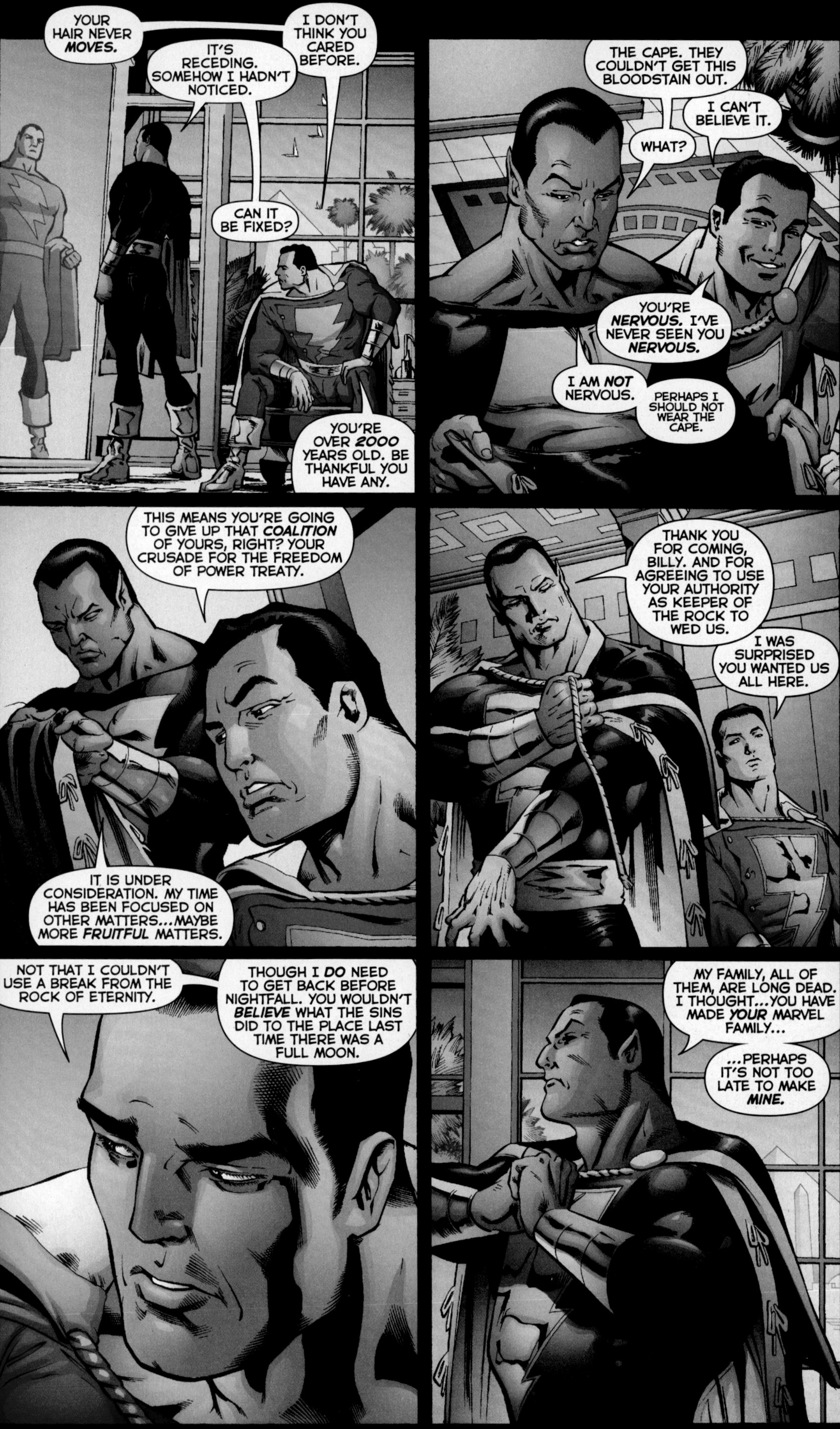
YOUR HAIR NEVER MOVES.
IT'S RECEDING. SOMEHOW I HADN'T NOTICED.
I DON'T THINK YOU CARED BEFORE.
CAN IT BE FIXED?
YOU'RE OVER 2000 YEARS OLD. BE THANKFUL YOU HAVE ANY.
THE CAPE. THEY COULDN'T GET THIS BLOODSTAIN OUT.
WHAT?
I CAN'T BELIEVE IT.
YOU'RE NERVOUS. I'VE NEVER SEEN YOU NERVOUS.
I AM NOT NERVOUS.
PERHAPS I SHOULD NOT WEAR THE CAPE.
THIS MEANS YOU'RE GOING TO GIVE UP THAT COALITION OF YOURS, RIGHT? YOUR CRUSADE FOR THE FREEDOM OF POWER TREATY.
IT IS UNDER CONSIDERATION. MY TIME HAS BEEN FOCUSED ON OTHER MATTERS...MAYBE MORE FRUITFUL MATTERS.
THANK YOU FOR COMING, BILLY. AND FOR AGREEING TO USE YOUR AUTHORITY AS KEEPER OF THE ROCK TO WED US.
I WAS SURPRISED YOU WANTED US ALL HERE.
NOT THAT I COULDN'T USE A BREAK FROM THE ROCK OF ETERNITY.
THOUGH I DO NEED TO GET BACK BEFORE NIGHTFALL. YOU WOULDN'T BELIEVE WHAT THE SINS DID TO THE PLACE LAST TIME THERE WAS A FULL MOON.
MY FAMILY, ALL OF THEM, ARE LONG DEAD. I THOUGHT...YOU HAVE MADE YOUR MARVEL FAMILY...
...PERHAPS IT'S NOT TOO LATE TO MAKE MINE.

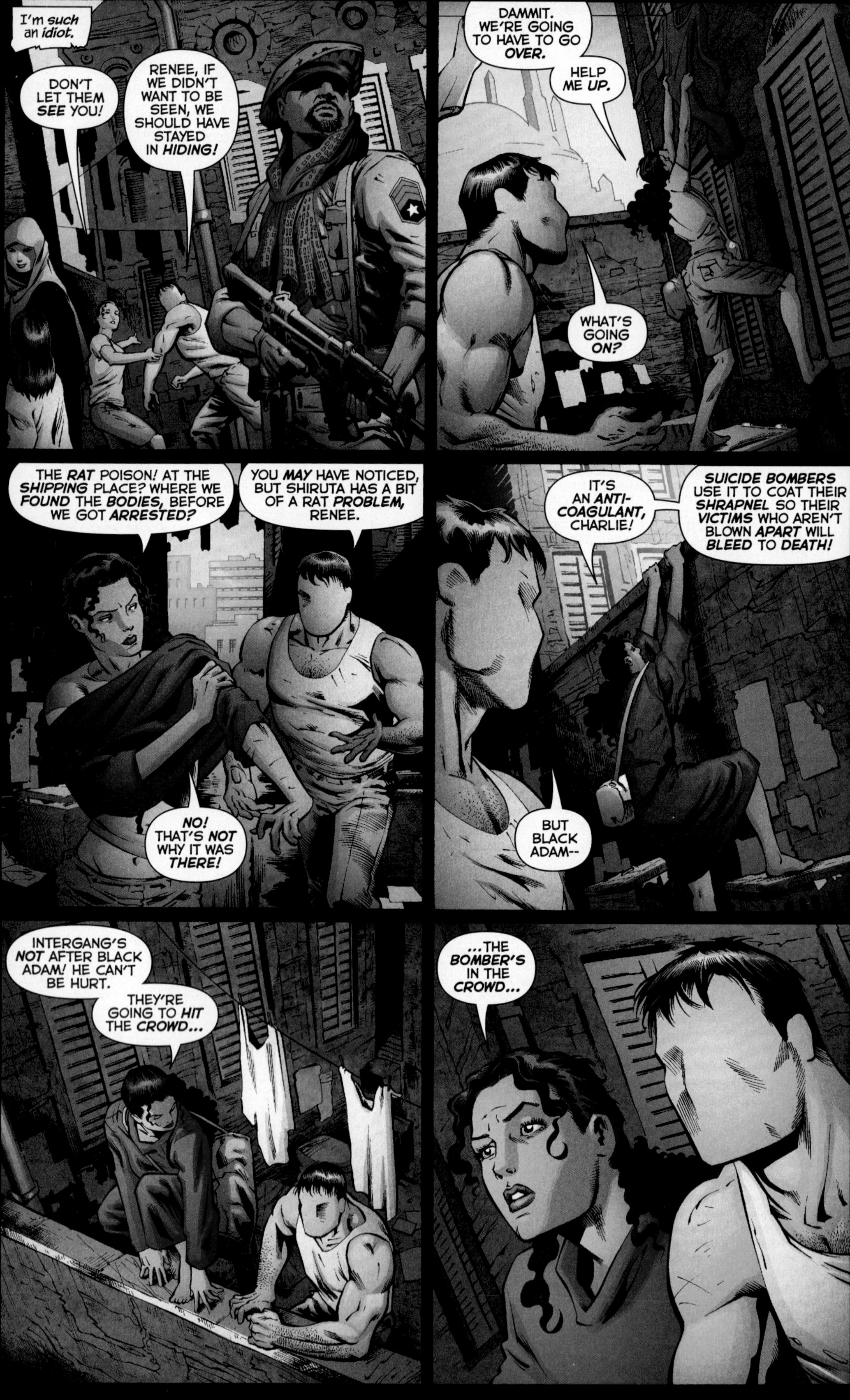
I'm such an idiot.
DON'T LET THEM SEE YOU!
RENEE, IF WE DIDN'T WANT TO BE SEEN, WE SHOULD HAVE STAYED IN HIDING!
DAMMIT. WE'RE GOING TO HAVE TO GO OVER.
HELP ME UP.
WHAT'S GOING ON?
THE RAT POISON! AT THE SHIPPING PLACE? WHERE WE FOUND THE BODIES, BEFORE WE GOT ARRESTED?
YOU MAY HAVE NOTICED, BUT SHIRUTA HAS A BIT OF A RAT PROBLEM, RENEE.
NO! THAT'S NOT WHY IT WAS THERE!
IT'S AN ANTI-COAGULANT, CHARLIE!
SUICIDE BOMBERS USE IT TO COAT THEIR SHRAPNEL SO THEIR VICTIMS WHO AREN'T BLOWN APART WILL BLEED TO DEATH!
BUT BLACK ADAM--
INTERGANG'S NOT AFTER BLACK ADAM! HE CAN'T BE HURT.
THEY'RE GOING TO HIT THE CROWD...
...THE BOMBER'S IN THE CROWD...

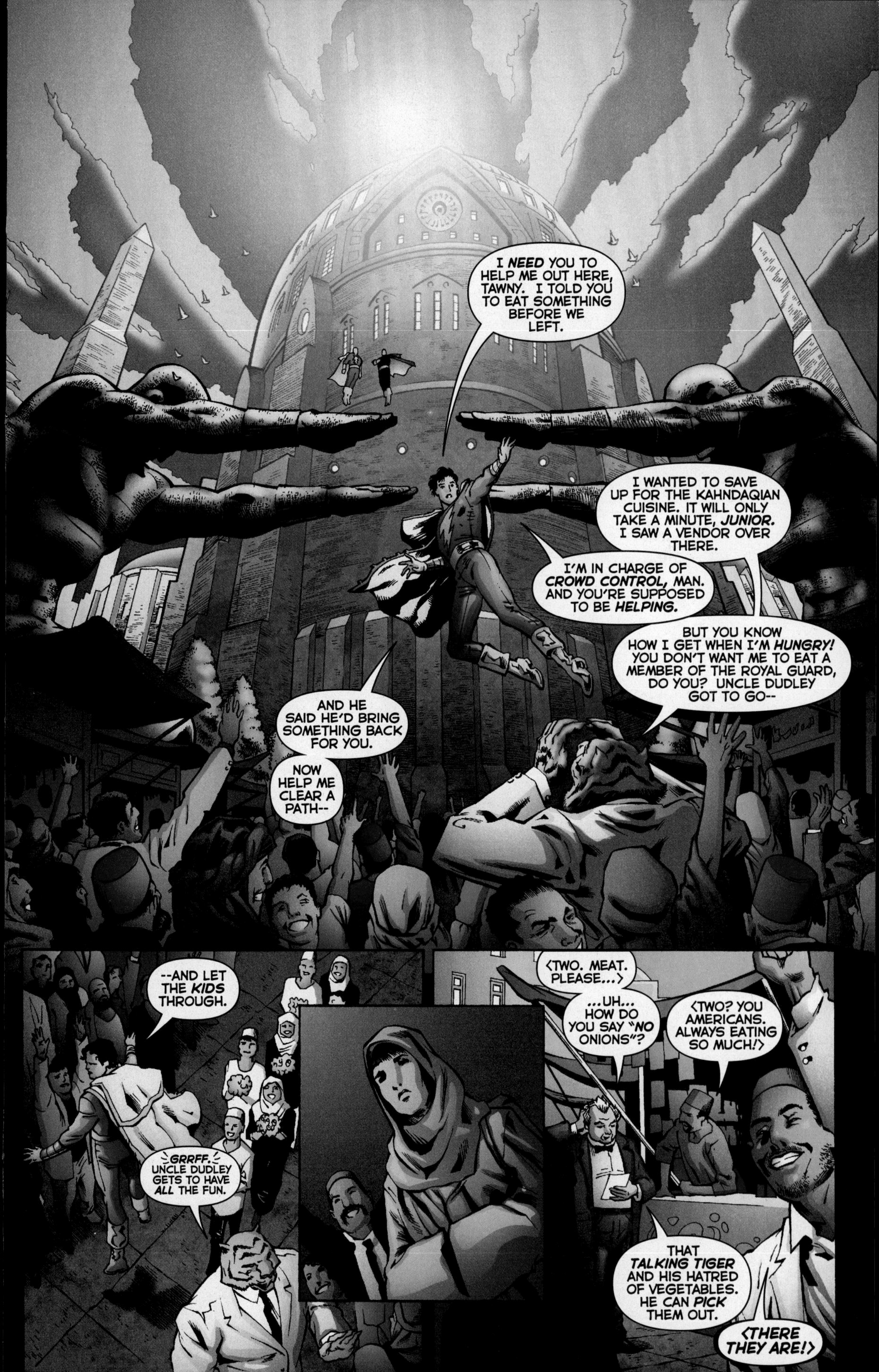
I NEED YOU TO HELP ME OUT HERE, TAWNY. I TOLD YOU TO EAT SOMETHING BEFORE WE LEFT.
I WANTED TO SAVE UP FOR THE KAHNDAQIAN CUISINE. IT WILL ONLY TAKE A MINUTE, JUNIOR. I SAW A VENDOR OVER THERE.
I'M IN CHARGE OF CROWD CONTROL, MAN. AND YOU'RE SUPPOSED TO BE HELPING.
BUT YOU KNOW HOW I GET WHEN I'M HUNGRY! YOU DON'T WANT ME TO EAT A MEMBER OF THE ROYAL GUARD, DO YOU? UNCLE DUDLEY GOT TO GO--
AND HE SAID HE'D BRING SOMETHING BACK FOR YOU.
NOW HELP ME CLEAR A PATH--
--AND LET THE KIDS THROUGH.
GRRFF. UNCLE DUDLEY GETS TO HAVE ALL THE FUN.
<TWO. MEAT. PLEASE...>
...UH... HOW DO YOU SAY "NO ONIONS"?
<TWO? YOU AMERICANS. ALWAYS EATING SO MUCH!>
THAT TALKING TIGER AND HIS HATRED OF VEGETABLES. HE CAN PICK THEM OUT.
<THERE THEY ARE!>

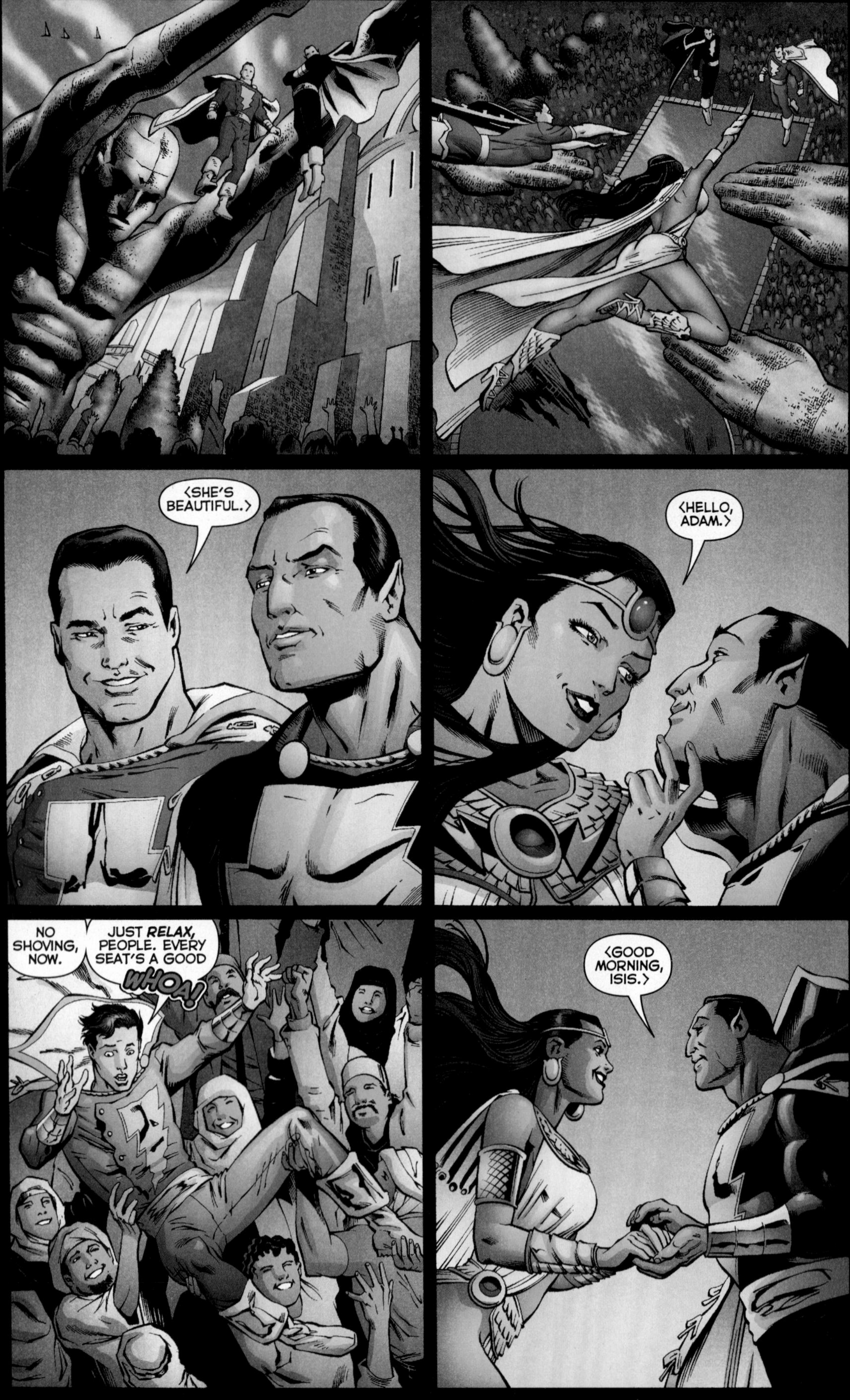

<SHE'S BEAUTIFUL.>
<HELLO, ADAM.>
NO SHOVING, NOW.
JUST RELAX, PEOPLE. EVERY SEAT'S A GOOD
WHOA!
<GOOD MORNING, ISIS.>

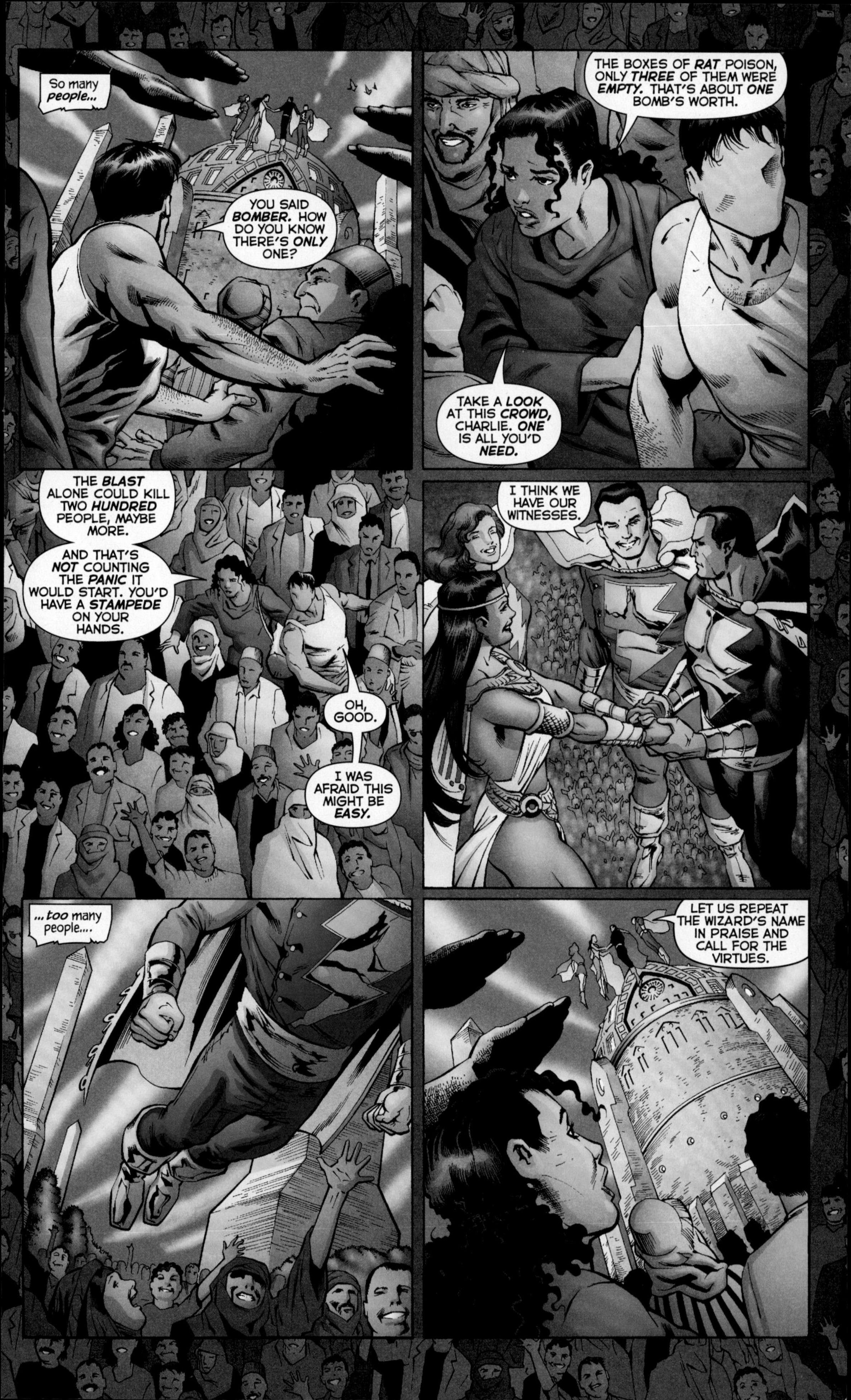
So many *people*...
YOU SAID *BOMBER*. HOW DO YOU KNOW THERE'S *ONLY* ONE?
THE BOXES OF *RAT* POISON, ONLY *THREE* OF THEM WERE *EMPTY*. THAT'S ABOUT *ONE* BOMB'S WORTH.
TAKE A *LOOK* AT THIS *CROWD*, CHARLIE. *ONE* IS ALL YOU'D *NEED*.
THE *BLAST* ALONE COULD KILL TWO *HUNDRED* PEOPLE, MAYBE MORE.
AND THAT'S *NOT* COUNTING THE *PANIC* IT WOULD START. YOU'D HAVE A *STAMPEDE* ON YOUR HANDS.
OH, GOOD.
I WAS AFRAID THIS MIGHT BE *EASY*.
I THINK WE HAVE OUR WITNESSES.
...*too* many people....
LET US REPEAT THE WIZARD'S NAME IN PRAISE AND CALL FOR THE VIRTUES.

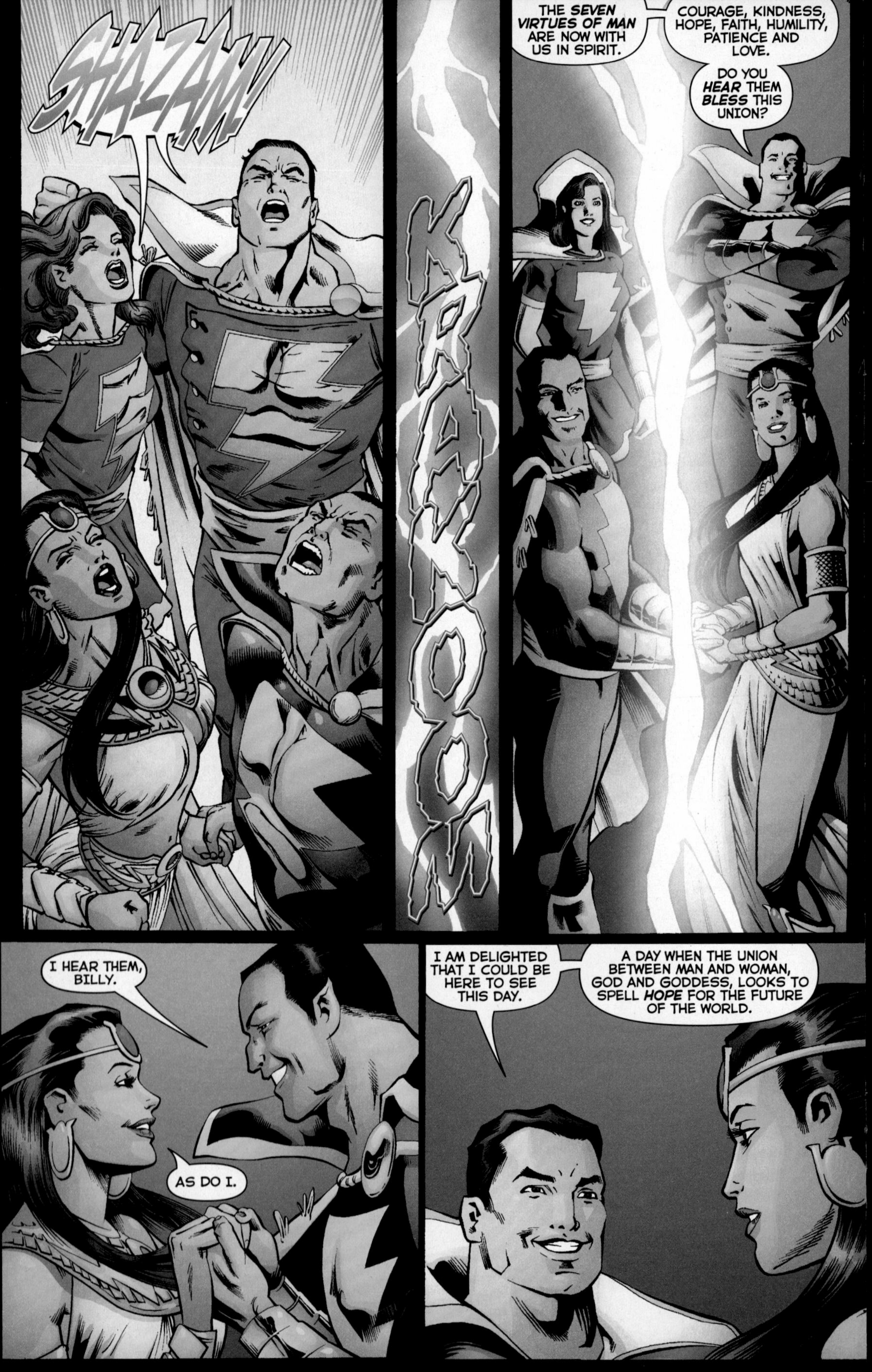
SHAZAM!
KRAKOOOM
THE SEVEN VIRTUES OF MAN ARE NOW WITH US IN SPIRIT.
COURAGE, KINDNESS, HOPE, FAITH, HUMILITY, PATIENCE AND LOVE.
DO YOU HEAR THEM BLESS THIS UNION?
I HEAR THEM, BILLY.
AS DO I.
I AM DELIGHTED THAT I COULD BE HERE TO SEE THIS DAY.
A DAY WHEN THE UNION BETWEEN MAN AND WOMAN, GOD AND GODDESS, LOOKS TO SPELL HOPE FOR THE FUTURE OF THE WORLD.

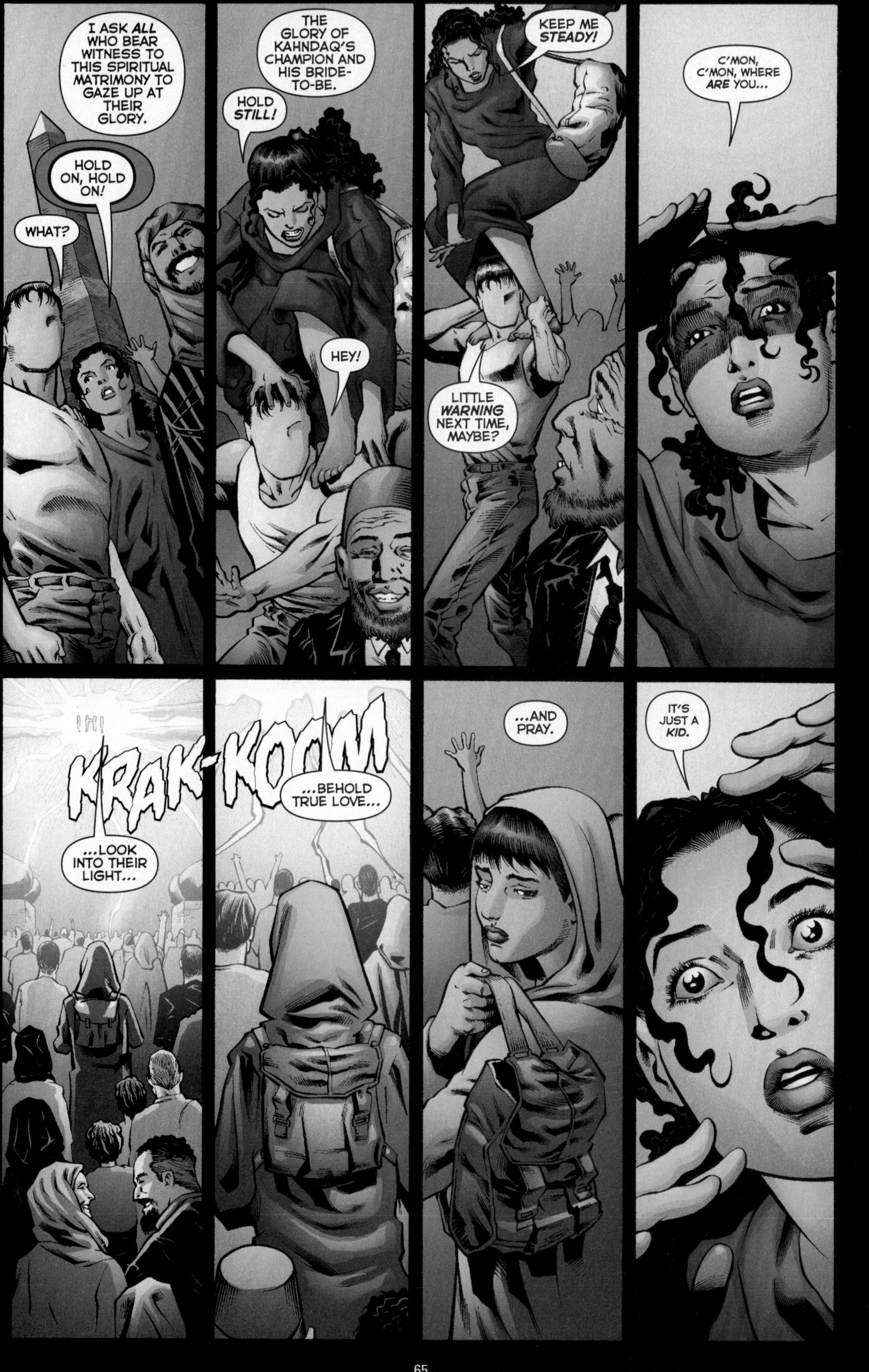
I ASK ALL WHO BEAR WITNESS TO THIS SPIRITUAL MATRIMONY TO GAZE UP AT THEIR GLORY.
HOLD ON, HOLD ON!
WHAT?
THE GLORY OF KAHNDAQ'S CHAMPION AND HIS BRIDE-TO-BE.
HOLD STILL!
HEY!
KEEP ME STEADY!
LITTLE WARNING NEXT TIME, MAYBE?
C'MON, C'MON, WHERE ARE YOU...
KRAK-KOOM
...LOOK INTO THEIR LIGHT...
...BEHOLD TRUE LOVE...
...AND PRAY.
IT'S JUST A KID.

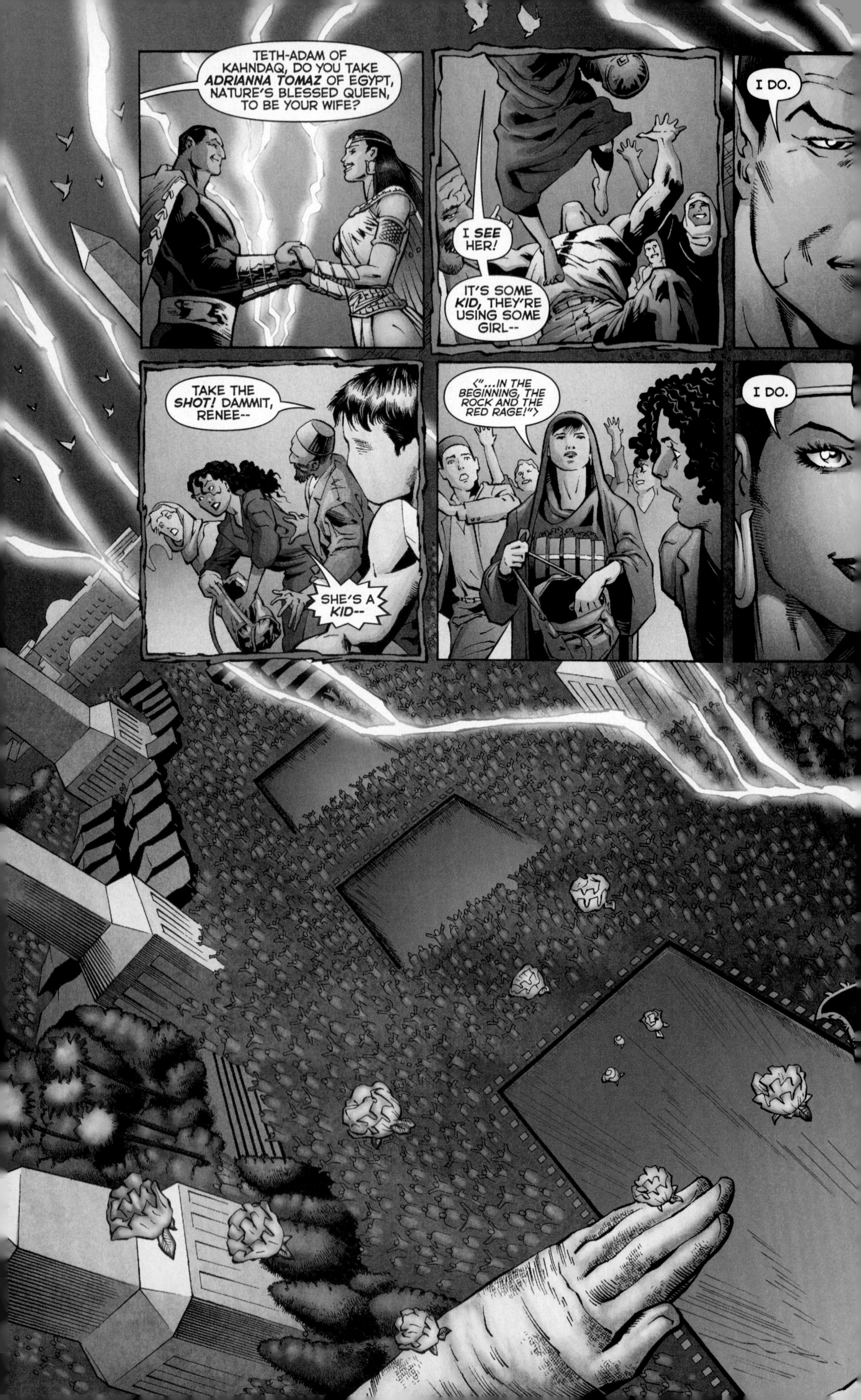
TETH-ADAM OF KAHNDAQ, DO YOU TAKE ADRIANNA TOMAZ OF EGYPT, NATURE'S BLESSED QUEEN, TO BE YOUR WIFE?
I SEE HER!
IT'S SOME KID, THEY'RE USING SOME GIRL--
I DO.
TAKE THE SHOT! DAMMIT, RENEE--
SHE'S A KID--
<"...IN THE BEGINNING, THE ROCK AND THE RED RAGE!">
I DO.

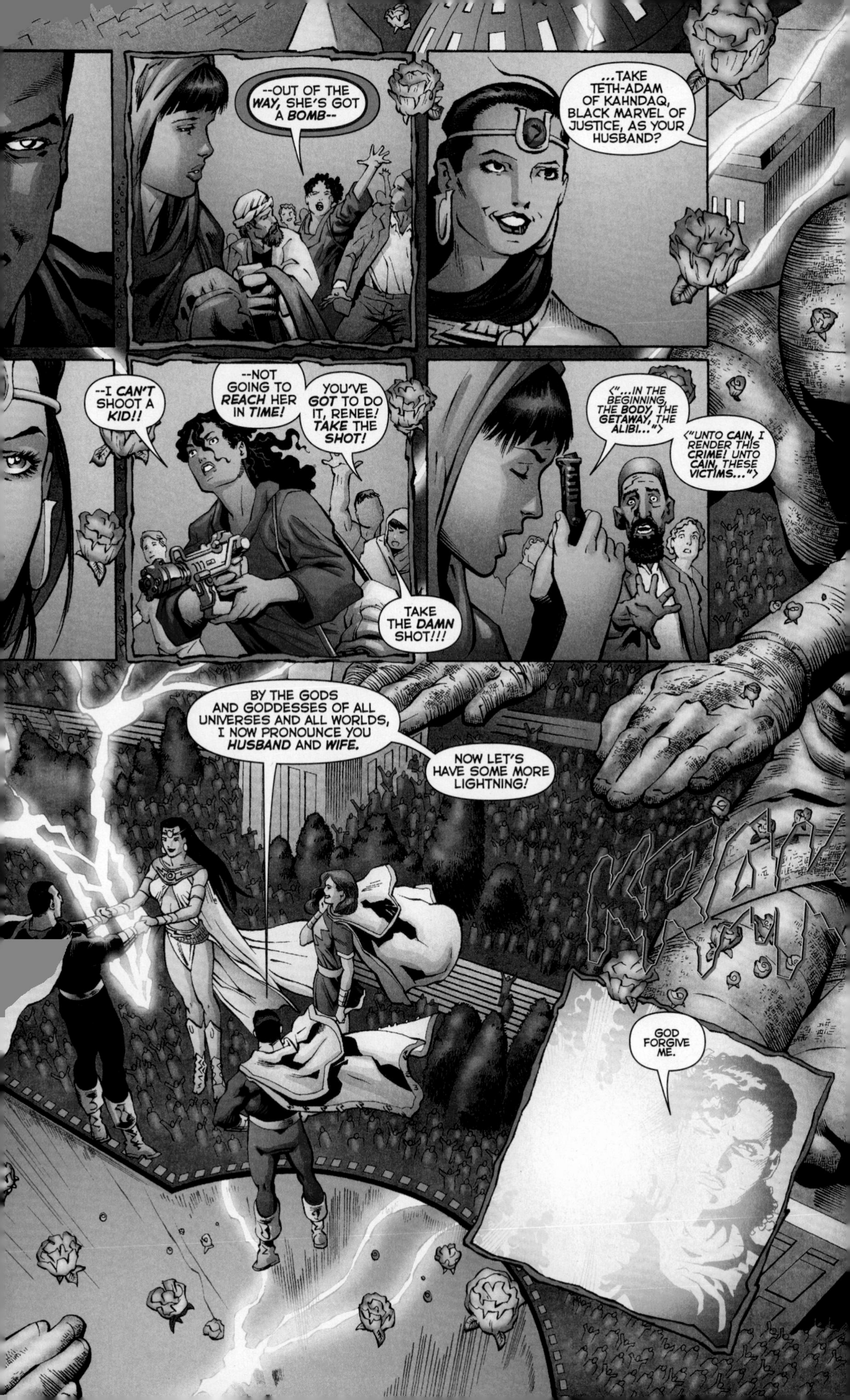

--OUT OF THE WAY, SHE'S GOT A BOMB--
...TAKE TETH-ADAM OF KAHNDAQ, BLACK MARVEL OF JUSTICE, AS YOUR HUSBAND?
--I CAN'T SHOOT A KID!!
--NOT GOING TO REACH HER IN TIME!
YOU'VE GOT TO DO IT, RENEE! TAKE THE SHOT!
TAKE THE DAMN SHOT!!!
<"...IN THE BEGINNING, THE BODY, THE GETAWAY, THE ALIBI...">
<"UNTO CAIN, I RENDER THIS CRIME! UNTO CAIN, THESE VICTIMS...">
BY THE GODS AND GODDESSES OF ALL UNIVERSES AND ALL WORLDS, I NOW PRONOUNCE YOU HUSBAND AND WIFE.
NOW LET'S HAVE SOME MORE LIGHTNING!
KRAKOOM
GOD FORGIVE ME.

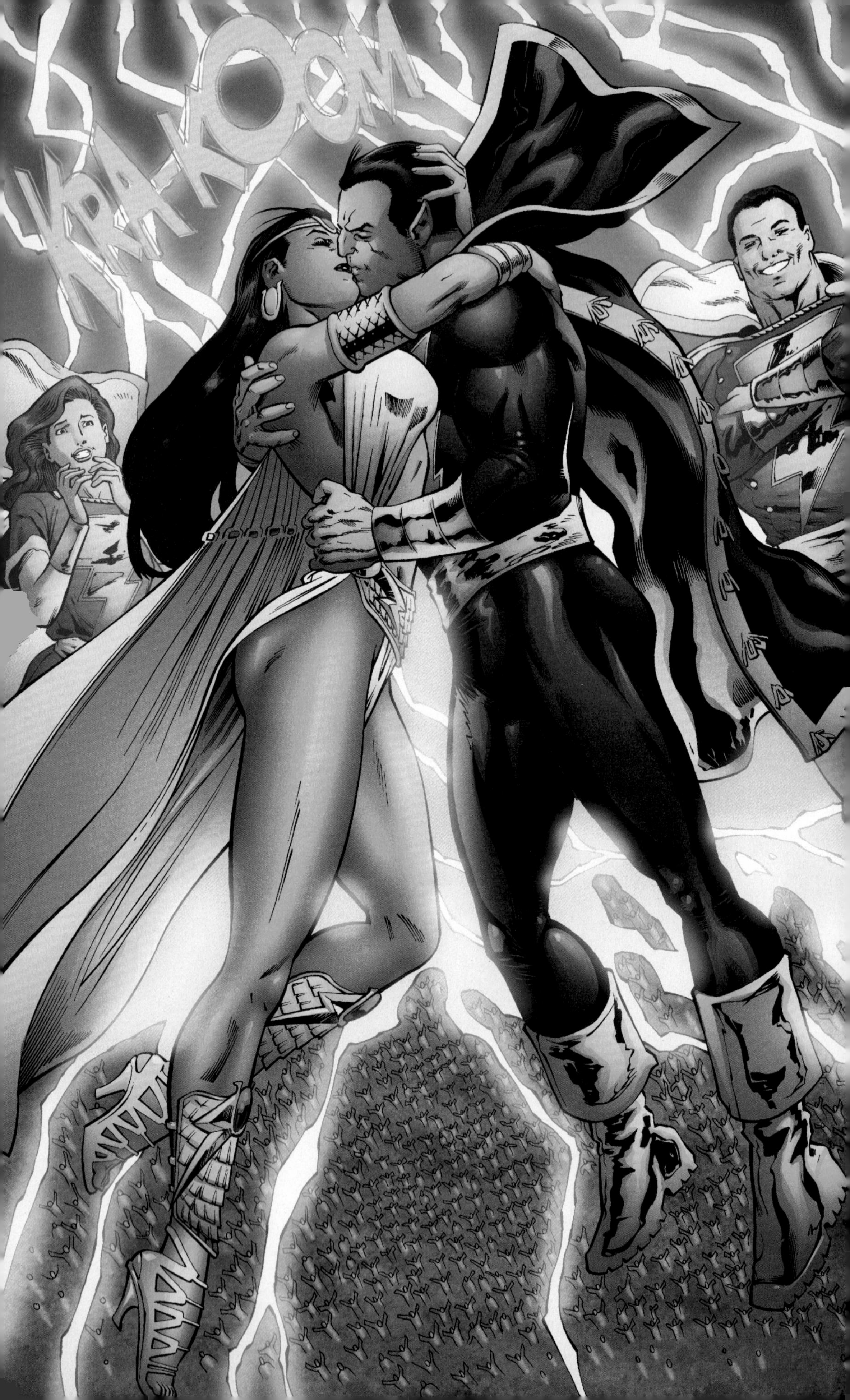
KRA-KOOM

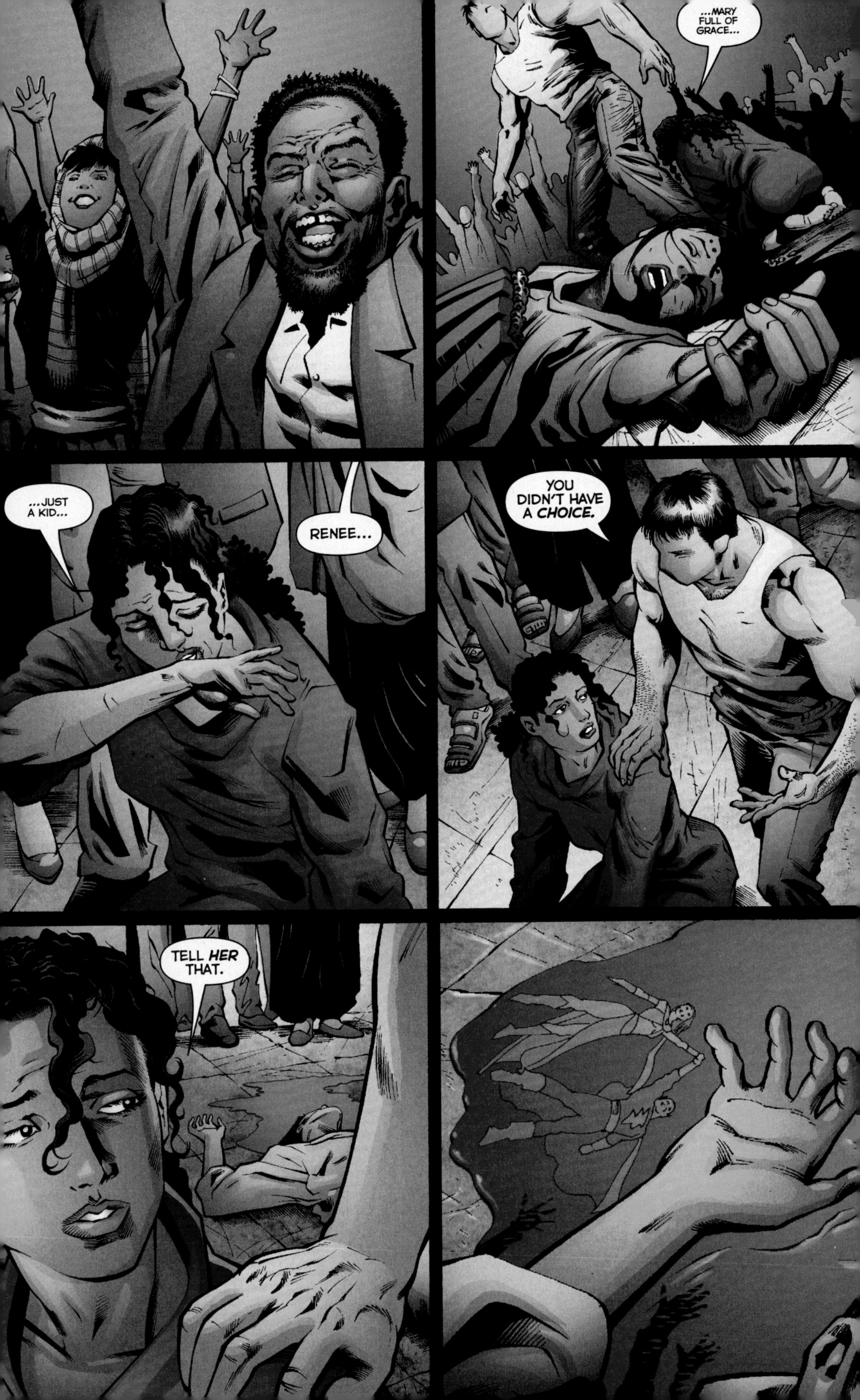
...MARY FULL OF GRACE...
...JUST A KID...
RENEE...
YOU DIDN'T HAVE A CHOICE.
TELL HER THAT.

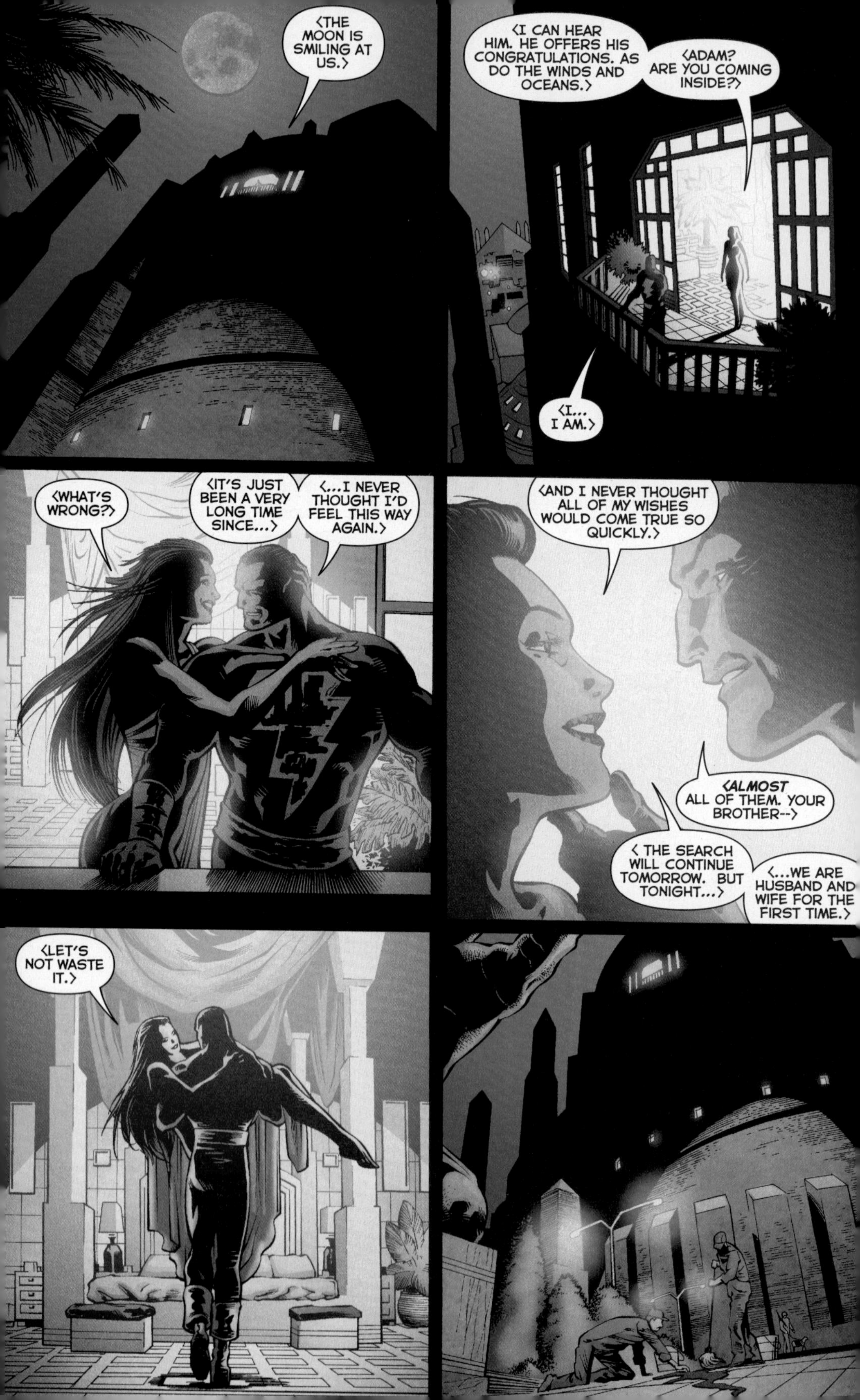
<THE MOON IS SMILING AT US.>
<I CAN HEAR HIM. HE OFFERS HIS CONGRATULATIONS. AS DO THE WINDS AND OCEANS.>
<ADAM? ARE YOU COMING INSIDE?>
<I... I AM.>
<WHAT'S WRONG?>
<IT'S JUST BEEN A VERY LONG TIME SINCE...>
<...I NEVER THOUGHT I'D FEEL THIS WAY AGAIN.>
<AND I NEVER THOUGHT ALL OF MY WISHES WOULD COME TRUE SO QUICKLY.>
<*ALMOST* ALL OF THEM. YOUR BROTHER-->
< THE SEARCH WILL CONTINUE TOMORROW. BUT TONIGHT...>
<...WE ARE HUSBAND AND WIFE FOR THE FIRST TIME.>
<LET'S NOT WASTE IT.>

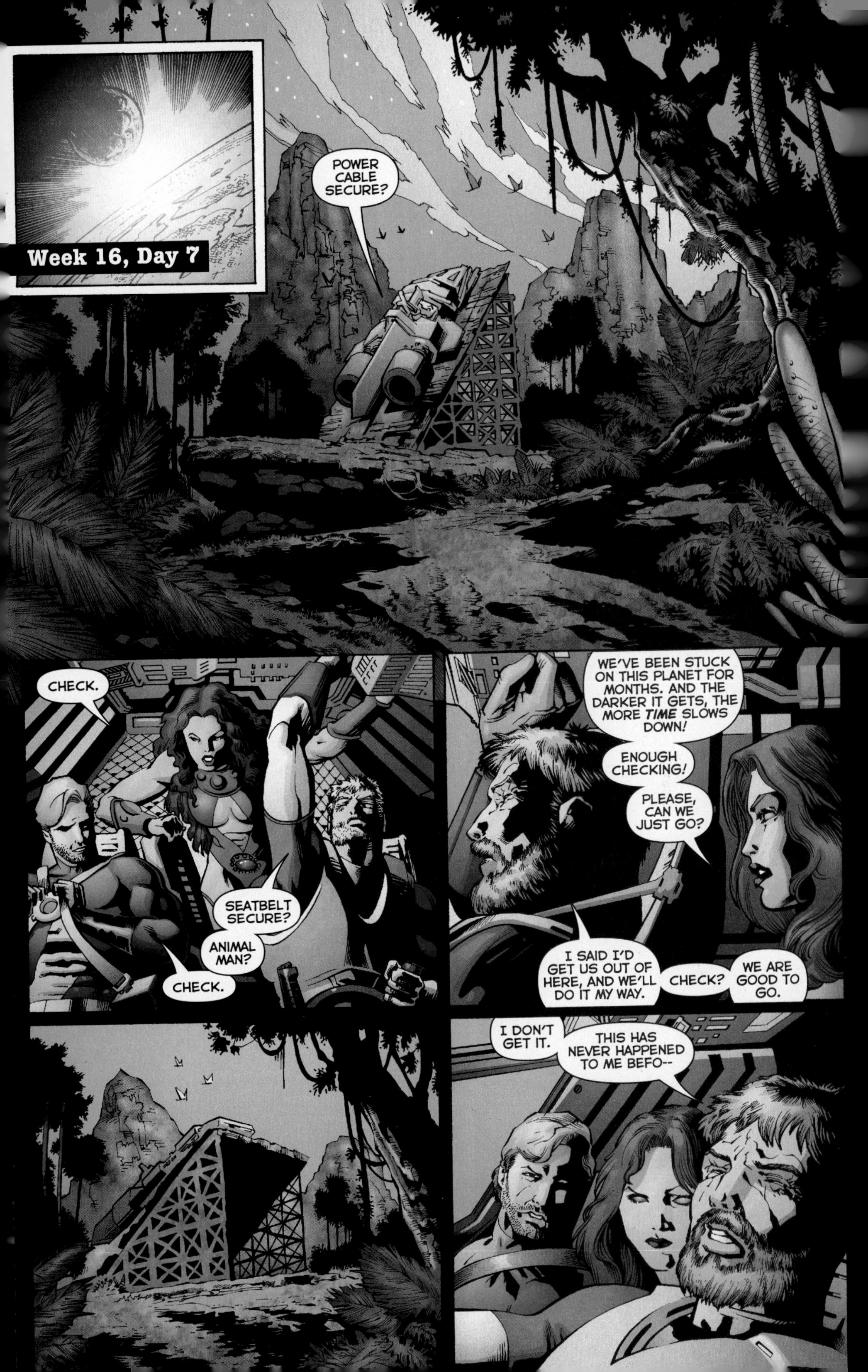
Week 16, Day 7
POWER CABLE SECURE?
CHECK.
SEATBELT SECURE?
ANIMAL MAN?
CHECK.
WE'VE BEEN STUCK ON THIS PLANET FOR MONTHS. AND THE DARKER IT GETS, THE MORE TIME SLOWS DOWN!
ENOUGH CHECKING!
PLEASE, CAN WE JUST GO?
I SAID I'D GET US OUT OF HERE, AND WE'LL DO IT MY WAY.
CHECK?
WE ARE GOOD TO GO.
I DON'T GET IT.
THIS HAS NEVER HAPPENED TO ME BEFO--

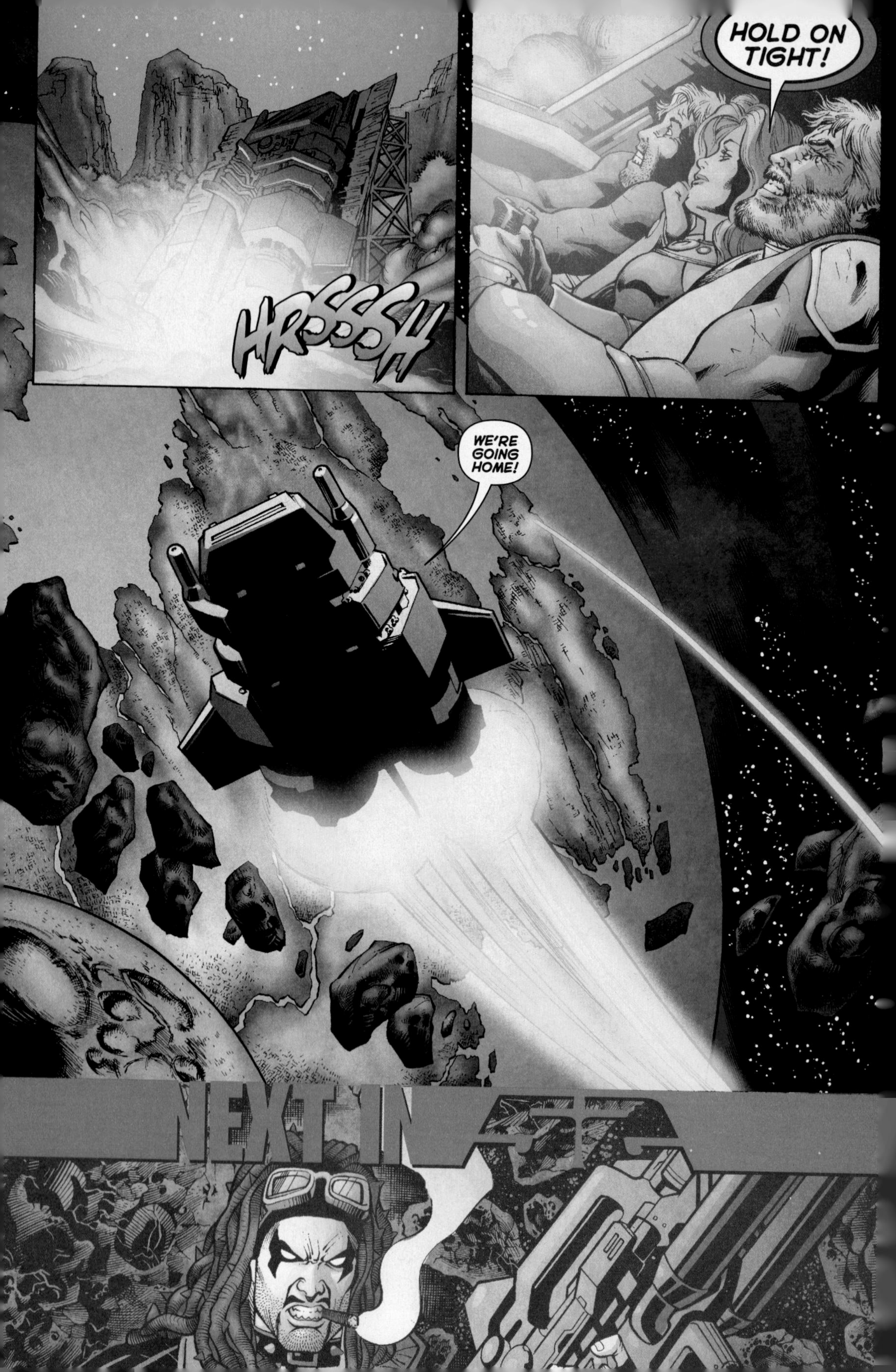
HRSSSH
HOLD ON TIGHT!
WE'RE GOING HOME!
NEXT IN 52

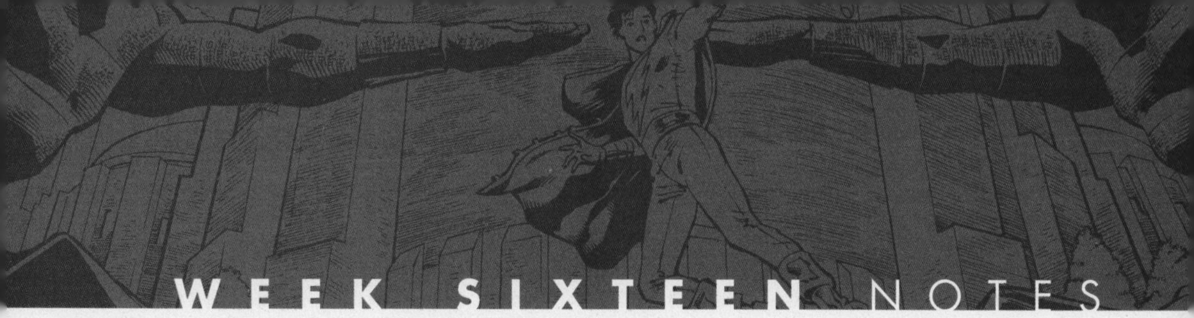

WEEK SIXTEEN NOTES

GREG RUCKA

Okay, here it is. I've spent a few of these talking about how everything went right and well and swimmingly and so on. We were having our weekly conference calls, we were turning in our pages, we were a Pit Team at Indianapolis, we were working so well.

So, of course, something had to slip through the cracks, and what slipped through was an error in storytelling that arose more out of the constraints of the process (how we wrote what we wrote, why we wrote what we wrote, and when we wrote what we wrote) than a mistake on the part of any one person or position. At the time this issue came out, it bothered me something fierce, mostly because I'd worked so darn hard on maintaining internal logic and consistency. Now, it bothers me less so, because — honestly — I don't think it truly detracts from the story.

Here's the deal: issues, you see, were sometimes written out of order. Which is to say that while Grant would be, potentially, writing eight pages for Week 10, I would be writing six pages in Week 12 potentially influenced by what he was covering. In this instance, I was writing the Kahndaq sequences before Geoff had written much of the intervening Isis/Black Adam beats. Until this point, working in this way hadn't been a problem, because we all knew *what* we were supposed to be doing, even if we didn't know specifically *how* we were going to accomplish it on the page. To put it plainly, I was writing Charlie and Renee in Kahndaq knowing that Black Adam and Isis were getting married in Week 16.

What I didn't know was that Geoff had postponed Black Adam *proposing* to Isis until, yes, the start of Week 16.

Which meant that when I wrote Week 14, it was with the plan that the wedding *had already been announced*. Hence the celebrations in the streets, the lack of hotel rooms, and — most crucially as far as I was concerned — Intergang's suicide bombing plot. As it stands now, you read the issues and it looks like Intergang knew the wedding was coming even before Black Adam did.

Bugged me like you wouldn't believe at the time. Like. You. Wouldn't. Believe.

Now?

Not so much. Go figure.

The rat poison thing is a True Fact, by the way.

Last note. The original art following the splash page of Adam and Isis smooching had Renee vomiting as a result of what she'd had to do, something that I hated the moment I saw it. Wacker's solution was inspired, and totally in character for Renee. See if you can spot it.

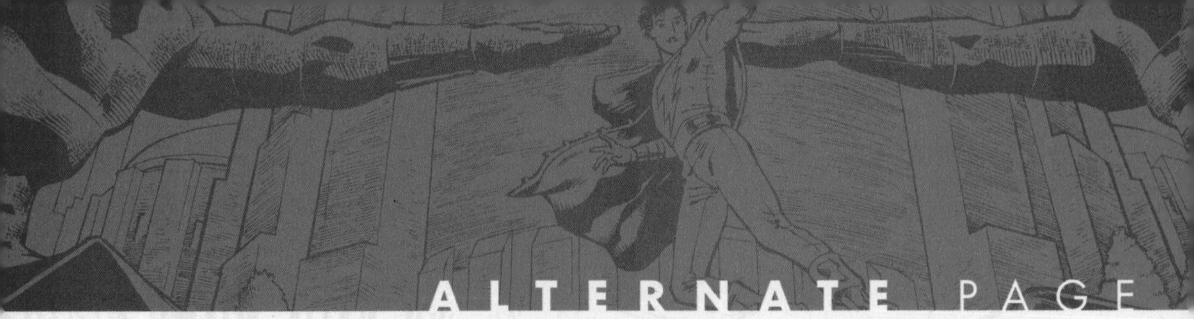

ALTERNATE PAGE

(COMPARE WITH PAGE 64 OF THIS COLLECTION)

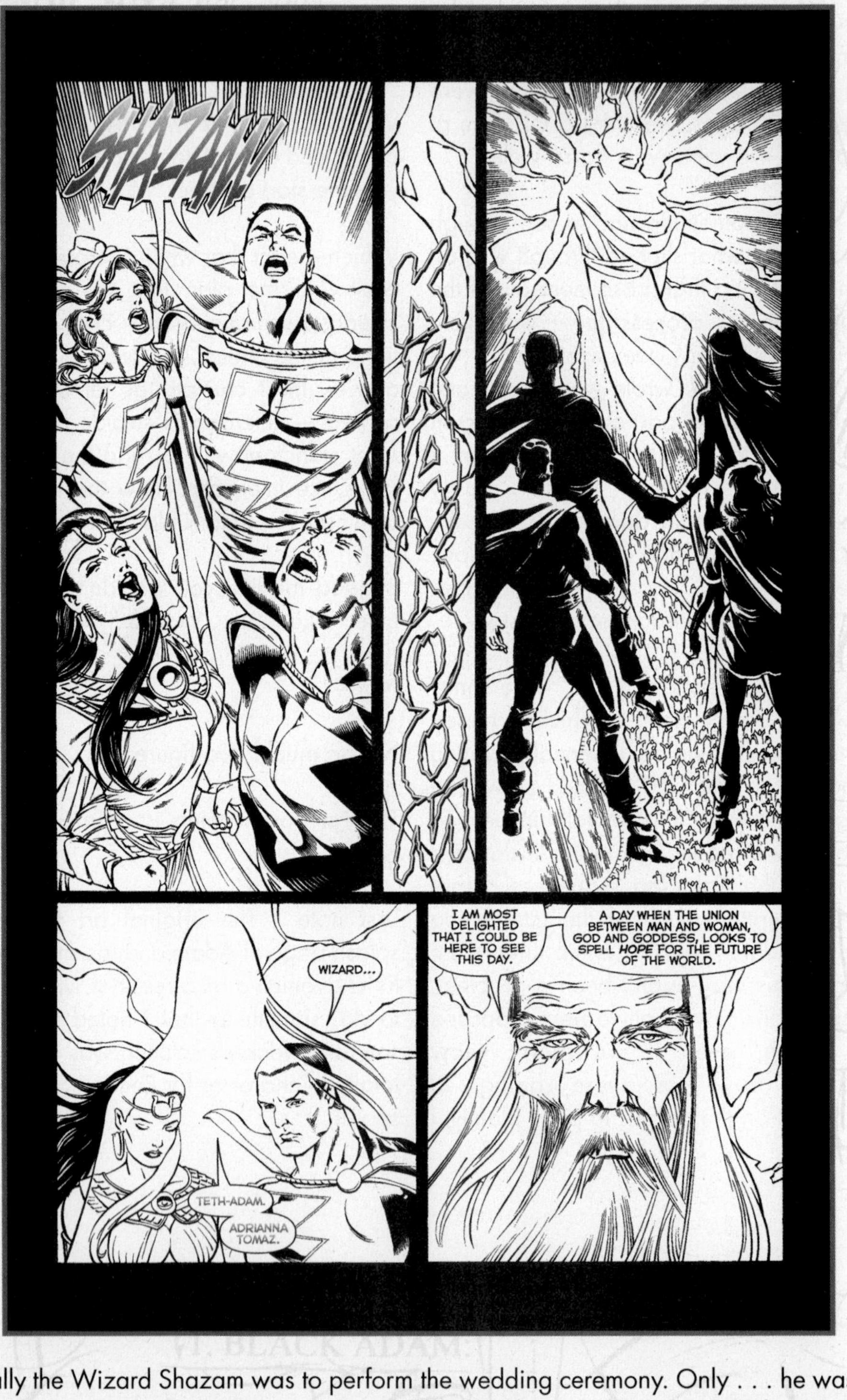
SHAZAM!
KRAKOOOM
WIZARD...
TETH-ADAM.
ADRIANNA TOMAZ.
I AM MOST DELIGHTED THAT I COULD BE HERE TO SEE THIS DAY.
A DAY WHEN THE UNION BETWEEN MAN AND WOMAN, GOD AND GODDESS, LOOKS TO SPELL *HOPE* FOR THE FUTURE OF THE WORLD.

Originally the Wizard Shazam was to perform the wedding ceremony. Only . . . he was dead by this time in continuity. So Captain Marvel ended up being a last-minute replacement.

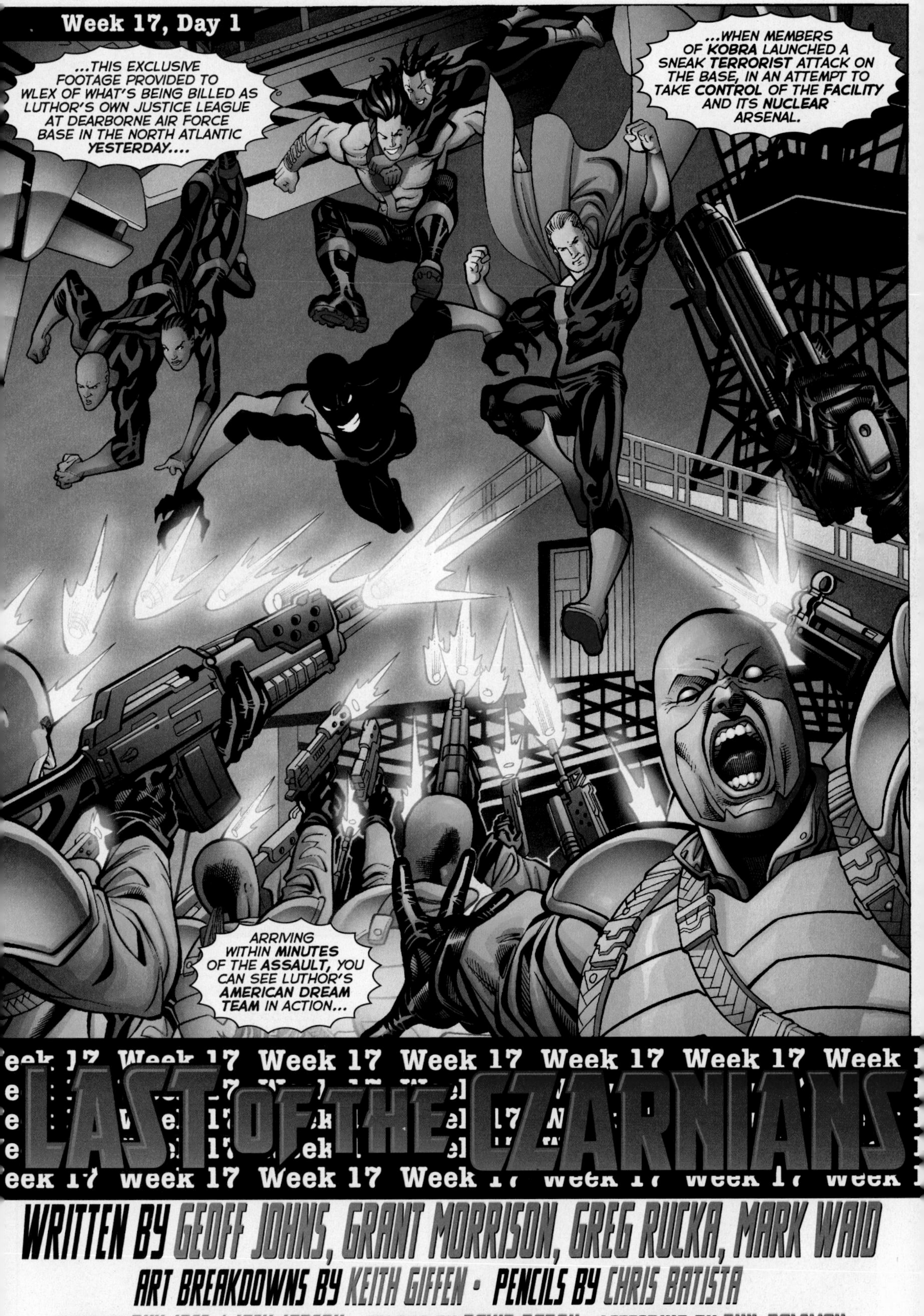
Week 17, Day 1
...THIS EXCLUSIVE FOOTAGE PROVIDED TO WLEX OF WHAT'S BEING BILLED AS LUTHOR'S OWN JUSTICE LEAGUE AT DEARBORNE AIR FORCE BASE IN THE NORTH ATLANTIC YESTERDAY....
...WHEN MEMBERS OF KOBRA LAUNCHED A SNEAK TERRORIST ATTACK ON THE BASE, IN AN ATTEMPT TO TAKE CONTROL OF THE FACILITY AND ITS NUCLEAR ARSENAL.
ARRIVING WITHIN MINUTES OF THE ASSAULT, YOU CAN SEE LUTHOR'S AMERICAN DREAM TEAM IN ACTION...

Week 17 Week 17 Week 17 Week 17 Week 17

LAST OF THE CZARNIANS

WRITTEN BY GEOFF JOHNS, GRANT MORRISON, GREG RUCKA, MARK WAID
ART BREAKDOWNS BY KEITH GIFFEN • PENCILS BY CHRIS BATISTA
INKS BY RUY JOSE & JACK JADSON • COLORS BY DAVID BARON • LETTERING BY PHIL BALSMAN
ASSISTANT EDITORS JANN JONES & HARVEY RICHARDS
EDITED BY STEPHEN WACKER • COVER BY J.G. JONES & ALEX SINCLAIR

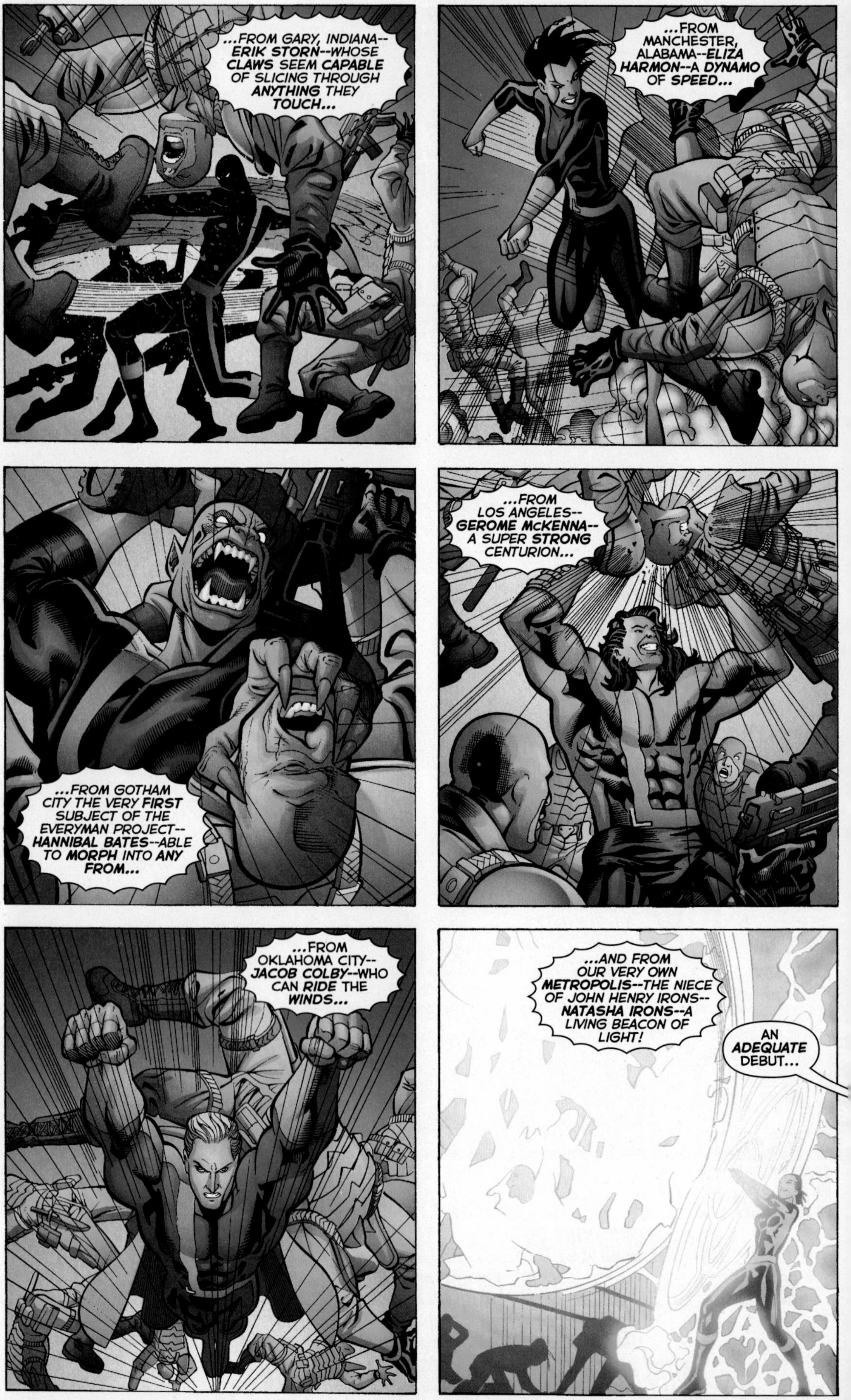
...FROM GARY, INDIANA--ERIK STORN--WHOSE CLAWS SEEM CAPABLE OF SLICING THROUGH ANYTHING THEY TOUCH...
...FROM MANCHESTER, ALABAMA--ELIZA HARMON--A DYNAMO OF SPEED...
...FROM GOTHAM CITY THE VERY FIRST SUBJECT OF THE EVERYMAN PROJECT--HANNIBAL BATES--ABLE TO MORPH INTO ANY FROM...
...FROM LOS ANGELES--GEROME McKENNA--A SUPER STRONG CENTURION...
...FROM OKLAHOMA CITY--JACOB COLBY--WHO CAN RIDE THE WINDS...
...AND FROM OUR VERY OWN METROPOLIS--THE NIECE OF JOHN HENRY IRONS--NATASHA IRONS--A LIVING BEACON OF LIGHT!
AN ADEQUATE DEBUT...

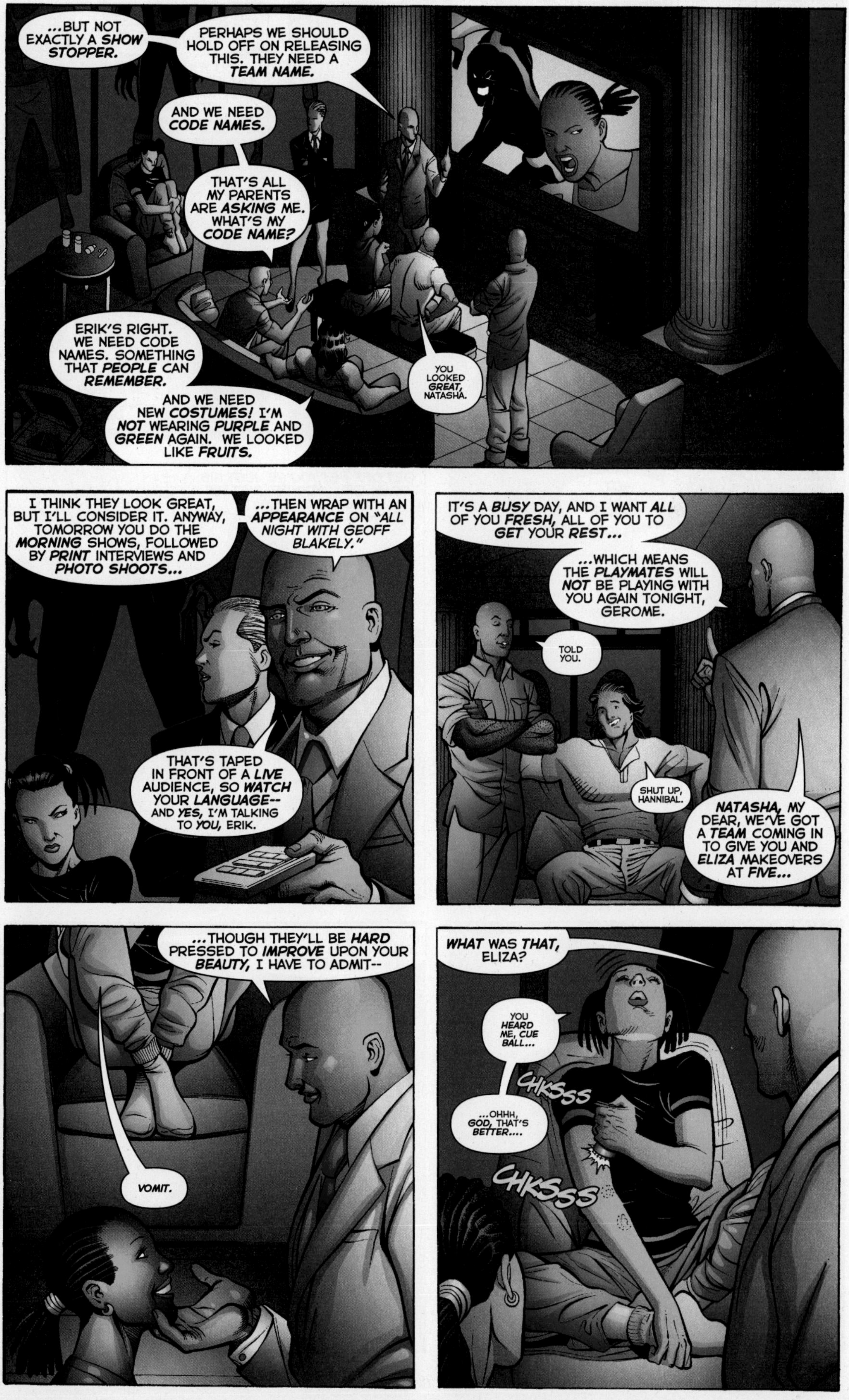
...BUT NOT EXACTLY A SHOW STOPPER.
PERHAPS WE SHOULD HOLD OFF ON RELEASING THIS. THEY NEED A TEAM NAME.
AND WE NEED CODE NAMES.
THAT'S ALL MY PARENTS ARE ASKING ME. WHAT'S MY CODE NAME?
ERIK'S RIGHT. WE NEED CODE NAMES. SOMETHING THAT PEOPLE CAN REMEMBER.
AND WE NEED NEW COSTUMES! I'M NOT WEARING PURPLE AND GREEN AGAIN. WE LOOKED LIKE FRUITS.
YOU LOOKED GREAT, NATASHA.
I THINK THEY LOOK GREAT, BUT I'LL CONSIDER IT. ANYWAY, TOMORROW YOU DO THE MORNING SHOWS, FOLLOWED BY PRINT INTERVIEWS AND PHOTO SHOOTS...
...THEN WRAP WITH AN APPEARANCE ON "ALL NIGHT WITH GEOFF BLAKELY."
THAT'S TAPED IN FRONT OF A LIVE AUDIENCE, SO WATCH YOUR LANGUAGE-- AND YES, I'M TALKING TO YOU, ERIK.
IT'S A BUSY DAY, AND I WANT ALL OF YOU FRESH, ALL OF YOU TO GET YOUR REST...
...WHICH MEANS THE PLAYMATES WILL NOT BE PLAYING WITH YOU AGAIN TONIGHT, GEROME.
TOLD YOU.
SHUT UP, HANNIBAL.
NATASHA, MY DEAR, WE'VE GOT A TEAM COMING IN TO GIVE YOU AND ELIZA MAKEOVERS AT FIVE...
...THOUGH THEY'LL BE HARD PRESSED TO IMPROVE UPON YOUR BEAUTY, I HAVE TO ADMIT--
VOMIT.
WHAT WAS THAT, ELIZA?
YOU HEARD ME, CUE BALL...
CHKSSS
...OHHH, GOD, THAT'S BETTER....
CHKSSS

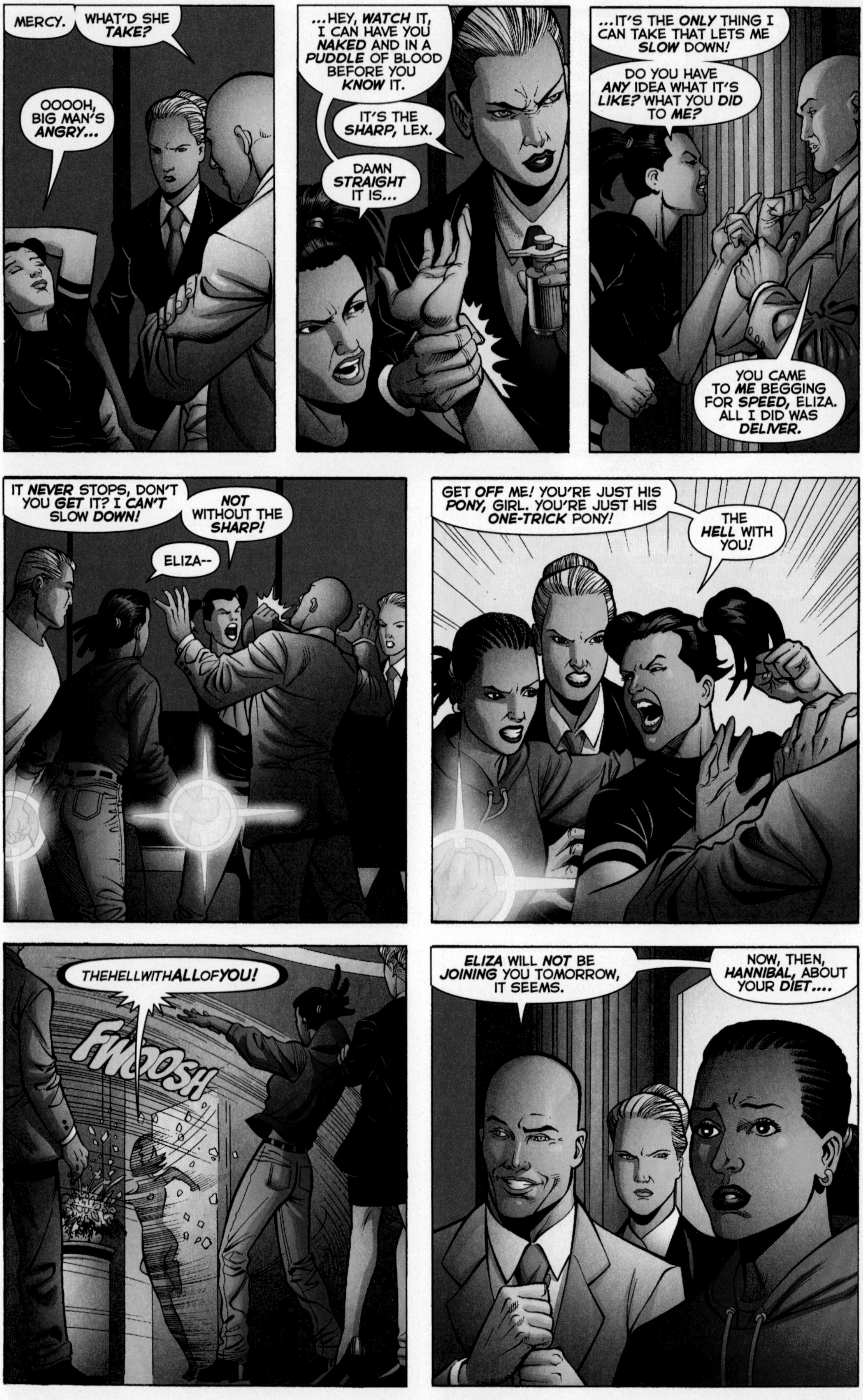
MERCY.
WHAT'D SHE TAKE?
OOOOH, BIG MAN'S ANGRY...
...HEY, WATCH IT, I CAN HAVE YOU NAKED AND IN A PUDDLE OF BLOOD BEFORE YOU KNOW IT.
IT'S THE SHARP, LEX.
DAMN STRAIGHT IT IS...
...IT'S THE ONLY THING I CAN TAKE THAT LETS ME SLOW DOWN!
DO YOU HAVE ANY IDEA WHAT IT'S LIKE? WHAT YOU DID TO ME?
YOU CAME TO ME BEGGING FOR SPEED, ELIZA. ALL I DID WAS DELIVER.
IT NEVER STOPS, DON'T YOU GET IT? I CAN'T SLOW DOWN!
NOT WITHOUT THE SHARP!
ELIZA--
GET OFF ME! YOU'RE JUST HIS PONY, GIRL. YOU'RE JUST HIS ONE-TRICK PONY!
THE HELL WITH YOU!
THEHELLWITHALLOFYOU!
FWOOSH
ELIZA WILL NOT BE JOINING YOU TOMORROW, IT SEEMS.
NOW, THEN, HANNIBAL, ABOUT YOUR DIET....

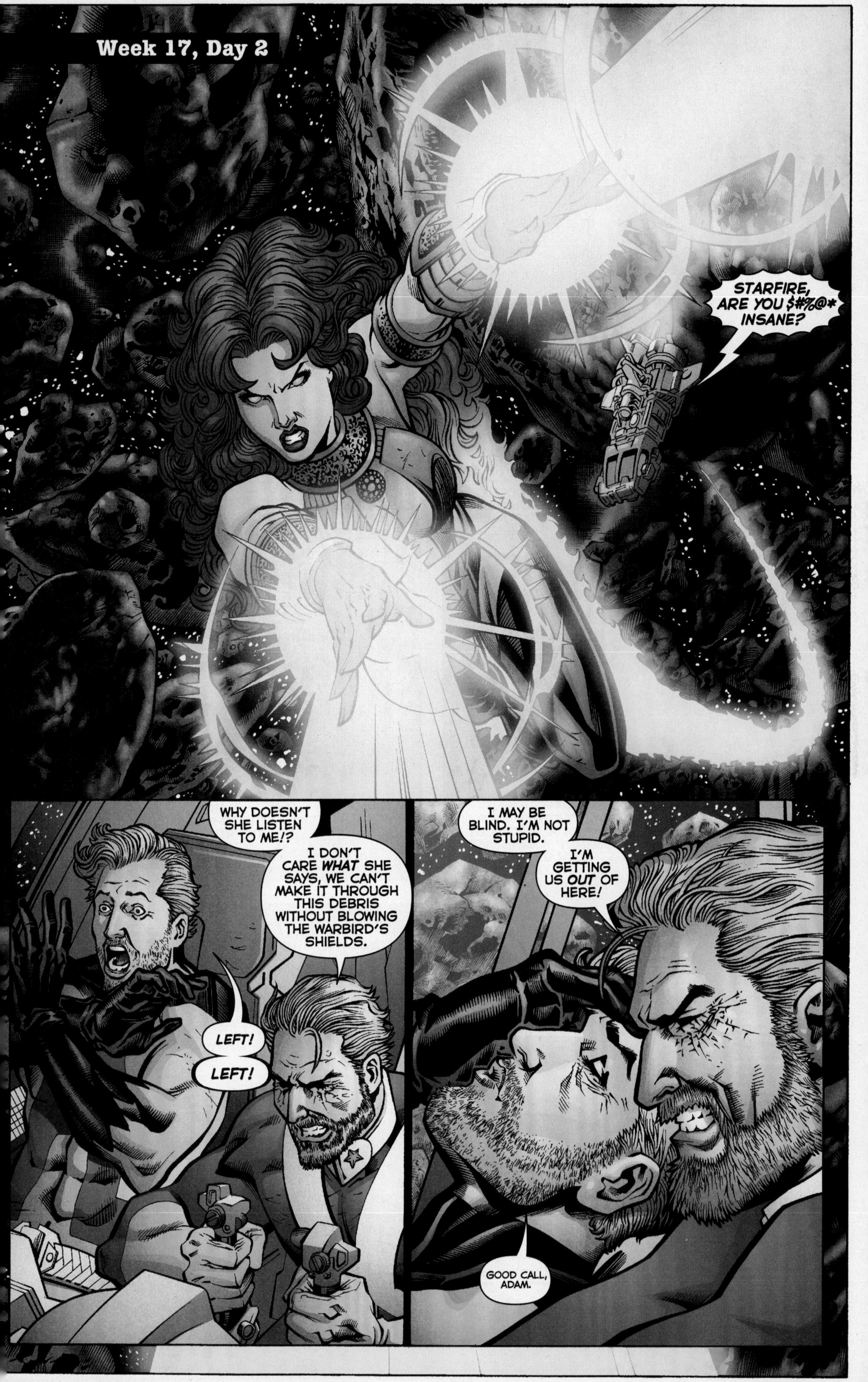

Week 17, Day 2
STARFIRE, ARE YOU $#%@* INSANE?
WHY DOESN'T SHE LISTEN TO ME!?
I DON'T CARE WHAT SHE SAYS, WE CAN'T MAKE IT THROUGH THIS DEBRIS WITHOUT BLOWING THE WARBIRD'S SHIELDS.
LEFT!
LEFT!
I MAY BE BLIND. I'M NOT STUPID.
I'M GETTING US OUT OF HERE!
GOOD CALL, ADAM.

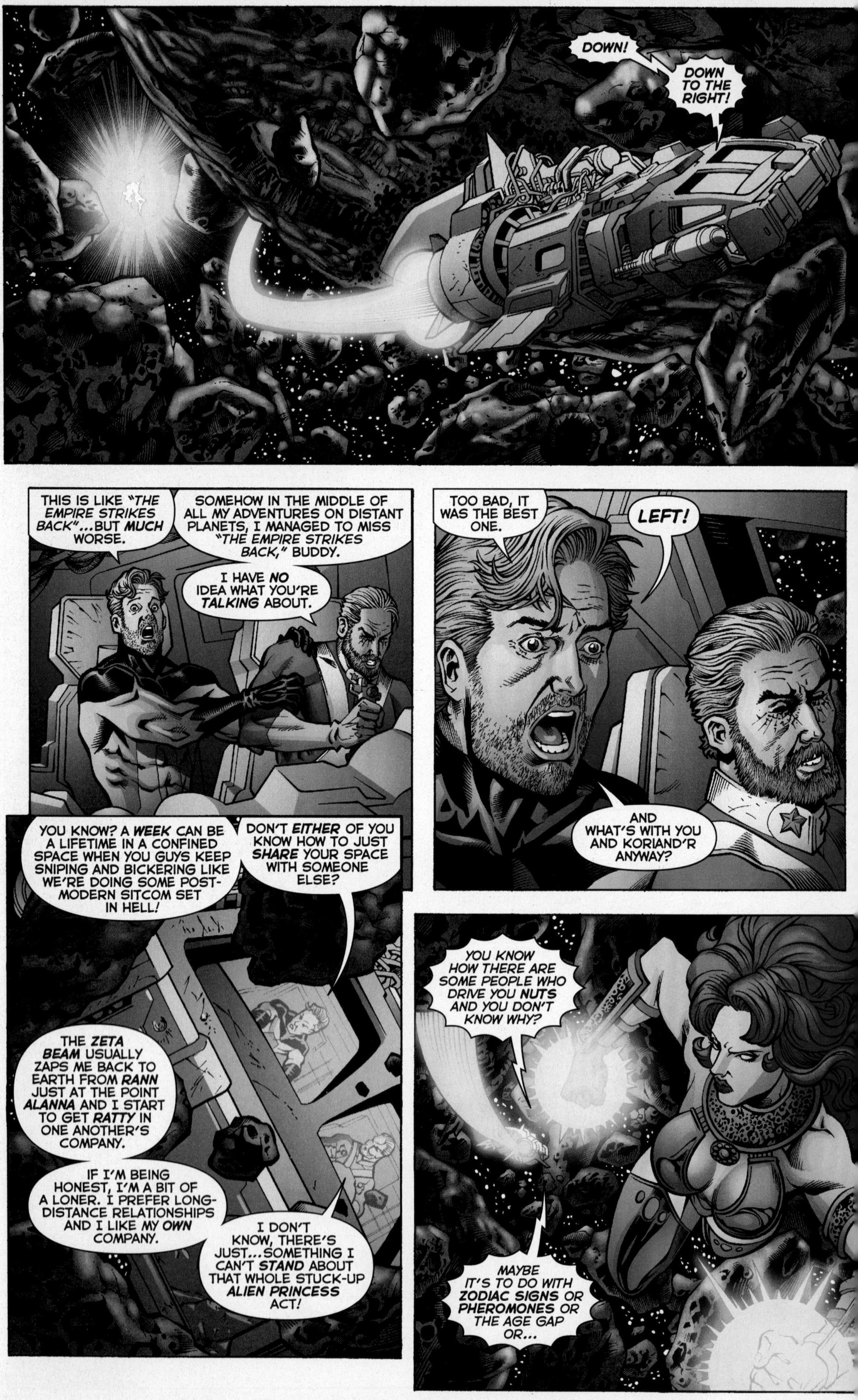
DOWN!
DOWN TO THE RIGHT!
THIS IS LIKE "THE EMPIRE STRIKES BACK"...BUT MUCH WORSE.
SOMEHOW IN THE MIDDLE OF ALL MY ADVENTURES ON DISTANT PLANETS, I MANAGED TO MISS "THE EMPIRE STRIKES BACK," BUDDY.
I HAVE NO IDEA WHAT YOU'RE TALKING ABOUT.
TOO BAD, IT WAS THE BEST ONE.
LEFT!
AND WHAT'S WITH YOU AND KORIAND'R ANYWAY?
YOU KNOW? A WEEK CAN BE A LIFETIME IN A CONFINED SPACE WHEN YOU GUYS KEEP SNIPING AND BICKERING LIKE WE'RE DOING SOME POST-MODERN SITCOM SET IN HELL!
DON'T EITHER OF YOU KNOW HOW TO JUST SHARE YOUR SPACE WITH SOMEONE ELSE?
THE ZETA BEAM USUALLY ZAPS ME BACK TO EARTH FROM RANN JUST AT THE POINT ALANNA AND I START TO GET RATTY IN ONE ANOTHER'S COMPANY.
IF I'M BEING HONEST, I'M A BIT OF A LONER. I PREFER LONG-DISTANCE RELATIONSHIPS AND I LIKE MY OWN COMPANY.
I DON'T KNOW, THERE'S JUST...SOMETHING I CAN'T STAND ABOUT THAT WHOLE STUCK-UP ALIEN PRINCESS ACT!
YOU KNOW HOW THERE ARE SOME PEOPLE WHO DRIVE YOU NUTS AND YOU DON'T KNOW WHY?
MAYBE IT'S TO DO WITH ZODIAC SIGNS OR PHEROMONES OR THE AGE GAP OR...

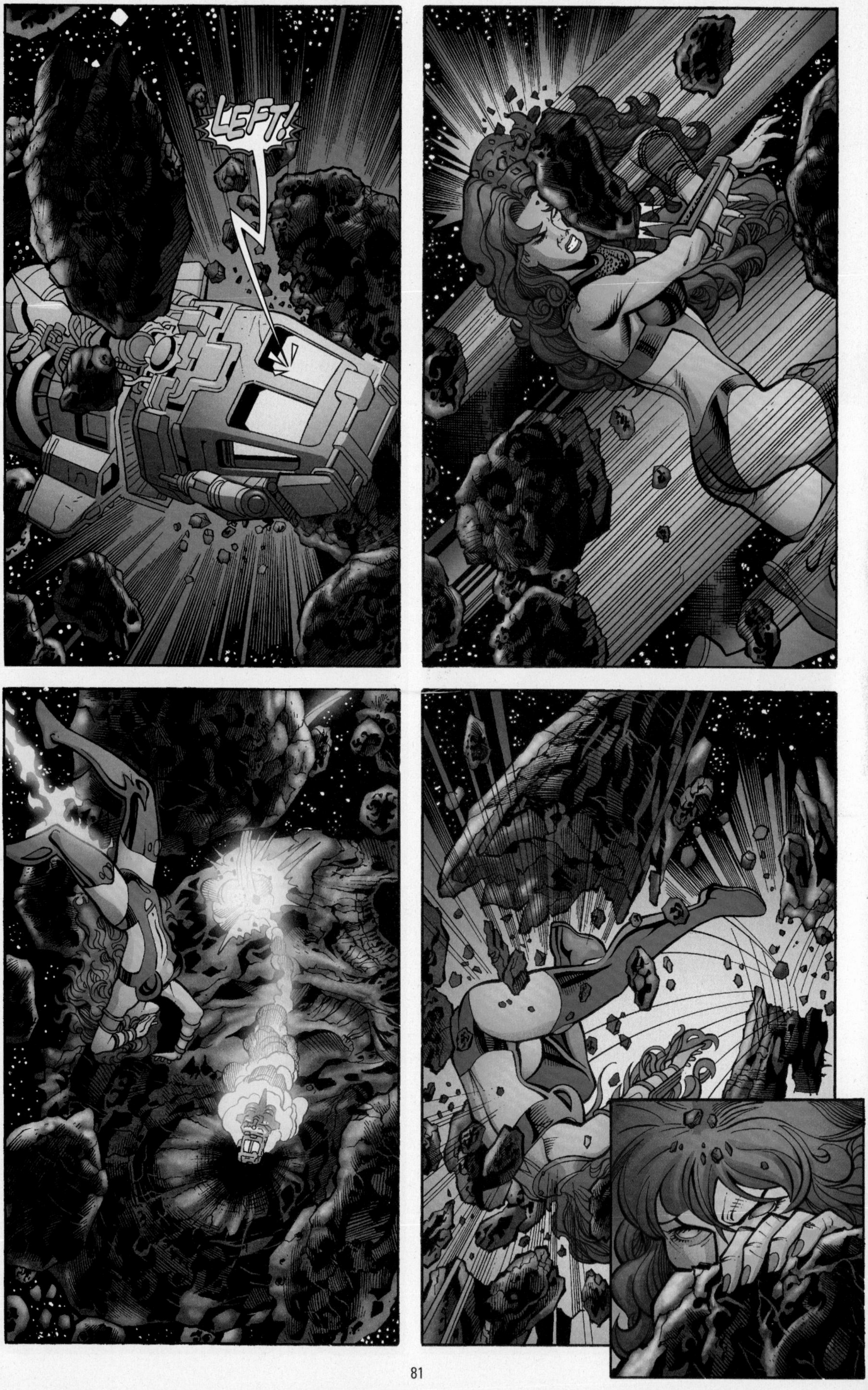
LEFT!

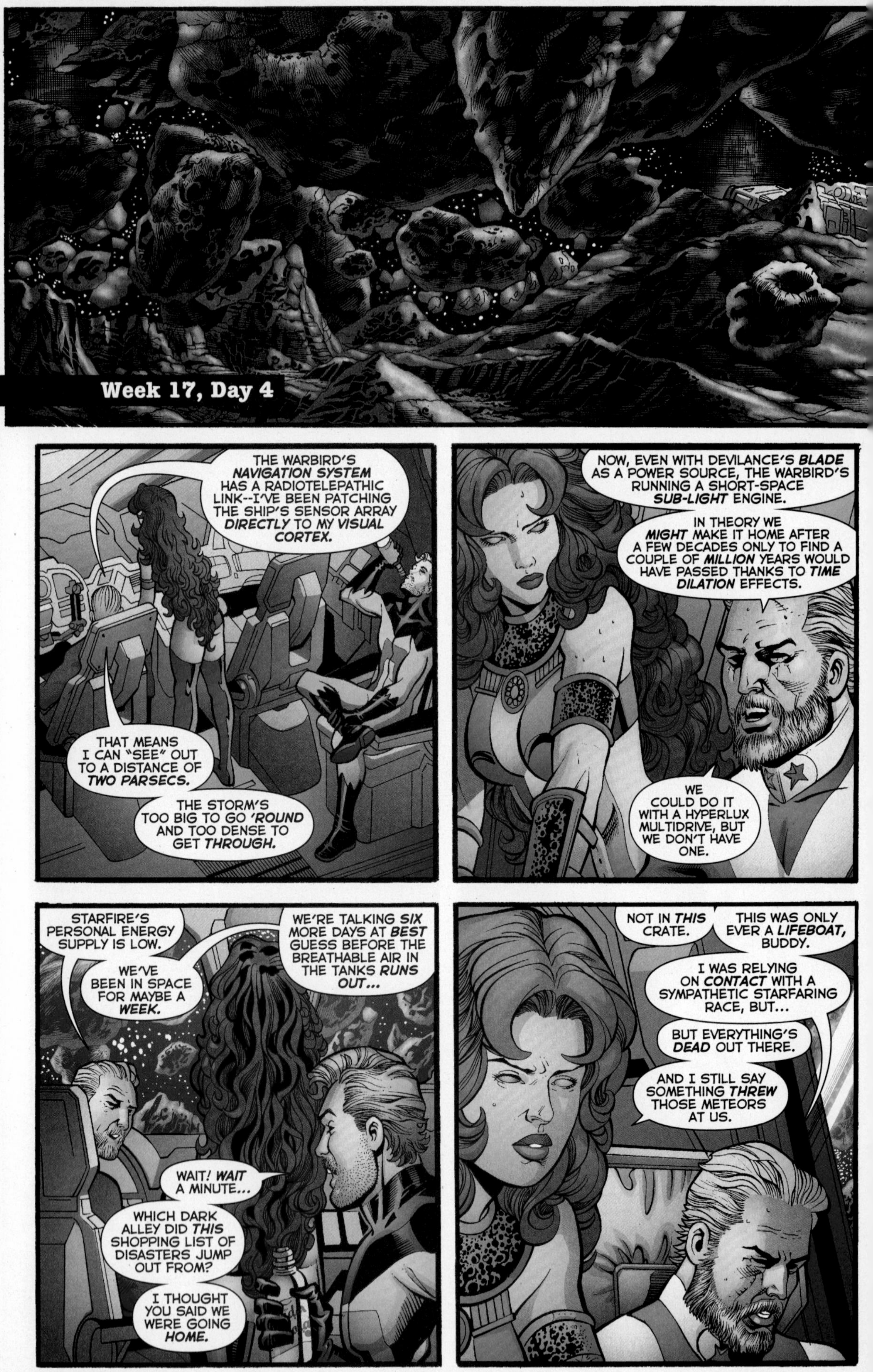
Week 17, Day 4
THE WARBIRD'S NAVIGATION SYSTEM HAS A RADIOTELEPATHIC LINK--I'VE BEEN PATCHING THE SHIP'S SENSOR ARRAY DIRECTLY TO MY VISUAL CORTEX.
THAT MEANS I CAN "SEE" OUT TO A DISTANCE OF TWO PARSECS.
THE STORM'S TOO BIG TO GO 'ROUND AND TOO DENSE TO GET THROUGH.
NOW, EVEN WITH DEVILANCE'S BLADE AS A POWER SOURCE, THE WARBIRD'S RUNNING A SHORT-SPACE SUB-LIGHT ENGINE.
IN THEORY WE MIGHT MAKE IT HOME AFTER A FEW DECADES ONLY TO FIND A COUPLE OF MILLION YEARS WOULD HAVE PASSED THANKS TO TIME DILATION EFFECTS.
WE COULD DO IT WITH A HYPERLUX MULTIDRIVE, BUT WE DON'T HAVE ONE.
STARFIRE'S PERSONAL ENERGY SUPPLY IS LOW.
WE'VE BEEN IN SPACE FOR MAYBE A WEEK.
WE'RE TALKING SIX MORE DAYS AT BEST GUESS BEFORE THE BREATHABLE AIR IN THE TANKS RUNS OUT...
WAIT! WAIT A MINUTE...
WHICH DARK ALLEY DID THIS SHOPPING LIST OF DISASTERS JUMP OUT FROM?
I THOUGHT YOU SAID WE WERE GOING HOME.
NOT IN THIS CRATE.
THIS WAS ONLY EVER A LIFEBOAT, BUDDY.
I WAS RELYING ON CONTACT WITH A SYMPATHETIC STARFARING RACE, BUT...
BUT EVERYTHING'S DEAD OUT THERE.
AND I STILL SAY SOMETHING THREW THOSE METEORS AT US.

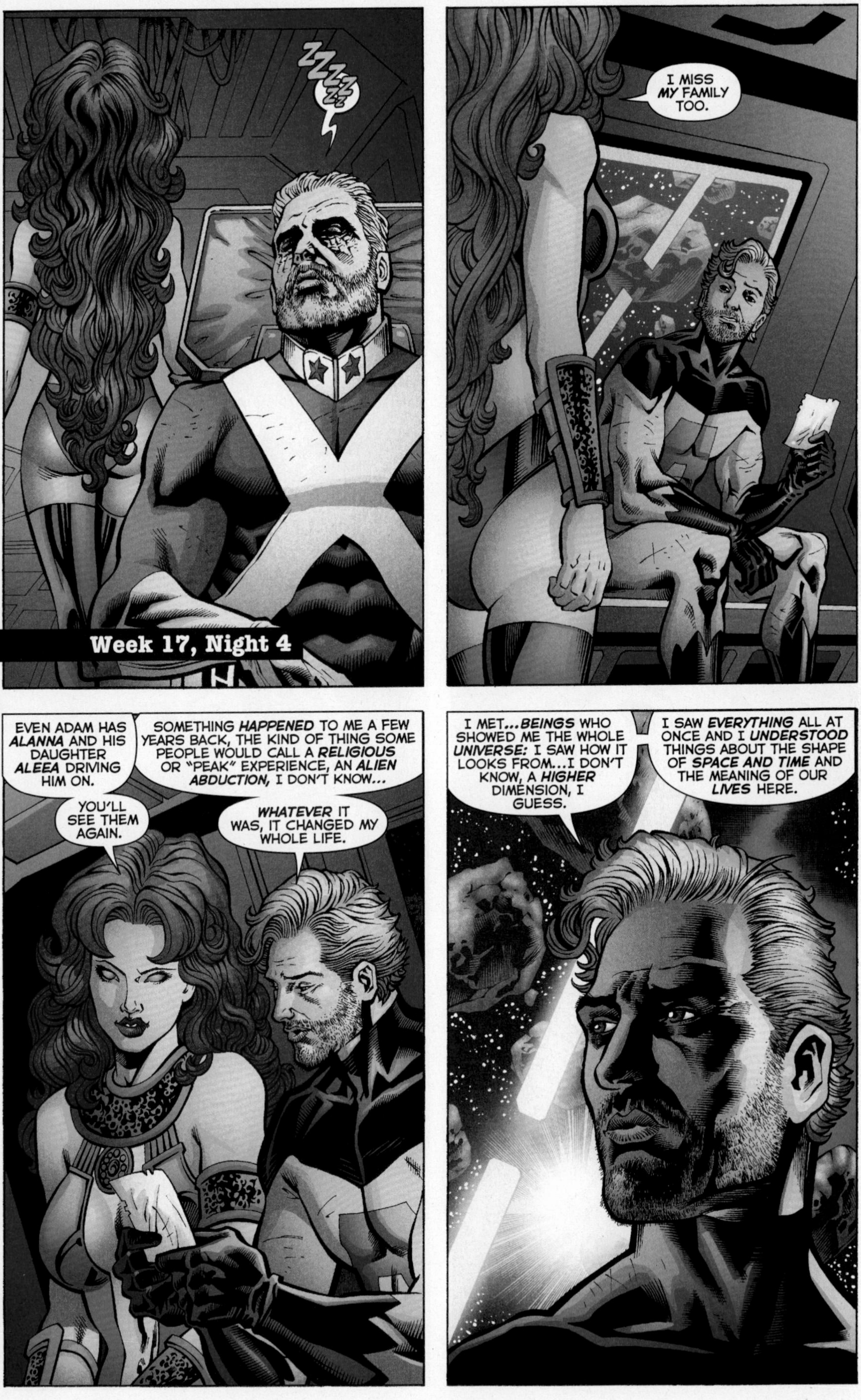
ZZZZZ
Week 17, Night 4
I MISS MY FAMILY TOO.
EVEN ADAM HAS ALANNA AND HIS DAUGHTER ALEEA DRIVING HIM ON.
YOU'LL SEE THEM AGAIN.
SOMETHING HAPPENED TO ME A FEW YEARS BACK, THE KIND OF THING SOME PEOPLE WOULD CALL A RELIGIOUS OR "PEAK" EXPERIENCE, AN ALIEN ABDUCTION, I DON'T KNOW...
WHATEVER IT WAS, IT CHANGED MY WHOLE LIFE.
I MET...BEINGS WHO SHOWED ME THE WHOLE UNIVERSE: I SAW HOW IT LOOKS FROM...I DON'T KNOW, A HIGHER DIMENSION, I GUESS.
I SAW EVERYTHING ALL AT ONCE AND I UNDERSTOOD THINGS ABOUT THE SHAPE OF SPACE AND TIME AND THE MEANING OF OUR LIVES HERE.

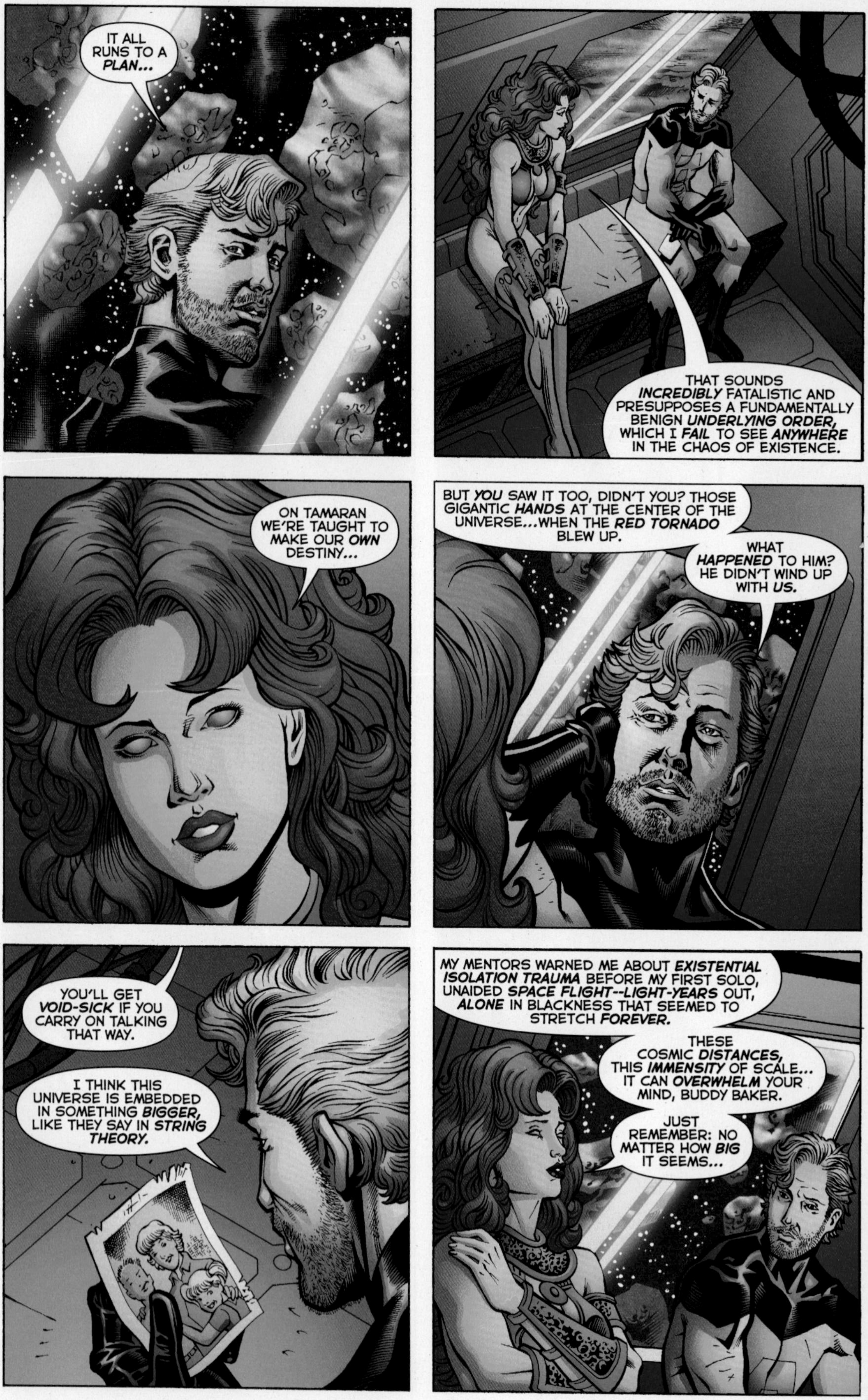
IT ALL RUNS TO A PLAN...
THAT SOUNDS INCREDIBLY FATALISTIC AND PRESUPPOSES A FUNDAMENTALLY BENIGN UNDERLYING ORDER, WHICH I FAIL TO SEE ANYWHERE IN THE CHAOS OF EXISTENCE.
ON TAMARAN WE'RE TAUGHT TO MAKE OUR OWN DESTINY...
BUT YOU SAW IT TOO, DIDN'T YOU? THOSE GIGANTIC HANDS AT THE CENTER OF THE UNIVERSE...WHEN THE RED TORNADO BLEW UP.
WHAT HAPPENED TO HIM? HE DIDN'T WIND UP WITH US.
YOU'LL GET VOID-SICK IF YOU CARRY ON TALKING THAT WAY.
I THINK THIS UNIVERSE IS EMBEDDED IN SOMETHING BIGGER, LIKE THEY SAY IN STRING THEORY.
MY MENTORS WARNED ME ABOUT EXISTENTIAL ISOLATION TRAUMA BEFORE MY FIRST SOLO, UNAIDED SPACE FLIGHT--LIGHT-YEARS OUT, ALONE IN BLACKNESS THAT SEEMED TO STRETCH FOREVER.
THESE COSMIC DISTANCES, THIS IMMENSITY OF SCALE... IT CAN OVERWHELM YOUR MIND, BUDDY BAKER.
JUST REMEMBER: NO MATTER HOW BIG IT SEEMS...

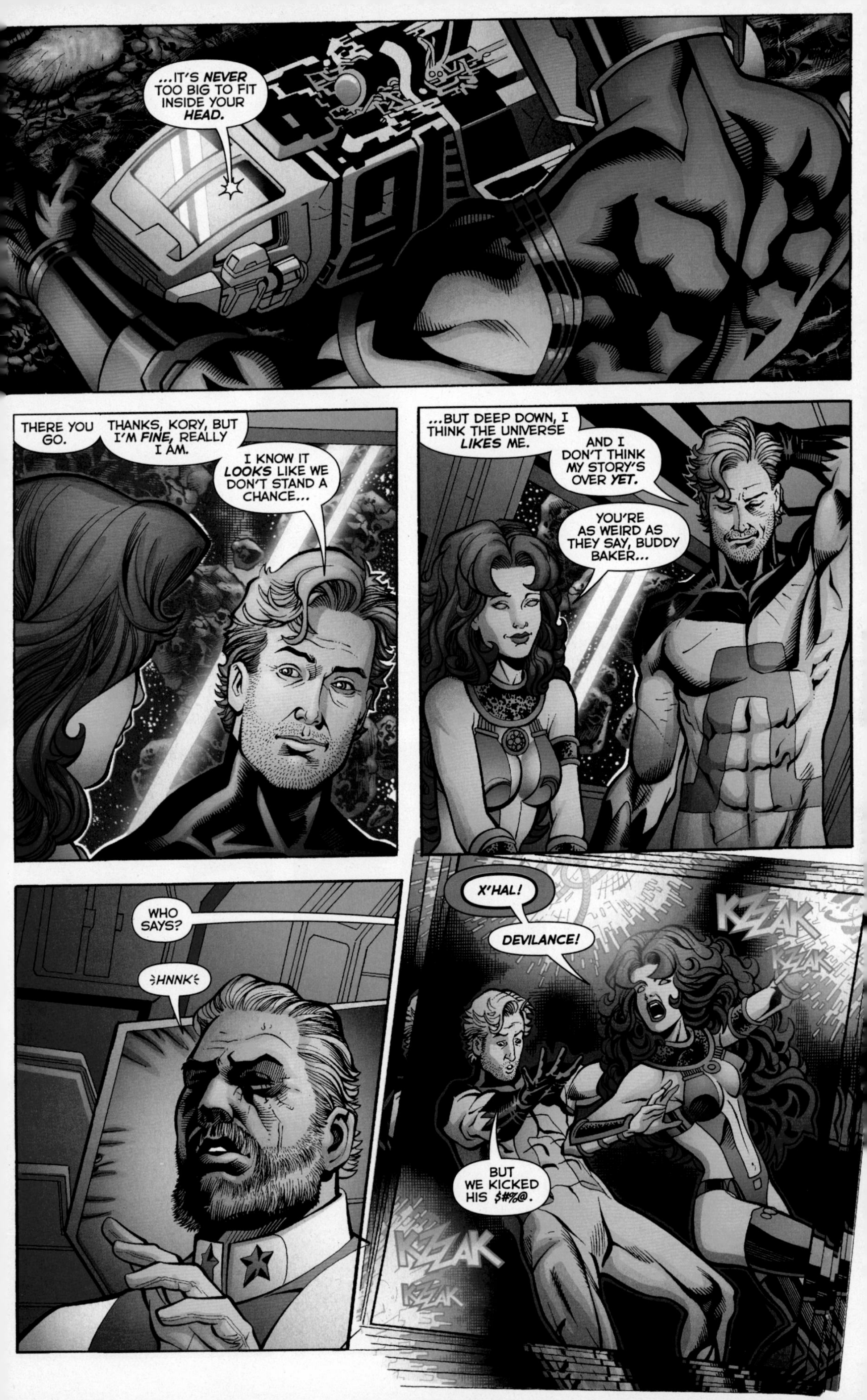
...IT'S NEVER TOO BIG TO FIT INSIDE YOUR HEAD.
THERE YOU GO.
THANKS, KORY, BUT I'M FINE, REALLY I AM.
I KNOW IT LOOKS LIKE WE DON'T STAND A CHANCE...
...BUT DEEP DOWN, I THINK THE UNIVERSE LIKES ME.
AND I DON'T THINK MY STORY'S OVER YET.
YOU'RE AS WEIRD AS THEY SAY, BUDDY BAKER...
WHO SAYS?
HNNK
X'HAL!
DEVILANCE!
KZZAK
KZZAK
BUT WE KICKED HIS $#%@.
KZZAK
KZZAK

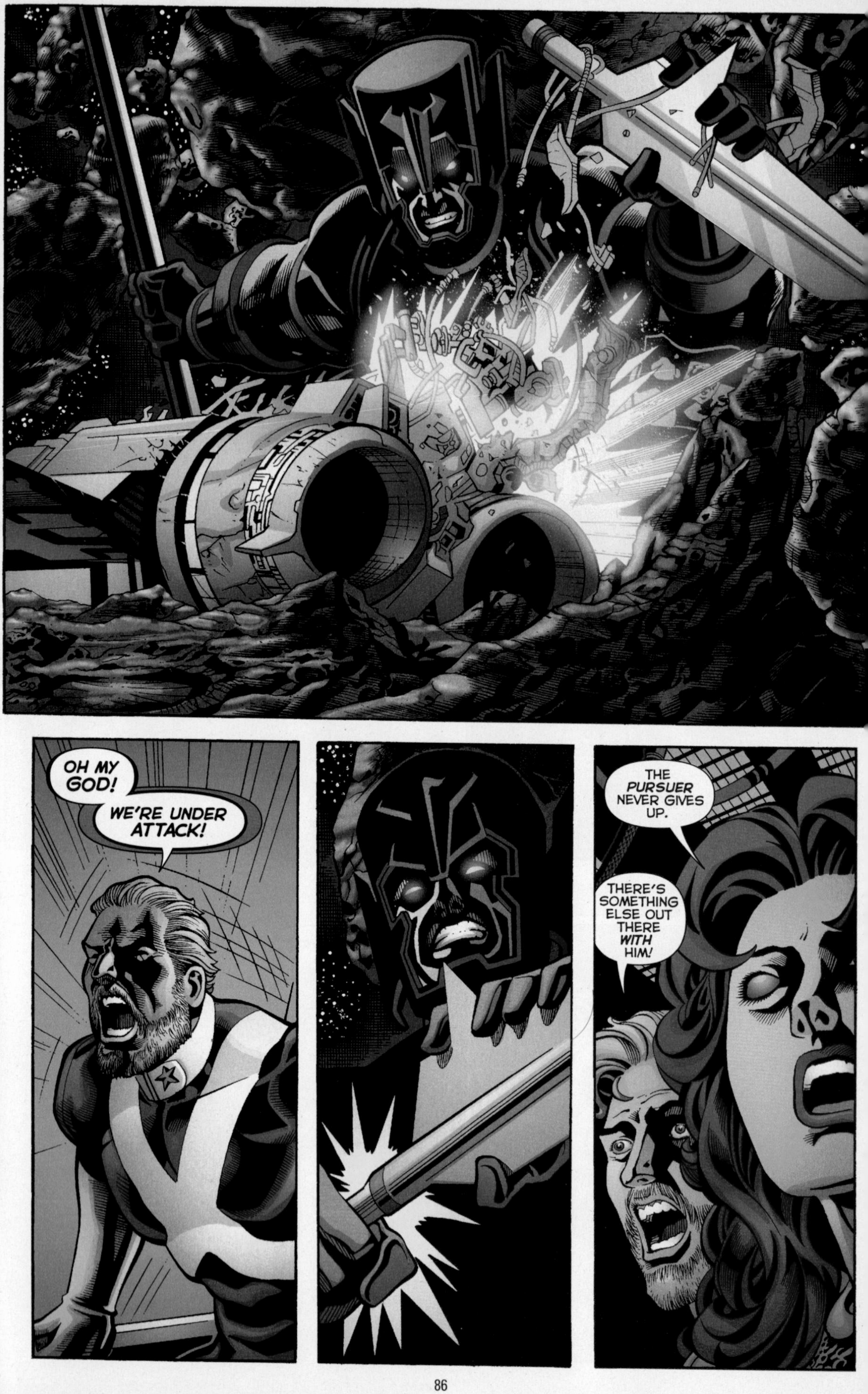
OH MY GOD!
WE'RE UNDER ATTACK!
THE PURSUER NEVER GIVES UP.
THERE'S SOMETHING ELSE OUT THERE WITH HIM!

A HUGE ENERGY SPIKE!

WHAT THE HELL IS IT?

WHAT CAN YOU SEE?

JUST ABOUT EVERYTHING... FROM THE INSIDE OUT.

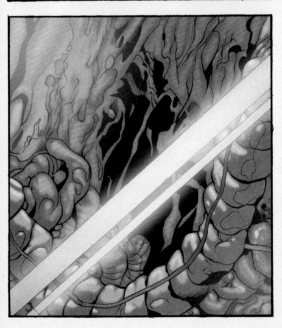

WHO'S THERE?

X'HAL!

LOBO.

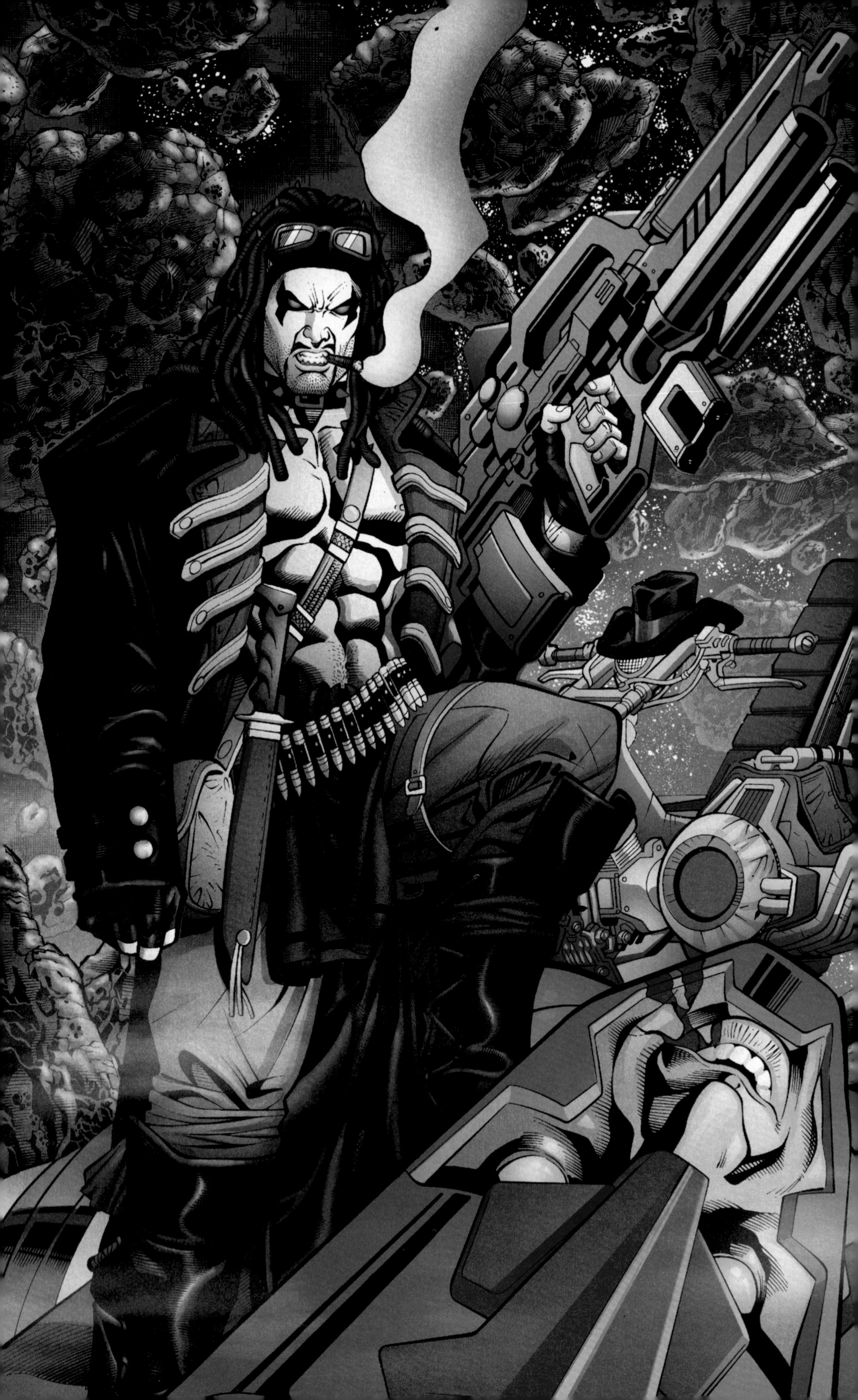

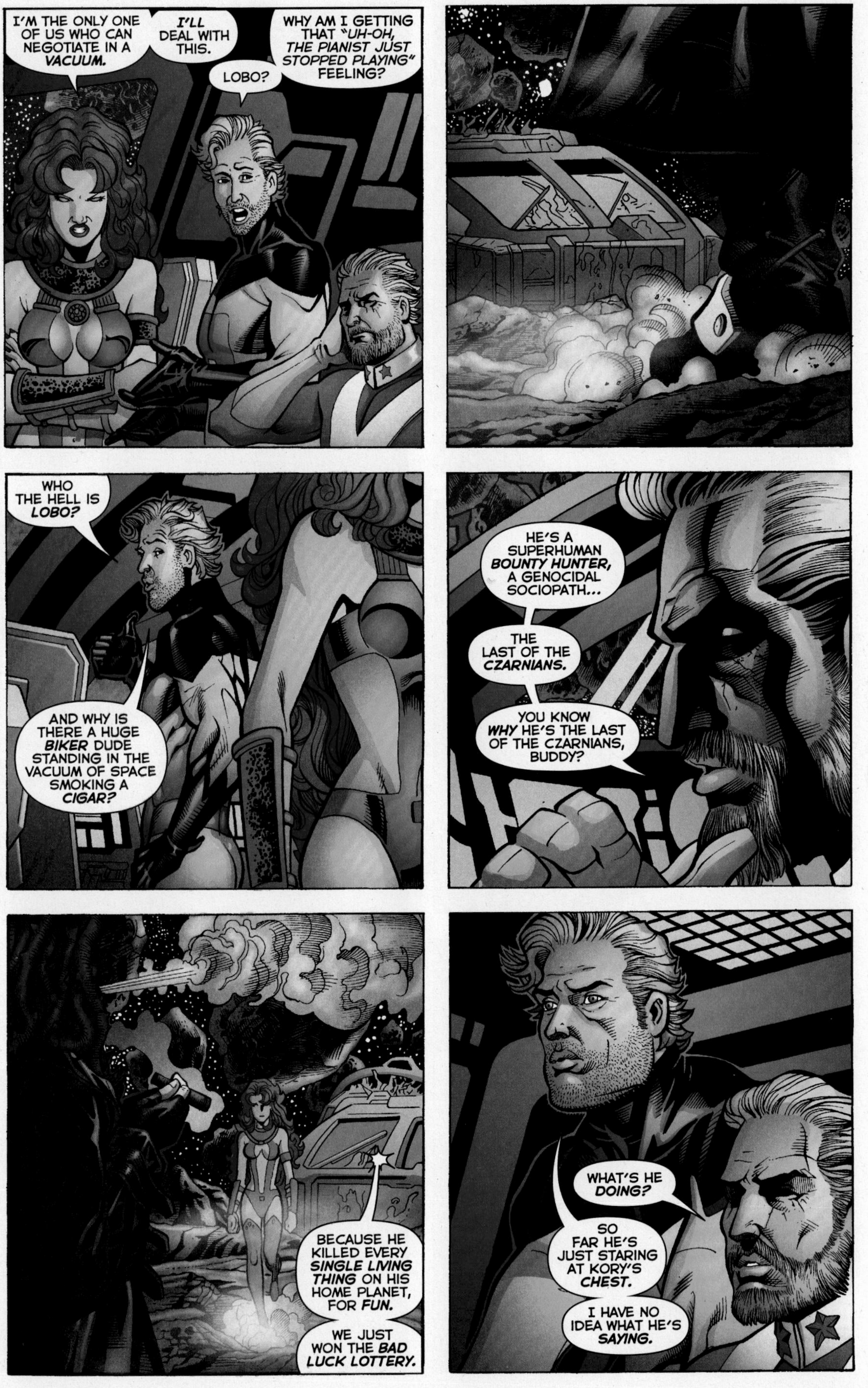
I'M THE ONLY ONE OF US WHO CAN NEGOTIATE IN A VACUUM.
I'LL DEAL WITH THIS.
LOBO?
WHY AM I GETTING THAT "UH-OH, THE PIANIST JUST STOPPED PLAYING" FEELING?
WHO THE HELL IS LOBO?
AND WHY IS THERE A HUGE BIKER DUDE STANDING IN THE VACUUM OF SPACE SMOKING A CIGAR?
HE'S A SUPERHUMAN BOUNTY HUNTER, A GENOCIDAL SOCIOPATH...
THE LAST OF THE CZARNIANS.
YOU KNOW WHY HE'S THE LAST OF THE CZARNIANS, BUDDY?
BECAUSE HE KILLED EVERY SINGLE LIVING THING ON HIS HOME PLANET, FOR FUN.
WE JUST WON THE BAD LUCK LOTTERY.
WHAT'S HE DOING?
SO FAR HE'S JUST STARING AT KORY'S CHEST.
I HAVE NO IDEA WHAT HE'S SAYING.

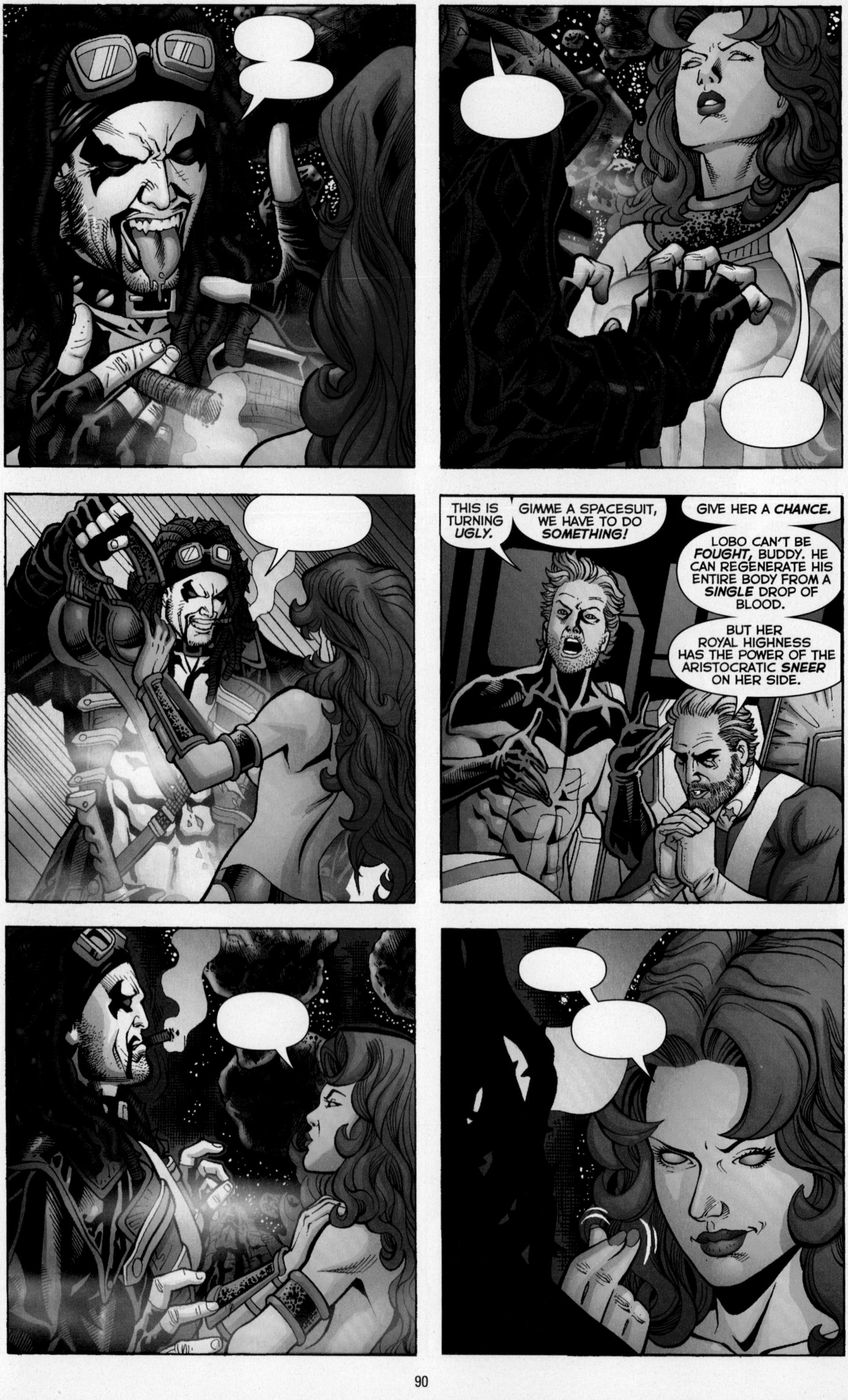

THIS IS TURNING *UGLY.*
GIMME A SPACESUIT, WE HAVE TO DO *SOMETHING!*
GIVE HER A *CHANCE.*
LOBO CAN'T BE *FOUGHT,* BUDDY. HE CAN REGENERATE HIS ENTIRE BODY FROM A *SINGLE* DROP OF BLOOD.
BUT HER ROYAL HIGHNESS HAS THE POWER OF THE ARISTOCRATIC *SNEER* ON HER SIDE.

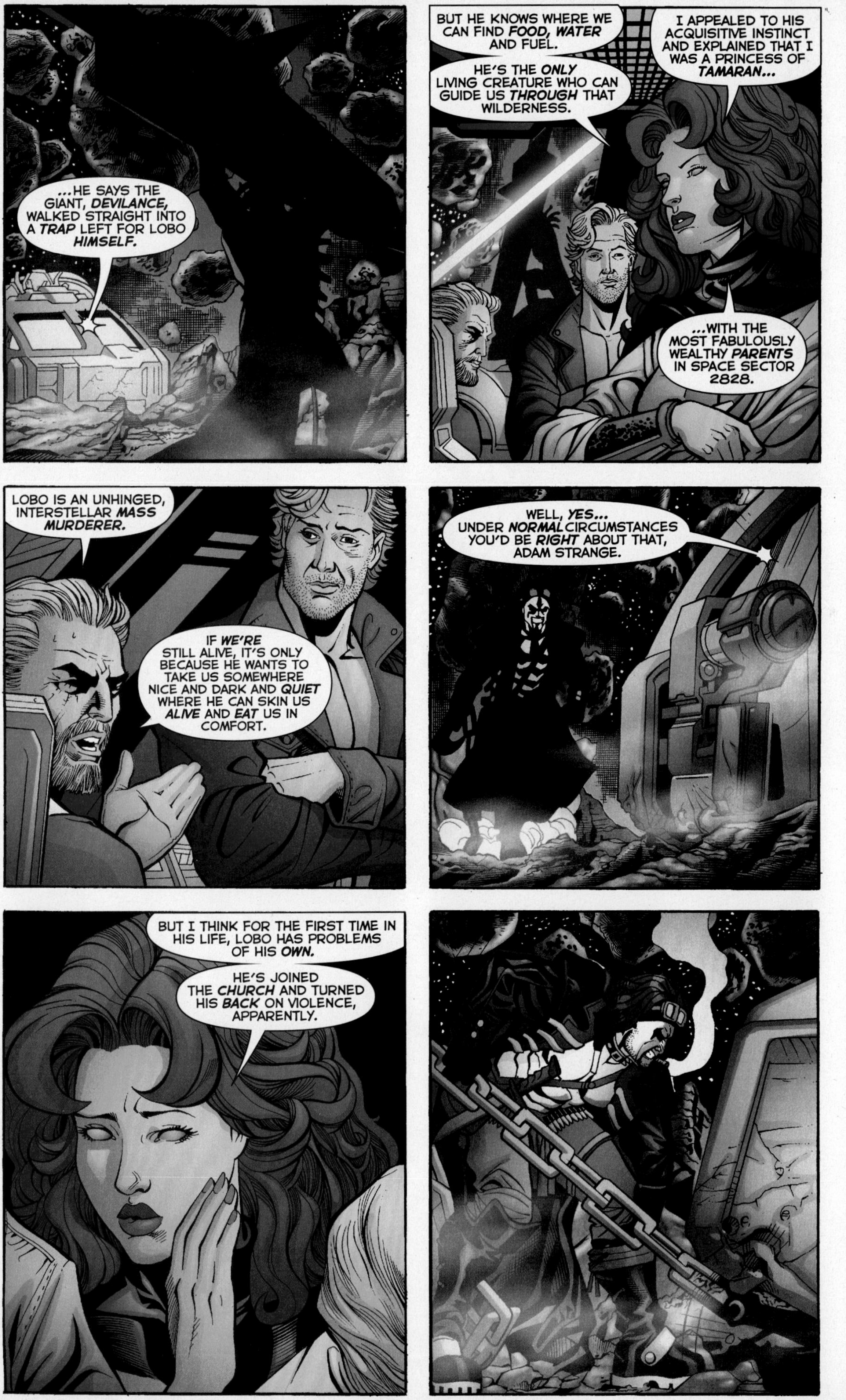
...HE SAYS THE GIANT, DEVILANCE, WALKED STRAIGHT INTO A TRAP LEFT FOR LOBO HIMSELF.
BUT HE KNOWS WHERE WE CAN FIND FOOD, WATER AND FUEL.
HE'S THE ONLY LIVING CREATURE WHO CAN GUIDE US THROUGH THAT WILDERNESS.
I APPEALED TO HIS ACQUISITIVE INSTINCT AND EXPLAINED THAT I WAS A PRINCESS OF TAMARAN...
...WITH THE MOST FABULOUSLY WEALTHY PARENTS IN SPACE SECTOR 2828.
LOBO IS AN UNHINGED, INTERSTELLAR MASS MURDERER.
IF WE'RE STILL ALIVE, IT'S ONLY BECAUSE HE WANTS TO TAKE US SOMEWHERE NICE AND DARK AND QUIET WHERE HE CAN SKIN US ALIVE AND EAT US IN COMFORT.
WELL, YES... UNDER NORMAL CIRCUMSTANCES YOU'D BE RIGHT ABOUT THAT, ADAM STRANGE.
BUT I THINK FOR THE FIRST TIME IN HIS LIFE, LOBO HAS PROBLEMS OF HIS OWN.
HE'S JOINED THE CHURCH AND TURNED HIS BACK ON VIOLENCE, APPARENTLY.

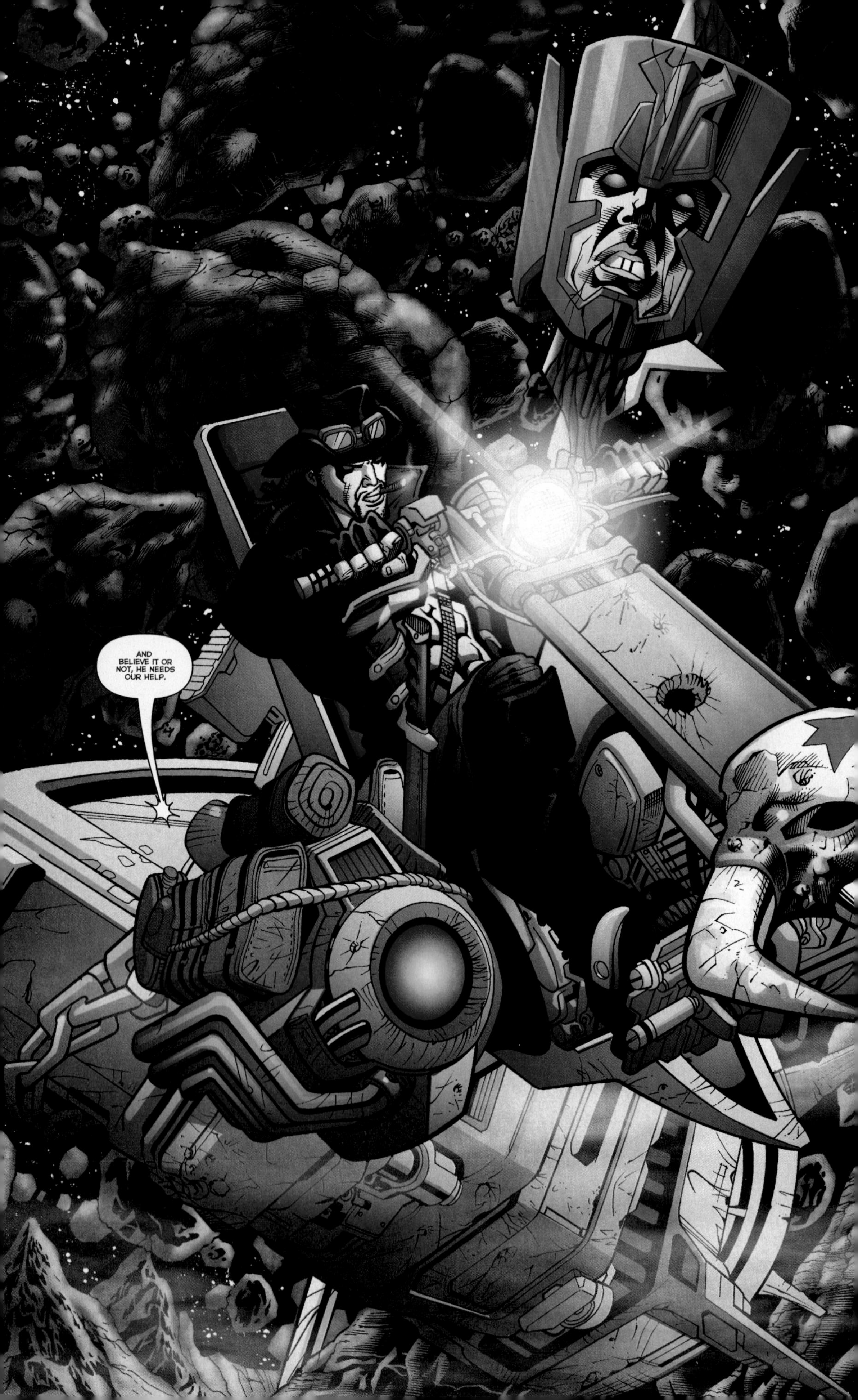
AND BELIEVE IT OR NOT, HE NEEDS OUR HELP.

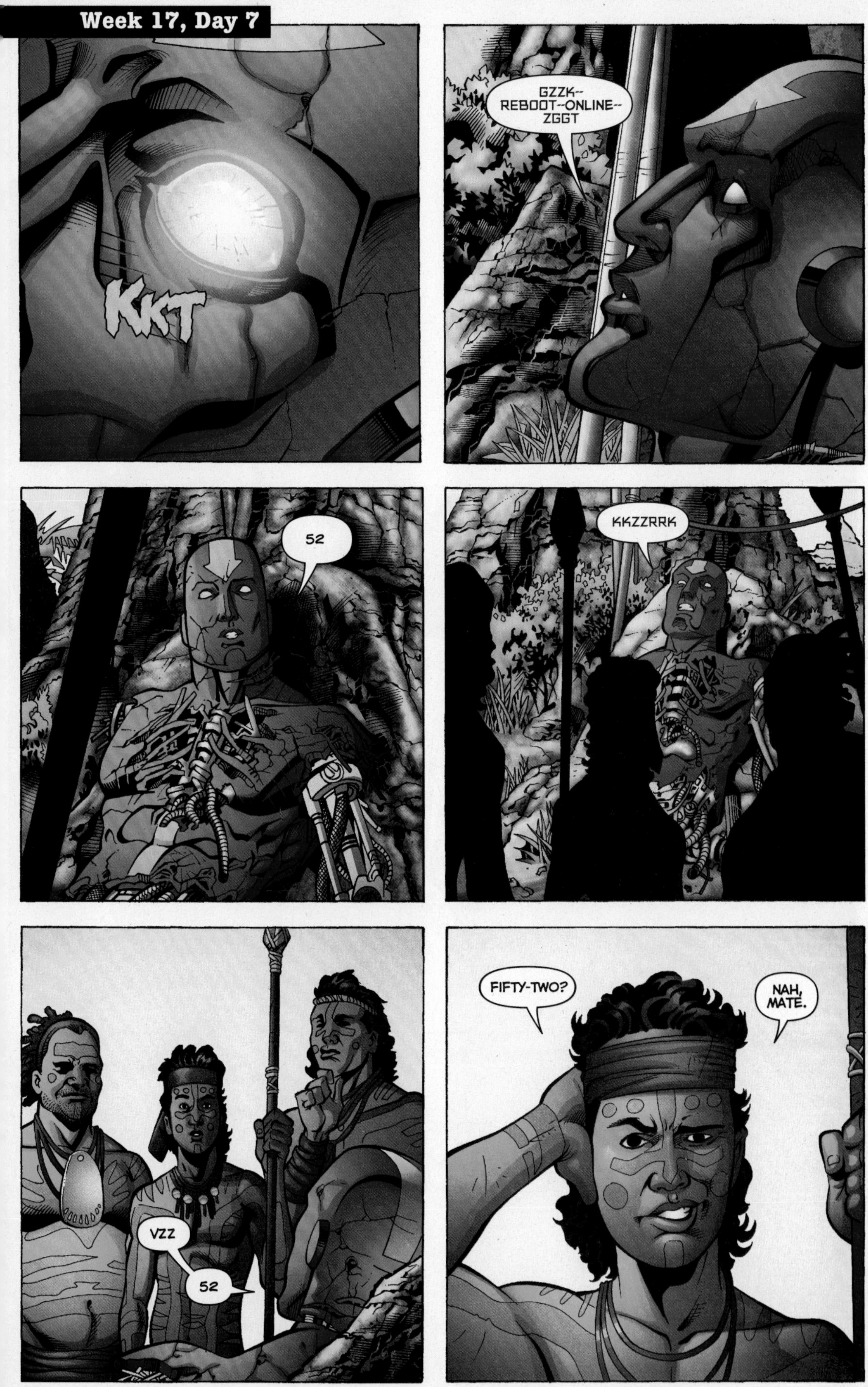
Week 17, Day 7
KKT
GZZK--
REBOOT--ONLINE--
ZGGT
52
KKZZRRK
VZZ
52
FIFTY-TWO?
NAH, MATE.

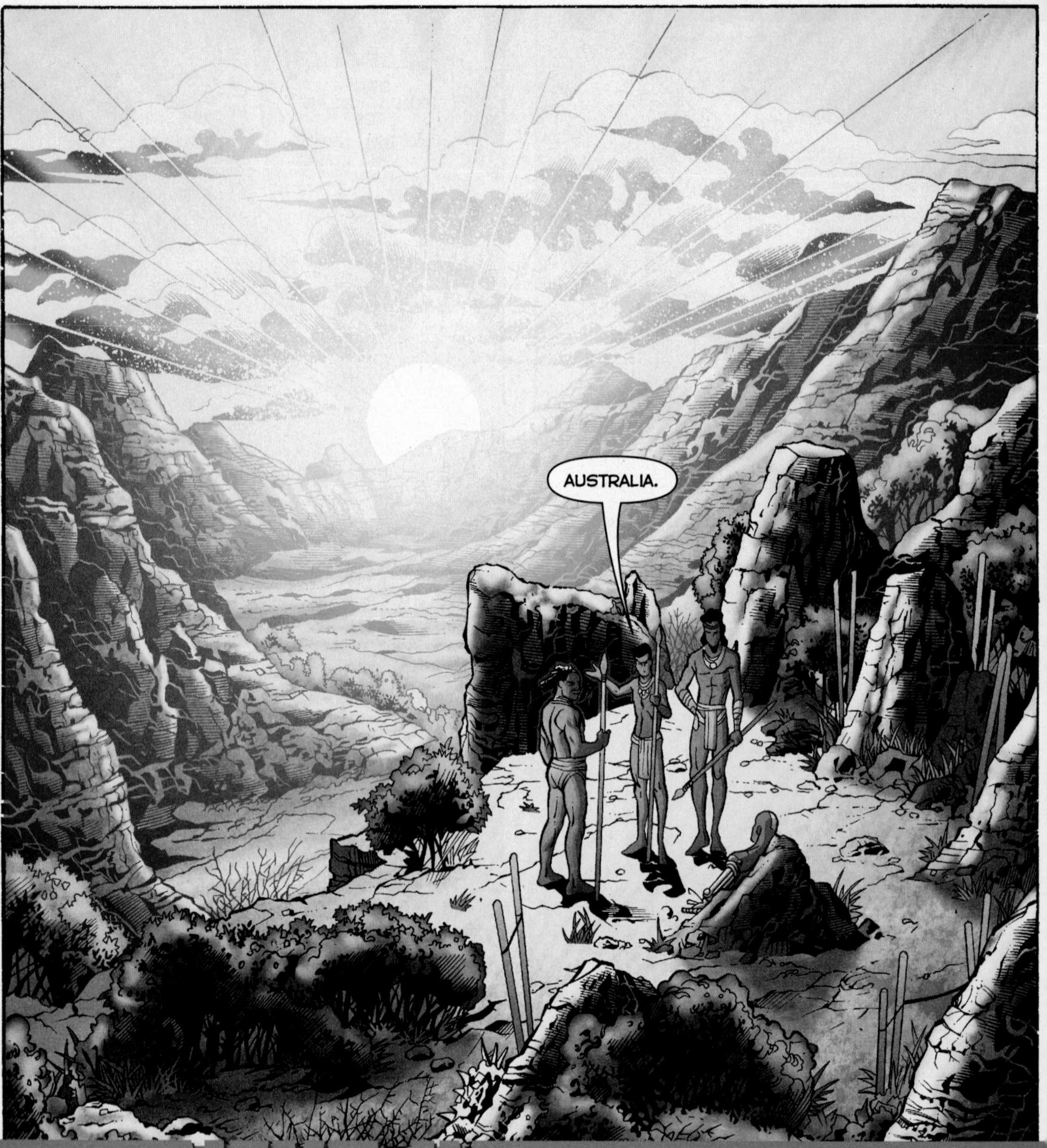
AUSTRALIA.

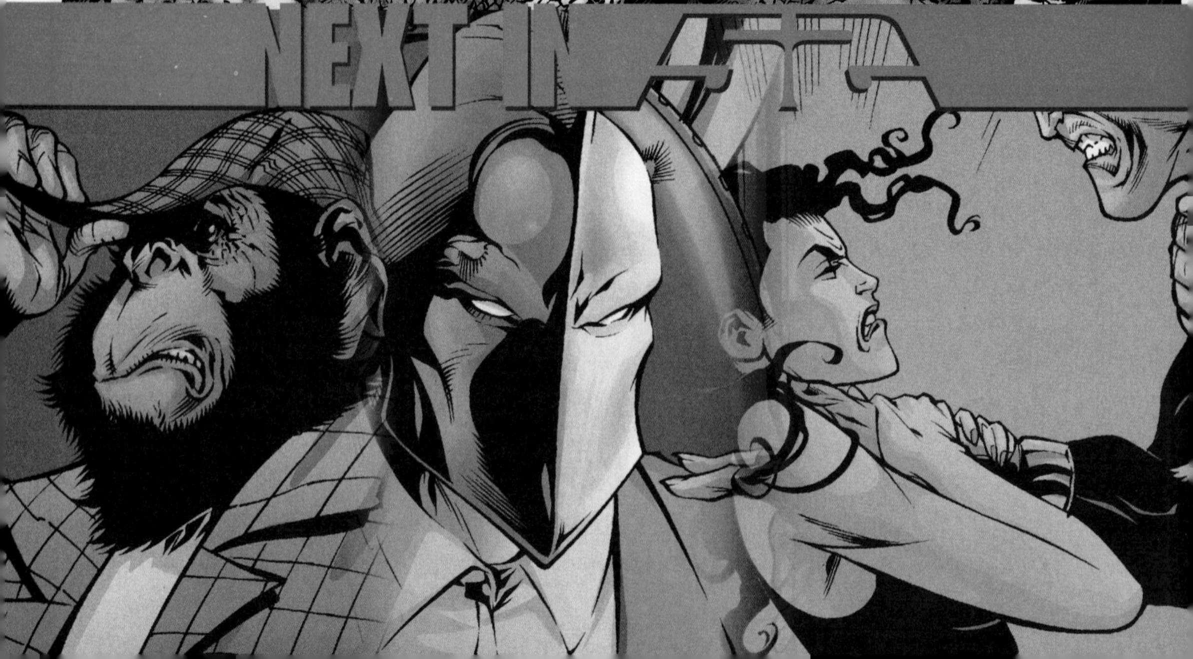
NEXT IN

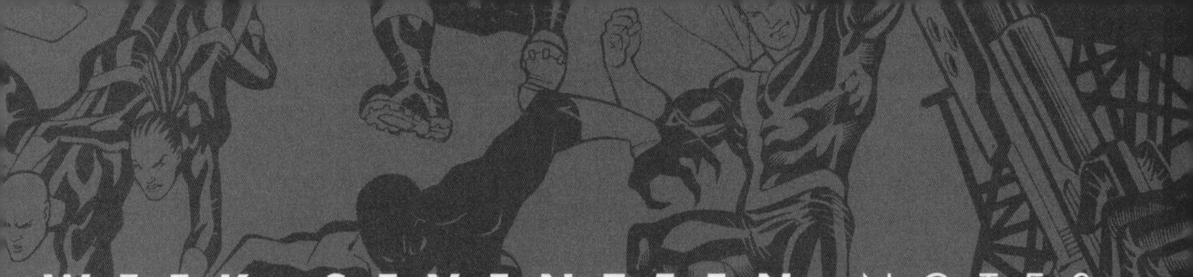

WEEK SEVENTEEN NOTES

KEITH GIFFEN

Aww... Fer the luvva... Who let him in?

For the record, Lobo was not my idea. In fact, I distinctly remember cringing at the "52" summit when his name was brought up and all eyes locked on me. Not that I don't like the character...the Czarnian's been pretty good to me, it's just...I had nothing else I wanted to say with the character and, truth be told, I was more than a little bored with all of the mindless mayhem.

Then I remembered, as if one could ever forget, that Grant was in the room. I all but begged him to take Lobo and make the character his own, to sprinkle some of that rather suspect Morrison magic dust and take the character in a bold, new direction, one as far from me as possible. Grant's reaction?

"I don't know...I've never really liked Lobo."

That's when I knew I had him.

I could practically see the gears turning as he mulled the character over. The end result? Pope Lobo and his trusty space dolphin companion. Pure Morrison. Oh, and, as it turned out, once Grant did a bit of research into the character, he found that he did, in his own unfathomable way, respond to Lobo. Am I the only one who finds that deeply disturbing?

And, just like that, I was Lobo free! Or so I thought.

As it turned out, fate...okay, Steve Wacker...wasn't about to let me walk away from the character that easily.

I'd been shooting my mouth off for some months before about wanting to pick up the pencil again and draw the occasional backup, short inventory issue, whatever. Be careful what you wish for.

Wacker called me on it, told me there'd be enough time for me to pencil one of Mark's origin backups if I was still interested. I immediately accepted. I immediately, knowing full well Wacker's Machiavellian nature, accepted. I never was the brightest bulb in the chandelier.

Which brings us to the Lobo origin pencilled by yours truly [to be collected in another trade paperback down the line]. I'd say it was fun to do, but I refuse to give Wacker the satisfaction. Petty? You bet, but I wouldn't judge too harshly until you've worked with the man. Then you'd understand.

Oh, and I still think that word balloon on the cover, "Only 35 more ta go," was a direct stab at me. We were seventeen weeks in and I was still sounding off about lead time and ship dates and hitting each week. OCD doesn't begin to describe it. And having Lobo deliver the line?

Well, that...that was just cruel.

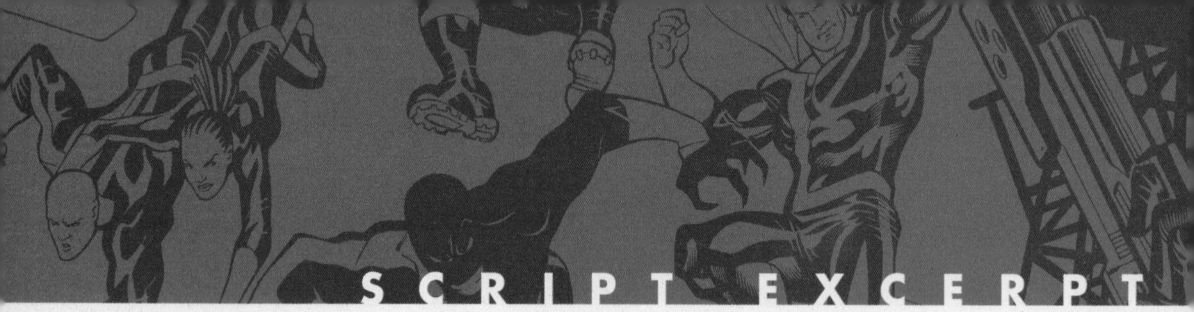

S C R I P T E X C E R P T

(COMPARE WITH PAGE 87 OF THIS COLLECTION)

WEEK SEVENTEEN - PAGE THIRTEEN

PANEL ONE
Looking down over Devilance's shoulders. He lifts his lance as if to strike down through the cockpit of the Warbird, at the people within...

> **ADAM:** There's something else out there WITH him. A HUGE energy spike!

PANEL TWO
Something distracts him and he begins to turn his head.

PANEL THREE
Starfire brings her hand to her mouth, Buddy's eyes bulge with complete shock as he sees something he's never seen before — the evisceration of a God is occurring offscreen... Adam sees nothing but is sensing the action through the ship's systems.

> **ADAM:** What the hell IS it?

> **ADAM:** What can you SEE?

PANEL FOUR
Looking over the shoulders of our heroes at Devilance's guts, which are now sliding down the window like intricate butcher's offal. We can see all sorts of gloopy coils and glassy mechanism and the sort of bloody bowel machinery only New Gods have.

> **BUDDY (small):** Just about everything...from the inside out.

PANEL FIVE
Move close — the mess of innards slides in a heap down the glass of the cockpit to reveal a shape behind. Silhouetted against the light of his bike is a big, shaggy figure, standing out there in the depths of space without a protective suit. The eyes of the silhouette are narrow red slits. In one hand he lefts a gigantic gun/cannon from which trailing smoke rises. The other hand lifts a bottle to his lips. All backlit, so we don't see him in all his glory yet.
[Editor's note: Don't show figure yet? Save for dramatic splash page]

PANEL SIX
Buddy and Starfire look out. Adam still listening to the radar, yelling.

> **ADAM (big):** WHO'S THERE?

> **STARFIRE (small):** X'Hal!

> **STARFIRE (small):** Lobo.

DC COMICS 52

The House of Mystery.

Week 18, Day 1

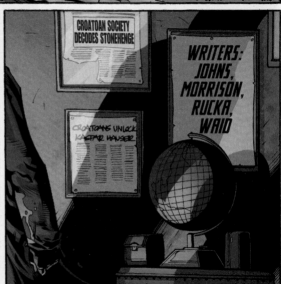

CROATOAN SOCIETY
DECODES STONEHENGE

CROATOANS UNLOCK
KASPAR HAUSER

WRITERS:
JOHNS,
MORRISON,
RUCKA,
WAID

CROATOANS 1
EASTER ISLANDO

MYSTER
RENNES

LAYOUTS:
KEITH GIFFEN
PENCILS:
EDDY BARROWS
INKS:
ROB STULL

PICTURED, L-R: EDOGAWA SANGAKU, TERRI THIRTEEN,
RALPH "ELONGATED MAN" DIBNY, DETECTIVE B.T. CHIMP,
TIM TRENCHO

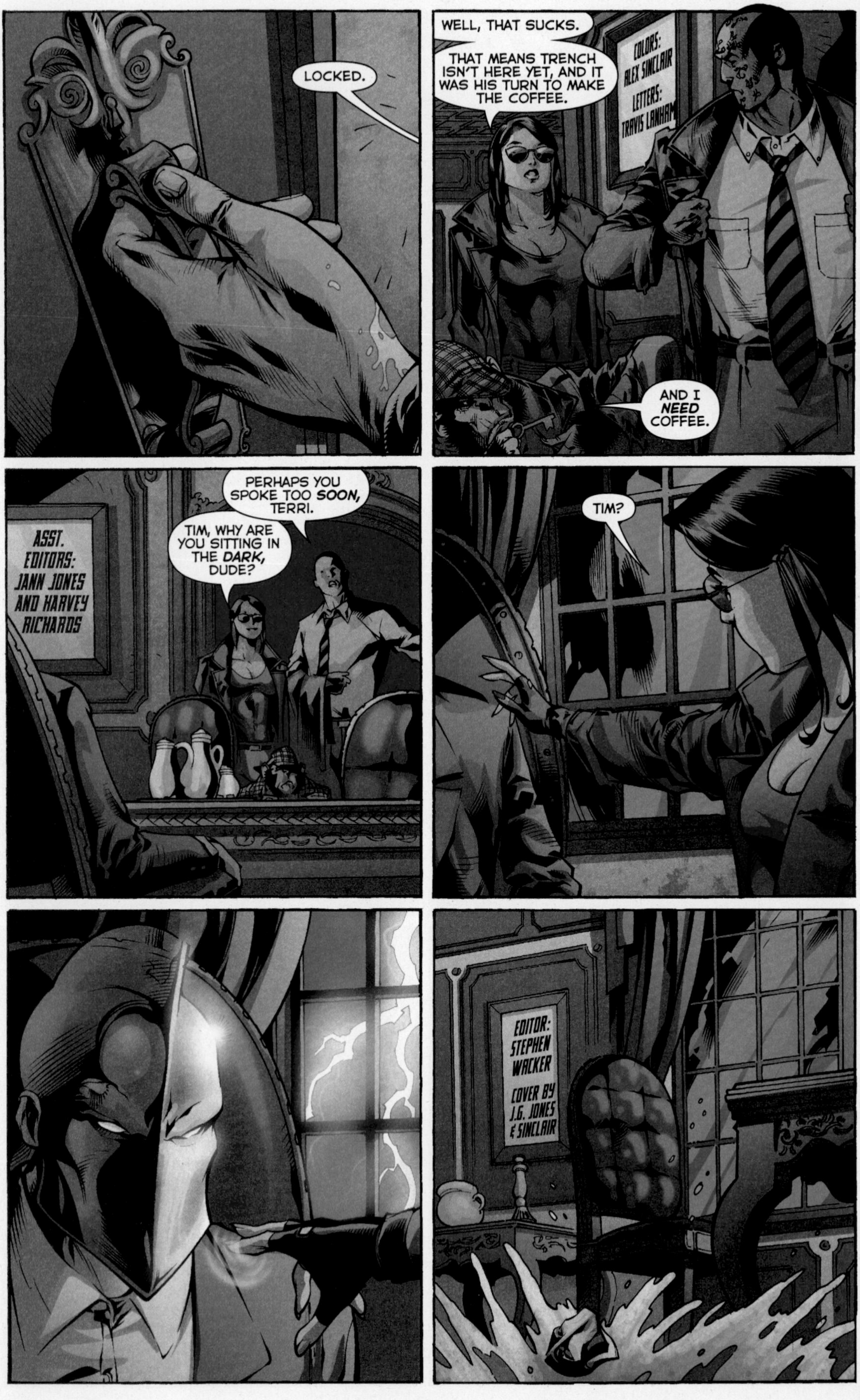
LOCKED.
WELL, THAT SUCKS.
THAT MEANS TRENCH ISN'T HERE YET, AND IT WAS HIS TURN TO MAKE THE COFFEE.
COLORS: ALEX SINCLAIR
LETTERS: TRAVIS LANHAM
AND I NEED COFFEE.
ASST. EDITORS: JANN JONES AND HARVEY RICHARDS
PERHAPS YOU SPOKE TOO SOON, TERRI.
TIM, WHY ARE YOU SITTING IN THE DARK, DUDE?
TIM?
EDITOR: STEPHEN WACKER
COVER BY J.G. JONES & SINCLAIR

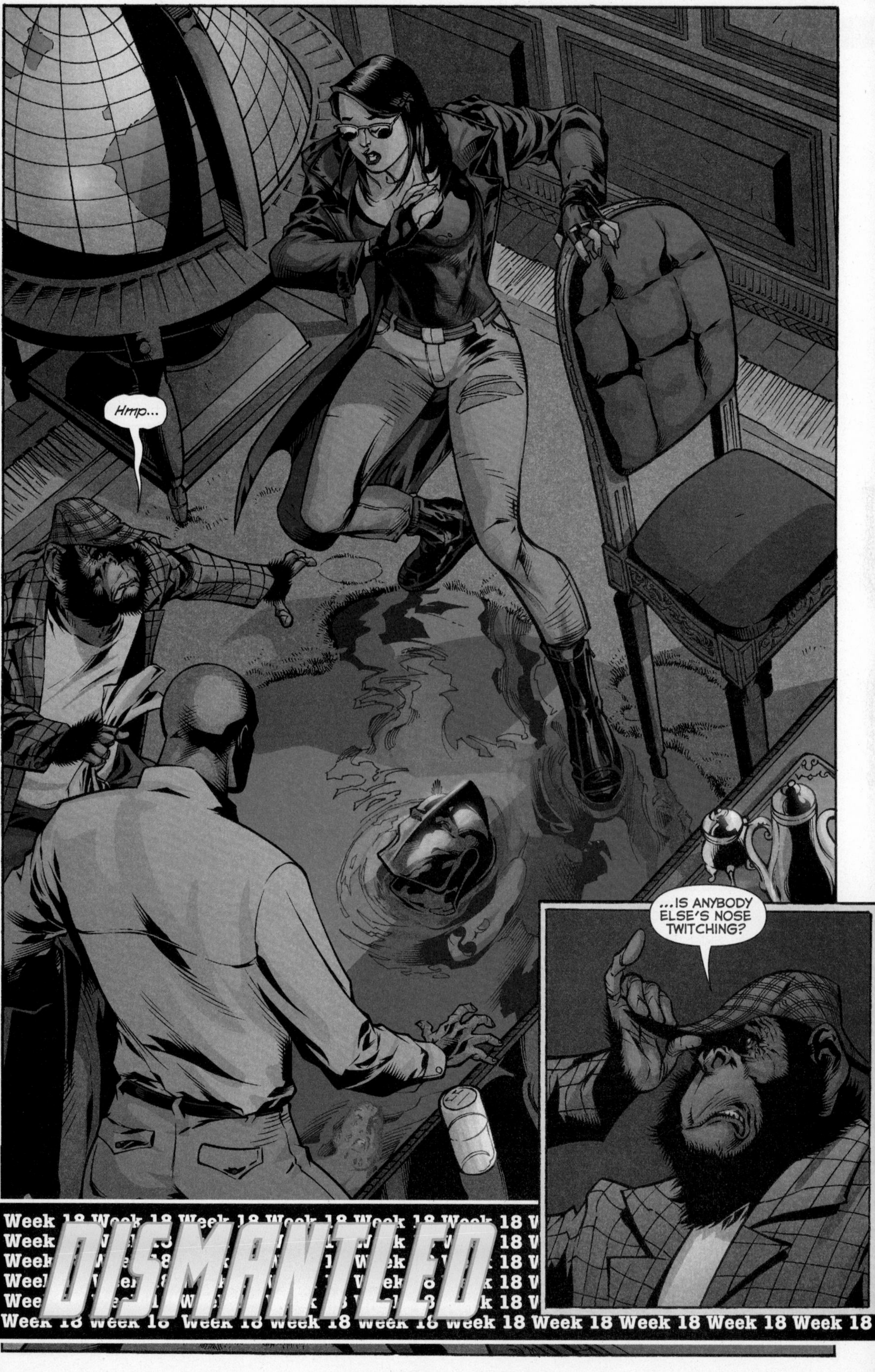
Hmp...
...IS ANYBODY ELSE'S NOSE TWITCHING?
Week 18 Week 18 Week 18 Week 18 Week 18 Week 18 Week 18 Week 18 Week 18 Week 18
DISMANTLED

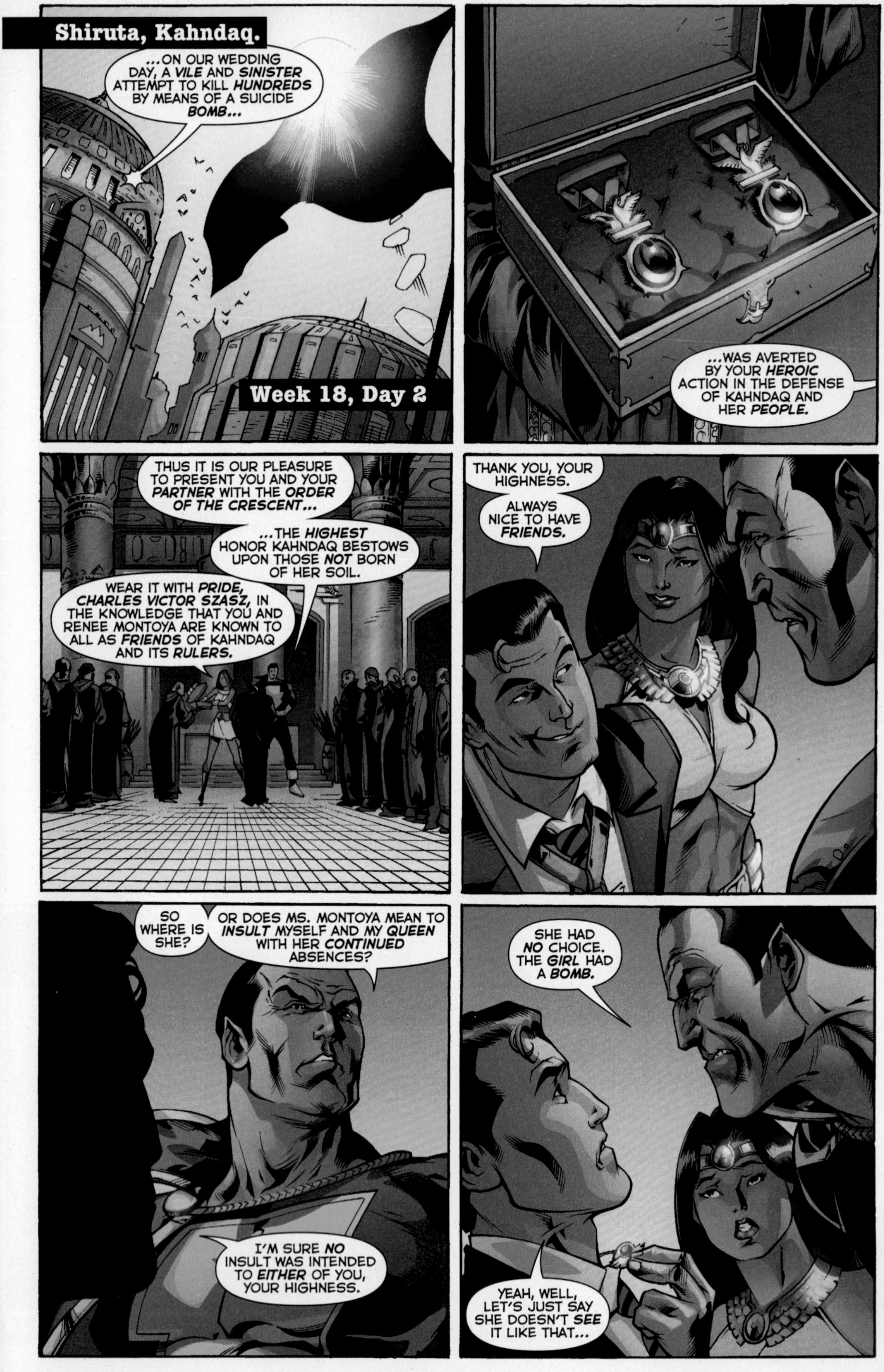
Shiruta, Kahndaq.
...ON OUR WEDDING DAY, A VILE AND SINISTER ATTEMPT TO KILL HUNDREDS BY MEANS OF A SUICIDE BOMB...
Week 18, Day 2
...WAS AVERTED BY YOUR HEROIC ACTION IN THE DEFENSE OF KAHNDAQ AND HER PEOPLE.
THUS IT IS OUR PLEASURE TO PRESENT YOU AND YOUR PARTNER WITH THE ORDER OF THE CRESCENT...
...THE HIGHEST HONOR KAHNDAQ BESTOWS UPON THOSE NOT BORN OF HER SOIL.
WEAR IT WITH PRIDE, CHARLES VICTOR SZASZ, IN THE KNOWLEDGE THAT YOU AND RENEE MONTOYA ARE KNOWN TO ALL AS FRIENDS OF KAHNDAQ AND ITS RULERS.
THANK YOU, YOUR HIGHNESS.
ALWAYS NICE TO HAVE FRIENDS.
SO WHERE IS SHE?
OR DOES MS. MONTOYA MEAN TO INSULT MYSELF AND MY QUEEN WITH HER CONTINUED ABSENCES?
I'M SURE NO INSULT WAS INTENDED TO EITHER OF YOU, YOUR HIGHNESS.
SHE HAD NO CHOICE. THE GIRL HAD A BOMB.
YEAH, WELL, LET'S JUST SAY SHE DOESN'T SEE IT LIKE THAT...

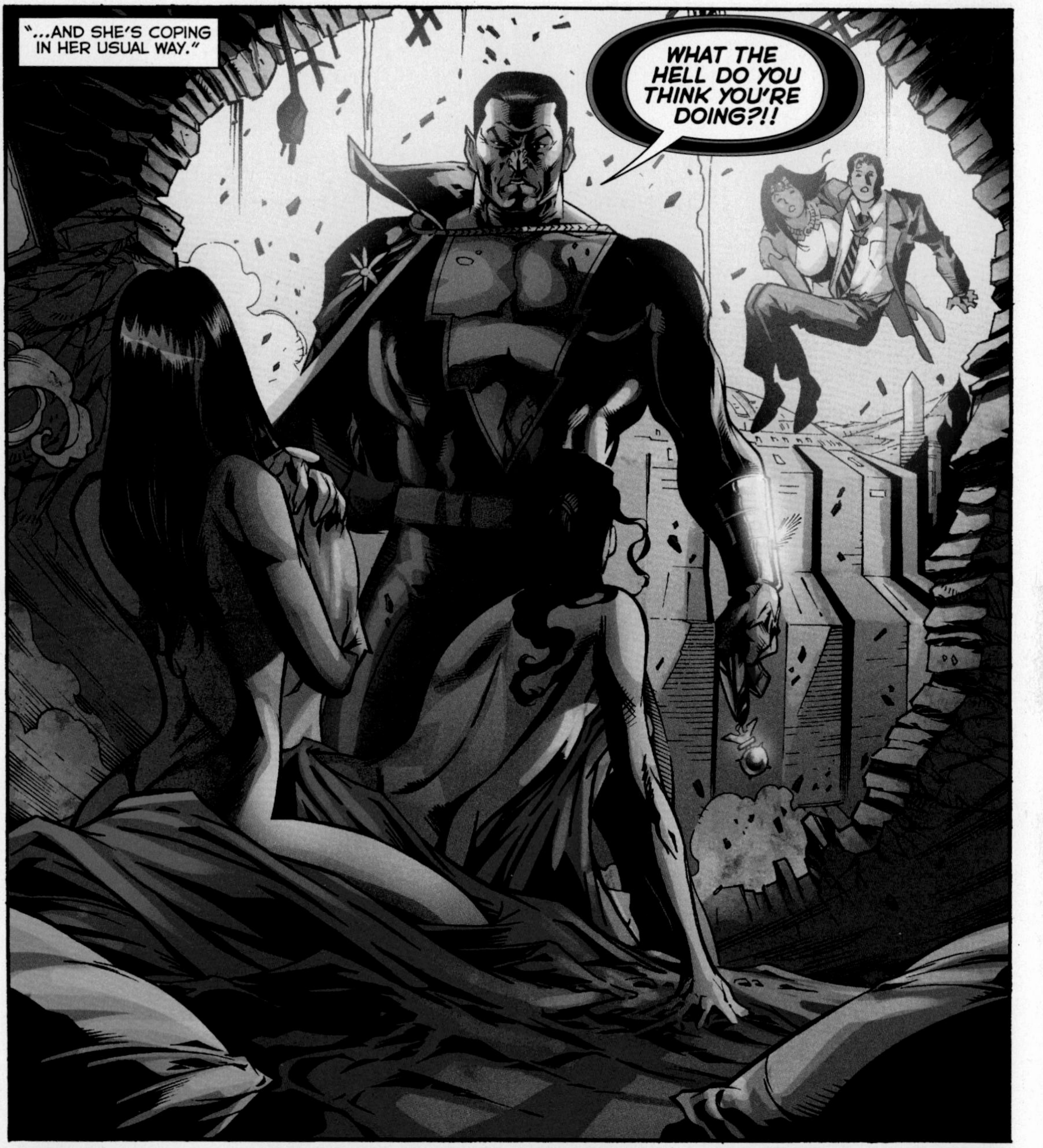
"...AND SHE'S COPING IN HER USUAL WAY."
WHAT THE HELL DO YOU THINK YOU'RE DOING?!!

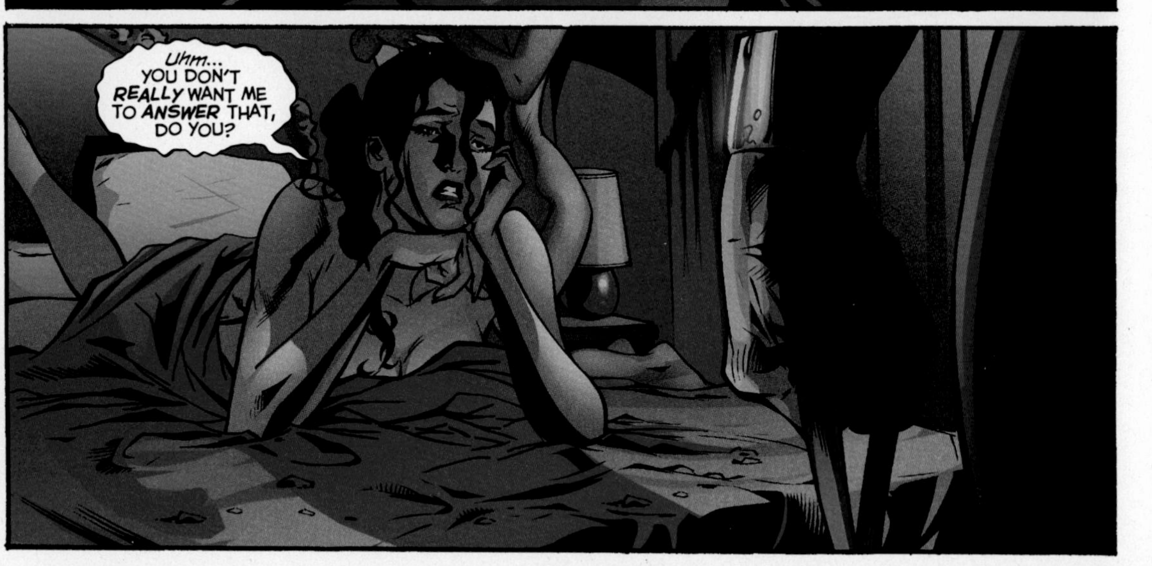
Uhm... YOU DON'T REALLY WANT ME TO ANSWER THAT, DO YOU?

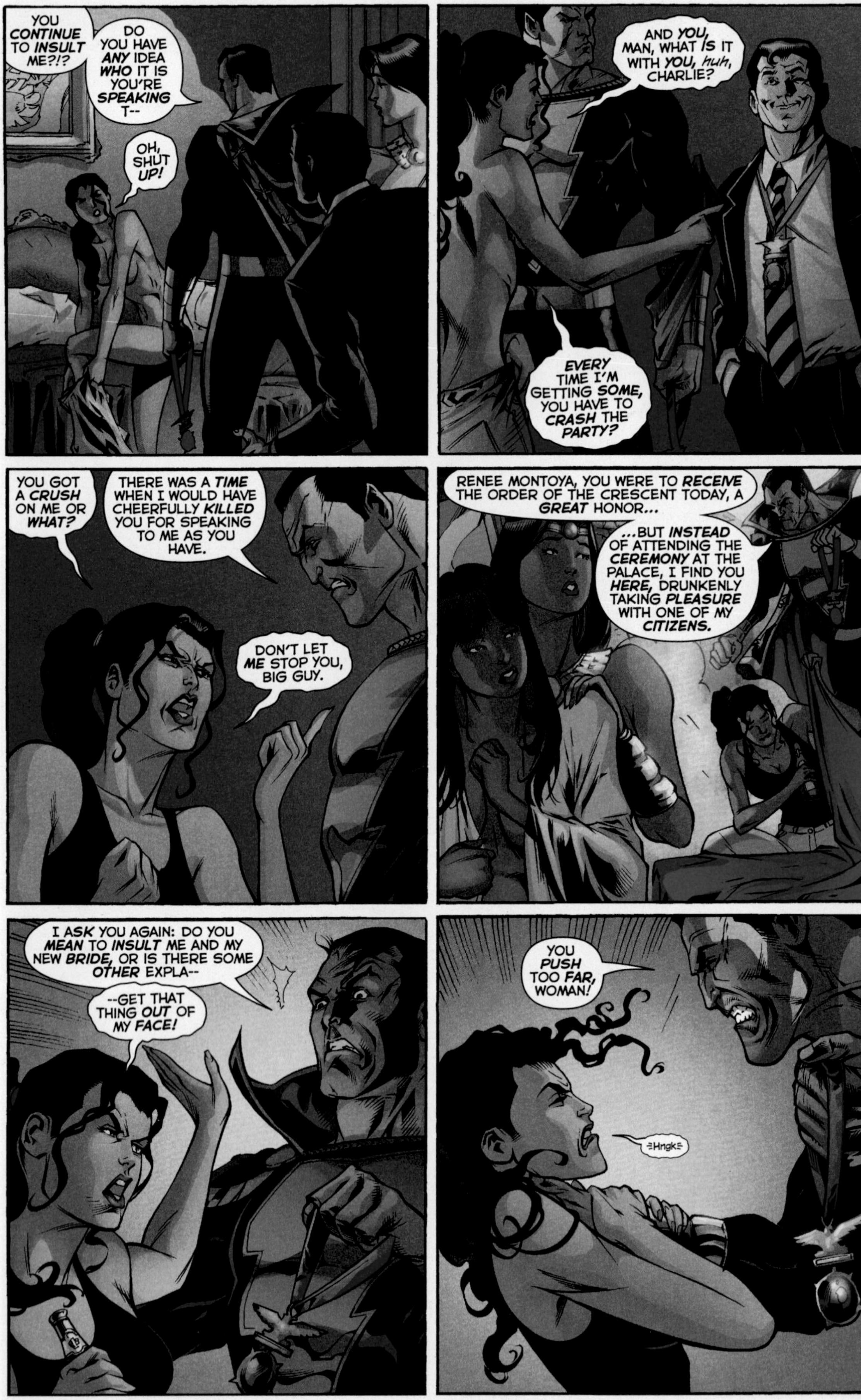
YOU CONTINUE TO INSULT ME?!?
DO YOU HAVE ANY IDEA WHO IT IS YOU'RE SPEAKING T--
OH, SHUT UP!
AND YOU, MAN, WHAT IS IT WITH YOU, huh, CHARLIE?
EVERY TIME I'M GETTING SOME, YOU HAVE TO CRASH THE PARTY?
YOU GOT A CRUSH ON ME OR WHAT?
THERE WAS A TIME WHEN I WOULD HAVE CHEERFULLY KILLED YOU FOR SPEAKING TO ME AS YOU HAVE.
DON'T LET ME STOP YOU, BIG GUY.
RENEE MONTOYA, YOU WERE TO RECEIVE THE ORDER OF THE CRESCENT TODAY, A GREAT HONOR...
...BUT INSTEAD OF ATTENDING THE CEREMONY AT THE PALACE, I FIND YOU HERE, DRUNKENLY TAKING PLEASURE WITH ONE OF MY CITIZENS.
I ASK YOU AGAIN: DO YOU MEAN TO INSULT ME AND MY NEW BRIDE, OR IS THERE SOME OTHER EXPLA--
--GET THAT THING OUT OF MY FACE!
YOU PUSH TOO FAR, WOMAN!
Hngk

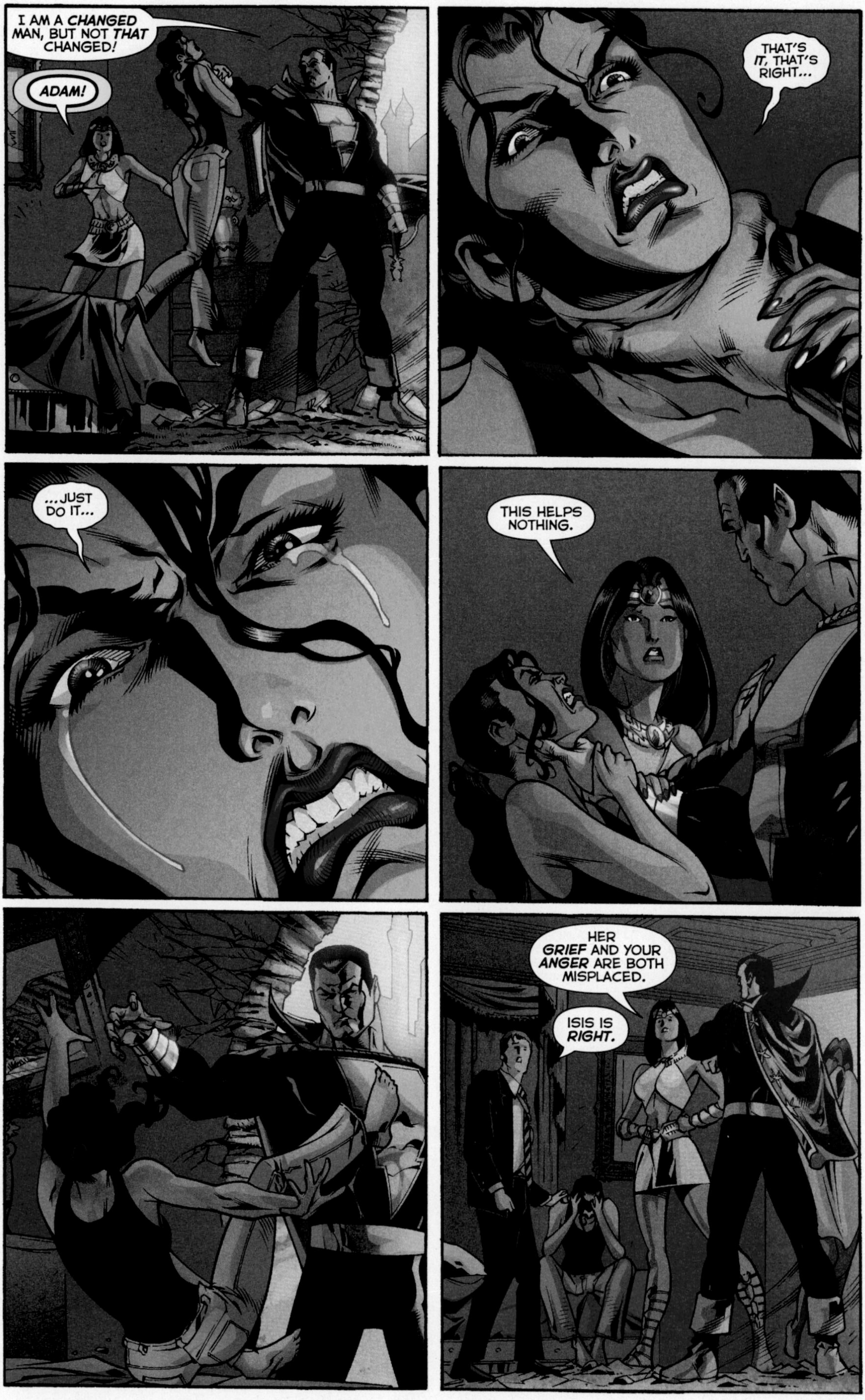
I AM A CHANGED MAN, BUT NOT THAT CHANGED!
ADAM!
THAT'S IT, THAT'S RIGHT...
...JUST DO IT...
THIS HELPS NOTHING.
HER GRIEF AND YOUR ANGER ARE BOTH MISPLACED.
ISIS IS RIGHT.

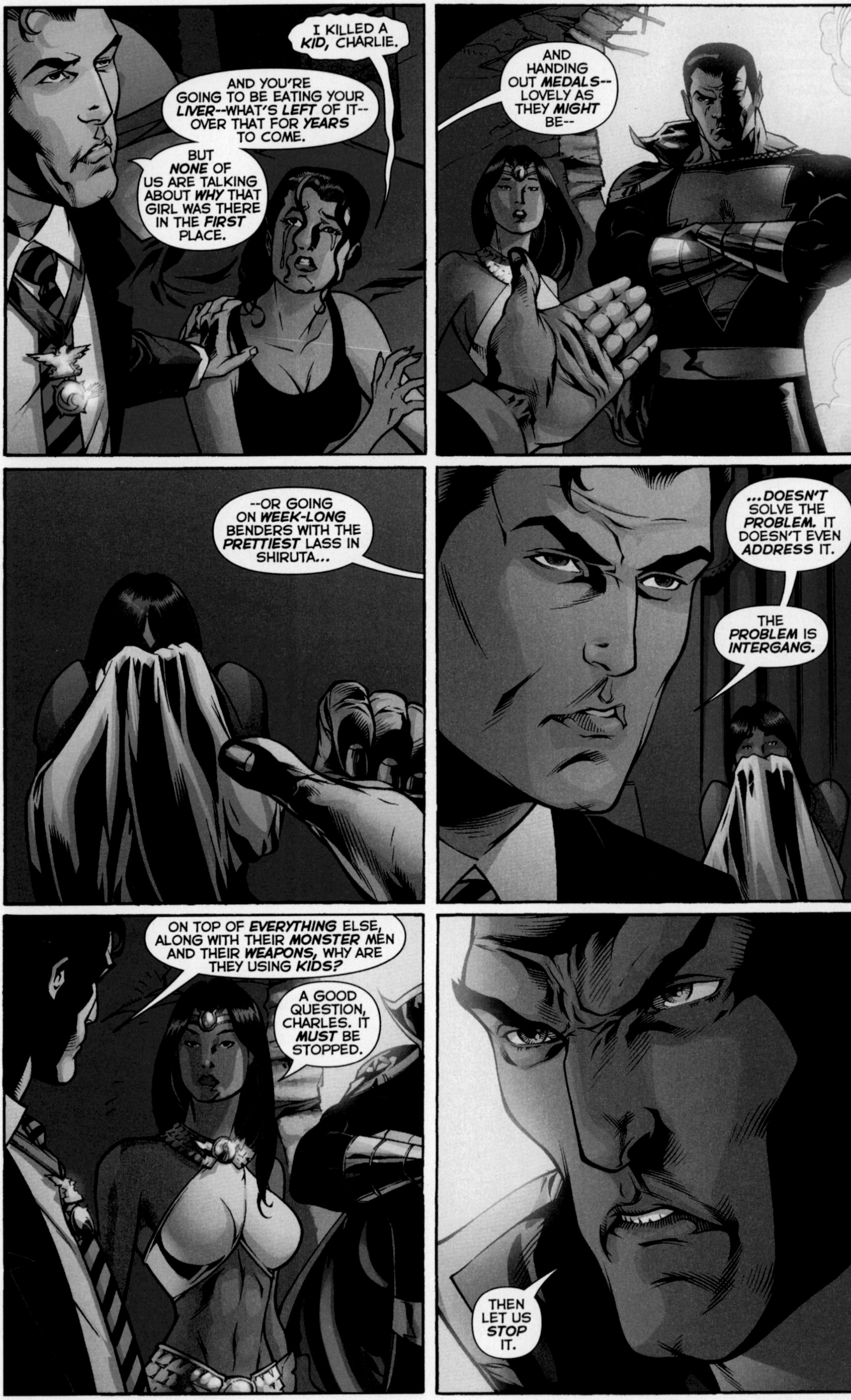
I KILLED A KID, CHARLIE.
AND YOU'RE GOING TO BE EATING YOUR LIVER--WHAT'S LEFT OF IT--OVER THAT FOR YEARS TO COME.
BUT NONE OF US ARE TALKING ABOUT WHY THAT GIRL WAS THERE IN THE FIRST PLACE.
AND HANDING OUT MEDALS--LOVELY AS THEY MIGHT BE--
--OR GOING ON WEEK-LONG BENDERS WITH THE PRETTIEST LASS IN SHIRUTA...
...DOESN'T SOLVE THE PROBLEM. IT DOESN'T EVEN ADDRESS IT.
THE PROBLEM IS INTERGANG.
ON TOP OF EVERYTHING ELSE, ALONG WITH THEIR MONSTER MEN AND THEIR WEAPONS, WHY ARE THEY USING KIDS?
A GOOD QUESTION, CHARLES. IT MUST BE STOPPED.
THEN LET US STOP IT.

AND THERE'S NO EVIDENCE AS TO EXACTLY WHAT CAUSED THE TRANSFORMATION.

Marseilles, France.

NOPE. THAT'S WHAT MAKES THIS ONE A *RALPH DIBNY* SPECIAL.

LOCKED ROOM MYSTERY WITH A SEVERE TOUCH OF THE *WEIRD*.

Week 18, Day 3

SOON AS WE SEALED THE CRIME SCENE, TERRI PUT A SPELL OF PROTECTION ON *THAT* THING, BUT I'M SURE YOU RECOGNIZE IT.

DR. FATE'S HELMET.

LAST TIME *I* SAW IT, CAPTAIN MARVEL WAS LOBBIN' IT INTO THE *SKY*, HOPIN' IT'D LAND NEAR A SUITABLE NEW *HOST*.

OBVIOUSLY, *THAT* WAS A MISCALCULATION.

WHICH LEAVES US WITH FOUR QUESTIONS.

ONE, HOW WAS TIM *LIQUEFIED* INSIDE A *SEALED* ROOM...

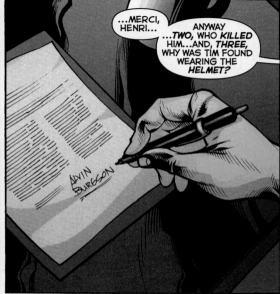

...MERCI, HENRI...

...*TWO*, WHO *KILLED* HIM...AND, *THREE*, WHY WAS TIM FOUND WEARING THE *HELMET*?

ALVIN BURGSON

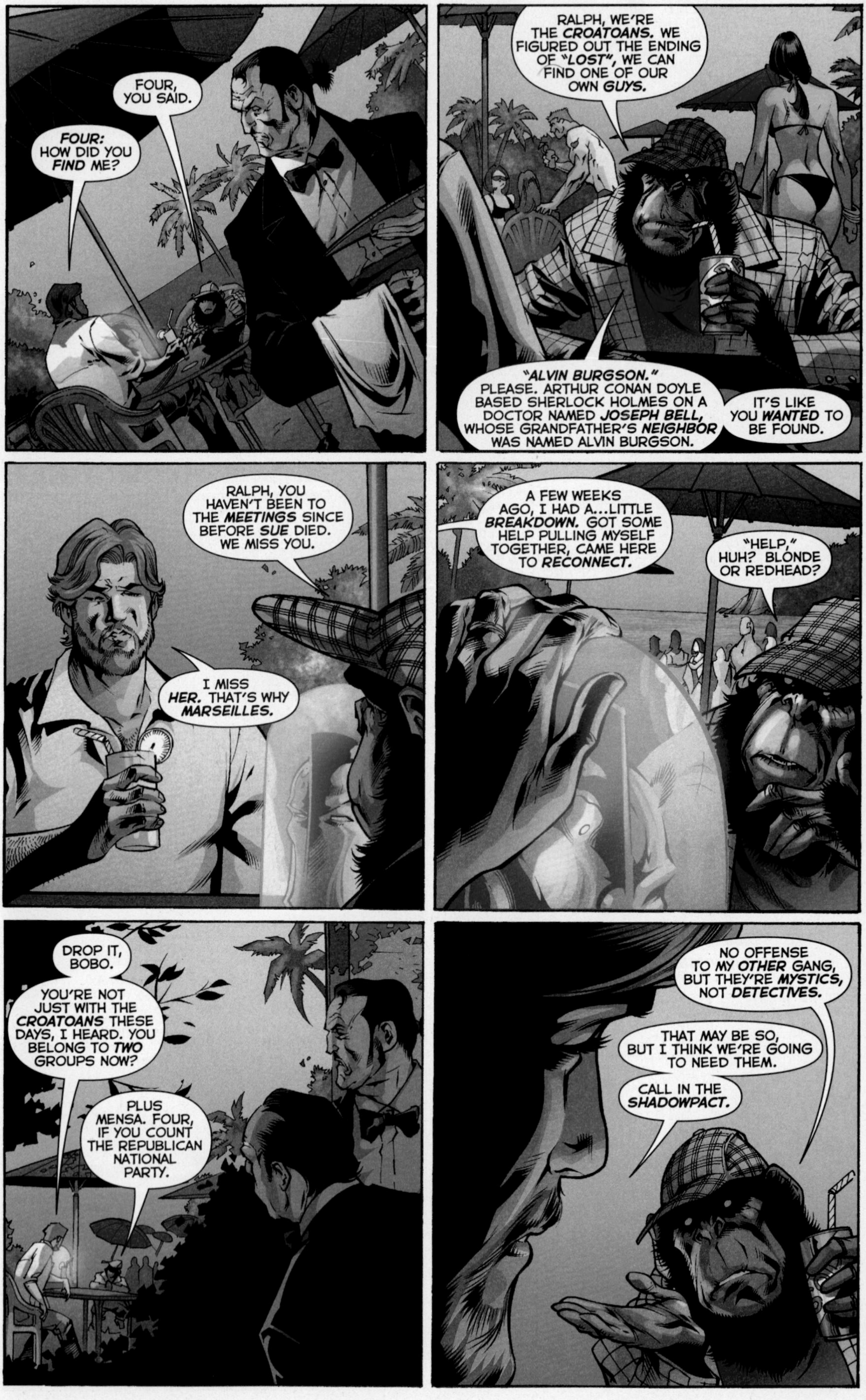
FOUR: HOW DID YOU FIND ME?
FOUR, YOU SAID.
RALPH, WE'RE THE CROATOANS. WE FIGURED OUT THE ENDING OF "LOST", WE CAN FIND ONE OF OUR OWN GUYS.
"ALVIN BURGSON." PLEASE. ARTHUR CONAN DOYLE BASED SHERLOCK HOLMES ON A DOCTOR NAMED JOSEPH BELL, WHOSE GRANDFATHER'S NEIGHBOR WAS NAMED ALVIN BURGSON.
IT'S LIKE YOU WANTED TO BE FOUND.
RALPH, YOU HAVEN'T BEEN TO THE MEETINGS SINCE BEFORE SUE DIED. WE MISS YOU.
I MISS HER. THAT'S WHY MARSEILLES.
A FEW WEEKS AGO, I HAD A...LITTLE BREAKDOWN. GOT SOME HELP PULLING MYSELF TOGETHER, CAME HERE TO RECONNECT.
"HELP," HUH? BLONDE OR REDHEAD?
DROP IT, BOBO.
YOU'RE NOT JUST WITH THE CROATOANS THESE DAYS, I HEARD. YOU BELONG TO TWO GROUPS NOW?
PLUS MENSA. FOUR, IF YOU COUNT THE REPUBLICAN NATIONAL PARTY.
NO OFFENSE TO MY OTHER GANG, BUT THEY'RE MYSTICS, NOT DETECTIVES.
THAT MAY BE SO, BUT I THINK WE'RE GOING TO NEED THEM.
CALL IN THE SHADOWPACT.

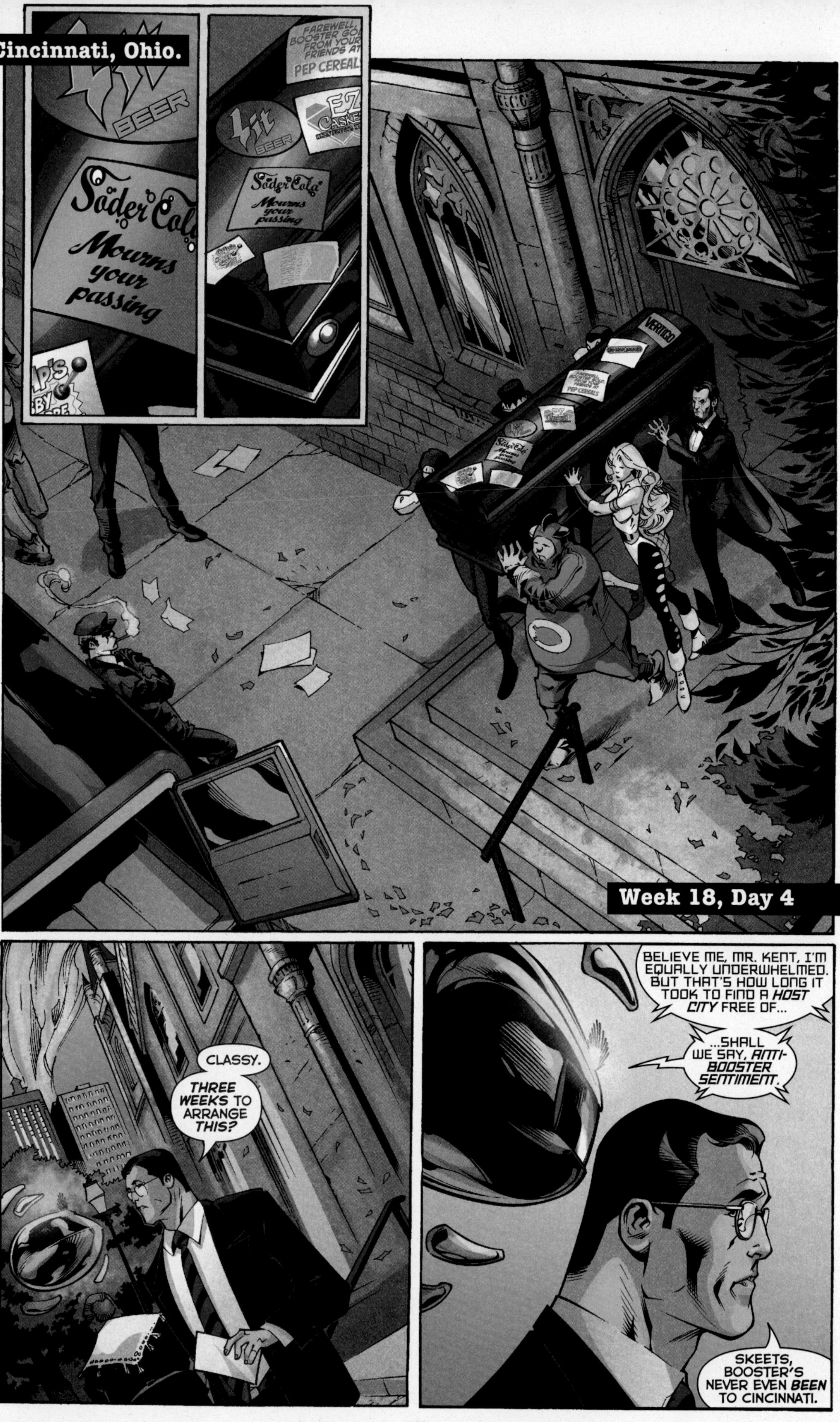
Cincinnati, Ohio.
BEER
Soder Cola
Mourns your passing
PEP CEREALS
VERTIGO
Week 18, Day 4
CLASSY.
THREE WEEKS TO ARRANGE THIS?
BELIEVE ME, MR. KENT, I'M EQUALLY UNDERWHELMED. BUT THAT'S HOW LONG IT TOOK TO FIND A HOST CITY FREE OF...
...SHALL WE SAY, ANTI-BOOSTER SENTIMENT.
SKEETS, BOOSTER'S NEVER EVEN BEEN TO CINCINNATI.

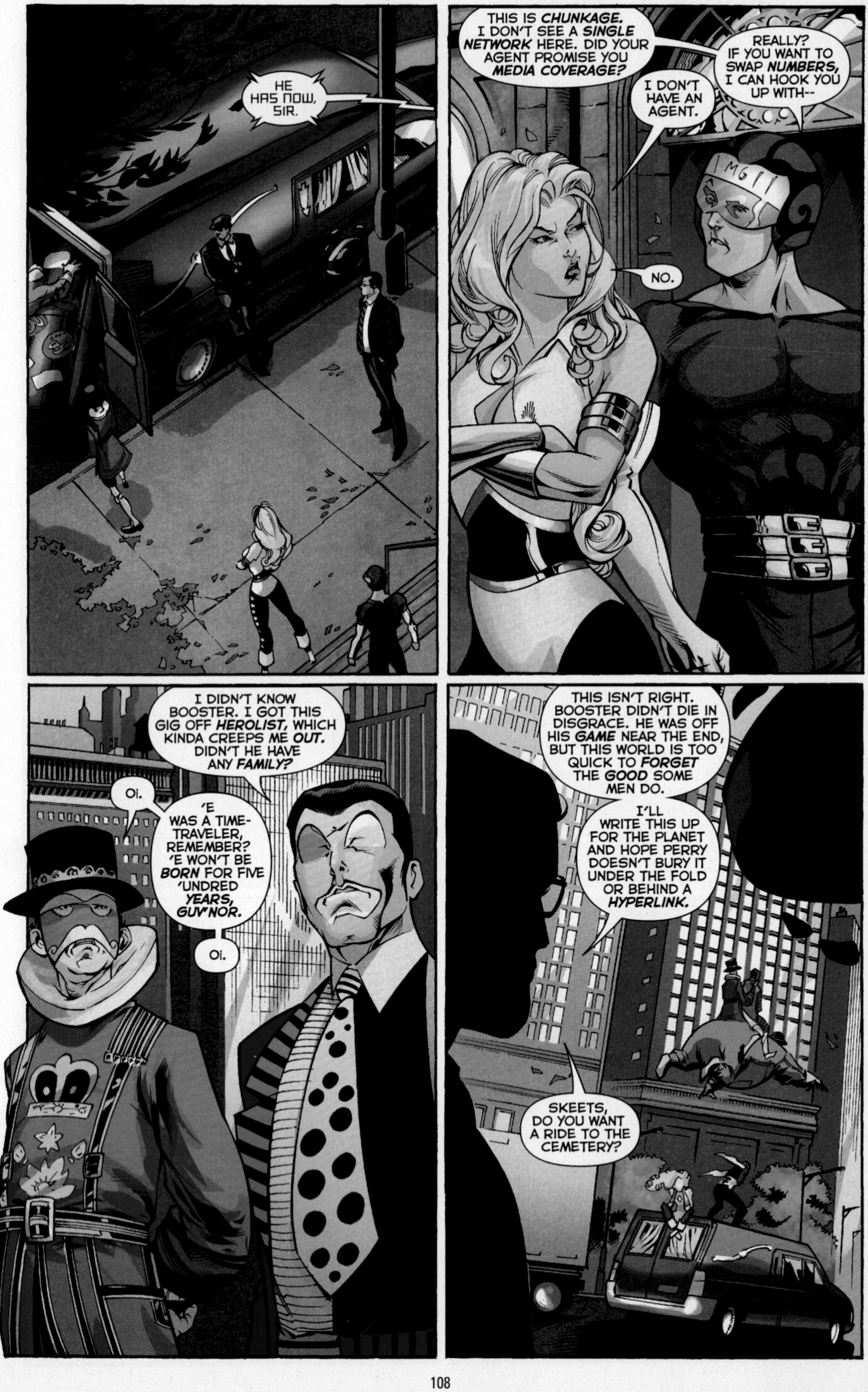
HE HAS NOW, SIR.
THIS IS CHUNKAGE. I DON'T SEE A SINGLE NETWORK HERE. DID YOUR AGENT PROMISE YOU MEDIA COVERAGE?
I DON'T HAVE AN AGENT.
REALLY? IF YOU WANT TO SWAP NUMBERS, I CAN HOOK YOU UP WITH--
NO.
I DIDN'T KNOW BOOSTER. I GOT THIS GIG OFF HEROLIST, WHICH KINDA CREEPS ME OUT. DIDN'T HE HAVE ANY FAMILY?
Oi.
'E WAS A TIME-TRAVELER, REMEMBER? 'E WON'T BE BORN FOR FIVE 'UNDRED YEARS, GUV'NOR.
Oi.
THIS ISN'T RIGHT. BOOSTER DIDN'T DIE IN DISGRACE. HE WAS OFF HIS GAME NEAR THE END, BUT THIS WORLD IS TOO QUICK TO FORGET THE GOOD SOME MEN DO.
I'LL WRITE THIS UP FOR THE PLANET AND HOPE PERRY DOESN'T BURY IT UNDER THE FOLD OR BEHIND A HYPERLINK.
SKEETS, DO YOU WANT A RIDE TO THE CEMETERY?

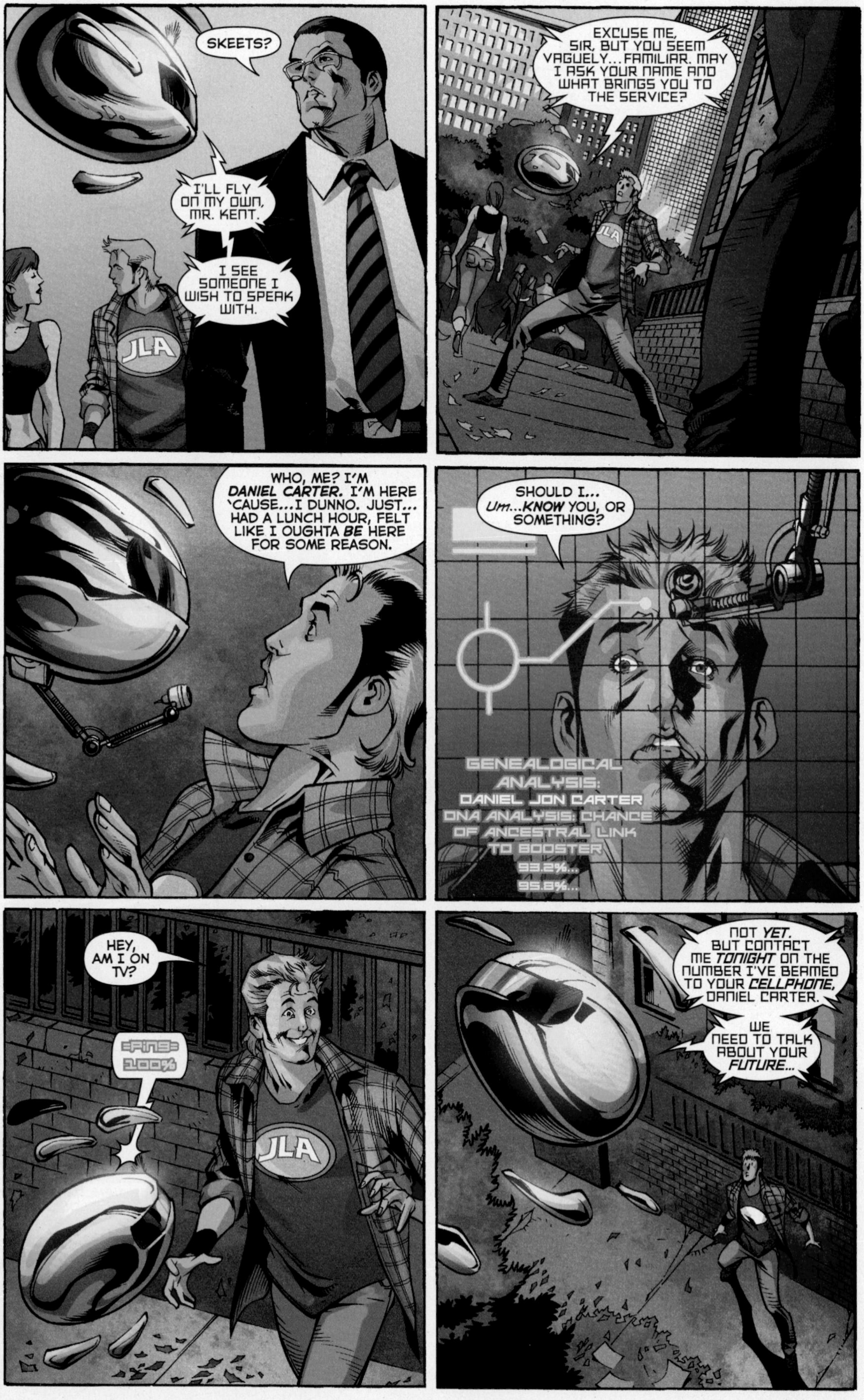
SKEETS?
I'LL FLY ON MY OWN, MR. KENT.
I SEE SOMEONE I WISH TO SPEAK WITH.
JLA
EXCUSE ME, SIR, BUT YOU SEEM VAGUELY...FAMILIAR. MAY I ASK YOUR NAME AND WHAT BRINGS YOU TO THE SERVICE?
JLA
WHO, ME? I'M DANIEL CARTER. I'M HERE 'CAUSE...I DUNNO. JUST... HAD A LUNCH HOUR, FELT LIKE I OUGHTA BE HERE FOR SOME REASON.
SHOULD I... Um...KNOW YOU, OR SOMETHING?
GENEALOGICAL ANALYSIS: DANIEL JON CARTER DNA ANALYSIS: CHANCE OF ANCESTRAL LINK TO BOOSTER 93.2%... 95.8%...
HEY, AM I ON TV?
=PING= 100%
JLA
NOT YET. BUT CONTACT ME TONIGHT ON THE NUMBER I'VE BEAMED TO YOUR CELLPHONE, DANIEL CARTER.
WE NEED TO TALK ABOUT YOUR FUTURE...

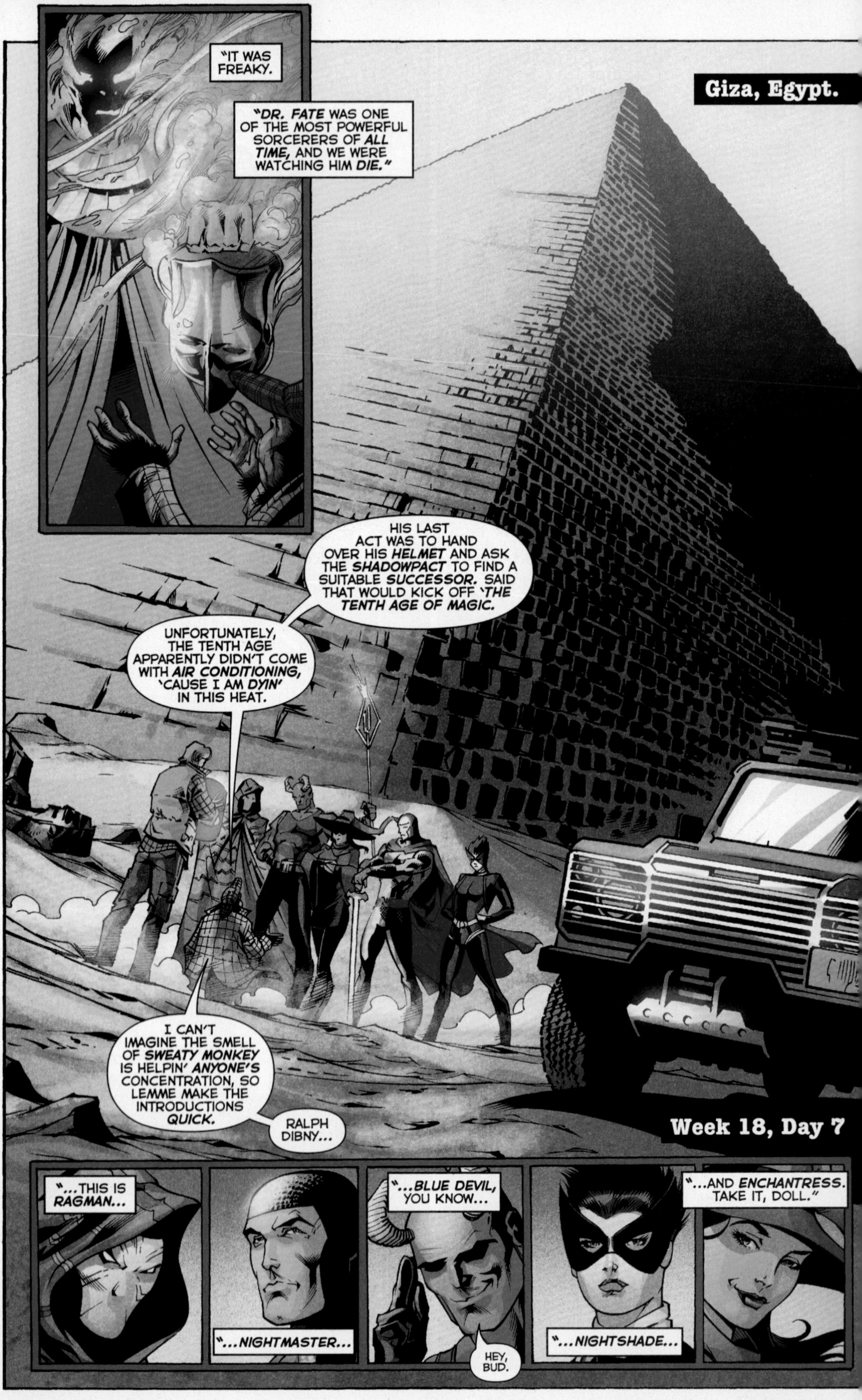
"IT WAS FREAKY.
"DR. FATE WAS ONE OF THE MOST POWERFUL SORCERERS OF ALL TIME, AND WE WERE WATCHING HIM DIE."
Giza, Egypt.
HIS LAST ACT WAS TO HAND OVER HIS HELMET AND ASK THE SHADOWPACT TO FIND A SUITABLE SUCCESSOR. SAID THAT WOULD KICK OFF 'THE TENTH AGE OF MAGIC.
UNFORTUNATELY, THE TENTH AGE APPARENTLY DIDN'T COME WITH AIR CONDITIONING, 'CAUSE I AM DYIN' IN THIS HEAT.
I CAN'T IMAGINE THE SMELL OF SWEATY MONKEY IS HELPIN' ANYONE'S CONCENTRATION, SO LEMME MAKE THE INTRODUCTIONS QUICK.
RALPH DIBNY...
Week 18, Day 7
"...THIS IS RAGMAN...
"...NIGHTMASTER...
"...BLUE DEVIL, YOU KNOW...
HEY, BUD.
"...NIGHTSHADE...
"...AND ENCHANTRESS. TAKE IT, DOLL."

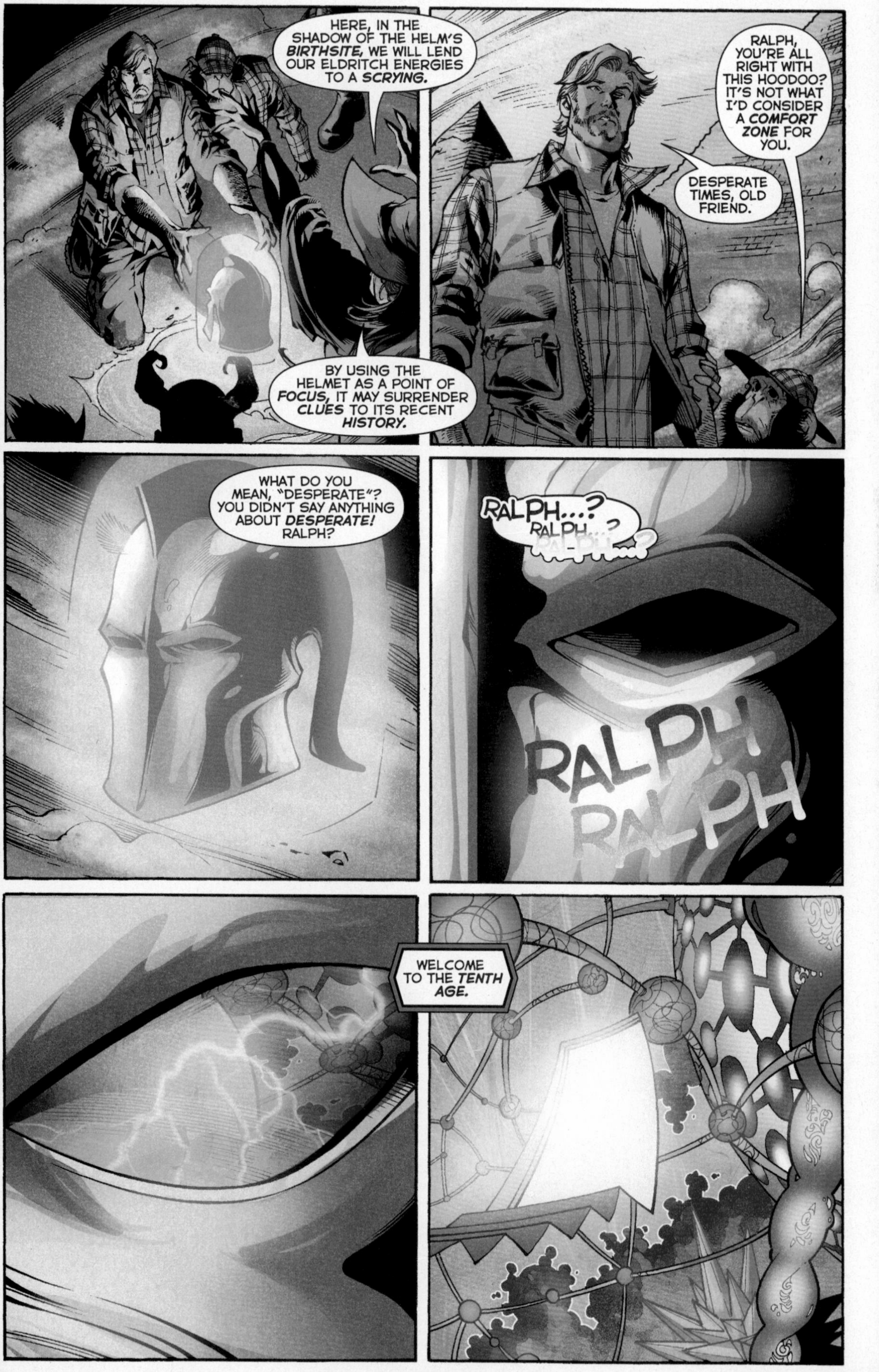
HERE, IN THE SHADOW OF THE HELM'S BIRTHSITE, WE WILL LEND OUR ELDRITCH ENERGIES TO A SCRYING.
BY USING THE HELMET AS A POINT OF FOCUS, IT MAY SURRENDER CLUES TO ITS RECENT HISTORY.
RALPH, YOU'RE ALL RIGHT WITH THIS HOODOO? IT'S NOT WHAT I'D CONSIDER A COMFORT ZONE FOR YOU.
DESPERATE TIMES, OLD FRIEND.
WHAT DO YOU MEAN, "DESPERATE"? YOU DIDN'T SAY ANYTHING ABOUT DESPERATE! RALPH?
RALPH...? RALPH...? RALPH...?
RALPH RALPH
WELCOME TO THE TENTH AGE.

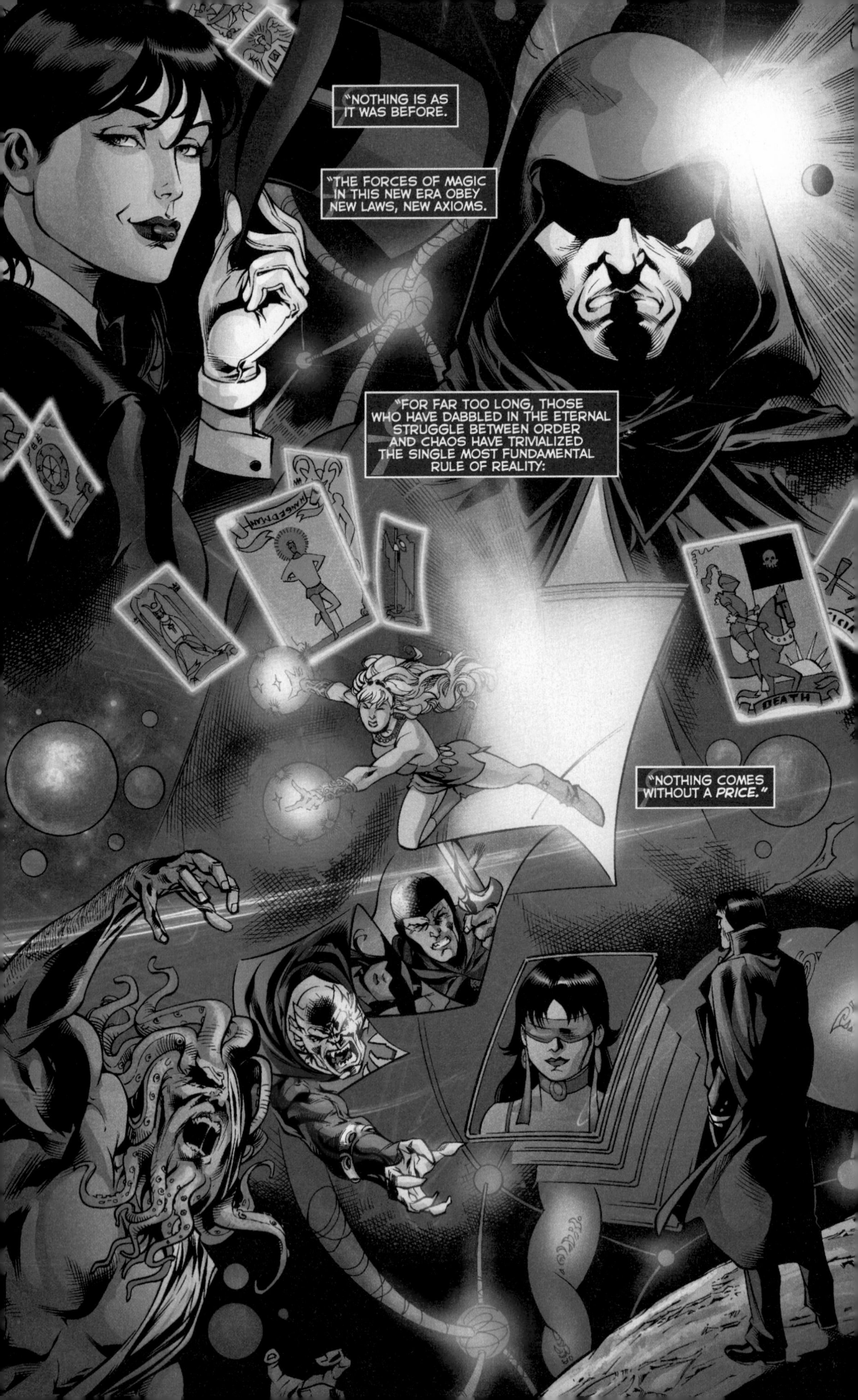
"NOTHING IS AS IT WAS BEFORE.
"THE FORCES OF MAGIC IN THIS NEW ERA OBEY NEW LAWS, NEW AXIOMS.
"FOR FAR TOO LONG, THOSE WHO HAVE DABBLED IN THE ETERNAL STRUGGLE BETWEEN ORDER AND CHAOS HAVE TRIVIALIZED THE SINGLE MOST FUNDAMENTAL RULE OF REALITY:
DEATH
"NOTHING COMES WITHOUT A *PRICE.*"

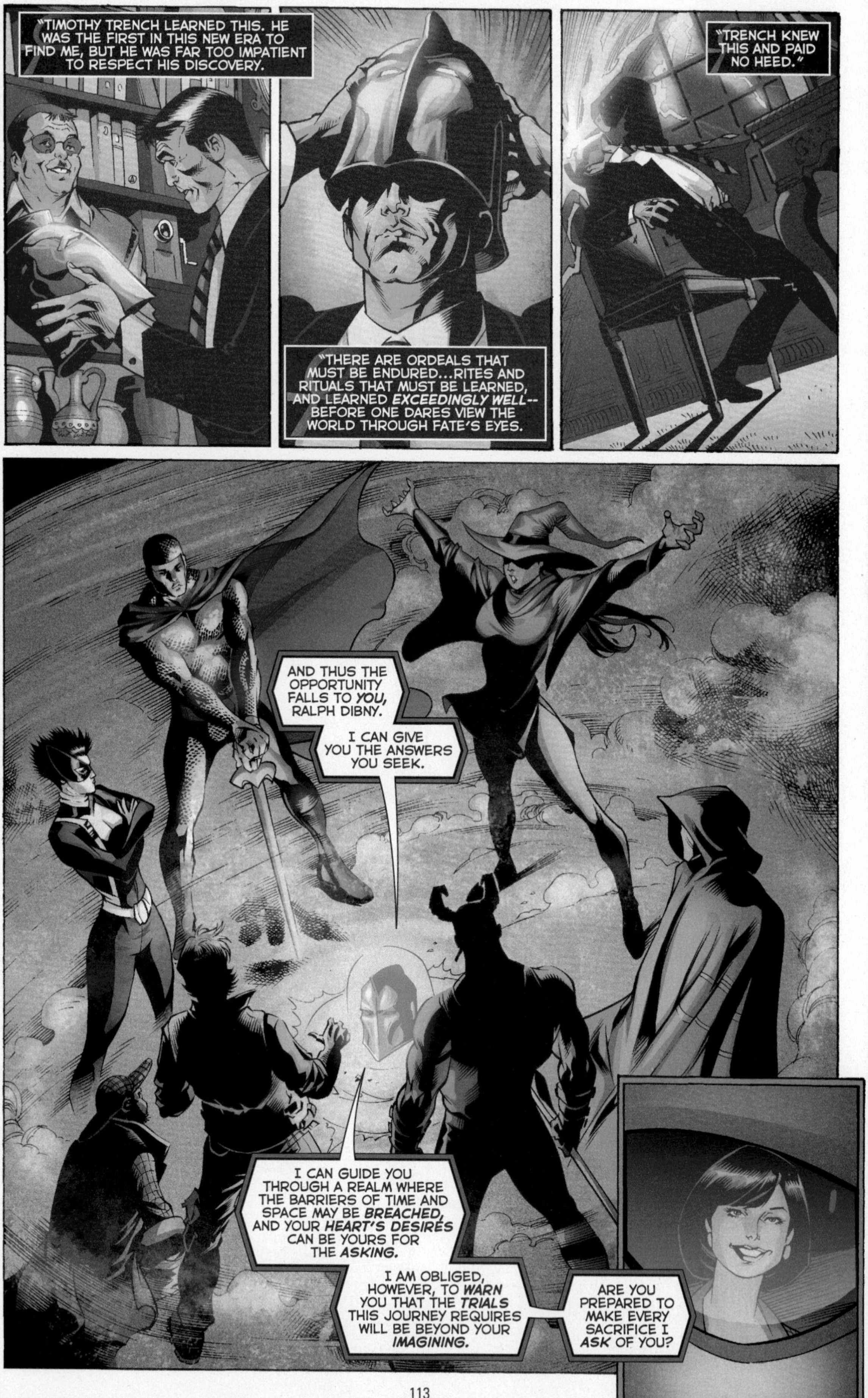
"TIMOTHY TRENCH LEARNED THIS. HE WAS THE FIRST IN THIS NEW ERA TO FIND ME, BUT HE WAS FAR TOO IMPATIENT TO RESPECT HIS DISCOVERY.
"THERE ARE ORDEALS THAT MUST BE ENDURED...RITES AND RITUALS THAT MUST BE LEARNED, AND LEARNED EXCEEDINGLY WELL-- BEFORE ONE DARES VIEW THE WORLD THROUGH FATE'S EYES.
"TRENCH KNEW THIS AND PAID NO HEED."
AND THUS THE OPPORTUNITY FALLS TO YOU, RALPH DIBNY.
I CAN GIVE YOU THE ANSWERS YOU SEEK.
I CAN GUIDE YOU THROUGH A REALM WHERE THE BARRIERS OF TIME AND SPACE MAY BE BREACHED, AND YOUR HEART'S DESIRES CAN BE YOURS FOR THE ASKING.
I AM OBLIGED, HOWEVER, TO WARN YOU THAT THE TRIALS THIS JOURNEY REQUIRES WILL BE BEYOND YOUR IMAGINING.
ARE YOU PREPARED TO MAKE EVERY SACRIFICE I ASK OF YOU?

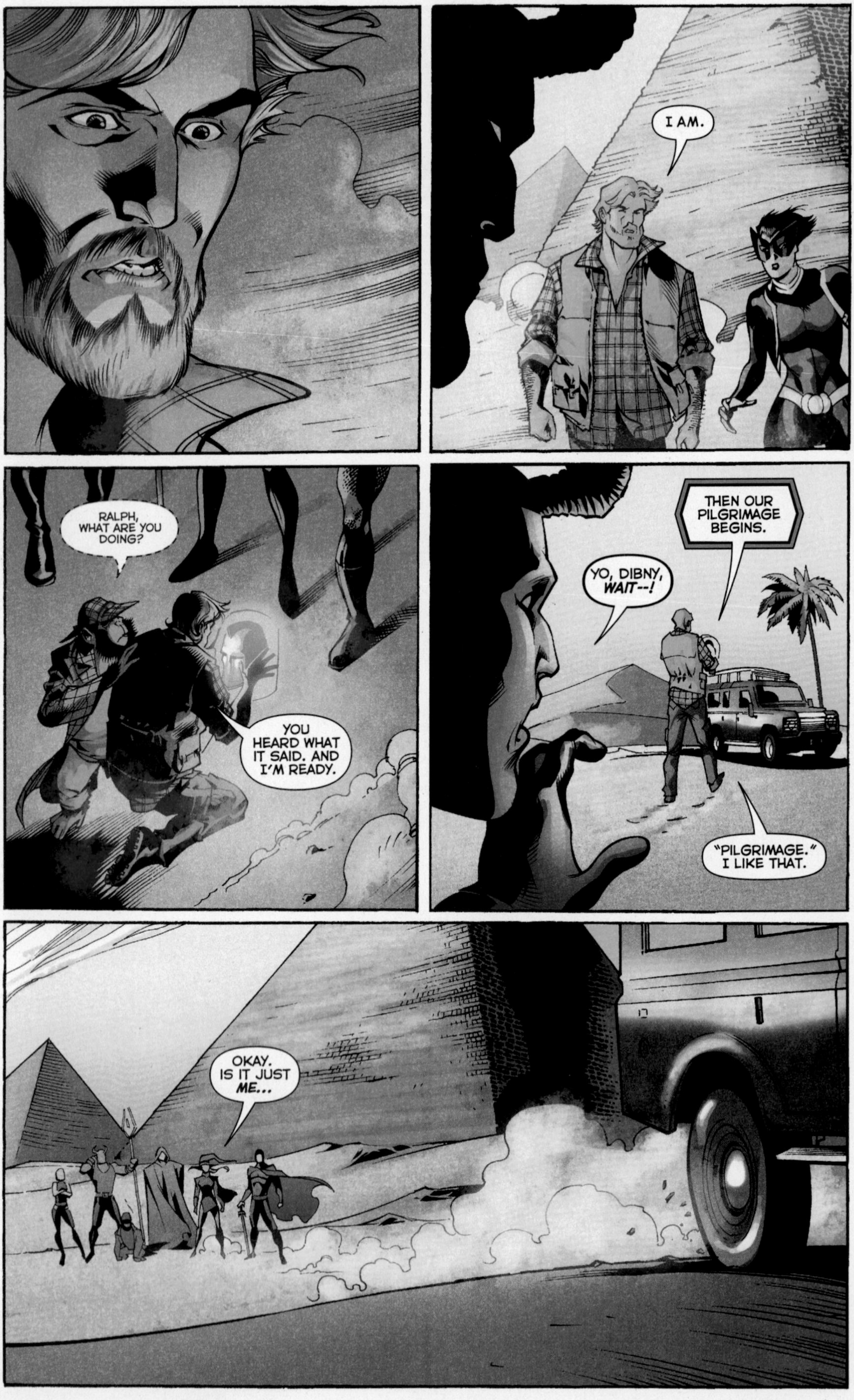
I AM.
RALPH, WHAT ARE YOU DOING?
YOU HEARD WHAT IT SAID. AND I'M READY.
THEN OUR PILGRIMAGE BEGINS.
YO, DIBNY, WAIT--!
"PILGRIMAGE." I LIKE THAT.
OKAY. IS IT JUST ME...

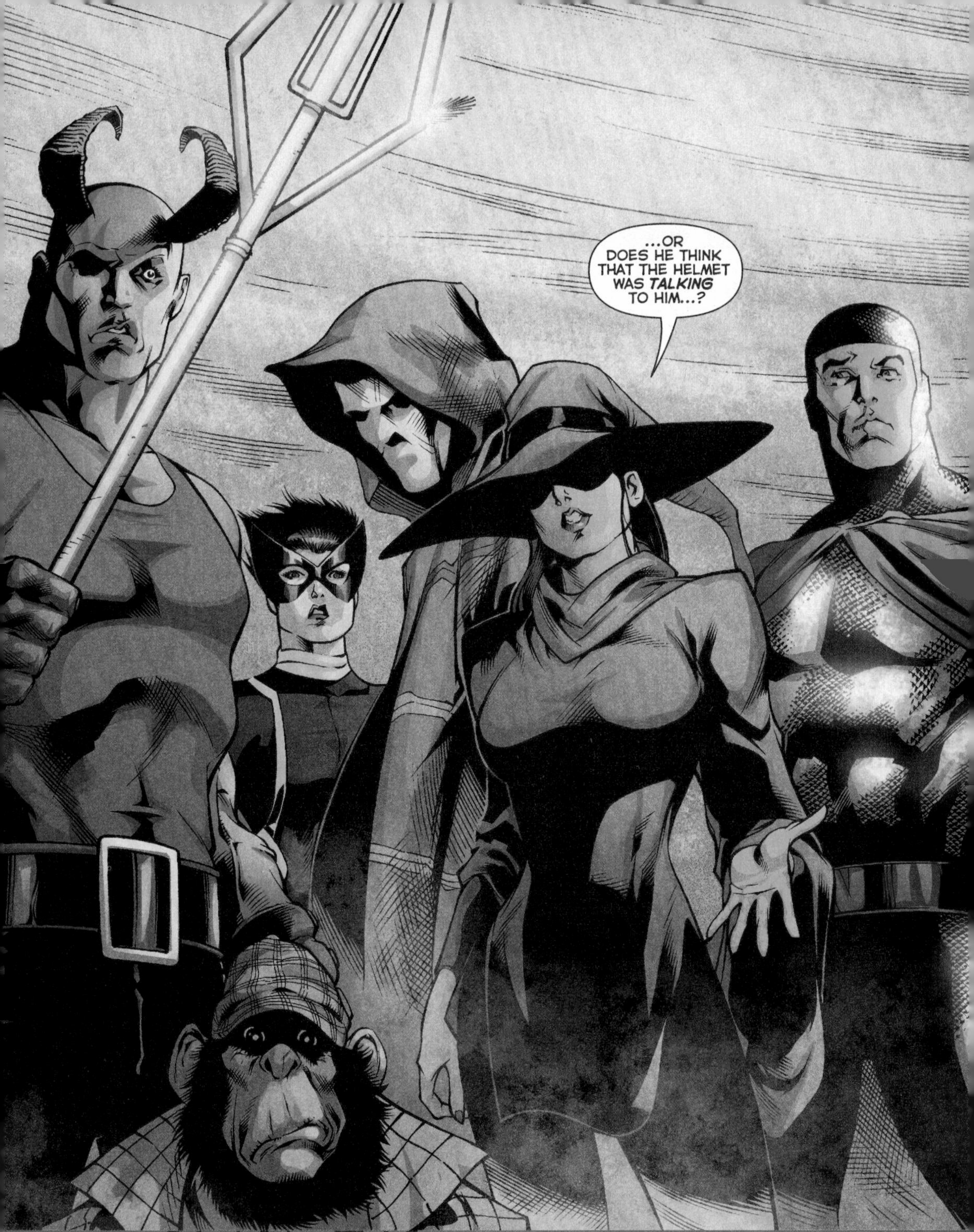
...OR DOES HE THINK THAT THE HELMET WAS *TALKING* TO HIM...?

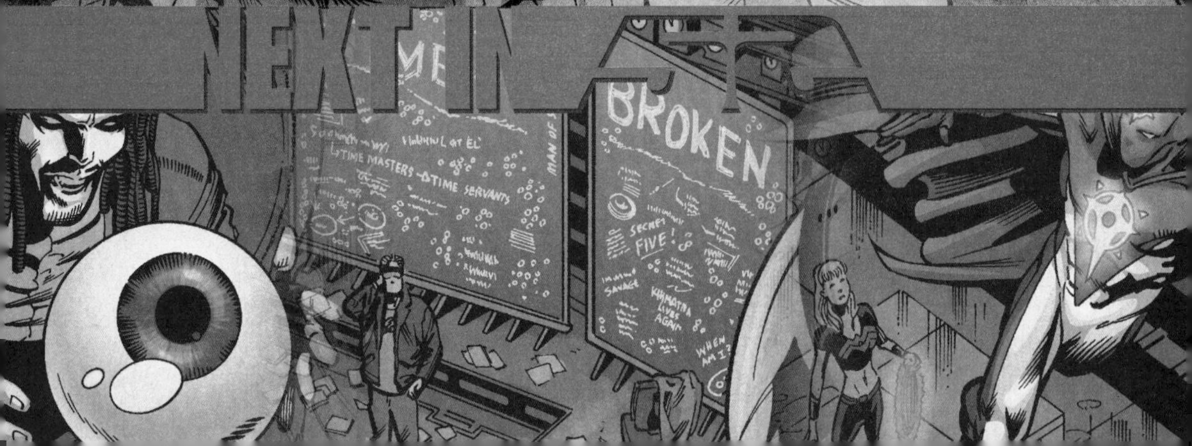
NEXT IN
BROKEN
SECRET FIVE!

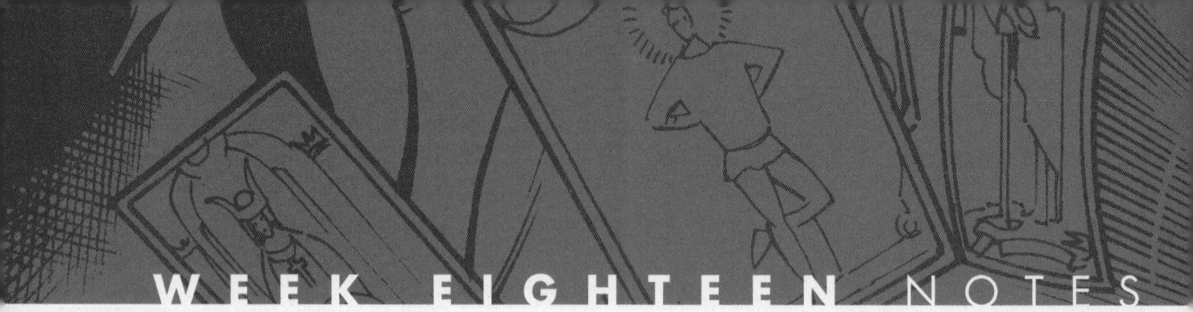

WEEK EIGHTEEN NOTES

MARK WAID

In the interest of full disclosure, I was probably the best man to take point on Ralph not because I so love the character...not because we're both such resolute devotees of science and logic and detective work...but because his spiritual journey is something I very much understand. Ralph has his worldview forcibly opened to the realities of magic once he encounters the Helmet of Fate. I started hanging out with Grant Morrison. Same difference.

If you look closely, you'll note that Ralph is now (and throughout the rest of the series) wearing a wedding ring made of wicker.

The introduction of the Shadowpact into our story — one of our early attempts to show, as promised, what was going on with some of the other players in the DC Universe during this year — blew up in our collective face when the SHADOWPACT writer inadvertently but simultaneously wrote them OUT of the DC Universe during this year. No good deed goes unpunished. I bring this up in case devoted Shadowpact fans think we didn't notice. Believe me, we noticed.

Tim Trench was a late substitution. Originally, I'd written a 1950s DETECTIVE COMICS hero, Mysto the Magician, into the Croatoans (tip of the hat to Geoff for the group name). Only as the art was being finished did I, the walking DC encyclopedia, remember that Mysto's secret identity was Rick Carter and that the absolute last thing this issue needed in it was yet another guy named "Carter."

For those still keeping cameo scorecards, the pallbearers at Booster's service — chosen mostly by editor Steve Wacker — are the Blimp (from the Inferior Five), Mind-Grabber Man (an old JLA comedy go-to revived by Grant in SEVEN SOLDIERS: BULLETEER, about whom more later), Yellow Peri (who grew up in Smallville), the Odd Man (a one-shot Steve Ditko hero), Beefeater (from JUSTICE LEAGUE EUROPE), and, yes, Abraham Lincoln (from — my hand to God — an unpublished Justice League story I once wrote for Steve on a dare). This, I might add, is pretty much what I expect my own funeral to look like.

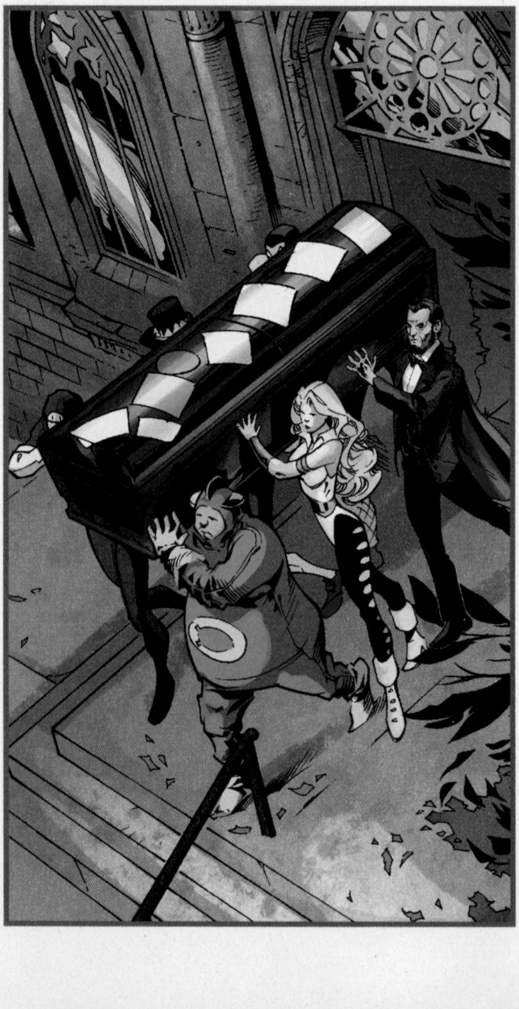

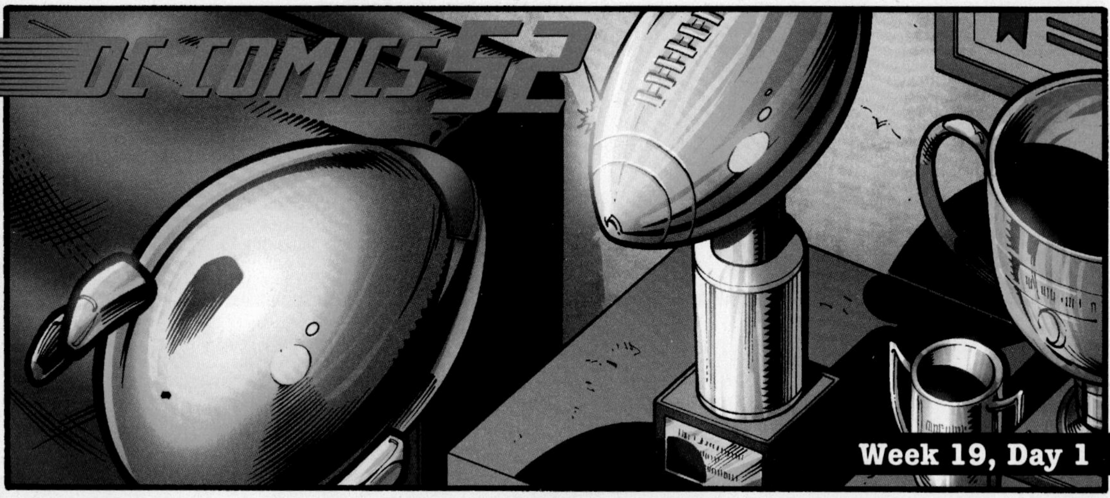
DC COMICS 52
Week 19, Day 1

WRITTEN BY GEOFF JOHNS, GRANT MORRISON, GREG RUCKA, MARK WAID

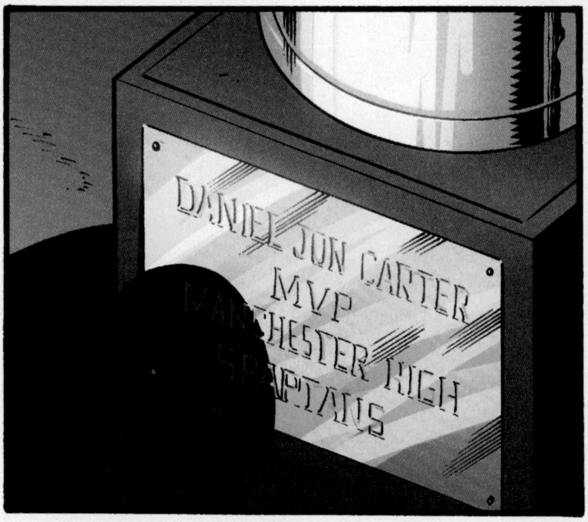
DANIEL JON CARTER
MVP

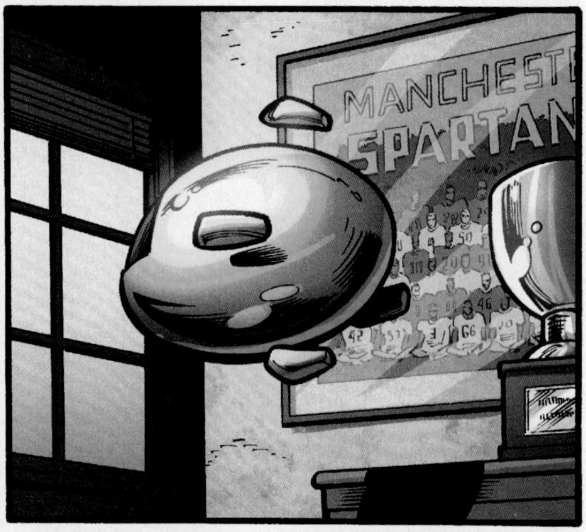

ART BREAKDOWNS BY KEITH GIFFEN • PENCILS BY PATRICK OLLIFFE
INKS BY DREW GERACI • COLORS BY ALEX SINCLAIR • LETTERING BY PAT BROSSEAU

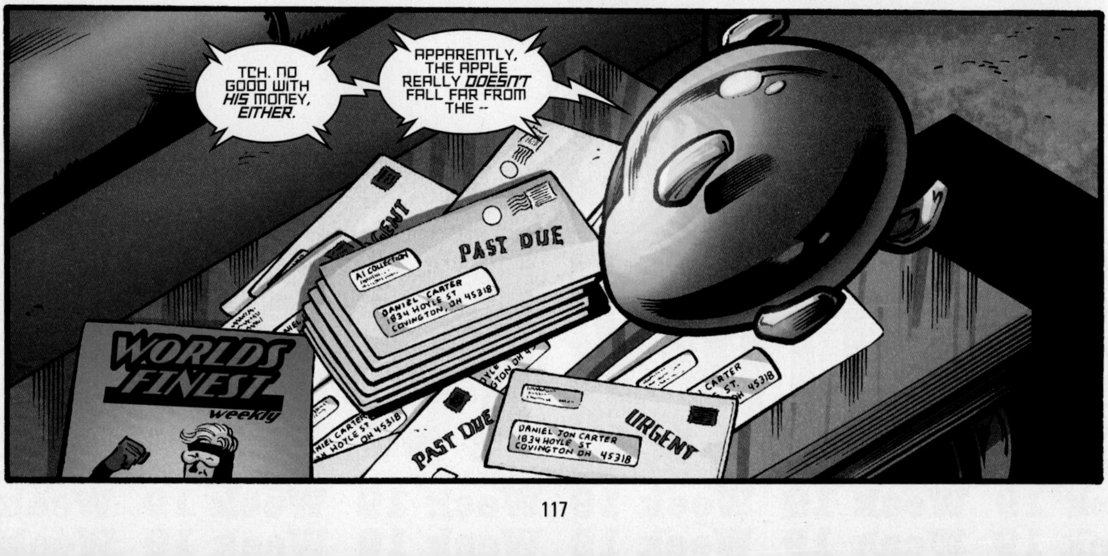
TCH. NO GOOD WITH *HIS* MONEY, *EITHER*.
APPARENTLY, THE APPLE REALLY *DOESN'T* FALL FAR FROM THE --
PAST DUE
DANIEL CARTER
1834 HOYLE ST
COVINGTON, OH 45318
URGENT
PAST DUE
DANIEL JON CARTER
1834 HOYLE ST
COVINGTON OH 45318
WORLDS FINEST
weekly

ASSISTANT EDITORS *HARVEY RICHARDS & JEANINE SCHAEFER*
EDITED BY *STEPHEN WACKER* **COVER BY** *J.G. JONES & ALEX SINCLAIR*

HISTORY REPEATS

Week 19 Week 19 Week 19 Week 19 Week 19 Week
Week 19 Week 19 Week 19 Week 19 Week 19 Week
Week 19 Week 19 Week 19 Week 19 Week 19 Week
Week 19 Week 19 Week 19 Week 19 Week 19 Week
Week 19 Week 19 Week 19 Week 19 Week 19 Week
Week 19 Week 19 Week 19 Week 19 Week 19 Week
Week 19 Week 19 Week 19 Week 19 Week 19 Week

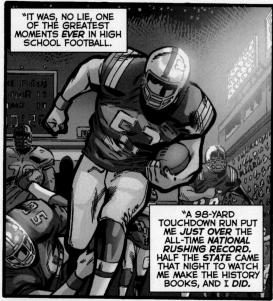

"IT WAS, NO LIE, ONE OF THE GREATEST MOMENTS *EVER* IN HIGH SCHOOL FOOTBALL.

"A 98-YARD TOUCHDOWN RUN PUT ME *JUST OVER* THE ALL-TIME *NATIONAL RUSHING RECORD.* HALF THE *STATE* CAME THAT NIGHT TO WATCH ME MAKE THE HISTORY BOOKS, AND I *DID.*

"AND DIDN'T EVEN GET TO SCORE WITH THE *HEAD CHEERLEADER* AFTER."

BROKE MY LEG IN *FOUR PLACES,* SKEETS. BLEW MY KNEE *AND MY* SCHOLARSHIP.

BUT ALL WAS NOT LOST. I GREW UP TO BE EVERGREEN INSURANCE COMPANY'S *FIFTH-BEST TERM-LIFE SALESMAN!*

FIFTH!

OUT OF SIX.

IT COULD HAVE BEEN *WORSE,* DANIEL CARTER.

YOU COULD HAVE ENDED UP A *MUSEUM JANITOR.*

UHH...THAT'S A PRETTY SPECIFIC REFERENCE.

IT'S THE PATH YOUR *DESCENDANT* FOLLOWED. *WILL* FOLLOW.

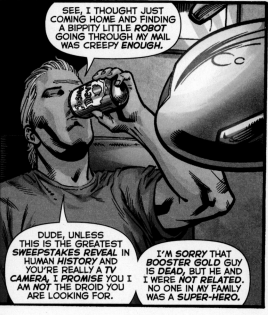

SEE, I THOUGHT JUST COMING HOME AND FINDING A BIPPITY LITTLE *ROBOT* GOING THROUGH MY MAIL WAS CREEPY *ENOUGH.*

DUDE, UNLESS THIS IS THE GREATEST *SWEEPSTAKES REVEAL* IN HUMAN *HISTORY* AND YOU'RE REALLY A TV CAMERA, I *PROMISE* YOU I AM *NOT* THE DROID YOU ARE LOOKING FOR.

I'M *SORRY* THAT *BOOSTER GOLD* GUY IS *DEAD,* BUT HE AND I WERE *NOT RELATED.* NO ONE IN MY FAMILY WAS A *SUPER-HERO.*

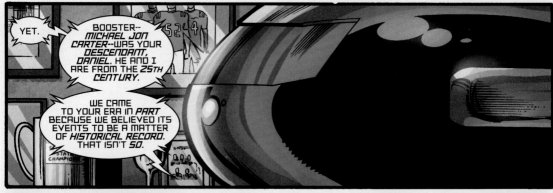

YET.

BOOSTER--*MICHAEL JON CARTER*--WAS YOUR *DESCENDANT, DANIEL.* HE AND I ARE FROM THE *25TH CENTURY.*

WE CAME TO YOUR ERA IN *PART* BECAUSE WE BELIEVED ITS EVENTS TO BE A MATTER OF *HISTORICAL RECORD.* THAT ISN'T *SO.*

"SOMETHING IS *AWRY* IN THE *TIMESTREAM.*

"BEFORE HE WAS *KILLED,* BOOSTER AND I INFILTRATED THE LAB OF A *CHRONONAUT* NAMED *RIP HUNTER* TO *INVESTIGATE* THE CAUSE OF THE *PARADOXES.*

WHAT DID YOU *FIND?*

I'M NOT *CERTAIN.* MY PRESENCE WAS REQUIRED TO KEEP THE *ATOMIC TIMELOCK* OPEN WHILE BOOSTER WENT *INSIDE.*

HE CLAIMED TO HAVE SEEN NOTHING OF *SIGNIFICANCE,* BUT I'M WONDERING IF HE DIDN'T *OVERLOOK* SOMETHING.

YOU ARE ONE OF BOOSTER'S *ANCESTORS.* YOU WILL *KNOW.*

THIS IS *CRAZY* TALK. WHEN DOES *SARAH CONNOR* SHOW UP TO STOP ME FROM INVENTING *TERMINATORS?*

DANIEL, IT'S *VITALLY IMPORTANT* THAT I REGAIN ACCESS TO THAT LAB. ITS SECURITY SENSORS *"KNOW"* MICHAEL NOW, AND YOU'RE ENOUGH OF A GENETIC *MATCH* TO *FOOL* THEM.

CAN'T HELP YOU. I HAVE PLANS THIS WEEK THAT DON'T INVOLVE *B-AND-E.*

I KNOW.

YOU'RE *AUDITIONING* FOR LEX LUTHOR'S *EVERYMAN SCHOLARSHIP.* YOU'RE HOPING HE'LL GRANT YOU A *SUPERGENE.*

PRESUMABLY SO YOU MIGHT ENJOY THE *LIMELIGHT* ONCE MORE IN YOUR LIFE.

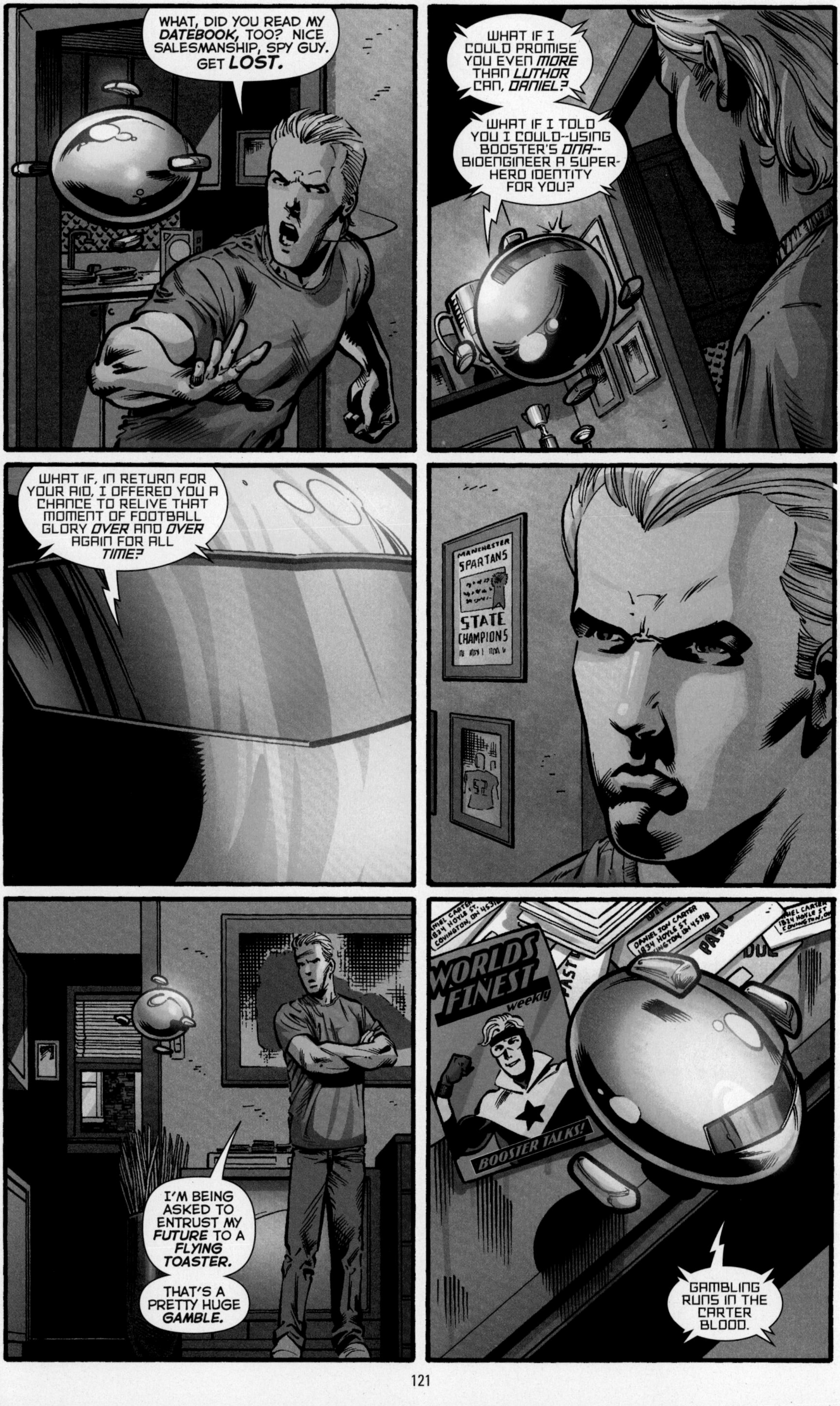
WHAT, DID YOU READ MY DATEBOOK, TOO? NICE SALESMANSHIP, SPY GUY. GET LOST.
WHAT IF I COULD PROMISE YOU EVEN MORE THAN LUTHOR CAN, DANIEL?
WHAT IF I TOLD YOU I COULD--USING BOOSTER'S DNA--BIOENGINEER A SUPER-HERO IDENTITY FOR YOU?
WHAT IF, IN RETURN FOR YOUR AID, I OFFERED YOU A CHANCE TO RELIVE THAT MOMENT OF FOOTBALL GLORY OVER AND OVER AGAIN FOR ALL TIME?
MANCHESTER
SPARTANS
STATE
CHAMPIONS
I'M BEING ASKED TO ENTRUST MY FUTURE TO A FLYING TOASTER.
THAT'S A PRETTY HUGE GAMBLE.
WORLDS FINEST
weekly
BOOSTER TALKS!
GAMBLING RUNS IN THE CARTER BLOOD.

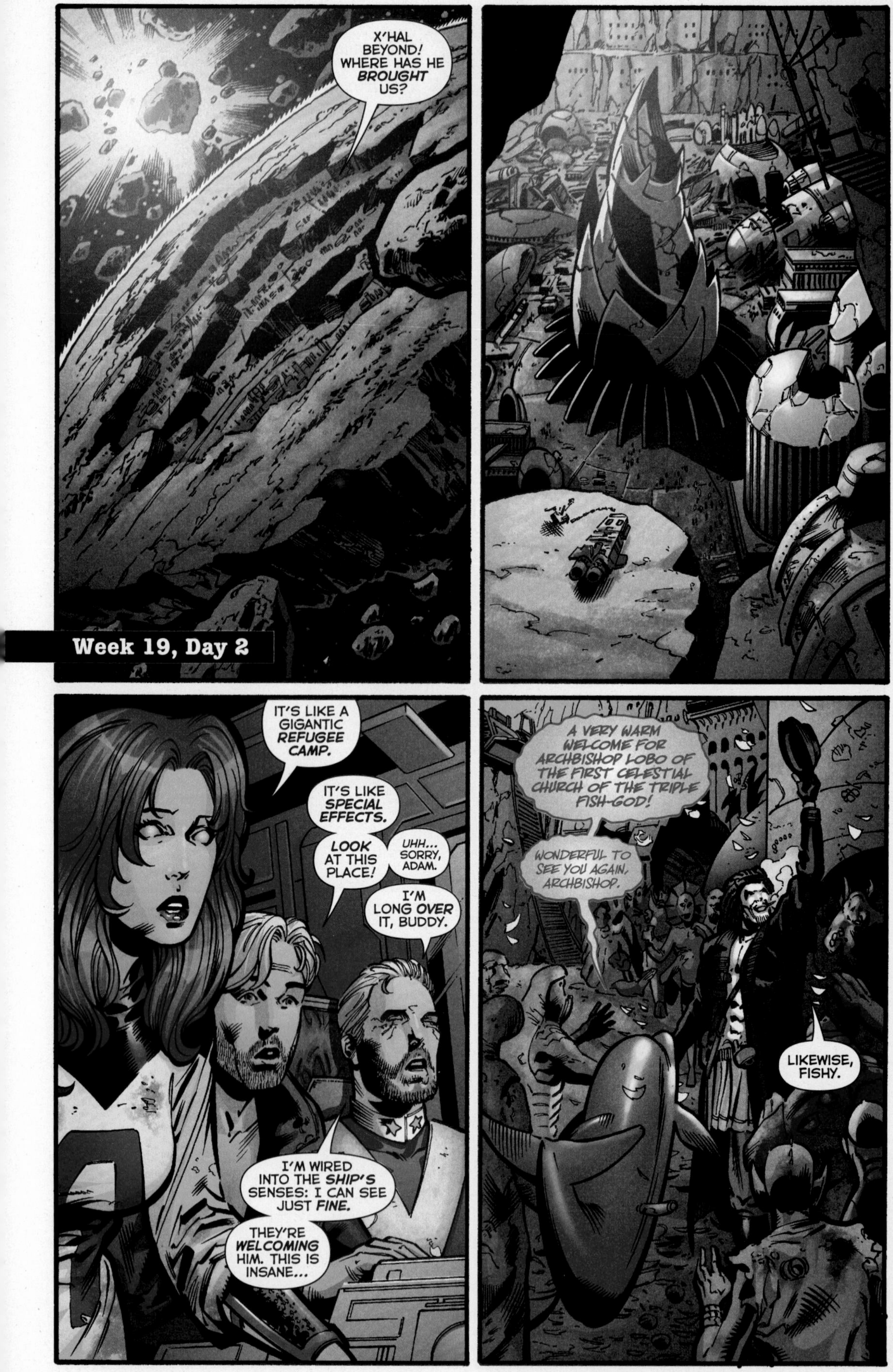
X'HAL BEYOND! WHERE HAS HE BROUGHT US?
Week 19, Day 2
IT'S LIKE A GIGANTIC REFUGEE CAMP.
IT'S LIKE SPECIAL EFFECTS.
LOOK AT THIS PLACE!
UHH... SORRY, ADAM.
I'M LONG OVER IT, BUDDY.
I'M WIRED INTO THE SHIP'S SENSES: I CAN SEE JUST FINE.
THEY'RE WELCOMING HIM. THIS IS INSANE...
A VERY WARM WELCOME FOR ARCHBISHOP LOBO OF THE FIRST CELESTIAL CHURCH OF THE TRIPLE FISH-GOD!
WONDERFUL TO SEE YOU AGAIN, ARCHBISHOP.
LIKEWISE, FISHY.

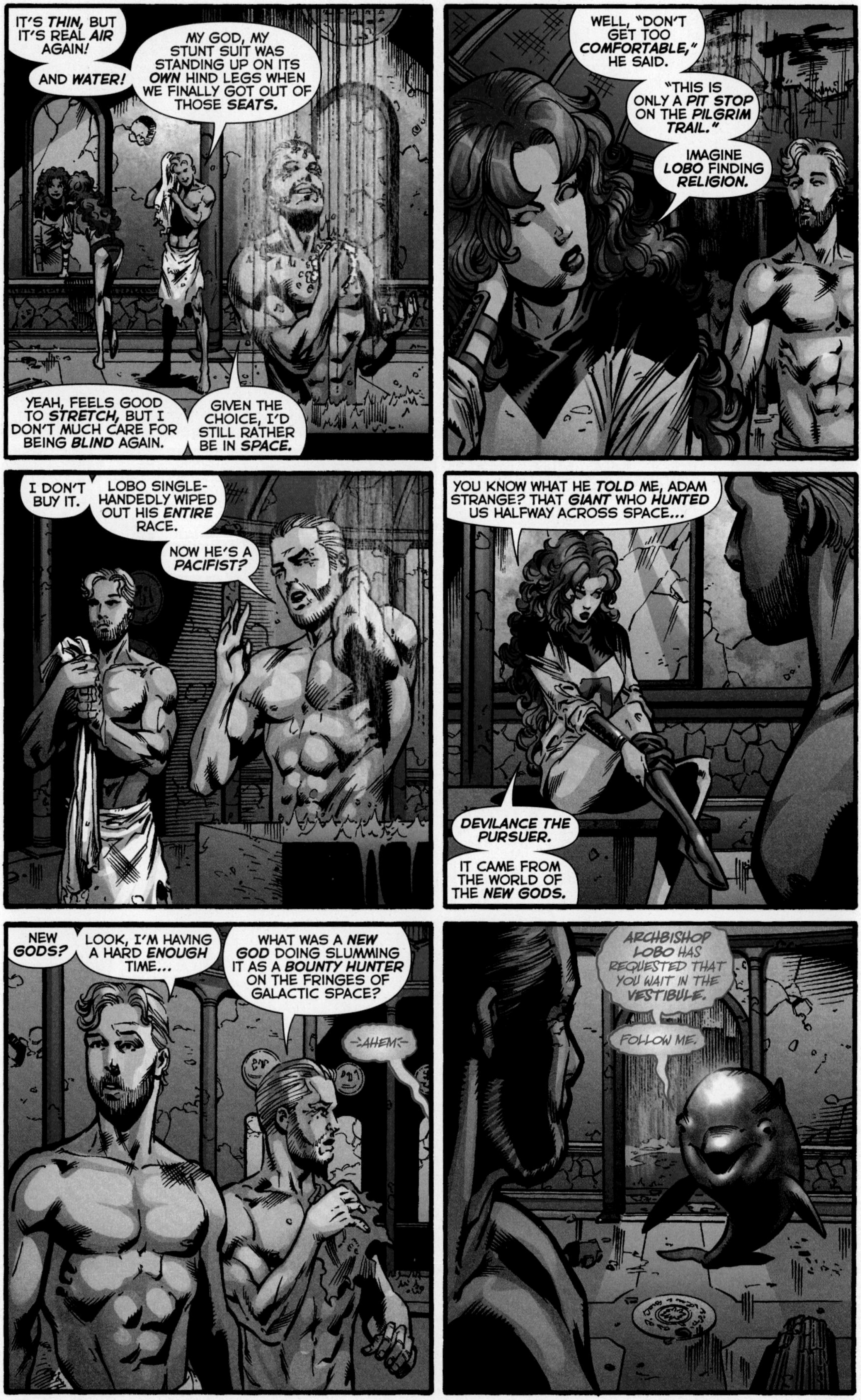
IT'S THIN, BUT IT'S REAL AIR AGAIN!
AND WATER!
MY GOD, MY STUNT SUIT WAS STANDING UP ON ITS OWN HIND LEGS WHEN WE FINALLY GOT OUT OF THOSE SEATS.
YEAH, FEELS GOOD TO STRETCH, BUT I DON'T MUCH CARE FOR BEING BLIND AGAIN.
GIVEN THE CHOICE, I'D STILL RATHER BE IN SPACE.
WELL, "DON'T GET TOO COMFORTABLE," HE SAID.
"THIS IS ONLY A PIT STOP ON THE PILGRIM TRAIL."
IMAGINE LOBO FINDING RELIGION.
I DON'T BUY IT.
LOBO SINGLE-HANDEDLY WIPED OUT HIS ENTIRE RACE.
NOW HE'S A PACIFIST?
YOU KNOW WHAT HE TOLD ME, ADAM STRANGE? THAT GIANT WHO HUNTED US HALFWAY ACROSS SPACE...
DEVILANCE THE PURSUER.
IT CAME FROM THE WORLD OF THE NEW GODS.
NEW GODS?
LOOK, I'M HAVING A HARD ENOUGH TIME...
WHAT WAS A NEW GOD DOING SLUMMING IT AS A BOUNTY HUNTER ON THE FRINGES OF GALACTIC SPACE?
-AHEM-
ARCHBISHOP LOBO HAS REQUESTED THAT YOU WAIT IN THE VESTIBULE.
FOLLOW ME.

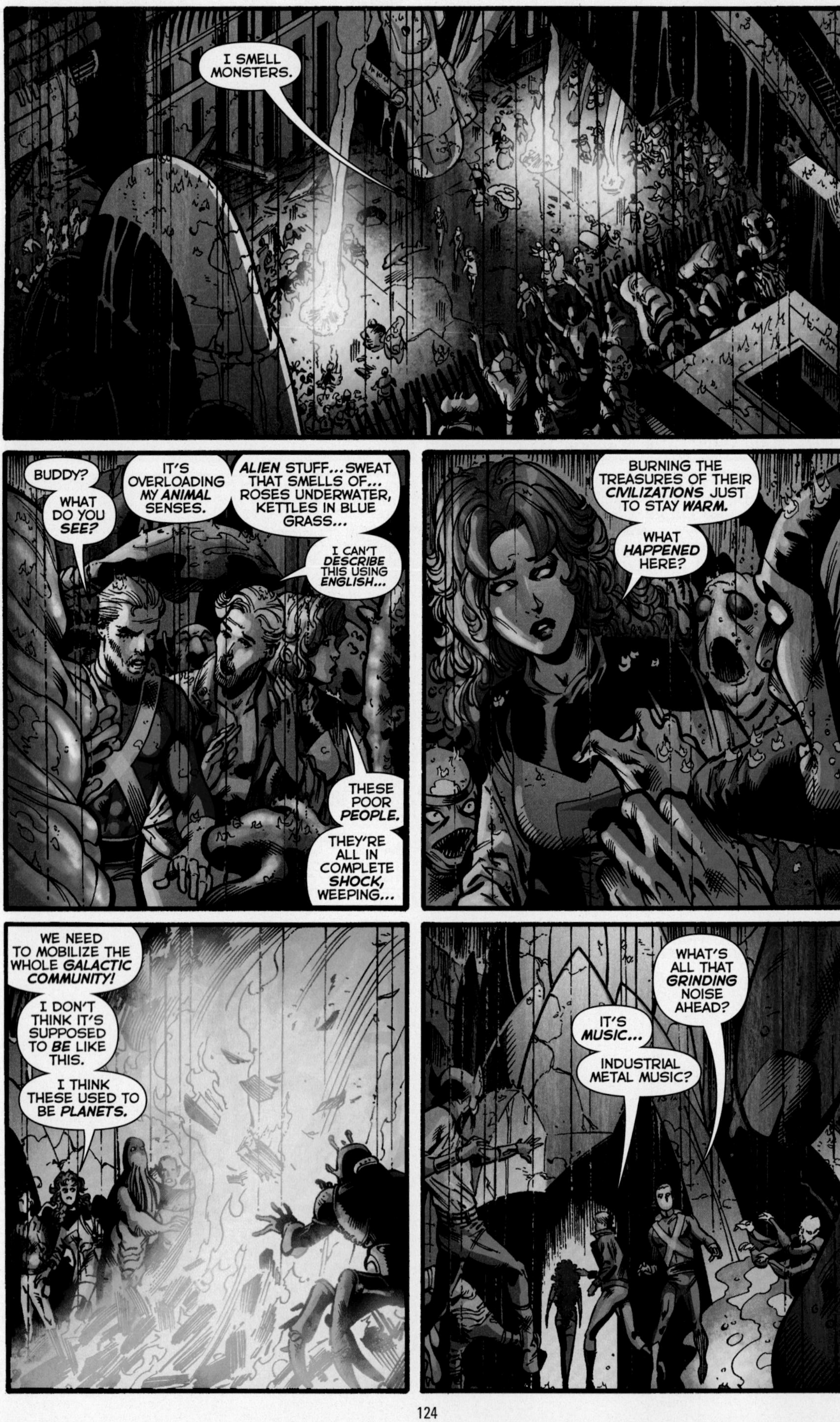
I SMELL MONSTERS.
BUDDY? WHAT DO YOU SEE?
IT'S OVERLOADING MY ANIMAL SENSES.
ALIEN STUFF... SWEAT THAT SMELLS OF... ROSES UNDERWATER, KETTLES IN BLUE GRASS...
I CAN'T DESCRIBE THIS USING ENGLISH...
THESE POOR PEOPLE.
THEY'RE ALL IN COMPLETE SHOCK, WEEPING...
BURNING THE TREASURES OF THEIR CIVILIZATIONS JUST TO STAY WARM.
WHAT HAPPENED HERE?
WE NEED TO MOBILIZE THE WHOLE GALACTIC COMMUNITY!
I DON'T THINK IT'S SUPPOSED TO BE LIKE THIS.
I THINK THESE USED TO BE PLANETS.
WHAT'S ALL THAT GRINDING NOISE AHEAD?
IT'S MUSIC...
INDUSTRIAL METAL MUSIC?

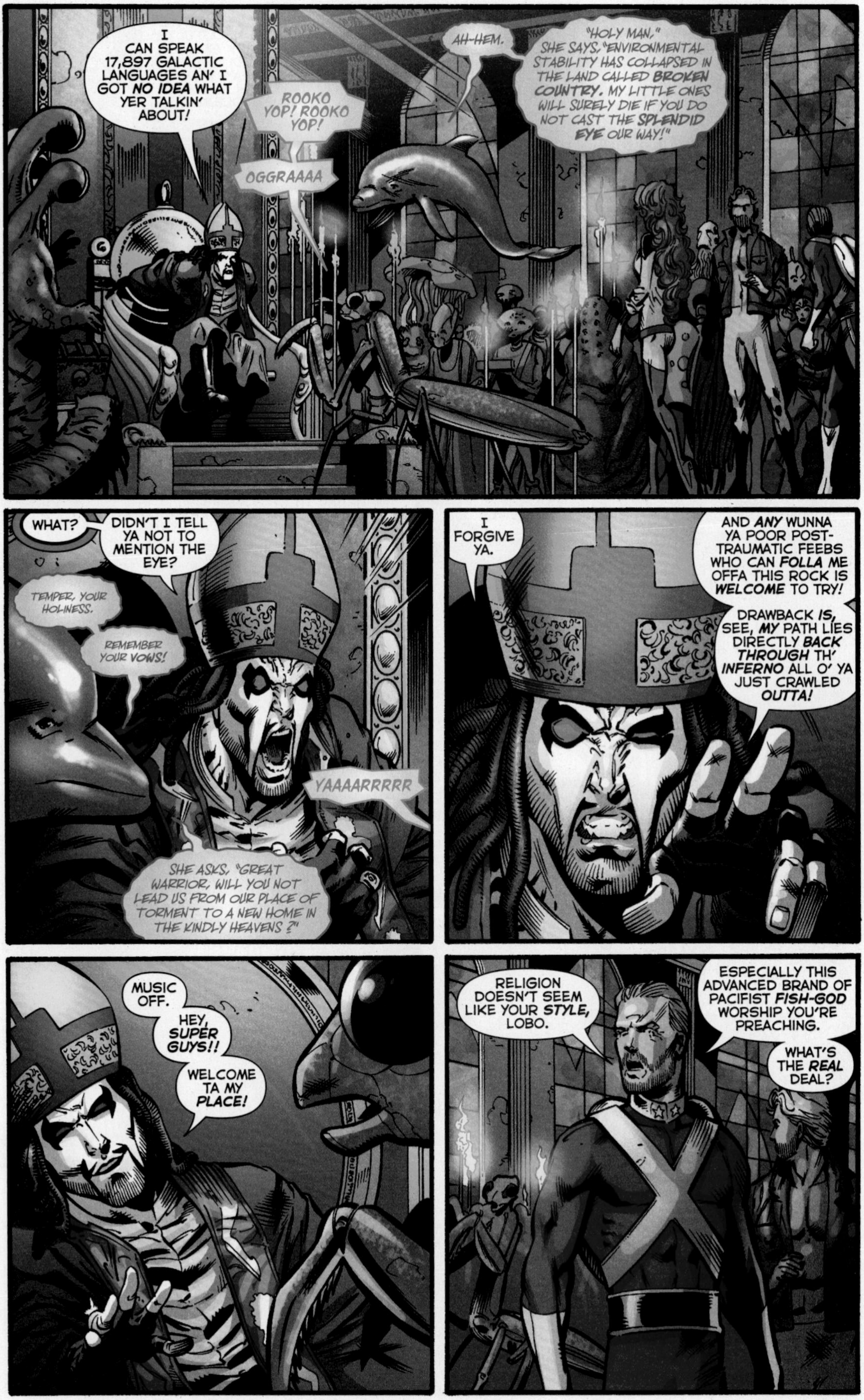
I CAN SPEAK 17,897 GALACTIC LANGUAGES AN' I GOT NO IDEA WHAT YER TALKIN' ABOUT!
ROOKO YOP! ROOKO YOP!
OGGRAAAA
AH-HEM.
"HOLY MAN," SHE SAYS, "ENVIRONMENTAL STABILITY HAS COLLAPSED IN THE LAND CALLED BROKEN COUNTRY. MY LITTLE ONES WILL SURELY DIE IF YOU DO NOT CAST THE SPLENDID EYE OUR WAY!"
WHAT?
DIDN'T I TELL YA NOT TO MENTION THE EYE?
TEMPER, YOUR HOLINESS.
REMEMBER YOUR VOWS!
YAAAARRRRR
SHE ASKS, "GREAT WARRIOR, WILL YOU NOT LEAD US FROM OUR PLACE OF TORMENT TO A NEW HOME IN THE KINDLY HEAVENS?"
I FORGIVE YA.
AND ANY WUNNA YA POOR POST-TRAUMATIC FEEBS WHO CAN FOLLA ME OFFA THIS ROCK IS WELCOME TO TRY!
DRAWBACK IS, SEE, MY PATH LIES DIRECTLY BACK THROUGH TH' INFERNO ALL O' YA JUST CRAWLED OUTTA!
MUSIC OFF.
HEY, SUPER GUYS!!
WELCOME TA MY PLACE!
RELIGION DOESN'T SEEM LIKE YOUR STYLE, LOBO.
ESPECIALLY THIS ADVANCED BRAND OF PACIFIST FISH-GOD WORSHIP YOU'RE PREACHING.
WHAT'S THE REAL DEAL?

I HAD MY VERY OWN MOMENT OF *ILLUMINATION*, MY SON.

THERE'S ME! UP TA MY *NOSTRILS* IN TH' STEAMIN' *OFFAL* OF ONE MORE *CONTRACT* HIT, THINKIN'...

"IS THIS REALLY THE BEST USE A YER TALENTS AS A PUBLIC SPEAKER, LOBO?"

AN' *LO!* A VOICE CAME FORTH, AS IF OUTTA TH' *GUTS* AN' *GIZZ*, SAYIN' "FOLLOW THE *FISH*," AN' WITH THAT...TH' MAIN MAN WAS REDEEMED!

SINCE THEN, I'VE TURNED MY BACK ON SWEARIN', VIOLENCE, *AN* TH' PLEASURES OF TH' *FLESH*.

LIQUOR, TOO... BUT IT'S A DIFFERENT STORY FOR THE HONORED *GUESTS* OF YOURS TRULY, *HIS HOLINESS*.

SPOILS OF A *HUNDRED* PLANETS WIND UP HERE, AN' PAMPERIN' *YOU* WITH AMBROSIAL *BREW*.

SO WHO ELSE *LIVES* ON THIS... FRAGMENT?

I'VE NEVER SEEN ANYTHING *LIKE* THIS, EXCEPT IN *MOVIES*.

I'M FINDING IT... KIND OF *OVERWHELMING*...

NOBODY *LIVES* HERE, MISTER ANIMAL MAN-- THESE ARE TH' *LAST* CRAWLIN', INSANE *SURVIVORS* OF TH' *STYGIAN PASSOVER*, SETTIN' UP TA DIE, NICE AN' *GRIM*.

CREEPY LITTLE *GUARDIANS A' TH' UNIVERSE* CALL IT *SECTOR 3500*. THIRTY PARSECS SOUTH FROM THE *VEGAN FRONTIER*. ONCE A *HUNDRED* COMPLEX, THRIVIN' SYSTEMS...

...NOW A BIG SKY FULLA SCREAMIN' *HEADSTONES*.

LOBO, I KNOW THE *PRINCESS* HERE TALKED ABOUT THIS ALREADY, BUT WE NEED YOUR *HELP* TO GET *PAST* THIS DEBRIS STORM AND BACK TO OUR *FAMILIES*.

YOU MAY BE *THE CLERGY* IN THESE PARTS, BUT YOU'RE STILL THE BEST TRACKER AND BOUNTY HUNTER IN THE *UNIVERSE* FROM WHAT I'VE HEARD.

HOW *MUCH*?

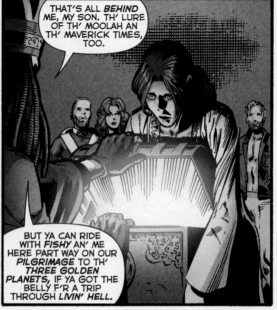

THAT'S ALL *BEHIND* ME, MY SON. TH' LURE OF TH' *MOOLAH* AN TH' *MAVERICK TIMES*, TOO.

BUT YA CAN RIDE WITH *FISHY* AN' ME HERE PART WAY ON OUR *PILGRIMAGE* TO TH' *THREE GOLDEN PLANETS*, IF YA GOT THE BELLY F'R A TRIP THROUGH *LIVIN' HELL*.

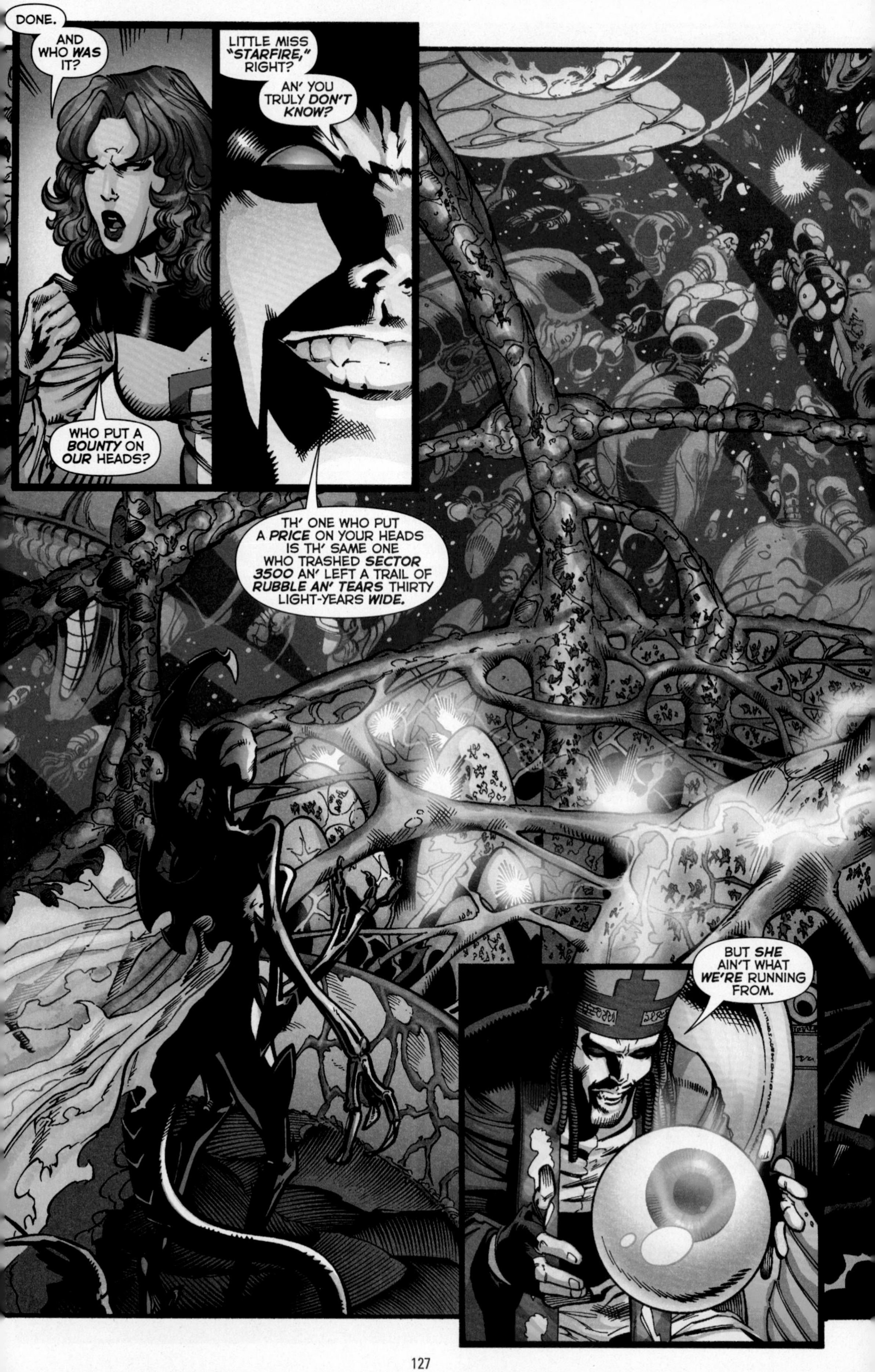

DONE.
AND WHO WAS IT?
LITTLE MISS "STARFIRE," RIGHT?
AN' YOU TRULY DON'T KNOW?
WHO PUT A BOUNTY ON OUR HEADS?
TH' ONE WHO PUT A PRICE ON YOUR HEADS IS TH' SAME ONE WHO TRASHED SECTOR 3500 AN' LEFT A TRAIL OF RUBBLE AN' TEARS THIRTY LIGHT-YEARS WIDE.
BUT SHE AIN'T WHAT WE'RE RUNNING FROM.

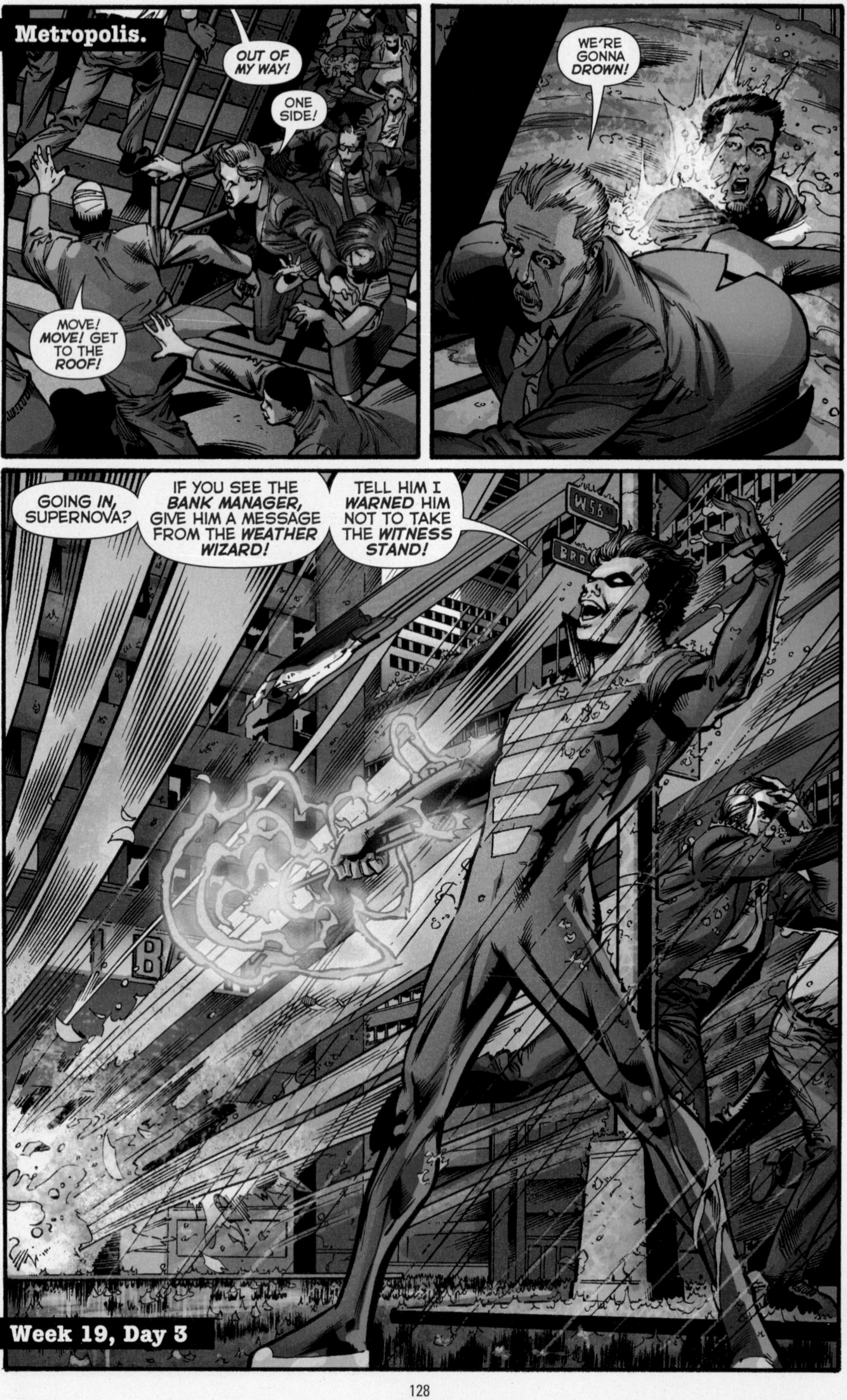
Metropolis.
OUT OF MY WAY!
ONE SIDE!
MOVE! MOVE! GET TO THE ROOF!
WE'RE GONNA DROWN!
GOING IN, SUPERNOVA?
IF YOU SEE THE BANK MANAGER, GIVE HIM A MESSAGE FROM THE WEATHER WIZARD!
TELL HIM I WARNED HIM NOT TO TAKE THE WITNESS STAND!
Week 19, Day 3

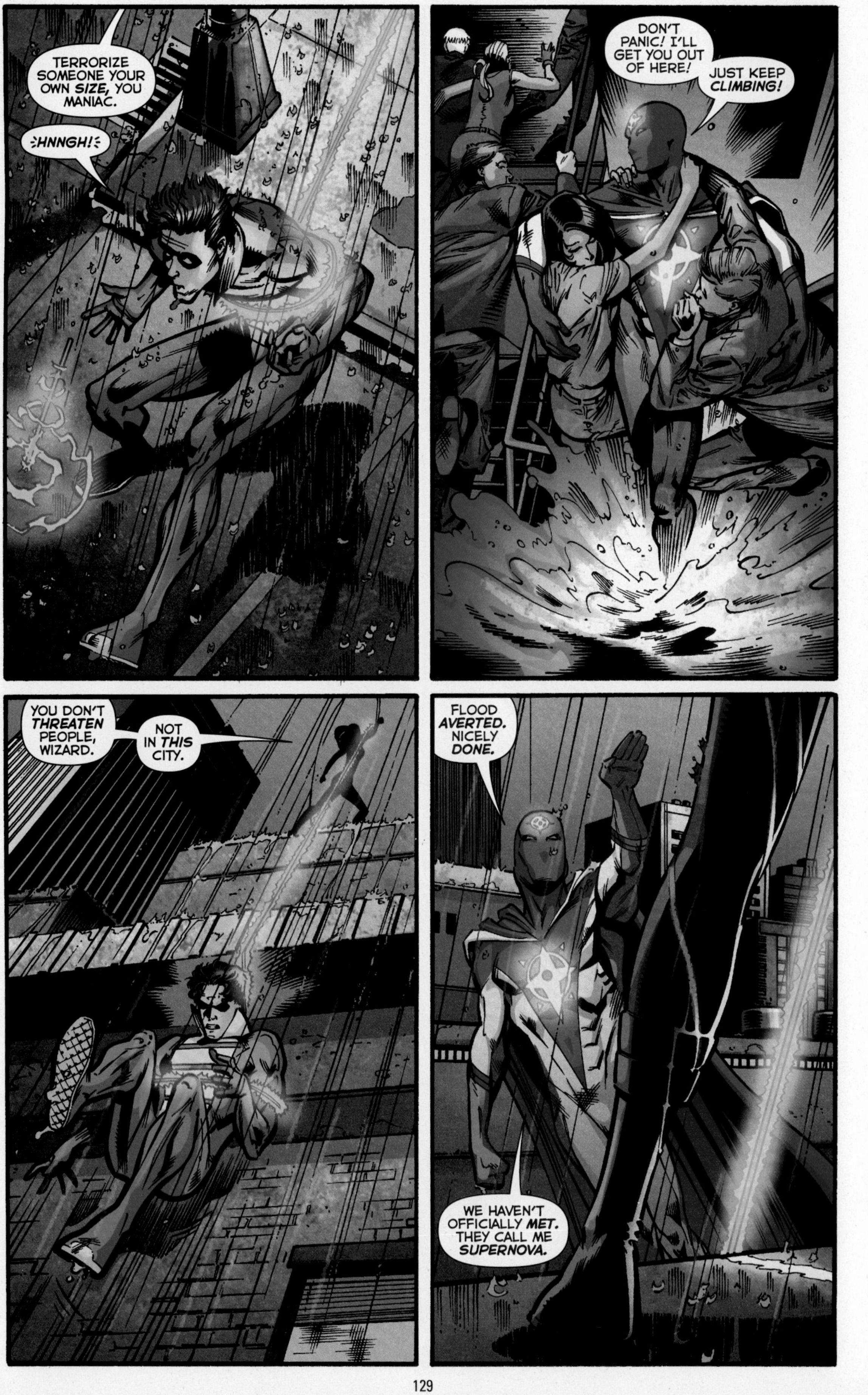

TERRORIZE SOMEONE YOUR OWN SIZE, YOU MANIAC.
HNNGH!
DON'T PANIC! I'LL GET YOU OUT OF HERE!
JUST KEEP CLIMBING!
YOU DON'T THREATEN PEOPLE, WIZARD.
NOT IN THIS CITY.
FLOOD AVERTED. NICELY DONE.
WE HAVEN'T OFFICIALLY MET. THEY CALL ME SUPERNOVA.

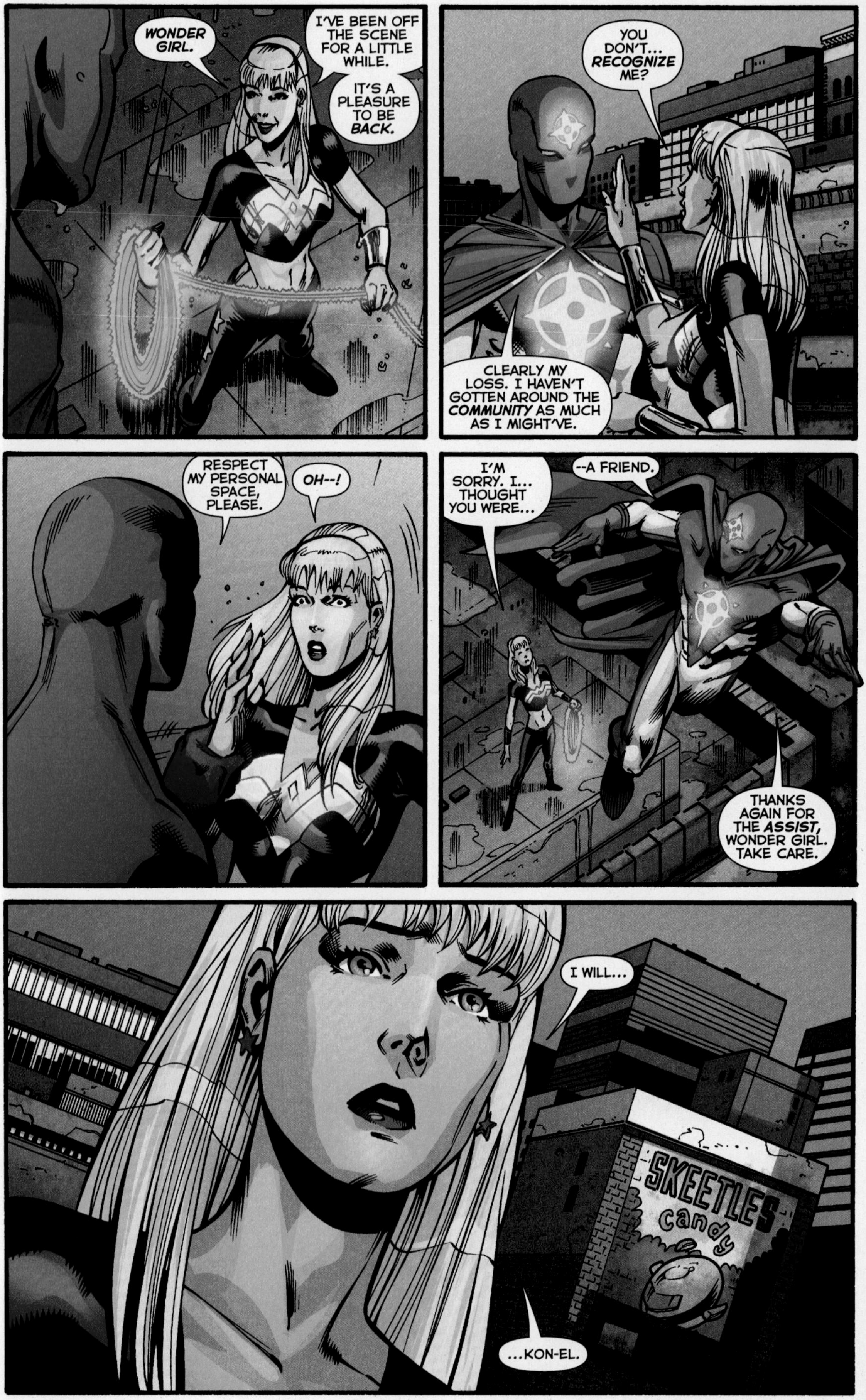
WONDER GIRL.
I'VE BEEN OFF THE SCENE FOR A LITTLE WHILE.
IT'S A PLEASURE TO BE BACK.
YOU DON'T... RECOGNIZE ME?
CLEARLY MY LOSS. I HAVEN'T GOTTEN AROUND THE COMMUNITY AS MUCH AS I MIGHT'VE.
RESPECT MY PERSONAL SPACE, PLEASE.
OH--!
I'M SORRY. I... THOUGHT YOU WERE...
--A FRIEND.
THANKS AGAIN FOR THE ASSIST, WONDER GIRL. TAKE CARE.
I WILL...
SKEETLES candy
...KON-EL.

"HOW DOES THE *VISOR* FEEL?"

Week 19, Day 4

Arizona.

FEATHERWEIGHT. MY *CONTACTS* ARE MORE TROUBLE THAN THIS.

YOU CAN SEE THROUGH 'EM, *TOO*, RIGHT?

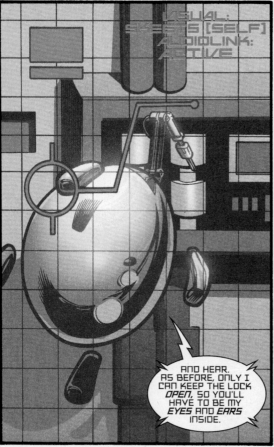

VISUAL: SKEETS [SELF] AUDIOLINK: ACTIVE

AND HEAR. AS BEFORE, ONLY I CAN KEEP THE LOCK *OPEN*, SO YOU'LL HAVE TO BE MY *EYES* AND *EARS* INSIDE.

WHAT DID YOU CALL THIS RIP HUNTER GUY, AGAIN?

A CHRONONAUT. A TIME TRAVELER.

JUST CHECKING.

WHAT THE HOLY LIVING HELL AM I GETTING *INTO...*?

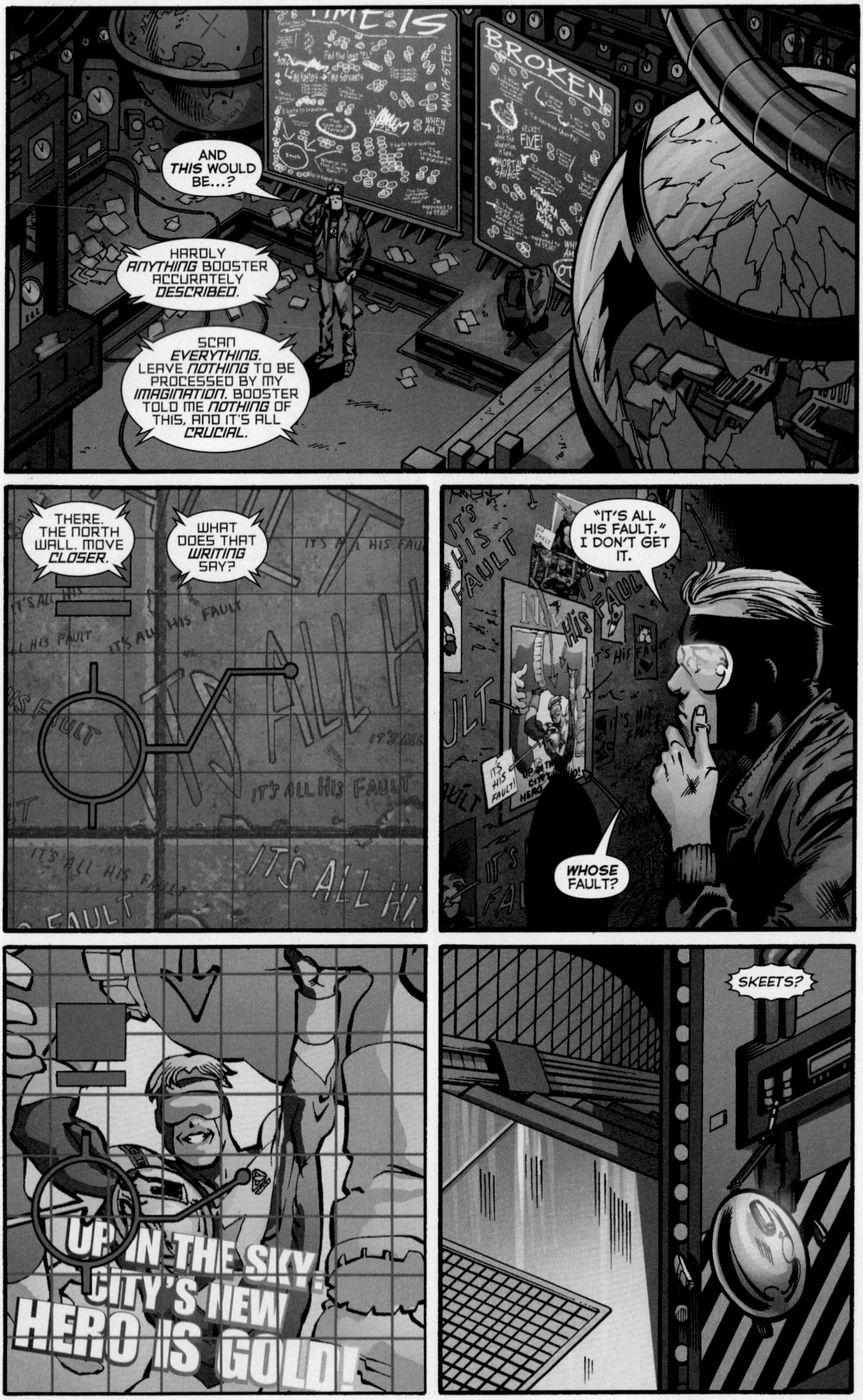
AND THIS WOULD BE...?
HARDLY ANYTHING BOOSTER ACCURATELY DESCRIBED.
SCAN EVERYTHING. LEAVE NOTHING TO BE PROCESSED BY MY IMAGINATION. BOOSTER TOLD ME NOTHING OF THIS, AND IT'S ALL CRUCIAL.
TIME IS
BROKEN
THERE. THE NORTH WALL. MOVE CLOSER.
WHAT DOES THAT WRITING SAY?
IT'S ALL HIS FAULT
"IT'S ALL HIS FAULT." I DON'T GET IT.
WHOSE FAULT?
UP IN THE SKY! CITY'S NEW HERO IS GOLD!
SKEETS?

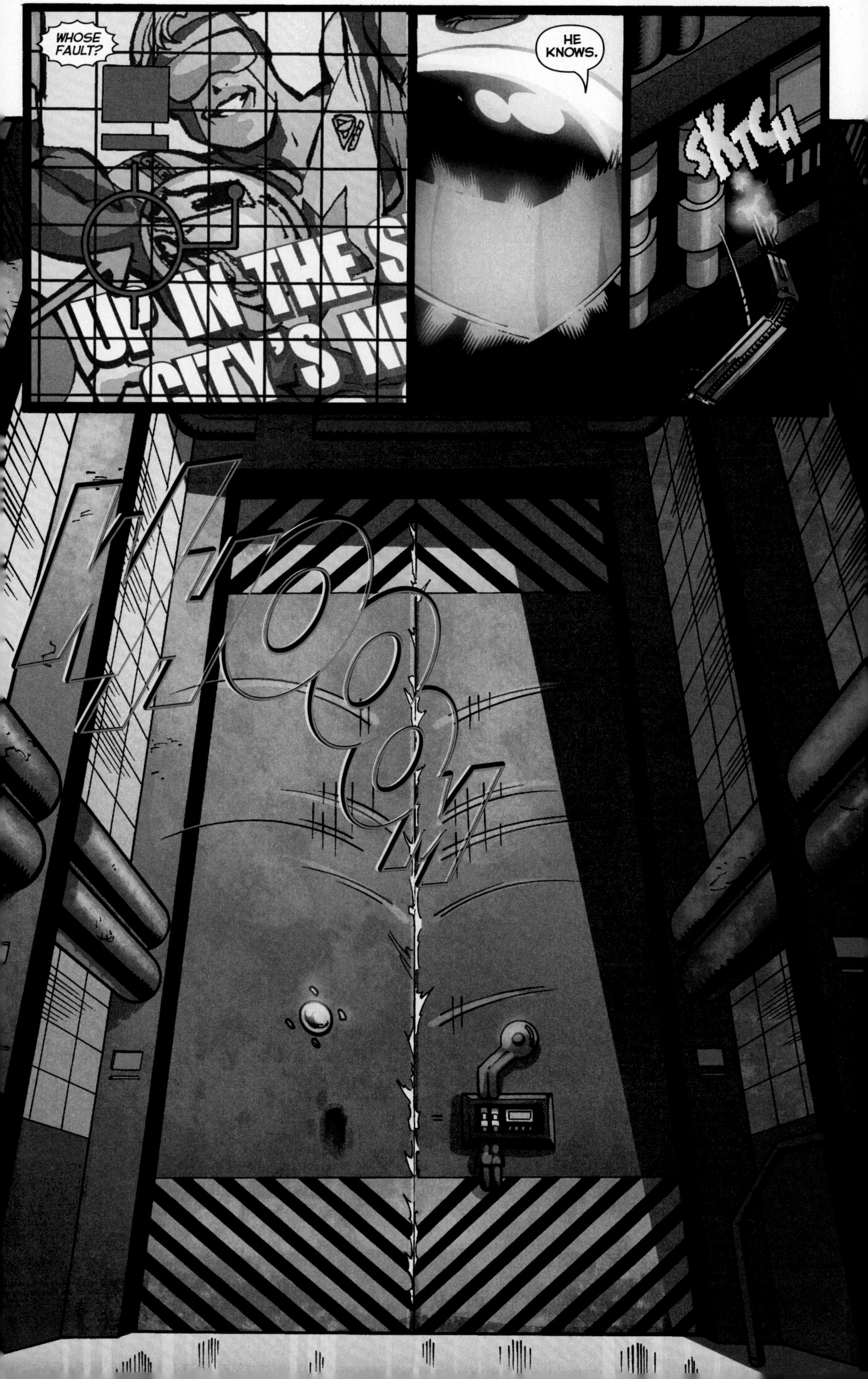
WHOSE FAULT?
UP IN THE
HE KNOWS.
SKTCH
WHOOOOM

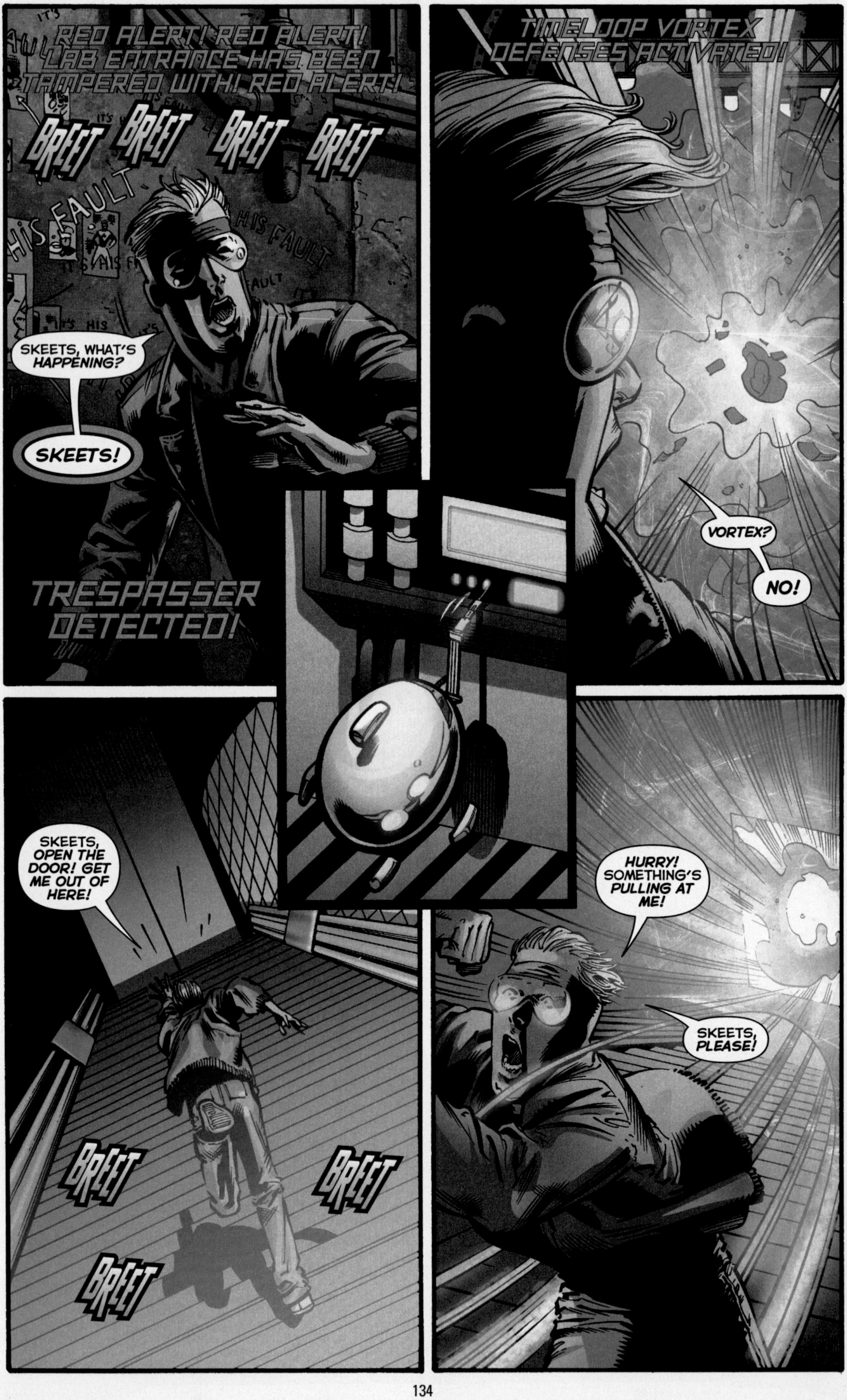
RED ALERT! RED ALERT! LAB ENTRANCE HAS BEEN TAMPERED WITH! RED ALERT!
BREET BREET BREET BREET
HIS FAULT
SKEETS, WHAT'S HAPPENING?
SKEETS!
TRESPASSER DETECTED!
TIMELOOP VORTEX DEFENSES ACTIVATED!
VORTEX?
NO!
SKEETS, OPEN THE DOOR! GET ME OUT OF HERE!
BREET
BREET
BREET
HURRY! SOMETHING'S PULLING AT ME!
SKEETS, PLEASE!

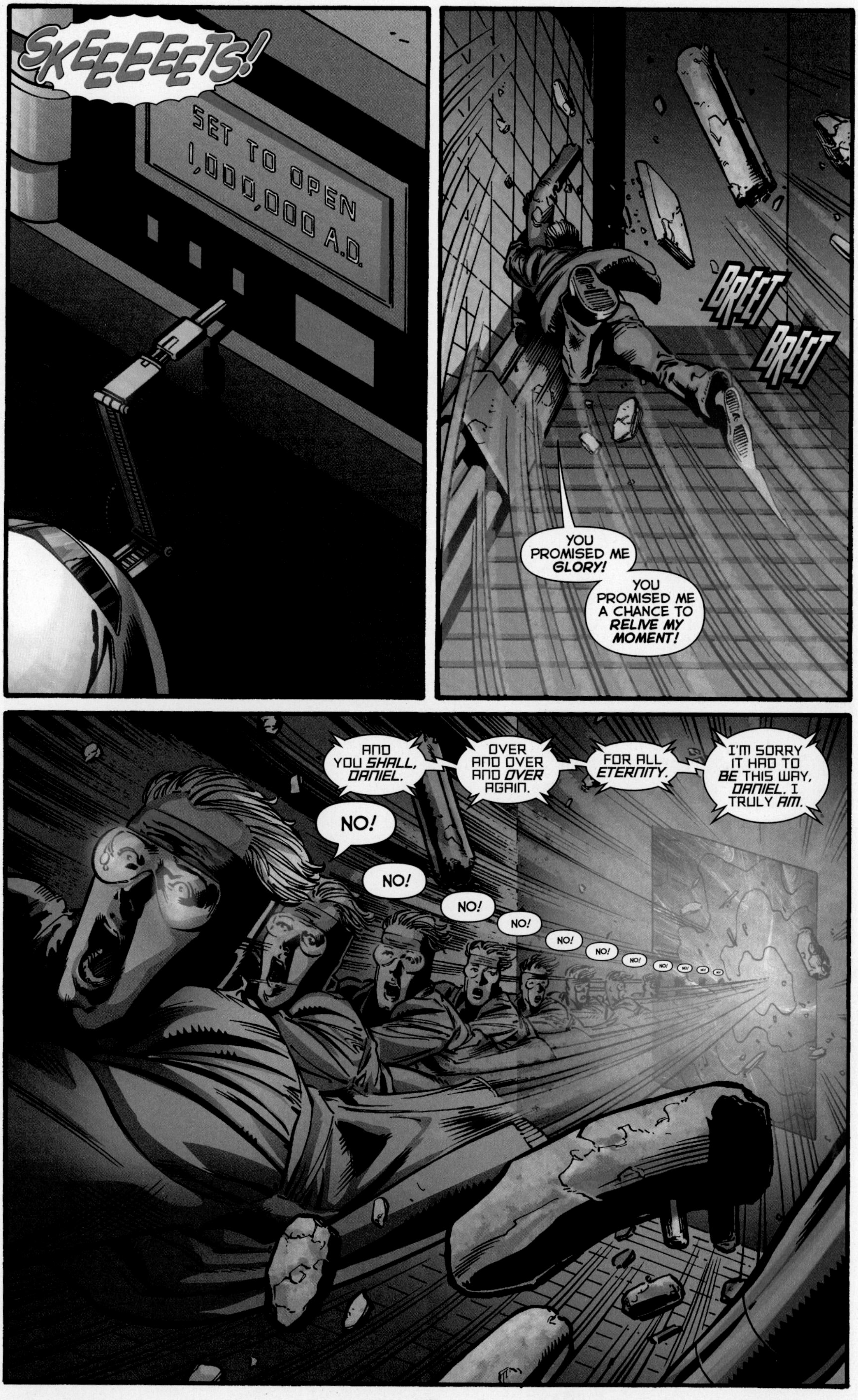
SKEEEEEETS!
SET TO OPEN 1,000,000 A.D.
BREET BREET
YOU PROMISED ME GLORY!
YOU PROMISED ME A CHANCE TO RELIVE MY MOMENT!
AND YOU SHALL, DANIEL.
OVER AND OVER AND OVER AGAIN.
FOR ALL ETERNITY.
I'M SORRY IT HAD TO BE THIS WAY, DANIEL. I TRULY AM.
NO!
NO!
NO!
NO!
NO!
NO!
NO!
NO!

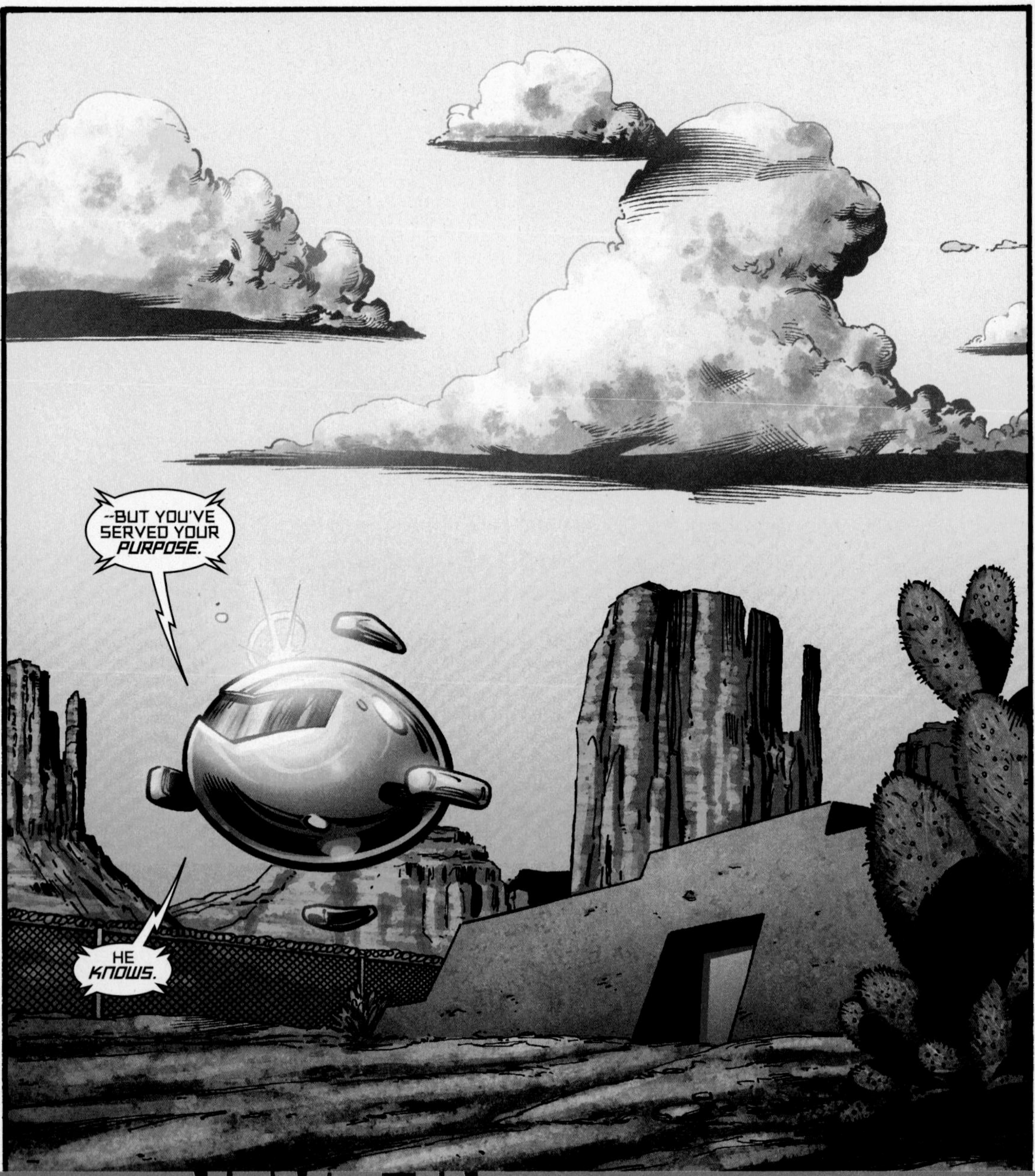
--BUT YOU'VE SERVED YOUR *PURPOSE.*
HE *KNOWS.*

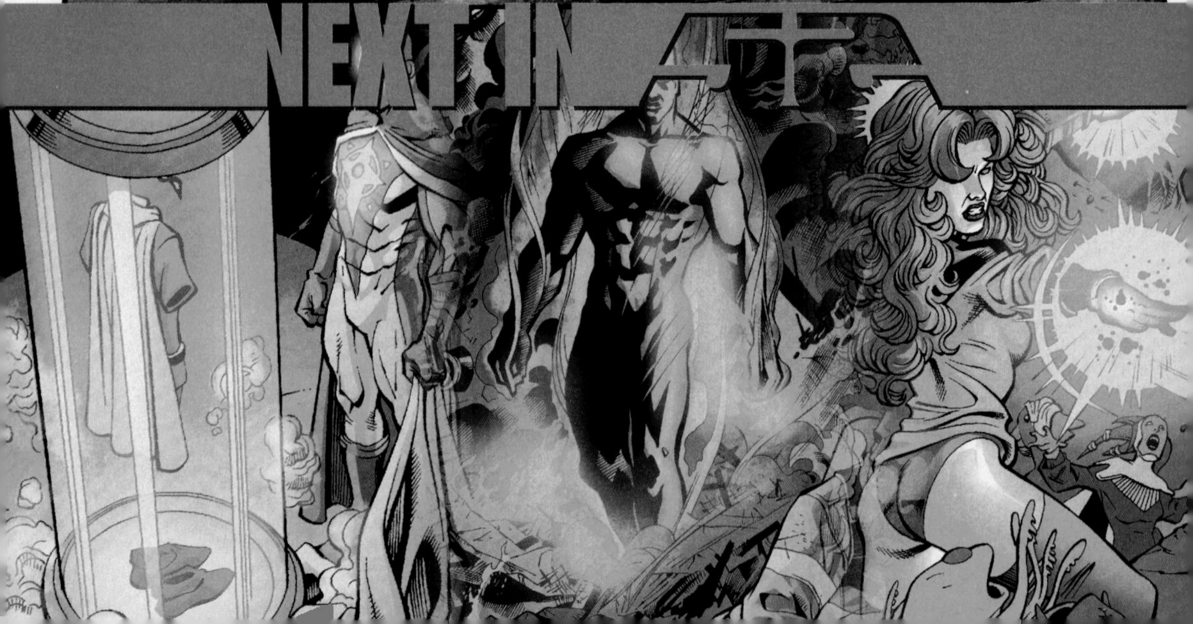
NEXT IN

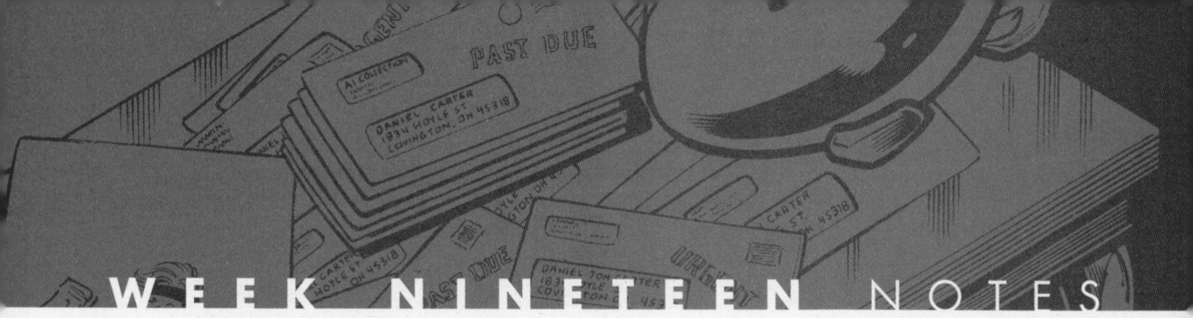
PAST DUE
DANIEL CARTER
1834 HOYLE ST
COVINGTON, OH 45318
PAST DUE

WEEK NINETEEN NOTES

MARK WAID

I realize much has already been said about this in interviews, and I know he's kinda sick of hearing about it by now, but I can't let this issue go by without reiterating what a brilliant infusion of energy to the whole series Grant delivered in the idle recasting of Skeets.

Originally, our group take on the plot threat that Skeets's historical knowledge was becoming gradually more corrupt had something or other to do with time itself being out of whack. Booster's big arc was supposed to be how he went about fixing that. But the further along we got in the actual storytelling, the duller and more familiar that all began to sound, and all four scripters realized simultaneously (almost, but not quite, too late) that none of us really wanted to write yet another super-hero story about someone repairing a corrupt timestream, not unless there were some sort of prize involved for being the millionth writers to do it.

However. If we changed Booster's quest — if we decided that time WASN'T screwy and set him a different goal — then the resultant, scary-huge plot hole was, "Okay, then why WAS Skeets giving bad information in earlier weeks?" I asked this question aloud during a meeting.

And THAT'S when Grant said, simply, "Because he's evil...?" and everyone else's jaws fell open.

Writers are easily bored, and we're always hungry for new ideas to alleviate that boredom, even if they're weird concepts that send us down unfamiliar roads. On a project this complex and this heavily mapped, however, even the really good new ideas have to be carefully weighed and studied and evaluated before they're integrated into the plot.

Not this one. This one, we all knew instantly and instinctively, was so absolutely perfect that we adopted it without hesitation, even though it meant we suddenly hadn't the first clue where a Skeets-as-villain story would take us or how it might integrate with all our other plans. See, Grant's big contribution to 52 wasn't that he was the "idea" guy. It was that he's fearless.

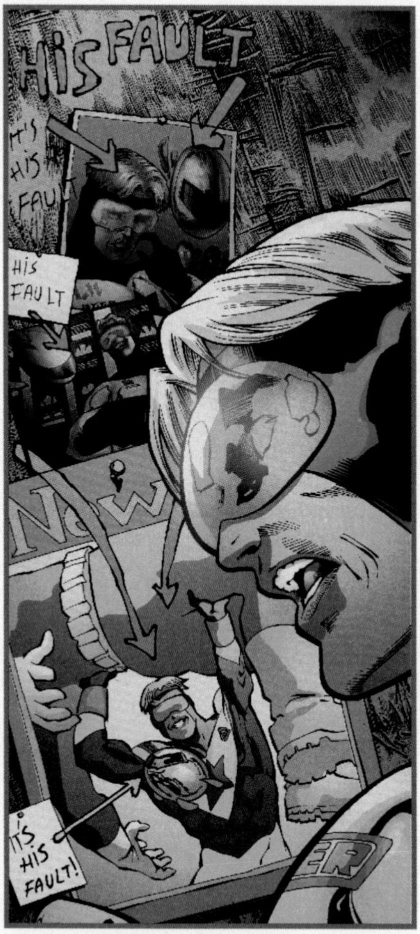
HIS FAULT
HIS FAULT
IT'S HIS FAULT!

The hints to Skeets's turn as a villain were seen as far back as Week Six.

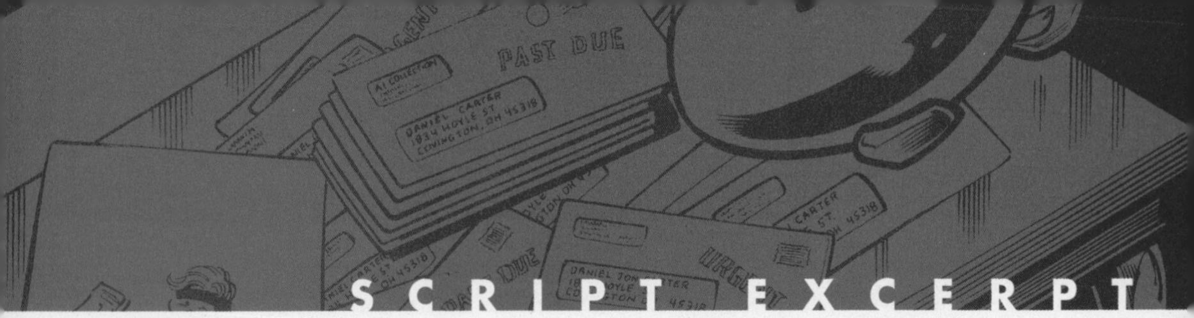
PAST DUE
DANIEL CARTER
1834 HOYLE ST.
COVINGTON, OH 45318

SCRIPT EXCERPT

(COMPARE WITH PAGE 122 OF THIS COLLECTION)

WEEK NINETEEN - PAGE SIX

PANEL ONE
A huge planetary chunk in the drifting array of debris. It's huge — like one of those Roger Dean floating continents. We can actually see the curvature of the horizon, it's so huge, and underneath there's a huge cone of cored-out planetary crust and mantle. Mountains, continental shelves and a thin atmosphere clinging to the spinning fragment's gravity.

STARFIRE: X'hal beyond! Where has he BROUGHT us?

PANEL TWO
Move in — the little ship that's carried our three brave space travellers across the void is now landing on a huge area outside the "cathedral." The ship has been towed by Lobo's space cycle. We're in a ramshackle DIY city — if a refugee camp were extended into a gigantic urban sprawl it might look a little like this. There are buildings made of salvaged spaceships combined with the shattered remnants of the original soaring, classical architecture of what was once a peaceful, advanced world dedicated to art and science. A whole planet — which was once like the Getty Center — is now in ruins, home to the ragged survivors of Lady Styx's apocalypse. There are thousands of aliens here, most suffering from the unimaginable post-traumatic stress of losing not only their homes but the PLANETS they lived on! Everybody here is nuts, doomed and haunted aliens shuffling around trying to pretend the ultimate apocalyptic end of all normal life has come.

PANEL THREE
Warbird cabin interior. Buddy Baker, Adam Strange and Starfire. They all look pretty rough. The guys are so grizzled as to be well-nigh bearded. Starfire's hair is lank and lacking in energy.

CAPTION: WEEK 19, DAY 2

STARFIRE: It's like a gigantic refugee camp. Look at this place. Uh...sorry, Adam.

ADAM: I'm long over it, Buddy. I'm wired into the SHIP's senses: I can see just fine. They're WELCOMING him. This is insane...

PANEL FOUR
Big pic. Pope Lobo walks between an aisle of supplicants — ragtag alien families of many different species (with body types that can go as crazy as you like as long as they're convincingly able to survive on this basically Earth-like fragment of planet. Maybe we could throw in some forgotten DC aliens from old Schwartz stories or whatever — any creatures that may qualify as coming from a region of space that's this far out from our Solar System.

They throw what gifts they can in front of Lobo as he marches forward. There are candles and bells and as much sci-fi Goth-y Heavy Metal imagery as we can safely handle. Lobo's being welcomed by a ragtag bunch who look to him as some kind of savior — at least for a little while. Lobo is being met by a floating dolphin-like creature (Keith, you know what these guys look like better than most, so here's a particularly mannered and mock-obsequious specimen).

FISHY: A very warm welcome for Archbishop Lobo of the First Celestial Church of the Triplefish-God!

FISHY: Wonderful to see you again, Archbishop.

LOBO: Likewise, Fishy.

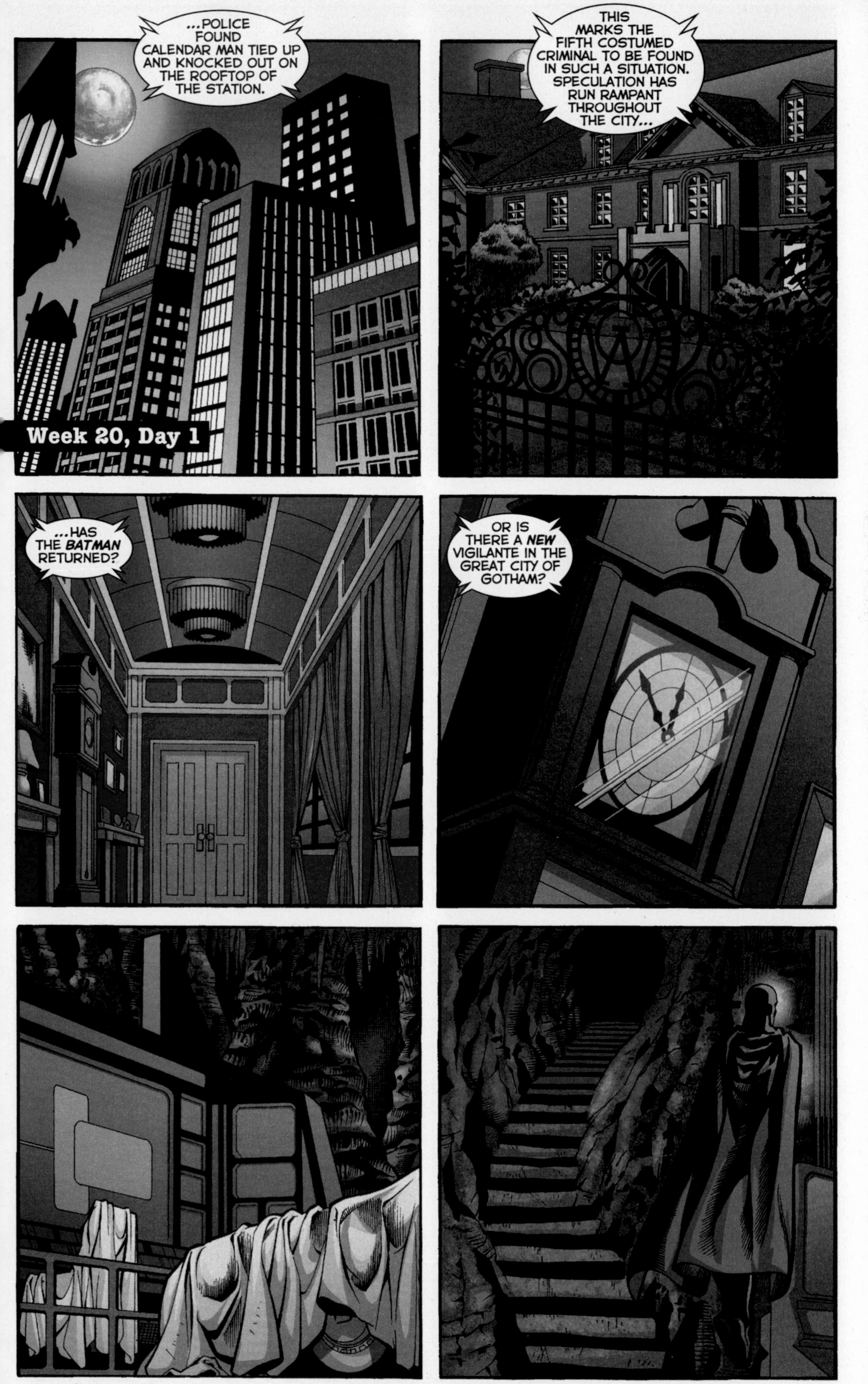

...POLICE FOUND CALENDAR MAN TIED UP AND KNOCKED OUT ON THE ROOFTOP OF THE STATION.
Week 20, Day 1
THIS MARKS THE FIFTH COSTUMED CRIMINAL TO BE FOUND IN SUCH A SITUATION. SPECULATION HAS RUN RAMPANT THROUGHOUT THE CITY...
...HAS THE *BATMAN* RETURNED?
OR IS THERE A *NEW* VIGILANTE IN THE GREAT CITY OF GOTHAM?

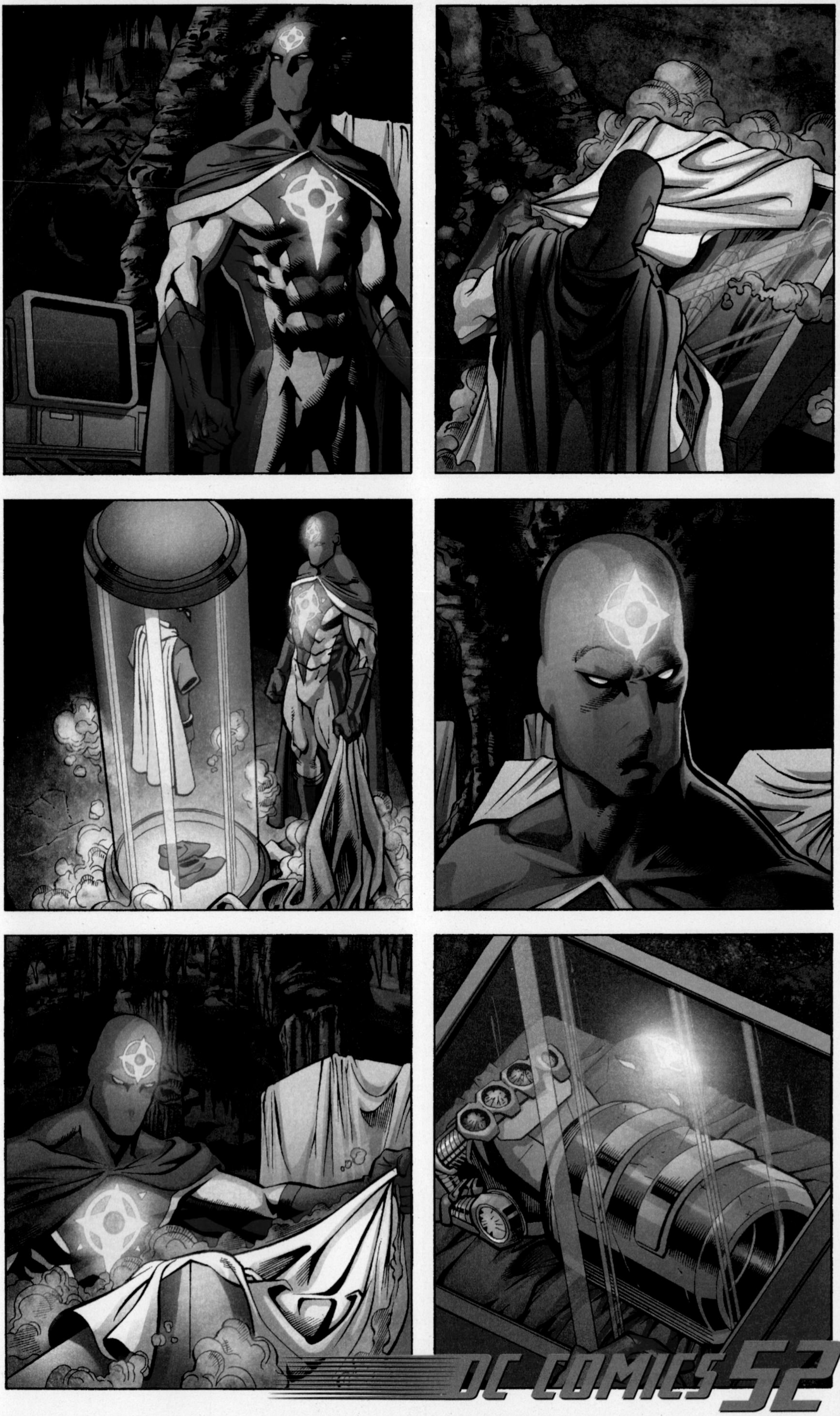
DC COMICS 52

WRITTEN BY GEOFF JOHNS, GRANT MORRISON, GREG RUCKA, MARK WAID

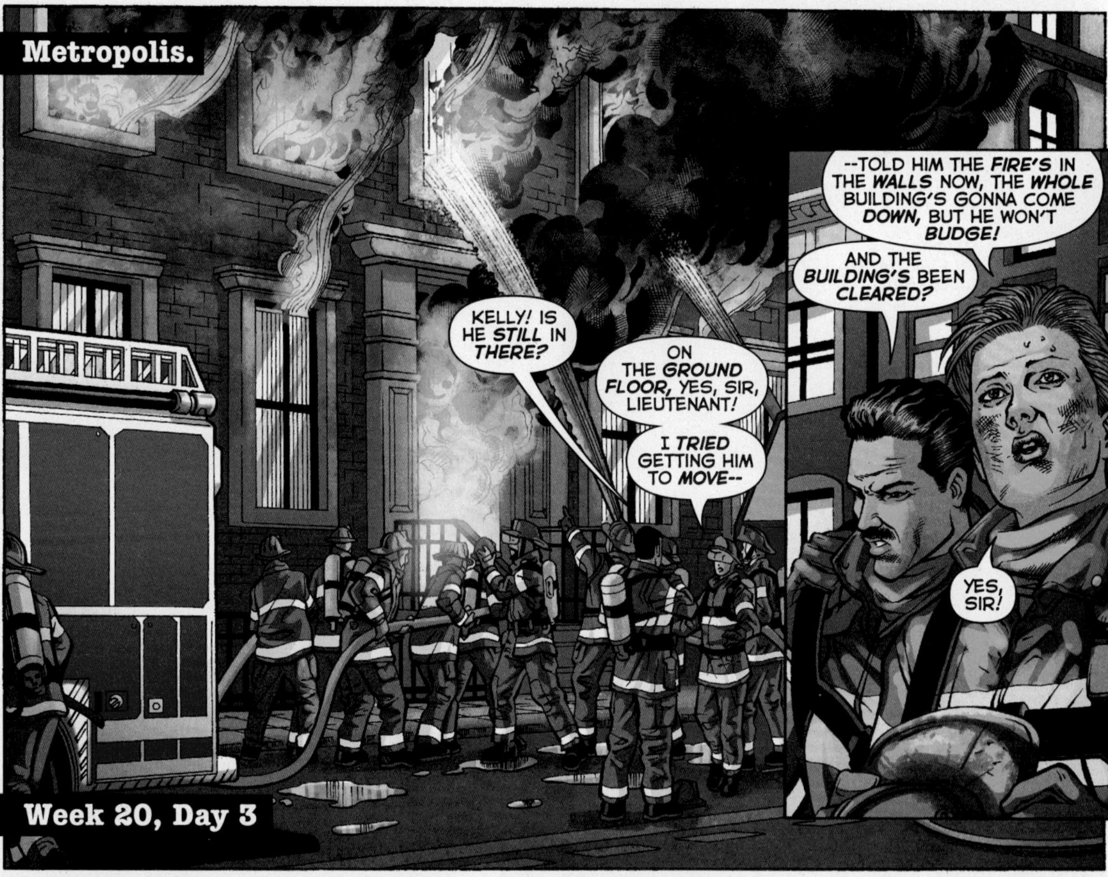
Metropolis.
KELLY! IS HE STILL IN THERE?
ON THE GROUND FLOOR, YES, SIR, LIEUTENANT!
I TRIED GETTING HIM TO MOVE--
--TOLD HIM THE FIRE'S IN THE WALLS NOW, THE WHOLE BUILDING'S GONNA COME DOWN, BUT HE WON'T BUDGE!
AND THE BUILDING'S BEEN CLEARED?
YES, SIR!
Week 20, Day 3

ART BREAKDOWNS BY KEITH GIFFEN • PENCILS BY CHRIS BATISTA • INKS BY RUY JOSE

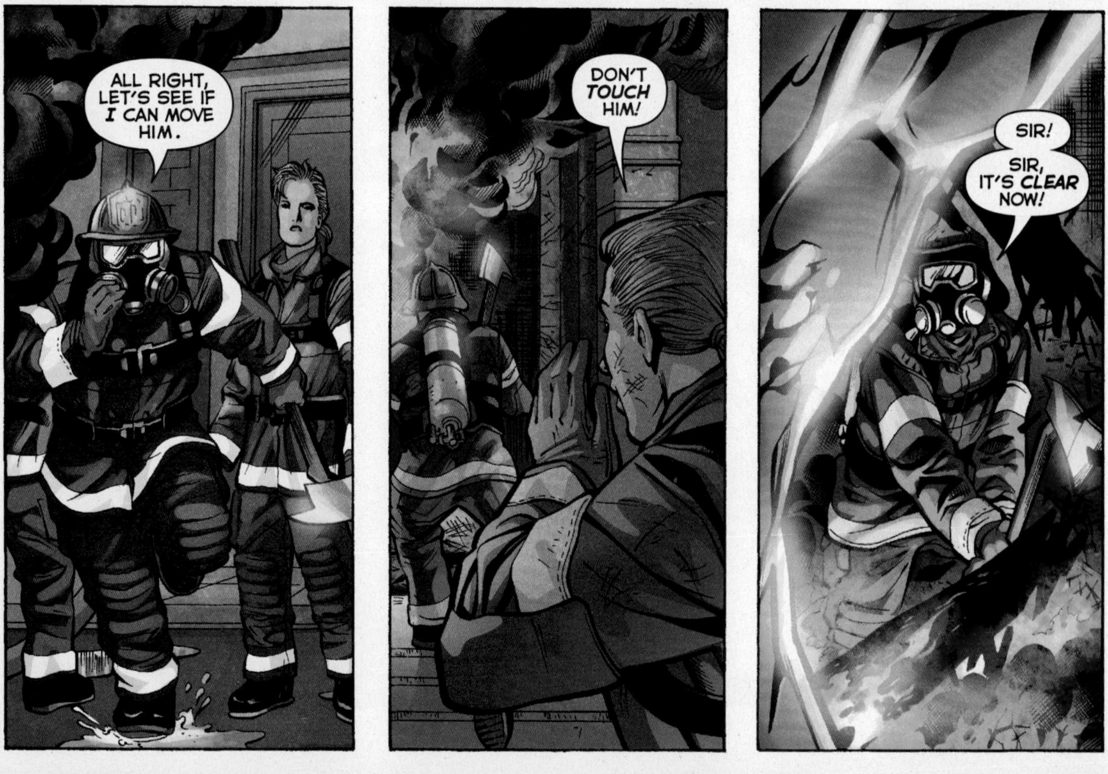
ALL RIGHT, LET'S SEE IF I CAN MOVE HIM.
DON'T TOUCH HIM!
SIR!
SIR, IT'S CLEAR NOW!

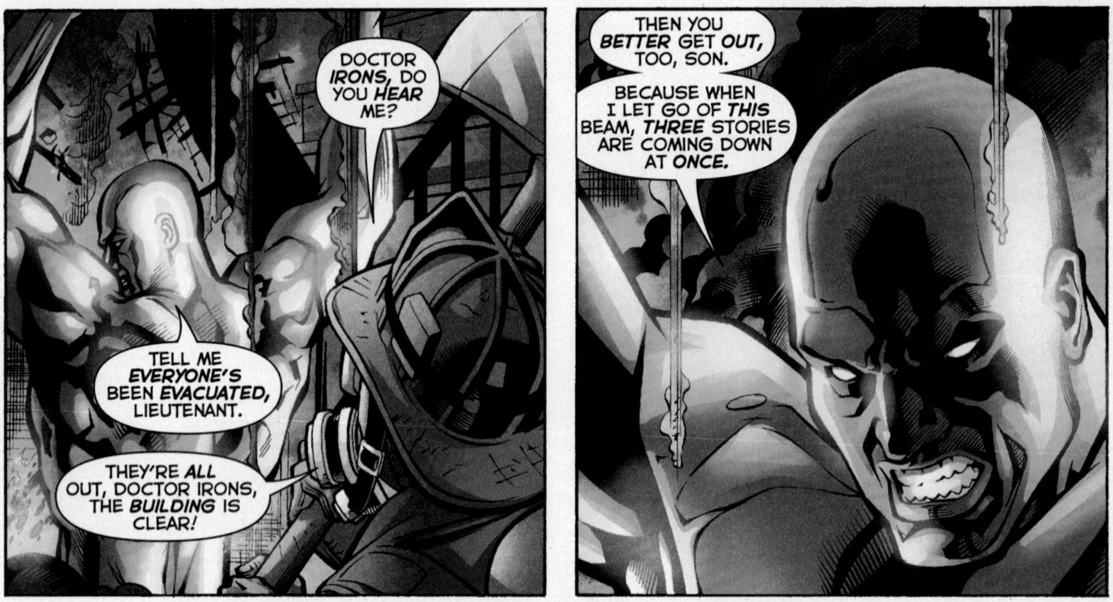
DOCTOR IRONS, DO YOU HEAR ME?
TELL ME EVERYONE'S BEEN EVACUATED, LIEUTENANT.
THEY'RE ALL OUT, DOCTOR IRONS, THE BUILDING IS CLEAR!
THEN YOU BETTER GET OUT, TOO, SON.
BECAUSE WHEN I LET GO OF THIS BEAM, THREE STORIES ARE COMING DOWN AT ONCE.

COLORS BY ALEX SINCLAIR • LETTERING BY TRAVIS LANHAM

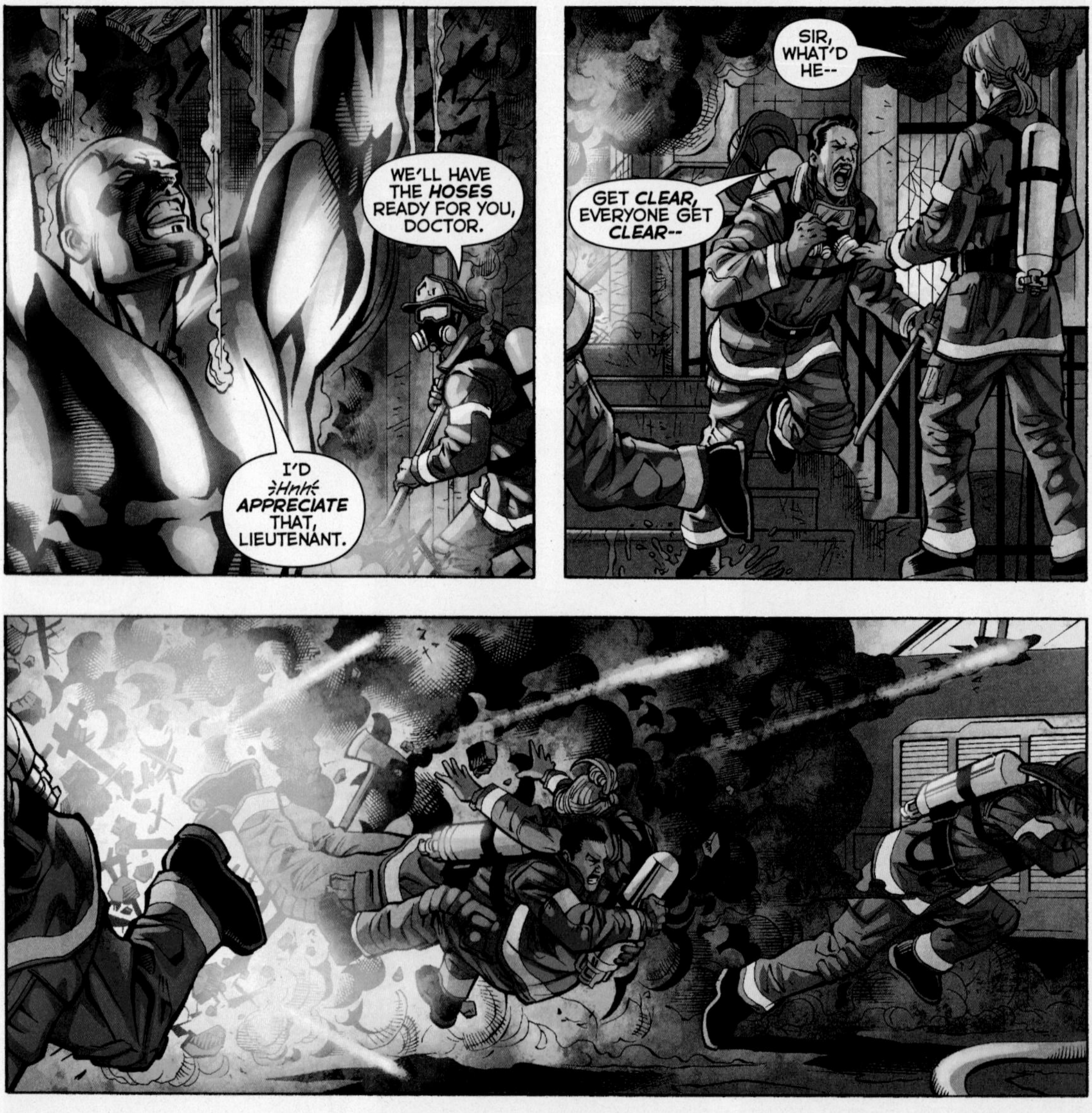
WE'LL HAVE THE HOSES READY FOR YOU, DOCTOR.
I'D Hnh APPRECIATE THAT, LIEUTENANT.
SIR, WHAT'D HE--
GET CLEAR, EVERYONE GET CLEAR--

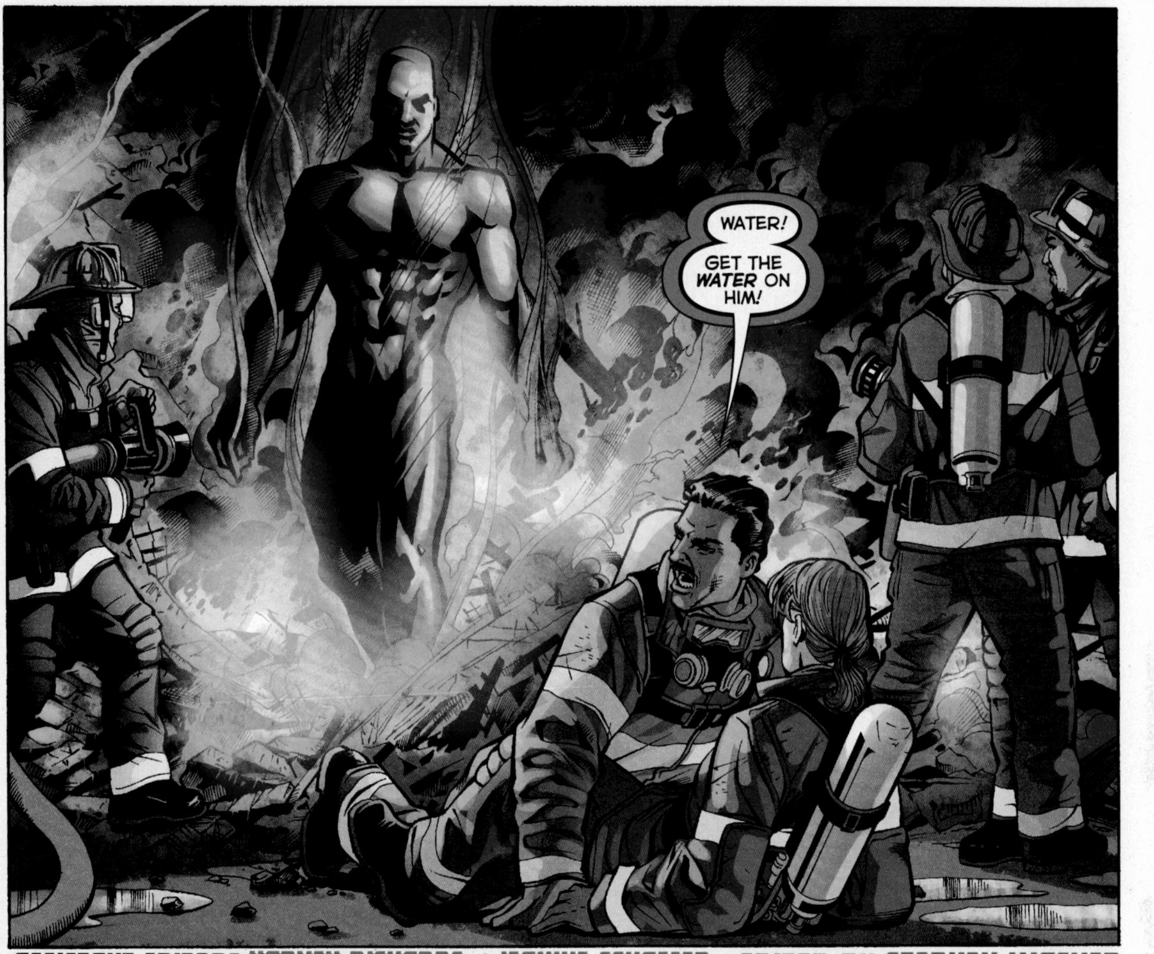
WATER!
GET THE WATER ON HIM!

ASSISTANT EDITORS HARVEY RICHARDS & JEANINE SCHAEFER EDITED BY STEPHEN WACKER
COVER BY J.G. JONES & ALEX SINCLAIR

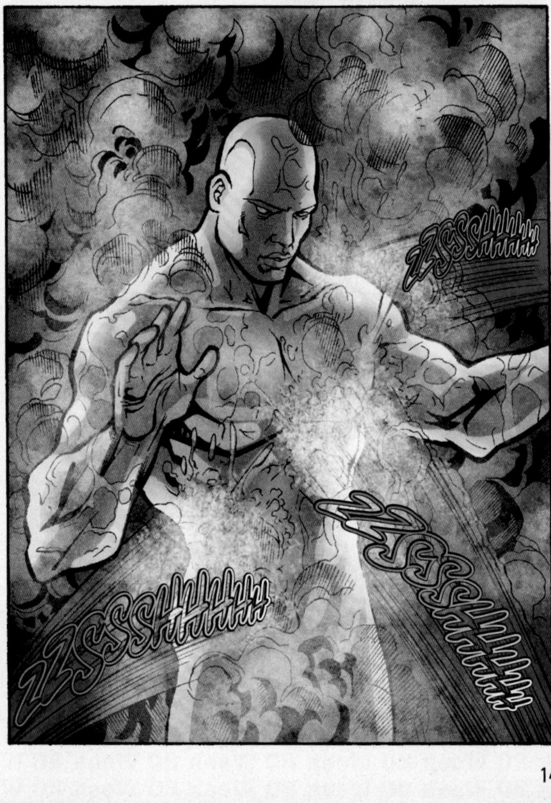

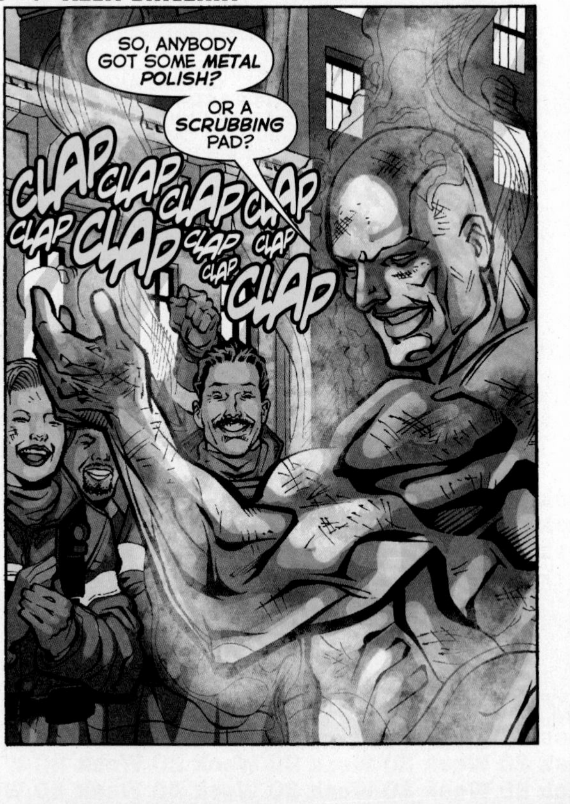
SO, ANYBODY GOT SOME METAL POLISH?
OR A SCRUBBING PAD?
CLAP CLAP CLAP CLAP CLAP CLAP clap clap clap clap CLAP

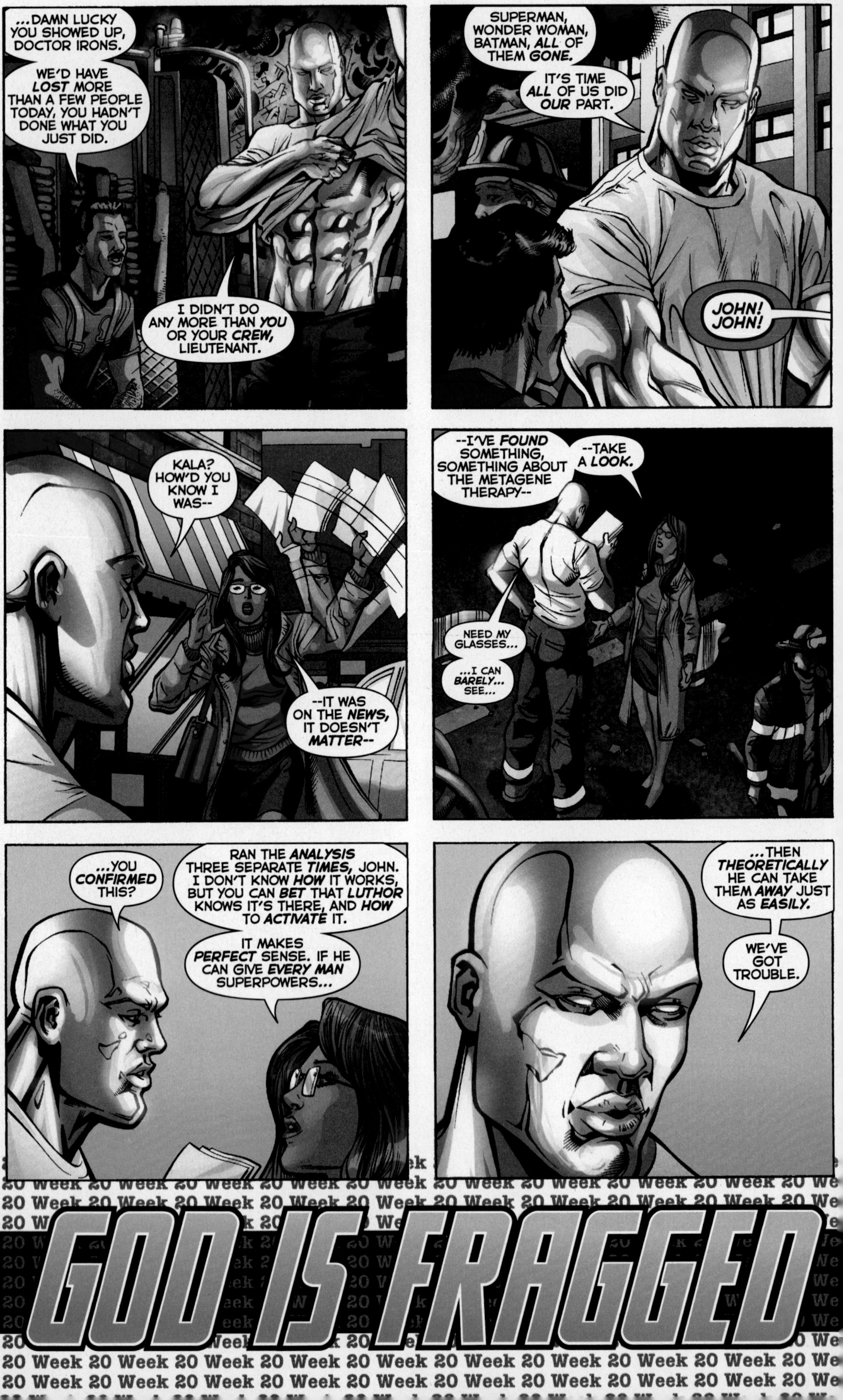
...DAMN LUCKY YOU SHOWED UP, DOCTOR IRONS.
WE'D HAVE LOST MORE THAN A FEW PEOPLE TODAY, YOU HADN'T DONE WHAT YOU JUST DID.
I DIDN'T DO ANY MORE THAN YOU OR YOUR CREW, LIEUTENANT.
SUPERMAN, WONDER WOMAN, BATMAN, ALL OF THEM GONE.
IT'S TIME ALL OF US DID OUR PART.
JOHN! JOHN!
KALA? HOW'D YOU KNOW I WAS--
--IT WAS ON THE NEWS, IT DOESN'T MATTER--
--I'VE FOUND SOMETHING, SOMETHING ABOUT THE METAGENE THERAPY--
--TAKE A LOOK.
NEED MY GLASSES...
...I CAN BARELY... SEE...
...YOU CONFIRMED THIS?
RAN THE ANALYSIS THREE SEPARATE TIMES, JOHN. I DON'T KNOW HOW IT WORKS, BUT YOU CAN BET THAT LUTHOR KNOWS IT'S THERE, AND HOW TO ACTIVATE IT.
IT MAKES PERFECT SENSE. IF HE CAN GIVE EVERY MAN SUPERPOWERS...
...THEN THEORETICALLY HE CAN TAKE THEM AWAY JUST AS EASILY.
WE'VE GOT TROUBLE.
Week 20 Week 20 Week 20 Week 20 Week 20 Week 20 Week 20 Week 20 Week 20 Week 20
GOD IS FRAGGED

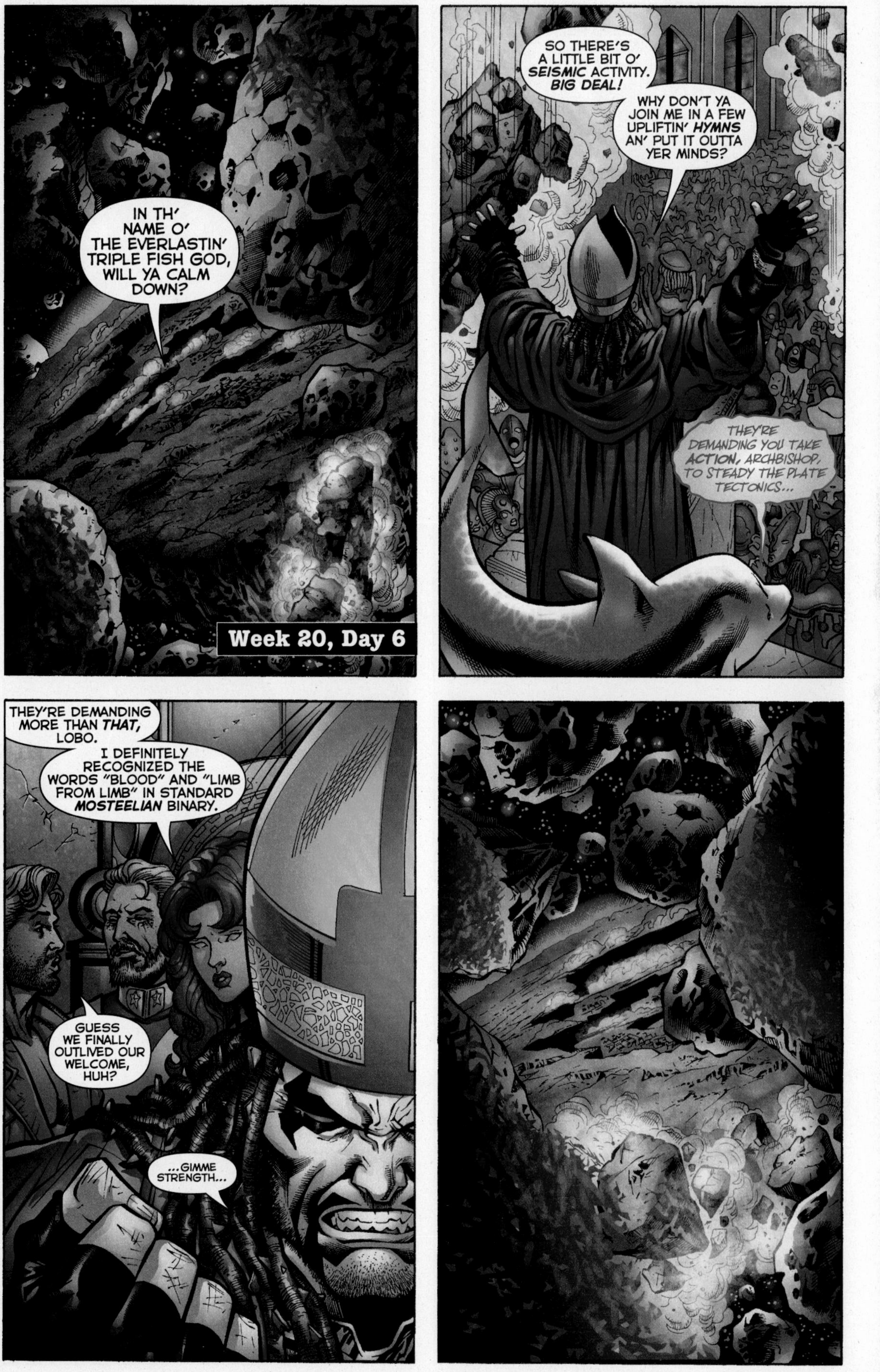
IN TH' NAME O' THE EVERLASTIN' TRIPLE FISH GOD, WILL YA CALM DOWN?
Week 20, Day 6
SO THERE'S A LITTLE BIT O' SEISMIC ACTIVITY. BIG DEAL!
WHY DON'T YA JOIN ME IN A FEW UPLIFTIN' HYMNS AN' PUT IT OUTTA YER MINDS?
THEY'RE DEMANDING YOU TAKE ACTION, ARCHBISHOP, TO STEADY THE PLATE TECTONICS...
THEY'RE DEMANDING MORE THAN THAT, LOBO.
I DEFINITELY RECOGNIZED THE WORDS "BLOOD" AND "LIMB FROM LIMB" IN STANDARD MOSTEELIAN BINARY.
GUESS WE FINALLY OUTLIVED OUR WELCOME, HUH?
...GIMME STRENGTH...

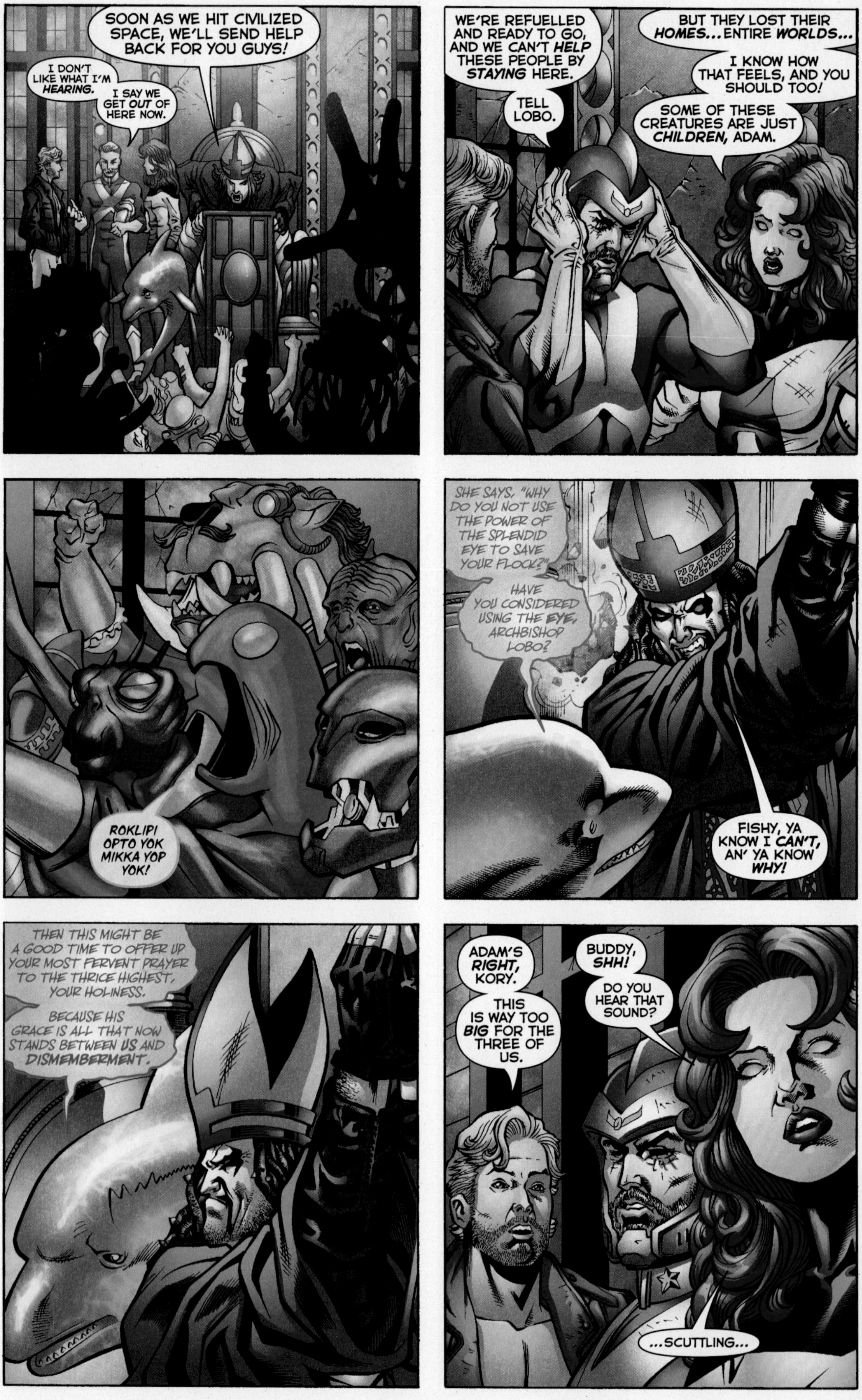
SOON AS WE HIT CIVILIZED SPACE, WE'LL SEND HELP BACK FOR YOU GUYS!
I DON'T LIKE WHAT I'M HEARING.
I SAY WE GET OUT OF HERE NOW.
WE'RE REFUELLED AND READY TO GO, AND WE CAN'T HELP THESE PEOPLE BY STAYING HERE.
TELL LOBO.
BUT THEY LOST THEIR HOMES... ENTIRE WORLDS...
I KNOW HOW THAT FEELS, AND YOU SHOULD TOO!
SOME OF THESE CREATURES ARE JUST CHILDREN, ADAM.
ROKLIPI OPTO YOK MIKKA YOP YOK!
SHE SAYS, "WHY DO YOU NOT USE THE POWER OF THE SPLENDID EYE TO SAVE YOUR FLOCK?"
HAVE YOU CONSIDERED USING THE EYE, ARCHBISHOP LOBO?
FISHY, YA KNOW I CAN'T, AN' YA KNOW WHY!
THEN THIS MIGHT BE A GOOD TIME TO OFFER UP YOUR MOST FERVENT PRAYER TO THE THRICE HIGHEST, YOUR HOLINESS.
BECAUSE HIS GRACE IS ALL THAT NOW STANDS BETWEEN US AND DISMEMBERMENT.
ADAM'S RIGHT, KORY.
THIS IS WAY TOO BIG FOR THE THREE OF US.
BUDDY, SHH!
DO YOU HEAR THAT SOUND?
...SCUTTLING...

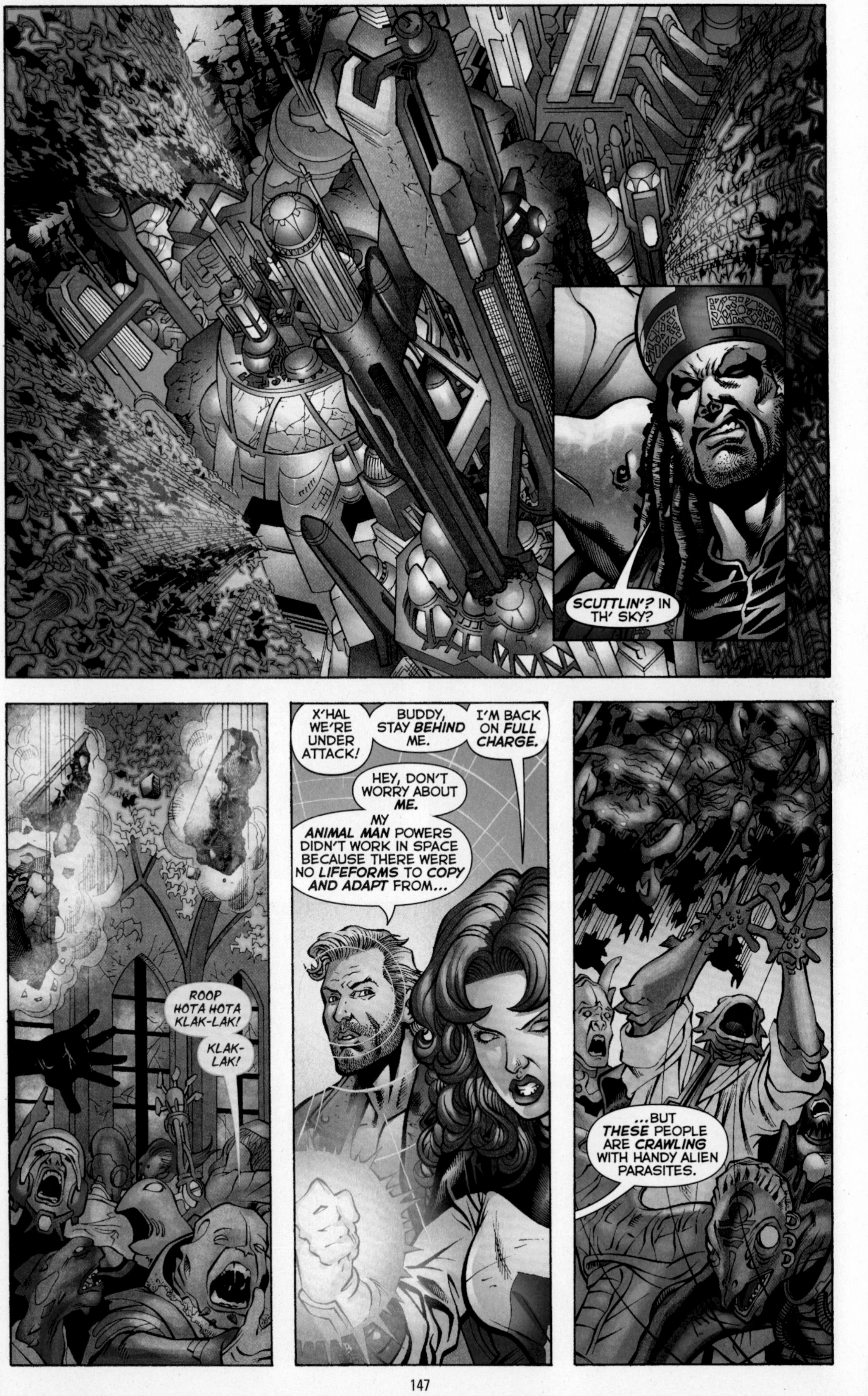
SCUTTLIN'? IN TH' SKY?
ROOP HOTA HOTA KLAK-LAK!
KLAK-LAK!
X'HAL WE'RE UNDER ATTACK!
BUDDY, STAY BEHIND ME.
I'M BACK ON FULL CHARGE.
HEY, DON'T WORRY ABOUT ME.
MY ANIMAL MAN POWERS DIDN'T WORK IN SPACE BECAUSE THERE WERE NO LIFEFORMS TO COPY AND ADAPT FROM...
...BUT THESE PEOPLE ARE CRAWLING WITH HANDY ALIEN PARASITES.

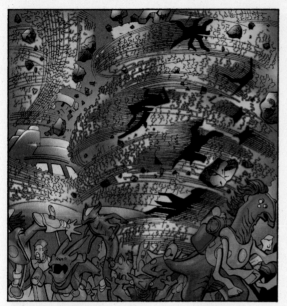

VRSSHT

...Unnh...

WEIRD.

WHAT ARE WE *UP* AGAINST, LOBO?

THE MIRACULOUS POWER O' *PRAYER*, MY SON, IN THE FORM OF INTERSTELLAR CARRION THAT *FEED* OFF DEAD AN' DYIN' PLANETS.

THEY'LL KILL AND EAT JUST ABOUT *ANYTHIN.'*

NOW WOULD BE A GOOD TIME TO STRUT YER SUPER-STUFF, GUYS!

THAT FISH GOD SURE MOVES IN MYSTERIOUS WAYS.

YEAH?

ME TOO!

SPR-OING

⟩Karrff⟨

FIREBALLS?

148

Phitt
Phitt-phitt
Phitt-phitt
Phitt
Phitt
Phitt
Phitt-phitt
COOL.
Kaff
RRRAAA

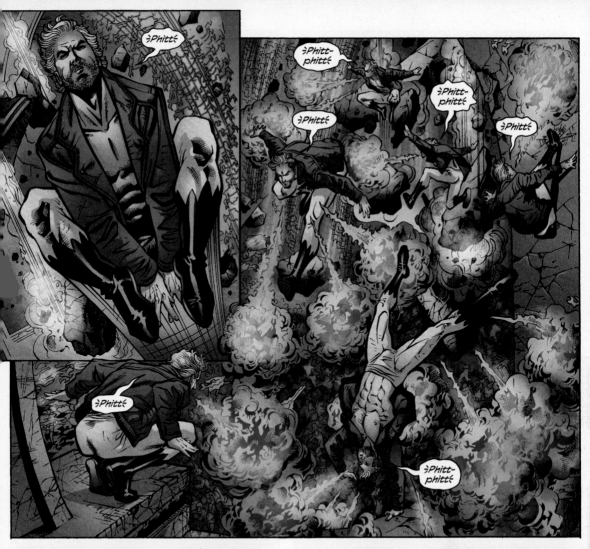

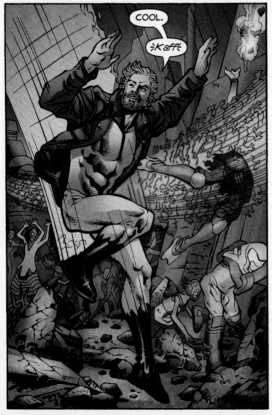

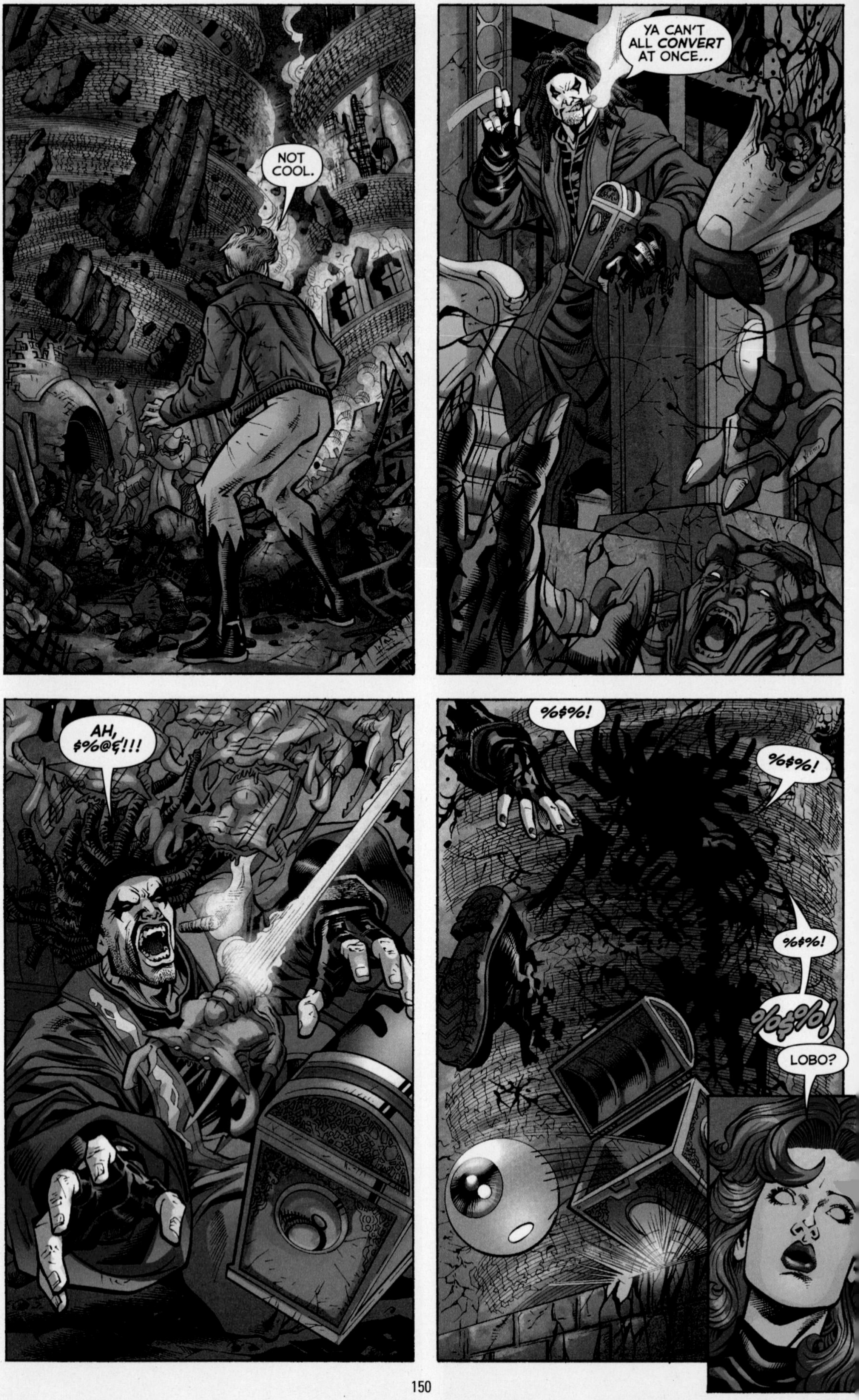
NOT COOL.
YA CAN'T ALL CONVERT AT ONCE...
AH, $%@€!!!
%$%!
%$%!
%$%!
%$%!
LOBO?

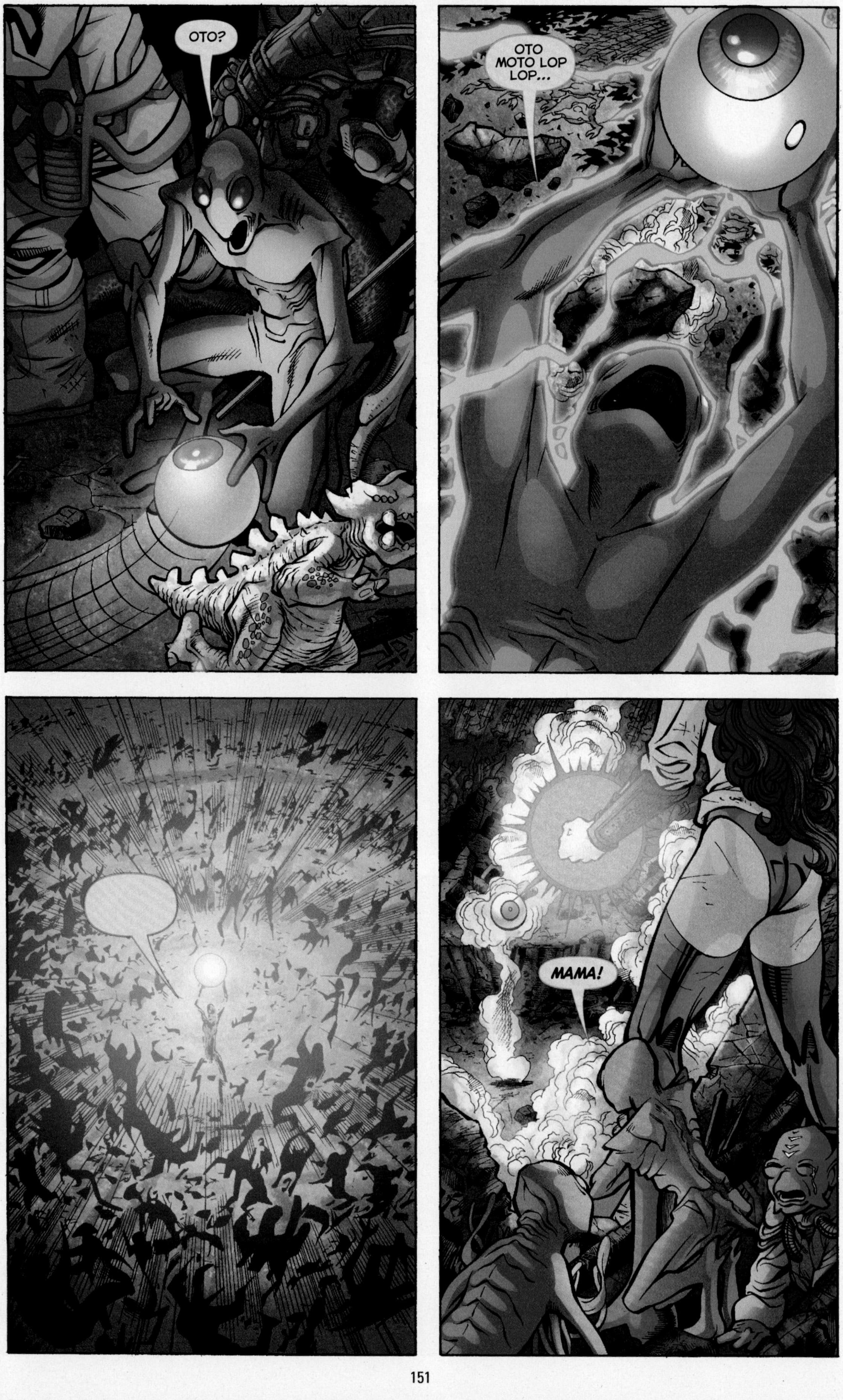
OTO?
OTO MOTO LOP LOP...
MAMA!

‡Gnnahh‡

GET OFF ME!

GET OFF ME!

‡Unnh‡

ADAM?

CHOOM

CHOOM

CHOOM

CHOOM

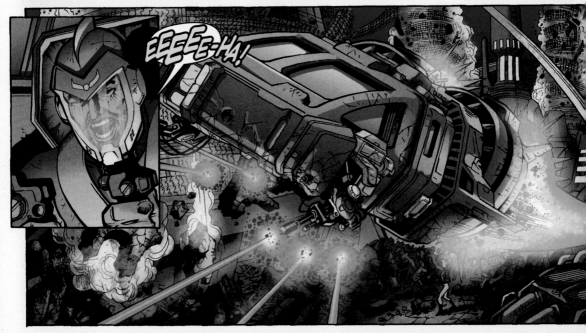

EEEEE-HA!

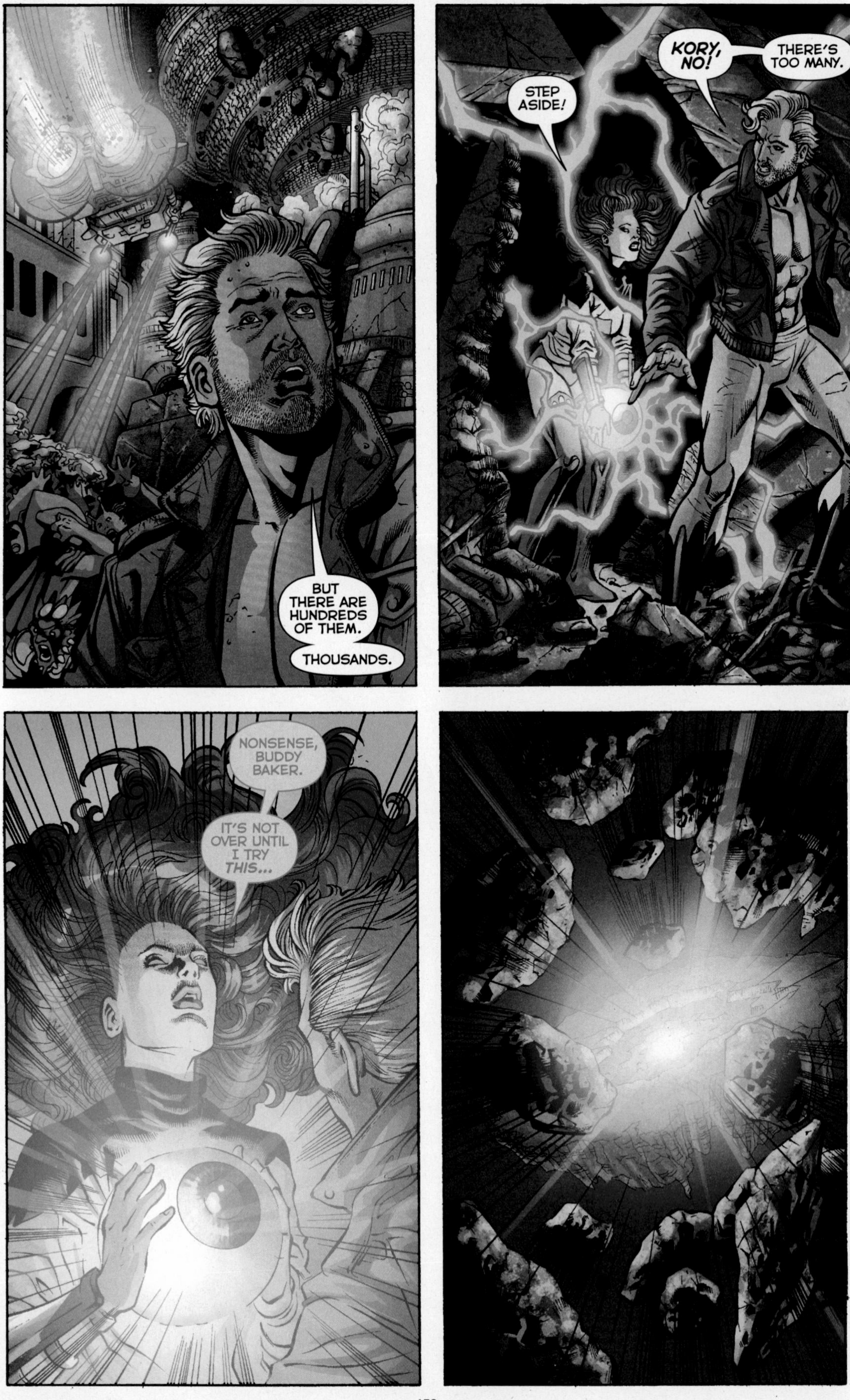
BUT THERE ARE HUNDREDS OF THEM.
THOUSANDS.
KORY, NO!
THERE'S TOO MANY.
STEP ASIDE!
NONSENSE, BUDDY BAKER.
IT'S NOT OVER UNTIL I TRY THIS...

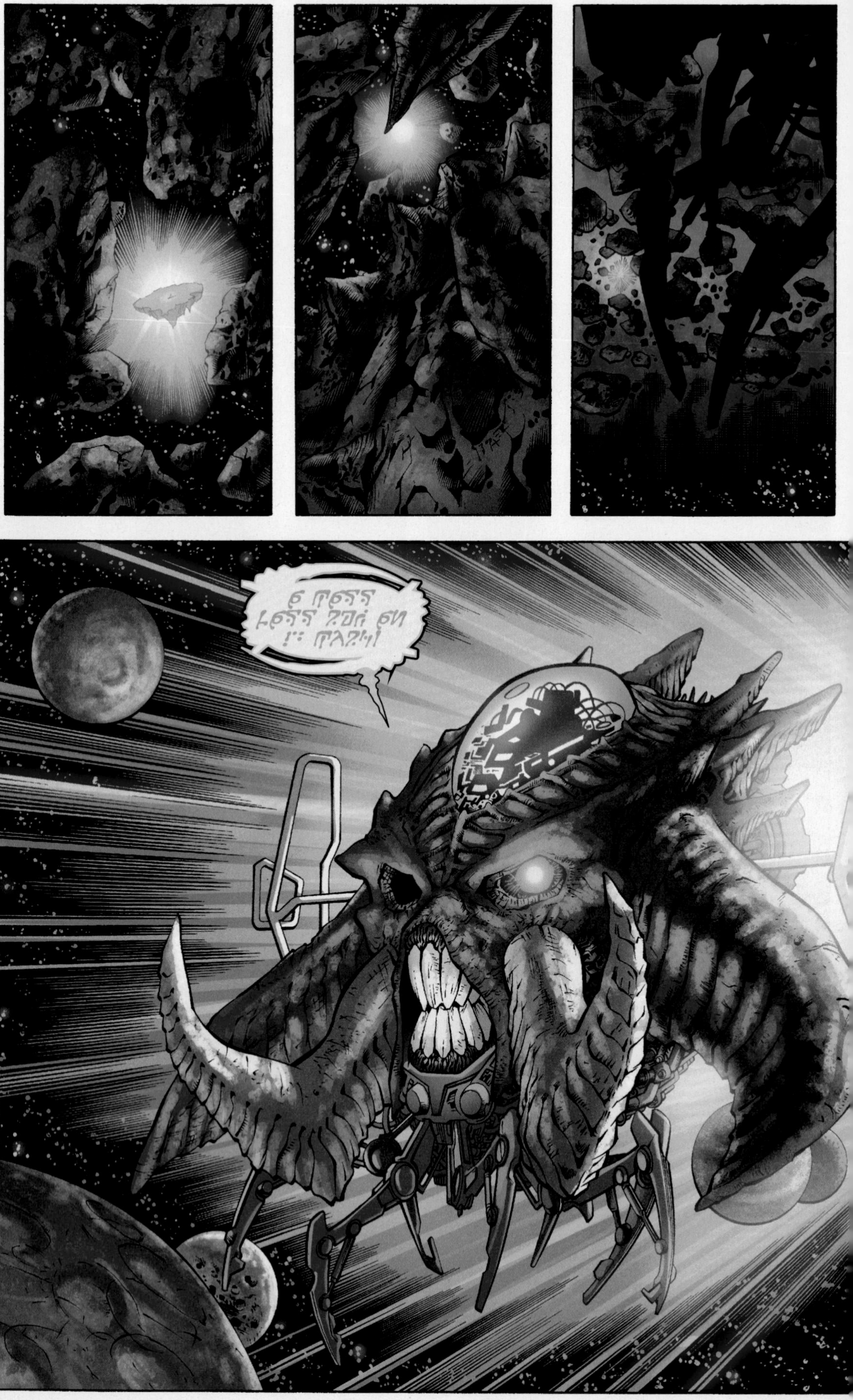

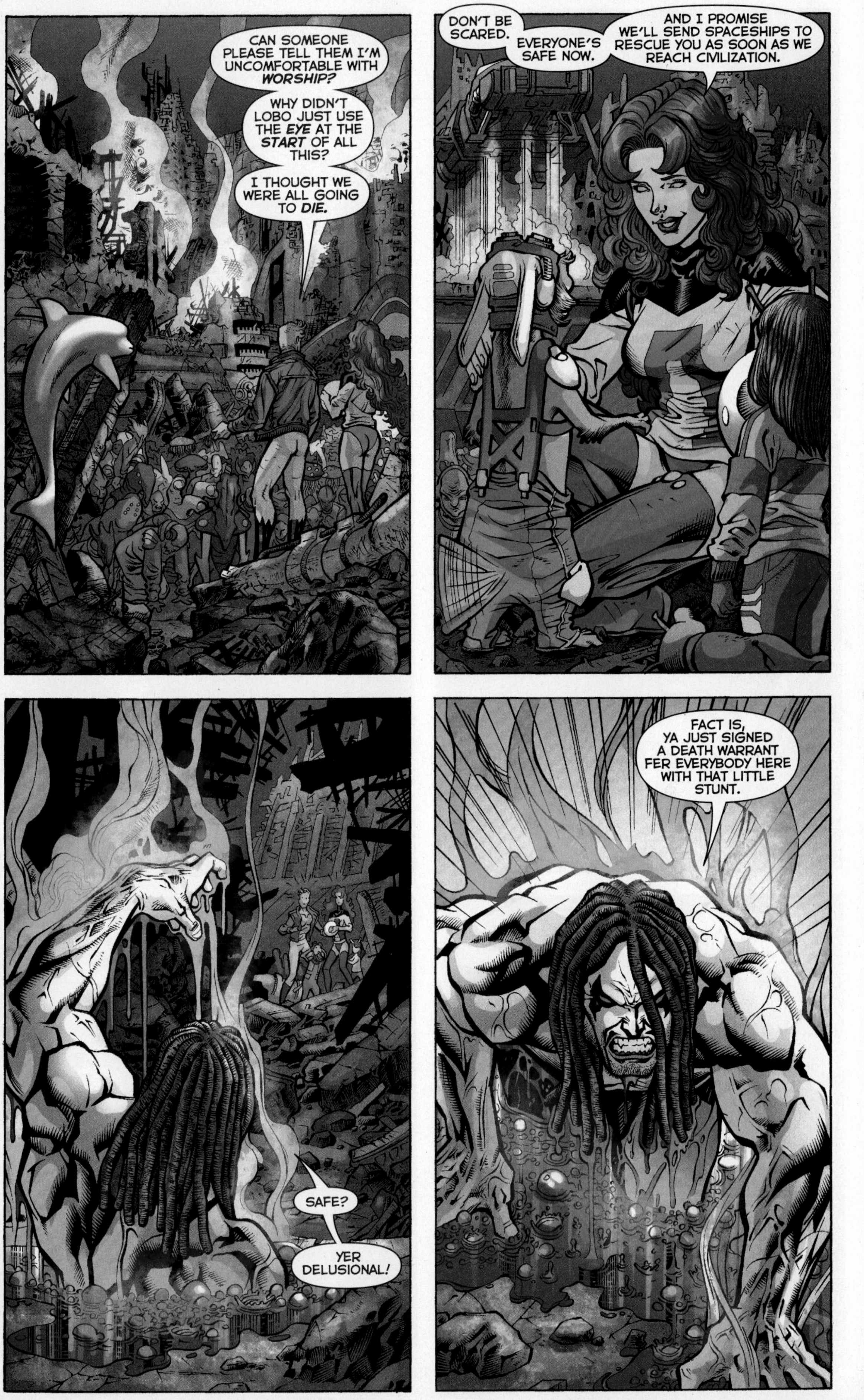
CAN SOMEONE PLEASE TELL THEM I'M UNCOMFORTABLE WITH WORSHIP?
WHY DIDN'T LOBO JUST USE THE EYE AT THE START OF ALL THIS?
I THOUGHT WE WERE ALL GOING TO DIE.
DON'T BE SCARED.
EVERYONE'S SAFE NOW.
AND I PROMISE WE'LL SEND SPACESHIPS TO RESCUE YOU AS SOON AS WE REACH CIVILIZATION.
SAFE?
YER DELUSIONAL!
FACT IS, YA JUST SIGNED A DEATH WARRANT FER EVERYBODY HERE WITH THAT LITTLE STUNT.

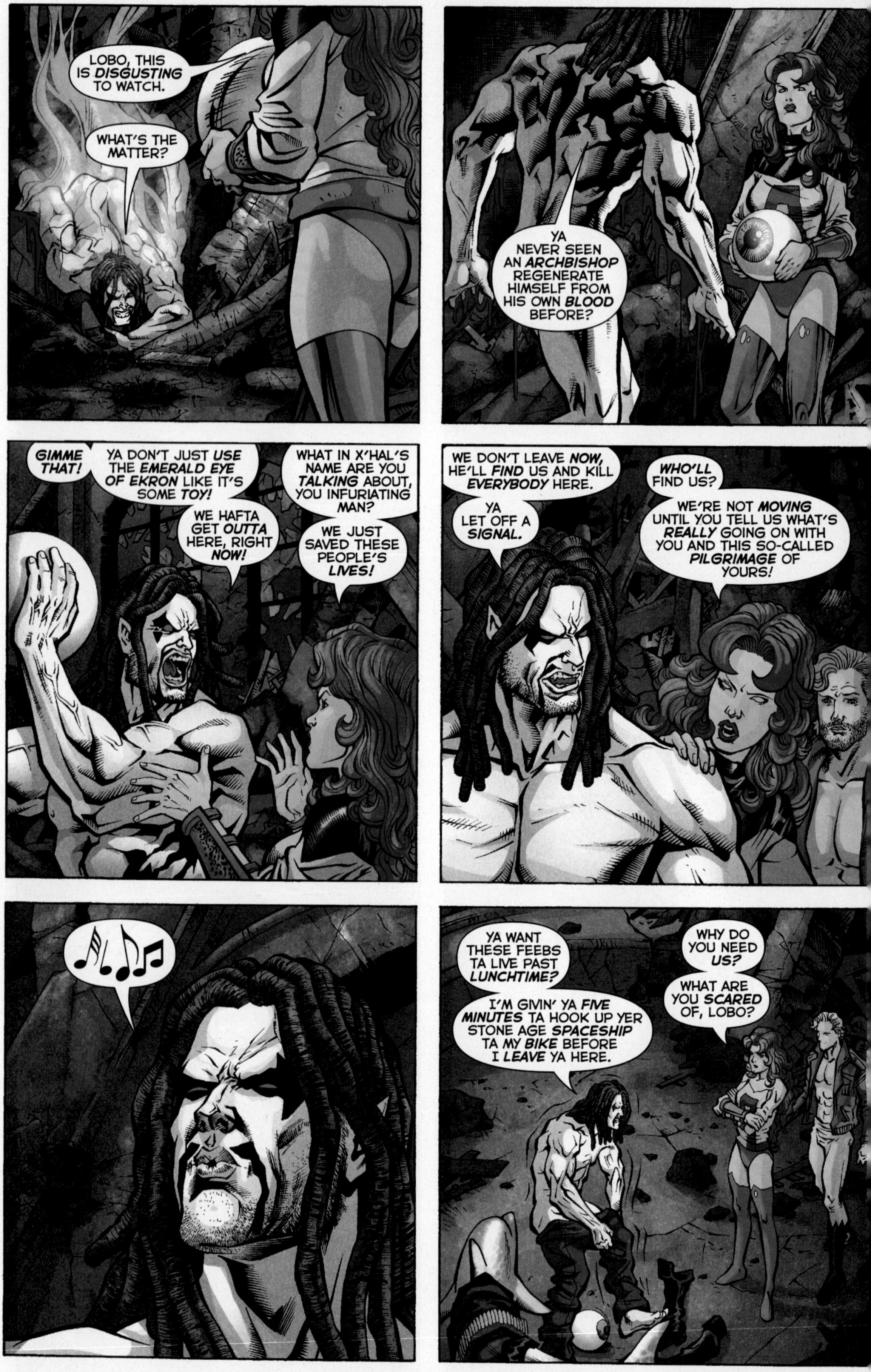
LOBO, THIS IS DISGUSTING TO WATCH.
WHAT'S THE MATTER?
YA NEVER SEEN AN ARCHBISHOP REGENERATE HIMSELF FROM HIS OWN BLOOD BEFORE?
GIMME THAT!
YA DON'T JUST USE THE EMERALD EYE OF EKRON LIKE IT'S SOME TOY!
WE HAFTA GET OUTTA HERE, RIGHT NOW!
WHAT IN X'HAL'S NAME ARE YOU TALKING ABOUT, YOU INFURIATING MAN?
WE JUST SAVED THESE PEOPLE'S LIVES!
WE DON'T LEAVE NOW, HE'LL FIND US AND KILL EVERYBODY HERE.
YA LET OFF A SIGNAL.
WHO'LL FIND US?
WE'RE NOT MOVING UNTIL YOU TELL US WHAT'S REALLY GOING ON WITH YOU AND THIS SO-CALLED PILGRIMAGE OF YOURS!
YA WANT THESE FEEBS TA LIVE PAST LUNCHTIME?
I'M GIVIN' YA FIVE MINUTES TA HOOK UP YER STONE AGE SPACESHIP TA MY BIKE BEFORE I LEAVE YA HERE.
WHY DO YOU NEED US?
WHAT ARE YOU SCARED OF, LOBO?

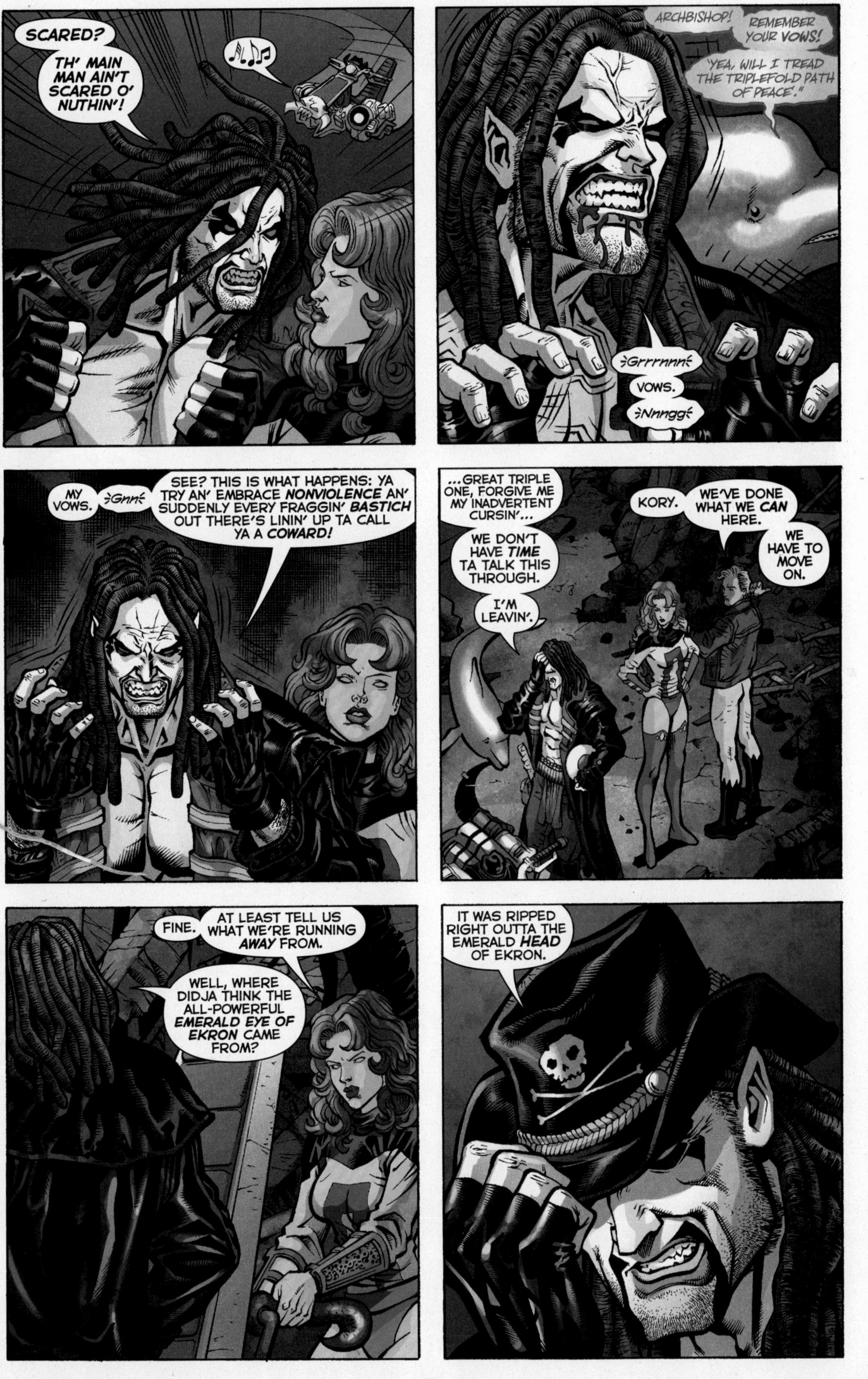
SCARED?
TH' MAIN MAN AIN'T SCARED O' NUTHIN'!
ARCHBISHOP!
REMEMBER YOUR VOWS!
"YEA, WILL I TREAD THE TRIPLEFOLD PATH OF PEACE."
Grrrnnn
VOWS.
Nnngg
MY VOWS.
Gnn
SEE? THIS IS WHAT HAPPENS: YA TRY AN' EMBRACE NONVIOLENCE AN' SUDDENLY EVERY FRAGGIN' BASTICH OUT THERE'S LININ' UP TA CALL YA A COWARD!
...GREAT TRIPLE ONE, FORGIVE ME MY INADVERTENT CURSIN'...
WE DON'T HAVE TIME TA TALK THIS THROUGH.
I'M LEAVIN'.
KORY.
WE'VE DONE WHAT WE CAN HERE.
WE HAVE TO MOVE ON.
FINE.
AT LEAST TELL US WHAT WE'RE RUNNING AWAY FROM.
WELL, WHERE DIDJA THINK THE ALL-POWERFUL EMERALD EYE OF EKRON CAME FROM?
IT WAS RIPPED RIGHT OUTTA THE EMERALD HEAD OF EKRON.

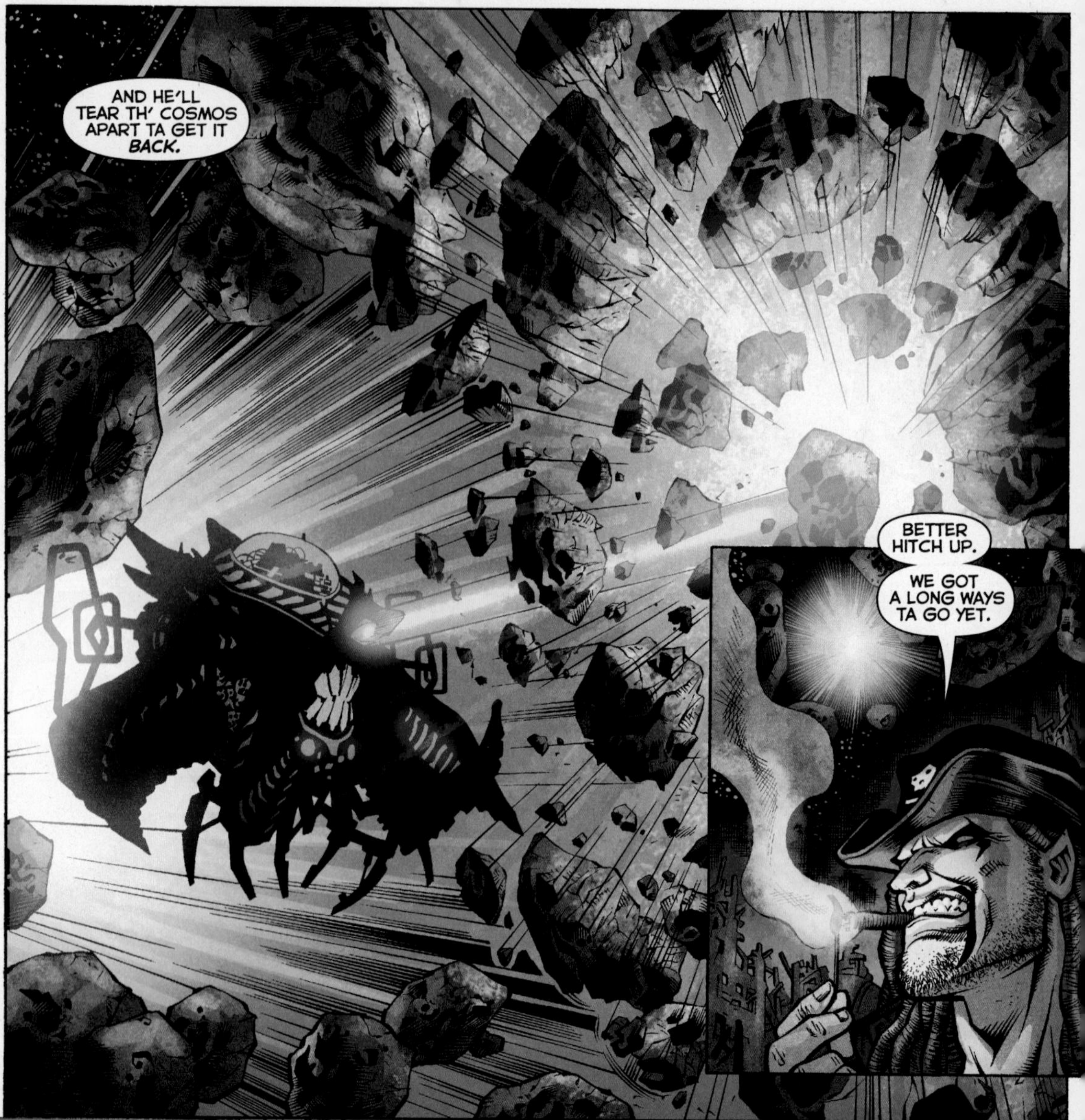
AND HE'LL TEAR TH' COSMOS APART TA GET IT *BACK*.
BETTER HITCH UP.
WE GOT A LONG WAYS TA GO YET.

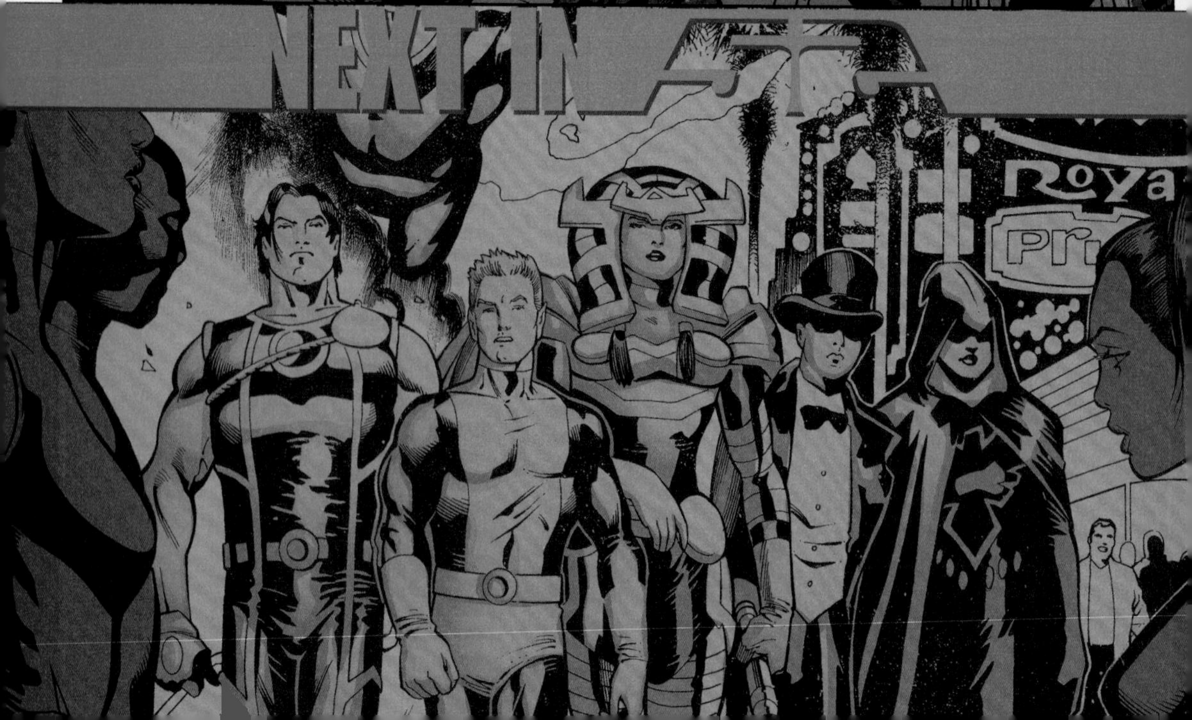
NEXT IN

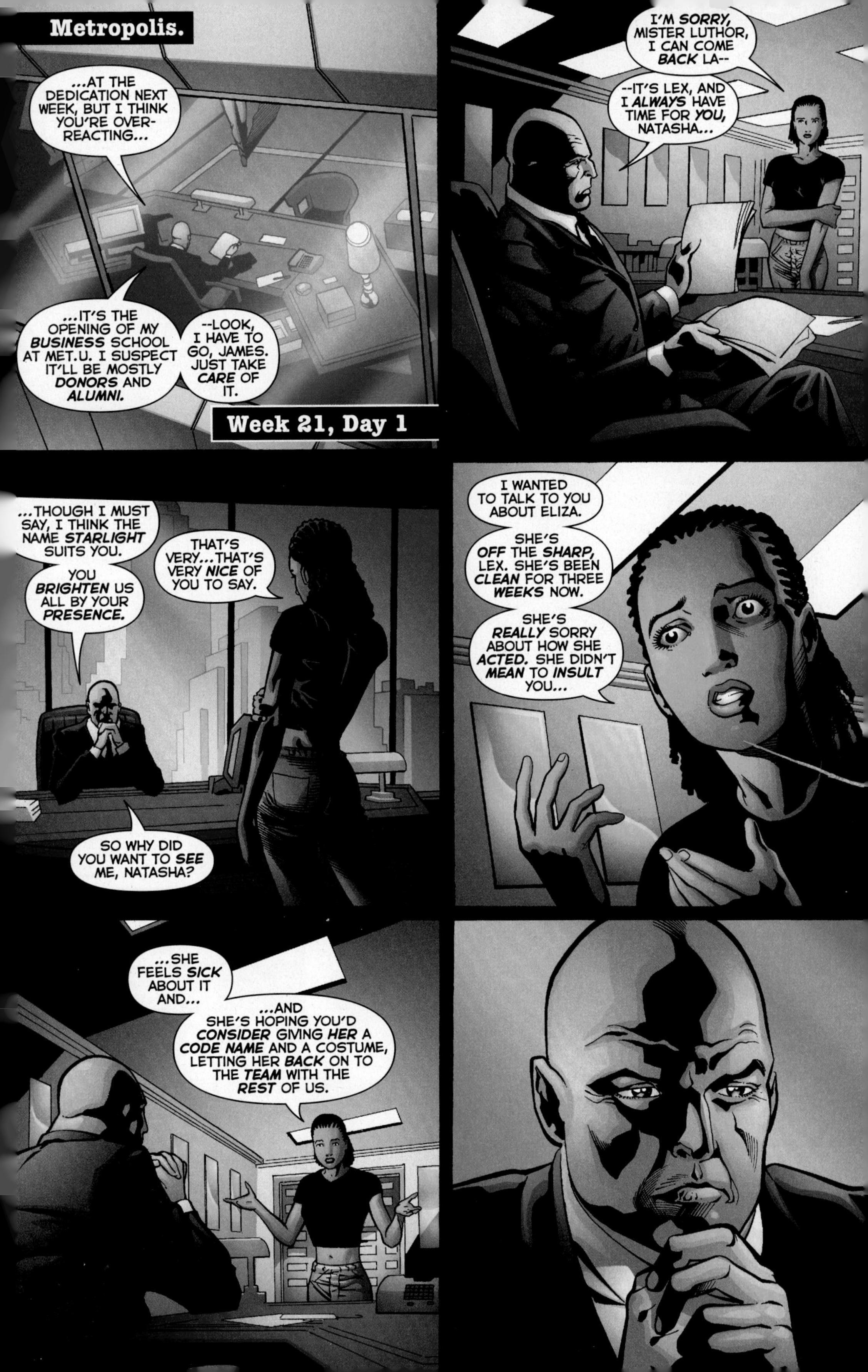
Metropolis.
...AT THE DEDICATION NEXT WEEK, BUT I THINK YOU'RE OVER-REACTING...
...IT'S THE OPENING OF MY BUSINESS SCHOOL AT MET.U. I SUSPECT IT'LL BE MOSTLY DONORS AND ALUMNI.
--LOOK, I HAVE TO GO, JAMES. JUST TAKE CARE OF IT.
Week 21, Day 1
I'M SORRY, MISTER LUTHOR, I CAN COME BACK LA--
--IT'S LEX, AND I ALWAYS HAVE TIME FOR YOU, NATASHA...
...THOUGH I MUST SAY, I THINK THE NAME STARLIGHT SUITS YOU.
YOU BRIGHTEN US ALL BY YOUR PRESENCE.
THAT'S VERY...THAT'S VERY NICE OF YOU TO SAY.
SO WHY DID YOU WANT TO SEE ME, NATASHA?
I WANTED TO TALK TO YOU ABOUT ELIZA.
SHE'S OFF THE SHARP, LEX. SHE'S BEEN CLEAN FOR THREE WEEKS NOW.
SHE'S REALLY SORRY ABOUT HOW SHE ACTED. SHE DIDN'T MEAN TO INSULT YOU...
...SHE FEELS SICK ABOUT IT AND...
...AND SHE'S HOPING YOU'D CONSIDER GIVING HER A CODE NAME AND A COSTUME, LETTING HER BACK ON TO THE TEAM WITH THE REST OF US.

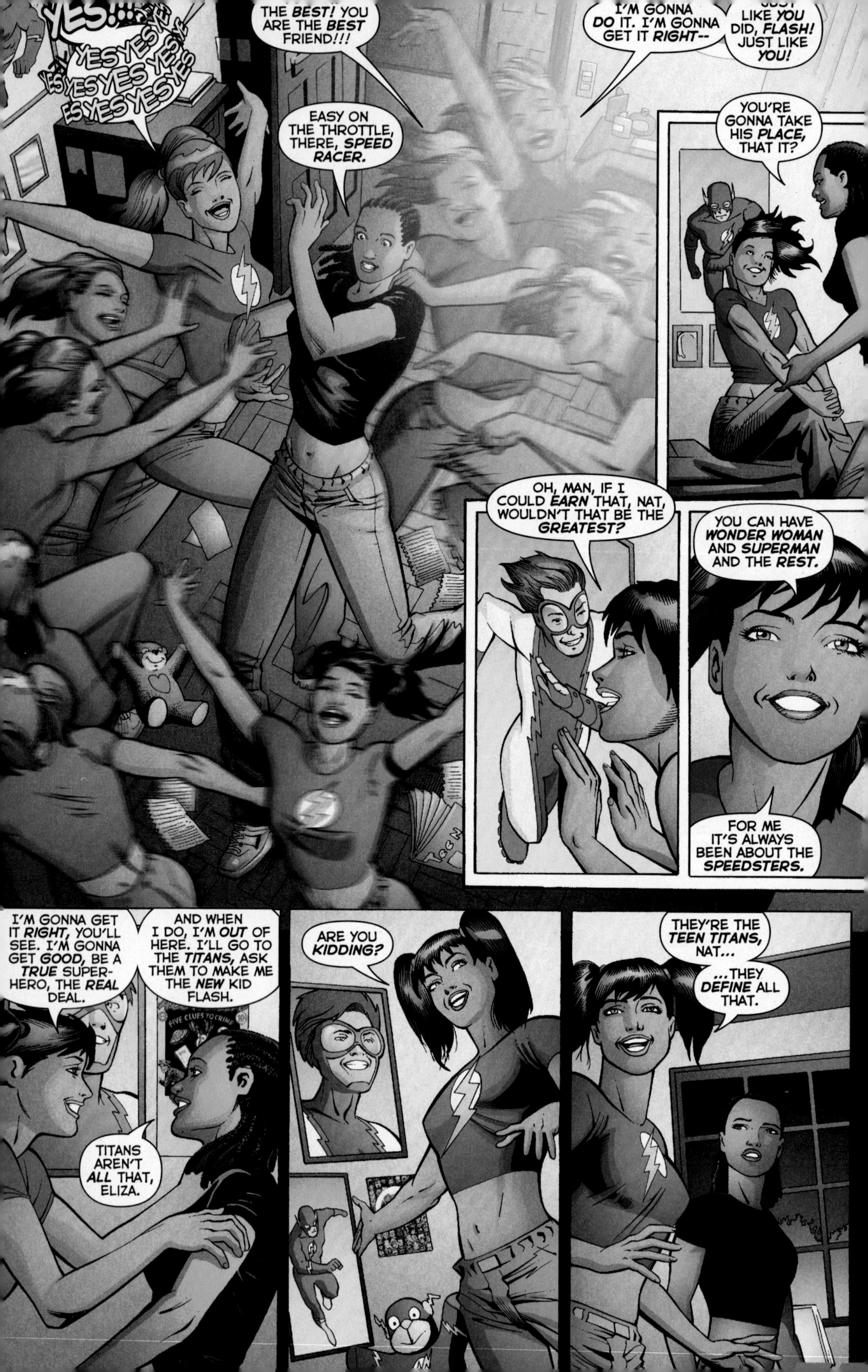
YES!!!
YESYESYES YESYES YESYES YESYESYES
THE *BEST!* YOU ARE THE *BEST* FRIEND!!!
EASY ON THE THROTTLE, THERE, *SPEED RACER.*
I'M GONNA *DO* IT. I'M GONNA GET IT *RIGHT*--
LIKE *YOU* DID, *FLASH!* JUST LIKE *YOU!*
YOU'RE GONNA TAKE HIS *PLACE,* THAT IT?
OH, MAN, IF I COULD *EARN* THAT, NAT, WOULDN'T THAT BE THE *GREATEST?*
YOU CAN HAVE *WONDER WOMAN* AND *SUPERMAN* AND THE *REST.*
FOR ME IT'S ALWAYS BEEN ABOUT THE *SPEEDSTERS.*
I'M GONNA GET IT *RIGHT,* YOU'LL SEE. I'M GONNA GET *GOOD,* BE A *TRUE* SUPER-HERO, THE *REAL* DEAL.
AND WHEN I DO, I'M *OUT* OF HERE. I'LL GO TO THE *TITANS,* ASK THEM TO MAKE ME THE *NEW* KID FLASH.
TITANS AREN'T *ALL* THAT, ELIZA.
ARE YOU *KIDDING?*
THEY'RE THE *TEEN TITANS,* NAT...
...THEY *DEFINE* ALL THAT.

WRITTEN BY GEOFF JOHNS, GRANT MORRISON, GREG RUCKA, MARK WAID

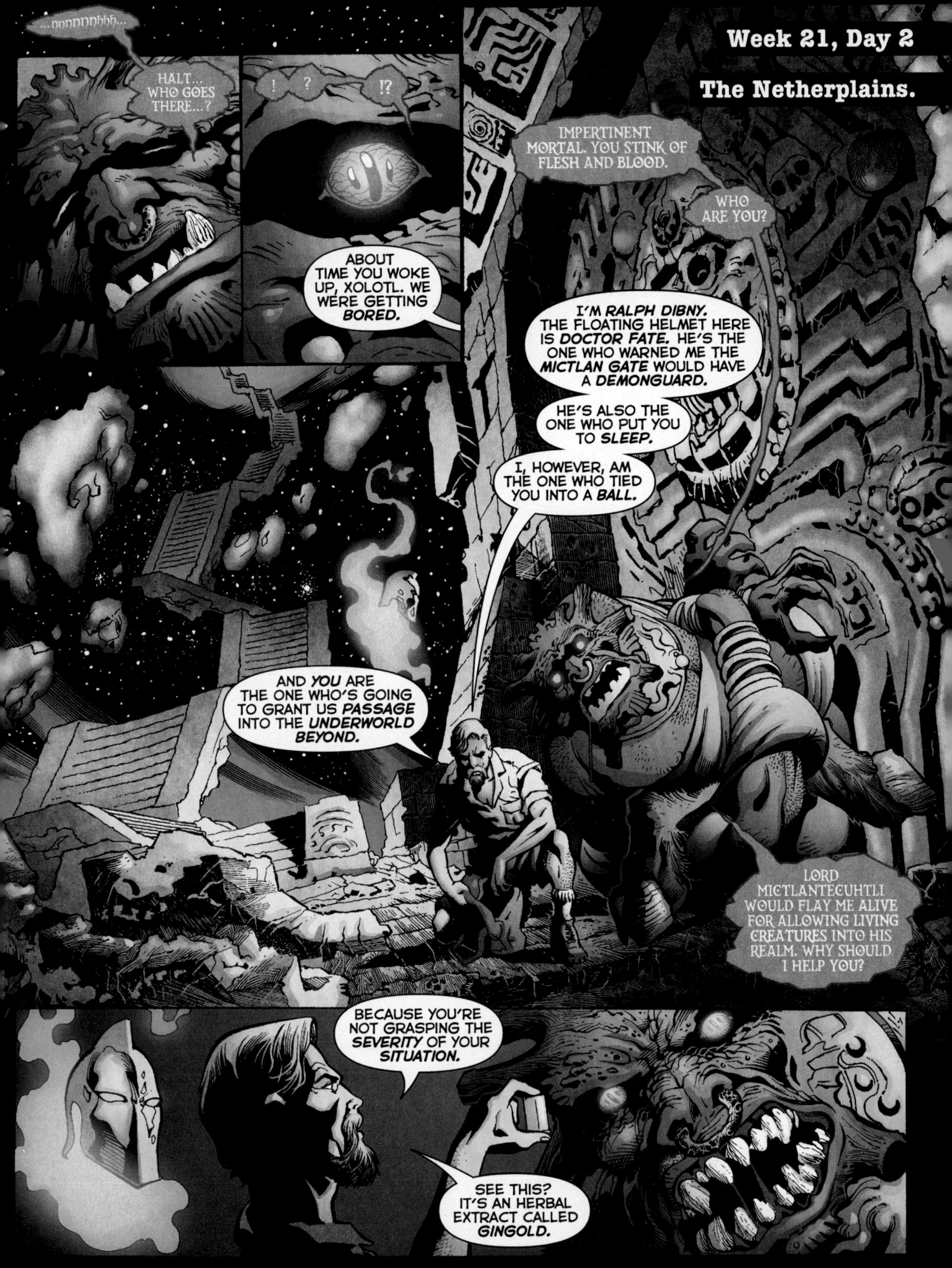
...nnnnnhhh...
HALT... WHO GOES THERE...?
! ? !?
ABOUT TIME YOU WOKE UP, XOLOTL. WE WERE GETTING BORED.
Week 21, Day 2
The Netherplains.
IMPERTINENT MORTAL. YOU STINK OF FLESH AND BLOOD.
WHO ARE YOU?
I'M RALPH DIBNY. THE FLOATING HELMET HERE IS DOCTOR FATE. HE'S THE ONE WHO WARNED ME THE MICTLAN GATE WOULD HAVE A DEMONGUARD.
HE'S ALSO THE ONE WHO PUT YOU TO SLEEP.
I, HOWEVER, AM THE ONE WHO TIED YOU INTO A BALL.
AND YOU ARE THE ONE WHO'S GOING TO GRANT US PASSAGE INTO THE UNDERWORLD BEYOND.
LORD MICTLANTECUHTLI WOULD FLAY ME ALIVE FOR ALLOWING LIVING CREATURES INTO HIS REALM. WHY SHOULD I HELP YOU?
BECAUSE YOU'RE NOT GRASPING THE SEVERITY OF YOUR SITUATION.
SEE THIS? IT'S AN HERBAL EXTRACT CALLED GINGOLD.

ART BREAKDOWNS BY KEITH GIFFEN • PENCILS BY JOE BENNETT • INKS BY JACK JADSON

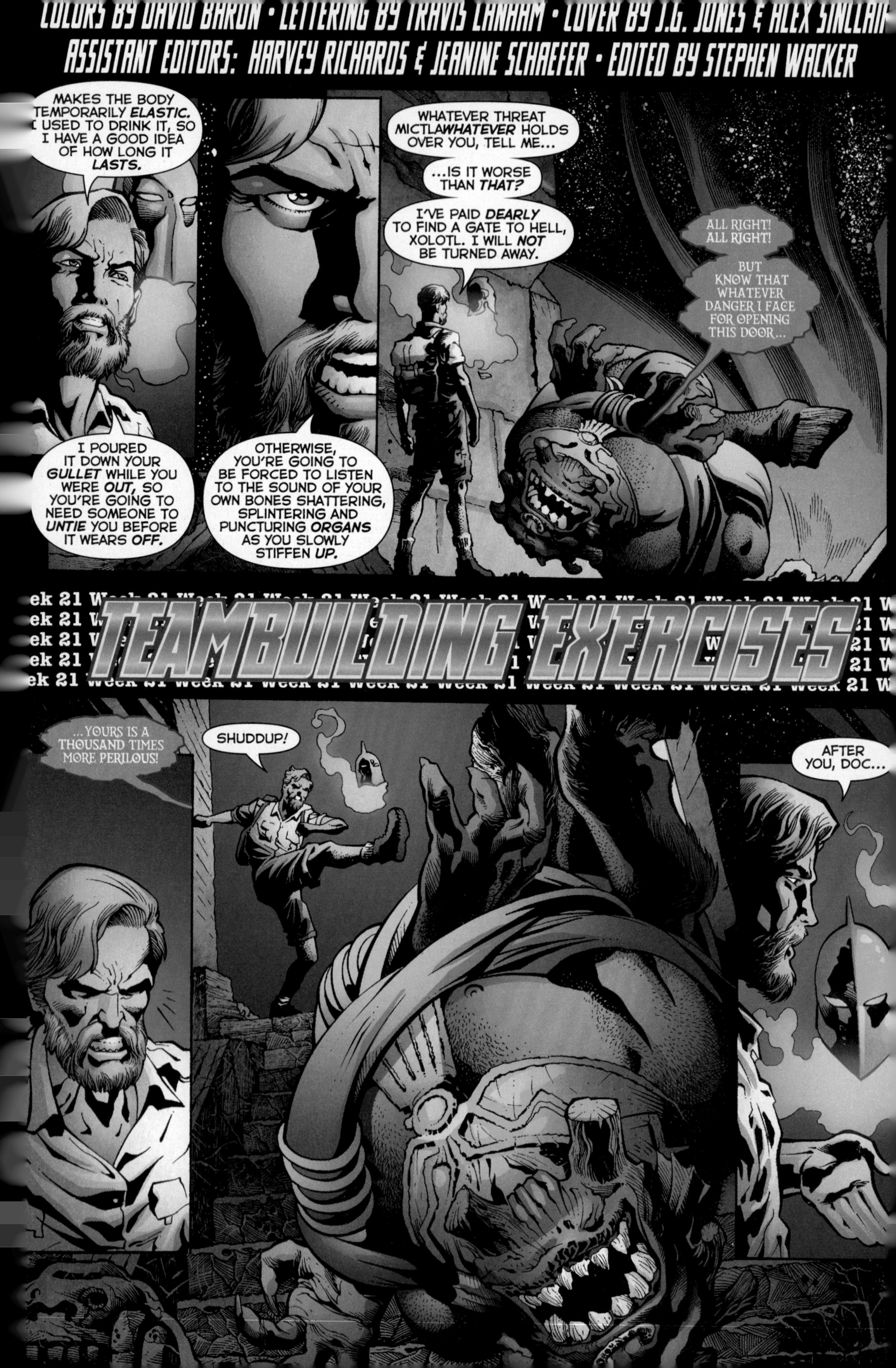
COLORS BY DAVID BARON • LETTERING BY TRAVIS LANHAM • COVER BY J.G. JONES & ALEX SINCLAIR
ASSISTANT EDITORS: HARVEY RICHARDS & JEANINE SCHAEFER • EDITED BY STEPHEN WACKER
MAKES THE BODY TEMPORARILY ELASTIC. I USED TO DRINK IT, SO I HAVE A GOOD IDEA OF HOW LONG IT LASTS.
I POURED IT DOWN YOUR GULLET WHILE YOU WERE OUT, SO YOU'RE GOING TO NEED SOMEONE TO UNTIE YOU BEFORE IT WEARS OFF.
OTHERWISE, YOU'RE GOING TO BE FORCED TO LISTEN TO THE SOUND OF YOUR OWN BONES SHATTERING, SPLINTERING AND PUNCTURING ORGANS AS YOU SLOWLY STIFFEN UP.
WHATEVER THREAT MICTLAWHATEVER HOLDS OVER YOU, TELL ME...
...IS IT WORSE THAN THAT?
I'VE PAID DEARLY TO FIND A GATE TO HELL, XOLOTL. I WILL NOT BE TURNED AWAY.
ALL RIGHT! ALL RIGHT!
BUT KNOW THAT WHATEVER DANGER I FACE FOR OPENING THIS DOOR...
Week 21
TEAMBUILDING EXERCISES
...YOURS IS A THOUSAND TIMES MORE PERILOUS!
SHUDDUP!
AFTER YOU, DOC...

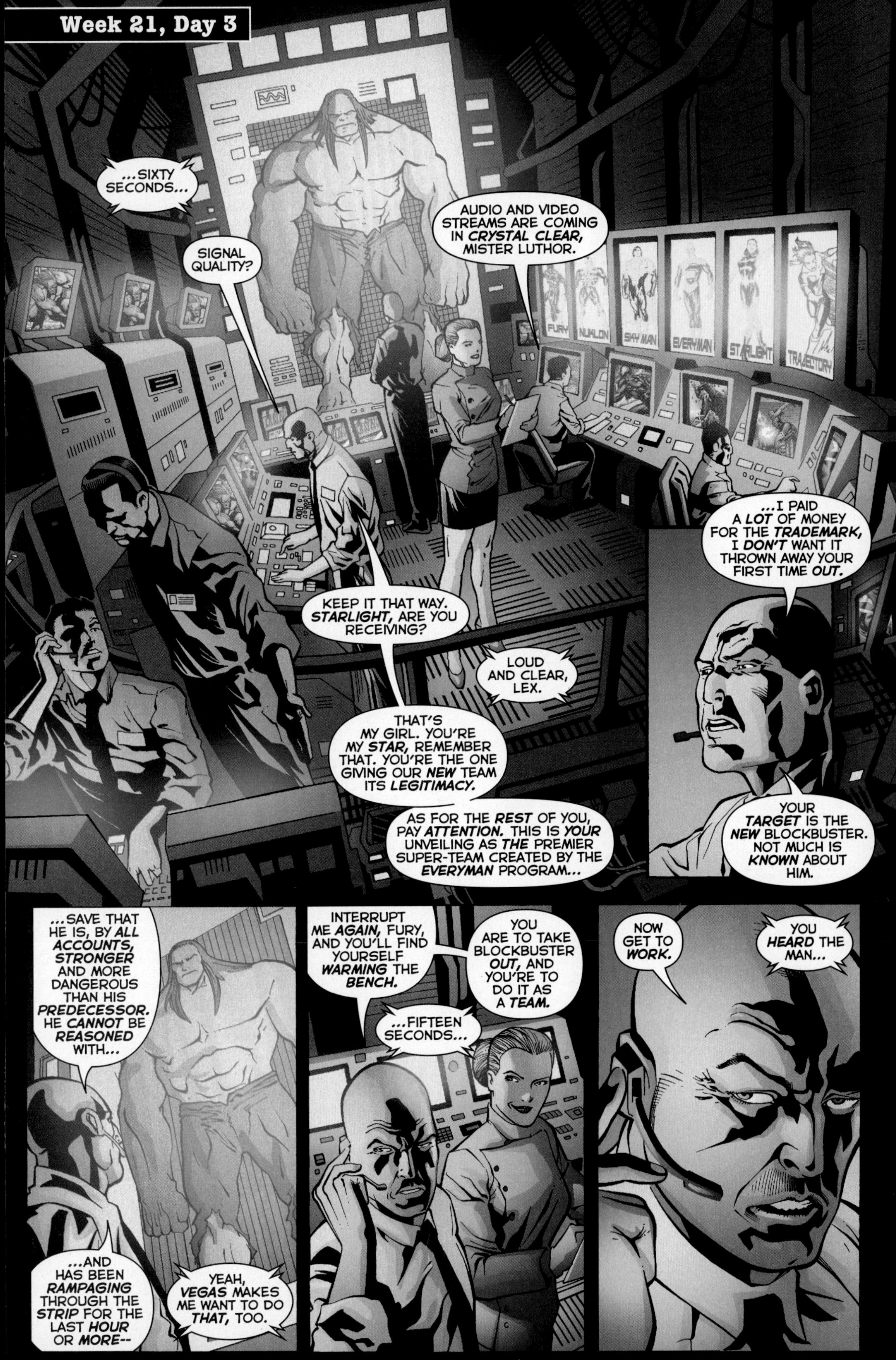
Week 21, Day 3
...SIXTY SECONDS...
SIGNAL QUALITY?
AUDIO AND VIDEO STREAMS ARE COMING IN CRYSTAL CLEAR, MISTER LUTHOR.
FURY
NUKLON
SKY MAN
EVERYMAN
STARLIGHT
TRAJECTORY
KEEP IT THAT WAY. STARLIGHT, ARE YOU RECEIVING?
LOUD AND CLEAR, LEX.
THAT'S MY GIRL. YOU'RE MY STAR, REMEMBER THAT. YOU'RE THE ONE GIVING OUR NEW TEAM ITS LEGITIMACY.
AS FOR THE REST OF YOU, PAY ATTENTION. THIS IS YOUR UNVEILING AS THE PREMIER SUPER-TEAM CREATED BY THE EVERYMAN PROGRAM...
...I PAID A LOT OF MONEY FOR THE TRADEMARK, I DON'T WANT IT THROWN AWAY YOUR FIRST TIME OUT.
YOUR TARGET IS THE NEW BLOCKBUSTER. NOT MUCH IS KNOWN ABOUT HIM.
...SAVE THAT HE IS, BY ALL ACCOUNTS, STRONGER AND MORE DANGEROUS THAN HIS PREDECESSOR. HE CANNOT BE REASONED WITH...
...AND HAS BEEN RAMPAGING THROUGH THE STRIP FOR THE LAST HOUR OR MORE--
YEAH, VEGAS MAKES ME WANT TO DO THAT, TOO.
INTERRUPT ME AGAIN, FURY, AND YOU'LL FIND YOURSELF WARMING THE BENCH.
YOU ARE TO TAKE BLOCKBUSTER OUT, AND YOU'RE TO DO IT AS A TEAM.
...FIFTEEN SECONDS...
NOW GET TO WORK.
YOU HEARD THE MAN...

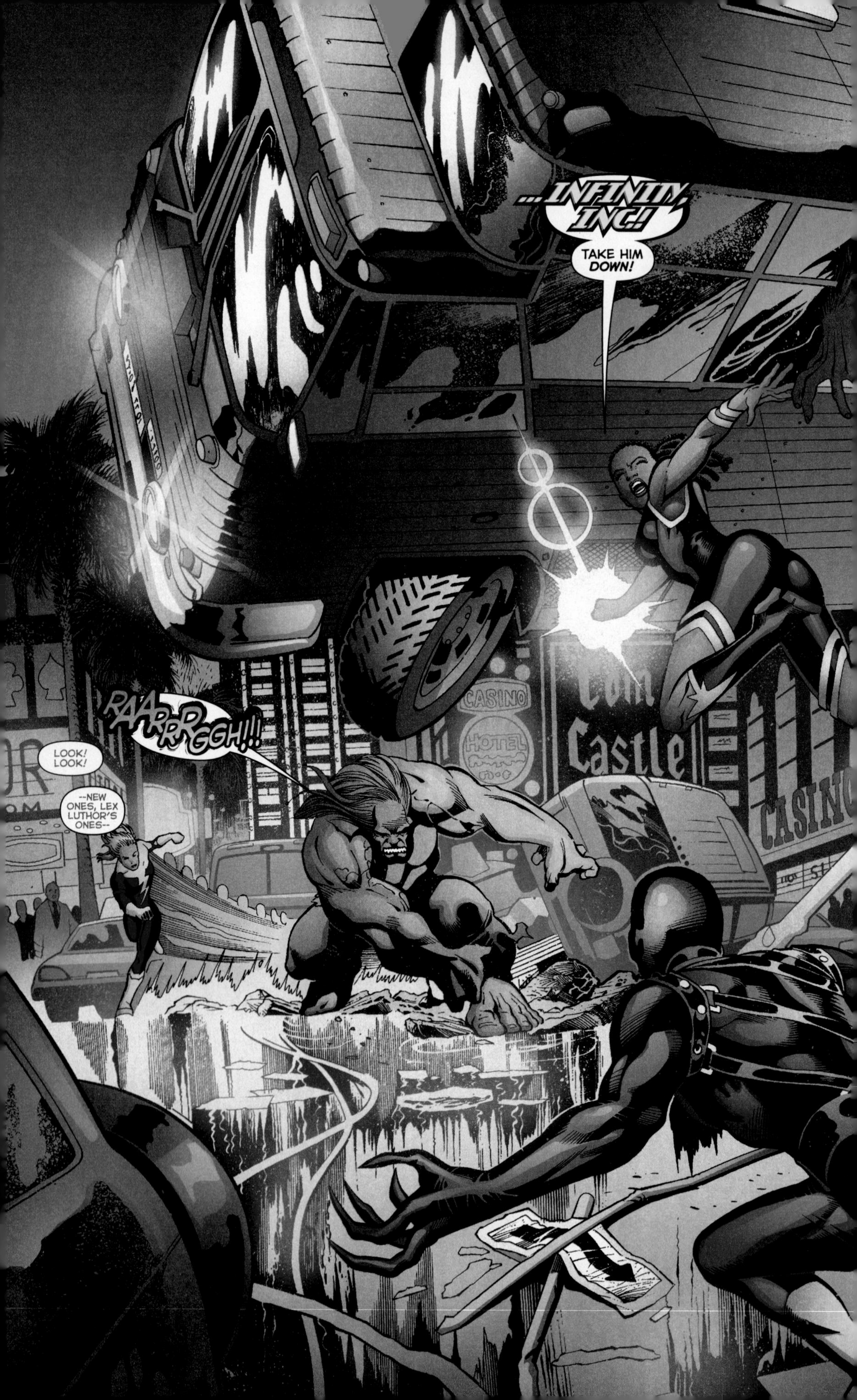
...INFINITY, INC.!
TAKE HIM DOWN!
RAARRRGGH!!!
LOOK! LOOK!
--NEW ONES, LEX LUTHOR'S ONES--
CASINO
HOTEL
Castle
CASINO

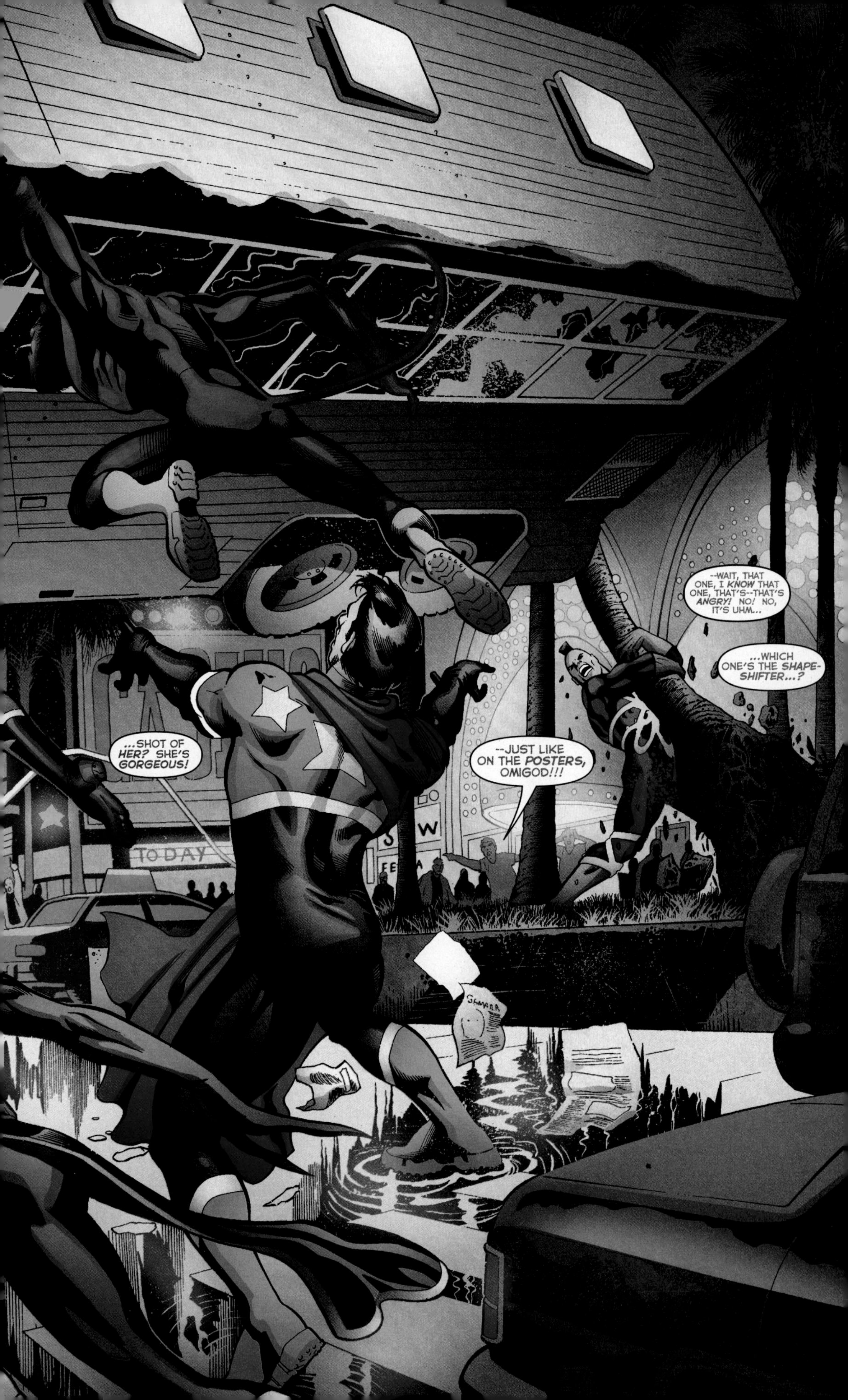

...SHOT OF HER? SHE'S GORGEOUS!
--JUST LIKE ON THE POSTERS, OMIGOD!!!
--WAIT, THAT ONE, I KNOW THAT ONE, THAT'S--THAT'S ANGRY! NO! NO, IT'S UHM...
...WHICH ONE'S THE SHAPE-SHIFTER...?
TODAY

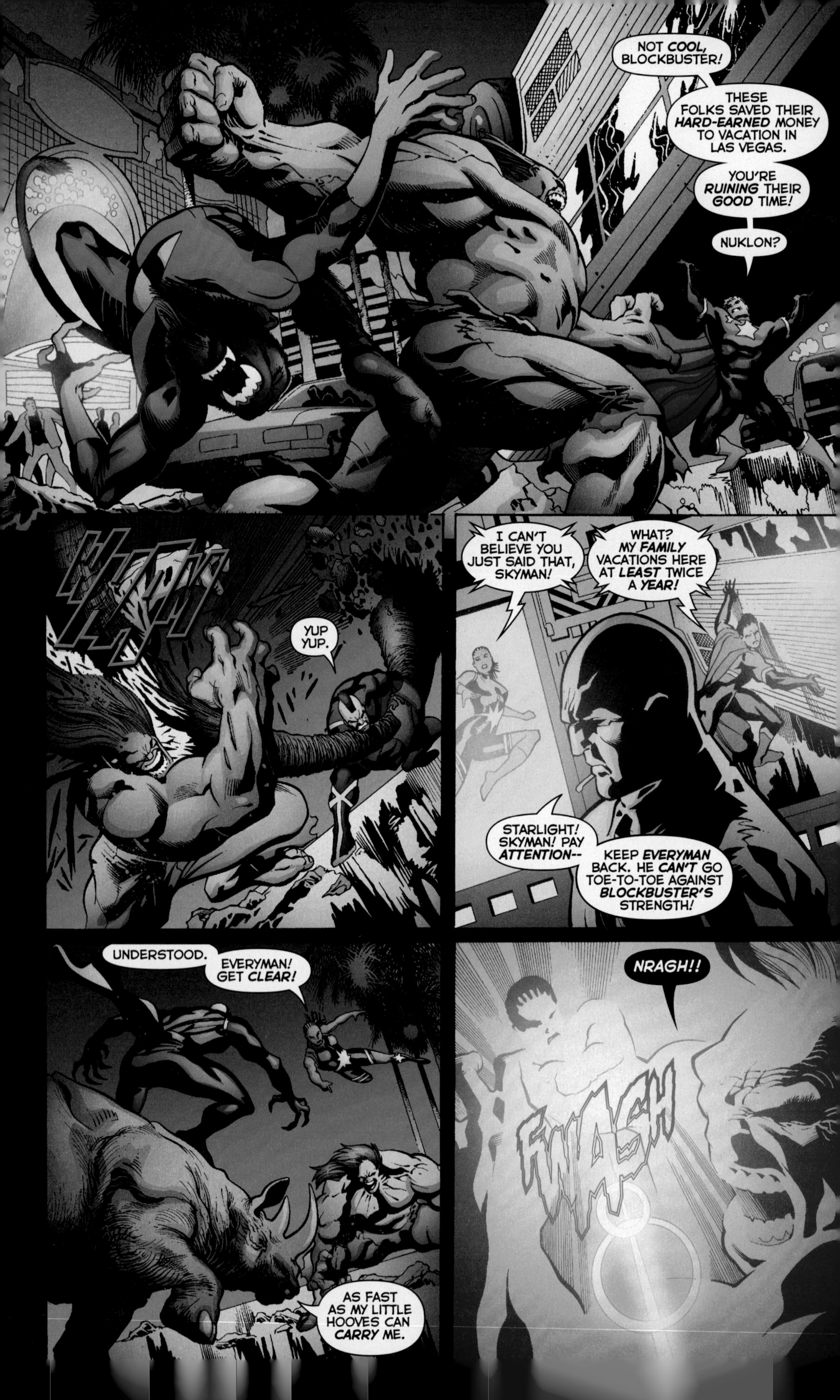
NOT *COOL*, BLOCKBUSTER!
THESE FOLKS SAVED THEIR *HARD-EARNED* MONEY TO VACATION IN LAS VEGAS.
YOU'RE *RUINING* THEIR *GOOD* TIME!
NUKLON?
YUP YUP.
I CAN'T BELIEVE YOU JUST SAID THAT, SKYMAN!
WHAT? *MY FAMILY* VACATIONS HERE AT *LEAST* TWICE A *YEAR!*
STARLIGHT! SKYMAN! PAY *ATTENTION--*
KEEP *EVERYMAN* BACK. HE *CAN'T* GO TOE-TO-TOE AGAINST *BLOCKBUSTER'S* STRENGTH!
UNDERSTOOD.
EVERYMAN! GET *CLEAR!*
AS FAST AS MY LITTLE HOOVES CAN *CARRY* ME.
NRAGH!!
FWASH

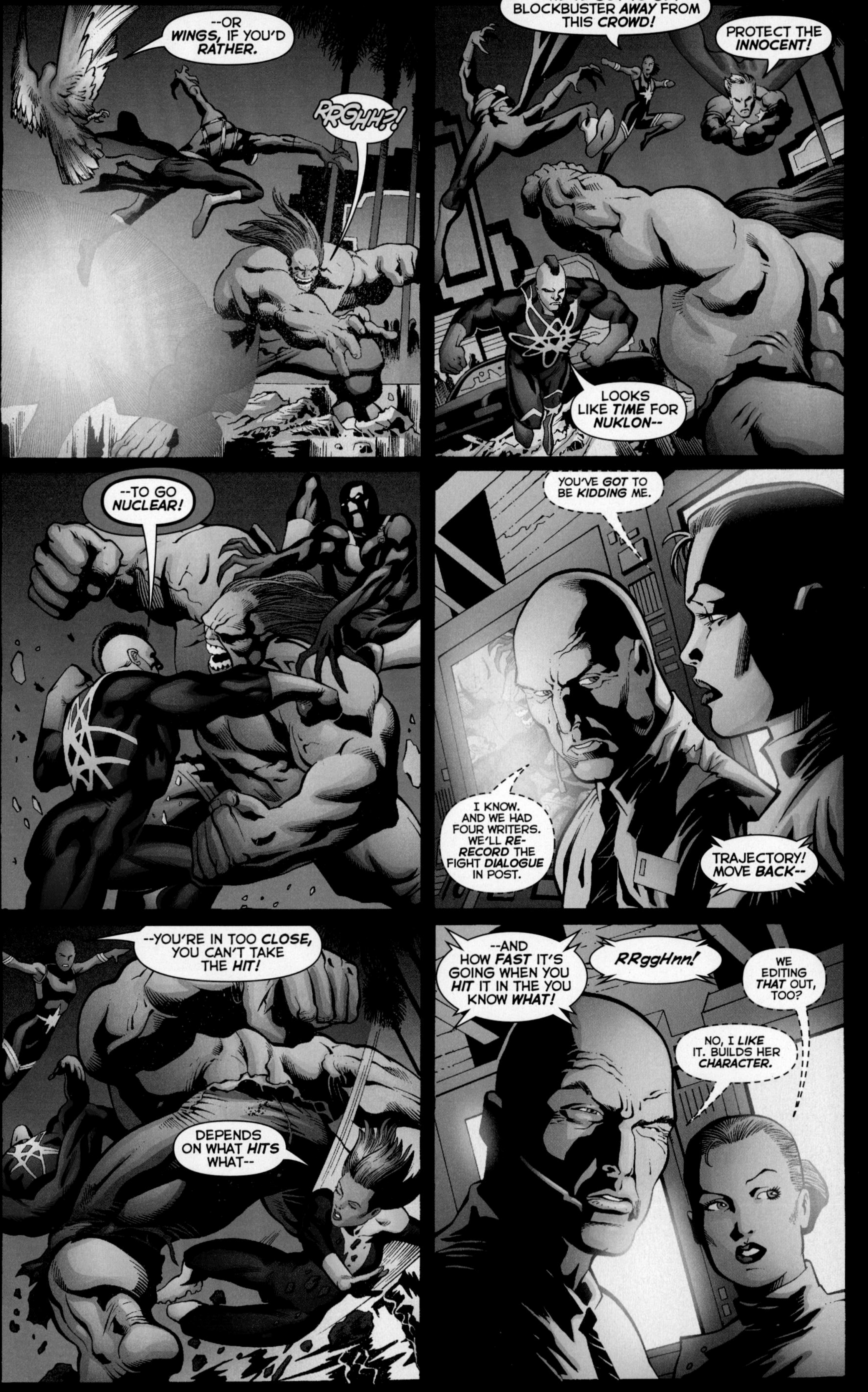
--OR WINGS, IF YOU'D RATHER.
RRGHH?!
--WE'VE GOT TO GET BLOCKBUSTER AWAY FROM THIS CROWD!
PROTECT THE INNOCENT!
LOOKS LIKE TIME FOR NUKLON--
--TO GO NUCLEAR!
YOU'VE GOT TO BE KIDDING ME.
I KNOW. AND WE HAD FOUR WRITERS. WE'LL RE-RECORD THE FIGHT DIALOGUE IN POST.
TRAJECTORY! MOVE BACK--
--YOU'RE IN TOO CLOSE, YOU CAN'T TAKE THE HIT!
DEPENDS ON WHAT HITS WHAT--
--AND HOW FAST IT'S GOING WHEN YOU HIT IT IN THE YOU KNOW WHAT!
RRggHnn!
WE EDITING THAT OUT, TOO?
NO, I LIKE IT. BUILDS HER CHARACTER.

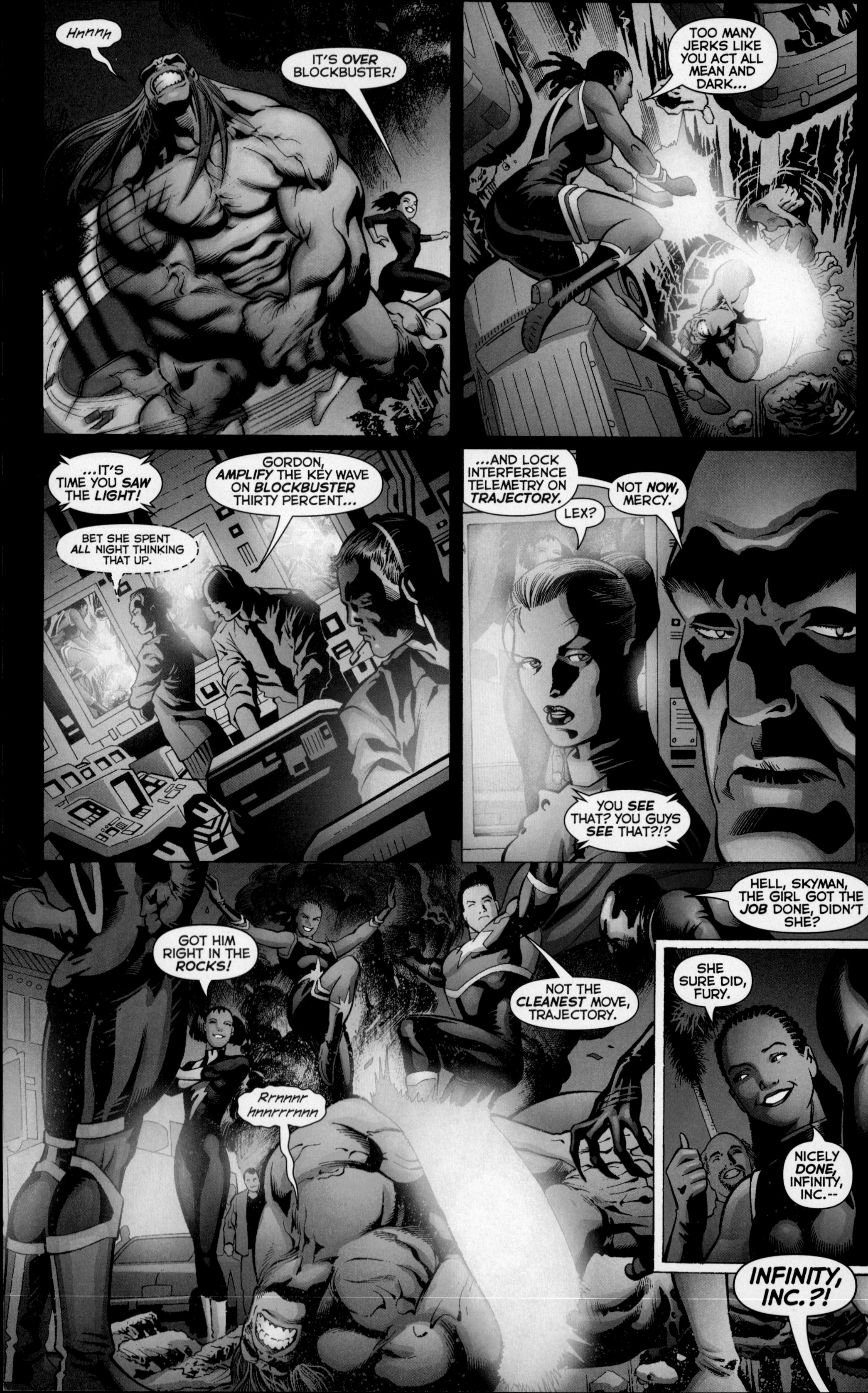

Hnnnh
IT'S OVER BLOCKBUSTER!
TOO MANY JERKS LIKE YOU ACT ALL MEAN AND DARK...
...IT'S TIME YOU SAW THE LIGHT!
GORDON, AMPLIFY THE KEY WAVE ON BLOCKBUSTER THIRTY PERCENT...
BET SHE SPENT ALL NIGHT THINKING THAT UP.
...AND LOCK INTERFERENCE TELEMETRY ON TRAJECTORY.
LEX?
NOT NOW, MERCY.
YOU SEE THAT? YOU GUYS SEE THAT?!?
GOT HIM RIGHT IN THE ROCKS!
NOT THE CLEANEST MOVE, TRAJECTORY.
HELL, SKYMAN, THE GIRL GOT THE JOB DONE, DIDN'T SHE?
Rrnnnr hnnrrrnnn
SHE SURE DID, FURY.
NICELY DONE, INFINITY, INC.--
INFINITY, INC.?!

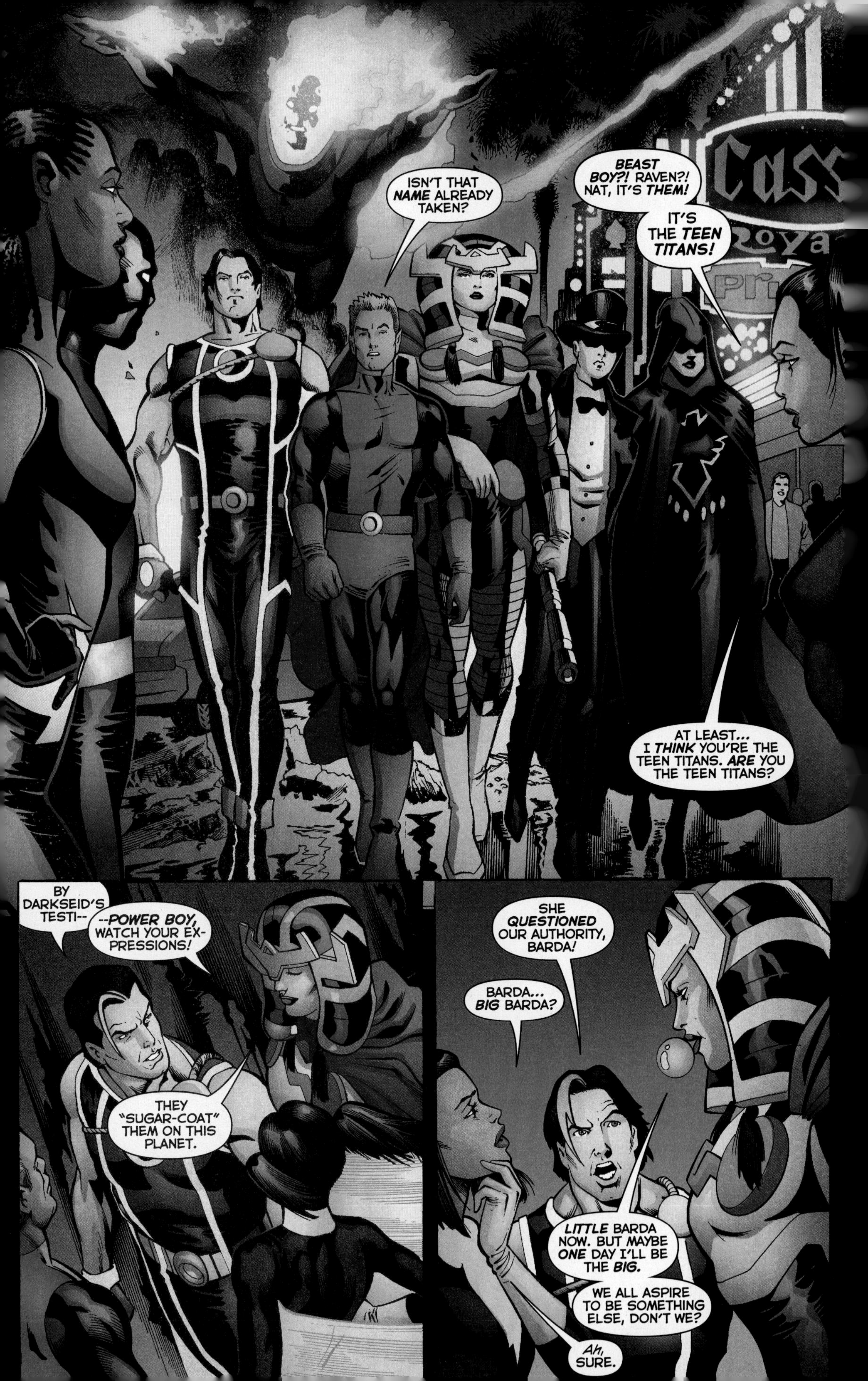
ISN'T THAT NAME ALREADY TAKEN?
BEAST BOY?! RAVEN?! NAT, IT'S THEM!
IT'S THE TEEN TITANS!
AT LEAST... I THINK YOU'RE THE TEEN TITANS. ARE YOU THE TEEN TITANS?
BY DARKSEID'S TESTI--
--POWER BOY, WATCH YOUR EX-PRESSIONS!
THEY "SUGAR-COAT" THEM ON THIS PLANET.
SHE QUESTIONED OUR AUTHORITY, BARDA!
BARDA... BIG BARDA?
LITTLE BARDA NOW. BUT MAYBE ONE DAY I'LL BE THE BIG.
WE ALL ASPIRE TO BE SOMETHING ELSE, DON'T WE?
Ah, SURE.

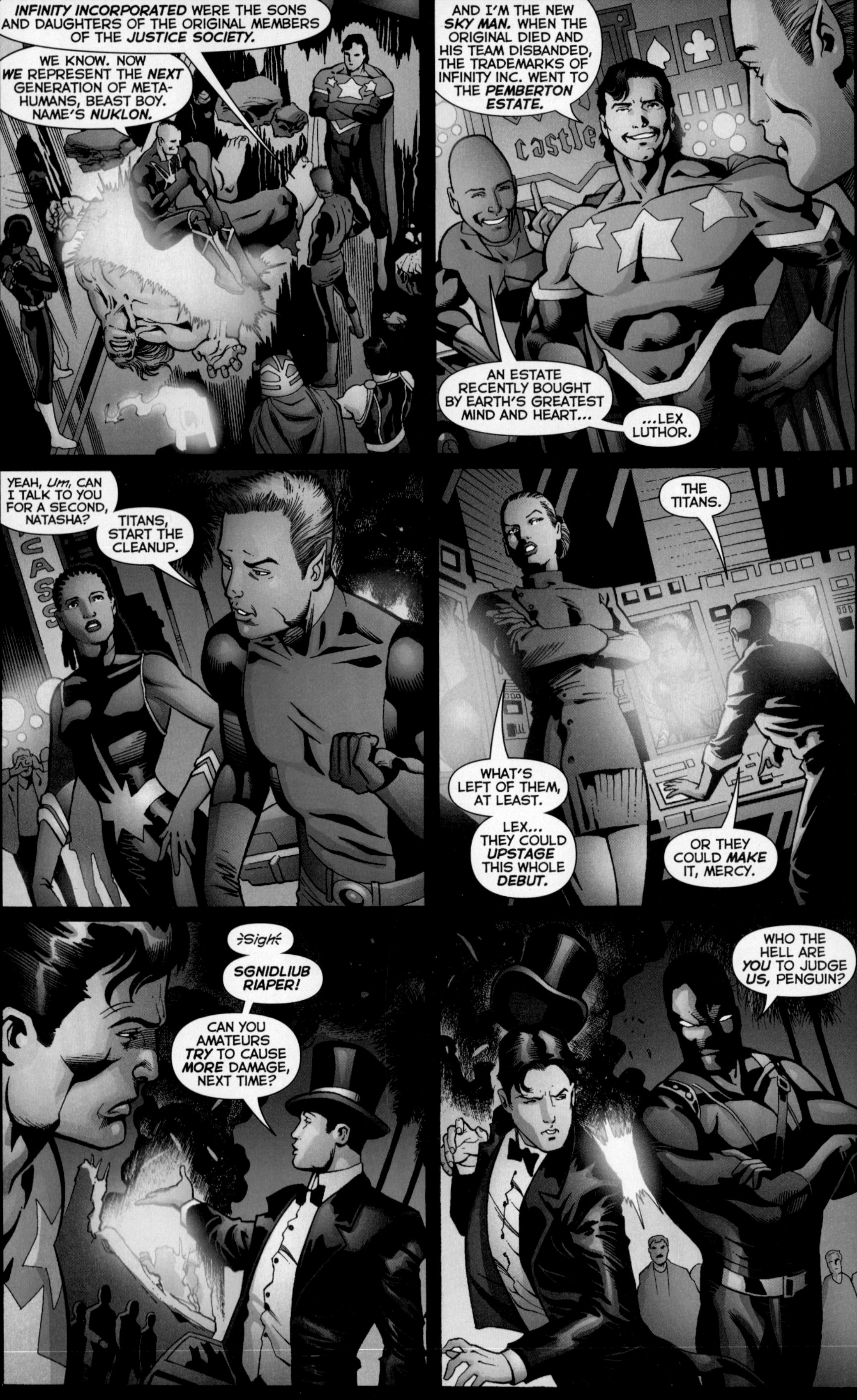
INFINITY INCORPORATED WERE THE SONS AND DAUGHTERS OF THE ORIGINAL MEMBERS OF THE JUSTICE SOCIETY.
WE KNOW. NOW WE REPRESENT THE NEXT GENERATION OF META-HUMANS, BEAST BOY. NAME'S NUKLON.
AND I'M THE NEW SKY MAN. WHEN THE ORIGINAL DIED AND HIS TEAM DISBANDED, THE TRADEMARKS OF INFINITY INC. WENT TO THE PEMBERTON ESTATE.
castle
AN ESTATE RECENTLY BOUGHT BY EARTH'S GREATEST MIND AND HEART...
...LEX LUTHOR.
YEAH, UM, CAN I TALK TO YOU FOR A SECOND, NATASHA?
TITANS, START THE CLEANUP.
THE TITANS.
WHAT'S LEFT OF THEM, AT LEAST.
LEX... THEY COULD UPSTAGE THIS WHOLE DEBUT.
OR THEY COULD MAKE IT, MERCY.
Sigh
SGNIDLIUB RIAPER!
CAN YOU AMATEURS TRY TO CAUSE MORE DAMAGE, NEXT TIME?
WHO THE HELL ARE YOU TO JUDGE US, PENGUIN?

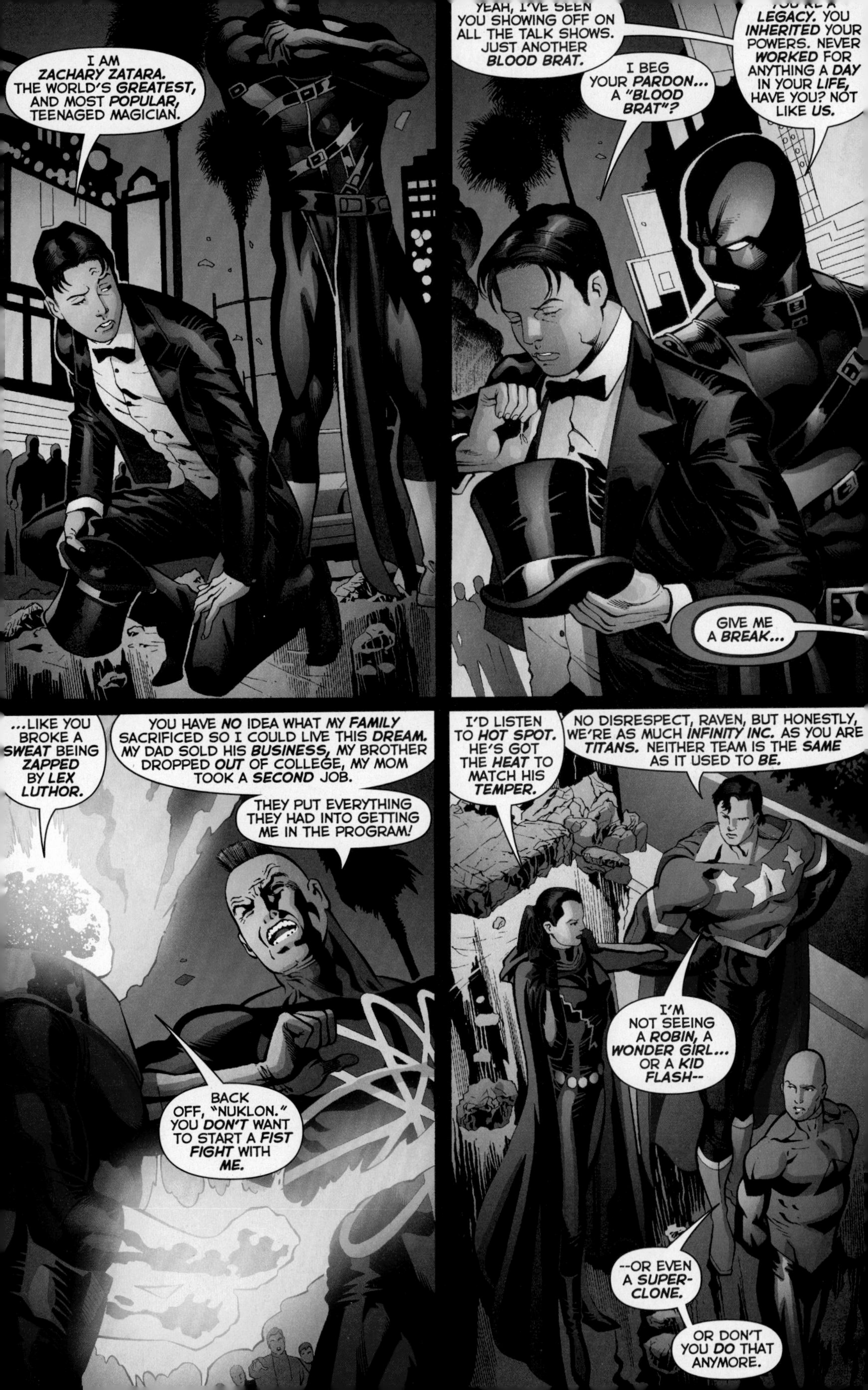
I AM ZACHARY ZATARA. THE WORLD'S GREATEST, AND MOST POPULAR, TEENAGED MAGICIAN.
YEAH, I'VE SEEN YOU SHOWING OFF ON ALL THE TALK SHOWS. JUST ANOTHER BLOOD BRAT.
I BEG YOUR PARDON... A "BLOOD BRAT"?
LEGACY. YOU INHERITED YOUR POWERS. NEVER WORKED FOR ANYTHING A DAY IN YOUR LIFE, HAVE YOU? NOT LIKE US.
GIVE ME A BREAK...
...LIKE YOU BROKE A SWEAT BEING ZAPPED BY LEX LUTHOR.
YOU HAVE NO IDEA WHAT MY FAMILY SACRIFICED SO I COULD LIVE THIS DREAM. MY DAD SOLD HIS BUSINESS, MY BROTHER DROPPED OUT OF COLLEGE, MY MOM TOOK A SECOND JOB.
THEY PUT EVERYTHING THEY HAD INTO GETTING ME IN THE PROGRAM!
BACK OFF, "NUKLON." YOU DON'T WANT TO START A FIST FIGHT WITH ME.
I'D LISTEN TO HOT SPOT. HE'S GOT THE HEAT TO MATCH HIS TEMPER.
NO DISRESPECT, RAVEN, BUT HONESTLY, WE'RE AS MUCH INFINITY INC. AS YOU ARE TITANS. NEITHER TEAM IS THE SAME AS IT USED TO BE.
I'M NOT SEEING A ROBIN, A WONDER GIRL... OR A KID FLASH--
--OR EVEN A SUPER-CLONE.
OR DON'T YOU DO THAT ANYMORE.

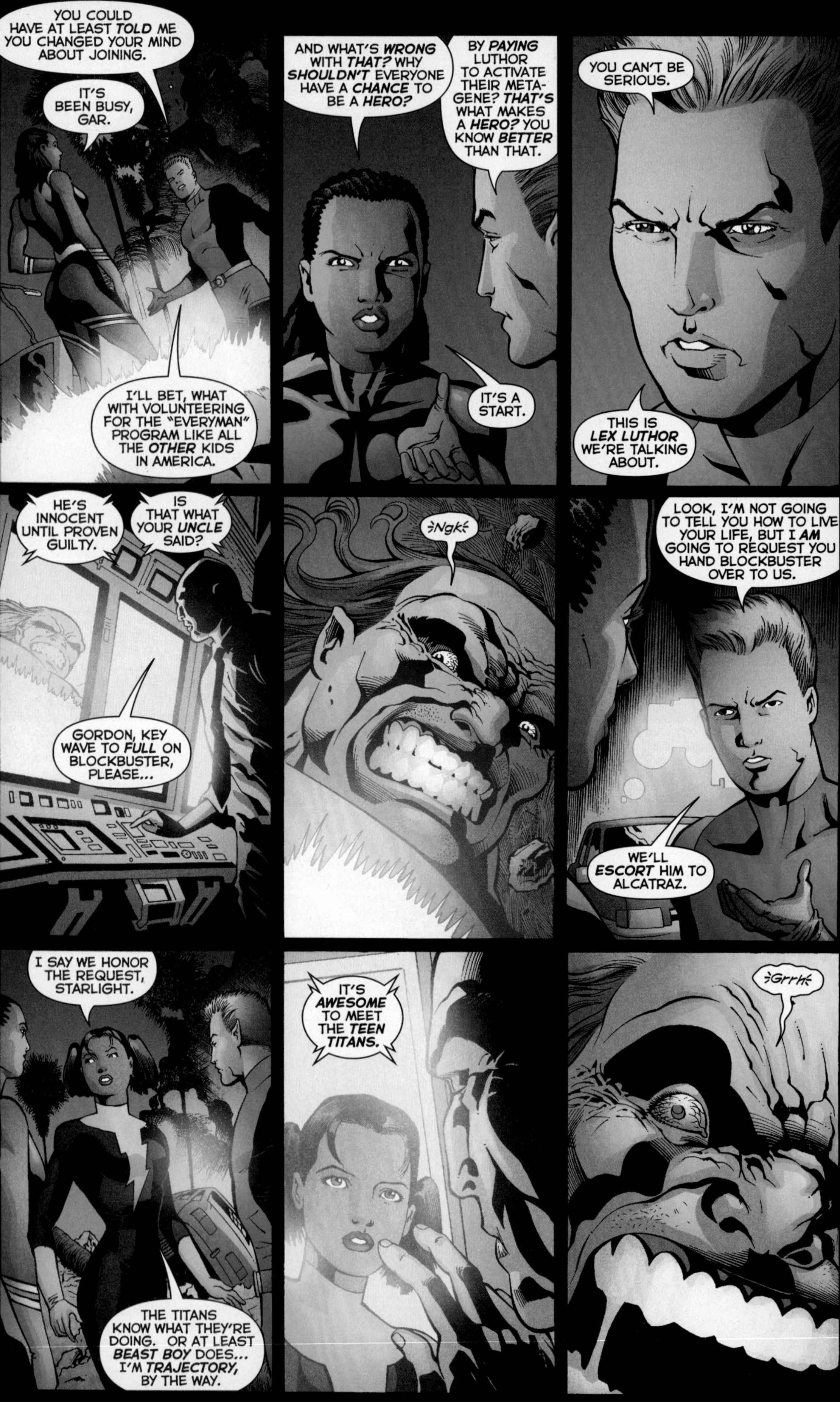
YOU COULD HAVE AT LEAST TOLD ME YOU CHANGED YOUR MIND ABOUT JOINING.
IT'S BEEN BUSY, GAR.
I'LL BET, WHAT WITH VOLUNTEERING FOR THE "EVERYMAN" PROGRAM LIKE ALL THE OTHER KIDS IN AMERICA.
AND WHAT'S WRONG WITH THAT? WHY SHOULDN'T EVERYONE HAVE A CHANCE TO BE A HERO?
BY PAYING LUTHOR TO ACTIVATE THEIR META-GENE? THAT'S WHAT MAKES A HERO? YOU KNOW BETTER THAN THAT.
IT'S A START.
YOU CAN'T BE SERIOUS.
THIS IS LEX LUTHOR WE'RE TALKING ABOUT.
HE'S INNOCENT UNTIL PROVEN GUILTY.
IS THAT WHAT YOUR UNCLE SAID?
GORDON, KEY WAVE TO FULL ON BLOCKBUSTER, PLEASE...
Ngk
LOOK, I'M NOT GOING TO TELL YOU HOW TO LIVE YOUR LIFE, BUT I AM GOING TO REQUEST YOU HAND BLOCKBUSTER OVER TO US.
WE'LL ESCORT HIM TO ALCATRAZ.
I SAY WE HONOR THE REQUEST, STARLIGHT.
THE TITANS KNOW WHAT THEY'RE DOING. OR AT LEAST BEAST BOY DOES... I'M TRAJECTORY, BY THE WAY.
IT'S AWESOME TO MEET THE TEEN TITANS.
Grrh

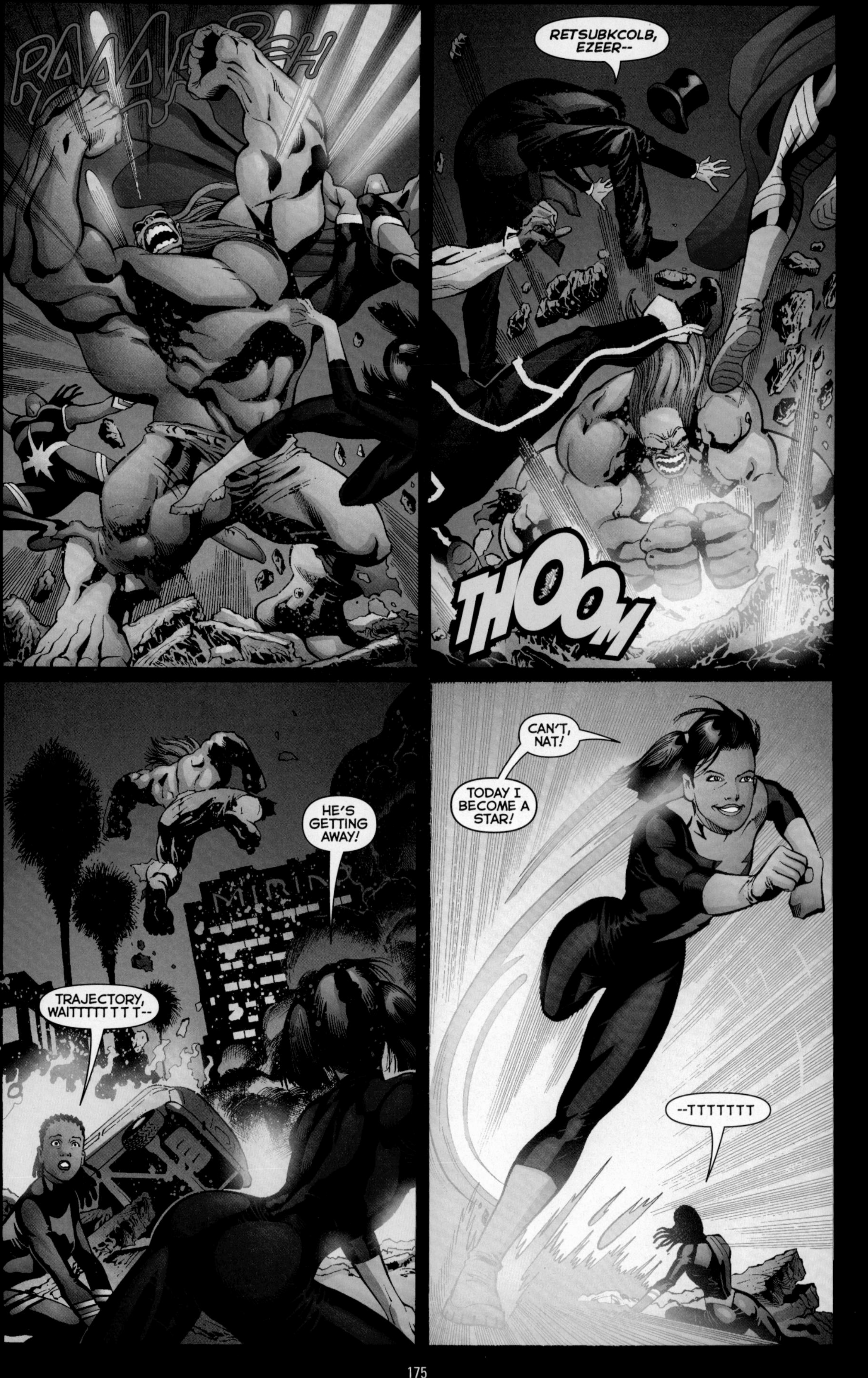
RETSUBKCOLB,
EZEER--
THOOM
HE'S GETTING AWAY!
TRAJECTORY, WAITTTTTT T T--
CAN'T, NAT!
TODAY I BECOME A STAR!
--TTTTTTT

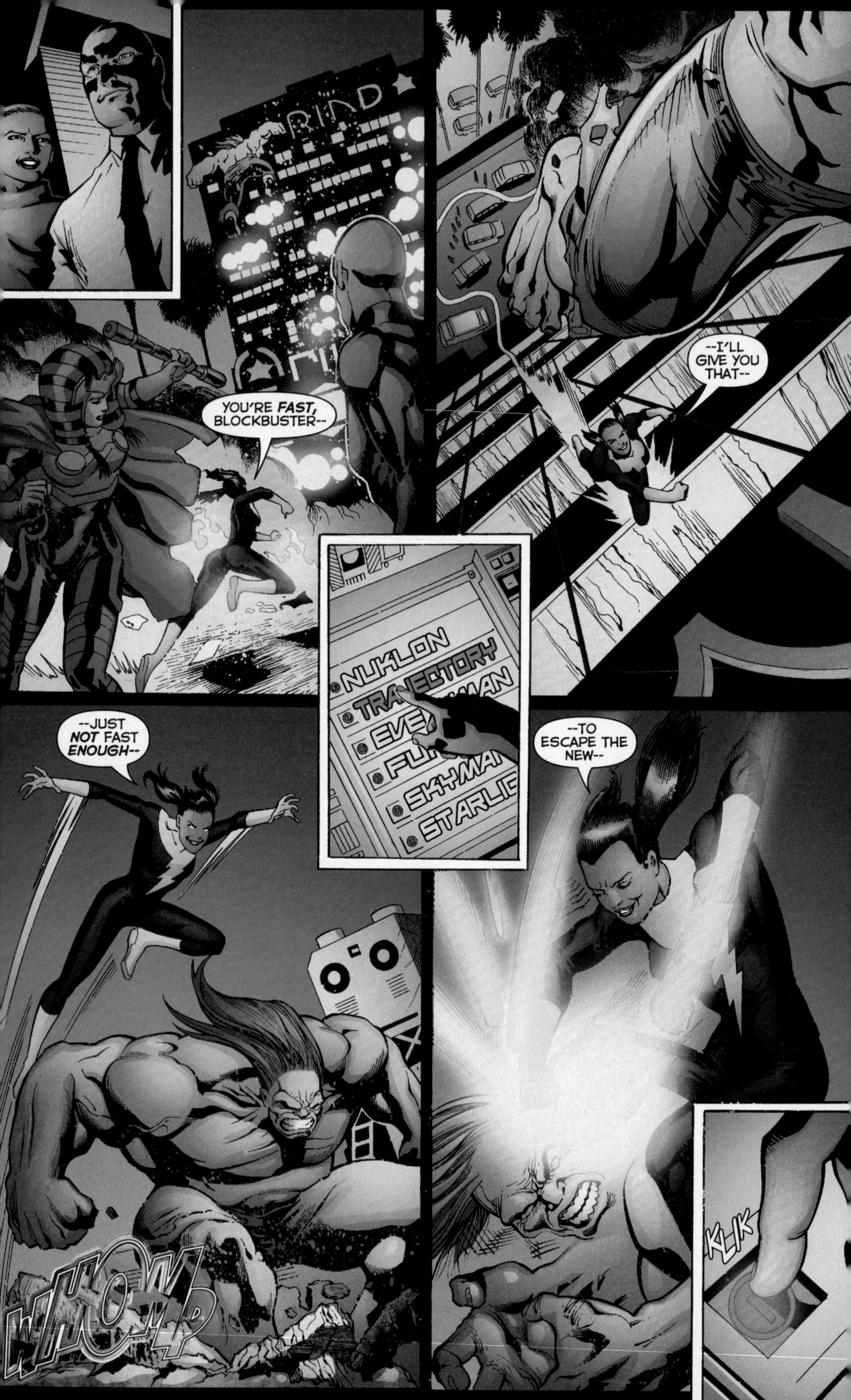
RIND
YOU'RE FAST, BLOCKBUSTER--
--I'LL GIVE YOU THAT--
NUKLON
TRAJECTORY
--JUST NOT FAST ENOUGH--
--TO ESCAPE THE NEW--
WHOOMP
KLIK

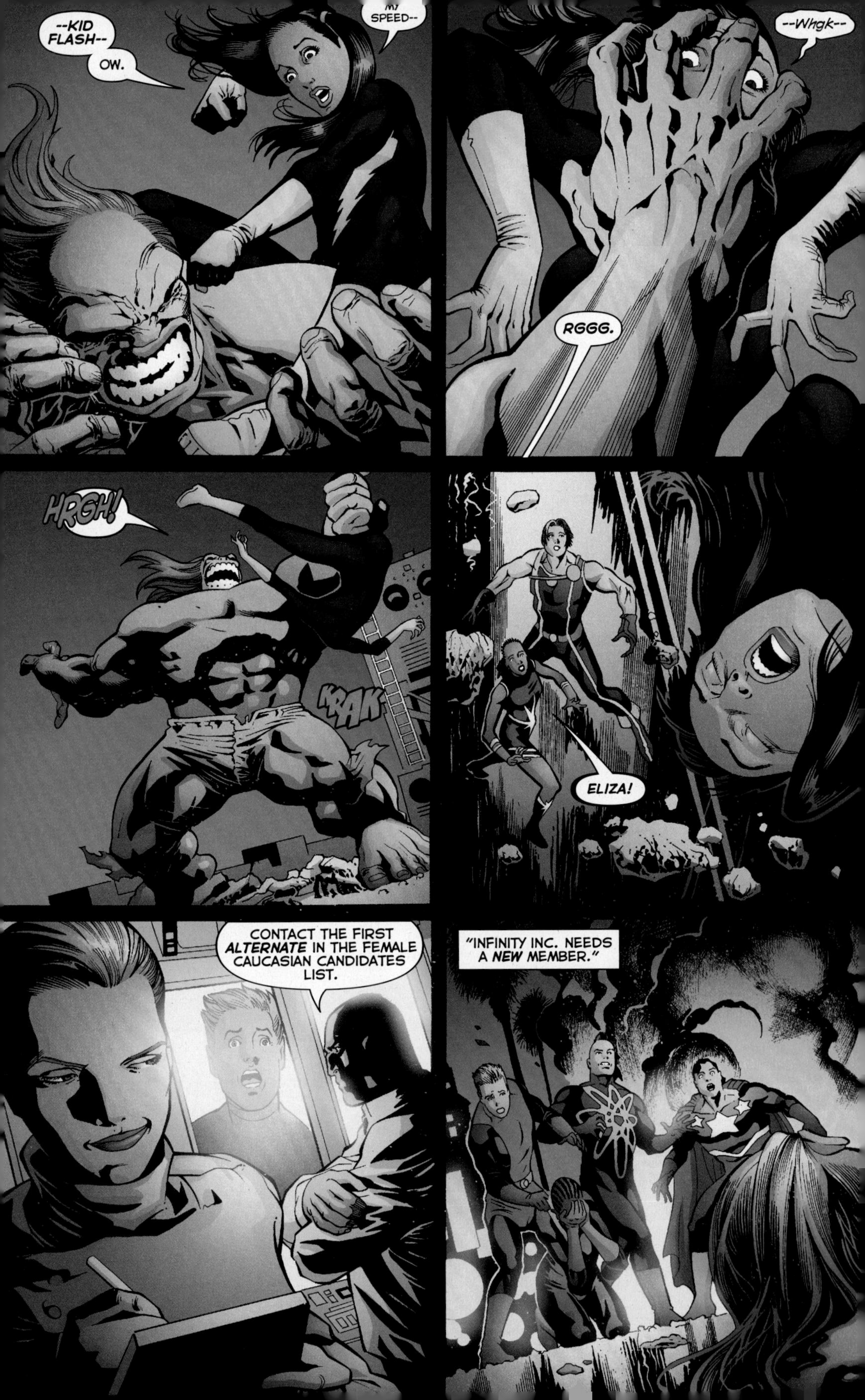

--KID FLASH--
OW.
MY SPEED--
--Whgk--
RGGG.
HRGH!
KRAK
ELIZA!
CONTACT THE FIRST ALTERNATE IN THE FEMALE CAUCASIAN CANDIDATES LIST.
"INFINITY INC. NEEDS A NEW MEMBER."

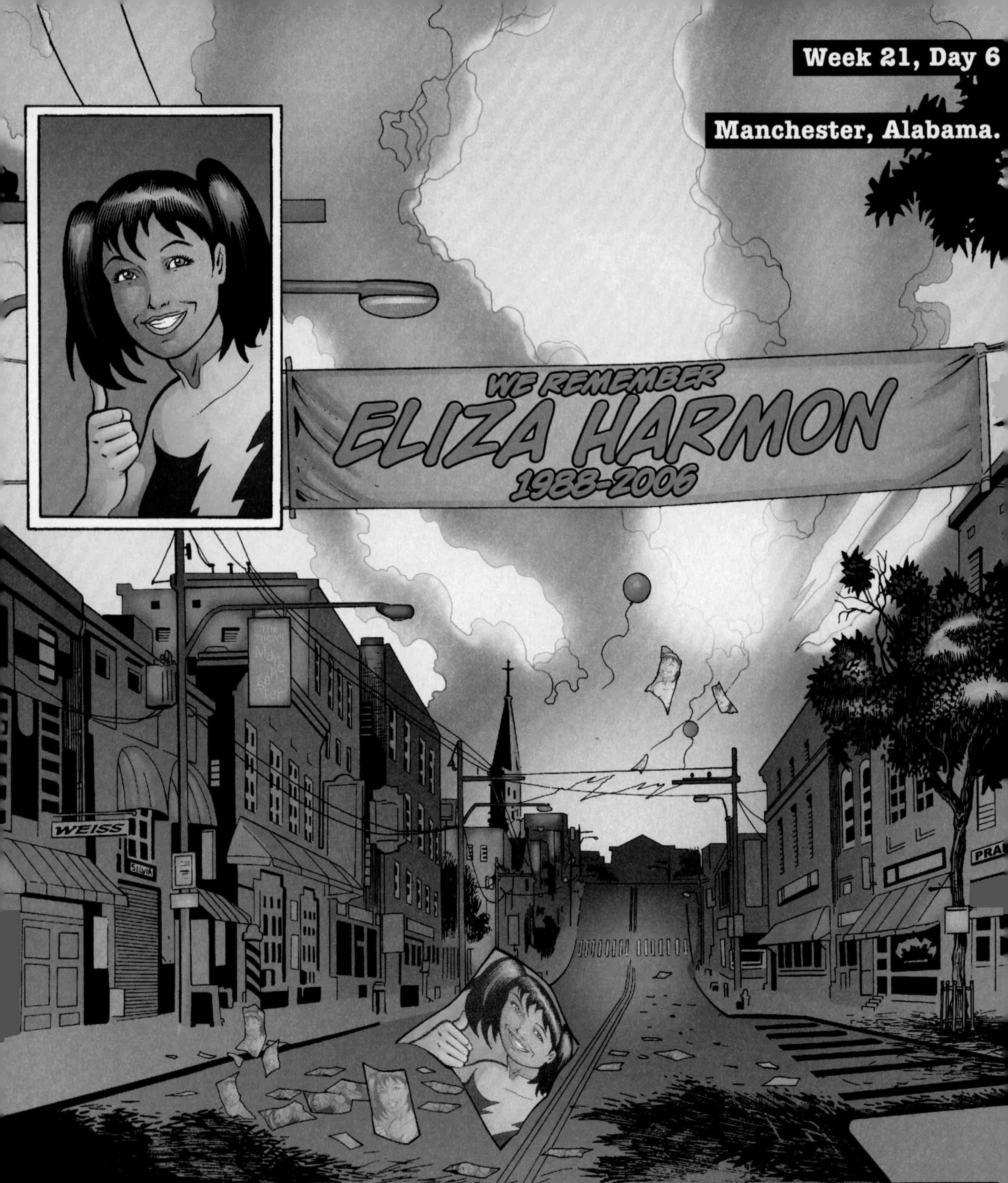
Week 21, Day 6
Manchester, Alabama.
WE REMEMBER
ELIZA HARMON
1988-2006
WEISS

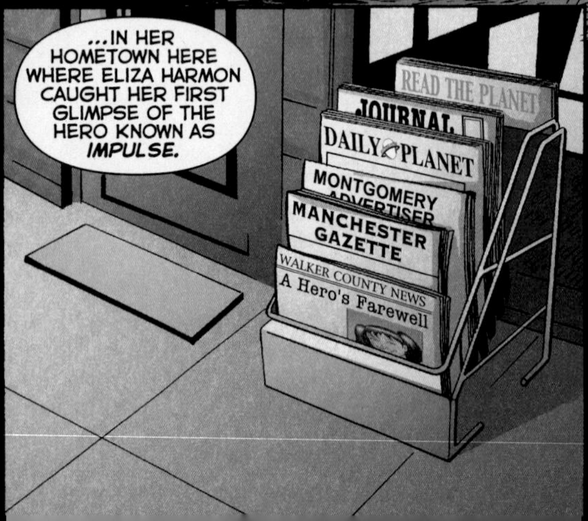
...IN HER HOMETOWN HERE WHERE ELIZA HARMON CAUGHT HER FIRST GLIMPSE OF THE HERO KNOWN AS *IMPULSE.*
READ THE PLANET
JOURNAL
DAILY PLANET
MONTGOMERY ADVERTISER
MANCHESTER GAZETTE
WALKER COUNTY NEWS
A Hero's Farewell

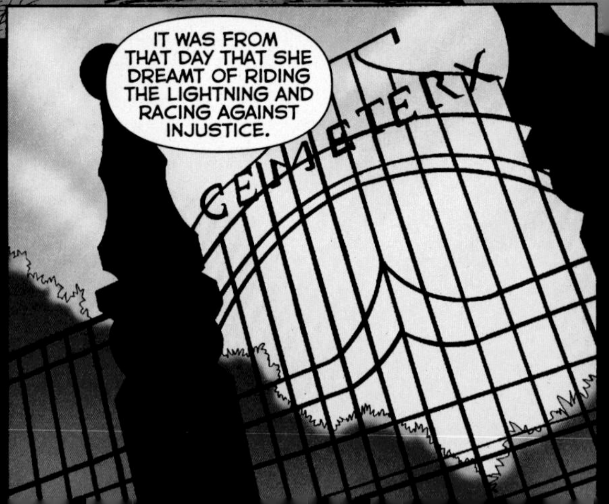
IT WAS FROM THAT DAY THAT SHE DREAMT OF RIDING THE LIGHTNING AND RACING AGAINST INJUSTICE.
CEMETERY

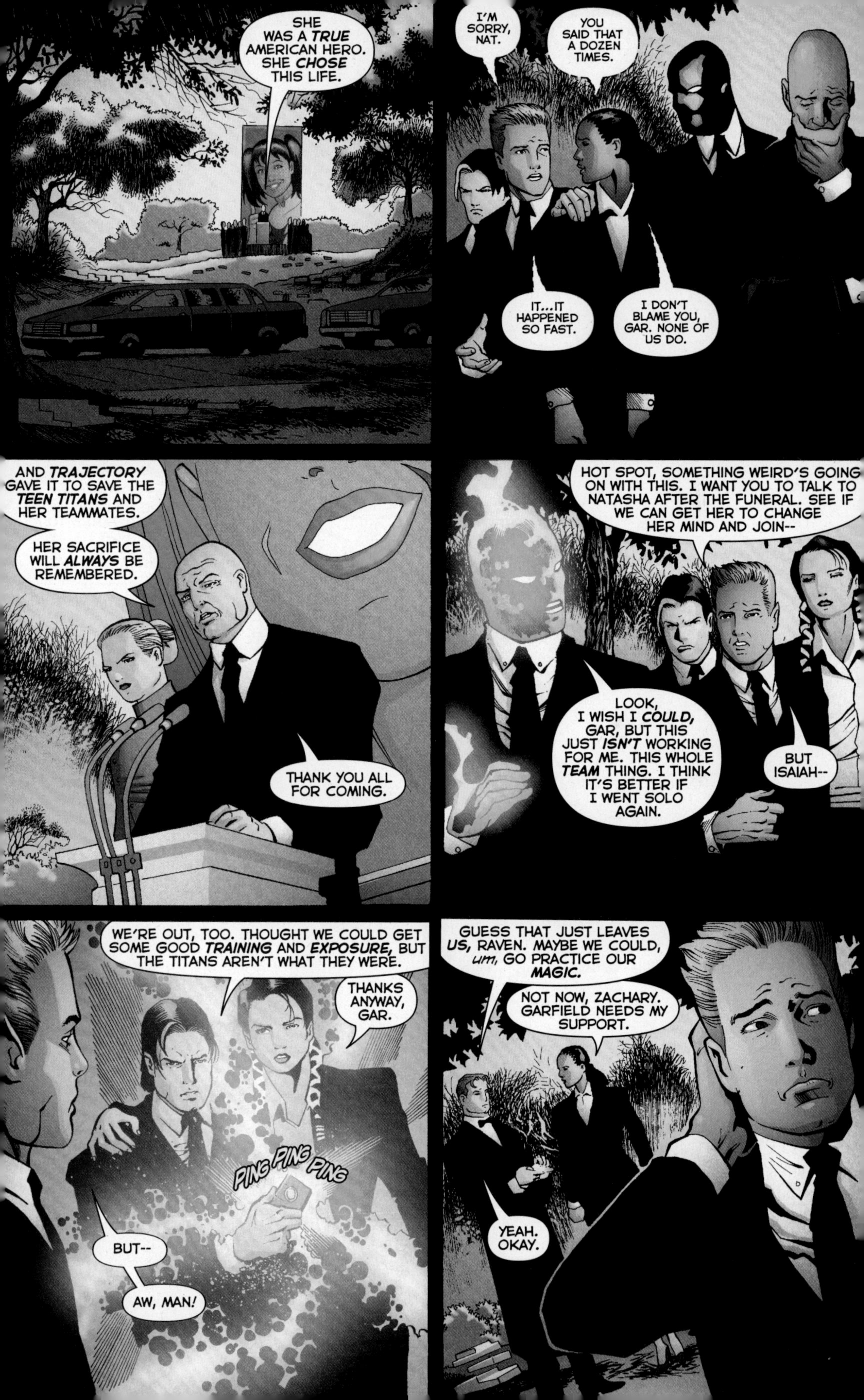
SHE WAS A TRUE AMERICAN HERO. SHE CHOSE THIS LIFE.
I'M SORRY, NAT.
YOU SAID THAT A DOZEN TIMES.
IT...IT HAPPENED SO FAST.
I DON'T BLAME YOU, GAR. NONE OF US DO.
AND TRAJECTORY GAVE IT TO SAVE THE TEEN TITANS AND HER TEAMMATES.
HER SACRIFICE WILL ALWAYS BE REMEMBERED.
THANK YOU ALL FOR COMING.
HOT SPOT, SOMETHING WEIRD'S GOING ON WITH THIS. I WANT YOU TO TALK TO NATASHA AFTER THE FUNERAL. SEE IF WE CAN GET HER TO CHANGE HER MIND AND JOIN--
LOOK, I WISH I COULD, GAR, BUT THIS JUST ISN'T WORKING FOR ME. THIS WHOLE TEAM THING. I THINK IT'S BETTER IF I WENT SOLO AGAIN.
BUT ISAIAH--
WE'RE OUT, TOO. THOUGHT WE COULD GET SOME GOOD TRAINING AND EXPOSURE, BUT THE TITANS AREN'T WHAT THEY WERE.
THANKS ANYWAY, GAR.
PING PING PING
BUT--
AW, MAN!
GUESS THAT JUST LEAVES US, RAVEN. MAYBE WE COULD, UM, GO PRACTICE OUR MAGIC.
NOT NOW, ZACHARY. GARFIELD NEEDS MY SUPPORT.
YEAH. OKAY.

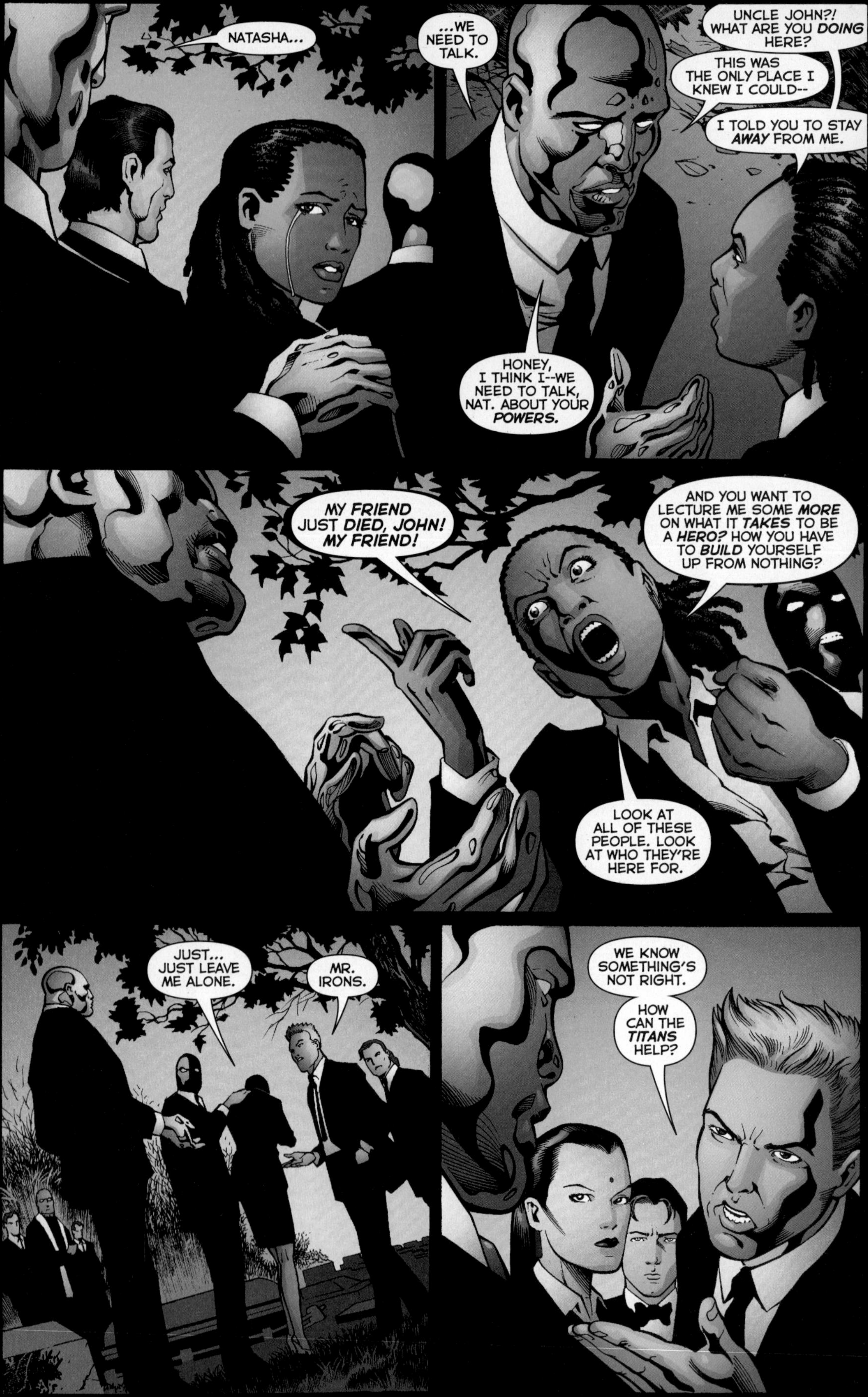
NATASHA...
...WE NEED TO TALK.
UNCLE JOHN?! WHAT ARE YOU DOING HERE?
THIS WAS THE ONLY PLACE I KNEW I COULD--
I TOLD YOU TO STAY AWAY FROM ME.
HONEY, I THINK I--WE NEED TO TALK, NAT. ABOUT YOUR POWERS.
MY FRIEND JUST DIED, JOHN! MY FRIEND!
AND YOU WANT TO LECTURE ME SOME MORE ON WHAT IT TAKES TO BE A HERO? HOW YOU HAVE TO BUILD YOURSELF UP FROM NOTHING?
LOOK AT ALL OF THESE PEOPLE. LOOK AT WHO THEY'RE HERE FOR.
JUST... JUST LEAVE ME ALONE.
MR. IRONS.
WE KNOW SOMETHING'S NOT RIGHT.
HOW CAN THE TITANS HELP?

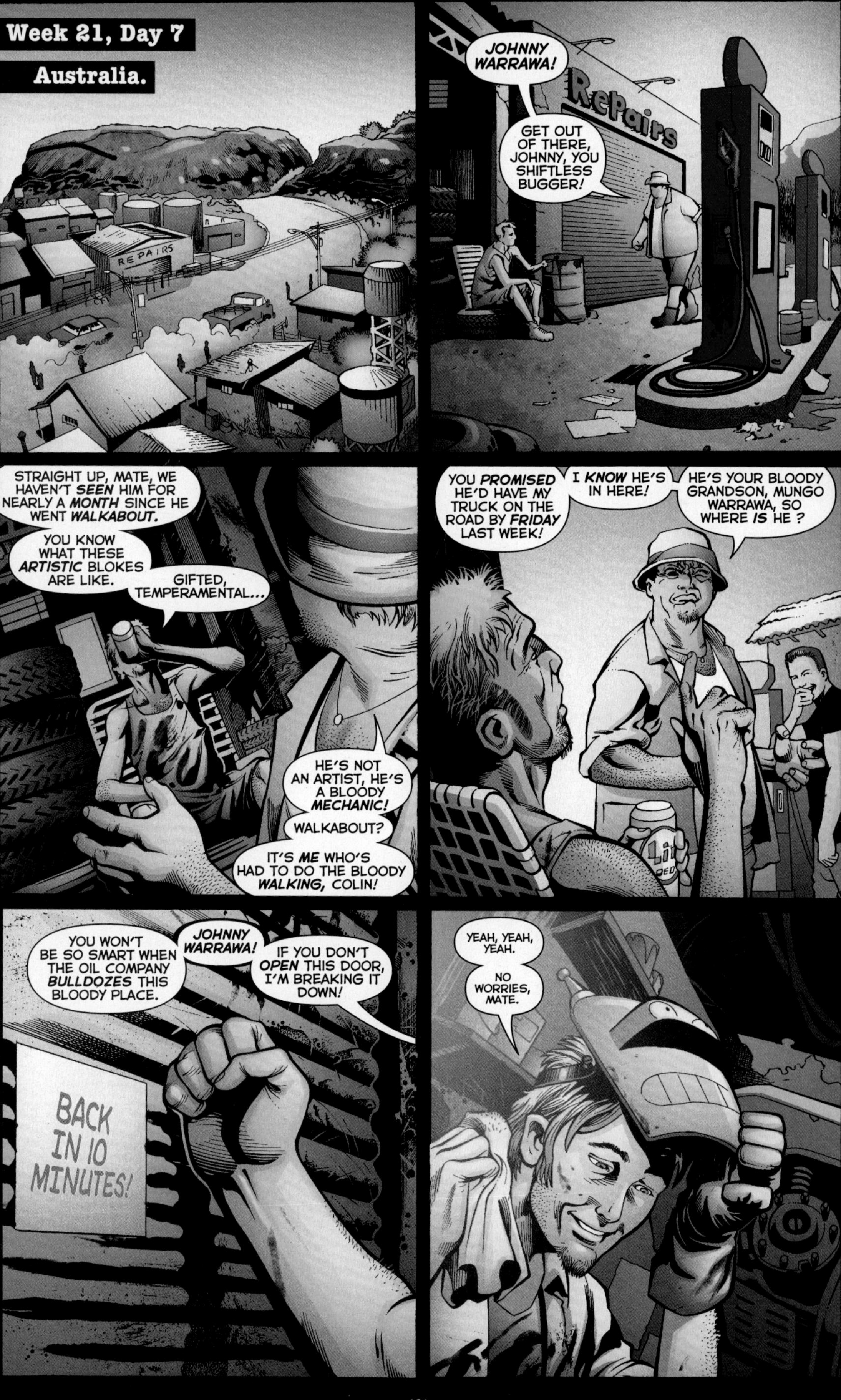
Week 21, Day 7
Australia.
REPAIRS
JOHNNY WARRAWA!
GET OUT OF THERE, JOHNNY, YOU SHIFTLESS BUGGER!
RePairs
STRAIGHT UP, MATE, WE HAVEN'T SEEN HIM FOR NEARLY A MONTH SINCE HE WENT WALKABOUT.
YOU KNOW WHAT THESE ARTISTIC BLOKES ARE LIKE.
GIFTED, TEMPERAMENTAL...
HE'S NOT AN ARTIST, HE'S A BLOODY MECHANIC!
WALKABOUT?
IT'S ME WHO'S HAD TO DO THE BLOODY WALKING, COLIN!
YOU PROMISED HE'D HAVE MY TRUCK ON THE ROAD BY FRIDAY LAST WEEK!
I KNOW HE'S IN HERE!
HE'S YOUR BLOODY GRANDSON, MUNGO WARRAWA, SO WHERE IS HE ?
YOU WON'T BE SO SMART WHEN THE OIL COMPANY BULLDOZES THIS BLOODY PLACE.
JOHNNY WARRAWA!
IF YOU DON'T OPEN THIS DOOR, I'M BREAKING IT DOWN!
BACK IN 10 MINUTES!
YEAH, YEAH, YEAH.
NO WORRIES, MATE.

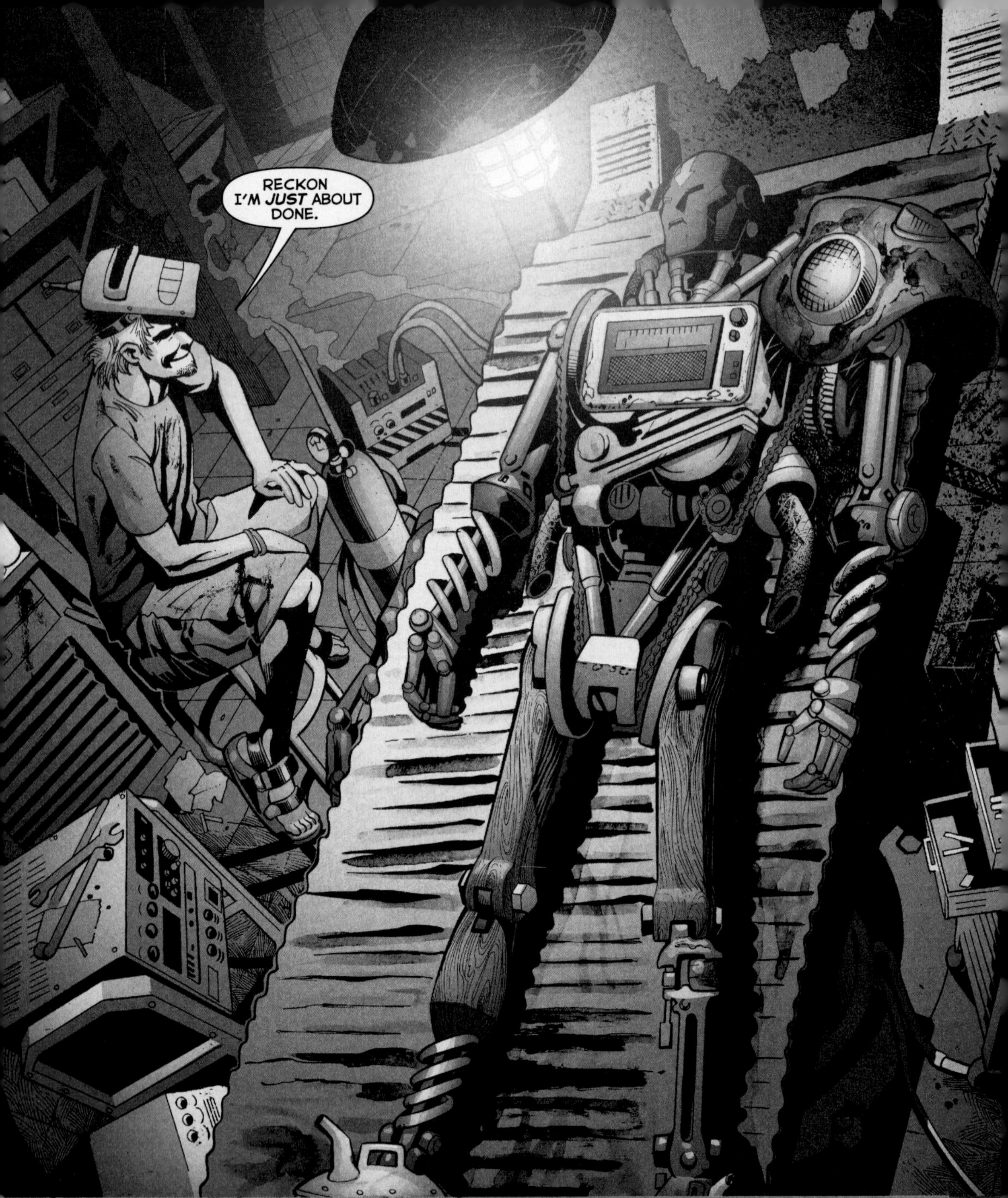
RECKON I'M *JUST* ABOUT DONE.

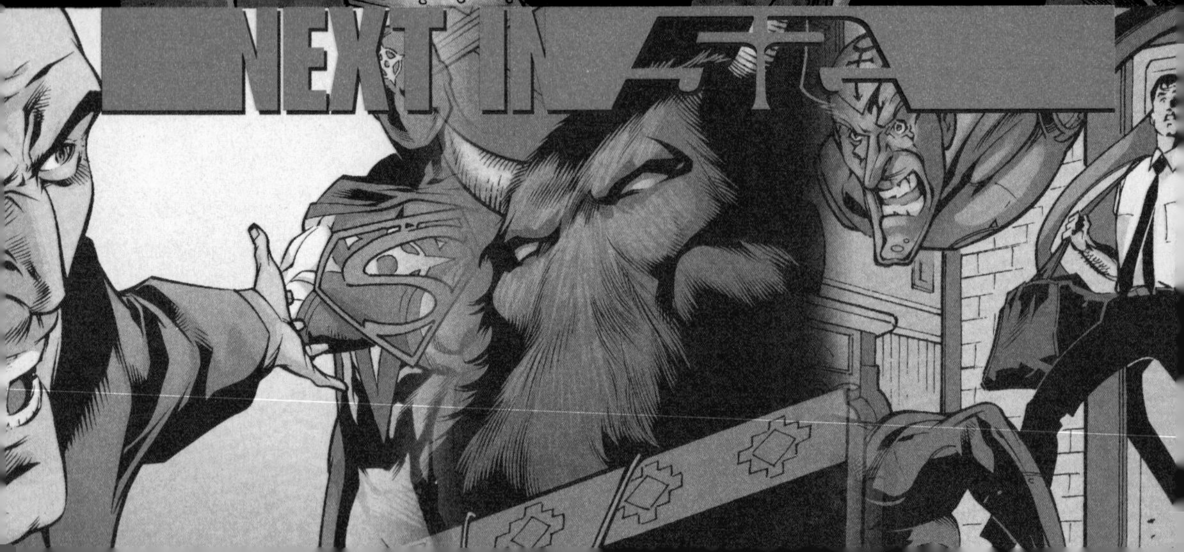
NEXT IN 52

WEEK TWENTY-ONE NOTES

GEOFF JOHNS

All right, this issue was one of the hardest we worked on. All of us were pretty vocal about the Steel story. We liked it, but our plans for it originally were much, much bigger and epic in scope. It felt like everything we were putting into it was too small. Including Luthor's team.

Originally, they didn't have a team name. They had green and purple uniforms that were nearly identical. And their code names were average. We knew we didn't have the space to really flesh out each and every one. Months earlier we spoke with Steve Wacker and discussed the possibility of finding a team name that wasn't in use. Steve hit us with "Infinity Inc."

It made sense. Luthor would know, just like comic readers, the public in the DCU would be more apt to remember a new "Nuklon" than "Starburst." It also dovetailed into exactly the right thematic element to pit these new kids who essentially bought their powers against the Justice Society of America. It added insult to injury.

This was also the first time we delved into the Teen Titans, which, according to the TEEN TITANS book, had gone through more than twenty members during this missing year. Power Boy, Little Barda, the new Zatara and Hot Spot (formerly Joto of Dan Jurgens's Teen Titans) made their debut. One of my favorite small details that Joe added was Little Barda chewing bubble gum. If I'd really noticed it when we got the black & white, I would've added a line about how wonderful food is on Earth compared to Apokolips. Gum is essentially an "entertainment" food since you never swallow it. The concept would be absolutely baffling to anyone from Apokolips. Another delightful detail, and one Keith might've filled you in on already, is that when he drew the layouts for this issue he put Zatara in fishnets, like his cousin Zatanna, as a joke. Joe had no idea who this Zatara was, so he actually drew him wearing fishnets. Due to the very looming deadlines, the Teen Titans nearly had a crossdresser on their team.

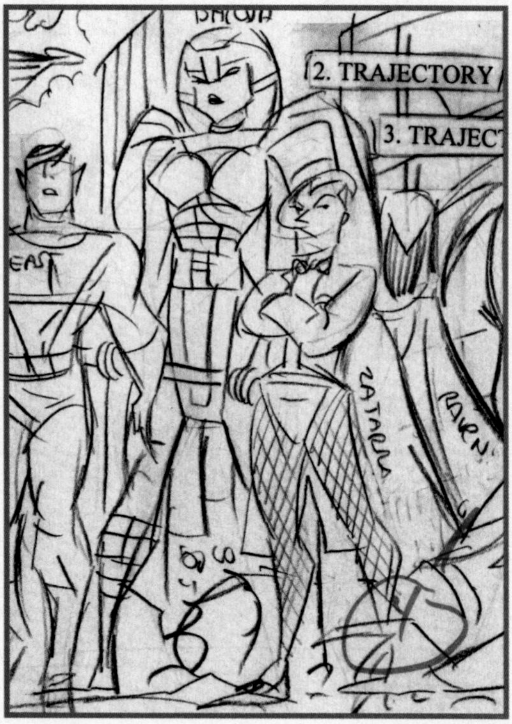
2. TRAJECTORY
3. TRAJECT
ZATARA

One other note: Mark and I are obviously massive Flash fans, so I find it a bit ironic now that Greg tackled the Trajectory scene of her hero-worshipping the speedsters.

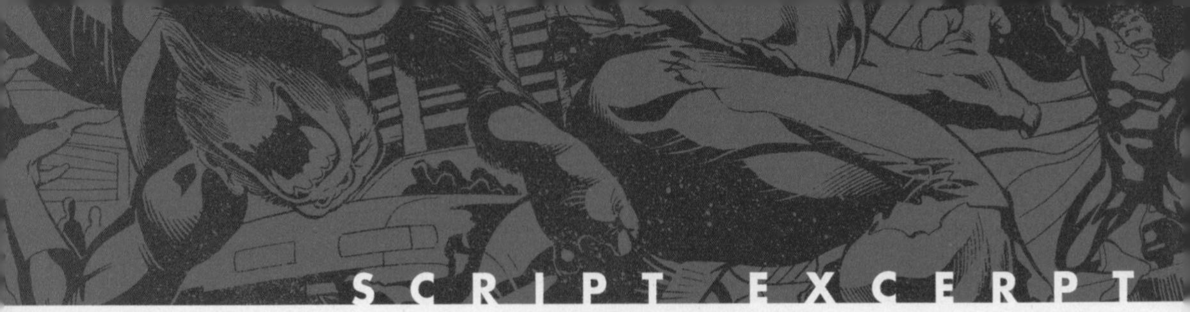

SCRIPT EXCERPT

(COMPARE WITH PAGES 166 & 167 OF THIS COLLECTION)

WEEK TWENTY-ONE — PAGES SIX & SEVEN

SPLASH
The new Infinity, Inc., as they attack BLOCKBUSTER on the Strip in Vegas, outside of one of the more garish, and probably not real at all, hotels. STARLIGHT, SKY MAN, TRAJECTORY, FURY, EVERYMAN, and NUKLON.

TOURISTS gape and gawk, snapping pictures, staring in amazement. BLOCKBUSTER is throwing a TOUR BUS. SKY MAN is CATCHING the BUS before it can do any damage. FURY and EVERYMAN are rushing towards BLOCKBUSTER — EVERYMAN is morphing into a HORSE, while FURY is vaulting onto his back, as if to ride him. TRAJECTORY is speeding along in semicircle, trying to form a perimeter. NUKLON is uprooting a PALM TREE to use as a bat. STARLIGHT floats above, shouting commands, riding on a nimbus of pure white light. ALL of the team wears small Bluetooth-like earpiece/camera units, sleek and barely noticeable.

STARLIGHT (large): ...INFINITY, INC.!
STARLIGHT (large): Take him DOWN!
BLOCKBUSTER: RRRAARRRRRRGGGGH!!!!
TAILLESS: Look! Look!
TAILLESS: — new ones, Lex Luthor's ones —
TAILLESS: — just like on the POSTERS, omygod!!!
TAILLESS: ...shot of HER? She's GORGEOUS!
TAILLESS: — wait, that one, I KNOW that one, that's-that's ANGRY! No! No, it's, uhm...
TAILLESS: ...which one's the SHAPE-SHIFTER...?

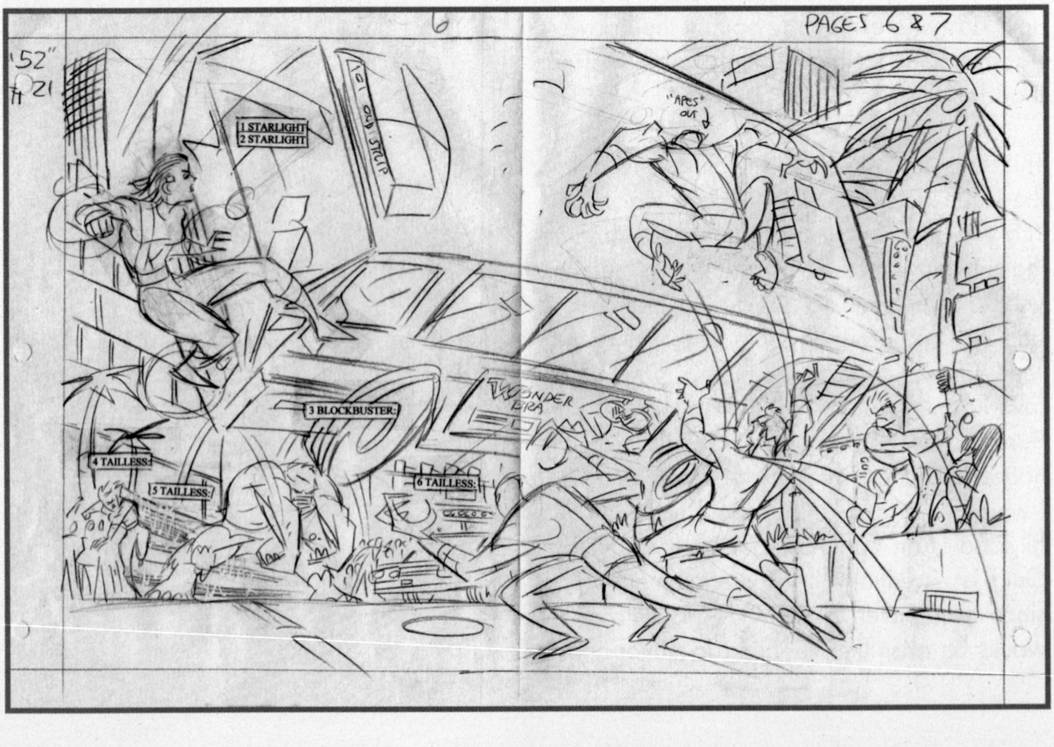
PAGES 6 & 7
6
"52" #21
1 STARLIGHT
2 STARLIGHT
"APES" out
3 BLOCKBUSTER:
WONDER BRA
4 TAILLESS:
5 TAILLESS:
6 TAILLESS:

DC COMICS 52

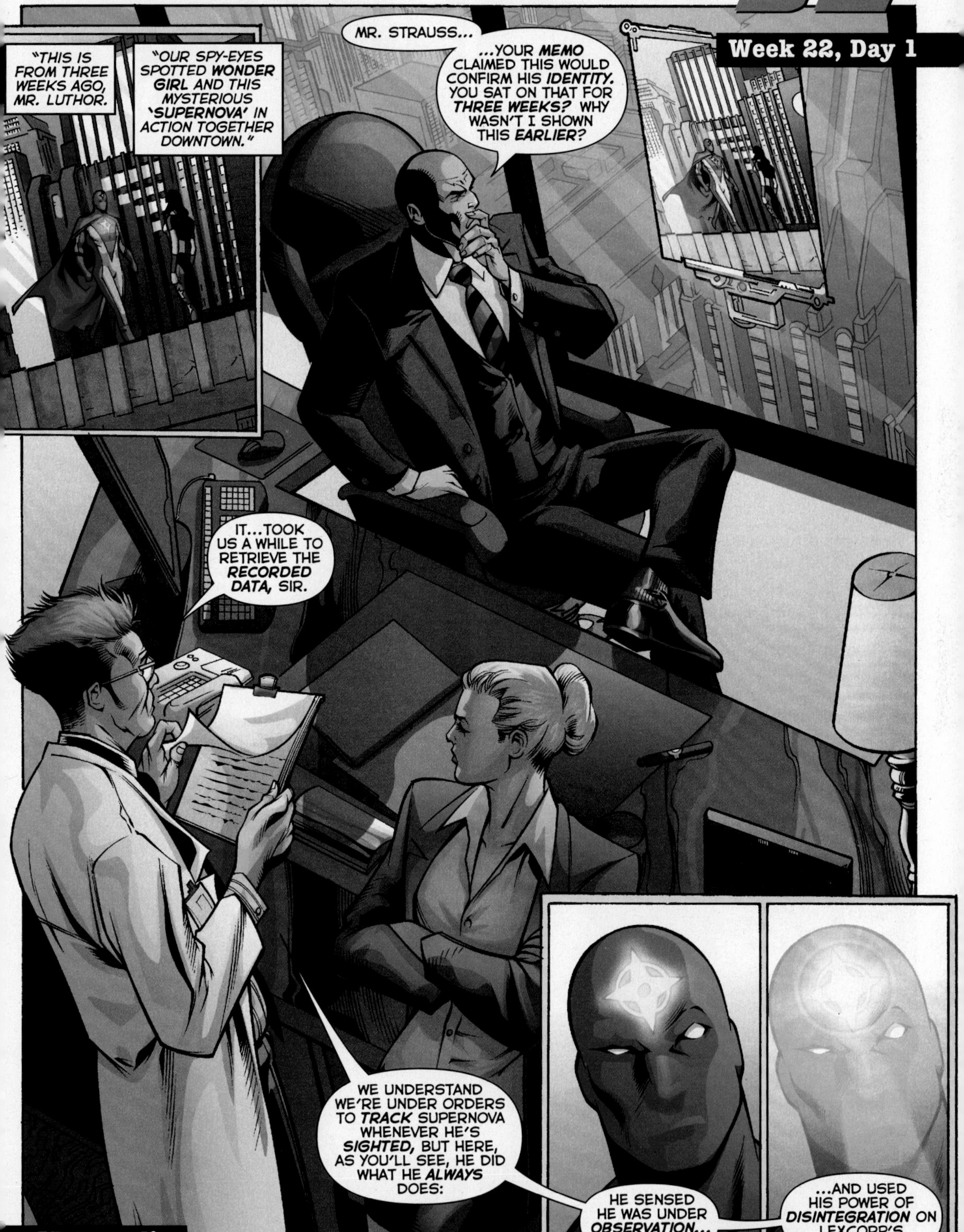
Week 22, Day 1
"THIS IS FROM THREE WEEKS AGO, MR. LUTHOR.
"OUR SPY-EYES SPOTTED WONDER GIRL AND THIS MYSTERIOUS 'SUPERNOVA' IN ACTION TOGETHER DOWNTOWN."
MR. STRAUSS...
...YOUR MEMO CLAIMED THIS WOULD CONFIRM HIS IDENTITY. YOU SAT ON THAT FOR THREE WEEKS? WHY WASN'T I SHOWN THIS EARLIER?
IT...TOOK US A WHILE TO RETRIEVE THE RECORDED DATA, SIR.
WE UNDERSTAND WE'RE UNDER ORDERS TO TRACK SUPERNOVA WHENEVER HE'S SIGHTED, BUT HERE, AS YOU'LL SEE, HE DID WHAT HE ALWAYS DOES:
HE SENSED HE WAS UNDER OBSERVATION... SOMEHOW...
...AND USED HIS POWER OF DISINTEGRATION ON LEXCORP'S CAMERAS.
Metropolis.

WRITTEN BY GEOFF JOHNS, GRANT MORRISON, GREG RUCKA, MARK WAID

LEXCORP'S BILLION DOLLAR *COMM* SATELLITE.

WHICH HE SAW FROM HUNDREDS OF MILES *AWAY.*

IT CERTAINLY *FITS*, DOESN'T IT?

EXCUSE ME?

NOTHING. GO ON.

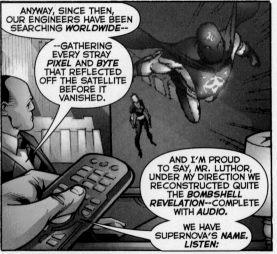

ANYWAY, SINCE THEN, OUR ENGINEERS HAVE BEEN SEARCHING *WORLDWIDE*--

--GATHERING EVERY STRAY *PIXEL* AND *BYTE* THAT REFLECTED OFF THE SATELLITE BEFORE IT VANISHED.

AND I'M PROUD TO SAY, MR. LUTHOR, UNDER MY DIRECTION WE RECONSTRUCTED QUITE THE *BOMBSHELL REVELATION*--COMPLETE WITH *AUDIO.*

WE HAVE SUPERNOVA'S *NAME.* LISTEN:

ART BREAKDOWNS BY KEITH GIFFEN • PENCILS BY EDDY BARROWS • INKS BY ROB STULL
COLORS BY ALEX SINCLAIR • LETTERING BY KEN LOPEZ • COVER BY J.G. JONES & ALEX SINCLAIR

...KON-EL.

GOOD NEWS, SIR. YOUR SON *KON-EL* DIDN'T *DIE* IN THE CRISIS AFTER ALL.

FOR WHATEVER REASON, HE *LIVES ON*--AS *SUPERNOVA.*

OF COURSE. AND HE'S BEEN SPOTTING OUR *SURVEILLANCE* WITH HIS *TELESCOPIC* VISION.

PRECISELY.

YOU'RE FIRED.

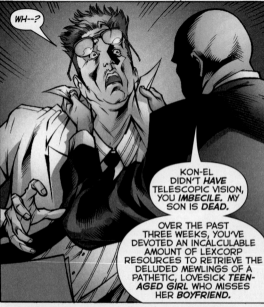

WH--?

KON-EL DIDN'T *HAVE* TELESCOPIC VISION, YOU *IMBECILE.* MY SON IS *DEAD.*

OVER THE PAST THREE WEEKS, YOU'VE DEVOTED AN INCALCULABLE AMOUNT OF LEXCORP RESOURCES TO RETRIEVE THE DELUDED MEWLINGS OF A PATHETIC, LOVESICK *TEEN-AGED GIRL* WHO MISSES HER *BOYFRIEND.*

ISN'T THAT *RIGHT*, "SUPERNOVA"?

SIR, WHO ARE YOU *TALKING* TO?

ASSISTANT EDITORS HARVEY RICHARDS & JEANINE SCHAEFER • EDITED BY STEPHEN WACKER

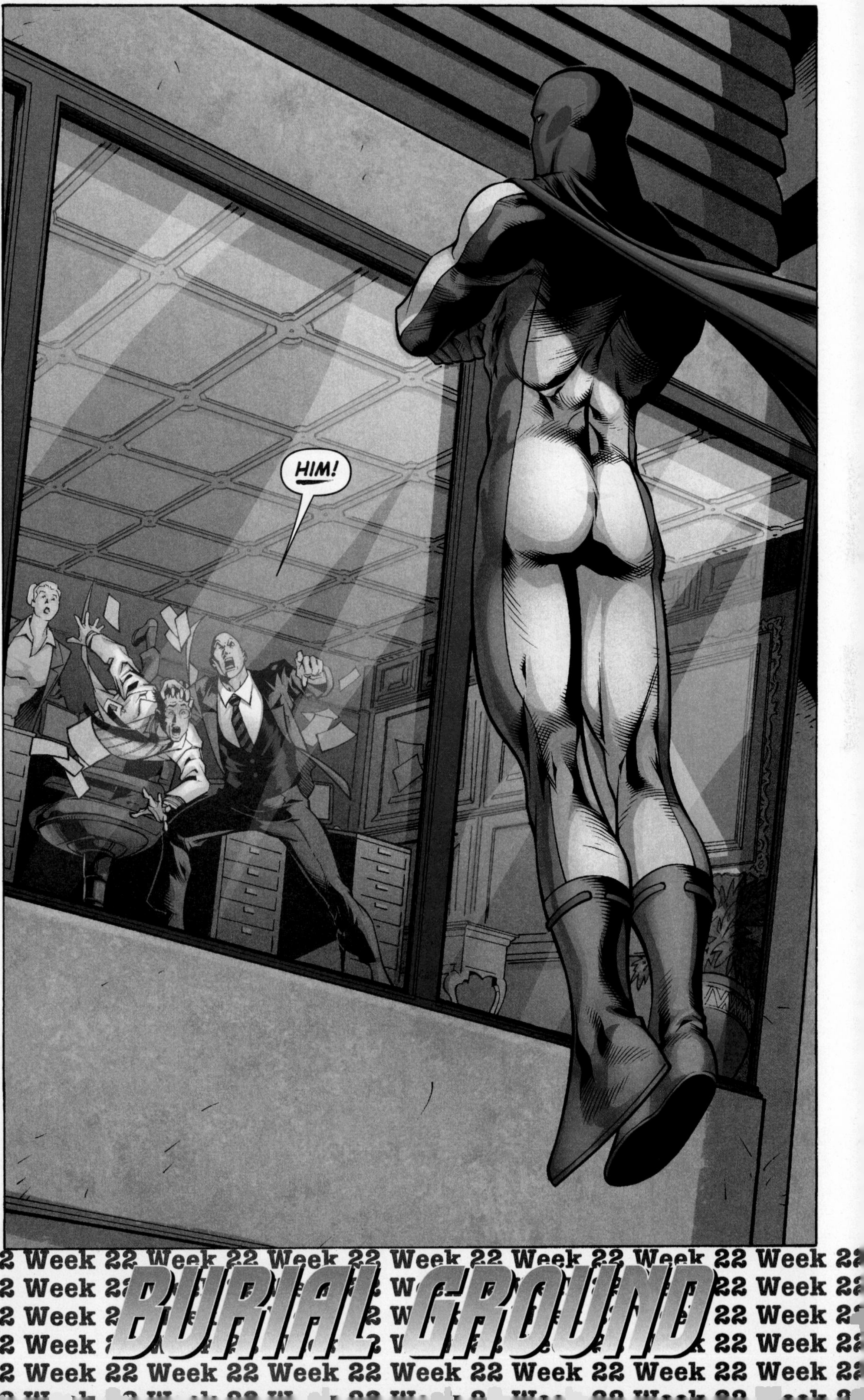
HIM!
BURIAL GROUND
Week 22

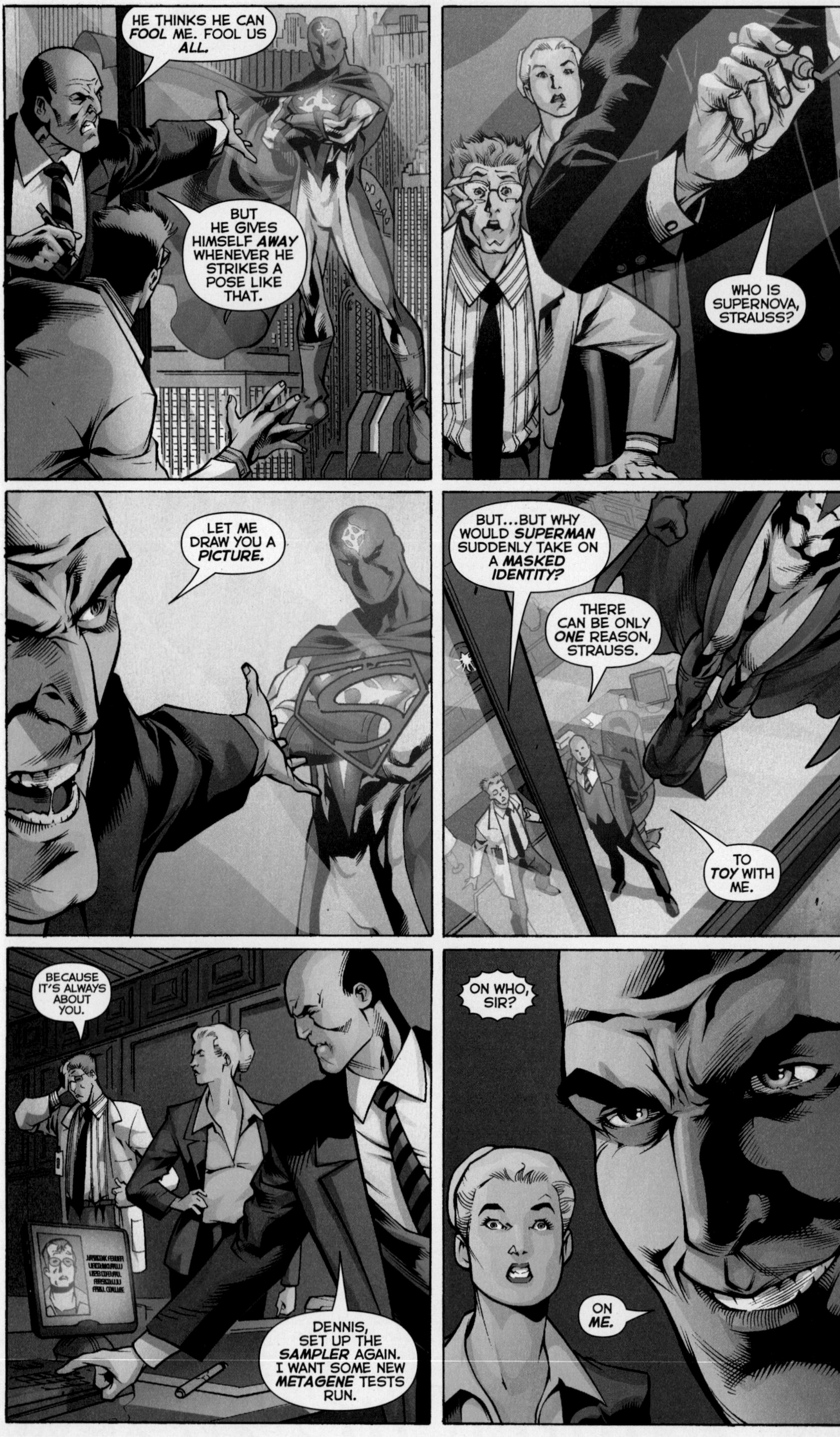
HE THINKS HE CAN FOOL ME. FOOL US ALL.
BUT HE GIVES HIMSELF AWAY WHENEVER HE STRIKES A POSE LIKE THAT.
WHO IS SUPERNOVA, STRAUSS?
LET ME DRAW YOU A PICTURE.
BUT...BUT WHY WOULD SUPERMAN SUDDENLY TAKE ON A MASKED IDENTITY?
THERE CAN BE ONLY ONE REASON, STRAUSS.
TO TOY WITH ME.
BECAUSE IT'S ALWAYS ABOUT YOU.
DENNIS, SET UP THE SAMPLER AGAIN. I WANT SOME NEW METAGENE TESTS RUN.
ON WHO, SIR?
ON ME.

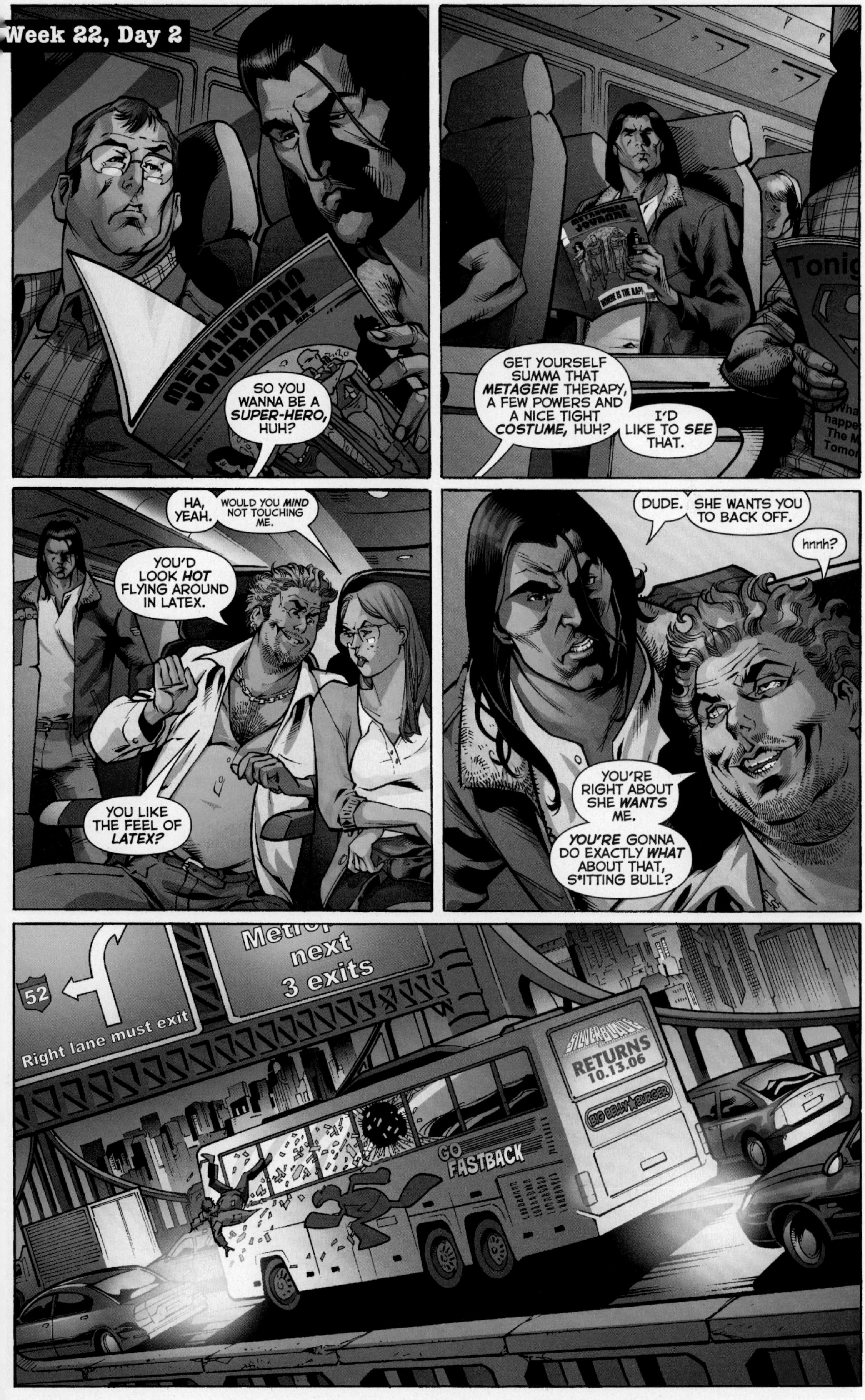
Week 22, Day 2
METAHUMAN JOURNAL
SO YOU WANNA BE A SUPER-HERO, HUH?
GET YOURSELF SUMMA THAT METAGENE THERAPY, A FEW POWERS AND A NICE TIGHT COSTUME, HUH?
I'D LIKE TO SEE THAT.
HA, YEAH.
WOULD YOU MIND NOT TOUCHING ME.
YOU'D LOOK HOT FLYING AROUND IN LATEX.
YOU LIKE THE FEEL OF LATEX?
DUDE.
SHE WANTS YOU TO BACK OFF.
hnnh?
YOU'RE RIGHT ABOUT SHE WANTS ME.
YOU'RE GONNA DO EXACTLY WHAT ABOUT THAT, S*ITTING BULL?
52
Right lane must exit
next
3 exits
RETURNS
10.13.06
BIG BELLY BURGER
GO FASTBACK

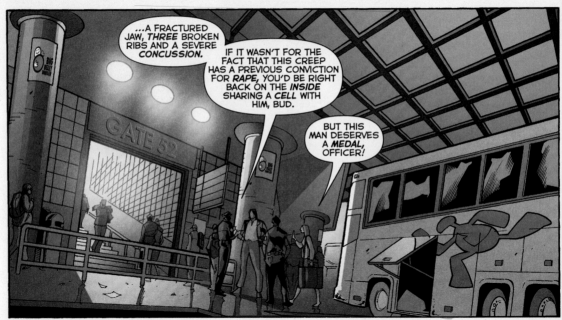

...A FRACTURED JAW, *THREE* BROKEN RIBS AND A SEVERE *CONCUSSION.*

IF IT WASN'T FOR THE FACT THAT THIS CREEP HAS A PREVIOUS CONVICTION FOR *RAPE,* YOU'D BE RIGHT BACK ON THE *INSIDE* SHARING A *CELL* WITH HIM, BUD.

BUT THIS MAN DESERVES A *MEDAL,* OFFICER!

YOU WOULDN'T BE SAYING THAT IF YOU'D SEEN HIS *SERVICE* RECORD.

ON YOUR *WAY,* SOLDIER.

AND AS FOR YOU, KID, THIS AIN'T *MISSOURI,* IT'S *METROPOLIS.*

IF YOU NEED A PLACE TO *STAY,* HERE'S THE *LIST.*

HEY!

WAIT UP!

LOOK, I ONLY *HIT* THE GUY 'CAUSE I HAVEN'T HIT ANYBODY *ELSE* IN TOO LONG A TIME.

GO BACK TO YOUR DREAMS.

YOU DON'T WANNA *KNOW* ME.

WHY NOT? YOU SEEM LIKE A NICE GUY, *JON STANDING BEAR.*

DON'T *YOU* WANT TO *FLY* TOO?

I'D ONLY *FALL.*

WATCH YOURSELF IN THE CLOUDS.

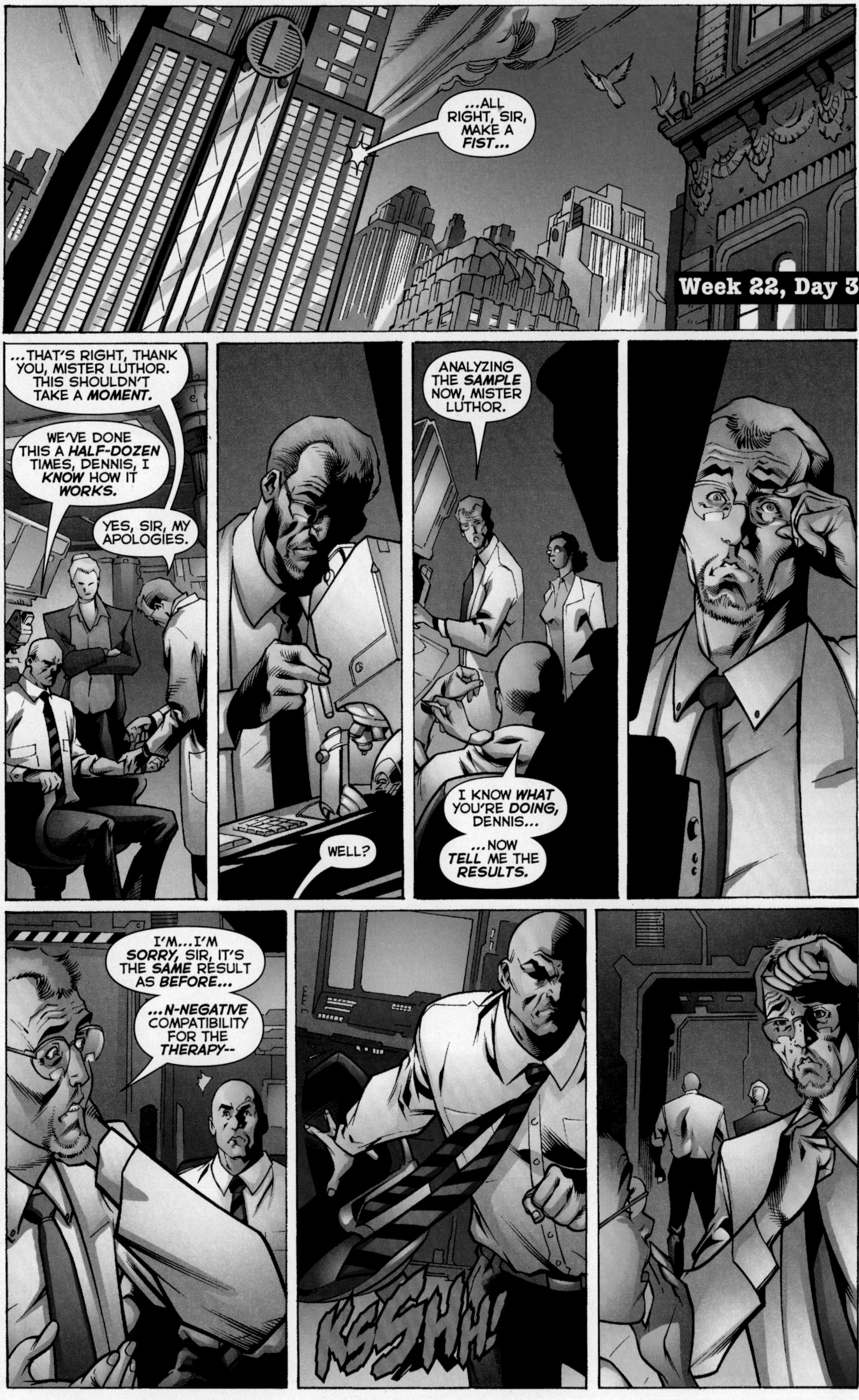
...ALL RIGHT, SIR, MAKE A FIST...
Week 22, Day 3
...THAT'S RIGHT, THANK YOU, MISTER LUTHOR. THIS SHOULDN'T TAKE A MOMENT.
WE'VE DONE THIS A HALF-DOZEN TIMES, DENNIS, I KNOW HOW IT WORKS.
YES, SIR, MY APOLOGIES.
ANALYZING THE SAMPLE NOW, MISTER LUTHOR.
WELL?
I KNOW WHAT YOU'RE DOING, DENNIS...
...NOW TELL ME THE RESULTS.
I'M...I'M SORRY, SIR, IT'S THE SAME RESULT AS BEFORE...
...N-NEGATIVE COMPATIBILITY FOR THE THERAPY--
KSSHH!

HE HAS LIVER FAILURE AND *I'M* STILL STANDING?

I'M SCREWED NOW.

YOUR FATHER? HE'S BEEN THE *ONLY* THING BETWEEN ME AND THE STREETS FOR THE LAST TWENTY YEARS.

IT'S MORE TIME THAN HE EVER GAVE *ME.*

YOU WANT *ME* TO WIPE YOUR ASS?

YOU TWO BASTARDS MADE MY LIFE *HELL,* OLD MAN.

WHAT DO *YOU* CARE ABOUT WHAT WE WENT THROUGH AFTER YOUR MOTHER DIED?

YOU WERE NEVER ANYTHING BUT *TROUBLE,* JON.

WHAT DO *YOU* GIVE A DAMN ABOUT *HERITAGE* AND YOUR OBLIGATIONS?

HERITAGE?

OBLIGATIONS?

TO TWO EVIL OLD MEN SHARING A DAMP APARTMENT?

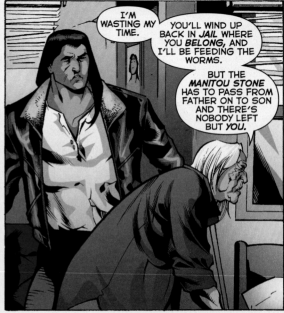

I'M WASTING MY TIME.

YOU'LL WIND UP BACK IN *JAIL* WHERE YOU *BELONG,* AND I'LL BE FEEDING THE WORMS.

BUT THE *MANITOU STONE* HAS TO PASS FROM FATHER ON TO SON AND THERE'S NOBODY LEFT BUT *YOU.*

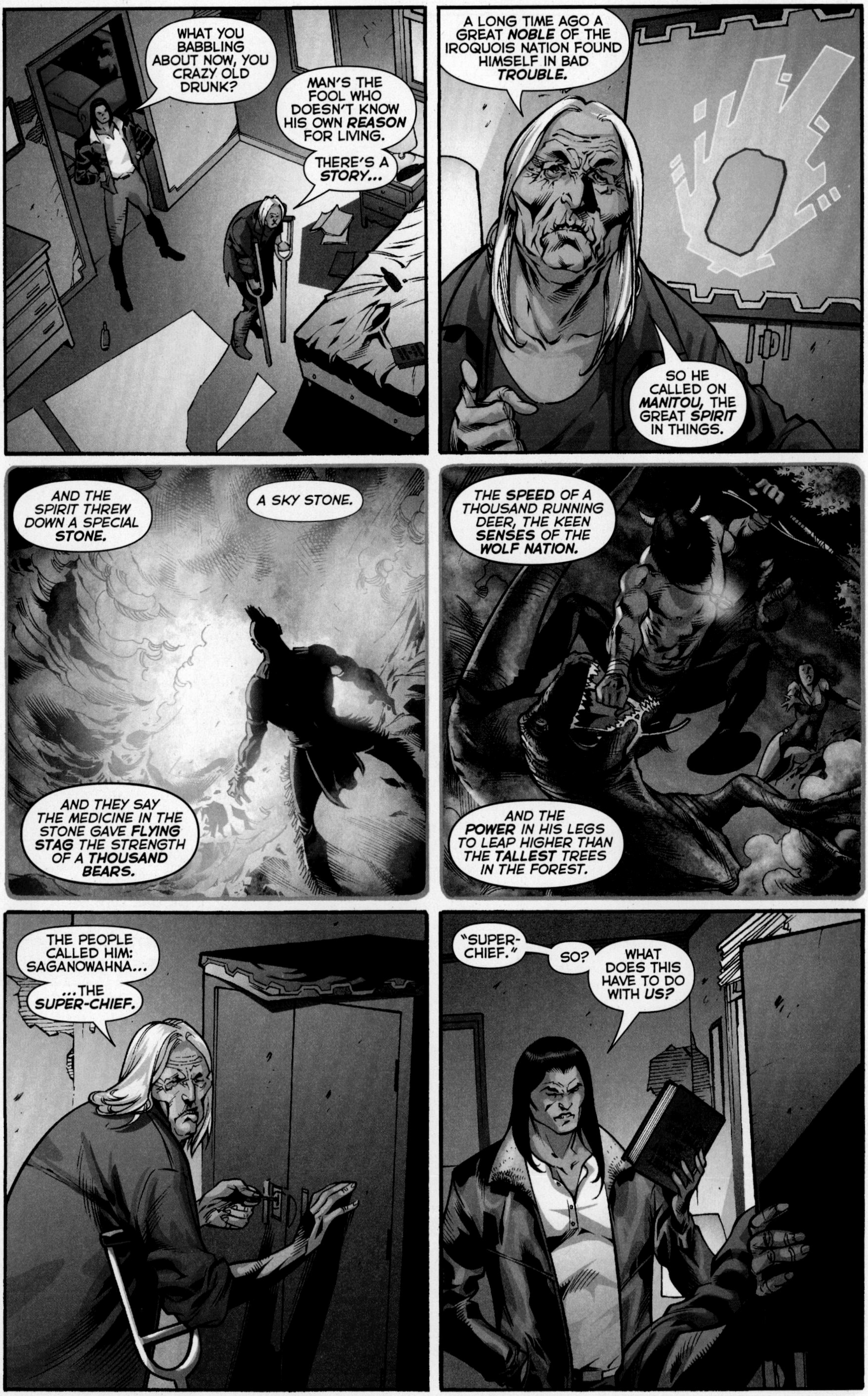
WHAT YOU BABBLING ABOUT NOW, YOU CRAZY OLD DRUNK?
MAN'S THE FOOL WHO DOESN'T KNOW HIS OWN REASON FOR LIVING.
THERE'S A STORY...
A LONG TIME AGO A GREAT NOBLE OF THE IROQUOIS NATION FOUND HIMSELF IN BAD TROUBLE.
SO HE CALLED ON MANITOU, THE GREAT SPIRIT IN THINGS.
AND THE SPIRIT THREW DOWN A SPECIAL STONE.
A SKY STONE.
AND THEY SAY THE MEDICINE IN THE STONE GAVE FLYING STAG THE STRENGTH OF A THOUSAND BEARS.
THE SPEED OF A THOUSAND RUNNING DEER, THE KEEN SENSES OF THE WOLF NATION.
AND THE POWER IN HIS LEGS TO LEAP HIGHER THAN THE TALLEST TREES IN THE FOREST.
THE PEOPLE CALLED HIM: SAGANOWAHNA...
...THE SUPER-CHIEF.
"SUPER-CHIEF."
SO?
WHAT DOES THIS HAVE TO DO WITH US?

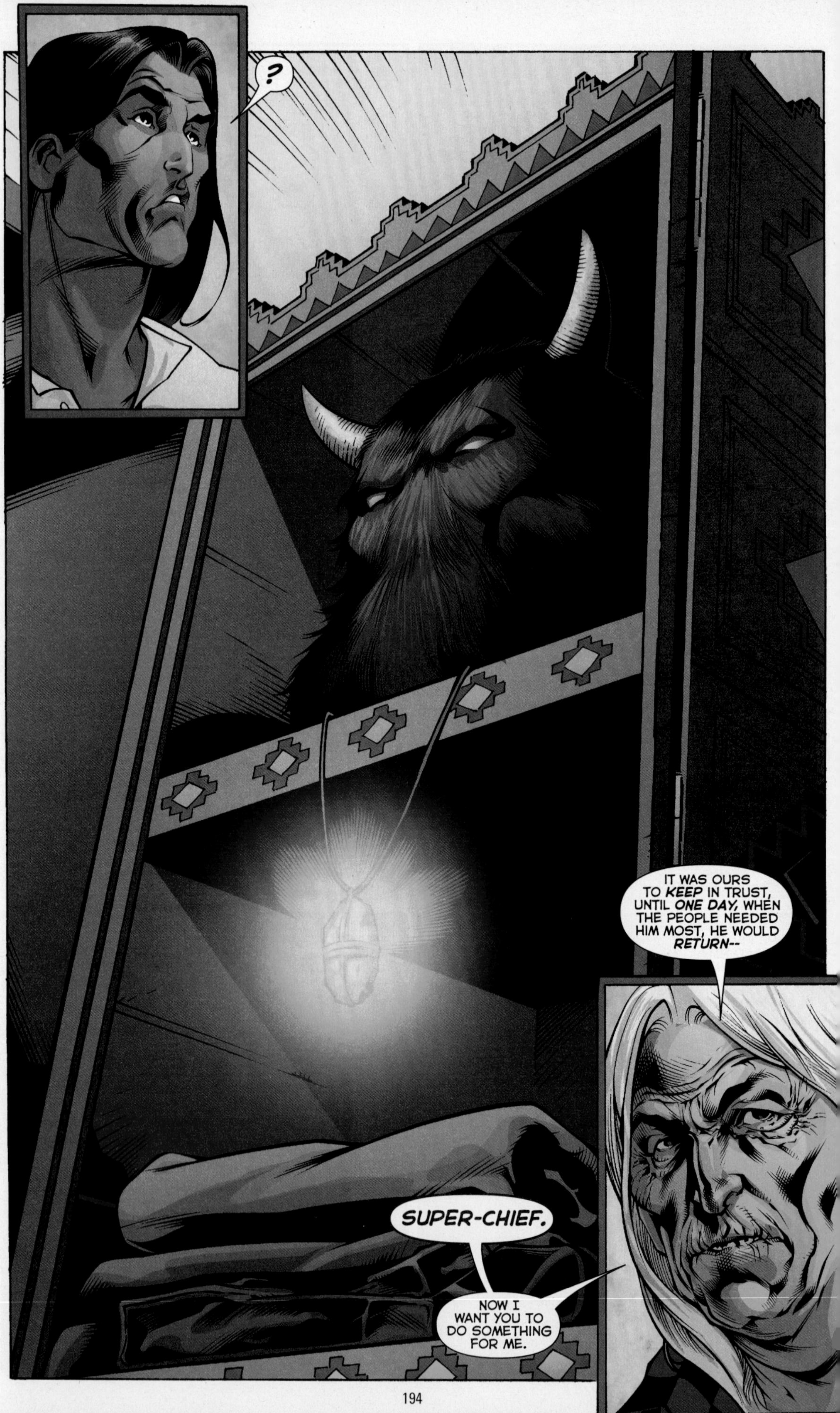
?
IT WAS OURS TO KEEP IN TRUST, UNTIL ONE DAY, WHEN THE PEOPLE NEEDED HIM MOST, HE WOULD RETURN--
SUPER-CHIEF.
NOW I WANT YOU TO DO SOMETHING FOR ME.

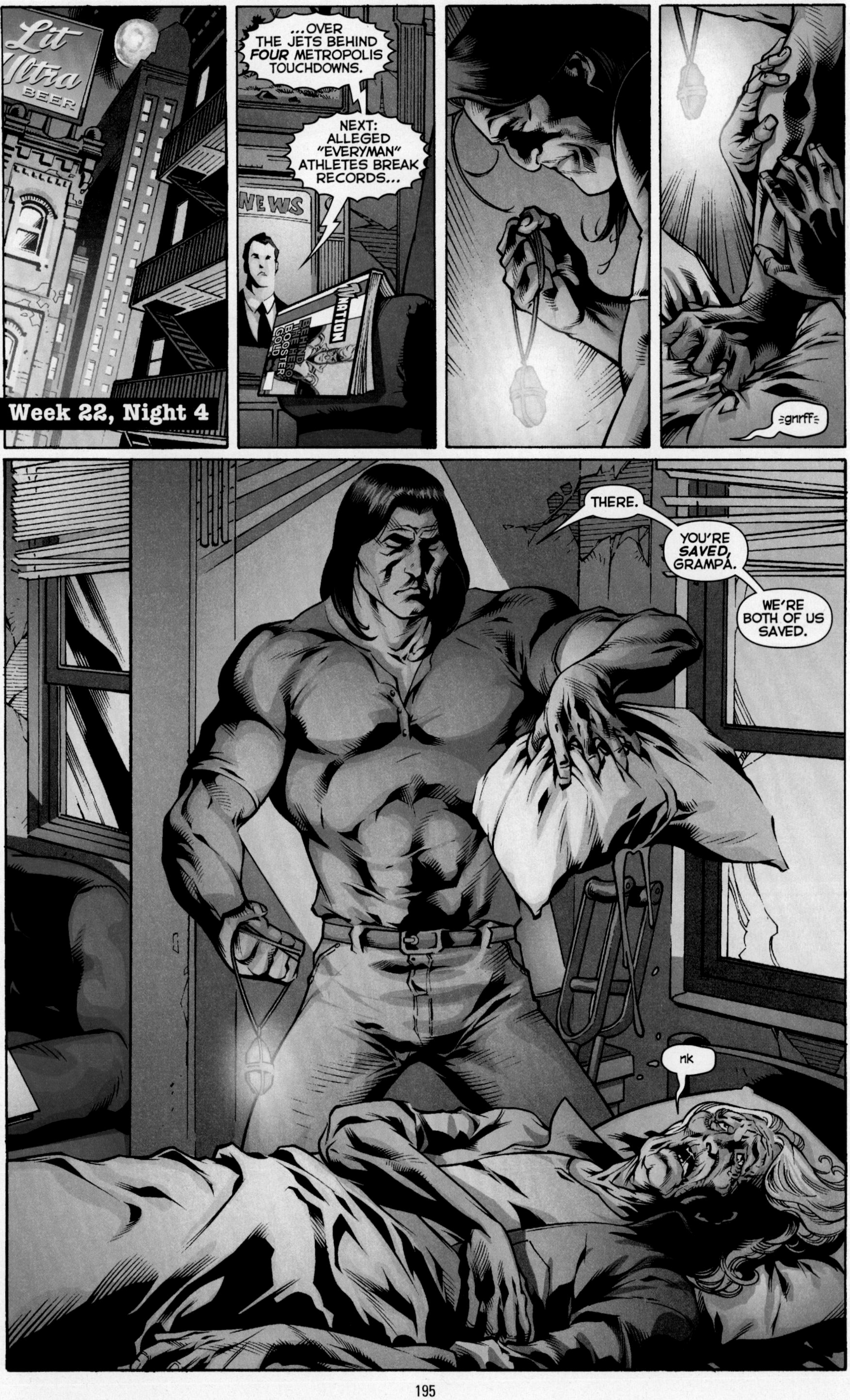

Lit Ultra BEER
Week 22, Night 4
...OVER THE JETS BEHIND FOUR METROPOLIS TOUCHDOWNS.
NEXT: ALLEGED "EVERYMAN" ATHLETES BREAK RECORDS...
NEWS
NATION
BEHIND THE HERO BOOSTER GOLD
gnrff
THERE.
YOU'RE SAVED, GRAMPA.
WE'RE BOTH OF US SAVED.
nk

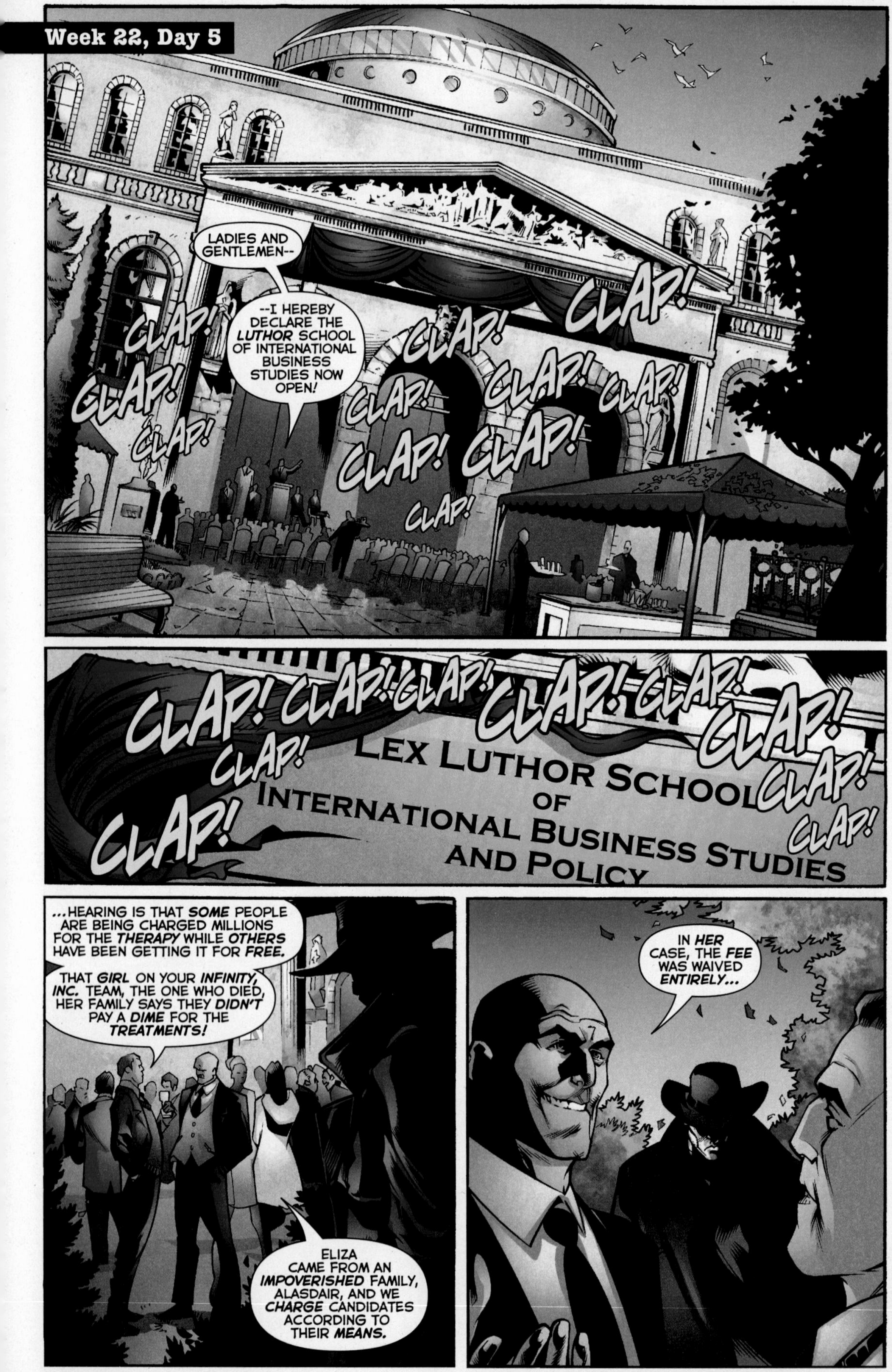
Week 22, Day 5
LADIES AND GENTLEMEN--
--I HEREBY DECLARE THE LUTHOR SCHOOL OF INTERNATIONAL BUSINESS STUDIES NOW OPEN!
CLAP! CLAP! CLAP! CLAP! CLAP! CLAP! CLAP! CLAP! CLAP! CLAP!
LEX LUTHOR SCHOOL OF INTERNATIONAL BUSINESS STUDIES AND POLICY
CLAP! CLAP! CLAP! CLAP! CLAP! CLAP! CLAP! CLAP! CLAP! CLAP!
...HEARING IS THAT SOME PEOPLE ARE BEING CHARGED MILLIONS FOR THE THERAPY WHILE OTHERS HAVE BEEN GETTING IT FOR FREE.
THAT GIRL ON YOUR INFINITY, INC. TEAM, THE ONE WHO DIED, HER FAMILY SAYS THEY DIDN'T PAY A DIME FOR THE TREATMENTS!
ELIZA CAME FROM AN IMPOVERISHED FAMILY, ALASDAIR, AND WE CHARGE CANDIDATES ACCORDING TO THEIR MEANS.
IN HER CASE, THE FEE WAS WAIVED ENTIRELY...

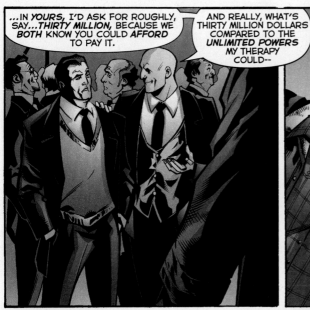

...IN *YOURS*, I'D ASK FOR ROUGHLY, SAY...*THIRTY MILLION*, BECAUSE WE *BOTH* KNOW YOU COULD *AFFORD* TO PAY IT.

AND REALLY, WHAT'S *THIRTY MILLION DOLLARS* COMPARED TO THE *UNLIMITED POWERS* MY THERAPY COULD--

LIAR!

UNLIMITED *POWER*, YEAH, FOR *YOU*, FOR *LEX LUTHOR!*

SCREW THE *REST* OF US! IT'S ABOUT *CONTROL!* HE *GIVES* YOU THESE *POWERS* AND THEN HE *TAKES* THEM *AWAY* AGAIN!

MISTER *FERRY*, WHAT A *PLEASURE* TO SEE YOU *AGAIN...*

...AND HERE I THOUGHT THE *RESTRAINING* ORDER REQUIRED THAT YOU KEEP A HUNDRED YARDS *AWAY* FROM ME AT *ALL* TIMES.

I'M *ON* TO YOU, LUTHOR, I'M GOING TO TELL THE *WORLD*--

GET *OUT* OF HERE, FERRY...

AHH!!!

...BEFORE I GET ALL *THEMYSCIRA* ON YOUR *ASS.*

≠HNFF≠

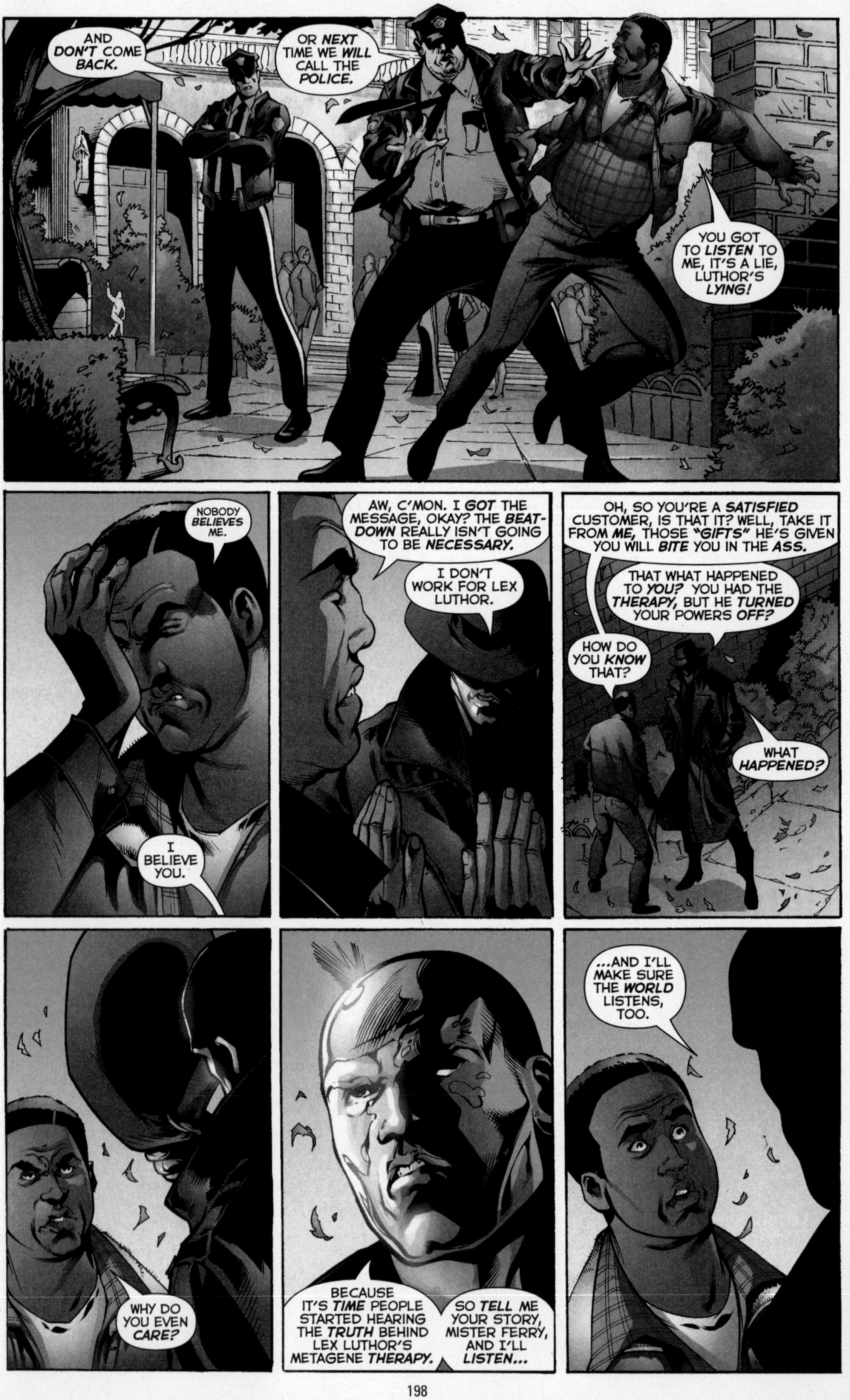
AND DON'T COME BACK.
OR NEXT TIME WE WILL CALL THE POLICE.
YOU GOT TO LISTEN TO ME, IT'S A LIE, LUTHOR'S LYING!
NOBODY BELIEVES ME.
I BELIEVE YOU.
AW, C'MON. I GOT THE MESSAGE, OKAY? THE BEAT-DOWN REALLY ISN'T GOING TO BE NECESSARY.
I DON'T WORK FOR LEX LUTHOR.
OH, SO YOU'RE A SATISFIED CUSTOMER, IS THAT IT? WELL, TAKE IT FROM ME, THOSE "GIFTS" HE'S GIVEN YOU WILL BITE YOU IN THE ASS.
THAT WHAT HAPPENED TO YOU? YOU HAD THE THERAPY, BUT HE TURNED YOUR POWERS OFF?
HOW DO YOU KNOW THAT?
WHAT HAPPENED?
WHY DO YOU EVEN CARE?
BECAUSE IT'S TIME PEOPLE STARTED HEARING THE TRUTH BEHIND LEX LUTHOR'S METAGENE THERAPY.
SO TELL ME YOUR STORY, MISTER FERRY, AND I'LL LISTEN...
...AND I'LL MAKE SURE THE WORLD LISTENS, TOO.

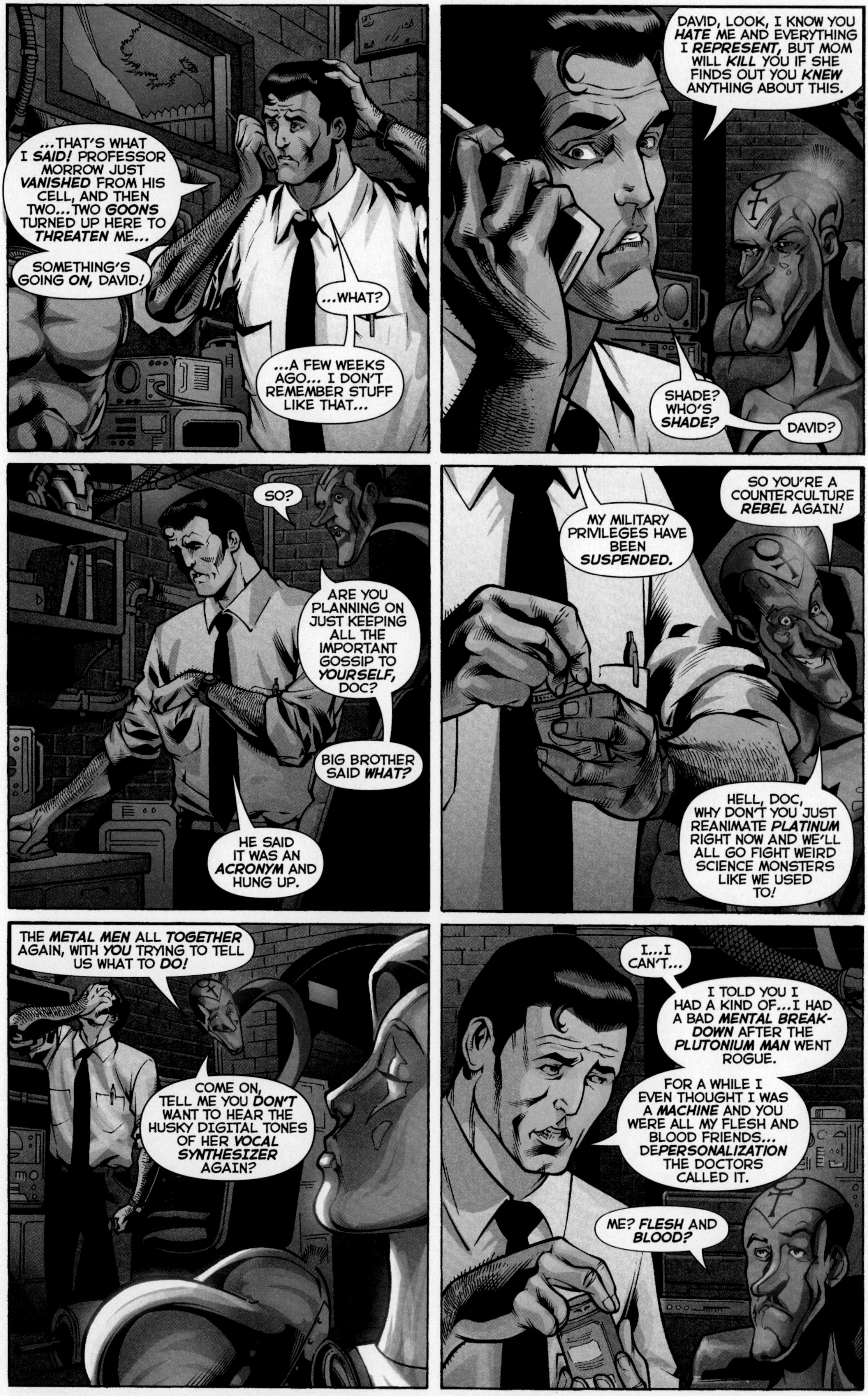
...THAT'S WHAT I SAID! PROFESSOR MORROW JUST VANISHED FROM HIS CELL, AND THEN TWO...TWO GOONS TURNED UP HERE TO THREATEN ME...
SOMETHING'S GOING ON, DAVID!
...WHAT?
...A FEW WEEKS AGO... I DON'T REMEMBER STUFF LIKE THAT...
DAVID, LOOK, I KNOW YOU HATE ME AND EVERYTHING I REPRESENT, BUT MOM WILL KILL YOU IF SHE FINDS OUT YOU KNEW ANYTHING ABOUT THIS.
SHADE? WHO'S SHADE?
DAVID?
SO?
ARE YOU PLANNING ON JUST KEEPING ALL THE IMPORTANT GOSSIP TO YOURSELF, DOC?
BIG BROTHER SAID WHAT?
HE SAID IT WAS AN ACRONYM AND HUNG UP.
MY MILITARY PRIVILEGES HAVE BEEN SUSPENDED.
SO YOU'RE A COUNTERCULTURE REBEL AGAIN!
HELL, DOC, WHY DON'T YOU JUST REANIMATE PLATINUM RIGHT NOW AND WE'LL ALL GO FIGHT WEIRD SCIENCE MONSTERS LIKE WE USED TO!
THE METAL MEN ALL TOGETHER AGAIN, WITH YOU TRYING TO TELL US WHAT TO DO!
COME ON, TELL ME YOU DON'T WANT TO HEAR THE HUSKY DIGITAL TONES OF HER VOCAL SYNTHESIZER AGAIN?
I...I CAN'T...
I TOLD YOU I HAD A KIND OF...I HAD A BAD MENTAL BREAK-DOWN AFTER THE PLUTONIUM MAN WENT ROGUE.
FOR A WHILE I EVEN THOUGHT I WAS A MACHINE AND YOU WERE ALL MY FLESH AND BLOOD FRIENDS... DEPERSONALIZATION THE DOCTORS CALLED IT.
ME? FLESH AND BLOOD?

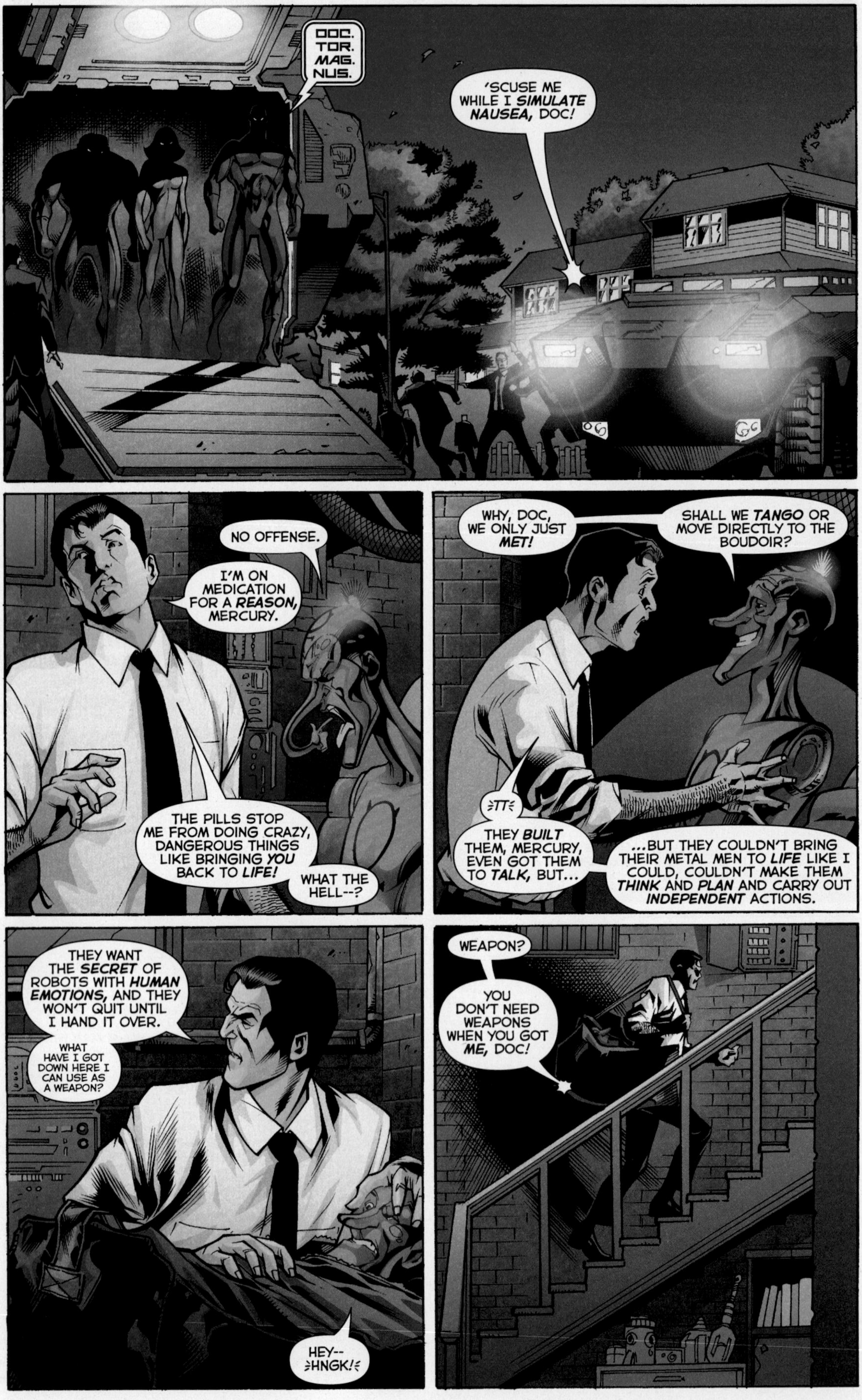
DOC. TOR. MAG. NUS.
'SCUSE ME WHILE I SIMULATE NAUSEA, DOC!
NO OFFENSE.
I'M ON MEDICATION FOR A REASON, MERCURY.
THE PILLS STOP ME FROM DOING CRAZY, DANGEROUS THINGS LIKE BRINGING YOU BACK TO LIFE!
WHAT THE HELL--?
WHY, DOC, WE ONLY JUST MET!
SHALL WE TANGO OR MOVE DIRECTLY TO THE BOUDOIR?
TT
THEY BUILT THEM, MERCURY, EVEN GOT THEM TO TALK, BUT...
...BUT THEY COULDN'T BRING THEIR METAL MEN TO LIFE LIKE I COULD, COULDN'T MAKE THEM THINK AND PLAN AND CARRY OUT INDEPENDENT ACTIONS.
THEY WANT THE SECRET OF ROBOTS WITH HUMAN EMOTIONS, AND THEY WON'T QUIT UNTIL I HAND IT OVER.
WHAT HAVE I GOT DOWN HERE I CAN USE AS A WEAPON?
HEY-- HNGK!
WEAPON?
YOU DON'T NEED WEAPONS WHEN YOU GOT ME, DOC!

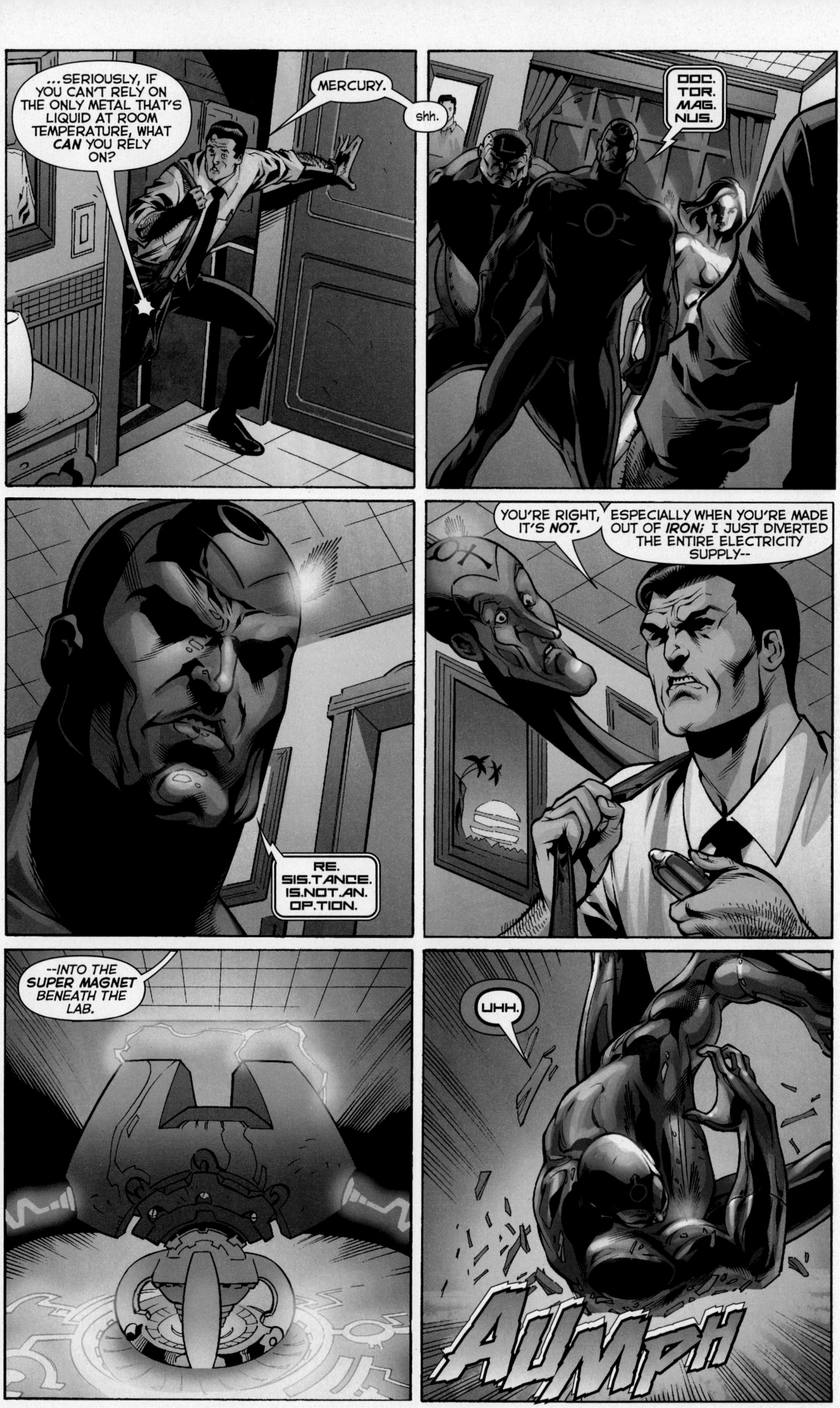
...SERIOUSLY, IF YOU CAN'T RELY ON THE ONLY METAL THAT'S LIQUID AT ROOM TEMPERATURE, WHAT CAN YOU RELY ON?
MERCURY.
shh.
DOC. TOR. MAG. NUS.
RE. SIS. TANCE. IS. NOT. AN. OP. TION.
YOU'RE RIGHT, IT'S NOT.
ESPECIALLY WHEN YOU'RE MADE OUT OF IRON; I JUST DIVERTED THE ENTIRE ELECTRICITY SUPPLY--
--INTO THE SUPER MAGNET BENEATH THE LAB.
UHH.
AUMPH

GO FOR IT, DOC!

THE FAT ONE'S MINE!

UNNH!

WHY?

AQUA REGIA.

A FRESH MIX OF CONCENTRATED HYDROCHLORIC AND NITRIC ACIDS.

IT DISSOLVES PLATINUM.

EEEEEE-11001010010

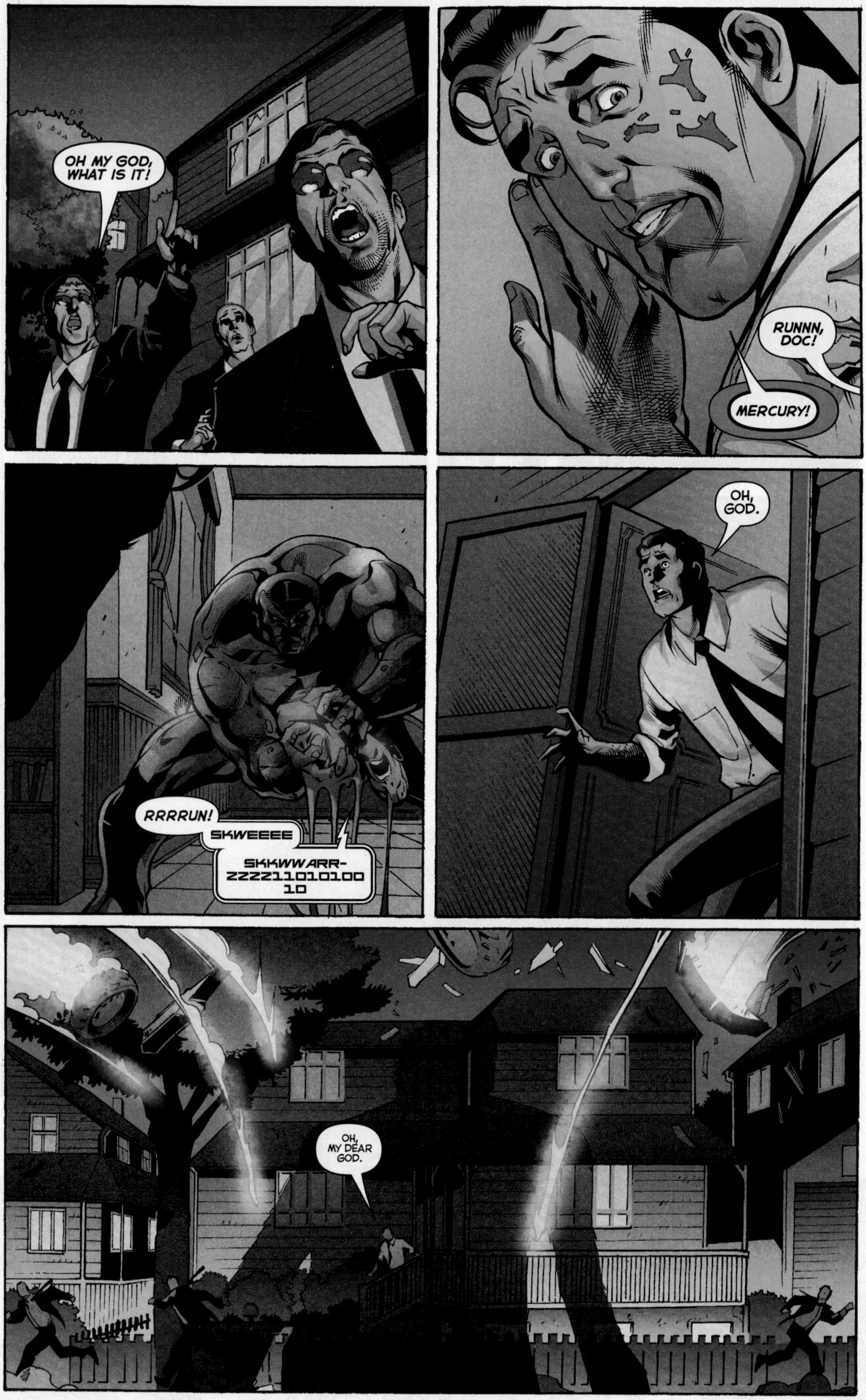
OH MY GOD, WHAT IS IT!
RUNNN, DOC!
MERCURY!
RRRRUN!
SKWEEEE
SKKWWARR-ZZZZ11010100 10
OH, GOD.
OH, MY DEAR GOD.

BY **EDDY BARROWS**

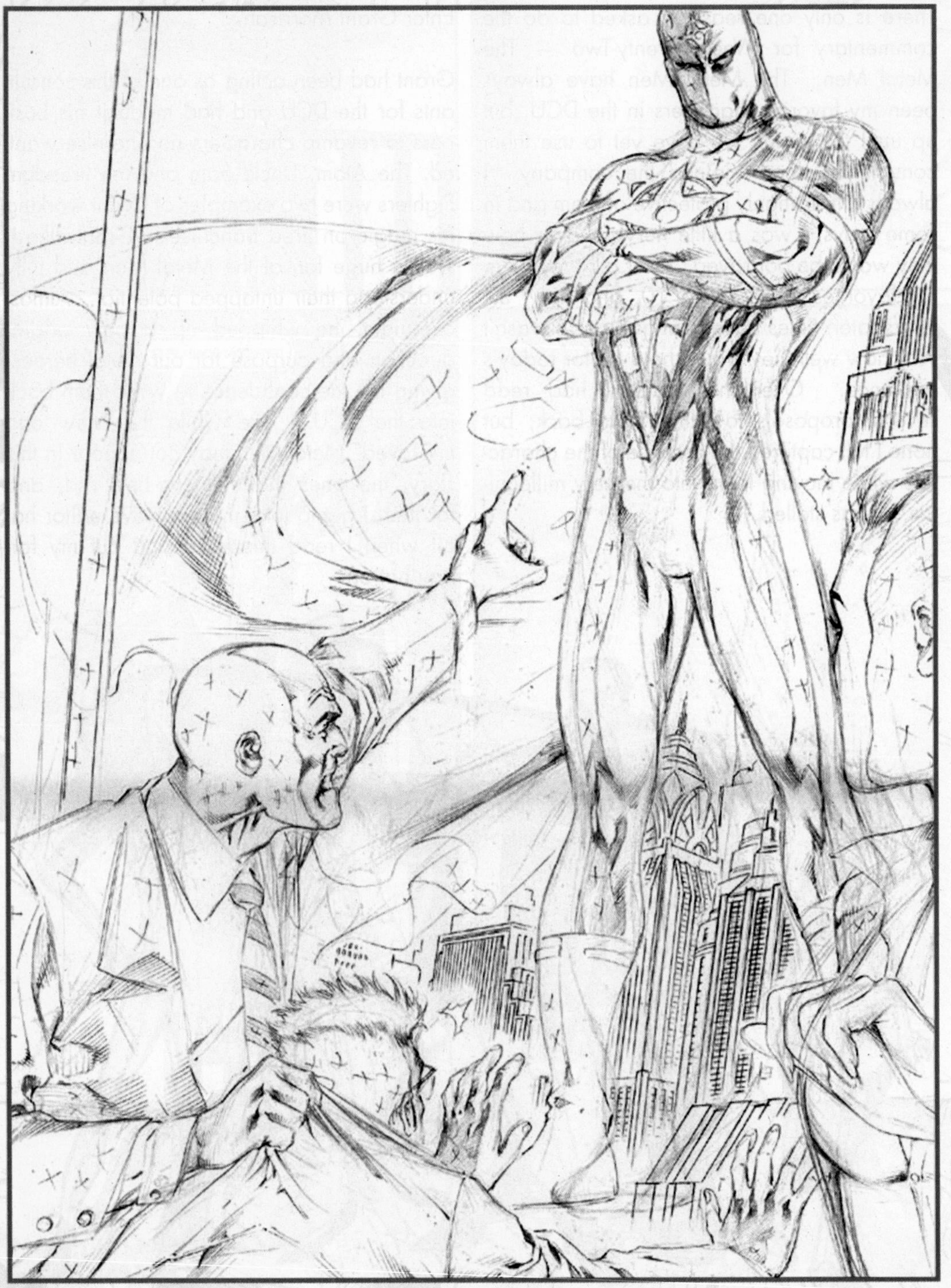

The original pencils to page 187 had a frontal-shot splash page of Supernova, before the decision was made to reverse the angle.

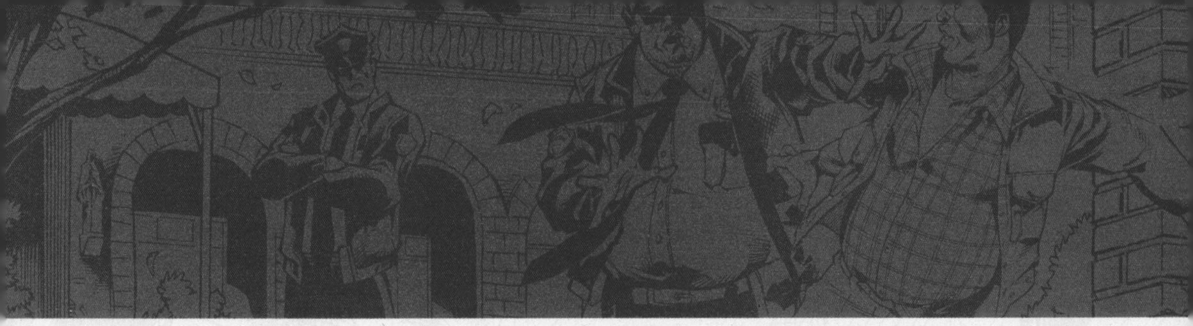

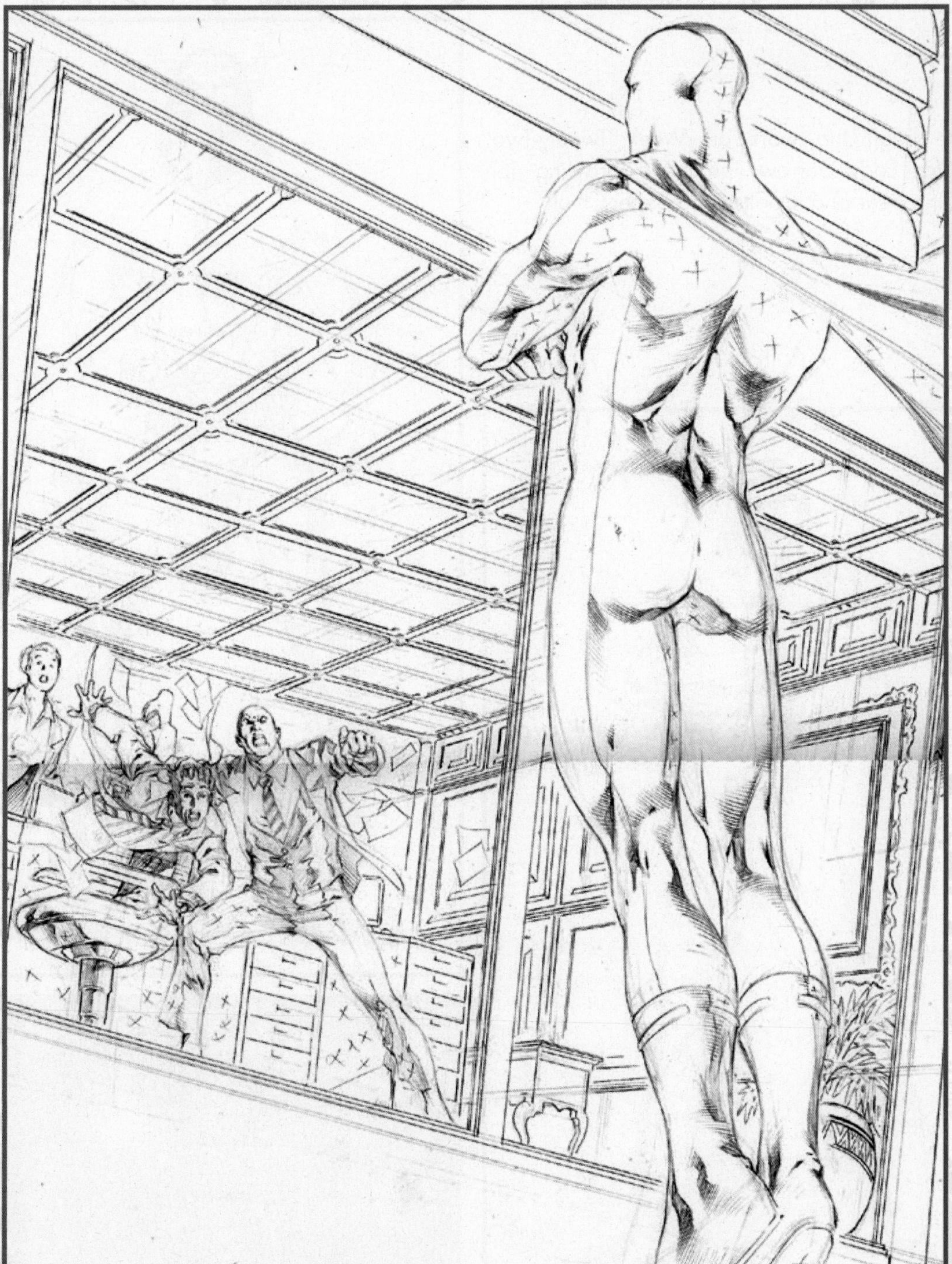

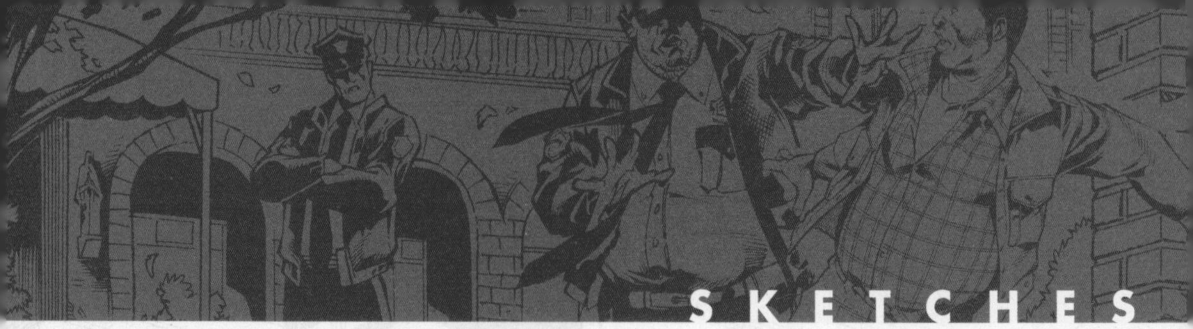

SKETCHES

BY **EDDY BARROWS**

Before beginning work on Week Twenty-Two, penciller Eddy Barrows practiced drawing Jon Standing Bear and his alter ego Super-Chief.

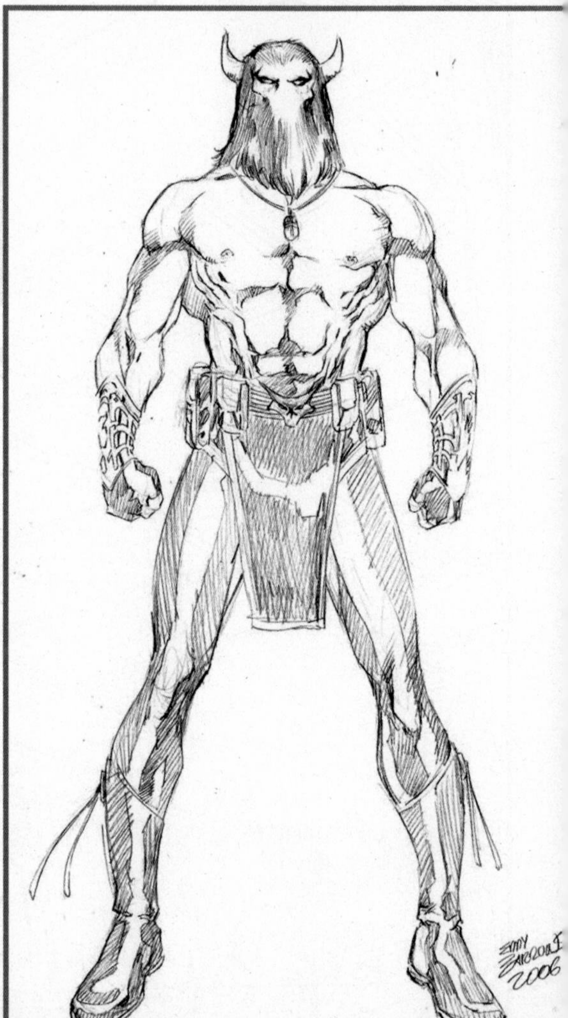
EDDY BARROWS 2006

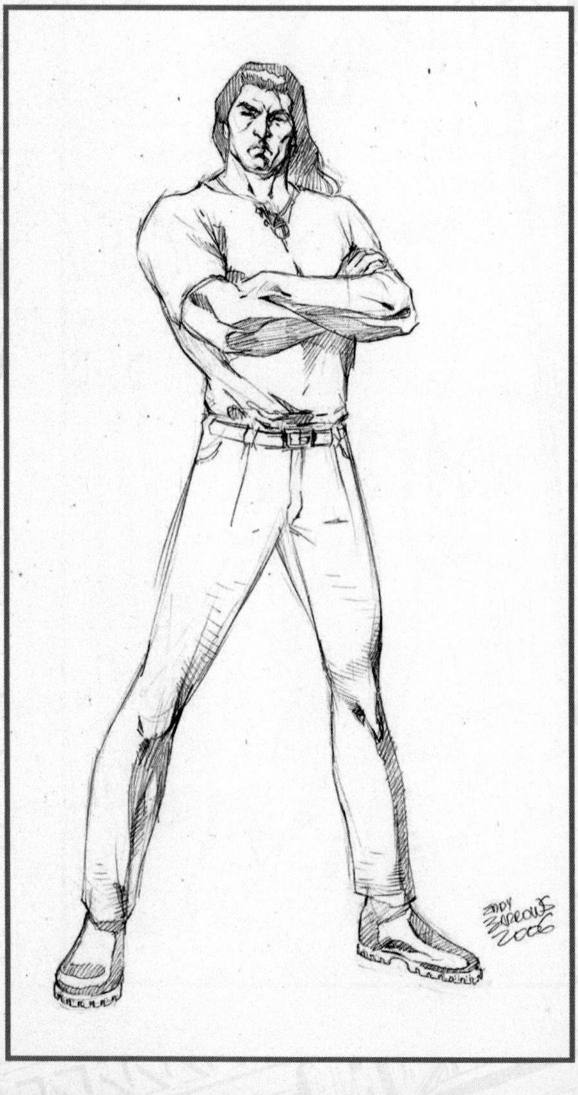
EDDY BARROWS 2006

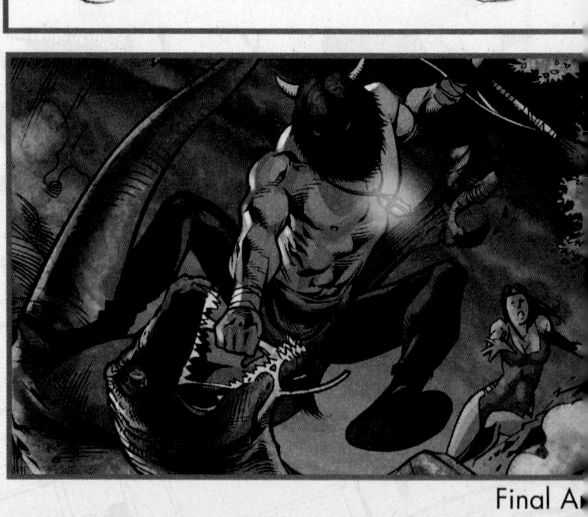

Final A

DC COMICS 5

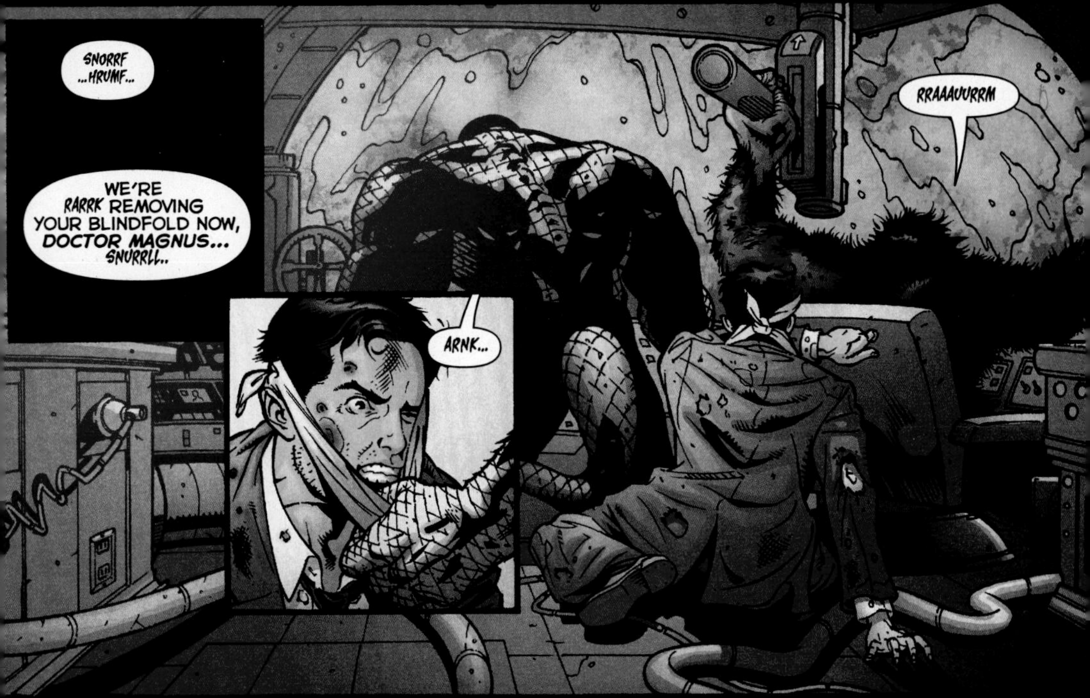

SNORRF ...HRUMF...
WE'RE RARRK REMOVING YOUR BLINDFOLD NOW, DOCTOR MAGNUS... SNURRLL..
RRAAAUURRM
ARNK...

RITTEN BY GEOFF JOHNS, GRANT MORRISON, GREG RUCKA, MARK WA

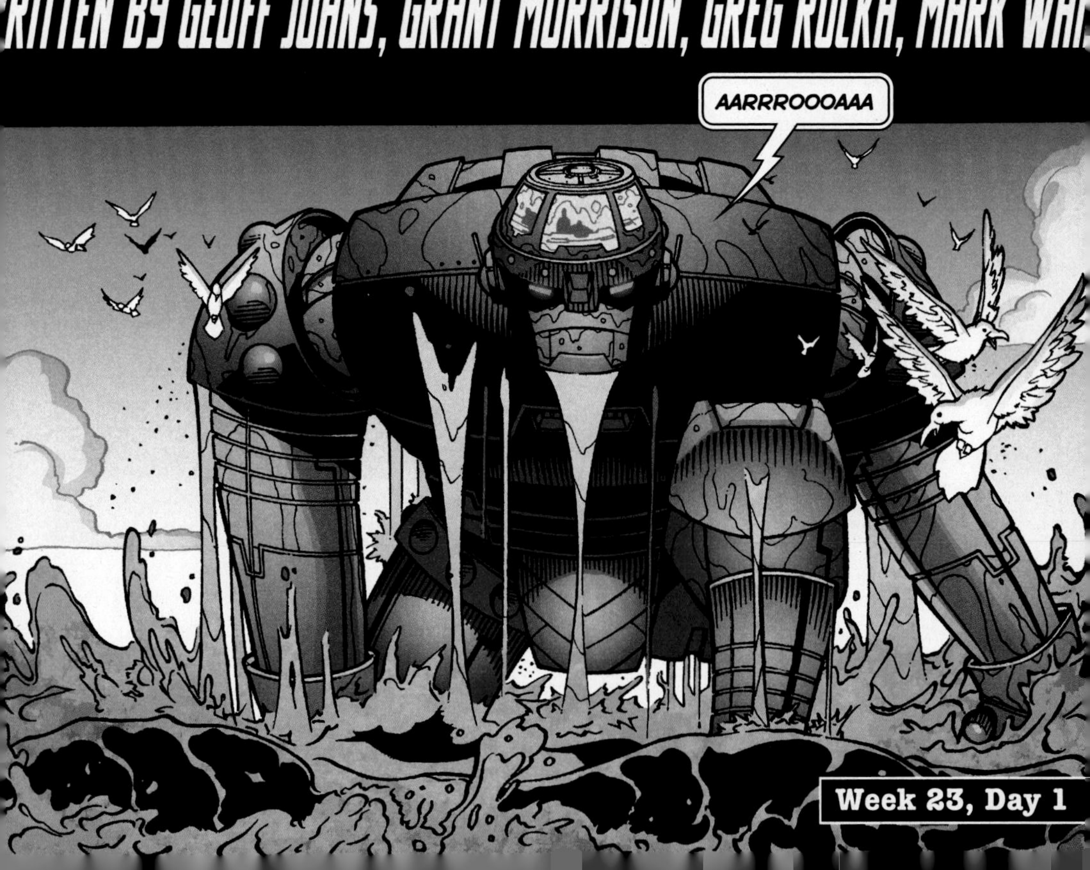

AARRROOOAAA
Week 23, Day 1

ART BREAKDOWNS BY KEITH GIFFEN • PENCILS BY DREW JOHNSON •
NKS BY RAY SNYDER • COLORS BY DAVID BARON • LETTERING BY TRAVIS LANHA

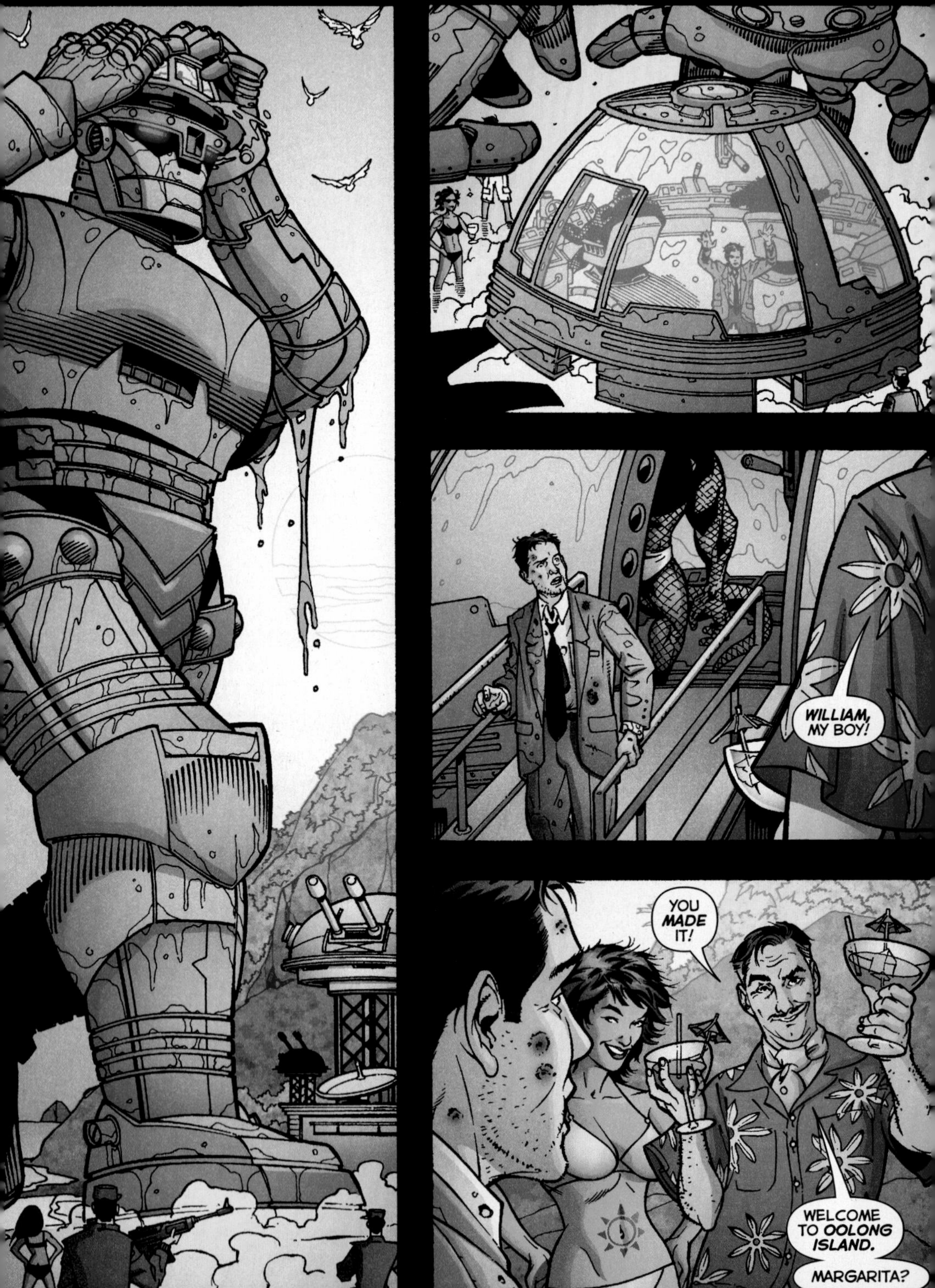

WILLIAM, MY BOY!
YOU MADE IT!
WELCOME TO OOLONG ISLAND.
MARGARITA?

ASSISTANT EDITORS HARVEY RICHARDS & JEANINE SCHAEFER
EDITED BY STEPHEN WACKER • COVER BY J.G. JONES & SINCLAIR

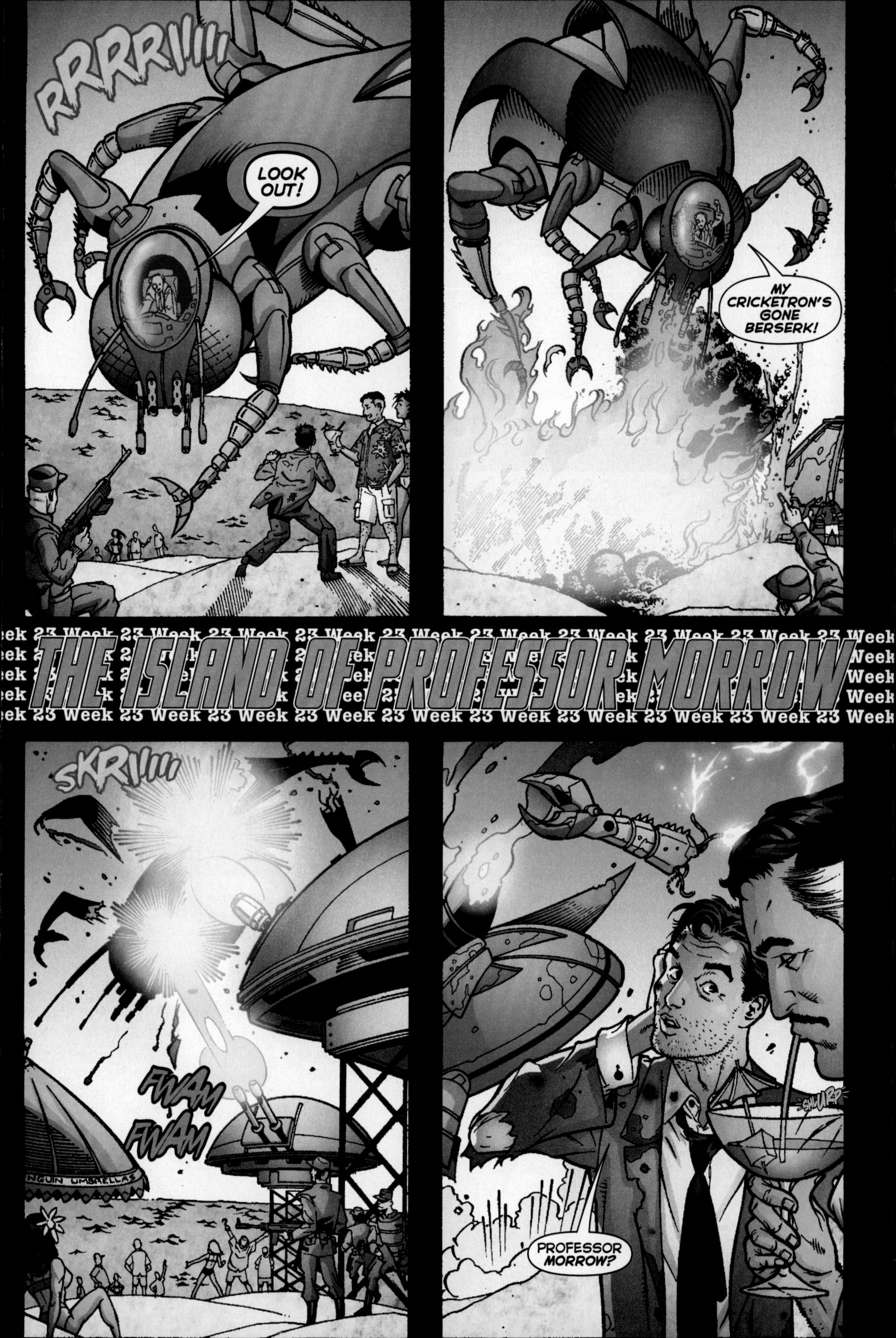
RRRR!!!!!
LOOK OUT!
MY CRICKETRON'S GONE BERSERK!
Week 23 Week 23 Week 23 Week 23 Week 23 Week 23 Week 23 Week
THE ISLAND OF PROFESSOR MORROW
SKRI!!!!
FWAM
FWAM
NGUIN UMBRELLAS
SHLURP
PROFESSOR MORROW?

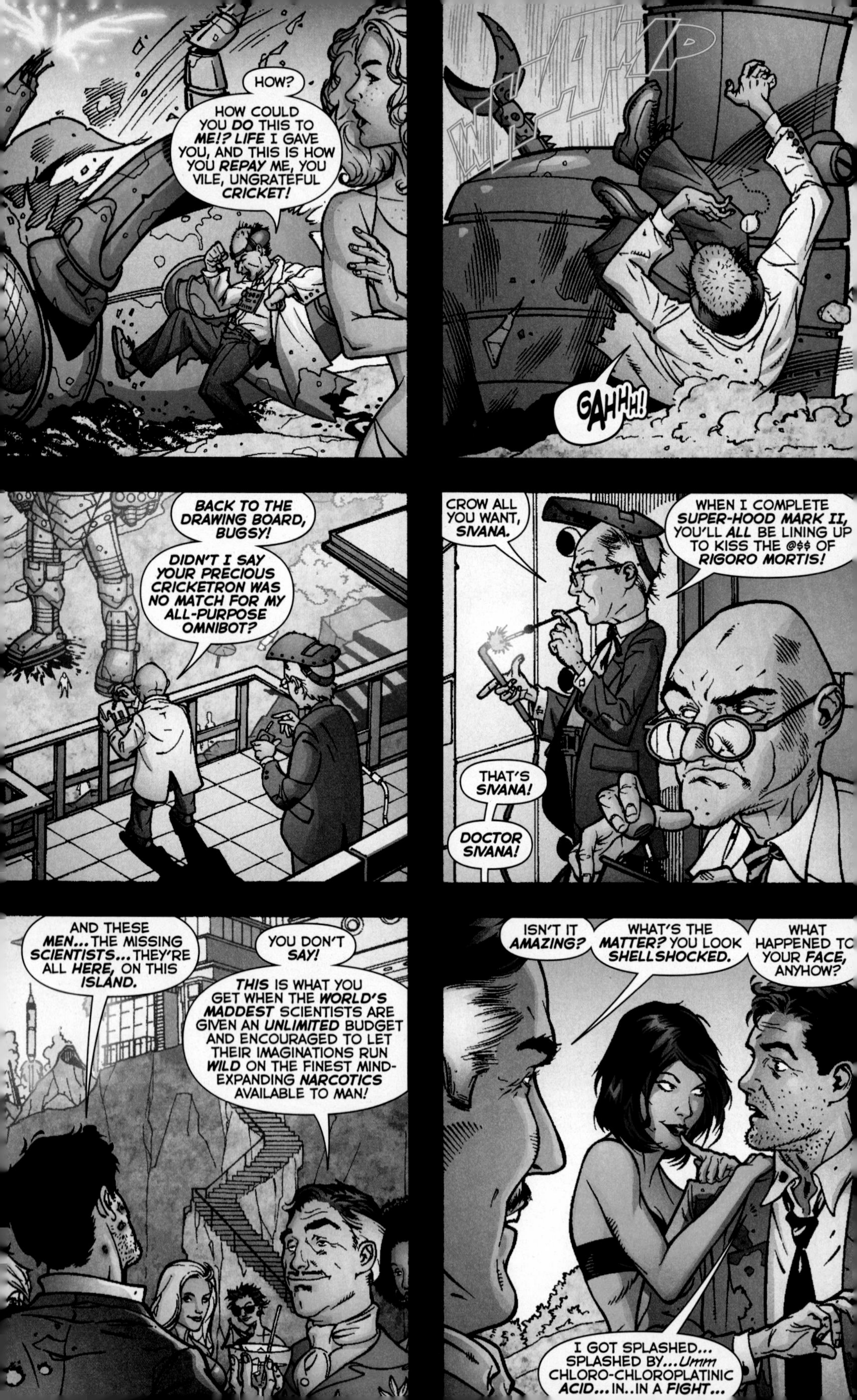
HOW?
HOW COULD YOU DO THIS TO ME!? LIFE I GAVE YOU, AND THIS IS HOW YOU REPAY ME, YOU VILE, UNGRATEFUL CRICKET!
GAHHH!
BACK TO THE DRAWING BOARD, BUGSY!
DIDN'T I SAY YOUR PRECIOUS CRICKETRON WAS NO MATCH FOR MY ALL-PURPOSE OMNIBOT?
CROW ALL YOU WANT, SIVANA.
WHEN I COMPLETE SUPER-HOOD MARK II, YOU'LL ALL BE LINING UP TO KISS THE @$$ OF RIGORO MORTIS!
THAT'S SIVANA!
DOCTOR SIVANA!
AND THESE MEN... THE MISSING SCIENTISTS... THEY'RE ALL HERE, ON THIS ISLAND.
YOU DON'T SAY!
THIS IS WHAT YOU GET WHEN THE WORLD'S MADDEST SCIENTISTS ARE GIVEN AN UNLIMITED BUDGET AND ENCOURAGED TO LET THEIR IMAGINATIONS RUN WILD ON THE FINEST MIND-EXPANDING NARCOTICS AVAILABLE TO MAN!
ISN'T IT AMAZING?
WHAT'S THE MATTER? YOU LOOK SHELLSHOCKED.
WHAT HAPPENED TO YOUR FACE, ANYHOW?
I GOT SPLASHED... SPLASHED BY... Umm CHLORO-CHLOROPLATINIC ACID... IN.. IN A FIGHT...

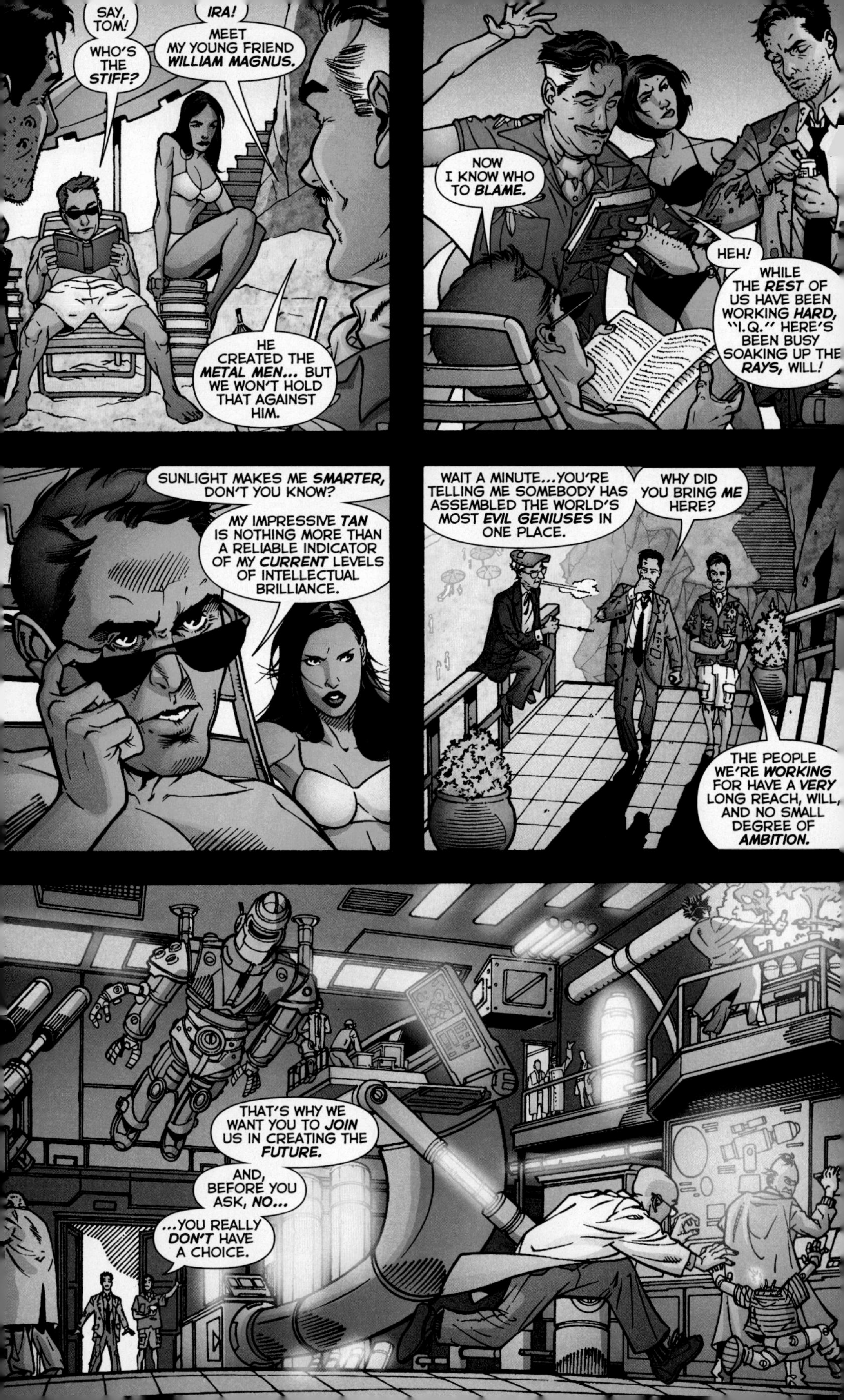
SAY, TOM!
WHO'S THE STIFF?
IRA!
MEET MY YOUNG FRIEND WILLIAM MAGNUS.
HE CREATED THE METAL MEN... BUT WE WON'T HOLD THAT AGAINST HIM.
NOW I KNOW WHO TO BLAME.
HEH!
WHILE THE REST OF US HAVE BEEN WORKING HARD, "I.Q." HERE'S BEEN BUSY SOAKING UP THE RAYS, WILL!
SUNLIGHT MAKES ME SMARTER, DON'T YOU KNOW?
MY IMPRESSIVE TAN IS NOTHING MORE THAN A RELIABLE INDICATOR OF MY CURRENT LEVELS OF INTELLECTUAL BRILLIANCE.
WAIT A MINUTE...YOU'RE TELLING ME SOMEBODY HAS ASSEMBLED THE WORLD'S MOST EVIL GENIUSES IN ONE PLACE.
WHY DID YOU BRING ME HERE?
THE PEOPLE WE'RE WORKING FOR HAVE A VERY LONG REACH, WILL, AND NO SMALL DEGREE OF AMBITION.
THAT'S WHY WE WANT YOU TO JOIN US IN CREATING THE FUTURE.
AND, BEFORE YOU ASK, NO...
...YOU REALLY DON'T HAVE A CHOICE.

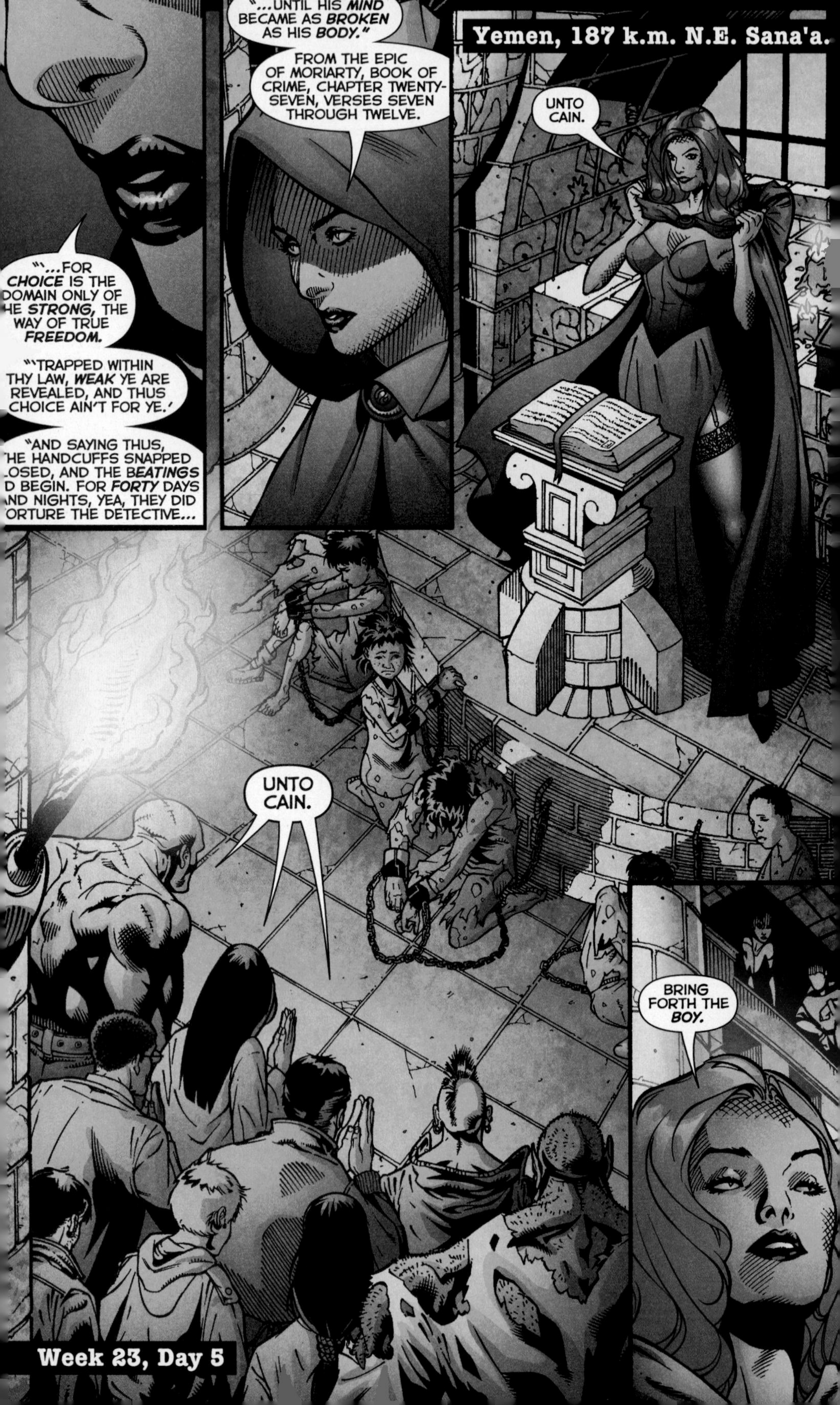
"'...FOR CHOICE IS THE DOMAIN ONLY OF THE STRONG, THE WAY OF TRUE FREEDOM.
"'TRAPPED WITHIN THY LAW, WEAK YE ARE REVEALED, AND THUS CHOICE AIN'T FOR YE.'
"AND SAYING THUS, THE HANDCUFFS SNAPPED CLOSED, AND THE BEATINGS DID BEGIN. FOR FORTY DAYS AND NIGHTS, YEA, THEY DID TORTURE THE DETECTIVE...
"...UNTIL HIS MIND BECAME AS BROKEN AS HIS BODY."
FROM THE EPIC OF MORIARTY, BOOK OF CRIME, CHAPTER TWENTY-SEVEN, VERSES SEVEN THROUGH TWELVE.
Yemen, 187 k.m. N.E. Sana'a.
UNTO CAIN.
UNTO CAIN.
BRING FORTH THE BOY.
Week 23, Day 5

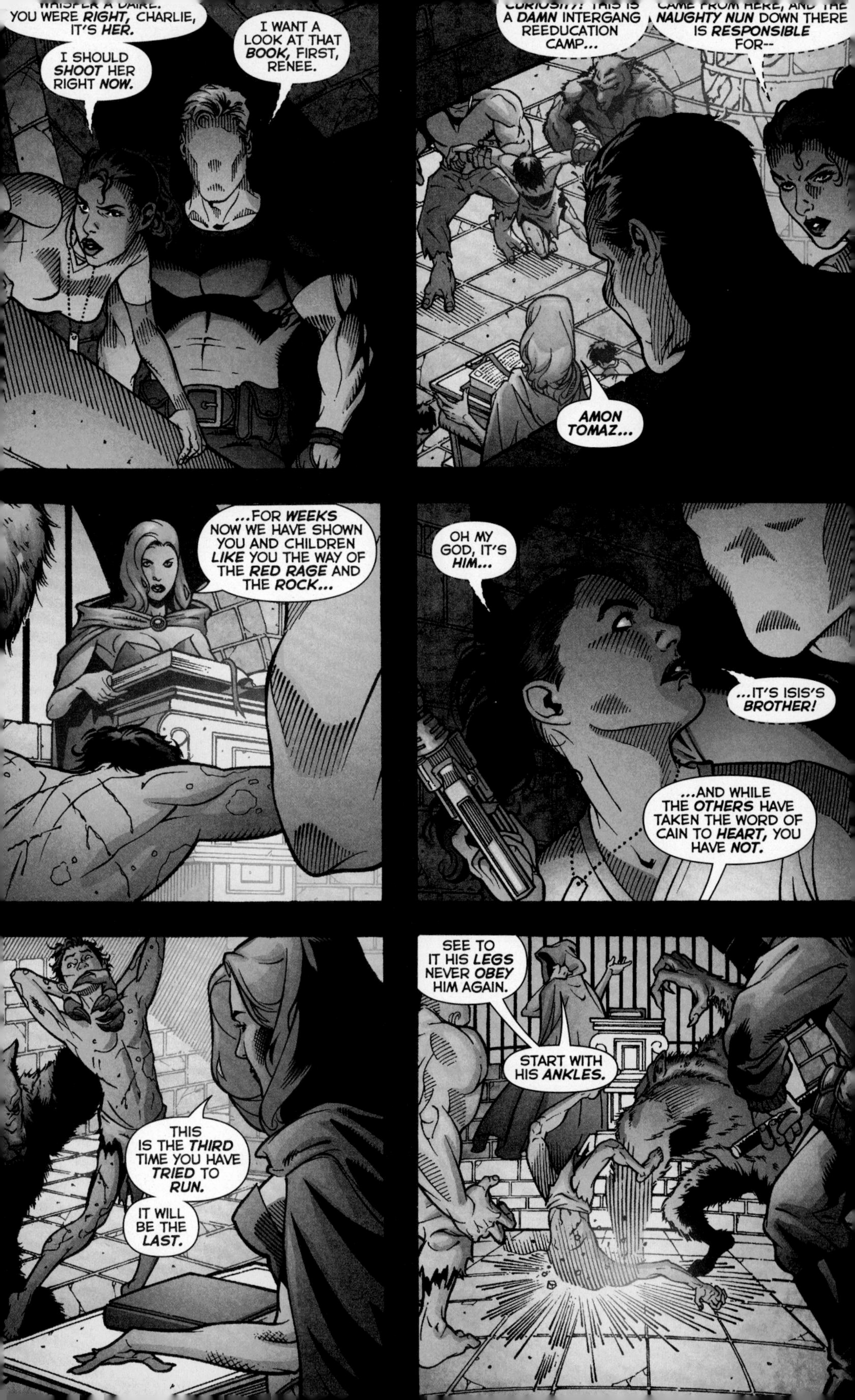
YOU WERE RIGHT, CHARLIE, IT'S HER.
I SHOULD SHOOT HER RIGHT NOW.
I WANT A LOOK AT THAT BOOK, FIRST, RENEE.
A DAMN INTERGANG REEDUCATION CAMP...
NAUGHTY NUN DOWN THERE IS RESPONSIBLE FOR--
AMON TOMAZ...
...FOR WEEKS NOW WE HAVE SHOWN YOU AND CHILDREN LIKE YOU THE WAY OF THE RED RAGE AND THE ROCK...
OH MY GOD, IT'S HIM...
...IT'S ISIS'S BROTHER!
...AND WHILE THE OTHERS HAVE TAKEN THE WORD OF CAIN TO HEART, YOU HAVE NOT.
THIS IS THE THIRD TIME YOU HAVE TRIED TO RUN.
IT WILL BE THE LAST.
SEE TO IT HIS LEGS NEVER OBEY HIM AGAIN.
START WITH HIS ANKLES.

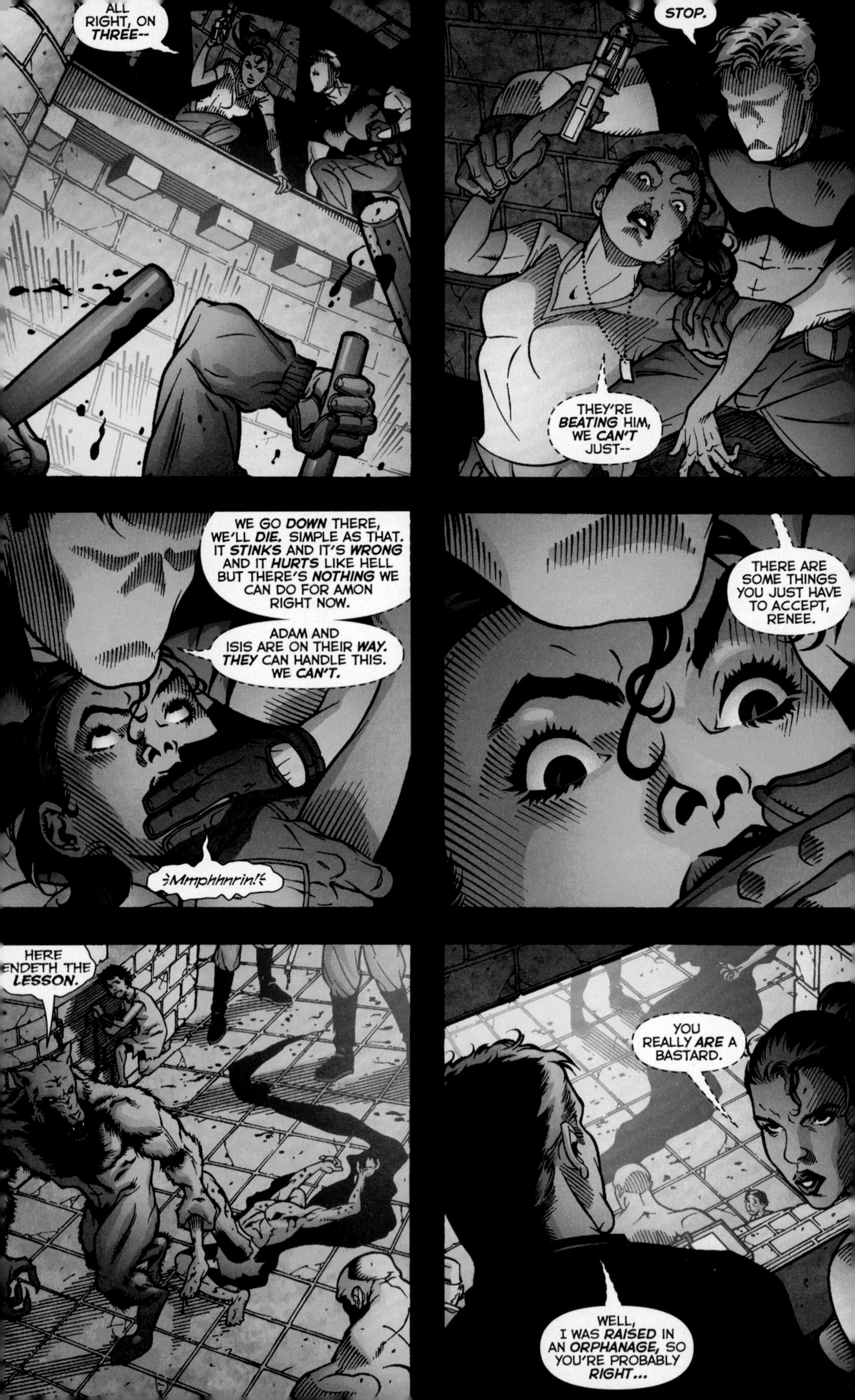
ALL RIGHT, ON THREE--
STOP.
THEY'RE BEATING HIM, WE CAN'T JUST--
WE GO DOWN THERE, WE'LL DIE. SIMPLE AS THAT. IT STINKS AND IT'S WRONG AND IT HURTS LIKE HELL BUT THERE'S NOTHING WE CAN DO FOR AMON RIGHT NOW.
ADAM AND ISIS ARE ON THEIR WAY. THEY CAN HANDLE THIS. WE CAN'T.
Mmphhnrin!
THERE ARE SOME THINGS YOU JUST HAVE TO ACCEPT, RENEE.
HERE ENDETH THE LESSON.
YOU REALLY ARE A BASTARD.
WELL, I WAS RAISED IN AN ORPHANAGE, SO YOU'RE PROBABLY RIGHT...

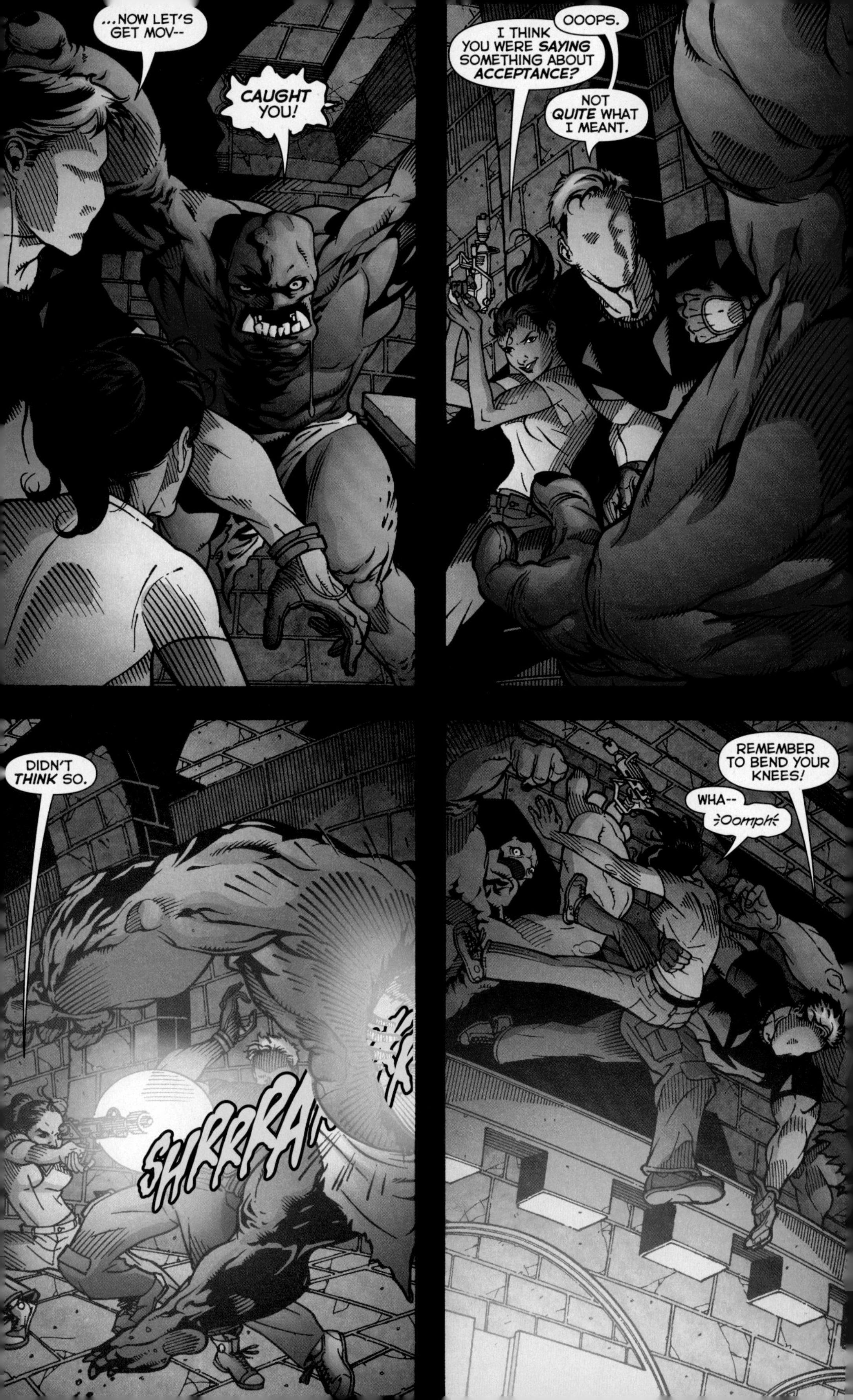
...NOW LET'S GET MOV--
CAUGHT YOU!
OOOPS.
I THINK YOU WERE SAYING SOMETHING ABOUT ACCEPTANCE?
NOT QUITE WHAT I MEANT.
DIDN'T THINK SO.
SKRRRA
REMEMBER TO BEND YOUR KNEES!
WHA--
Oomph

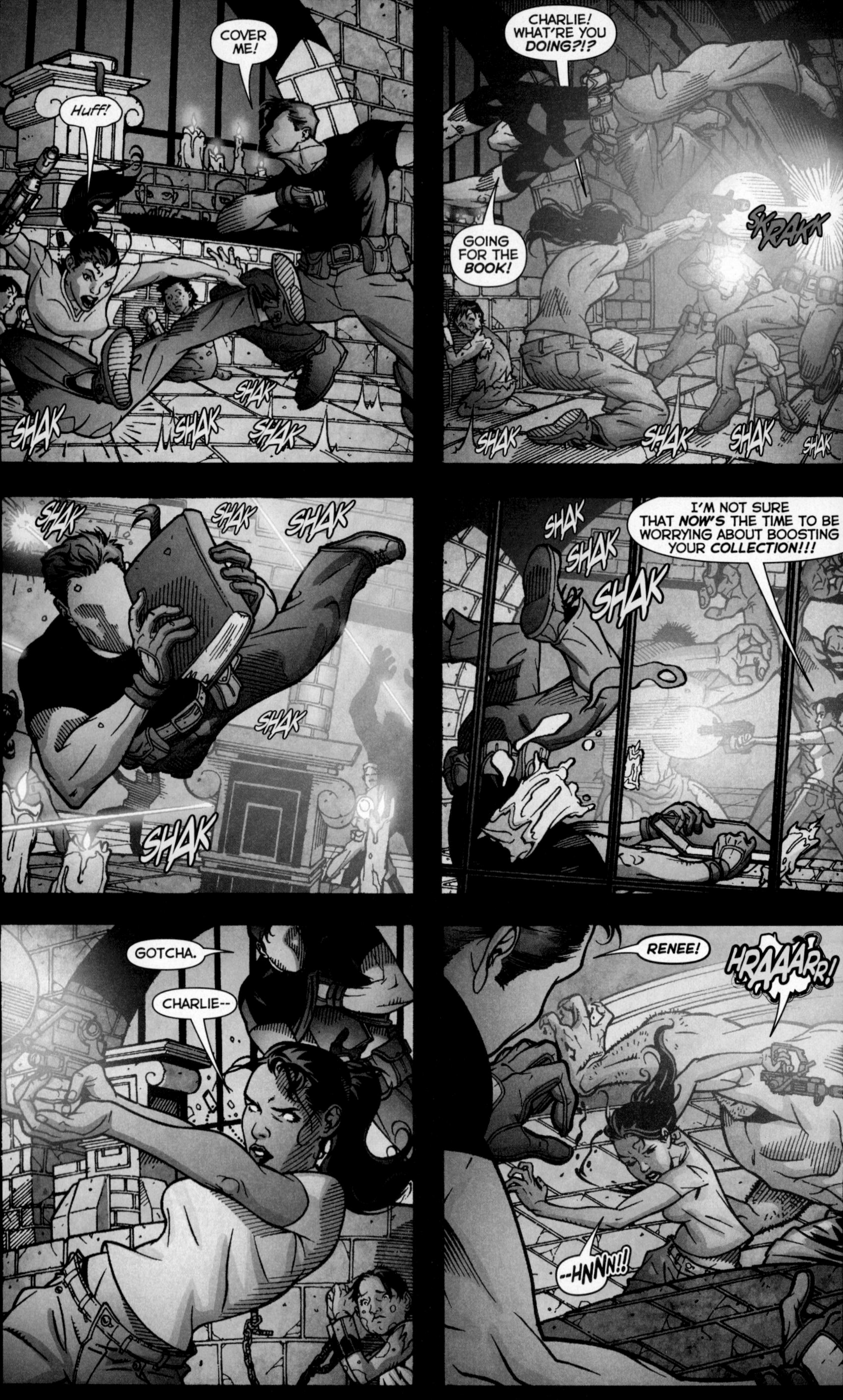
COVER ME!
Huff!
SHAK
SHAK
SHAK
SHAK
CHARLIE! WHAT'RE YOU DOING?!?
GOING FOR THE BOOK!
SKRAKK
SHAK
SHAK
SHAK
SHAK
SHAK
SHAK
SHAK
SHAK
SHAK
SHAK
SHAK
SHAK
I'M NOT SURE THAT NOW'S THE TIME TO BE WORRYING ABOUT BOOSTING YOUR COLLECTION!!!
GOTCHA.
CHARLIE--
RENEE!
HRAAARR!
--HNNN!!

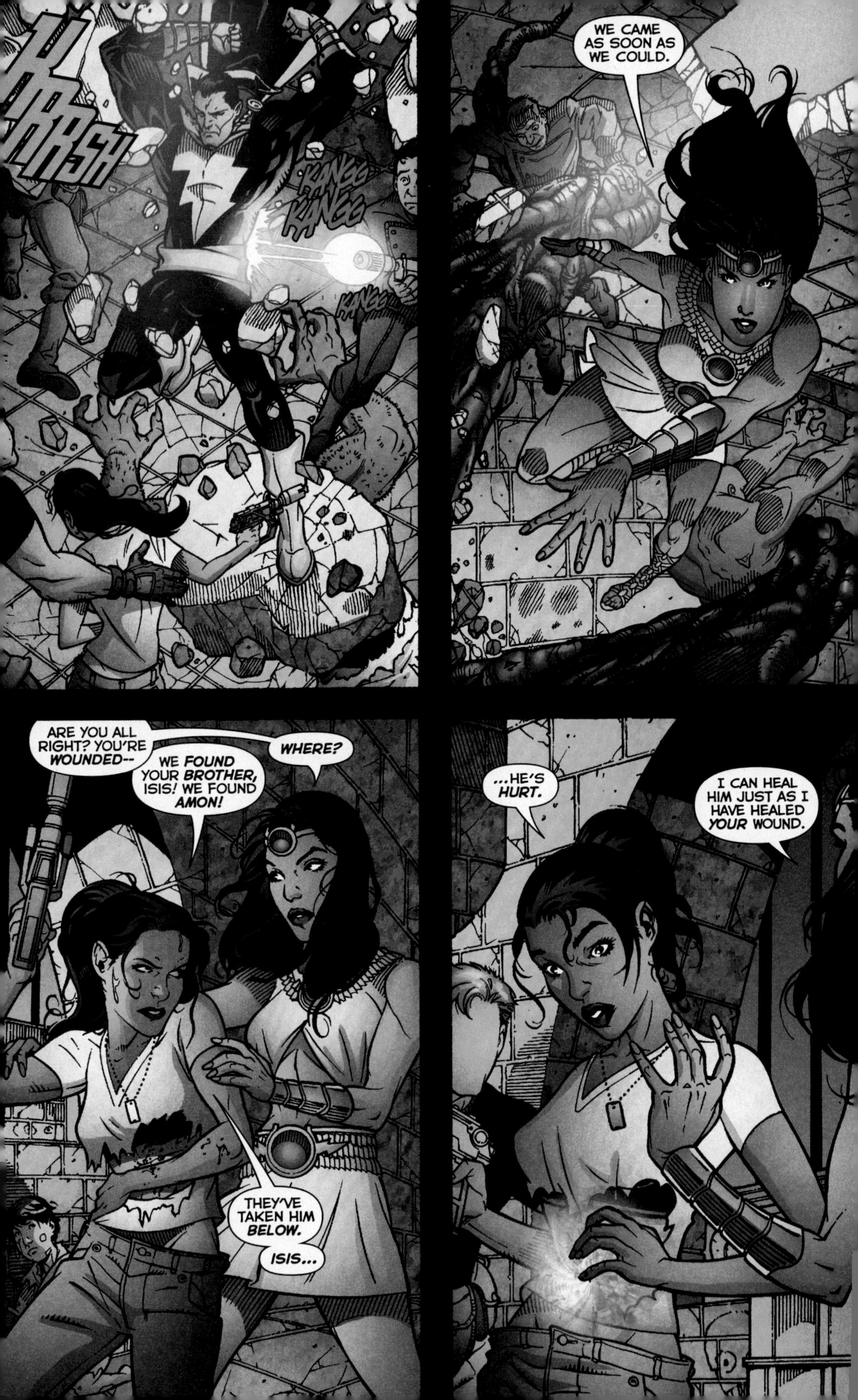
KRRRSH
KANGG KANGG
KANGG
WE CAME AS SOON AS WE COULD.
ARE YOU ALL RIGHT? YOU'RE *WOUNDED*--
WE *FOUND* YOUR *BROTHER*, ISIS! WE FOUND *AMON*!
WHERE?
THEY'VE TAKEN HIM *BELOW.*
ISIS...
...HE'S *HURT.*
I CAN HEAL HIM JUST AS I HAVE HEALED *YOUR* WOUND.

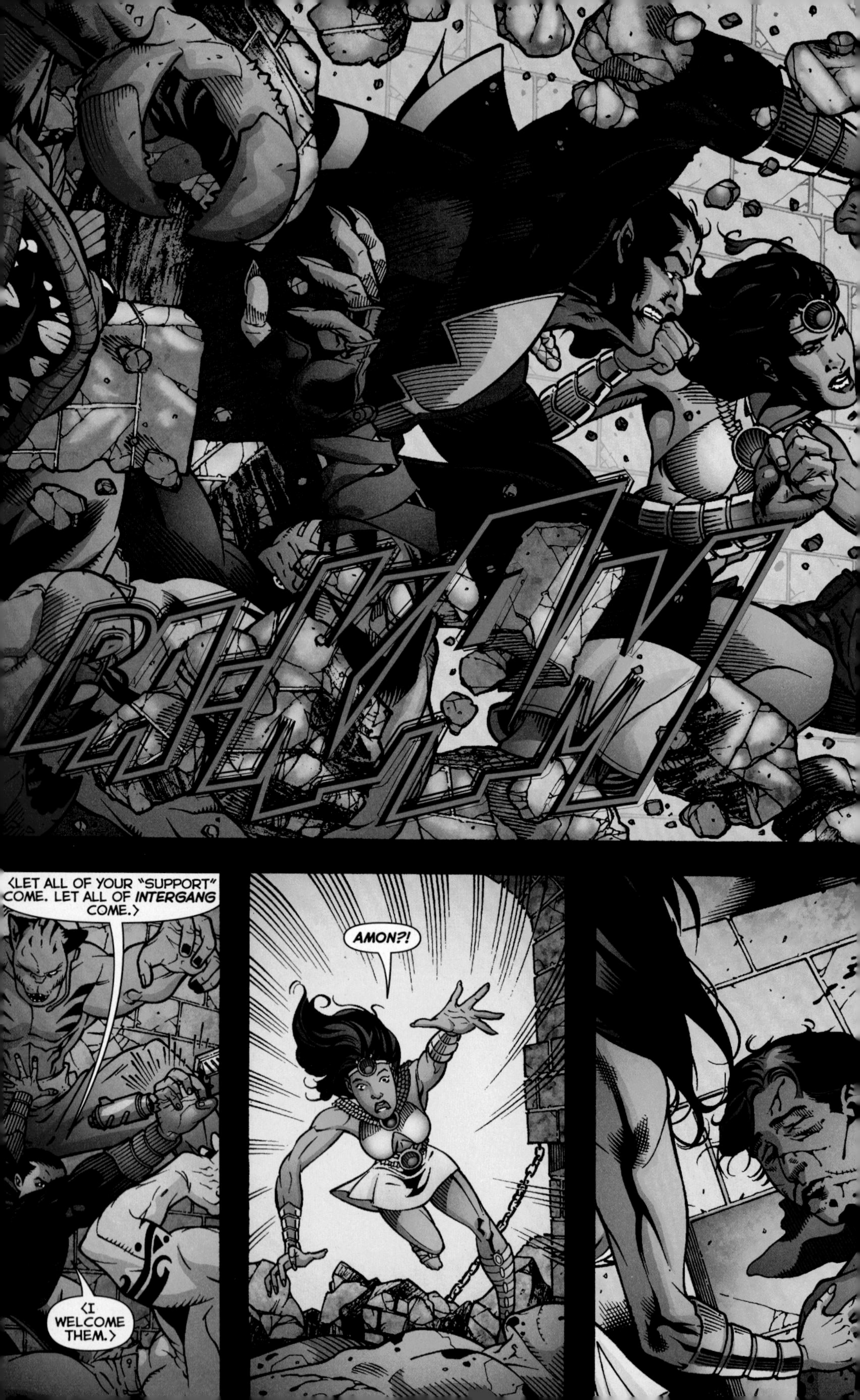

<LET ALL OF YOUR "SUPPORT" COME. LET ALL OF *INTERGANG* COME.>
AMON?!
<I WELCOME THEM.>

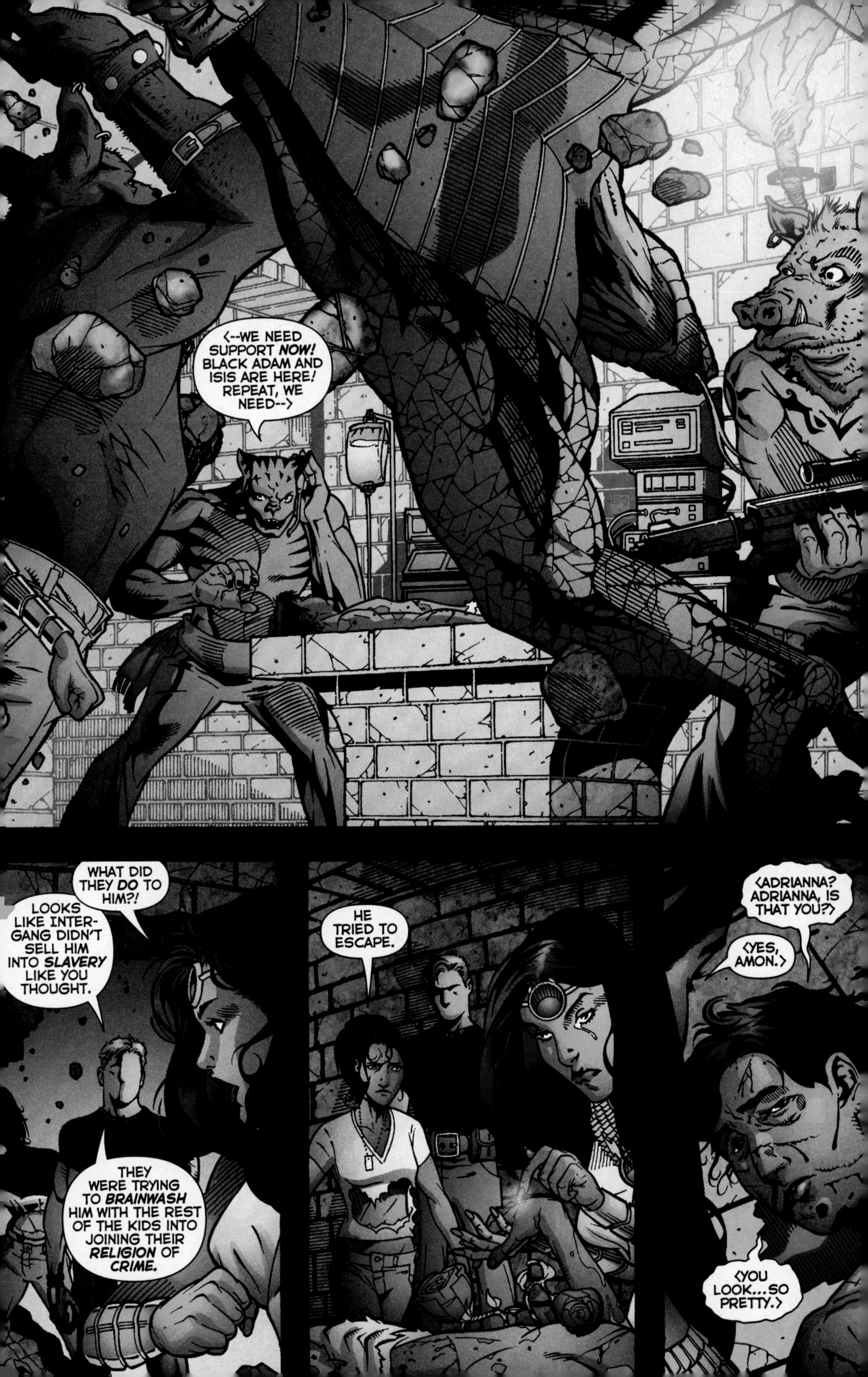

<--WE NEED SUPPORT NOW! BLACK ADAM AND ISIS ARE HERE! REPEAT, WE NEED-->
WHAT DID THEY DO TO HIM?!
LOOKS LIKE INTER-GANG DIDN'T SELL HIM INTO SLAVERY LIKE YOU THOUGHT.
THEY WERE TRYING TO BRAINWASH HIM WITH THE REST OF THE KIDS INTO JOINING THEIR RELIGION OF CRIME.
HE TRIED TO ESCAPE.
<ADRIANNA? ADRIANNA, IS THAT YOU?>
<YES, AMON.>
<YOU LOOK...SO PRETTY.>

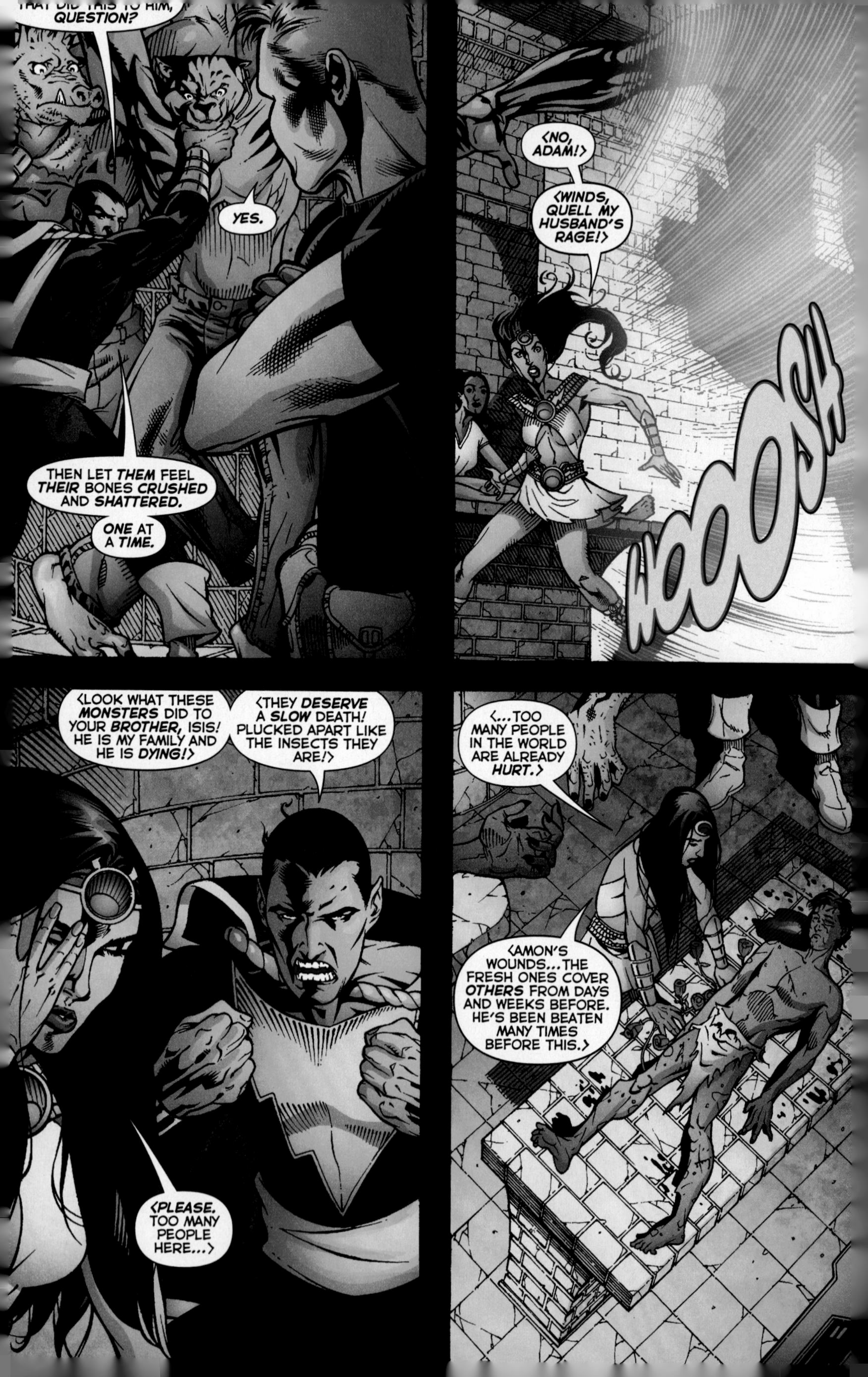
THAT DID THIS TO HIM, QUESTION?
YES.
THEN LET THEM FEEL THEIR BONES CRUSHED AND SHATTERED.
ONE AT A TIME.
<NO, ADAM!>
<WINDS, QUELL MY HUSBAND'S RAGE!>
WHOOOSH
<LOOK WHAT THESE MONSTERS DID TO YOUR BROTHER, ISIS! HE IS MY FAMILY AND HE IS DYING!>
<THEY DESERVE A SLOW DEATH! PLUCKED APART LIKE THE INSECTS THEY ARE!>
<PLEASE. TOO MANY PEOPLE HERE...>
<...TOO MANY PEOPLE IN THE WORLD ARE ALREADY HURT.>
<AMON'S WOUNDS... THE FRESH ONES COVER OTHERS FROM DAYS AND WEEKS BEFORE. HE'S BEEN BEATEN MANY TIMES BEFORE THIS.>

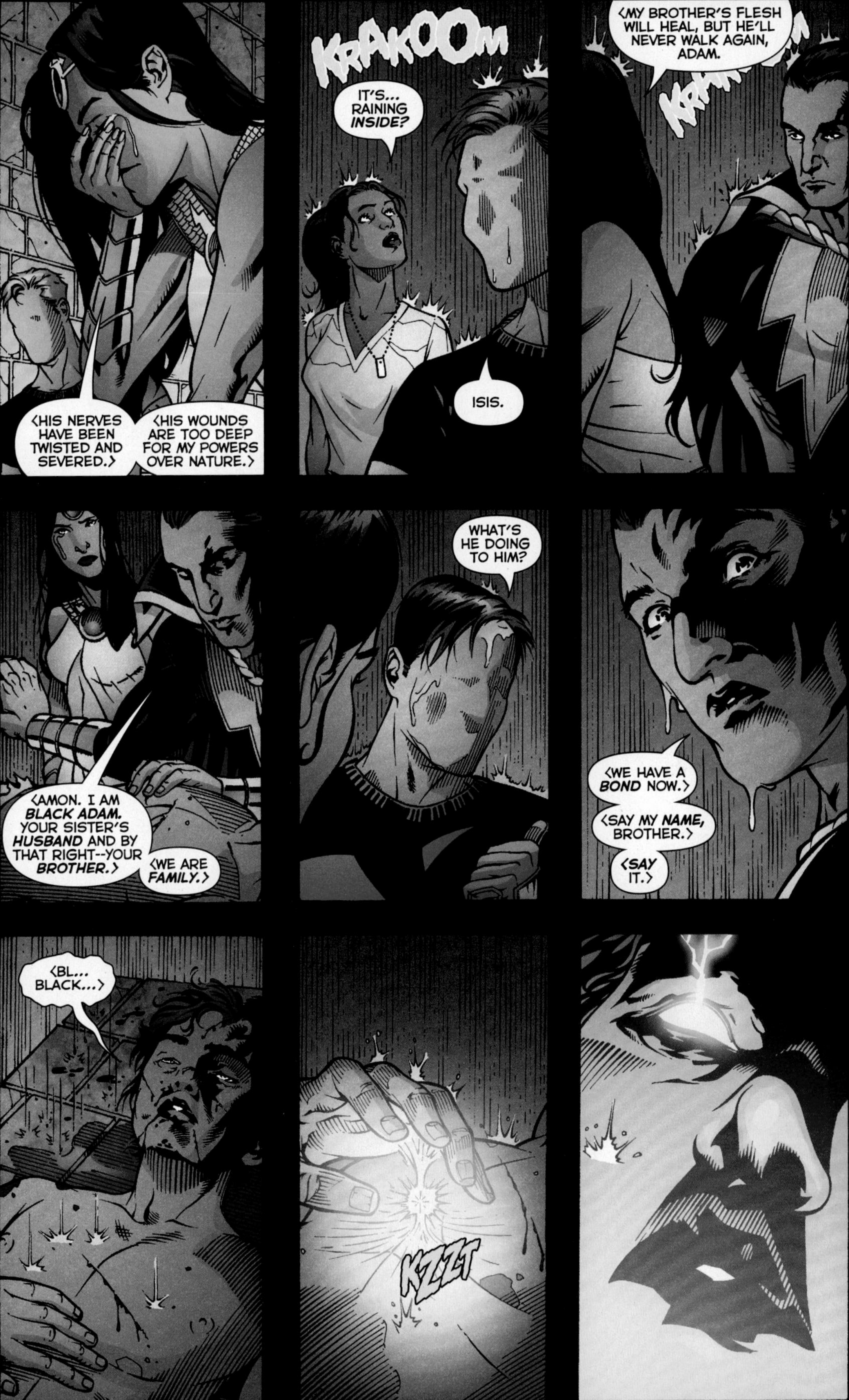

<HIS NERVES HAVE BEEN TWISTED AND SEVERED.>
<HIS WOUNDS ARE TOO DEEP FOR MY POWERS OVER NATURE.>
KRAKOOM
IT'S... RAINING INSIDE?
ISIS.
<MY BROTHER'S FLESH WILL HEAL, BUT HE'LL NEVER WALK AGAIN, ADAM.>
<AMON. I AM BLACK ADAM. YOUR SISTER'S HUSBAND AND BY THAT RIGHT--YOUR BROTHER.>
<WE ARE FAMILY.>
WHAT'S HE DOING TO HIM?
<WE HAVE A BOND NOW.>
<SAY MY NAME, BROTHER.>
<SAY IT.>
<BL... BLACK...>
KZZZT

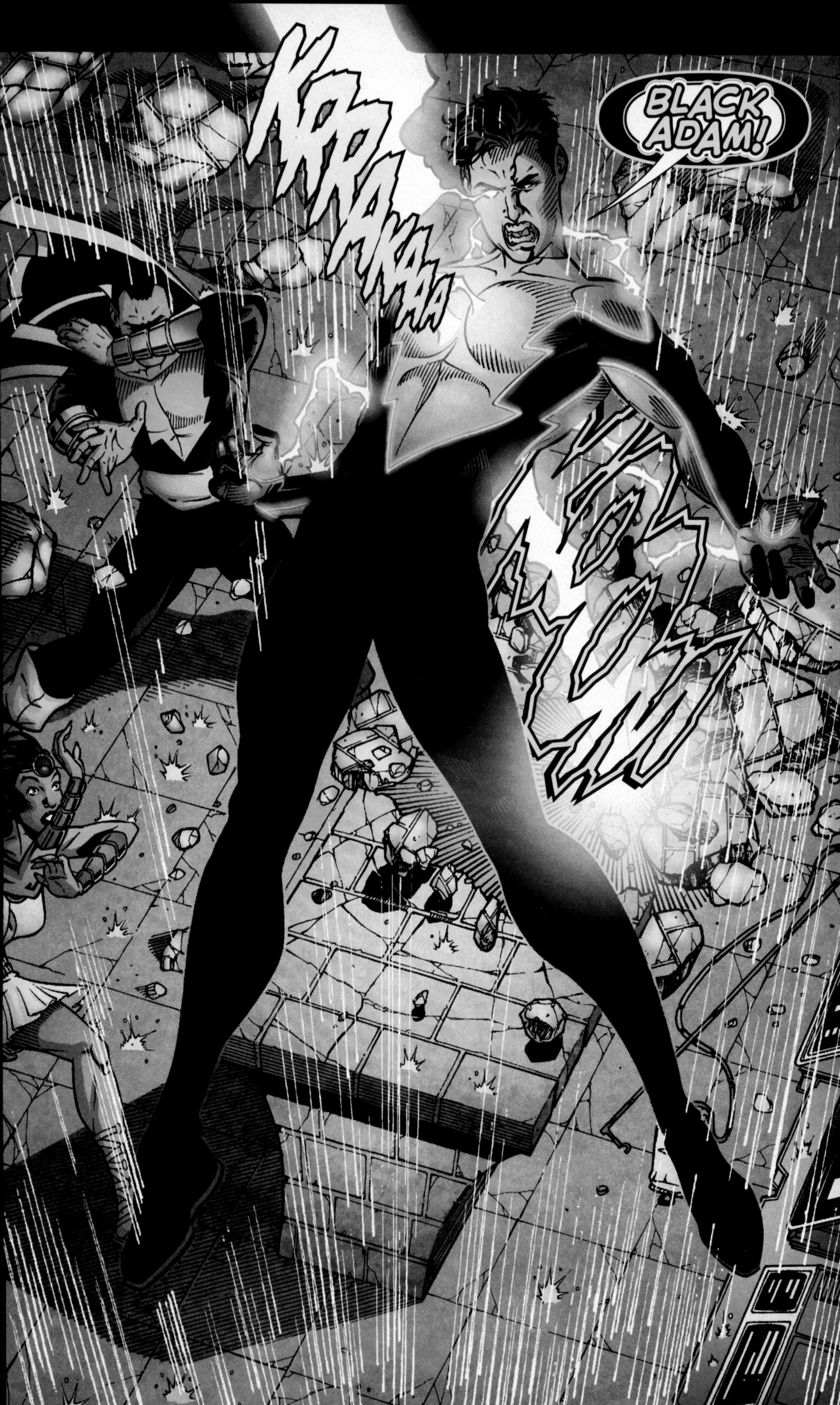
KRRAKAAA
BLACK ADAM!
VOOM

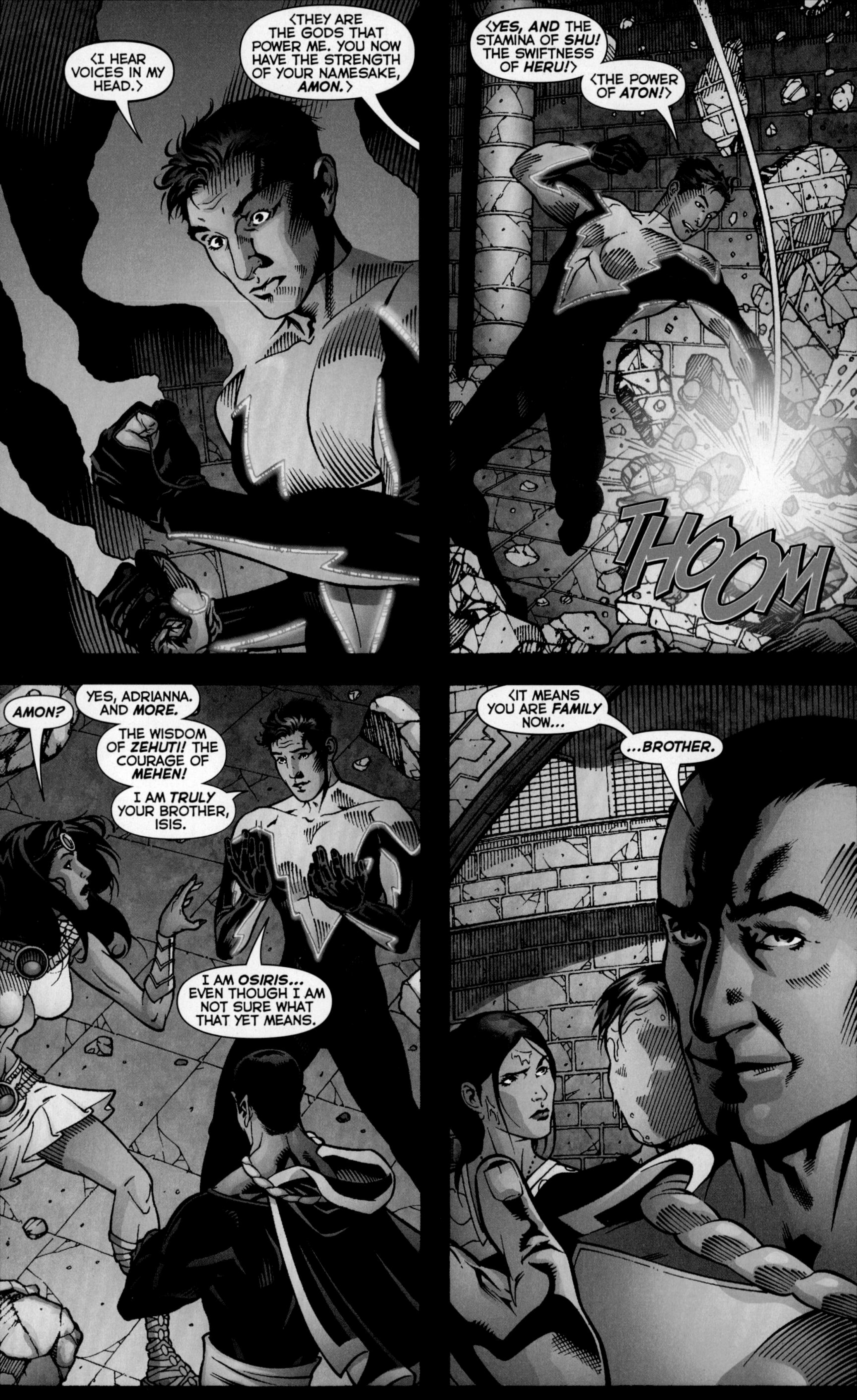

<I HEAR VOICES IN MY HEAD.>
<THEY ARE THE GODS THAT POWER ME. YOU NOW HAVE THE STRENGTH OF YOUR NAMESAKE, AMON.>
<YES, AND THE STAMINA OF SHU! THE SWIFTNESS OF HERU!>
<THE POWER OF ATON!>
THOOM
AMON?
YES, ADRIANNA. AND MORE.
THE WISDOM OF ZEHUTI! THE COURAGE OF MEHEN!
I AM TRULY YOUR BROTHER, ISIS.
I AM OSIRIS... EVEN THOUGH I AM NOT SURE WHAT THAT YET MEANS.
<IT MEANS YOU ARE FAMILY NOW...
...BROTHER.

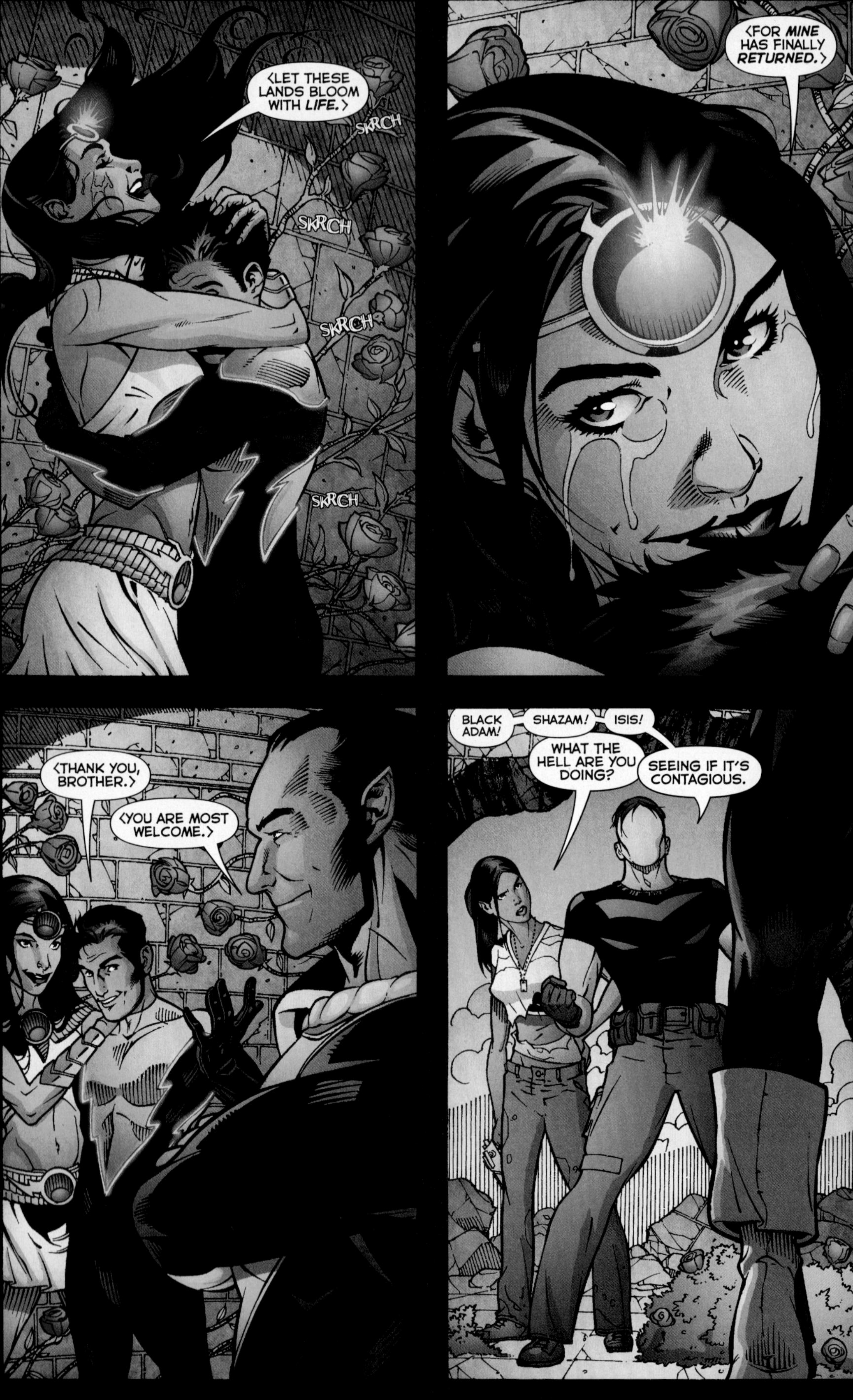

<LET THESE LANDS BLOOM WITH LIFE.>
SKRCH
SKRCH
SKRCH
SKRCH
<FOR MINE HAS FINALLY RETURNED.>
<THANK YOU, BROTHER.>
<YOU ARE MOST WELCOME.>
BLACK ADAM!
SHAZAM!
ISIS!
WHAT THE HELL ARE YOU DOING?
SEEING IF IT'S CONTAGIOUS.

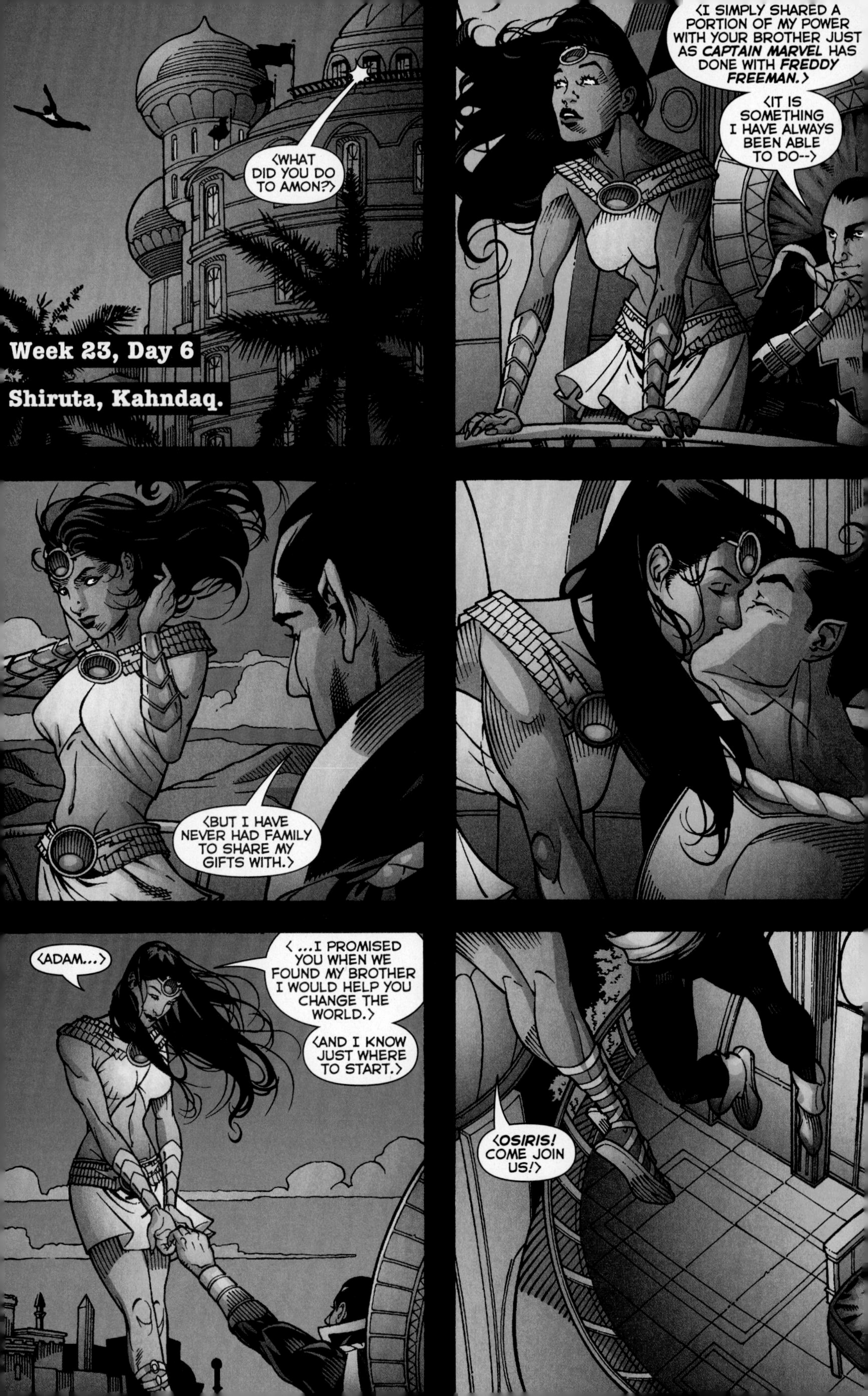

<WHAT DID YOU DO TO AMON?>
Week 23, Day 6
Shiruta, Kahndaq.
<I SIMPLY SHARED A PORTION OF MY POWER WITH YOUR BROTHER JUST AS CAPTAIN MARVEL HAS DONE WITH FREDDY FREEMAN.>
<IT IS SOMETHING I HAVE ALWAYS BEEN ABLE TO DO-->
<BUT I HAVE NEVER HAD FAMILY TO SHARE MY GIFTS WITH.>
<ADAM...>
<...I PROMISED YOU WHEN WE FOUND MY BROTHER I WOULD HELP YOU CHANGE THE WORLD.>
<AND I KNOW JUST WHERE TO START.>
<OSIRIS! COME JOIN US!>

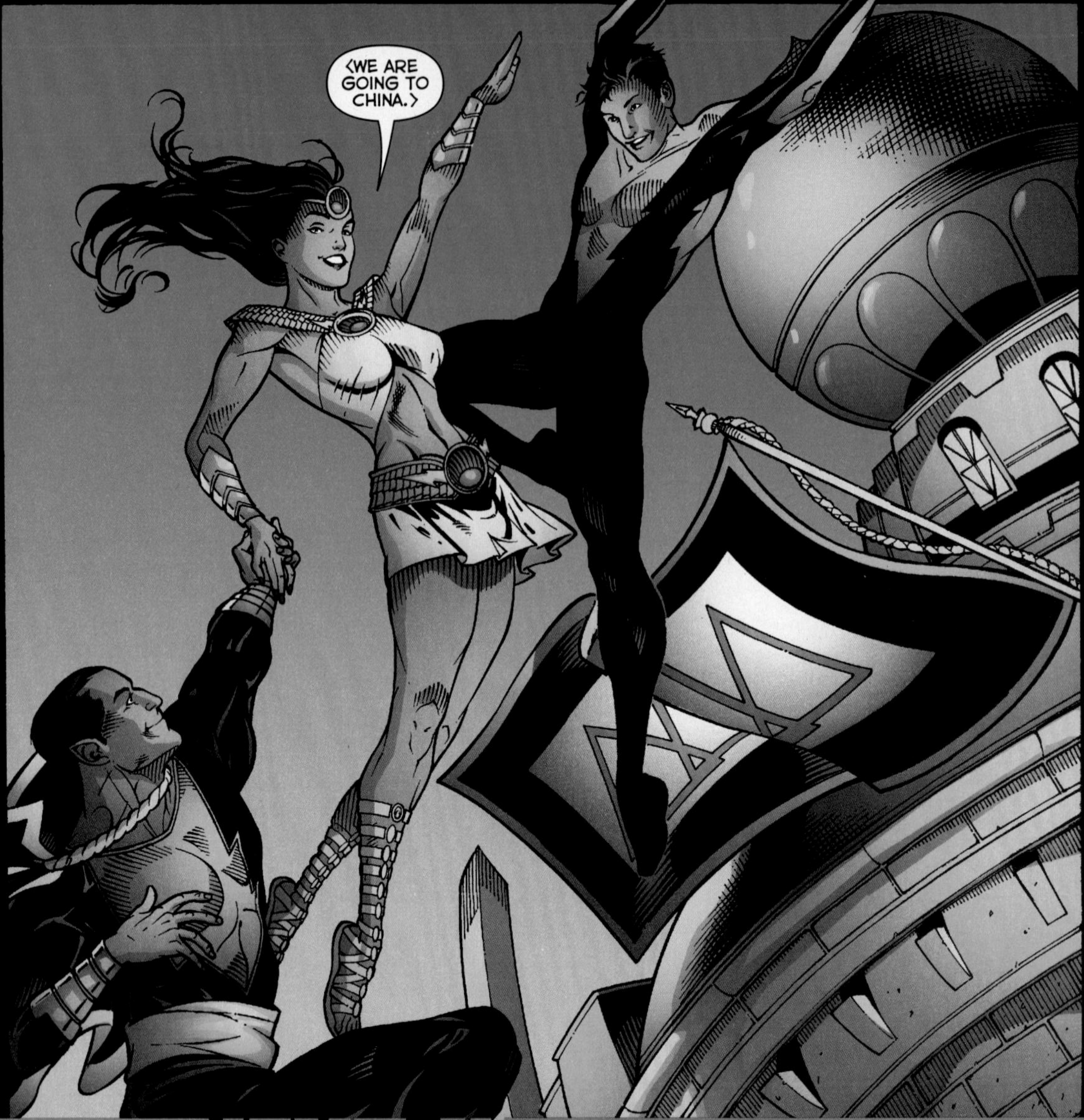

<WE ARE GOING TO CHINA.>

NEXT IN 52

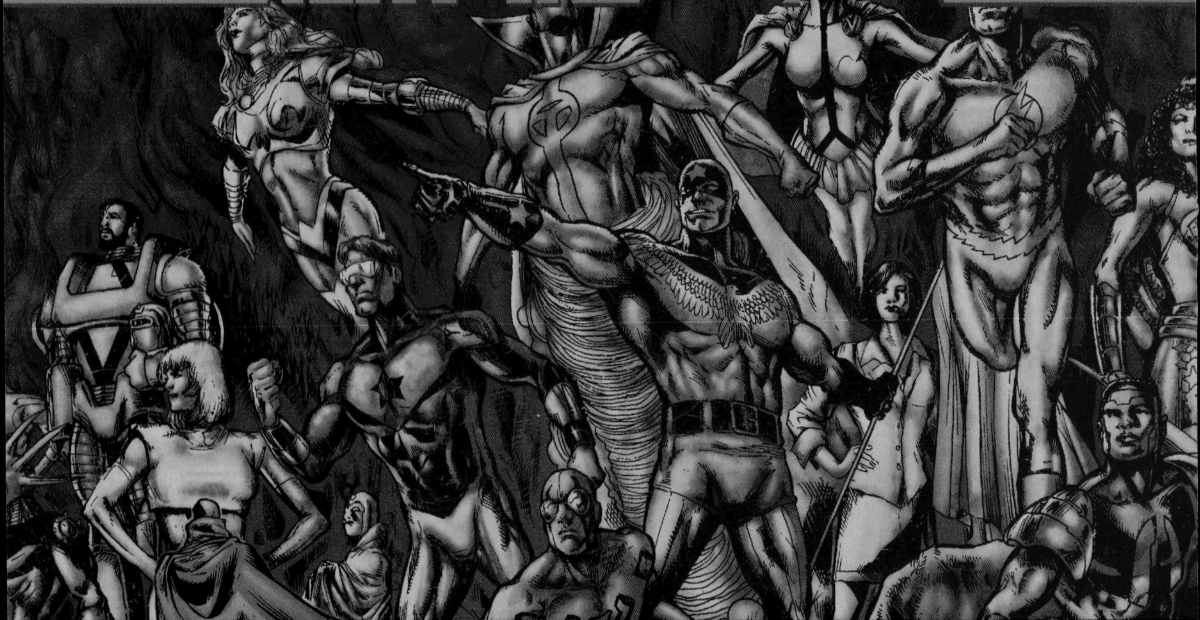

WEEK TWENTY-THREE NOTES

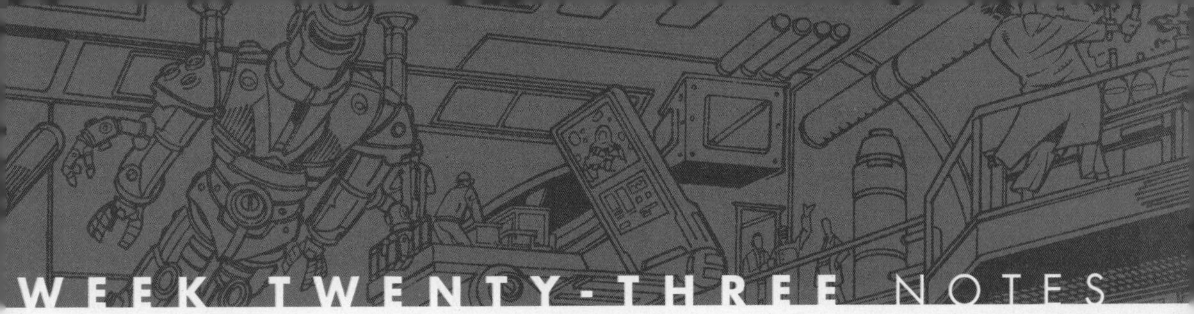

MARK WAID

A good number of the mad scientists on Oolong Island are cribbed from the Silver Age "Dial 'H' For Hero," my all-time favorite short-run DC series — and, yet, I didn't choose them, Grant did. I wouldn't have had the guts. I repeat: fearless.

GREG RUCKA

Personal recollections on this issue. I read Grant's pages for the start of the issue, and nearly bust a gut laughing. Oolong Island as the Home of All Things Mad Science had been, of course, his brainchild — and I knew that, but I hadn't realized the glee with which he'd been holding it in reserve. I read the script and after I finally stopped laughing, all I could think was that he'd been waiting *years* to write this sequence. I think it shows.

The other laugh-out-loud moment was the Charlie/Renee exchange at the end (Charlie: "Black Adam! Shazam! Isis!" Renee: "What the hell are you doing?" Charlie: "Seeing if it's contagious."). That was all Geoff, and, combined with the earlier exchange the two of them share while watching poor Amon's "punishment" (Charlie: "There are some things you just have to accept, Renee."), works quite elegantly as a foreshadowing of things yet to come in their shared story. Those reading this knowing the end read the joke as something a little less funny and a little more tragic.

This was the first week we really got to see the Religion of Crime as an organized body, and the ideas behind the religion — its structure, its doctrine, its beliefs — were still forming at the time. Grant had thrown down the idea of the "Red Rock and the Rage," and I tried to run with that, and we had some discussions about the patois of the actual book, about trying to work the language so it read as both properly liturgical while maintaining a sense of criminal slang. I think I even tried to work in some Cockney thieves cant, to no avail. Whisper A'Daire, serving as High Priestess of Sin, was supposed to have more of a "naughty nun" feel to her, another thing that, sadly, didn't quite translate.

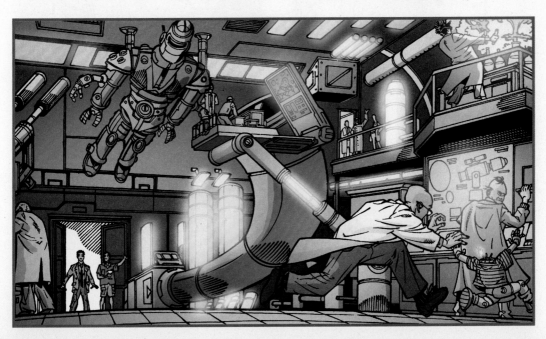

PENCILS

BY **DREW JOHNSON**

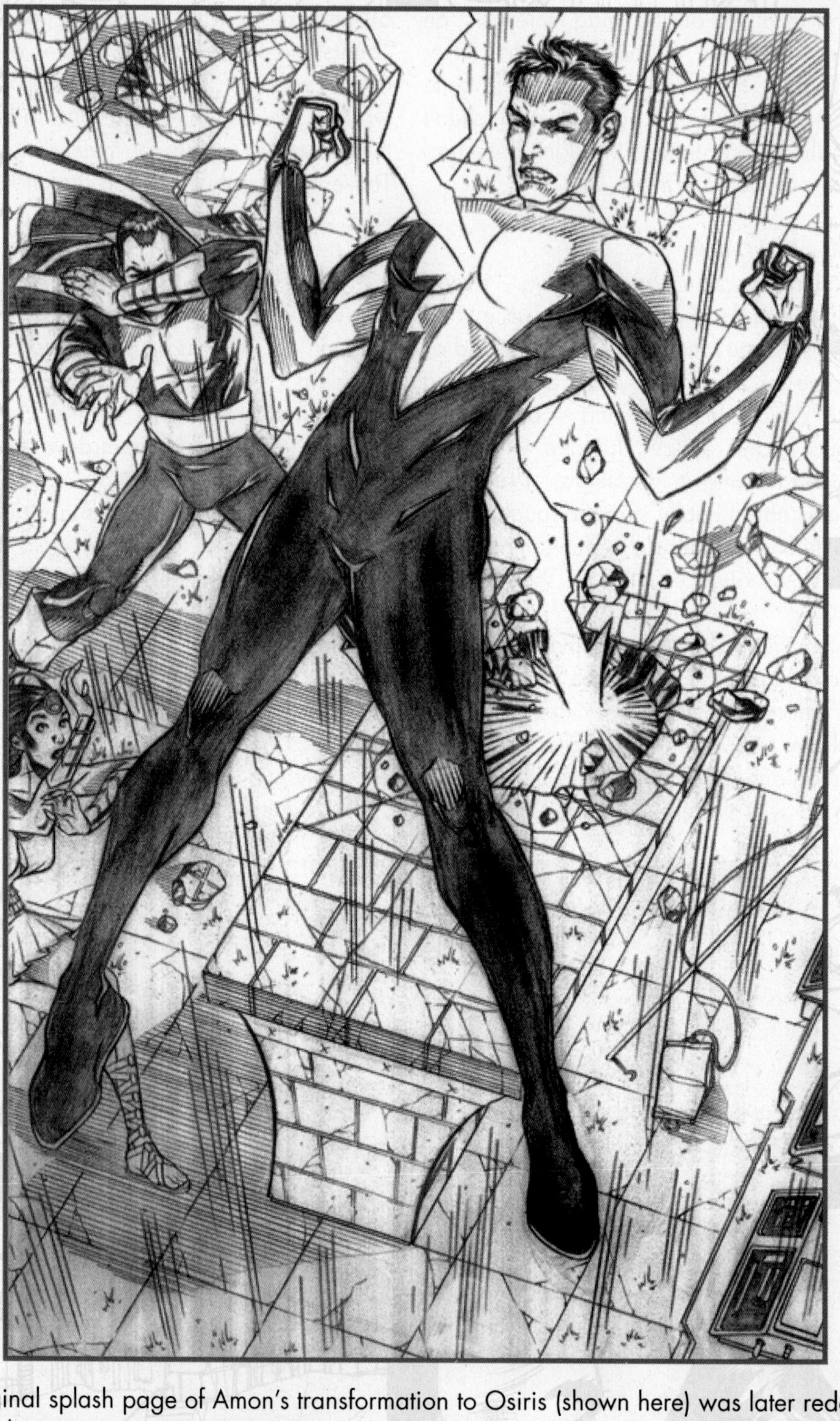

The original splash page of Amon's transformation to Osiris (shown here) was later redone in a more dramatic pose (see page 224).

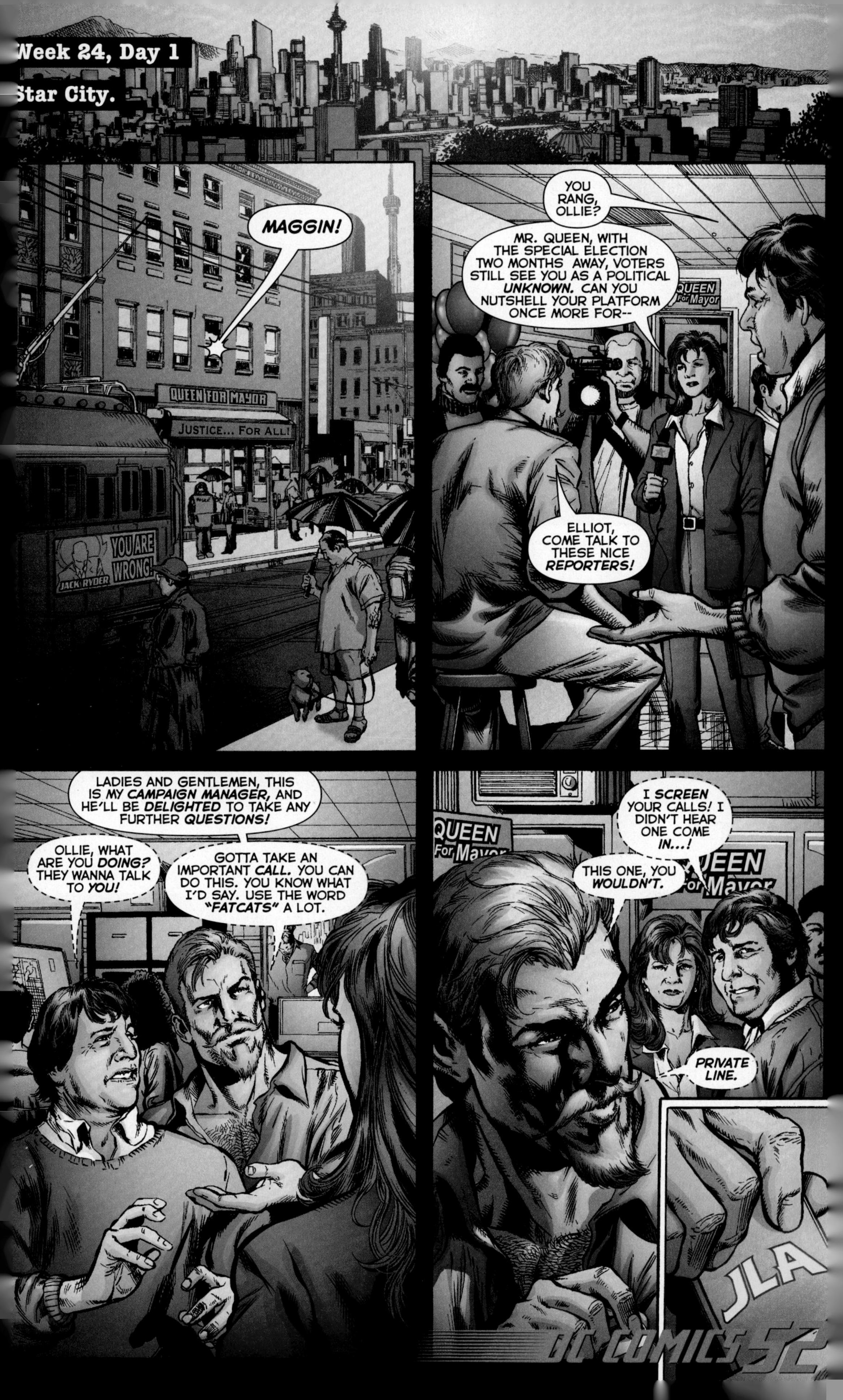
Week 24, Day 1
Star City.
MAGGIN!
QUEEN FOR MAYOR
JUSTICE... FOR ALL!
YOU ARE WRONG!
JACK RYDER
YOU RANG, OLLIE?
MR. QUEEN, WITH THE SPECIAL ELECTION TWO MONTHS AWAY, VOTERS STILL SEE YOU AS A POLITICAL UNKNOWN. CAN YOU NUTSHELL YOUR PLATFORM ONCE MORE FOR--
QUEEN For Mayor
ELLIOT, COME TALK TO THESE NICE REPORTERS!
LADIES AND GENTLEMEN, THIS IS MY CAMPAIGN MANAGER, AND HE'LL BE DELIGHTED TO TAKE ANY FURTHER QUESTIONS!
OLLIE, WHAT ARE YOU DOING? THEY WANNA TALK TO YOU!
GOTTA TAKE AN IMPORTANT CALL. YOU CAN DO THIS. YOU KNOW WHAT I'D SAY. USE THE WORD "FATCATS" A LOT.
I SCREEN YOUR CALLS! I DIDN'T HEAR ONE COME IN...!
THIS ONE, YOU WOULDN'T.
PRIVATE LINE.
JLA
DC COMICS 52

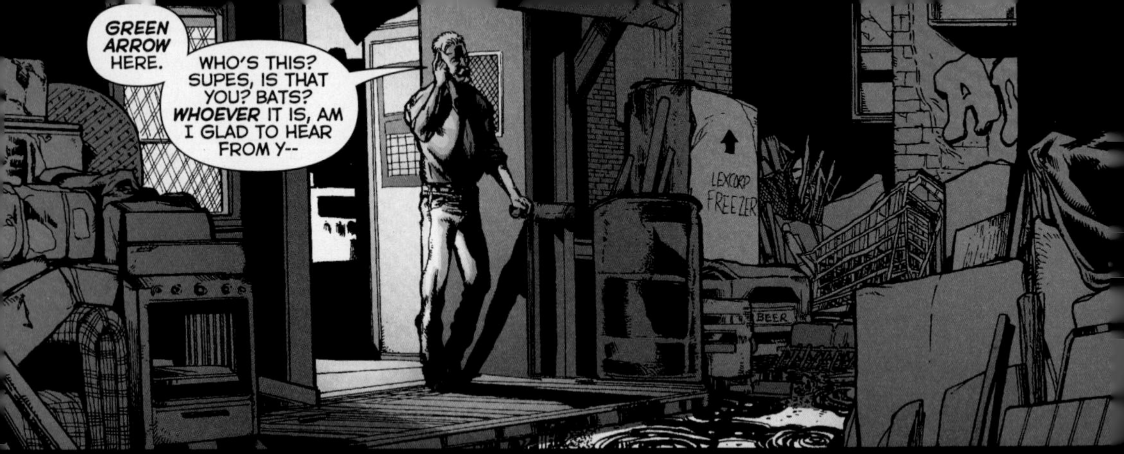
GREEN ARROW HERE.
WHO'S THIS? SUPES, IS THAT YOU? BATS? WHOEVER IT IS, AM I GLAD TO HEAR FROM Y--
LEXCORP FREEZER
BEER

WRITTEN BY GEOFF JOHNS, GRANT MORRISON, GREG RUCKA, MARK WAID

RT BREAKDOWNS BY KEITH GIFFEN • PENCILS BY PHIL JIMENEZ • INKS BY ANDY LANNIN

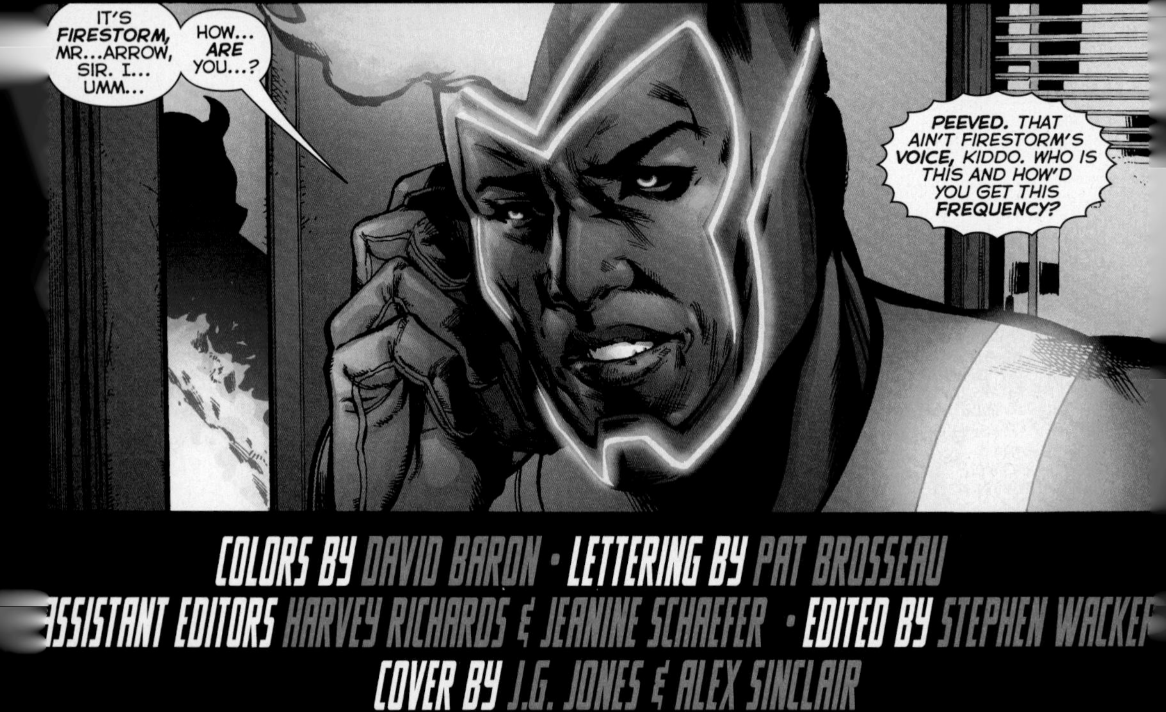
IT'S FIRESTORM, MR...ARROW, SIR. I... UMM...
HOW... ARE YOU...?
PEEVED. THAT AIN'T FIRESTORM'S VOICE, KIDDO. WHO IS THIS AND HOW'D YOU GET THIS FREQUENCY?

COLORS BY DAVID BARON • LETTERING BY PAT BROSSEAU

SSISTANT EDITORS HARVEY RICHARDS & JEANINE SCHAEFER • EDITED BY STEPHEN WACKE

COVER BY J.G. JONES & ALEX SINCLAIR

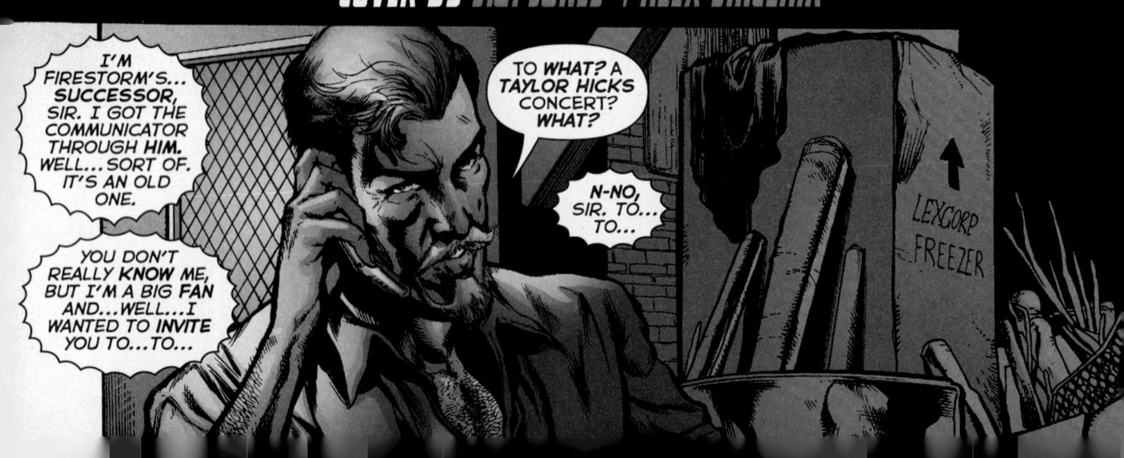
I'M FIRESTORM'S... SUCCESSOR, SIR. I GOT THE COMMUNICATOR THROUGH HIM. WELL... SORT OF. IT'S AN OLD ONE.
YOU DON'T REALLY KNOW ME, BUT I'M A BIG FAN AND...WELL...I WANTED TO INVITE YOU TO...TO...
TO WHAT? A TAYLOR HICKS CONCERT? WHAT?
N-NO, SIR. TO... TO...
LEXCORP FREEZER

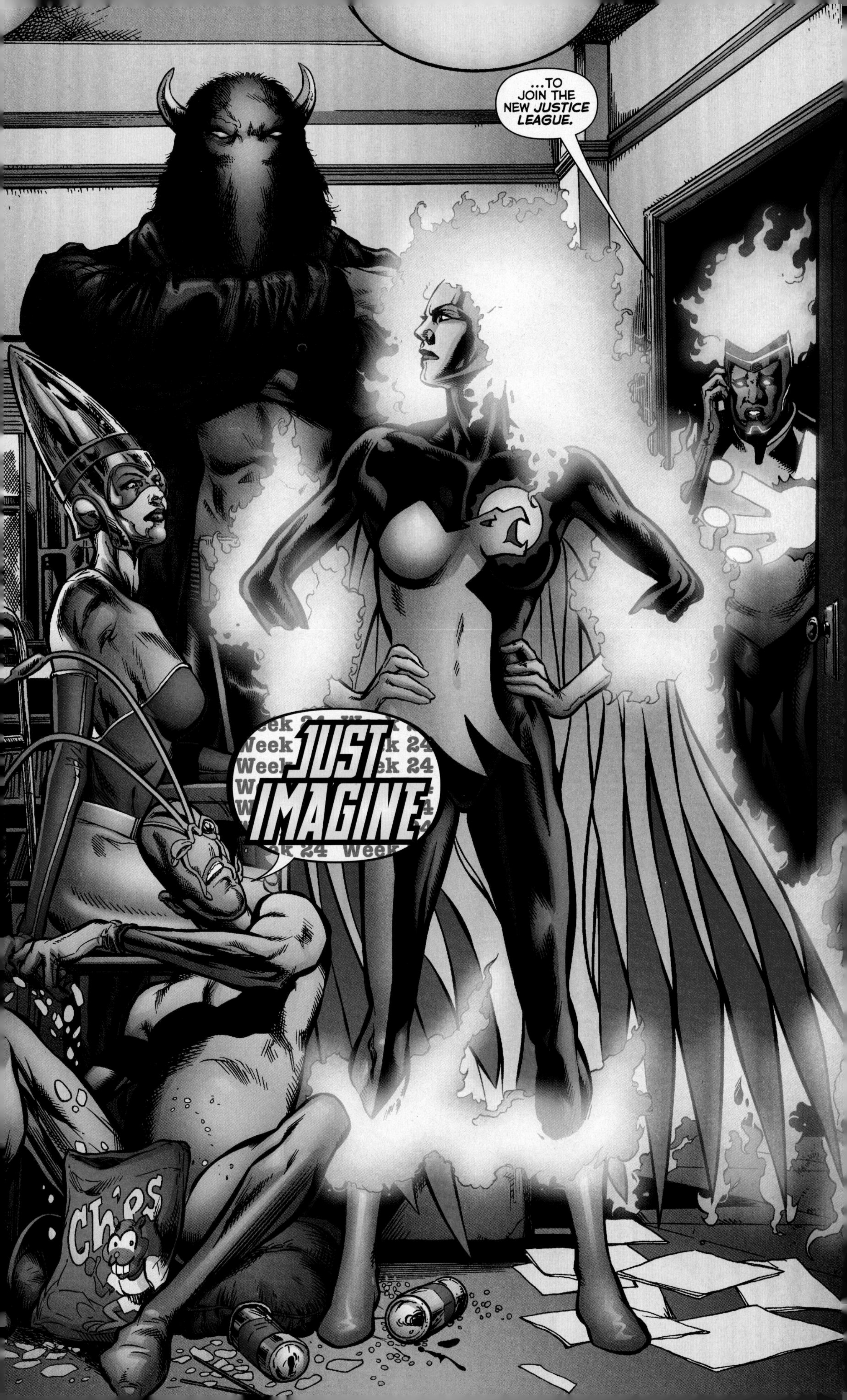
...TO JOIN THE NEW JUSTICE LEAGUE.
Week 24
JUST IMAGINE
Chips

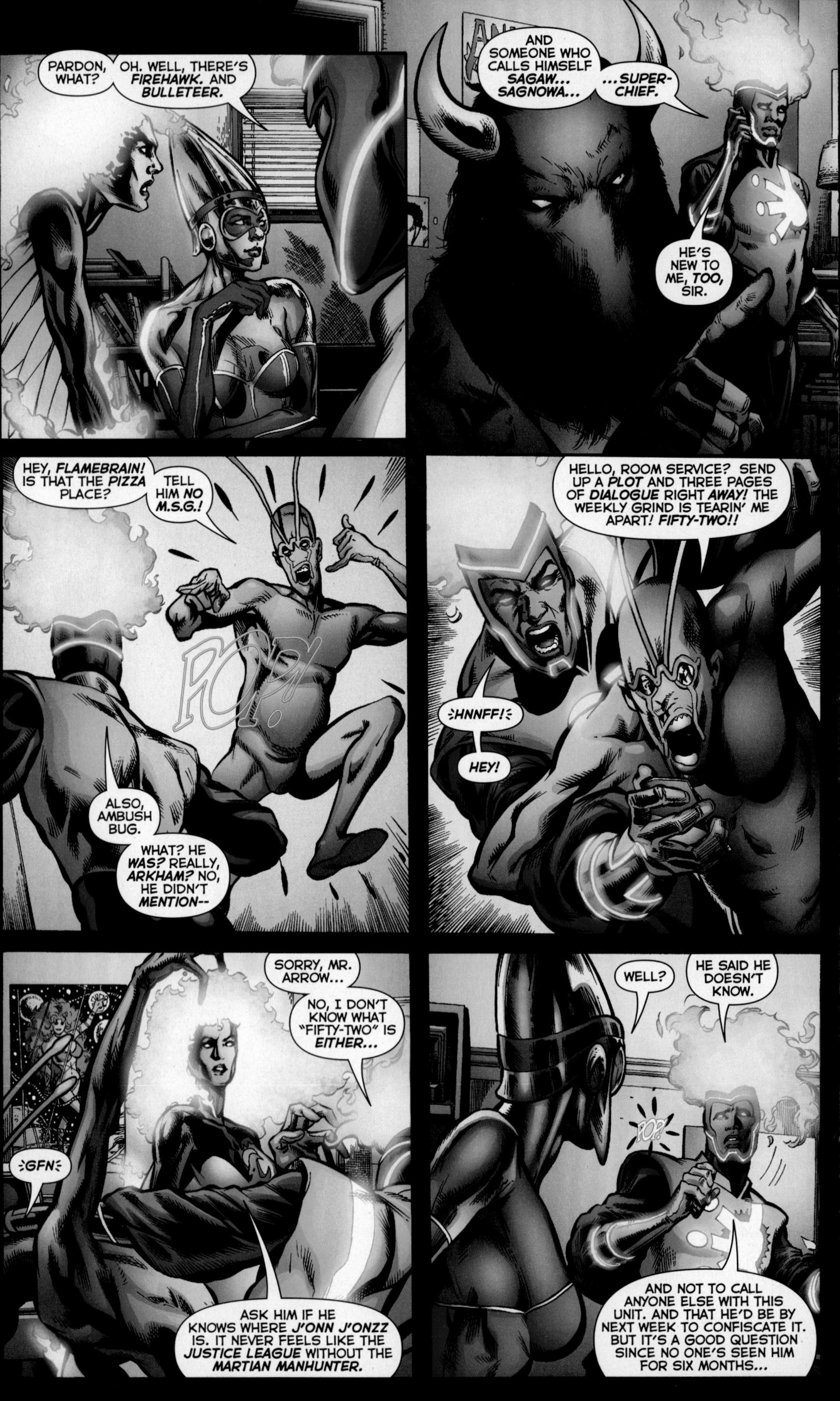
PARDON, WHAT?
OH. WELL, THERE'S FIREHAWK. AND BULLETEER.
AND SOMEONE WHO CALLS HIMSELF SAGAW... SAGNOWA...
...SUPER-CHIEF.
HE'S NEW TO ME, TOO, SIR.
HEY, FLAMEBRAIN! IS THAT THE PIZZA PLACE?
TELL HIM NO M.S.G.!
POP!
ALSO, AMBUSH BUG.
WHAT? HE WAS? REALLY, ARKHAM? NO, HE DIDN'T MENTION--
HELLO, ROOM SERVICE? SEND UP A PLOT AND THREE PAGES OF DIALOGUE RIGHT AWAY! THE WEEKLY GRIND IS TEARIN' ME APART! FIFTY-TWO!!
HNNFF!
HEY!
SORRY, MR. ARROW...
NO, I DON'T KNOW WHAT "FIFTY-TWO" IS EITHER...
GFN
ASK HIM IF HE KNOWS WHERE J'ONN J'ONZZ IS. IT NEVER FEELS LIKE THE JUSTICE LEAGUE WITHOUT THE MARTIAN MANHUNTER.
WELL?
HE SAID HE DOESN'T KNOW.
POP!
AND NOT TO CALL ANYONE ELSE WITH THIS UNIT. AND THAT HE'D BE BY NEXT WEEK TO CONFISCATE IT. BUT IT'S A GOOD QUESTION SINCE NO ONE'S SEEN HIM FOR SIX MONTHS...

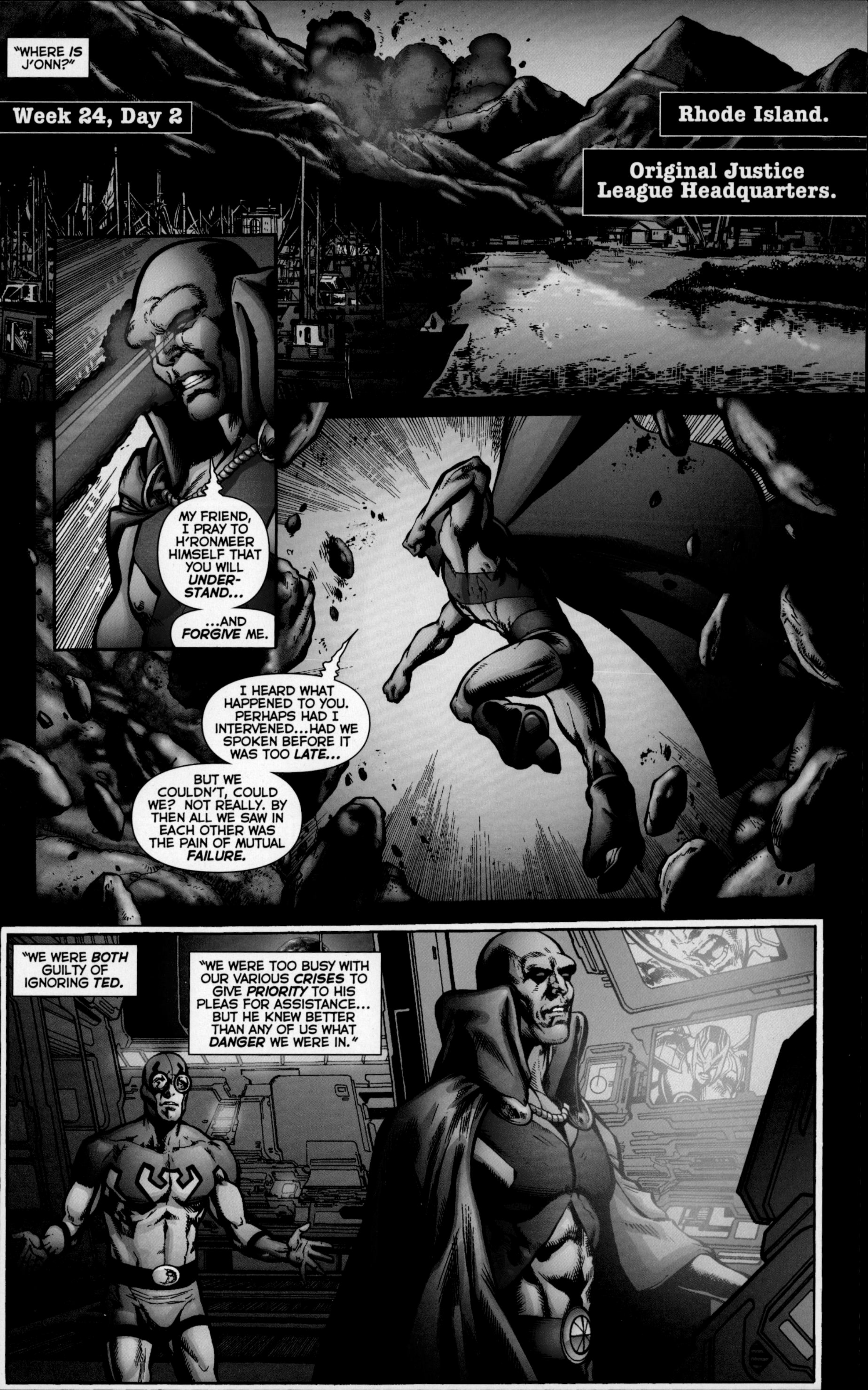
"WHERE *IS* J'ONN?"
Week 24, Day 2
Rhode Island.
Original Justice League Headquarters.
MY FRIEND, I PRAY TO H'RONMEER HIMSELF THAT YOU WILL *UNDER-STAND...*
...AND *FORGIVE* ME.
I HEARD WHAT HAPPENED TO YOU. PERHAPS HAD I INTERVENED...HAD WE SPOKEN BEFORE IT WAS TOO *LATE...*
BUT WE COULDN'T, COULD WE? NOT REALLY. BY THEN ALL WE SAW IN EACH OTHER WAS THE PAIN OF MUTUAL *FAILURE.*
"WE WERE *BOTH* GUILTY OF IGNORING *TED.*
"WE WERE TOO BUSY WITH OUR VARIOUS *CRISES* TO GIVE *PRIORITY* TO HIS PLEAS FOR ASSISTANCE... BUT HE KNEW BETTER THAN ANY OF US WHAT *DANGER* WE WERE IN."

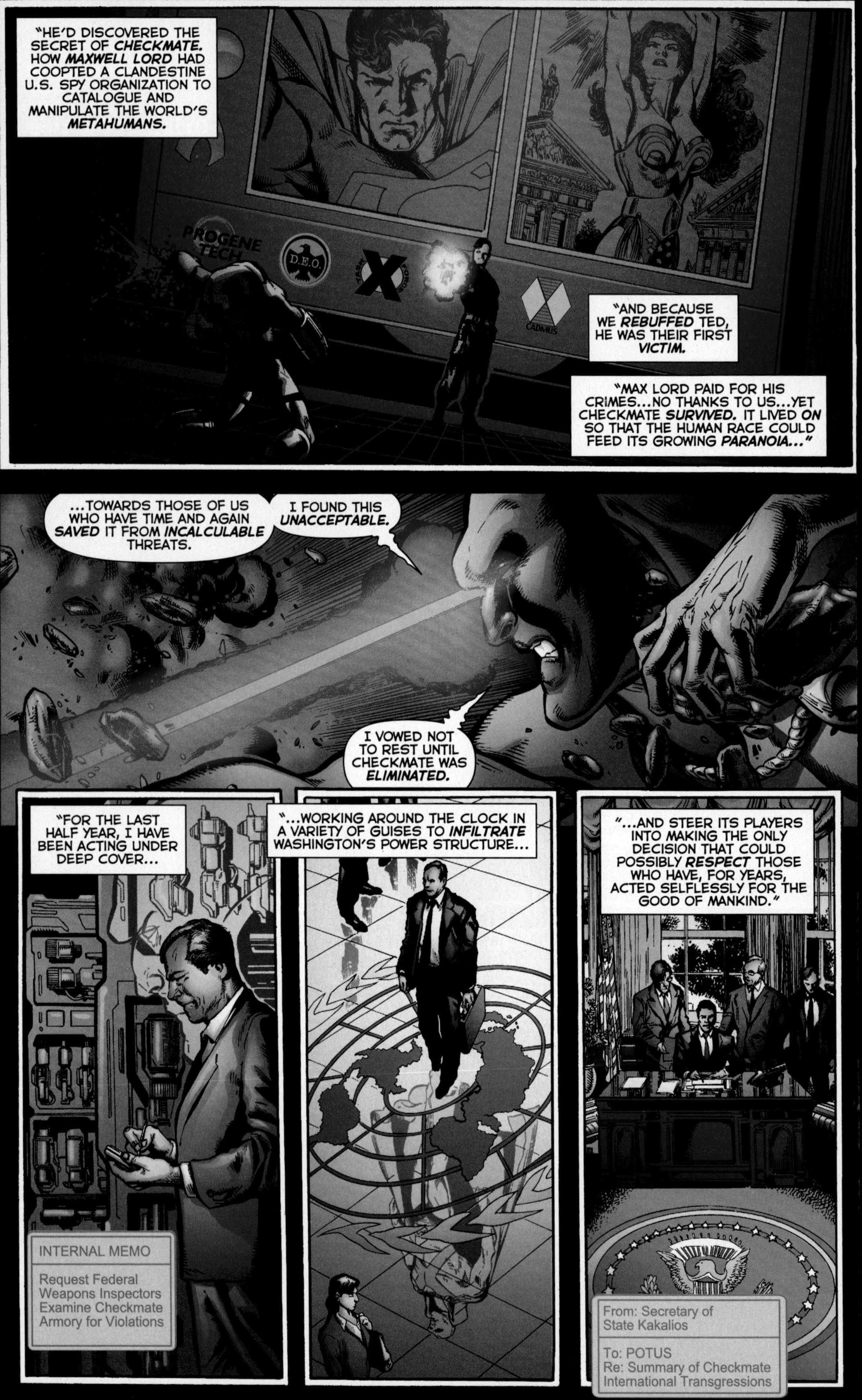
"HE'D DISCOVERED THE SECRET OF CHECKMATE. HOW MAXWELL LORD HAD COOPTED A CLANDESTINE U.S. SPY ORGANIZATION TO CATALOGUE AND MANIPULATE THE WORLD'S METAHUMANS.
PROGENE TECH
D.E.O.
X
CADMUS
"AND BECAUSE WE REBUFFED TED, HE WAS THEIR FIRST VICTIM.
"MAX LORD PAID FOR HIS CRIMES...NO THANKS TO US...YET CHECKMATE SURVIVED. IT LIVED ON SO THAT THE HUMAN RACE COULD FEED ITS GROWING PARANOIA..."
...TOWARDS THOSE OF US WHO HAVE TIME AND AGAIN SAVED IT FROM INCALCULABLE THREATS.
I FOUND THIS UNACCEPTABLE.
I VOWED NOT TO REST UNTIL CHECKMATE WAS ELIMINATED.
"FOR THE LAST HALF YEAR, I HAVE BEEN ACTING UNDER DEEP COVER...
INTERNAL MEMO
Request Federal Weapons Inspectors Examine Checkmate Armory for Violations
"...WORKING AROUND THE CLOCK IN A VARIETY OF GUISES TO INFILTRATE WASHINGTON'S POWER STRUCTURE...
"...AND STEER ITS PLAYERS INTO MAKING THE ONLY DECISION THAT COULD POSSIBLY RESPECT THOSE WHO HAVE, FOR YEARS, ACTED SELFLESSLY FOR THE GOOD OF MANKIND."
From: Secretary of State Kakalios
To: POTUS
Re: Summary of Checkmate International Transgressions

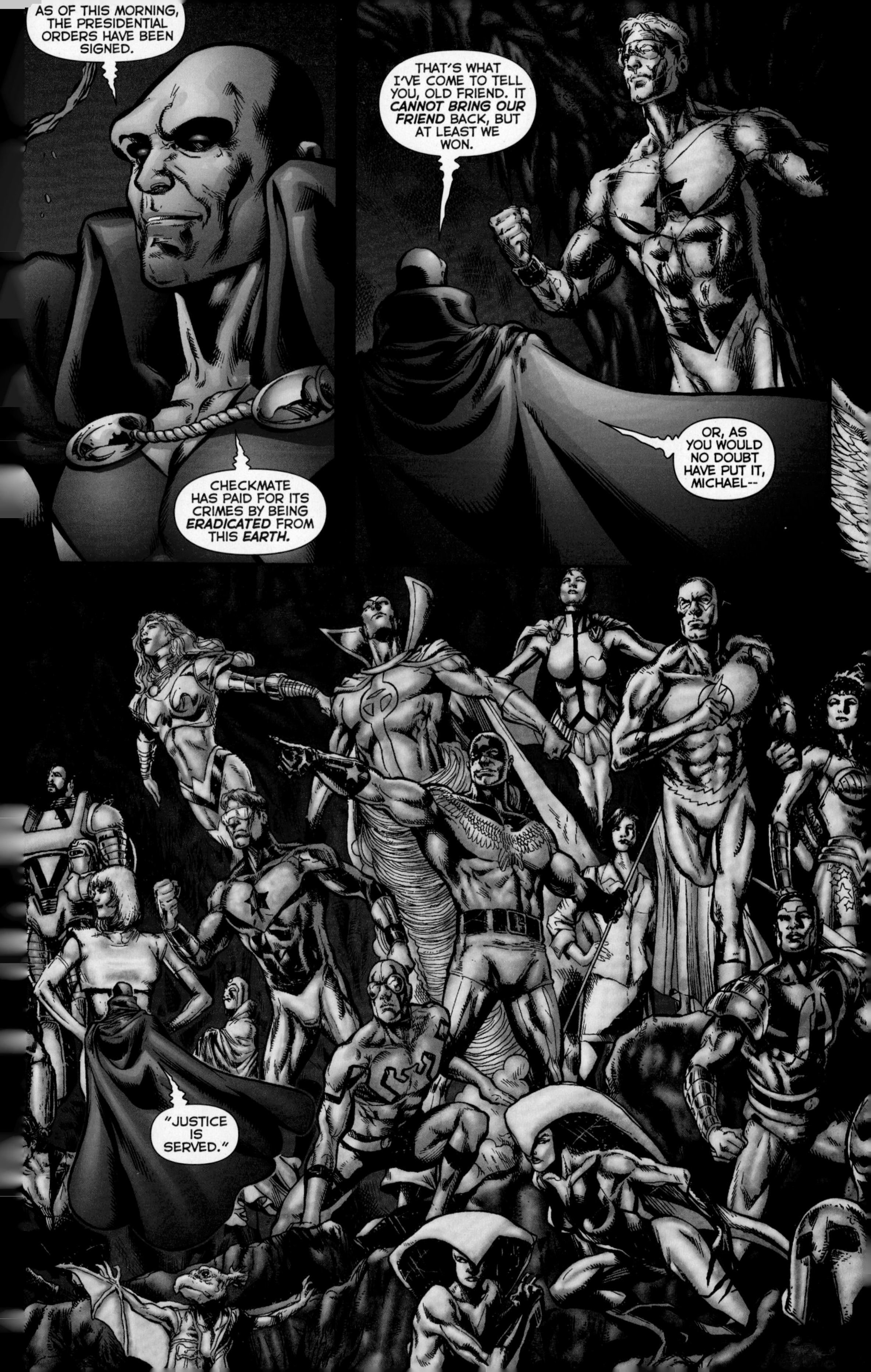
AS OF THIS MORNING, THE PRESIDENTIAL ORDERS HAVE BEEN SIGNED.
CHECKMATE HAS PAID FOR ITS CRIMES BY BEING ERADICATED FROM THIS EARTH.
THAT'S WHAT I'VE COME TO TELL YOU, OLD FRIEND. IT CANNOT BRING OUR FRIEND BACK, BUT AT LEAST WE WON.
OR, AS YOU WOULD NO DOUBT HAVE PUT IT, MICHAEL--
"JUSTICE IS SERVED."

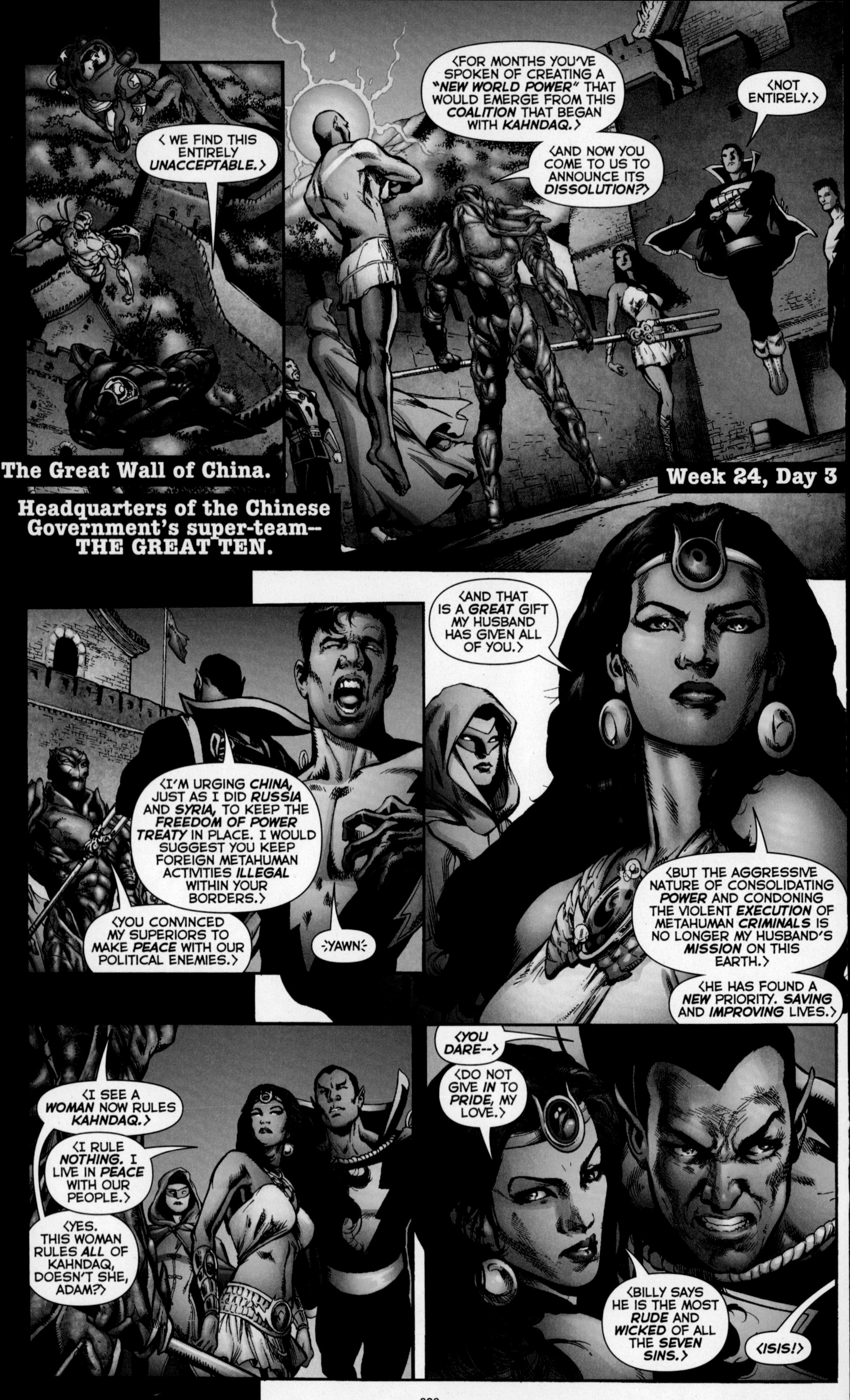

The Great Wall of China.
Headquarters of the Chinese Government's super-team-- THE GREAT TEN.
Week 24, Day 3
< WE FIND THIS ENTIRELY UNACCEPTABLE.>
<FOR MONTHS YOU'VE SPOKEN OF CREATING A "NEW WORLD POWER" THAT WOULD EMERGE FROM THIS COALITION THAT BEGAN WITH KAHNDAQ.>
<AND NOW YOU COME TO US TO ANNOUNCE ITS DISSOLUTION?>
<NOT ENTIRELY.>
<I'M URGING CHINA, JUST AS I DID RUSSIA AND SYRIA, TO KEEP THE FREEDOM OF POWER TREATY IN PLACE. I WOULD SUGGEST YOU KEEP FOREIGN METAHUMAN ACTIVITIES ILLEGAL WITHIN YOUR BORDERS.>
<YOU CONVINCED MY SUPERIORS TO MAKE PEACE WITH OUR POLITICAL ENEMIES.>
YAWN
<AND THAT IS A GREAT GIFT MY HUSBAND HAS GIVEN ALL OF YOU.>
<BUT THE AGGRESSIVE NATURE OF CONSOLIDATING POWER AND CONDONING THE VIOLENT EXECUTION OF METAHUMAN CRIMINALS IS NO LONGER MY HUSBAND'S MISSION ON THIS EARTH.>
<HE HAS FOUND A NEW PRIORITY. SAVING AND IMPROVING LIVES.>
<I SEE A WOMAN NOW RULES KAHNDAQ.>
<I RULE NOTHING. I LIVE IN PEACE WITH OUR PEOPLE.>
<YES. THIS WOMAN RULES ALL OF KAHNDAQ, DOESN'T SHE, ADAM?>
<YOU DARE-->
<DO NOT GIVE IN TO PRIDE, MY LOVE.>
<BILLY SAYS HE IS THE MOST RUDE AND WICKED OF ALL THE SEVEN SINS.>
<ISIS!>

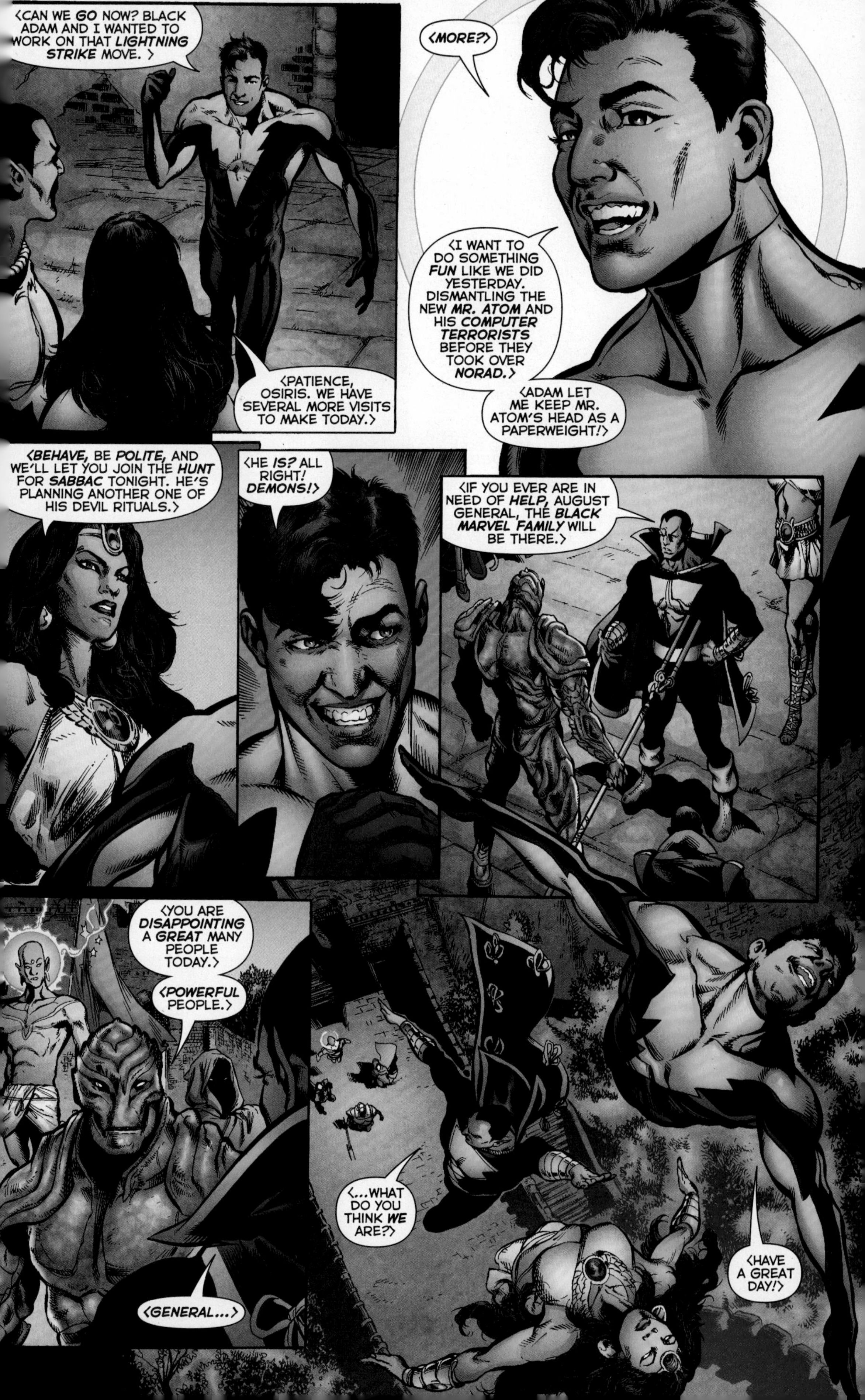
<CAN WE GO NOW? BLACK ADAM AND I WANTED TO WORK ON THAT LIGHTNING STRIKE MOVE. >
<PATIENCE, OSIRIS. WE HAVE SEVERAL MORE VISITS TO MAKE TODAY.>
<MORE?>
<I WANT TO DO SOMETHING FUN LIKE WE DID YESTERDAY. DISMANTLING THE NEW MR. ATOM AND HIS COMPUTER TERRORISTS BEFORE THEY TOOK OVER NORAD.>
<ADAM LET ME KEEP MR. ATOM'S HEAD AS A PAPERWEIGHT!>
<BEHAVE, BE POLITE, AND WE'LL LET YOU JOIN THE HUNT FOR SABBAC TONIGHT. HE'S PLANNING ANOTHER ONE OF HIS DEVIL RITUALS.>
<HE IS? ALL RIGHT! DEMONS!>
<IF YOU EVER ARE IN NEED OF HELP, AUGUST GENERAL, THE BLACK MARVEL FAMILY WILL BE THERE.>
<YOU ARE DISAPPOINTING A GREAT MANY PEOPLE TODAY.>
<POWERFUL PEOPLE.>
<GENERAL...>
<...WHAT DO YOU THINK WE ARE?>
<HAVE A GREAT DAY!>

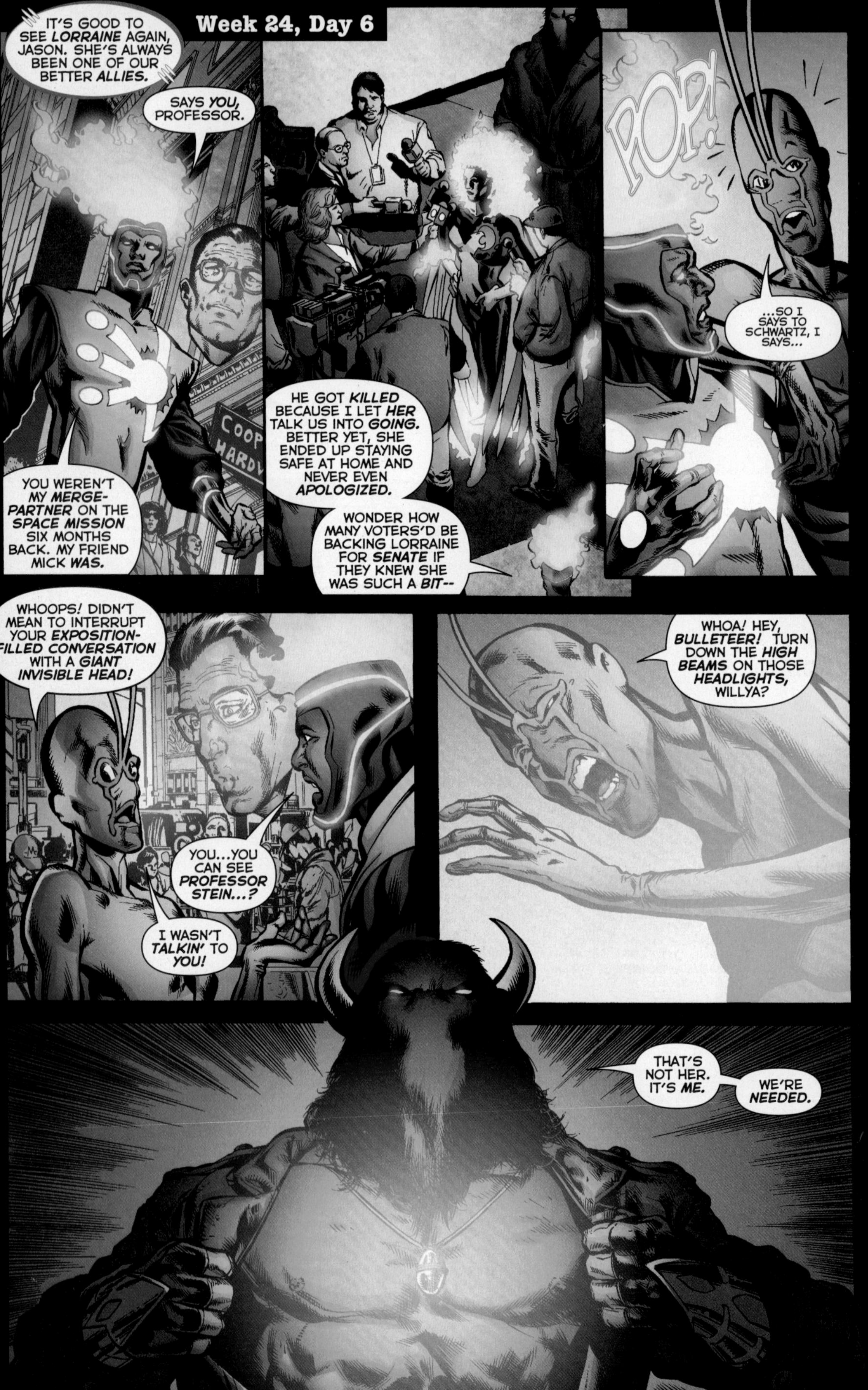
Week 24, Day 6
IT'S GOOD TO SEE LORRAINE AGAIN, JASON. SHE'S ALWAYS BEEN ONE OF OUR BETTER ALLIES.
SAYS YOU, PROFESSOR.
YOU WEREN'T MY MERGE-PARTNER ON THE SPACE MISSION SIX MONTHS BACK. MY FRIEND MICK WAS.
HE GOT KILLED BECAUSE I LET HER TALK US INTO GOING. BETTER YET, SHE ENDED UP STAYING SAFE AT HOME AND NEVER EVEN APOLOGIZED.
WONDER HOW MANY VOTERS'D BE BACKING LORRAINE FOR SENATE IF THEY KNEW SHE WAS SUCH A BIT--
POP!
...SO I SAYS TO SCHWARTZ, I SAYS...
WHOOPS! DIDN'T MEAN TO INTERRUPT YOUR EXPOSITION-FILLED CONVERSATION WITH A GIANT INVISIBLE HEAD!
YOU...YOU CAN SEE PROFESSOR STEIN...?
I WASN'T TALKIN' TO YOU!
WHOA! HEY, BULLETEER! TURN DOWN THE HIGH BEAMS ON THOSE HEADLIGHTS, WILLYA?
THAT'S NOT HER. IT'S ME.
WE'RE NEEDED.

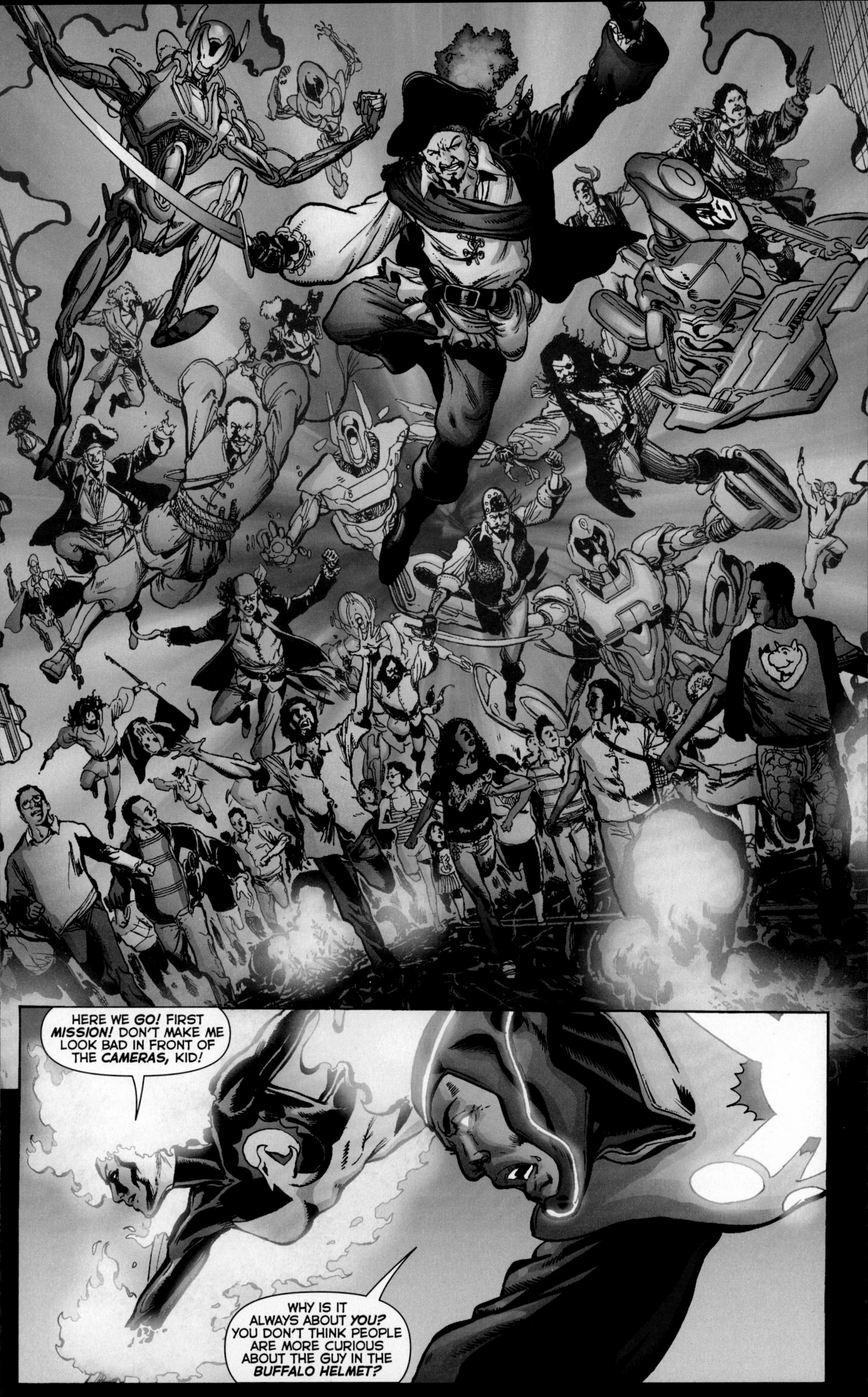

HERE WE GO! FIRST MISSION! DON'T MAKE ME LOOK BAD IN FRONT OF THE CAMERAS, KID!
WHY IS IT ALWAYS ABOUT YOU? YOU DON'T THINK PEOPLE ARE MORE CURIOUS ABOUT THE GUY IN THE BUFFALO HELMET?

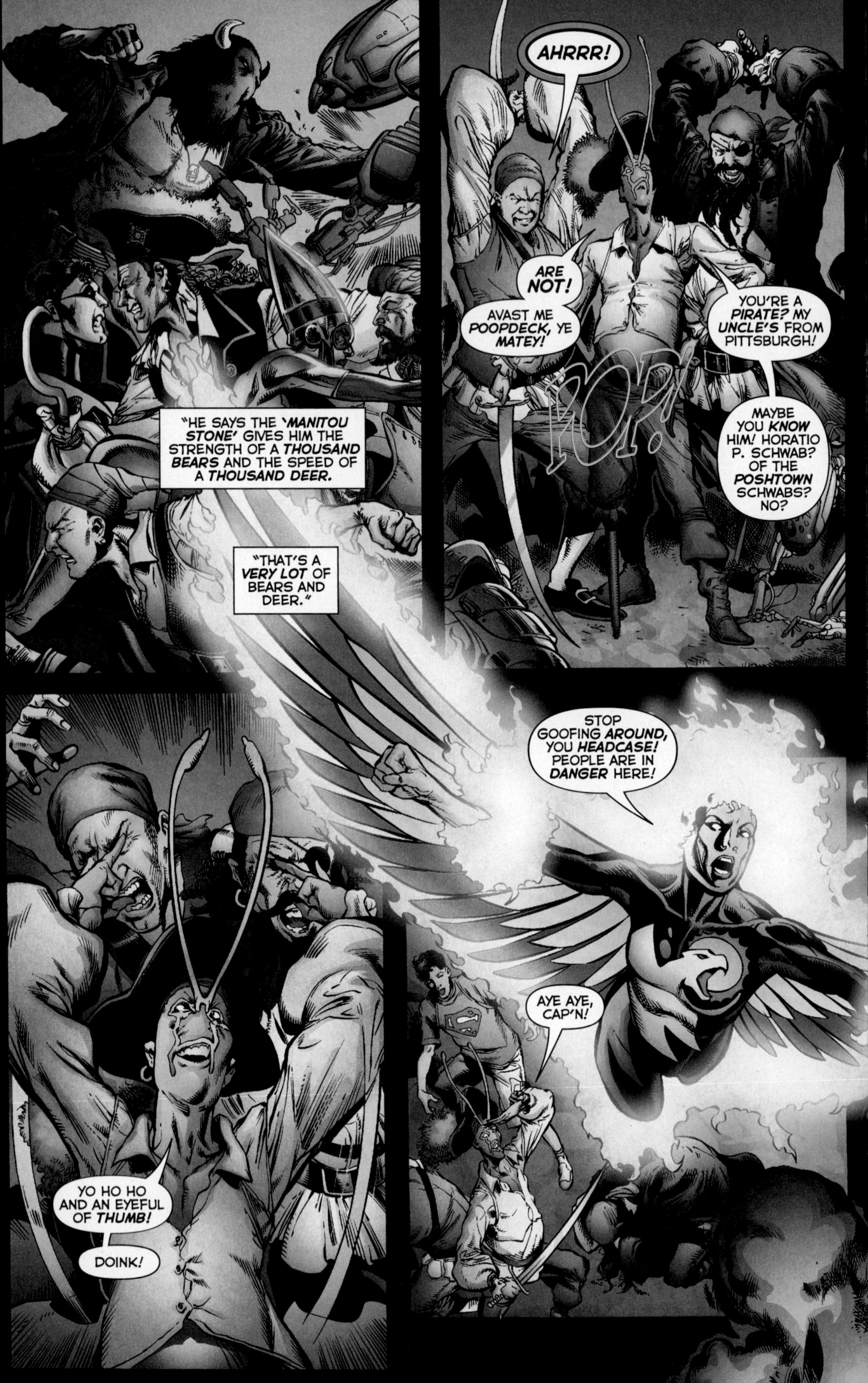
"HE SAYS THE 'MANITOU STONE' GIVES HIM THE STRENGTH OF A THOUSAND BEARS AND THE SPEED OF A THOUSAND DEER.
"THAT'S A VERY LOT OF BEARS AND DEER."
AHRRR!
ARE NOT!
AVAST ME POOPDECK, YE MATEY!
POP!
YOU'RE A PIRATE? MY UNCLE'S FROM PITTSBURGH!
MAYBE YOU KNOW HIM! HORATIO P. SCHWAB? OF THE POSHTOWN SCHWABS? NO?
YO HO HO AND AN EYEFUL OF THUMB!
DOINK!
STOP GOOFING AROUND, YOU HEADCASE! PEOPLE ARE IN DANGER HERE!
AYE AYE, CAP'N!

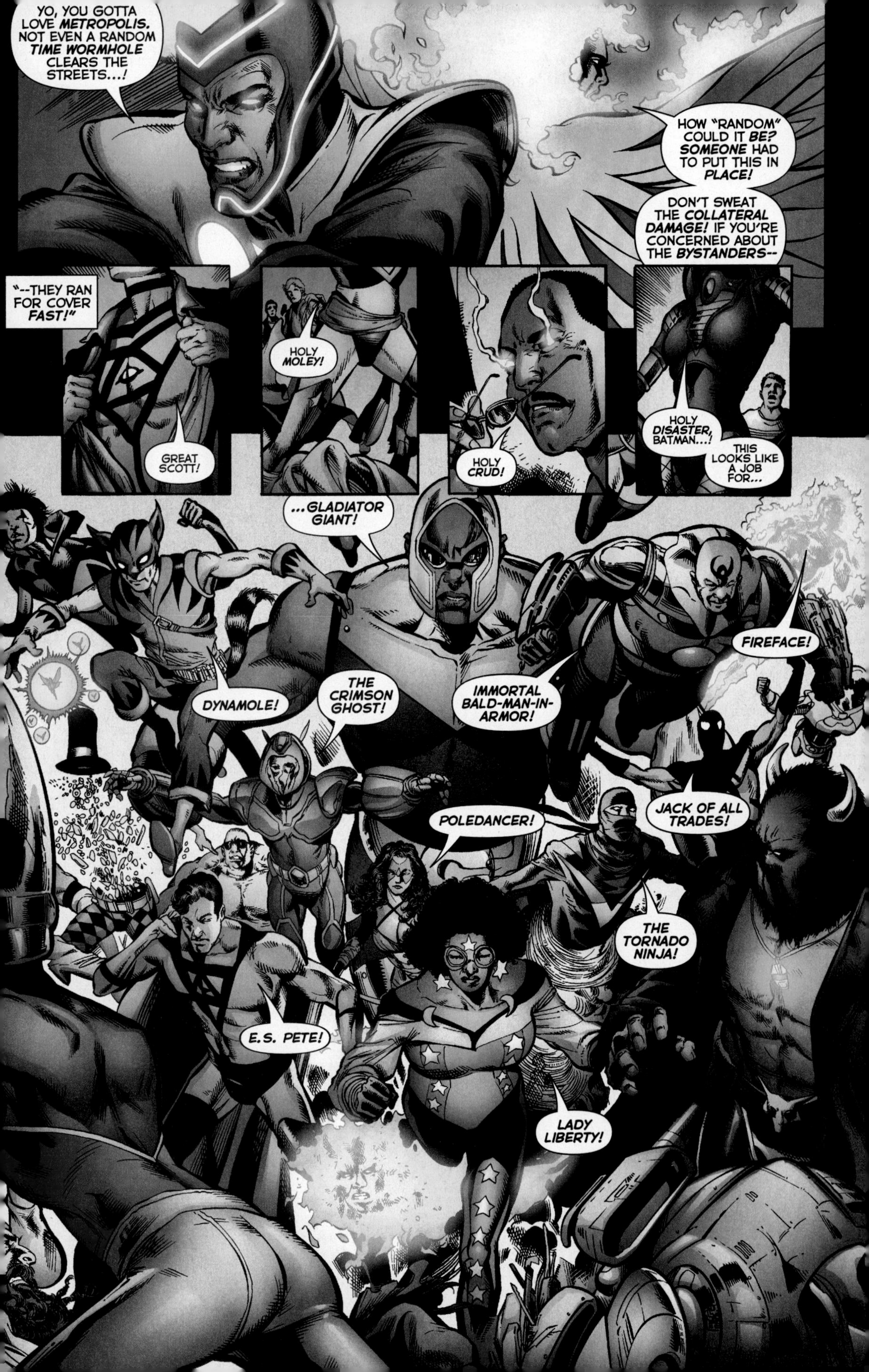
YO, YOU GOTTA LOVE METROPOLIS. NOT EVEN A RANDOM TIME WORMHOLE CLEARS THE STREETS...!
HOW "RANDOM" COULD IT BE? SOMEONE HAD TO PUT THIS IN PLACE!
DON'T SWEAT THE COLLATERAL DAMAGE! IF YOU'RE CONCERNED ABOUT THE BYSTANDERS--
"--THEY RAN FOR COVER FAST!"
GREAT SCOTT!
HOLY MOLEY!
HOLY CRUD!
HOLY DISASTER, BATMAN...!
THIS LOOKS LIKE A JOB FOR...
...GLADIATOR GIANT!
DYNAMOLE!
THE CRIMSON GHOST!
IMMORTAL BALD-MAN-IN-ARMOR!
FIREFACE!
JACK OF ALL TRADES!
POLEDANCER!
THE TORNADO NINJA!
E.S. PETE!
LADY LIBERTY!

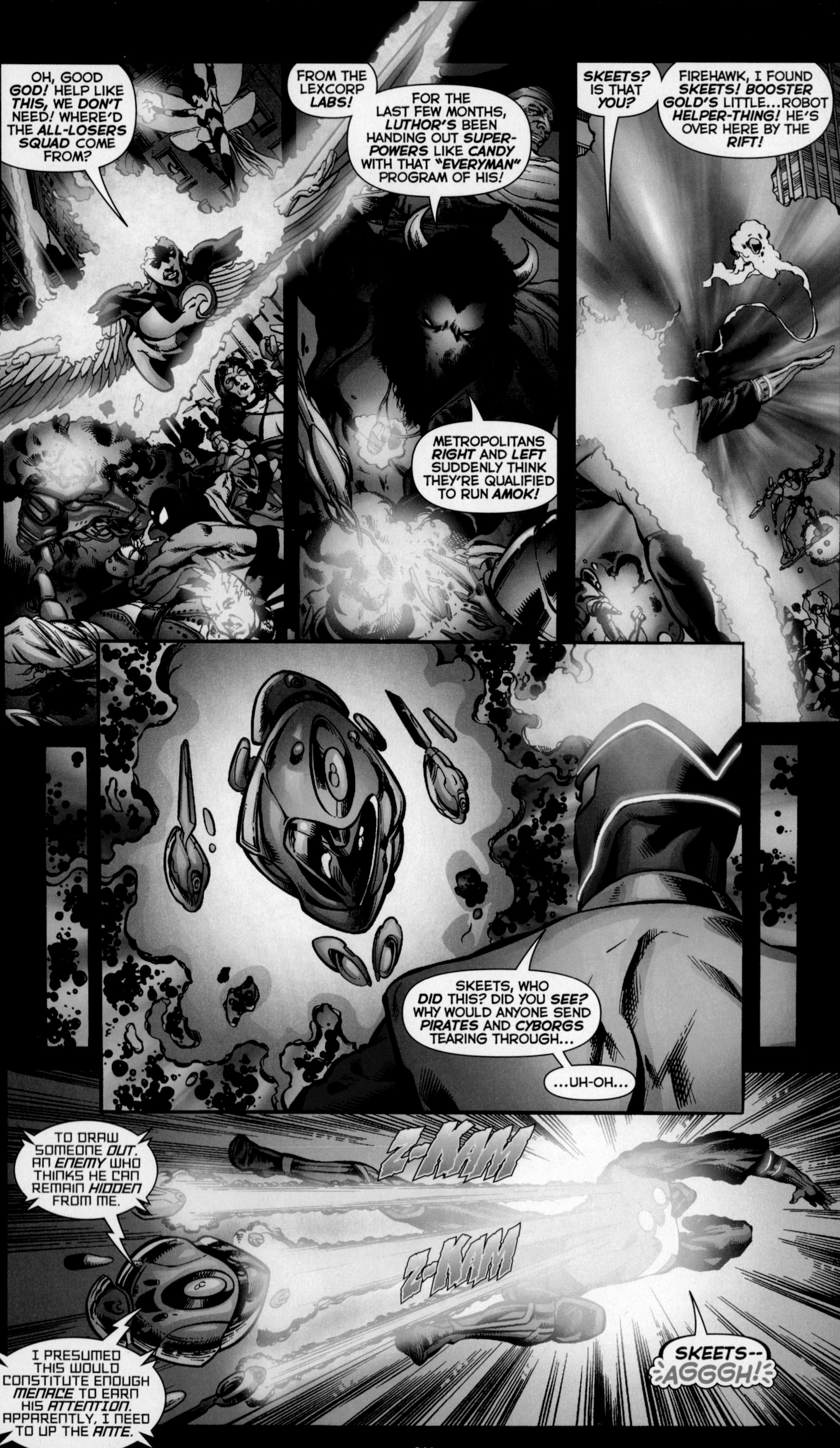

OH, GOOD GOD! HELP LIKE THIS, WE DON'T NEED! WHERE'D THE ALL-LOSERS SQUAD COME FROM?
FROM THE LEXCORP LABS!
FOR THE LAST FEW MONTHS, LUTHOR'S BEEN HANDING OUT SUPER-POWERS LIKE CANDY WITH THAT "EVERYMAN" PROGRAM OF HIS!
METROPOLITANS RIGHT AND LEFT SUDDENLY THINK THEY'RE QUALIFIED TO RUN AMOK!
SKEETS? IS THAT YOU?
FIREHAWK, I FOUND SKEETS! BOOSTER GOLD'S LITTLE...ROBOT HELPER-THING! HE'S OVER HERE BY THE RIFT!
SKEETS, WHO DID THIS? DID YOU SEE? WHY WOULD ANYONE SEND PIRATES AND CYBORGS TEARING THROUGH...
...UH-OH...
TO DRAW SOMEONE OUT. AN ENEMY WHO THINKS HE CAN REMAIN HIDDEN FROM ME.
Z-KAM
Z-KAM
I PRESUMED THIS WOULD CONSTITUTE ENOUGH MENACE TO EARN HIS ATTENTION. APPARENTLY, I NEED TO UP THE ANTE.
SKEETS--AGGGH!

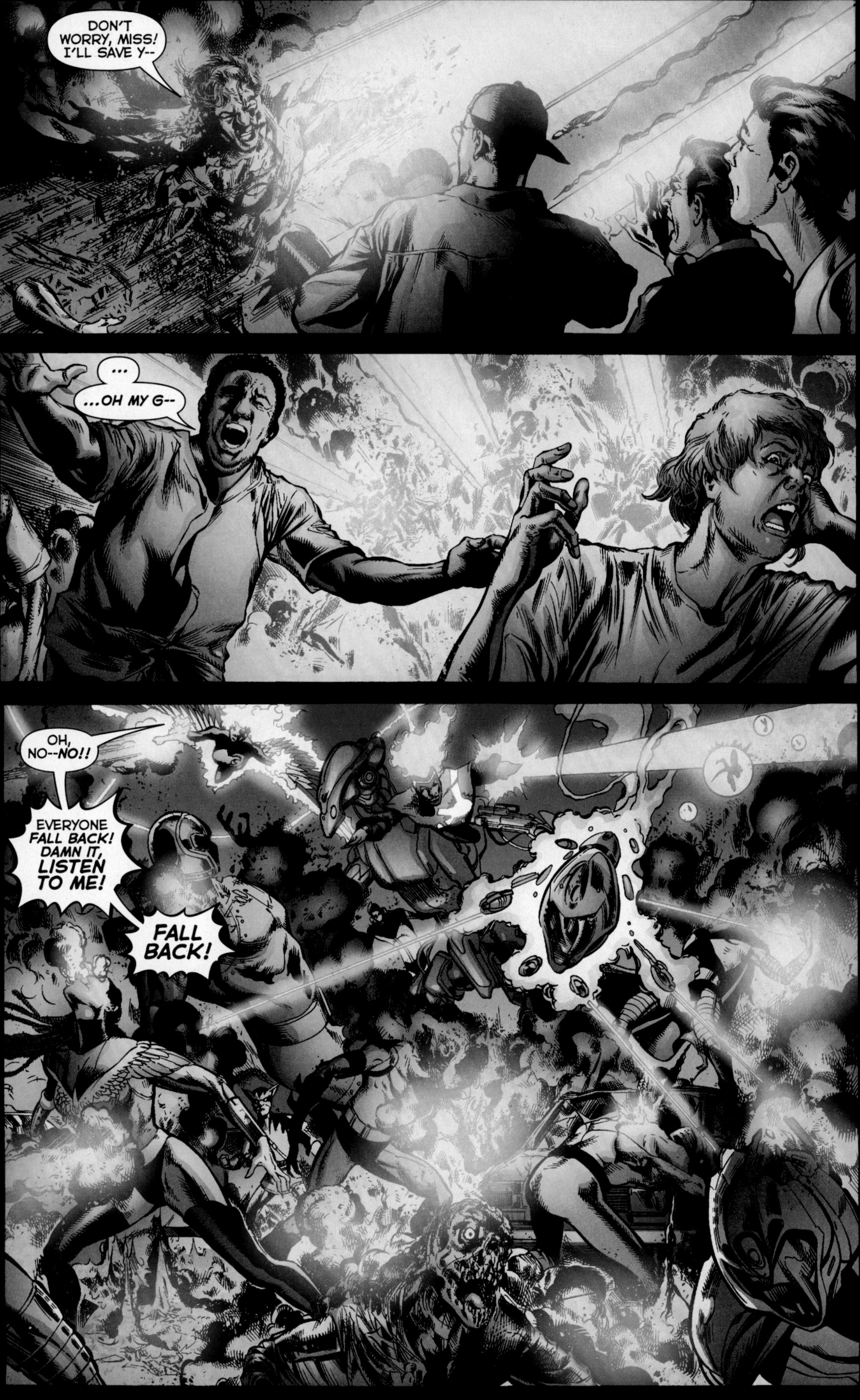
DON'T WORRY, MISS! I'LL SAVE Y--
...
...OH MY G--
OH, NO--NO!!
EVERYONE FALL BACK! DAMN IT, LISTEN TO ME!
FALL BACK!

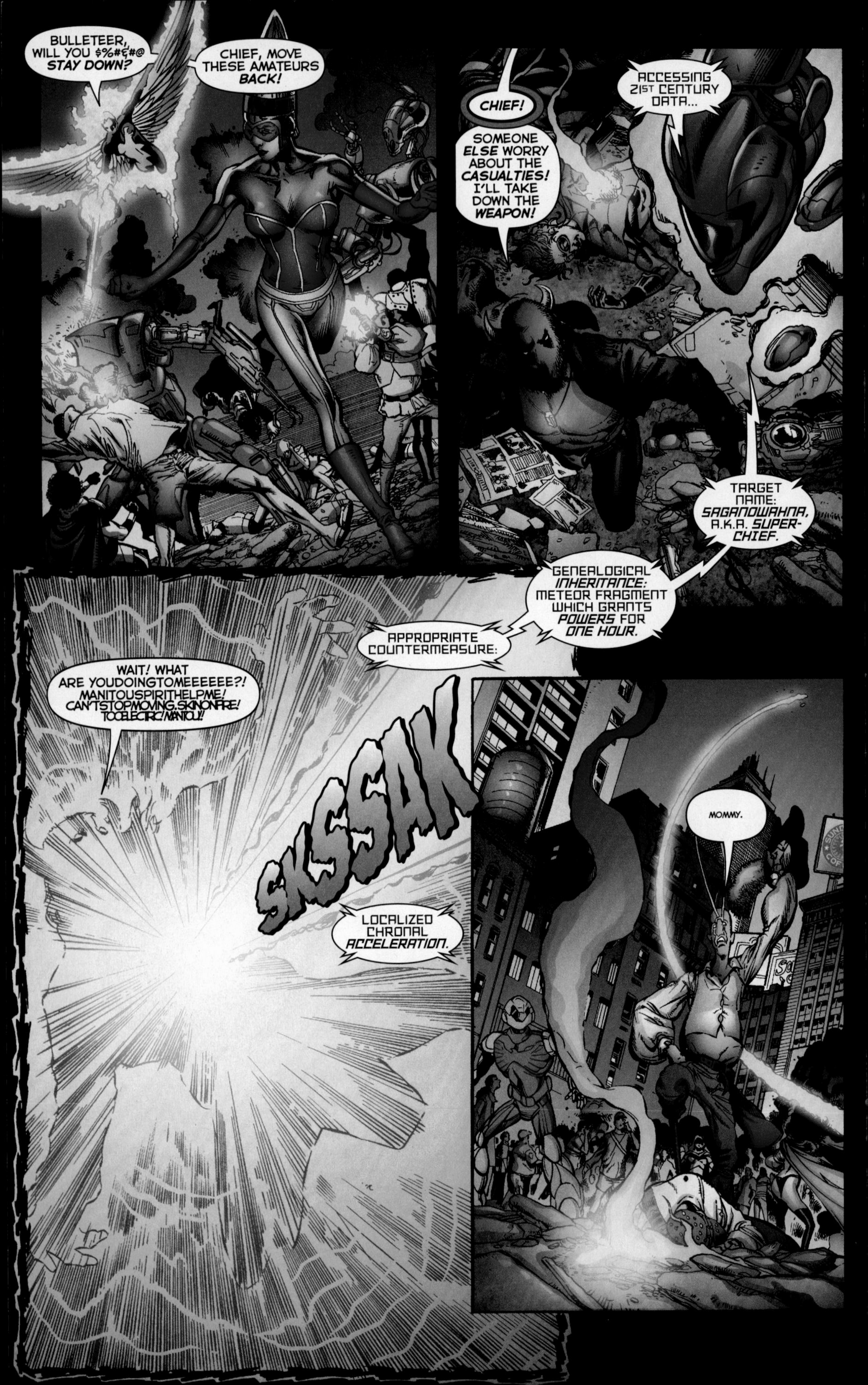
BULLETEER, WILL YOU $%#&#@ STAY DOWN?
CHIEF, MOVE THESE AMATEURS BACK!
CHIEF!
SOMEONE ELSE WORRY ABOUT THE CASUALTIES! I'LL TAKE DOWN THE WEAPON!
ACCESSING 21ST CENTURY DATA...
TARGET NAME: SAGANOWAHNA, A.K.A. SUPER-CHIEF.
GENEALOGICAL INHERITANCE: METEOR FRAGMENT WHICH GRANTS POWERS FOR ONE HOUR.
APPROPRIATE COUNTERMEASURE:
WAIT! WHAT ARE YOUDOINGTOMEEEEEE?! MANITOUSPIRITHELPME! CAN'TSTOPMOVING.SKINONFIRE! TOOELECTRIC!MANITOU!!
SKSSAK
LOCALIZED CHRONAL ACCELERATION.
MOMMY.

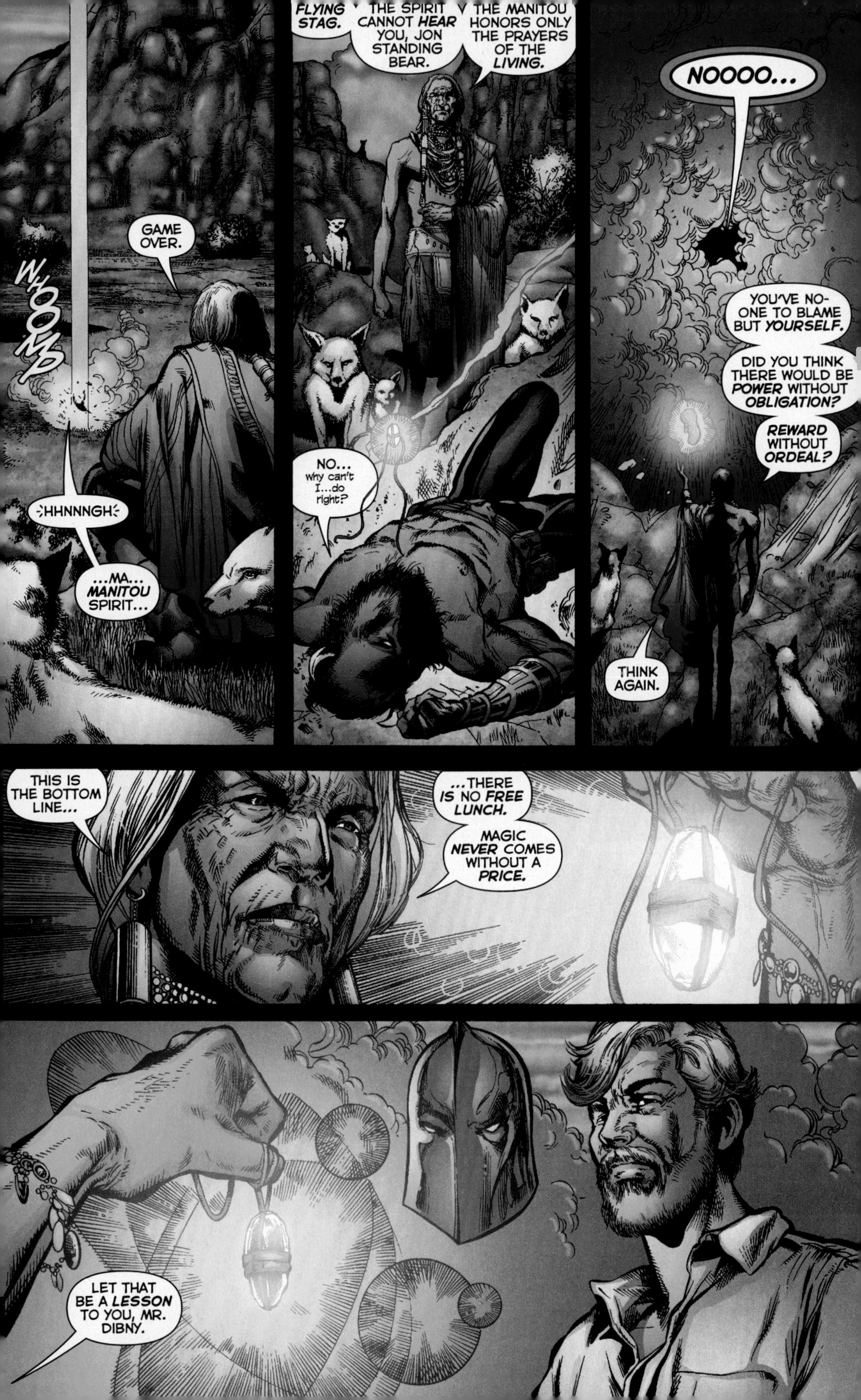

GAME OVER.
WHOOM
-HHNNNGH-
...MA... MANITOU SPIRIT...
FLYING STAG.
THE SPIRIT CANNOT HEAR YOU, JON STANDING BEAR.
THE MANITOU HONORS ONLY THE PRAYERS OF THE LIVING.
NO... why can't I...do right?
NOOOO...
YOU'VE NO-ONE TO BLAME BUT YOURSELF.
DID YOU THINK THERE WOULD BE POWER WITHOUT OBLIGATION?
REWARD WITHOUT ORDEAL?
THINK AGAIN.
THIS IS THE BOTTOM LINE...
...THERE IS NO FREE LUNCH.
MAGIC NEVER COMES WITHOUT A PRICE.
LET THAT BE A LESSON TO YOU, MR. DIBNY.

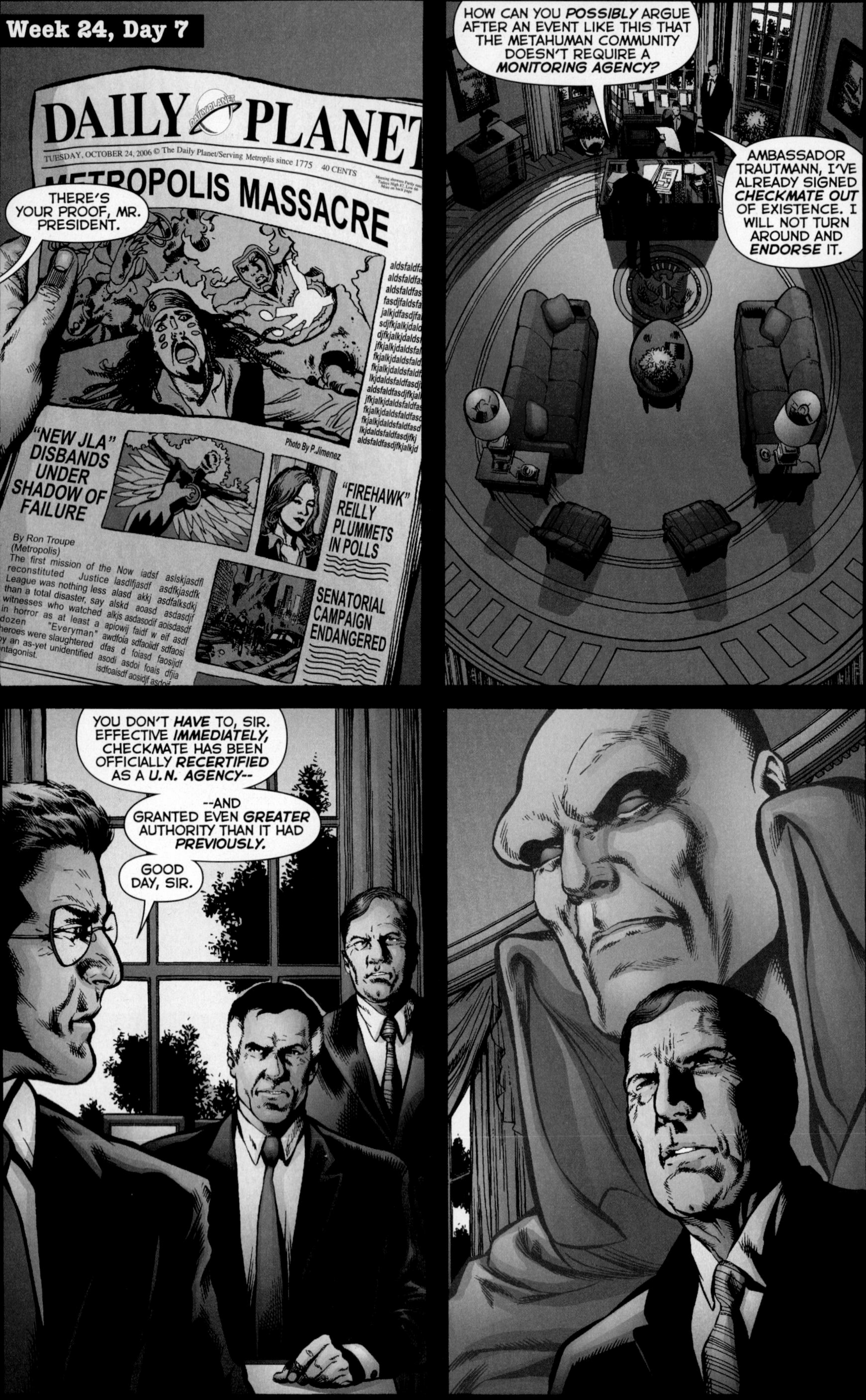
Week 24, Day 7
DAILY PLANET
TUESDAY, OCTOBER 24, 2006 © The Daily Planet/Serving Metropolis since 1775 40 CENTS
METROPOLIS MASSACRE
THERE'S YOUR PROOF, MR. PRESIDENT.
Photo By P. Jimenez
"NEW JLA" DISBANDS UNDER SHADOW OF FAILURE
By Ron Troupe (Metropolis)
The first mission of the Now reconstituted Justice League was nothing less than a total disaster, say witnesses who watched in horror as at least a dozen "Everyman" heroes were slaughtered by an as-yet unidentified antagonist.
"FIREHAWK" REILLY PLUMMETS IN POLLS
SENATORIAL CAMPAIGN ENDANGERED
HOW CAN YOU POSSIBLY ARGUE AFTER AN EVENT LIKE THIS THAT THE METAHUMAN COMMUNITY DOESN'T REQUIRE A MONITORING AGENCY?
AMBASSADOR TRAUTMANN, I'VE ALREADY SIGNED CHECKMATE OUT OF EXISTENCE. I WILL NOT TURN AROUND AND ENDORSE IT.
YOU DON'T HAVE TO, SIR. EFFECTIVE IMMEDIATELY, CHECKMATE HAS BEEN OFFICIALLY RECERTIFIED AS A U.N. AGENCY--
--AND GRANTED EVEN GREATER AUTHORITY THAN IT HAD PREVIOUSLY.
GOOD DAY, SIR.

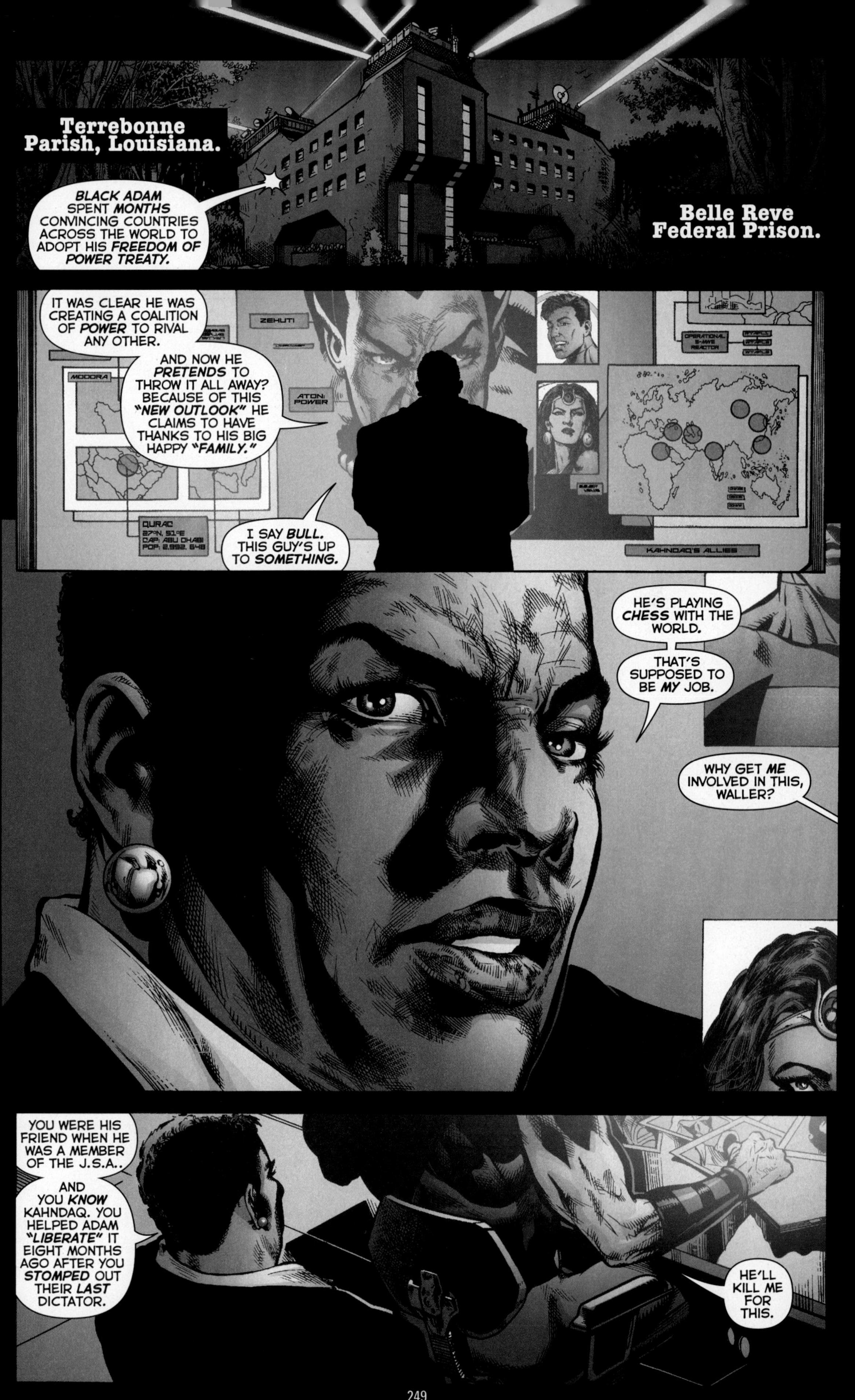
Terrebonne Parish, Louisiana.
BLACK ADAM SPENT MONTHS CONVINCING COUNTRIES ACROSS THE WORLD TO ADOPT HIS FREEDOM OF POWER TREATY.
Belle Reve Federal Prison.
IT WAS CLEAR HE WAS CREATING A COALITION OF POWER TO RIVAL ANY OTHER.
AND NOW HE PRETENDS TO THROW IT ALL AWAY? BECAUSE OF THIS "NEW OUTLOOK" HE CLAIMS TO HAVE THANKS TO HIS BIG HAPPY "FAMILY."
ZEHUTI
MODORA
ATON: POWER
QURAC 27°N, 51°E CAP: ABU DHABI POP: 2,992, 648
KAHNDAQ'S ALLIES
I SAY BULL. THIS GUY'S UP TO SOMETHING.
HE'S PLAYING CHESS WITH THE WORLD.
THAT'S SUPPOSED TO BE MY JOB.
WHY GET ME INVOLVED IN THIS, WALLER?
YOU WERE HIS FRIEND WHEN HE WAS A MEMBER OF THE J.S.A..
AND YOU KNOW KAHNDAQ. YOU HELPED ADAM "LIBERATE" IT EIGHT MONTHS AGO AFTER YOU STOMPED OUT THEIR LAST DICTATOR.
HE'LL KILL ME FOR THIS.

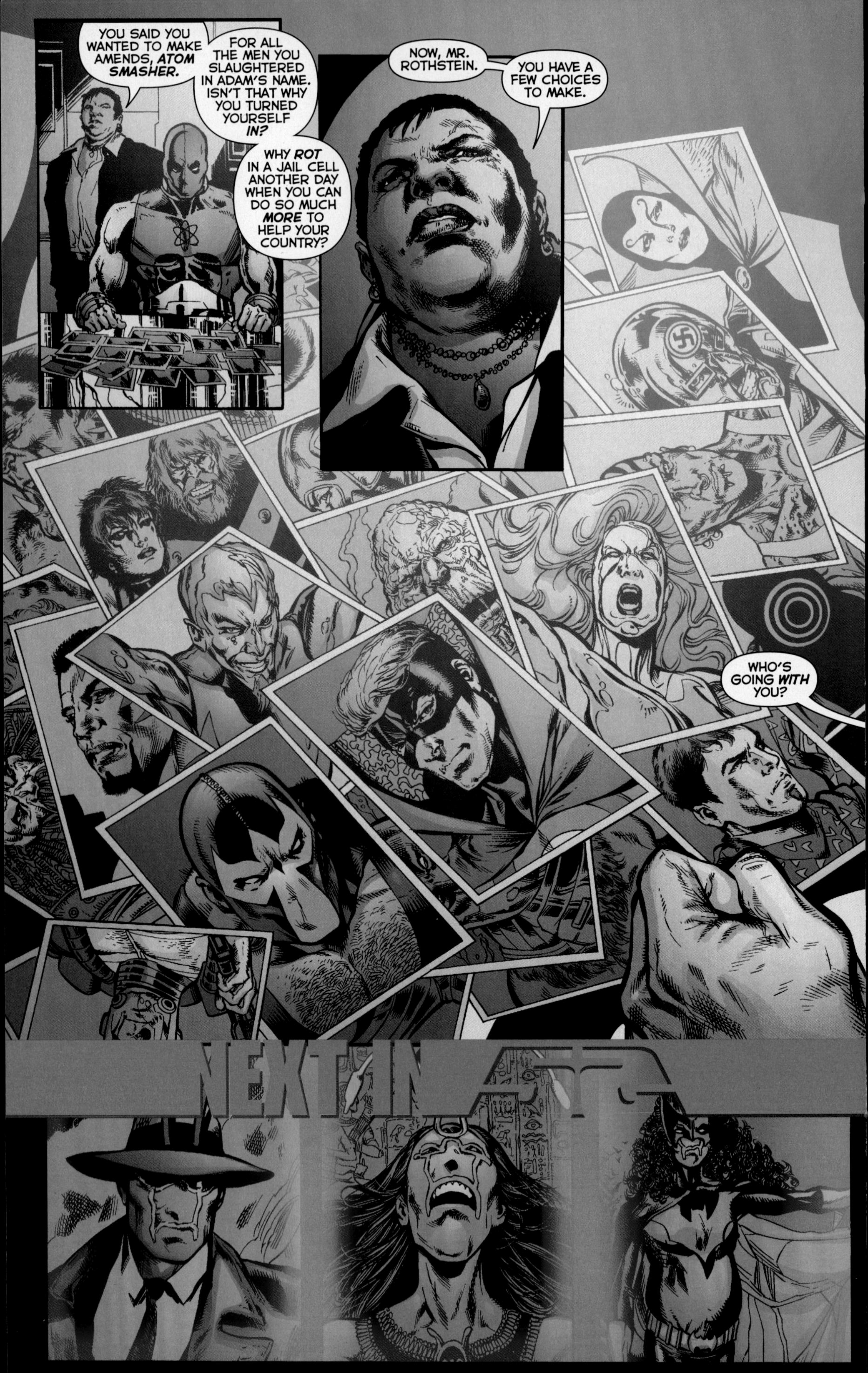
YOU SAID YOU WANTED TO MAKE AMENDS, ATOM SMASHER.
FOR ALL THE MEN YOU SLAUGHTERED IN ADAM'S NAME. ISN'T THAT WHY YOU TURNED YOURSELF IN?
WHY ROT IN A JAIL CELL ANOTHER DAY WHEN YOU CAN DO SO MUCH MORE TO HELP YOUR COUNTRY?
NOW, MR. ROTHSTEIN.
YOU HAVE A FEW CHOICES TO MAKE.
WHO'S GOING WITH YOU?
NEXT IN

WEEK TWENTY-FOUR NOTES

MARK WAID

Elliot Maggin was (and still is) a brilliant real-world comics writer. In the 1970s, he was the one who first envisioned Oliver Queen as a mayoral candidate, so it only seemed natural to make him Ollie's campaign manager in 52.

Ambush Bug — a Keith Giffen creation from the '80s — is here because we promised some convention-panel audience that we'd find a place for him, and, boy, I'm glad we did. I love occasionally writing characters who know they're in a comic book. In fact, in the original script for page four, his line is "Hello, room service? Send up a PLOT and three pages of DIALOGUE right AWAY! Giffen's getting BORED!," to which Firestorm says, "No, I don't know who 'Giffen' is, EITHER..." I was told that the Powers That Be at DC are nervous about characters who break the fourth wall, hence the change, but I suspect it was also a good way to work in another "52" reference.

I included Grant Morrison's new Bulleteer as a JLAer largely as a placeholder until we could come up with a more fitting character. You can tell because she has exactly one word of dialogue and no more. Unfortunately, Grant somehow overlooked the point in the script where I asked him specifically if she was available and okay to use (PAGE THREE, YOU DRUNKEN SCOT! SEE BELOW!) and, hearing no reply, we just went with her. Grant later complained in an interview that no one had alerted him to her presence, so I'm going to send him a copy of that script page every day for the rest of his life.

Only artist Phil Jimenez would put so much effort into designing two dozen new costumed heroes who have the life expectancy of one panel, one of the many reasons why we love him. Many of them, like "E.S. Pete" and "Immortal Bald-Man-In-Armor," are brainchildren of Steve Wacker's, but I have been waiting fifteen years to use the name "Poledancer."

I love Geoff's scene with the Black Marvel Family. Geoff has a gift for characterization, and within one page, you know who all these characters are and what motivates them.

SCRIPT EXCERPT

WEEK TWENTY-FOUR — PAGE THREE

PANEL ONE

Interior, Jason Rusch's college-student apartment. Firestorm's still on the "phone," and with him are Firehawk, Super-Chief (in an open trench coat, powerstone visible), Bulleteer (if available — Grant?) and Ambush Bug. The gathering has the air of a poker party — chips, sodas.

FIRESTORM: ...to join the new JUSTICE LEAGUE.

BREAKDOWNS

BY **KEITH GIFFEN**

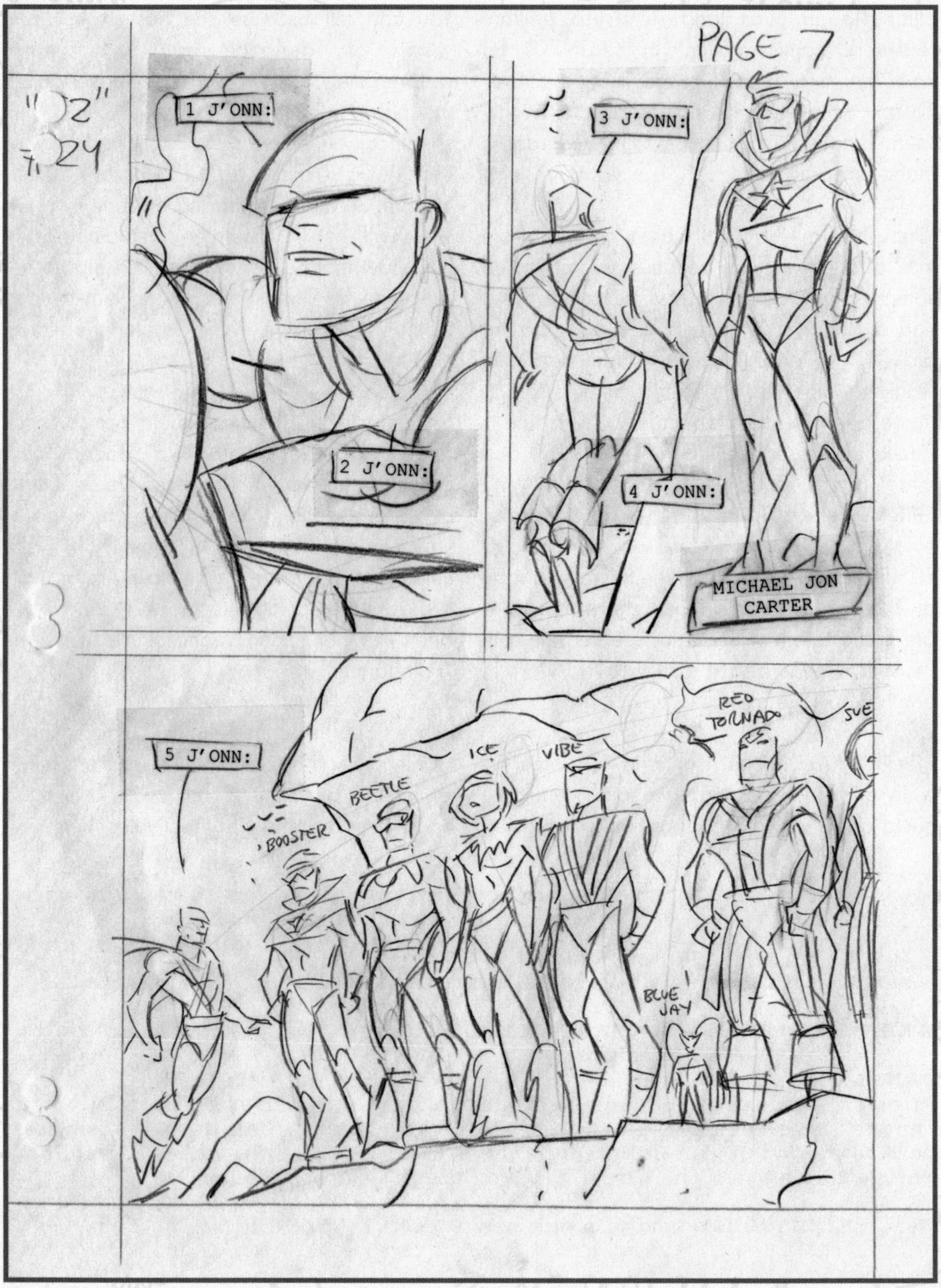

PAGE 7
1 J'ONN:
2 J'ONN:
3 J'ONN:
4 J'ONN:
MICHAEL JON CARTER
5 J'ONN:
BOOSTER
BEETLE
ICE
VIBE
RED TORNADO
SUE
BLUE JAY

P E N C I L S / I N K S

BY **PHIL JIMENEZ & ANDY LANNING**

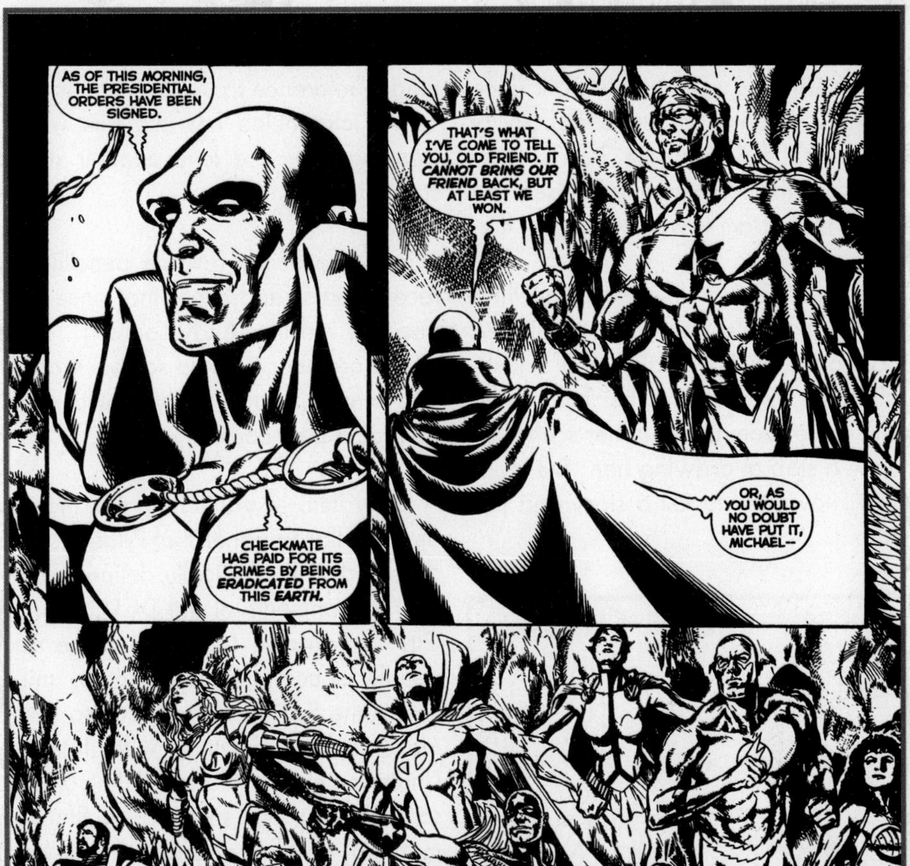
AS OF THIS MORNING, THE PRESIDENTIAL ORDERS HAVE BEEN SIGNED.
CHECKMATE HAS PAID FOR ITS CRIMES BY BEING *ERADICATED* FROM THIS *EARTH.*
THAT'S WHAT I'VE COME TO TELL YOU, OLD FRIEND. IT *CANNOT BRING OUR FRIEND* BACK, BUT AT LEAST WE WON.
OR, AS YOU WOULD NO DOUBT HAVE PUT IT, MICHAEL--
"JUSTICE IS SERVED."

Leave it to penciller Phil Jimenez to take Keith Giffen's modest panel of deceased Justice Leaguer statues and reinterpret it to encompass *every* JLAer who has been killed in action.

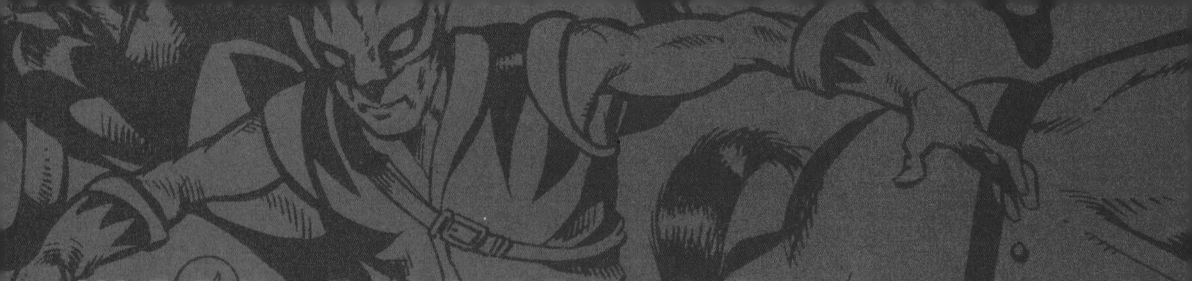

WEEK TWENTY-FOUR NOTES

PHIL JIMENEZ

The thing that excited me most about working on 52 was working with one of my artistic heroes, Keith Giffen. I've loved his work since I was 13 — his vision of the future in LEGION OF SUPER-HEROES defined the 30th century for me — so the opportunity to see his process and learn from it was thrilling to me.

Obviously, I do have a different storytelling style, so I did change some things — I flipped Firehawk around on the establishing splash, for example, so we could see her full frontal, and I gave more room to Isis in her scenes so I could take a stab at drawing her. But man, does Keith know how to tell a story and just get right to it.

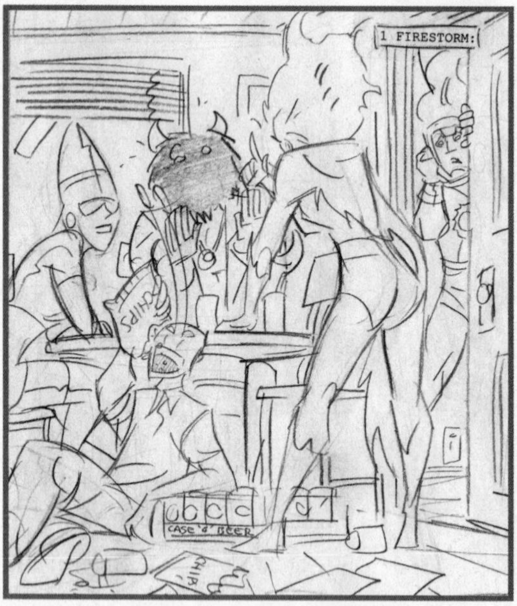
1 FIRESTORM:
CHIPS

Isis, ultimately, was my favorite character to draw — I love the regal, god-based characters — although drawing any member of the Great Ten was fantastic too. And never in my life did I think I'd have an opportunity to draw Ambush Bug...let alone on the Justice League. For some reason, I felt like Amy Sedaris's character "Jerri Blank" from *Strangers With Candy* was a great model/reference to use for Ambush Bug, and sort of channeled her into him when I was drawing him. I'd love another stab at him some day.

This is one of my favorite pencilling jobs in recent years, and proof that once again, no one inks me like Andy Lanning. I really do wish more people could see our work in black and white...I think Andy would win lots of awards if they could.

A funny item — you'll note that there are lots of umbrellas in panel 2 of Page 1. I'm sort of obsessed with artistically delineating the various environments of the DCU, from Gotham City to Paradise Island, to make each one visually special, unique. In my mind, Star City is the Seattle of the DCU, so I wanted to make it like Seattle, with lots of rain. Unfortunately, I failed to tell the colorist this — so there's lots of sunshine in Star City that morning, and lots of ordinary folk wandering around, for no apparent reason, with open umbrellas...

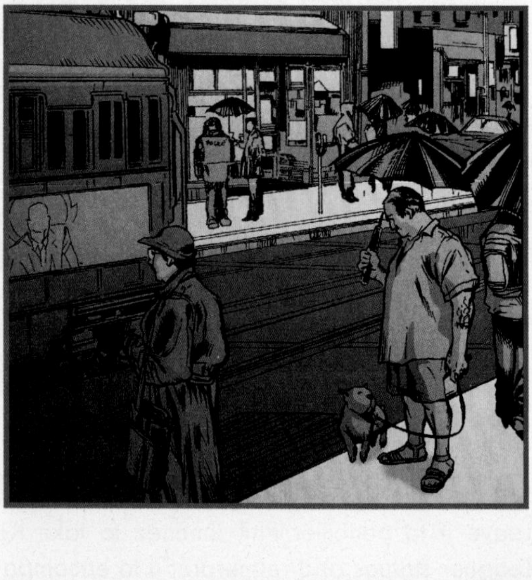

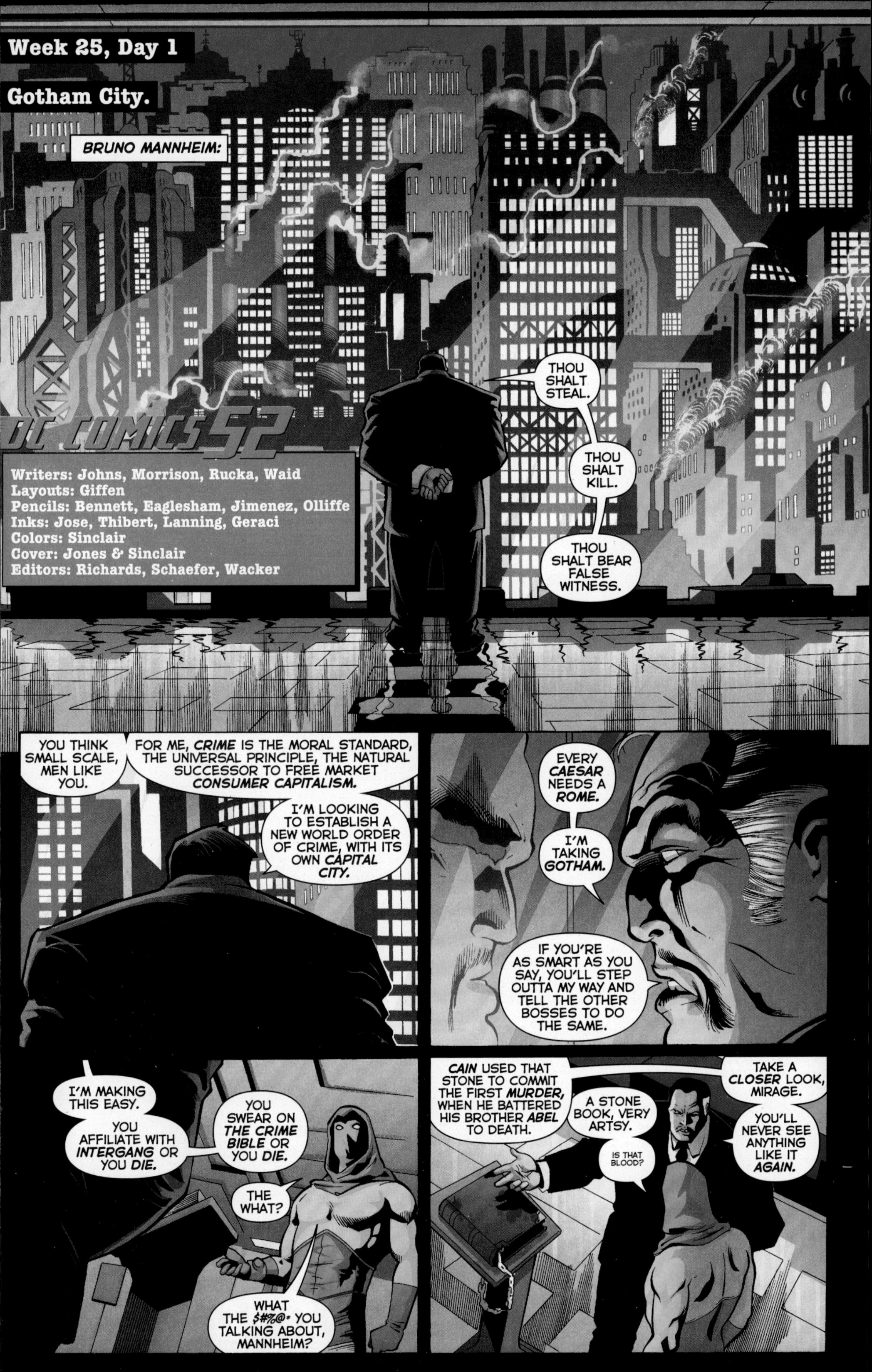
Week 25, Day 1
Gotham City.
BRUNO MANNHEIM:
THOU SHALT STEAL.
THOU SHALT KILL.
THOU SHALT BEAR FALSE WITNESS.
DC COMICS 52
Writers: Johns, Morrison, Rucka, Waid
Layouts: Giffen
Pencils: Bennett, Eaglesham, Jimenez, Olliffe
Inks: Jose, Thibert, Lanning, Geraci
Colors: Sinclair
Cover: Jones & Sinclair
Editors: Richards, Schaefer, Wacker
YOU THINK SMALL SCALE, MEN LIKE YOU.
FOR ME, CRIME IS THE MORAL STANDARD, THE UNIVERSAL PRINCIPLE, THE NATURAL SUCCESSOR TO FREE MARKET CONSUMER CAPITALISM.
I'M LOOKING TO ESTABLISH A NEW WORLD ORDER OF CRIME, WITH ITS OWN CAPITAL CITY.
EVERY CAESAR NEEDS A ROME.
I'M TAKING GOTHAM.
IF YOU'RE AS SMART AS YOU SAY, YOU'LL STEP OUTTA MY WAY AND TELL THE OTHER BOSSES TO DO THE SAME.
I'M MAKING THIS EASY.
YOU AFFILIATE WITH INTERGANG OR YOU DIE.
YOU SWEAR ON THE CRIME BIBLE OR YOU DIE.
THE WHAT?
WHAT THE $#%@* YOU TALKING ABOUT, MANNHEIM?
CAIN USED THAT STONE TO COMMIT THE FIRST MURDER, WHEN HE BATTERED HIS BROTHER ABEL TO DEATH.
A STONE BOOK, VERY ARTSY.
IS THAT BLOOD?
TAKE A CLOSER LOOK, MIRAGE.
YOU'LL NEVER SEE ANYTHING LIKE IT AGAIN.

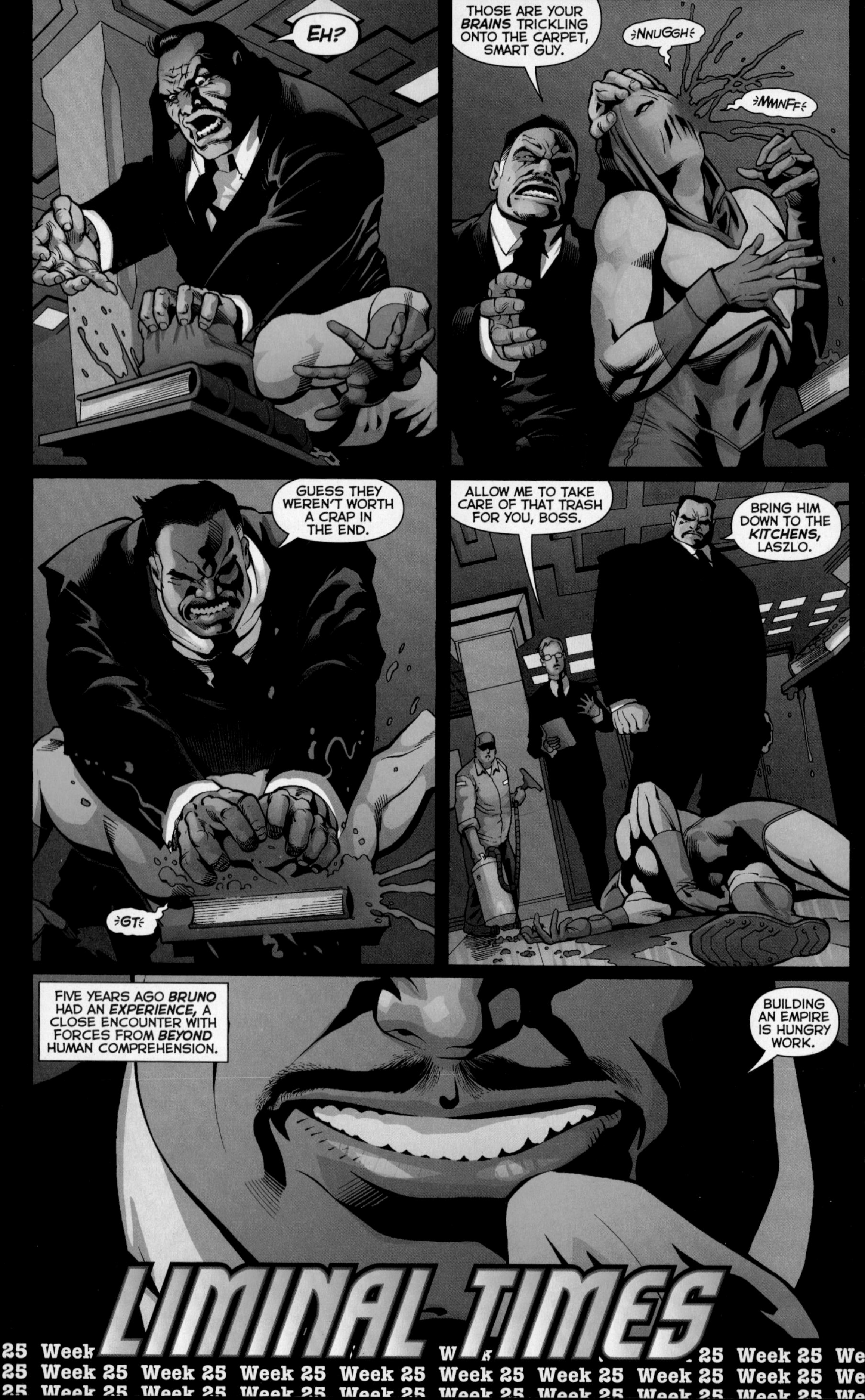
EH?
THOSE ARE YOUR BRAINS TRICKLING ONTO THE CARPET, SMART GUY.
NNUGGH
MMNFF
GUESS THEY WEREN'T WORTH A CRAP IN THE END.
GT
ALLOW ME TO TAKE CARE OF THAT TRASH FOR YOU, BOSS.
BRING HIM DOWN TO THE KITCHENS, LASZLO.
FIVE YEARS AGO BRUNO HAD AN EXPERIENCE, A CLOSE ENCOUNTER WITH FORCES FROM BEYOND HUMAN COMPREHENSION.
BUILDING AN EMPIRE IS HUNGRY WORK.
LIMINAL TIMES
25 Week 25 Week 25 Week 25 Week 25 Week 25 Week 25 Week 25 Week 25 We

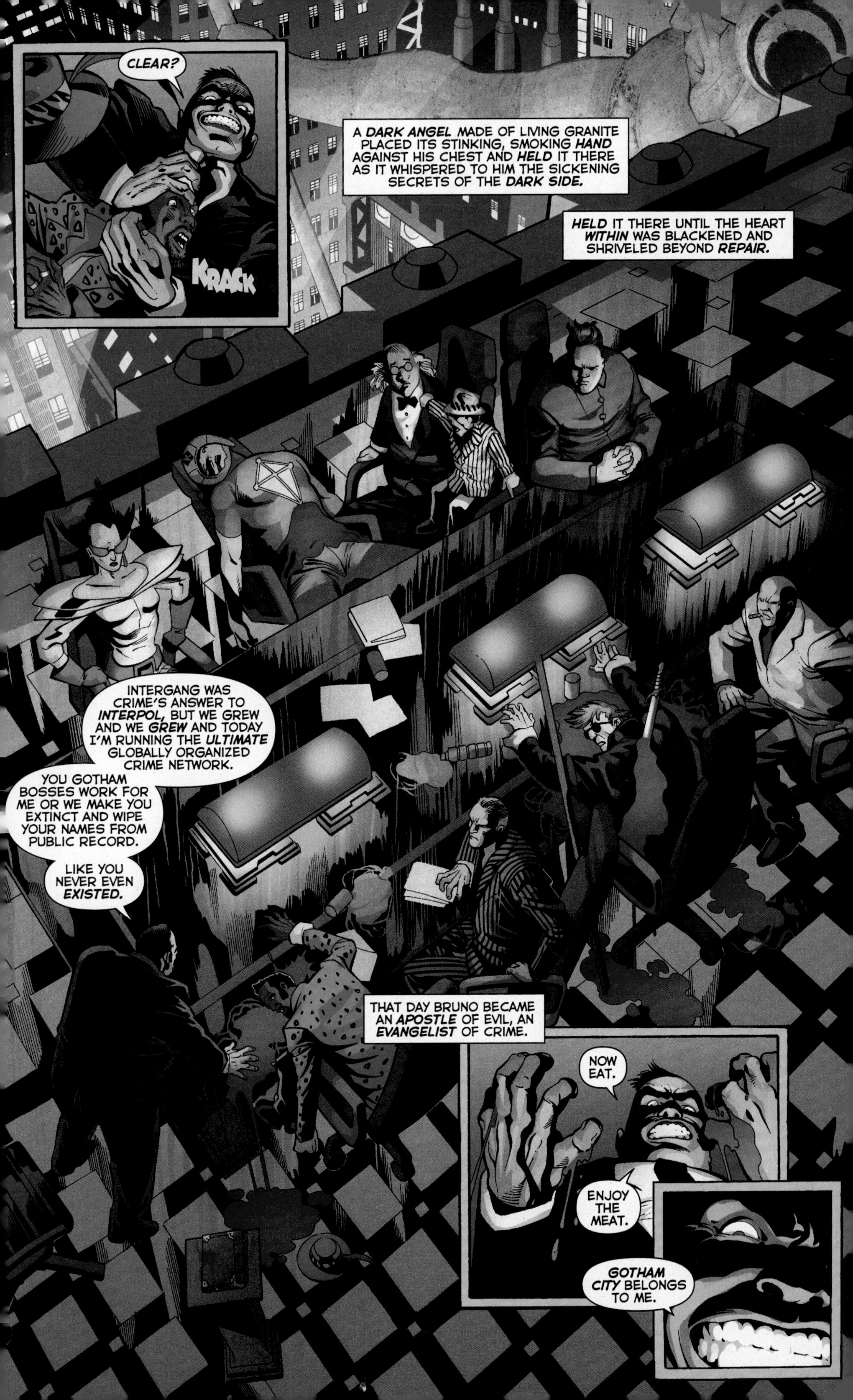
CLEAR?
KRACK
A DARK ANGEL MADE OF LIVING GRANITE PLACED ITS STINKING, SMOKING HAND AGAINST HIS CHEST AND HELD IT THERE AS IT WHISPERED TO HIM THE SICKENING SECRETS OF THE DARK SIDE.
HELD IT THERE UNTIL THE HEART WITHIN WAS BLACKENED AND SHRIVELED BEYOND REPAIR.
INTERGANG WAS CRIME'S ANSWER TO INTERPOL, BUT WE GREW AND WE GREW AND TODAY I'M RUNNING THE ULTIMATE GLOBALLY ORGANIZED CRIME NETWORK.
YOU GOTHAM BOSSES WORK FOR ME OR WE MAKE YOU EXTINCT AND WIPE YOUR NAMES FROM PUBLIC RECORD.
LIKE YOU NEVER EVEN EXISTED.
THAT DAY BRUNO BECAME AN APOSTLE OF EVIL, AN EVANGELIST OF CRIME.
NOW EAT.
ENJOY THE MEAT.
GOTHAM CITY BELONGS TO ME.

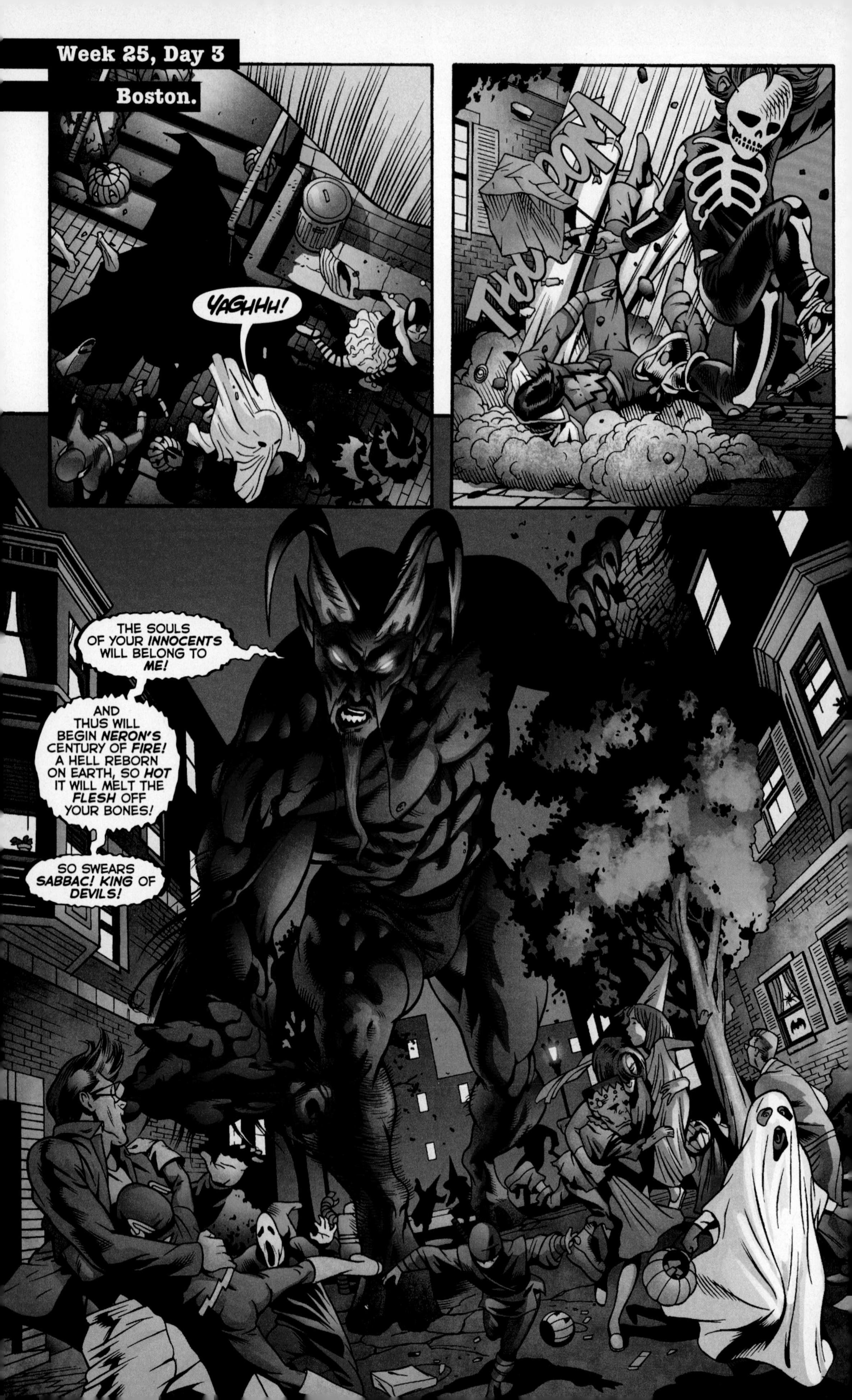
Week 25, Day 3
Boston.
YAGHHH!
THE SOULS OF YOUR INNOCENTS WILL BELONG TO ME!
AND THUS WILL BEGIN NERON'S CENTURY OF FIRE! A HELL REBORN ON EARTH, SO HOT IT WILL MELT THE FLESH OFF YOUR BONES!
SO SWEARS SABBAC! KING OF DEVILS!

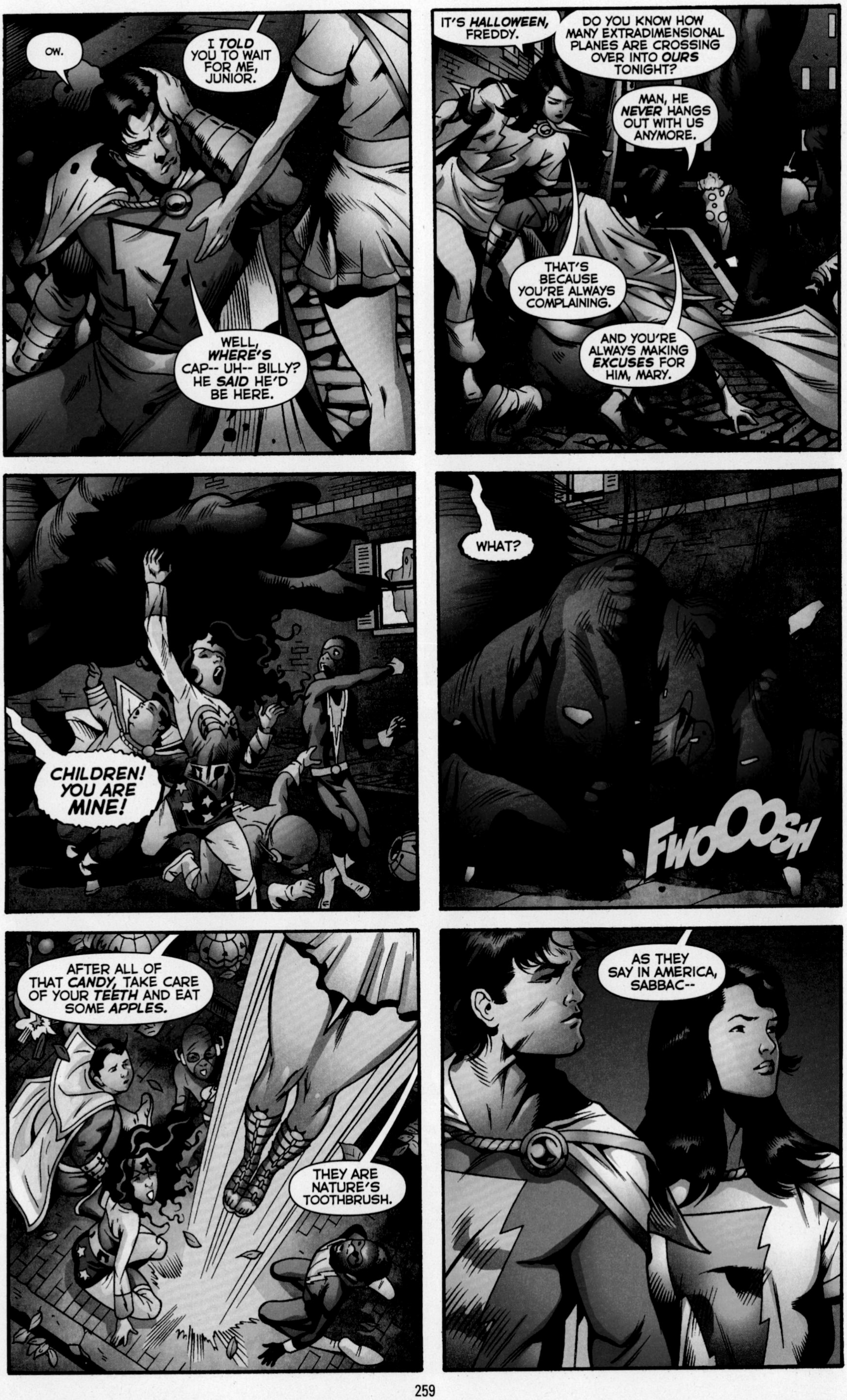
OW.
I TOLD YOU TO WAIT FOR ME, JUNIOR.
WELL, WHERE'S CAP-- UH-- BILLY? HE SAID HE'D BE HERE.
IT'S HALLOWEEN, FREDDY.
DO YOU KNOW HOW MANY EXTRADIMENSIONAL PLANES ARE CROSSING OVER INTO OURS TONIGHT?
MAN, HE NEVER HANGS OUT WITH US ANYMORE.
THAT'S BECAUSE YOU'RE ALWAYS COMPLAINING.
AND YOU'RE ALWAYS MAKING EXCUSES FOR HIM, MARY.
CHILDREN! YOU ARE MINE!
WHAT?
FWOOOSH
AFTER ALL OF THAT CANDY, TAKE CARE OF YOUR TEETH AND EAT SOME APPLES.
THEY ARE NATURE'S TOOTHBRUSH.
AS THEY SAY IN AMERICA, SABBAC--

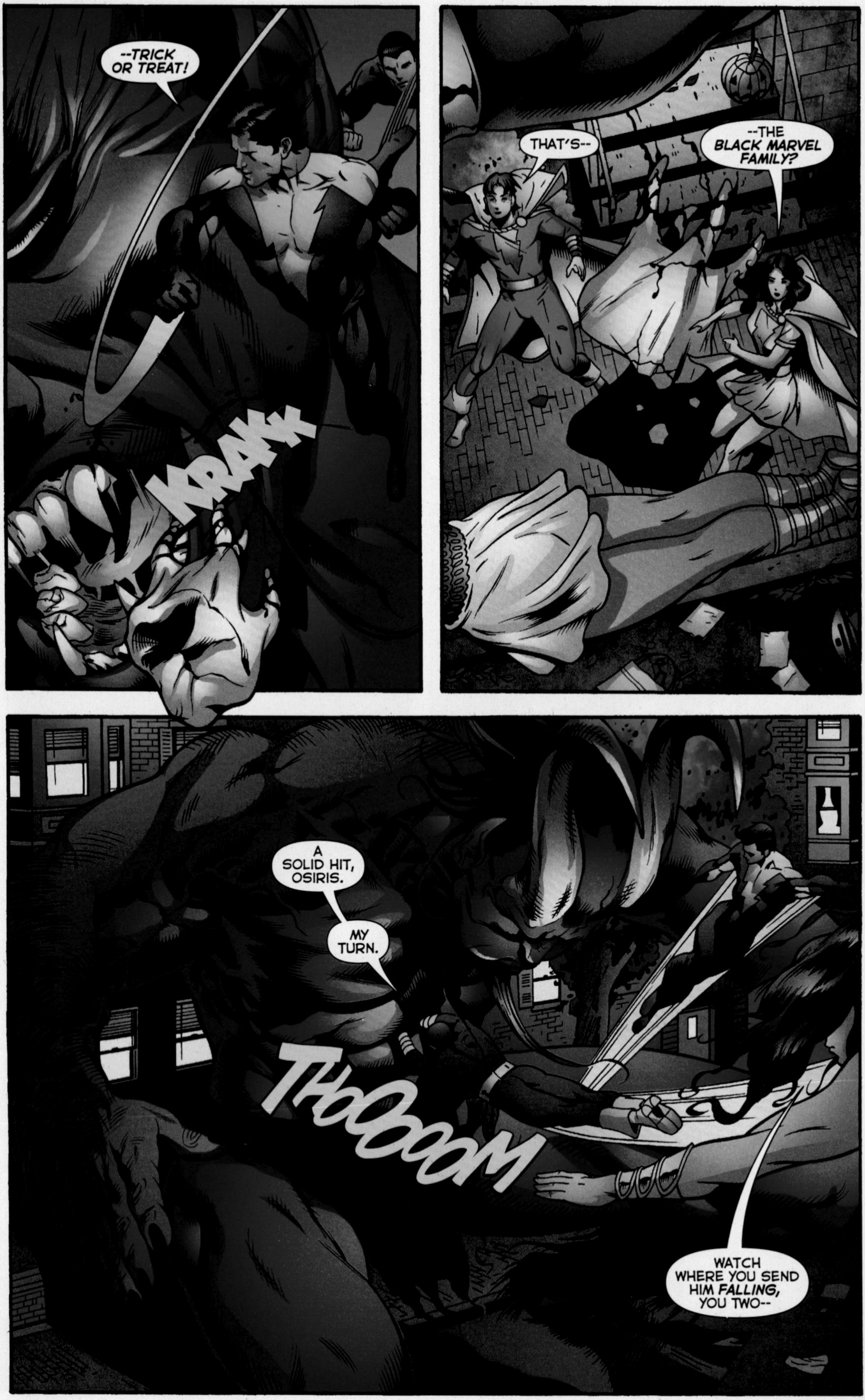
--TRICK OR TREAT!
KRAAK
THAT'S--
--THE BLACK MARVEL FAMILY?
A SOLID HIT, OSIRIS.
MY TURN.
THOOOOM
WATCH WHERE YOU SEND HIM FALLING, YOU TWO--

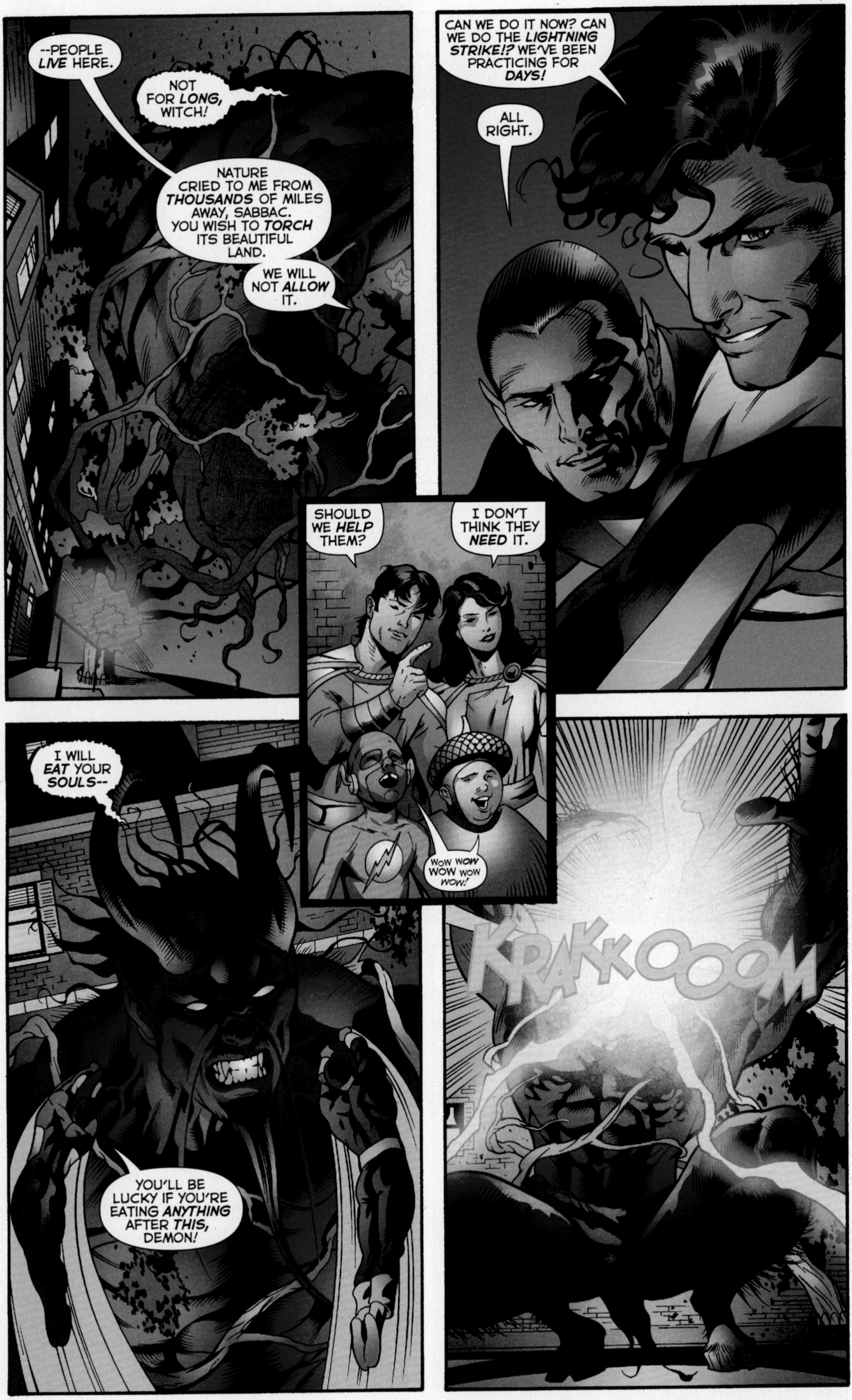
--PEOPLE LIVE HERE.
NOT FOR LONG, WITCH!
NATURE CRIED TO ME FROM THOUSANDS OF MILES AWAY, SABBAC. YOU WISH TO TORCH ITS BEAUTIFUL LAND.
WE WILL NOT ALLOW IT.
CAN WE DO IT NOW? CAN WE DO THE LIGHTNING STRIKE!? WE'VE BEEN PRACTICING FOR DAYS!
ALL RIGHT.
SHOULD WE HELP THEM?
I DON'T THINK THEY NEED IT.
WOW WOW WOW WOW WOW!
I WILL EAT YOUR SOULS--
YOU'LL BE LUCKY IF YOU'RE EATING ANYTHING AFTER THIS, DEMON!
KRAKKOOOM

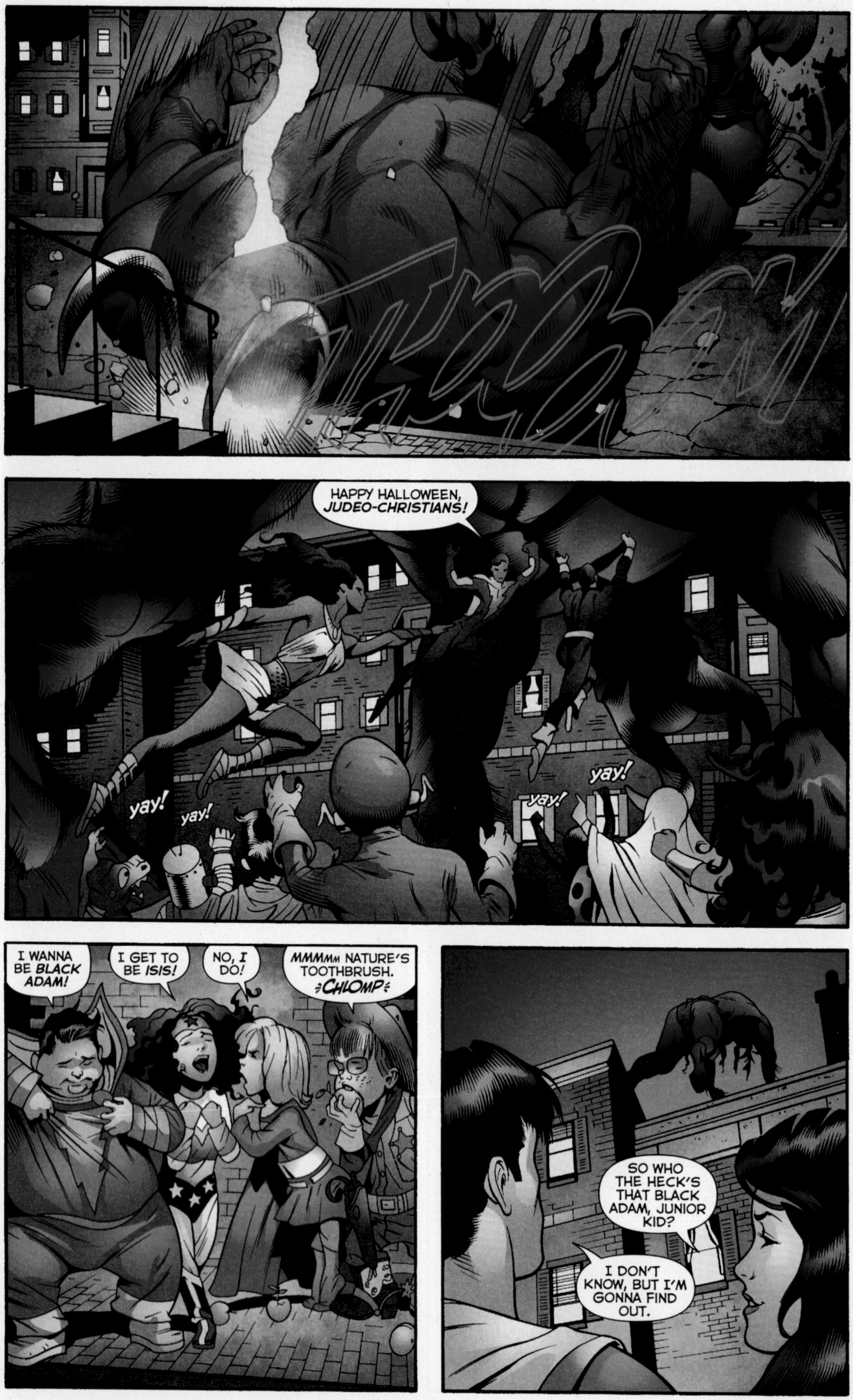
HAPPY HALLOWEEN, JUDEO-CHRISTIANS!
yay!
yay!
yay!
yay!
I WANNA BE BLACK ADAM!
I GET TO BE ISIS!
NO, I DO!
MMMMM NATURE'S TOOTHBRUSH.
CHLOMP
SO WHO THE HECK'S THAT BLACK ADAM, JUNIOR KID?
I DON'T KNOW, BUT I'M GONNA FIND OUT.

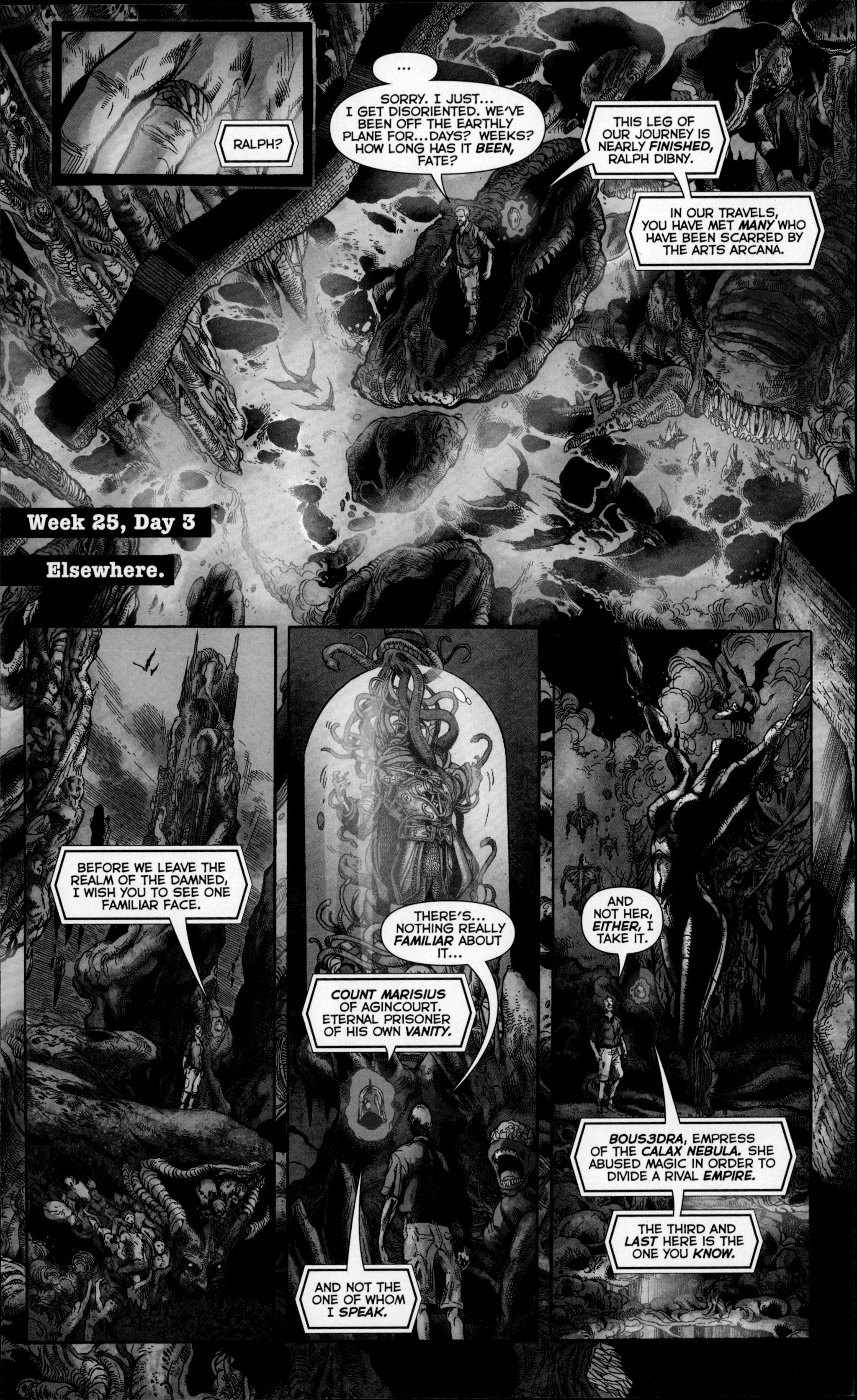
RALPH?
...
SORRY. I JUST... I GET DISORIENTED. WE'VE BEEN OFF THE EARTHLY PLANE FOR...DAYS? WEEKS? HOW LONG HAS IT BEEN, FATE?
THIS LEG OF OUR JOURNEY IS NEARLY FINISHED, RALPH DIBNY.
IN OUR TRAVELS, YOU HAVE MET MANY WHO HAVE BEEN SCARRED BY THE ARTS ARCANA.
Week 25, Day 3
Elsewhere.
BEFORE WE LEAVE THE REALM OF THE DAMNED, I WISH YOU TO SEE ONE FAMILIAR FACE.
THERE'S... NOTHING REALLY FAMILIAR ABOUT IT...
COUNT MARISIUS OF AGINCOURT. ETERNAL PRISONER OF HIS OWN VANITY.
AND NOT THE ONE OF WHOM I SPEAK.
AND NOT HER, EITHER, I TAKE IT.
BOUS3DRA, EMPRESS OF THE CALAX NEBULA. SHE ABUSED MAGIC IN ORDER TO DIVIDE A RIVAL EMPIRE.
THE THIRD AND LAST HERE IS THE ONE YOU KNOW.

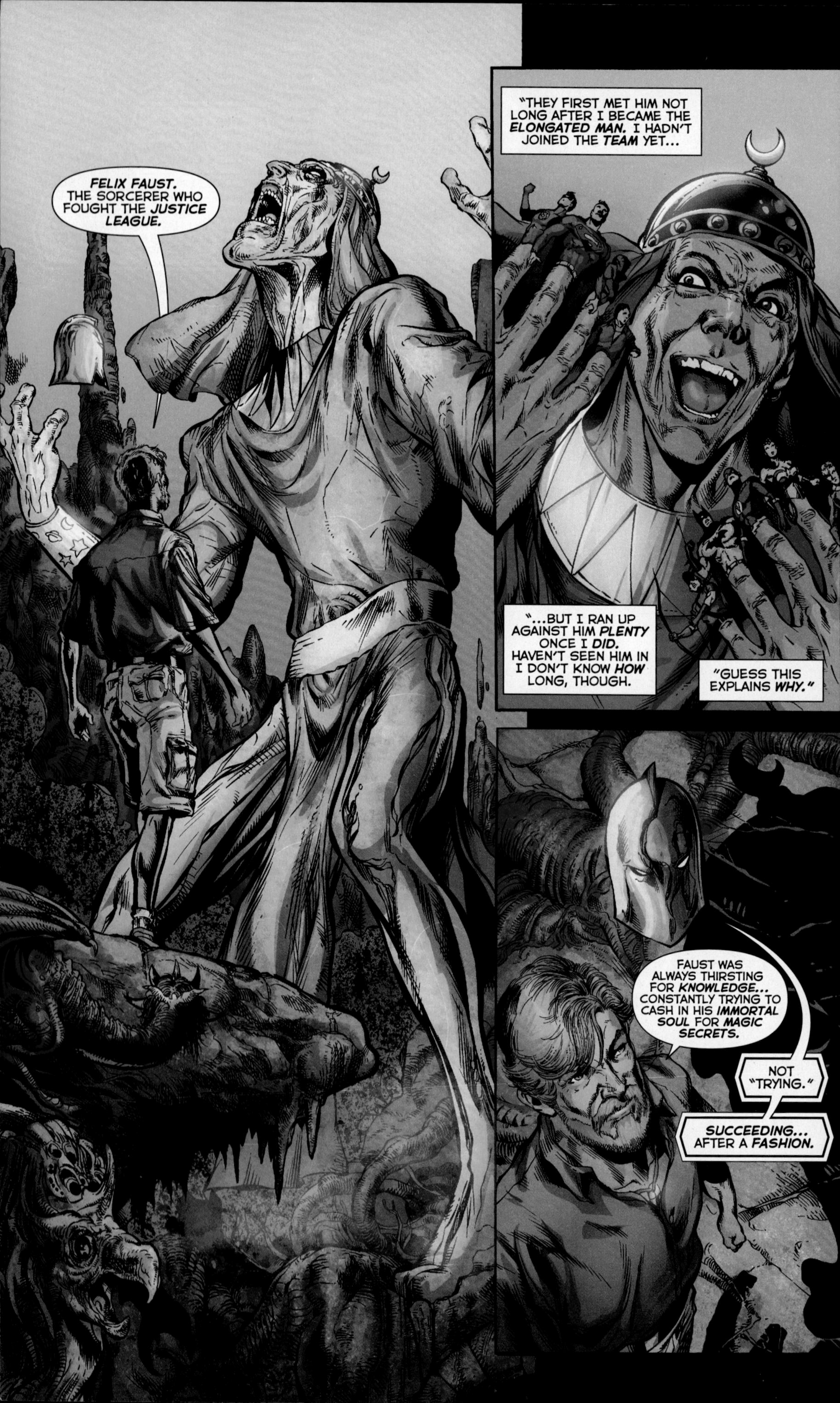
FELIX FAUST. THE SORCERER WHO FOUGHT THE JUSTICE LEAGUE.
"THEY FIRST MET HIM NOT LONG AFTER I BECAME THE ELONGATED MAN. I HADN'T JOINED THE TEAM YET...
"...BUT I RAN UP AGAINST HIM PLENTY ONCE I DID. HAVEN'T SEEN HIM IN I DON'T KNOW HOW LONG, THOUGH.
"GUESS THIS EXPLAINS WHY."
FAUST WAS ALWAYS THIRSTING FOR KNOWLEDGE... CONSTANTLY TRYING TO CASH IN HIS IMMORTAL SOUL FOR MAGIC SECRETS.
NOT "TRYING."
SUCCEEDING... AFTER A FASHION.

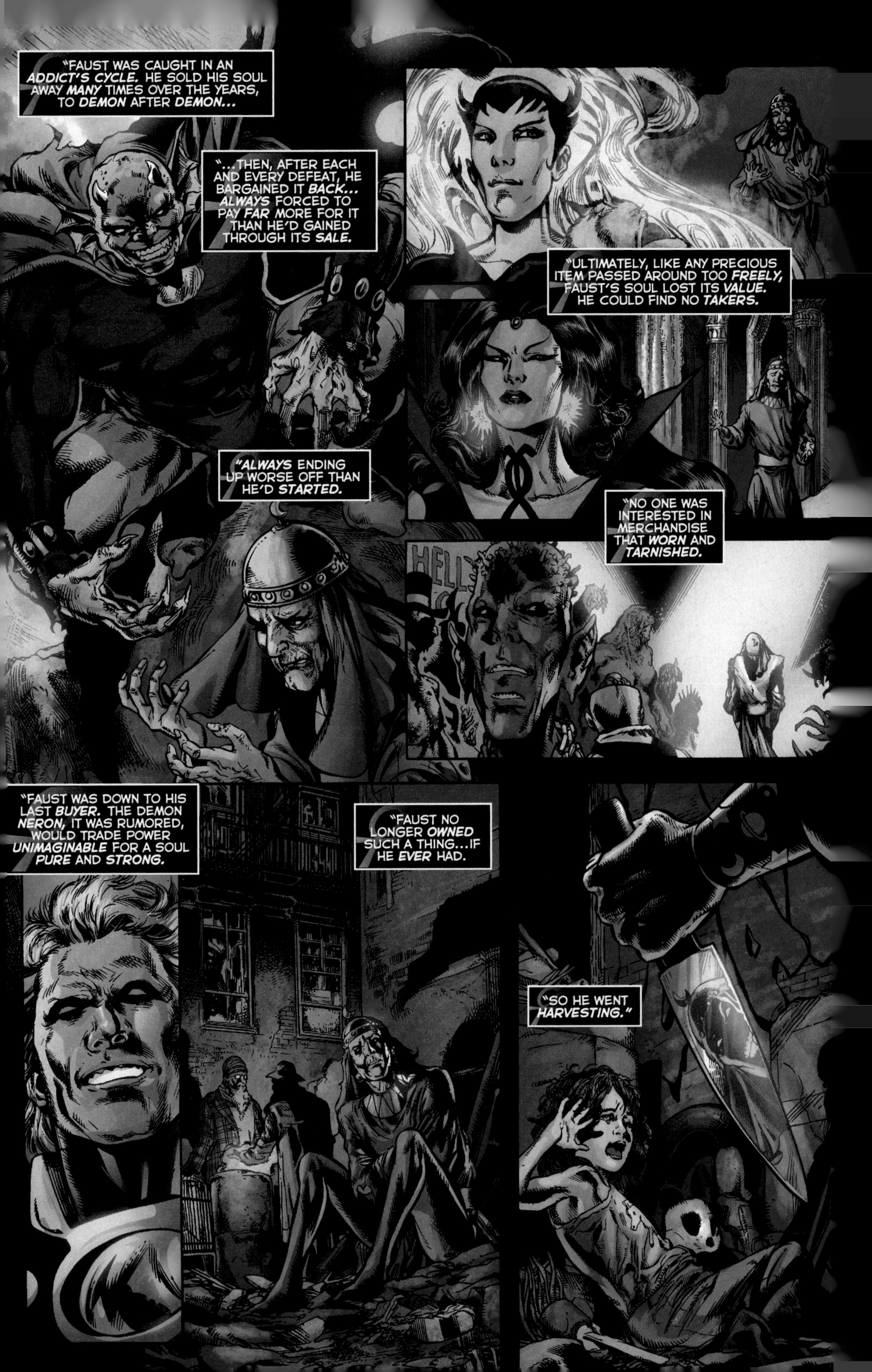
"FAUST WAS CAUGHT IN AN ADDICT'S CYCLE. HE SOLD HIS SOUL AWAY MANY TIMES OVER THE YEARS, TO DEMON AFTER DEMON...
"...THEN, AFTER EACH AND EVERY DEFEAT, HE BARGAINED IT BACK... ALWAYS FORCED TO PAY FAR MORE FOR IT THAN HE'D GAINED THROUGH ITS SALE.
"ULTIMATELY, LIKE ANY PRECIOUS ITEM PASSED AROUND TOO FREELY, FAUST'S SOUL LOST ITS VALUE. HE COULD FIND NO TAKERS.
"ALWAYS ENDING UP WORSE OFF THAN HE'D STARTED.
"NO ONE WAS INTERESTED IN MERCHANDISE THAT WORN AND TARNISHED.
"FAUST WAS DOWN TO HIS LAST BUYER. THE DEMON NERON, IT WAS RUMORED, WOULD TRADE POWER UNIMAGINABLE FOR A SOUL PURE AND STRONG.
"FAUST NO LONGER OWNED SUCH A THING...IF HE EVER HAD.
"SO HE WENT HARVESTING."

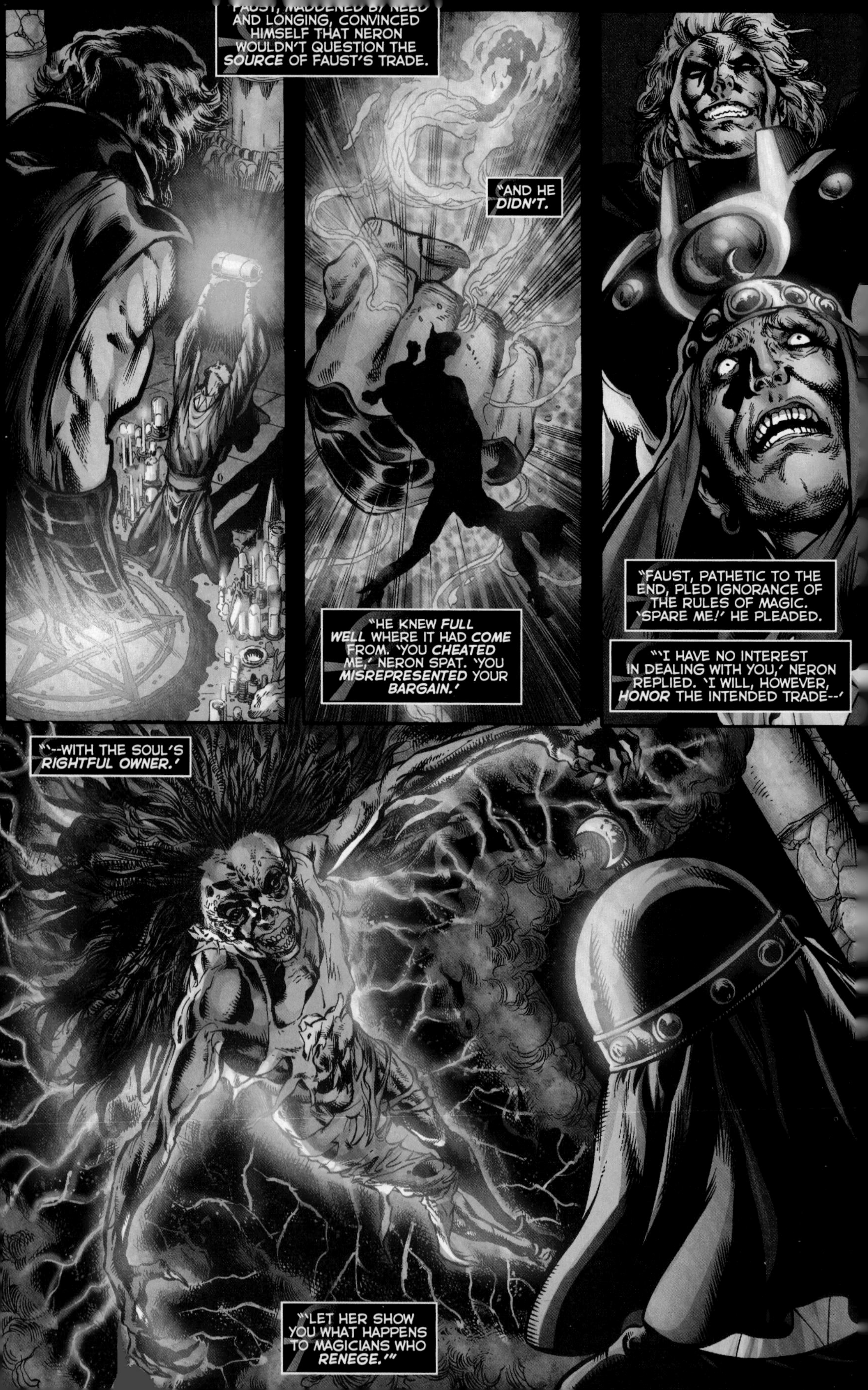
"FAUST, MADDENED BY NEED AND LONGING, CONVINCED HIMSELF THAT NERON WOULDN'T QUESTION THE SOURCE OF FAUST'S TRADE.
"AND HE DIDN'T.
"HE KNEW FULL WELL WHERE IT HAD COME FROM. 'YOU CHEATED ME,' NERON SPAT. 'YOU MISREPRESENTED YOUR BARGAIN.'
"FAUST, PATHETIC TO THE END, PLED IGNORANCE OF THE RULES OF MAGIC. 'SPARE ME!' HE PLEADED.
"'I HAVE NO INTEREST IN DEALING WITH YOU,' NERON REPLIED. 'I WILL, HOWEVER, HONOR THE INTENDED TRADE--'
"'--WITH THE SOUL'S RIGHTFUL OWNER.'
"'LET HER SHOW YOU WHAT HAPPENS TO MAGICIANS WHO RENEGE.'"

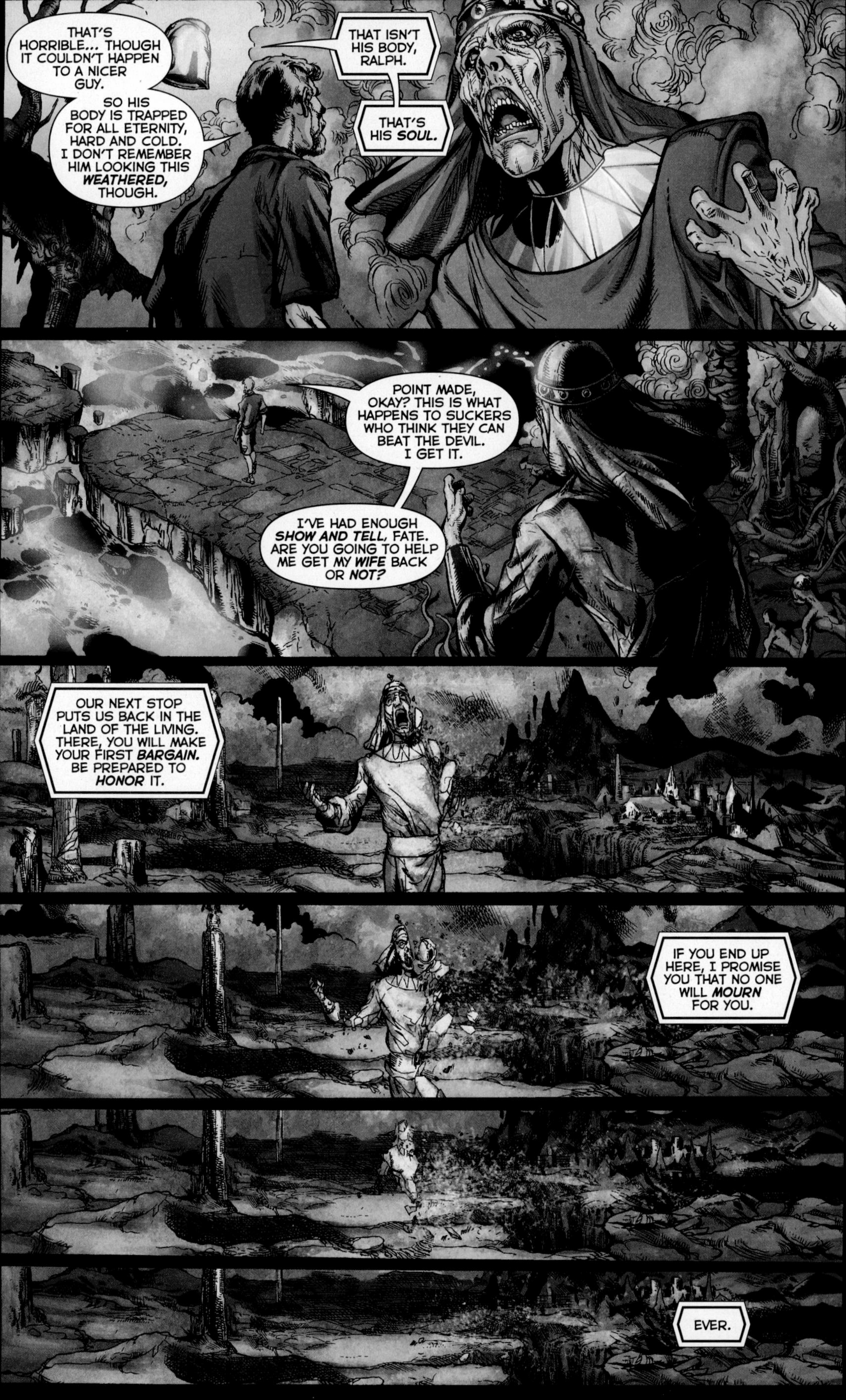
THAT'S HORRIBLE... THOUGH IT COULDN'T HAPPEN TO A NICER GUY.
SO HIS BODY IS TRAPPED FOR ALL ETERNITY, HARD AND COLD. I DON'T REMEMBER HIM LOOKING THIS WEATHERED, THOUGH.
THAT ISN'T HIS BODY, RALPH.
THAT'S HIS SOUL.
POINT MADE, OKAY? THIS IS WHAT HAPPENS TO SUCKERS WHO THINK THEY CAN BEAT THE DEVIL. I GET IT.
I'VE HAD ENOUGH SHOW AND TELL, FATE. ARE YOU GOING TO HELP ME GET MY WIFE BACK OR NOT?
OUR NEXT STOP PUTS US BACK IN THE LAND OF THE LIVING. THERE, YOU WILL MAKE YOUR FIRST BARGAIN. BE PREPARED TO HONOR IT.
IF YOU END UP HERE, I PROMISE YOU THAT NO ONE WILL MOURN FOR YOU.
EVER.

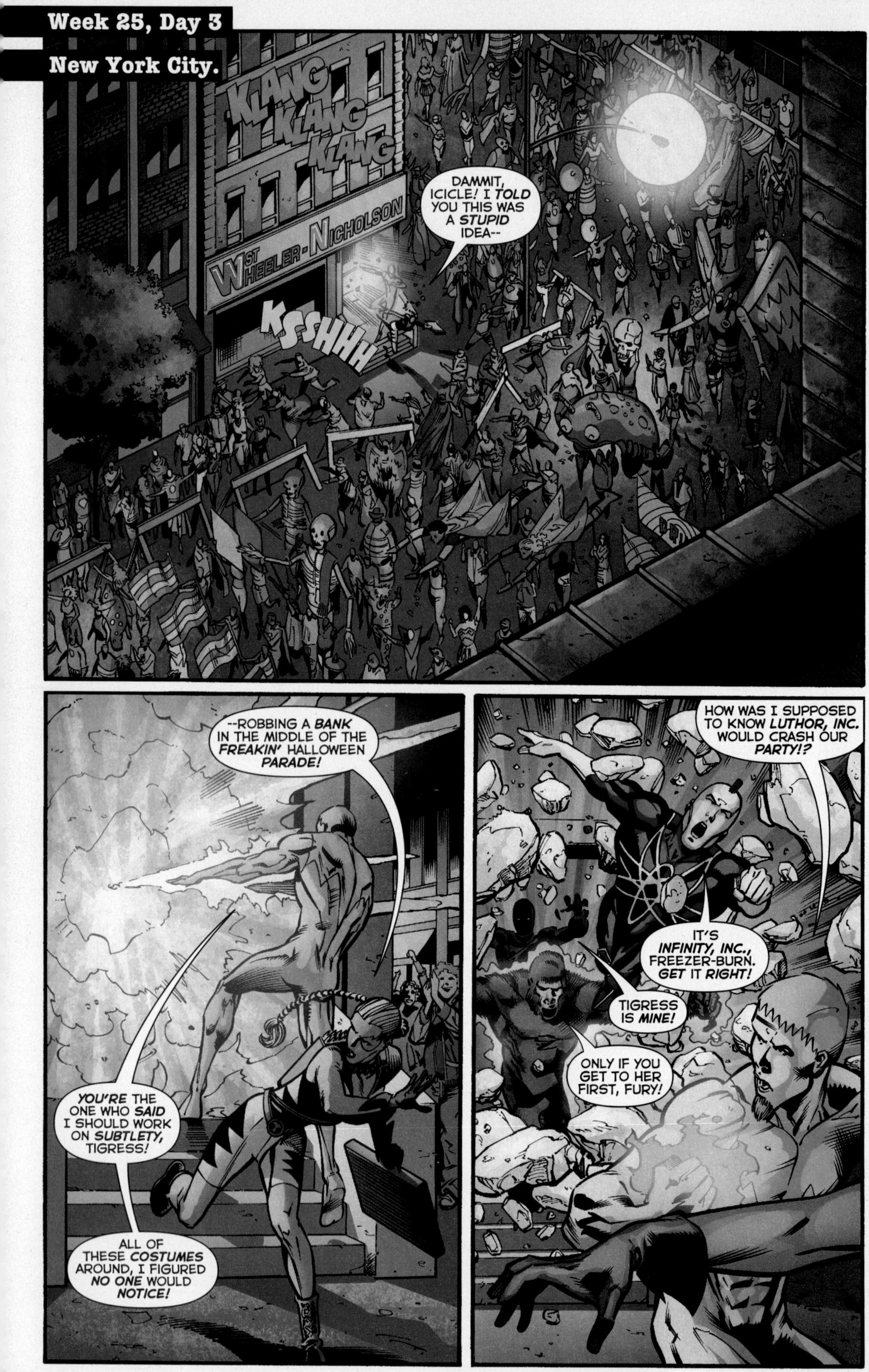
Week 25, Day 3
New York City.
KLANG KLANG KLANG
WST WHEELER-NICHOLSON
KSSHHH
DAMMIT, ICICLE! I TOLD YOU THIS WAS A STUPID IDEA--
--ROBBING A BANK IN THE MIDDLE OF THE FREAKIN' HALLOWEEN PARADE!
YOU'RE THE ONE WHO SAID I SHOULD WORK ON SUBTLETY, TIGRESS!
ALL OF THESE COSTUMES AROUND, I FIGURED NO ONE WOULD NOTICE!
HOW WAS I SUPPOSED TO KNOW LUTHOR, INC. WOULD CRASH OUR PARTY!?
IT'S INFINITY, INC., FREEZER-BURN. GET IT RIGHT!
TIGRESS IS MINE!
ONLY IF YOU GET TO HER FIRST, FURY!

KRAKK

TIGRESS AIN'T *NOBODY'S*, TOUGH-TALKER.

DOUBLE NEGATIVE, BABE--YOU'RE SAYING THAT YOU'RE *EVERYBODY'S*.

YOU *REALLY* THINK *NOW'S* THE TIME TO BE HANDING OUT *GRAMMAR* LESSONS?

WHM

GET US *OUT* OF HERE!

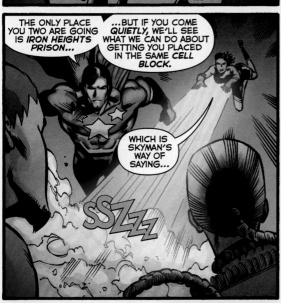

THE ONLY PLACE YOU TWO ARE GOING IS *IRON HEIGHTS PRISON*...

...BUT IF YOU COME *QUIETLY*, WE'LL SEE WHAT WE CAN DO ABOUT GETTING YOU PLACED IN THE SAME *CELL BLOCK*.

WHICH IS *SKYMAN'S* WAY OF SAYING...

SSZZZ

...YOU'RE *SURROUNDED* AND IT'S *TIME* TO *GIVE UP*.

CHECK IT OUT, ICE. *STARLIGHT'S* TRYING TO GIVE US *ADVICE*.

YEAH, IT'S *SWEET* OF HER. TOO *BAD* IT *WON'T* TAKE.

IT'S ALL RIGHT, I DIDN'T THINK IT WOULD.

MATRIX...

269

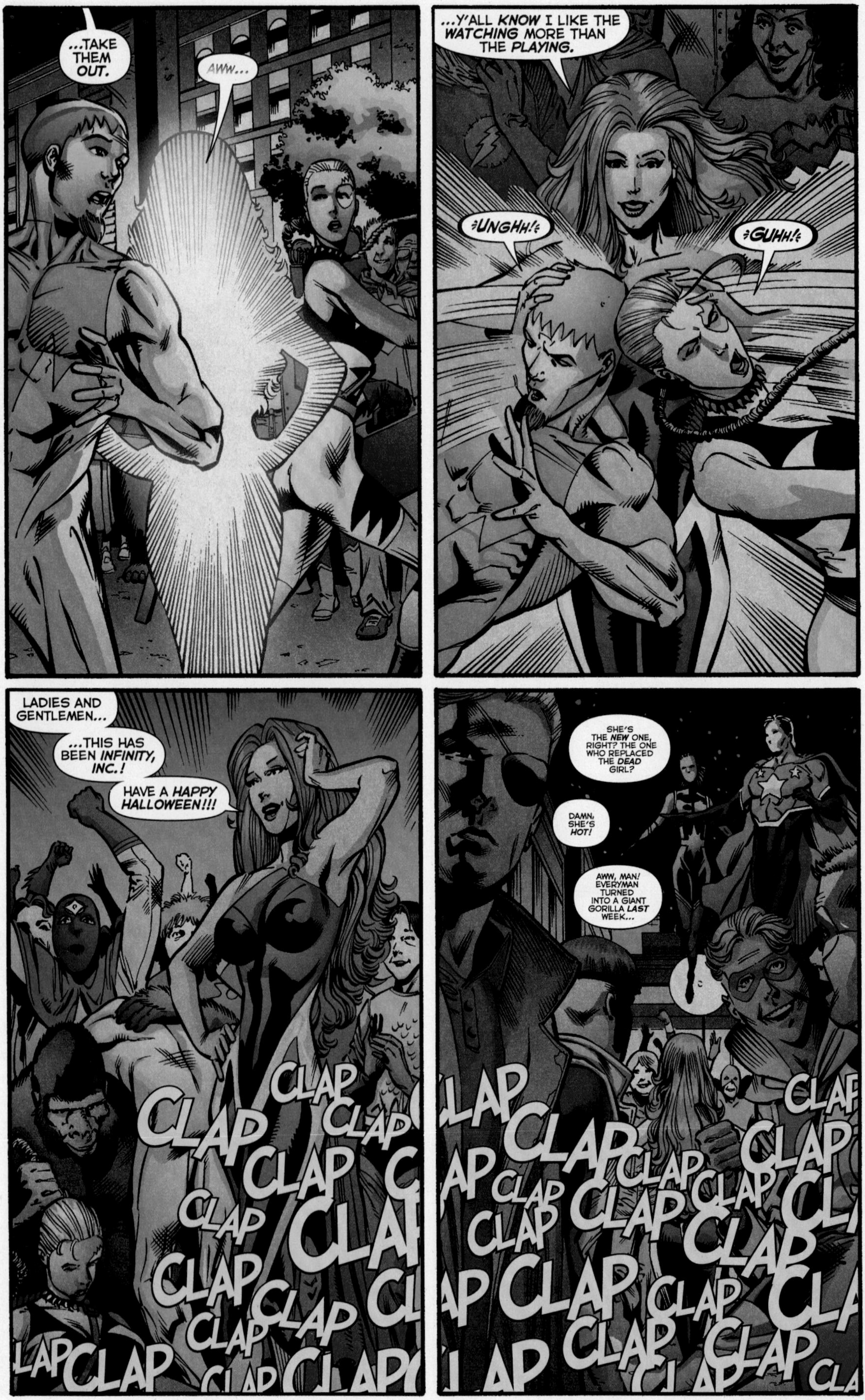
...TAKE THEM OUT.
AWW...
...Y'ALL KNOW I LIKE THE WATCHING MORE THAN THE PLAYING.
UNGHH!
GUHH!
LADIES AND GENTLEMEN...
...THIS HAS BEEN INFINITY, INC.!
HAVE A HAPPY HALLOWEEN!!!
SHE'S THE NEW ONE, RIGHT? THE ONE WHO REPLACED THE DEAD GIRL?
DAMN, SHE'S HOT!
AWW, MAN! EVERYMAN TURNED INTO A GIANT GORILLA LAST WEEK...
CLAP CLAP CLAP CLAP CLAP CLAP CLAP CLAP CLAP CLAP CLAP CLAP CLAP

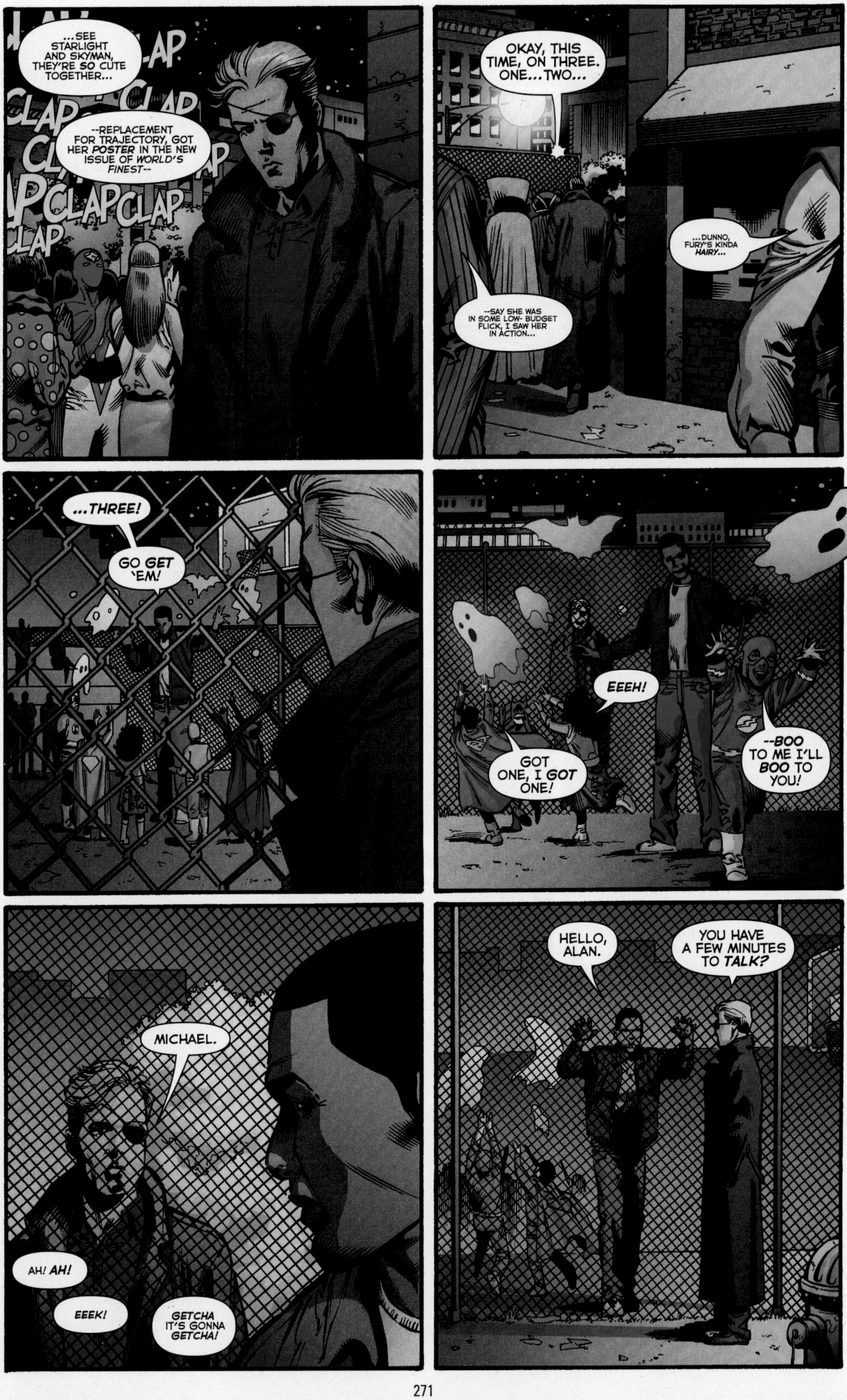
...SEE STARLIGHT AND SKYMAN, THEY'RE SO CUTE TOGETHER...
--REPLACEMENT FOR TRAJECTORY, GOT HER POSTER IN THE NEW ISSUE OF WORLD'S FINEST--
CLAP CLAP CLAP CLAP CLAP CLAP CLAP CLAP
OKAY, THIS TIME, ON THREE. ONE...TWO...
...DUNNO, FURY'S KINDA HAIRY...
--SAY SHE WAS IN SOME LOW- BUDGET FLICK, I SAW HER IN ACTION...
...THREE!
GO GET 'EM!
EEEH!
GOT ONE, I GOT ONE!
--BOO TO ME I'LL BOO TO YOU!
MICHAEL.
AH! AH!
EEEK!
GETCHA IT'S GONNA GETCHA!
HELLO, ALAN.
YOU HAVE A FEW MINUTES TO TALK?

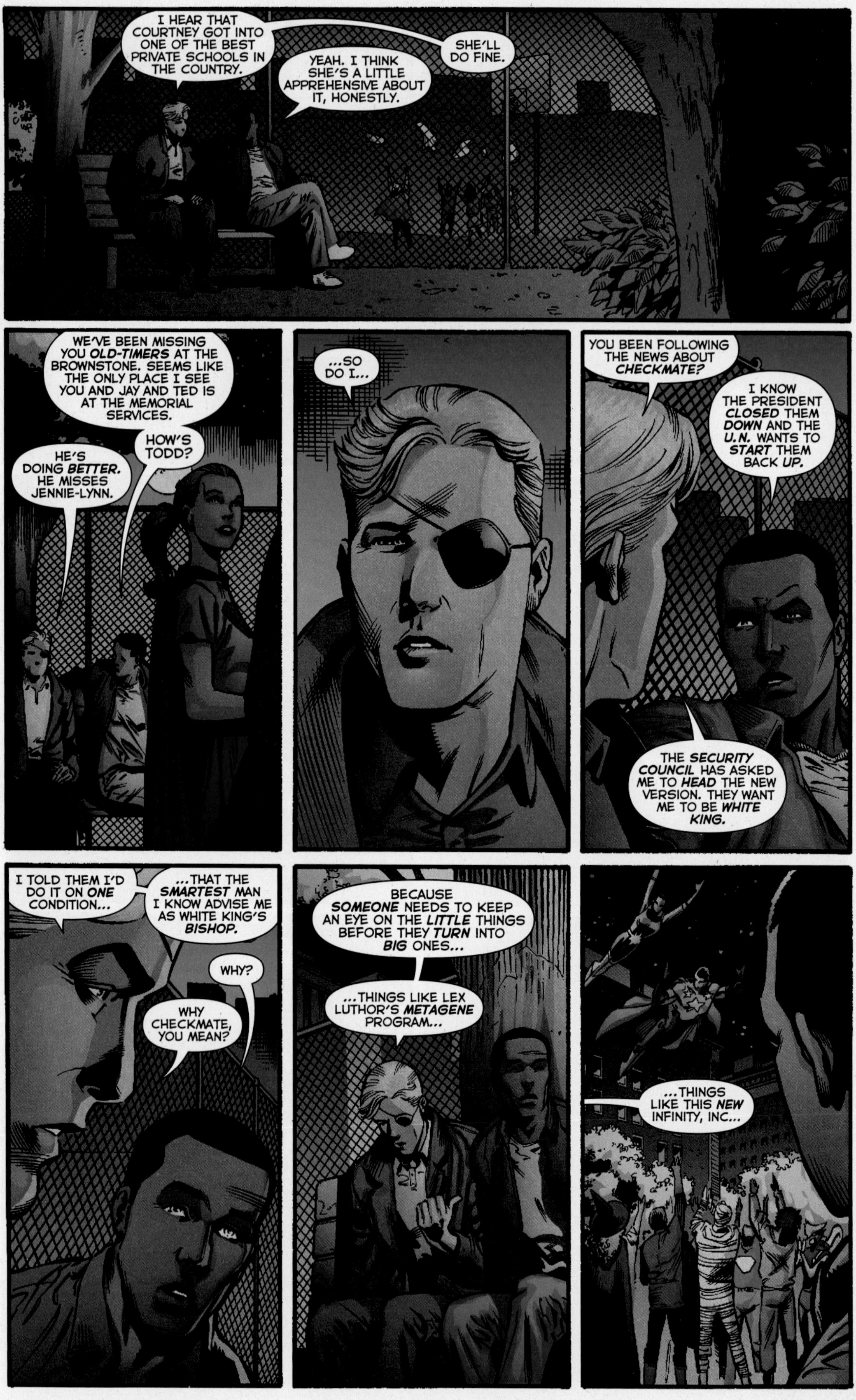
I HEAR THAT COURTNEY GOT INTO ONE OF THE BEST PRIVATE SCHOOLS IN THE COUNTRY.
YEAH. I THINK SHE'S A LITTLE APPREHENSIVE ABOUT IT, HONESTLY.
SHE'LL DO FINE.
WE'VE BEEN MISSING YOU OLD-TIMERS AT THE BROWNSTONE. SEEMS LIKE THE ONLY PLACE I SEE YOU AND JAY AND TED IS AT THE MEMORIAL SERVICES.
HOW'S TODD?
HE'S DOING BETTER. HE MISSES JENNIE-LYNN.
...SO DO I...
YOU BEEN FOLLOWING THE NEWS ABOUT CHECKMATE?
I KNOW THE PRESIDENT CLOSED THEM DOWN AND THE U.N. WANTS TO START THEM BACK UP.
THE SECURITY COUNCIL HAS ASKED ME TO HEAD THE NEW VERSION. THEY WANT ME TO BE WHITE KING.
I TOLD THEM I'D DO IT ON ONE CONDITION...
...THAT THE SMARTEST MAN I KNOW ADVISE ME AS WHITE KING'S BISHOP.
WHY?
WHY CHECKMATE, YOU MEAN?
BECAUSE SOMEONE NEEDS TO KEEP AN EYE ON THE LITTLE THINGS BEFORE THEY TURN INTO BIG ONES...
...THINGS LIKE LEX LUTHOR'S METAGENE PROGRAM...
...THINGS LIKE THIS NEW INFINITY, INC...

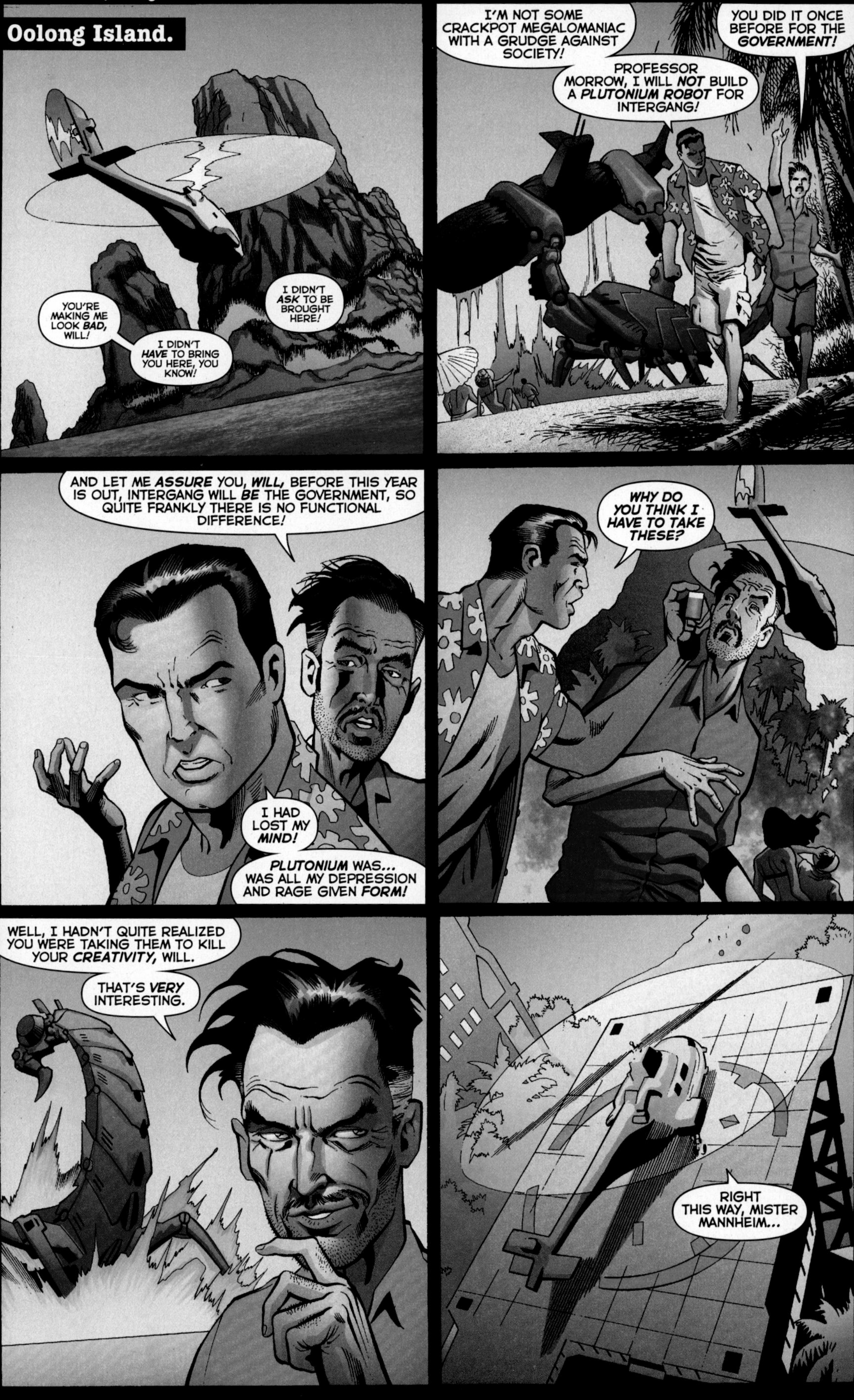
Oolong Island.
YOU'RE MAKING ME LOOK BAD, WILL!
I DIDN'T HAVE TO BRING YOU HERE, YOU KNOW!
I DIDN'T ASK TO BE BROUGHT HERE!
YOU DID IT ONCE BEFORE FOR THE GOVERNMENT!
I'M NOT SOME CRACKPOT MEGALOMANIAC WITH A GRUDGE AGAINST SOCIETY!
PROFESSOR MORROW, I WILL NOT BUILD A PLUTONIUM ROBOT FOR INTERGANG!
AND LET ME ASSURE YOU, WILL, BEFORE THIS YEAR IS OUT, INTERGANG WILL BE THE GOVERNMENT, SO QUITE FRANKLY THERE IS NO FUNCTIONAL DIFFERENCE!
I HAD LOST MY MIND!
PLUTONIUM WAS... WAS ALL MY DEPRESSION AND RAGE GIVEN FORM!
WHY DO YOU THINK I HAVE TO TAKE THESE?
WELL, I HADN'T QUITE REALIZED YOU WERE TAKING THEM TO KILL YOUR CREATIVITY, WILL.
THAT'S VERY INTERESTING.
RIGHT THIS WAY, MISTER MANNHEIM...

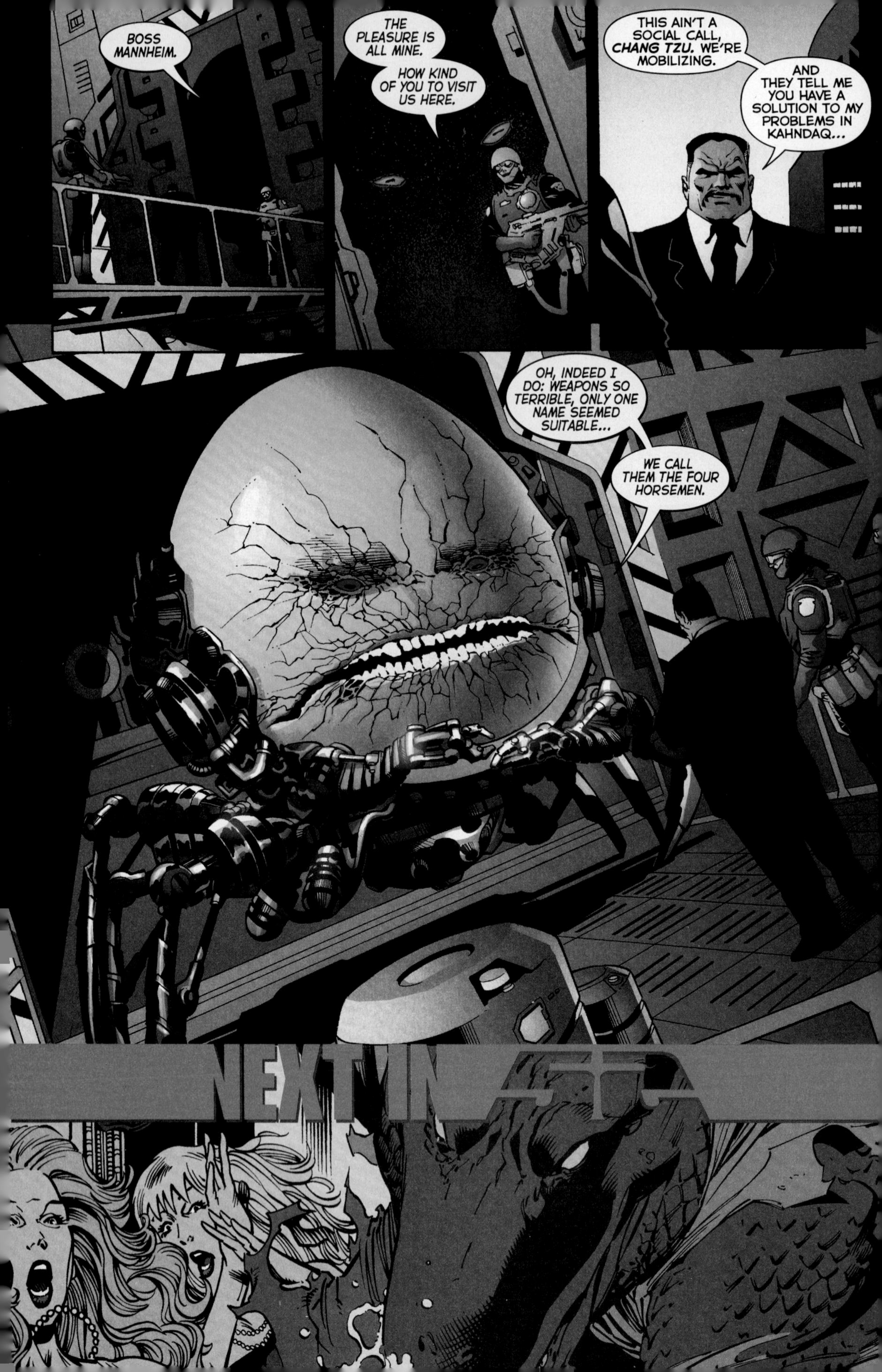

BOSS MANNHEIM.
THE PLEASURE IS ALL MINE.
HOW KIND OF YOU TO VISIT US HERE.
THIS AIN'T A SOCIAL CALL, CHANG TZU. WE'RE MOBILIZING.
AND THEY TELL ME YOU HAVE A SOLUTION TO MY PROBLEMS IN KAHNDAQ...
OH, INDEED I DO: WEAPONS SO TERRIBLE, ONLY ONE NAME SEEMED SUITABLE...
WE CALL THEM THE FOUR HORSEMEN.
NEXT IN 52

WRITTEN BY GEOFF JOHNS, GRANT MORRISON, GREG RUCKA, MARK WAID

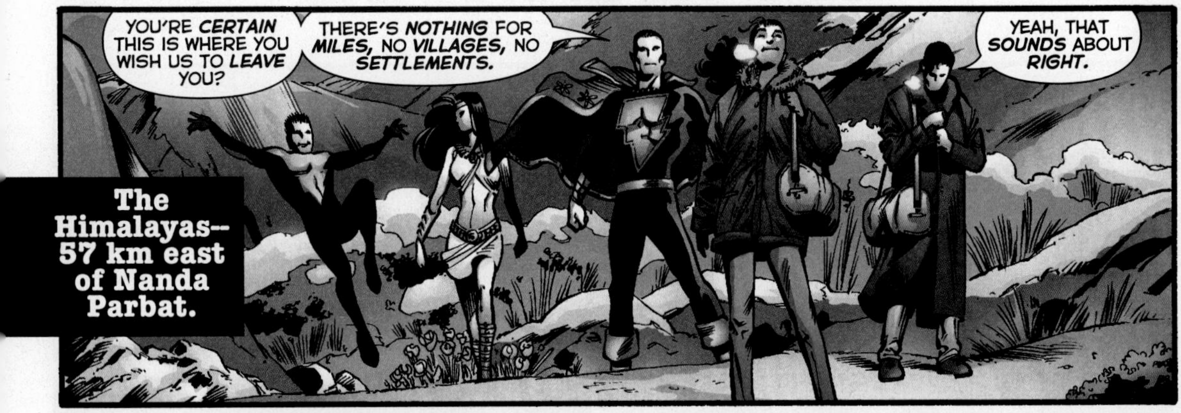

The Himalayas-- 57 km east of Nanda Parbat.
YOU'RE CERTAIN THIS IS WHERE YOU WISH US TO LEAVE YOU?
THERE'S NOTHING FOR MILES, NO VILLAGES, NO SETTLEMENTS.
YEAH, THAT SOUNDS ABOUT RIGHT.

ART BREAKDOWNS BY KEITH GIFFEN • PENCILS BY PATRICK OLLIFFE • INKS BY DREW GERACI
COLORS BY PETE PANTAZIS • LETTERING BY PAT BROSSEAU

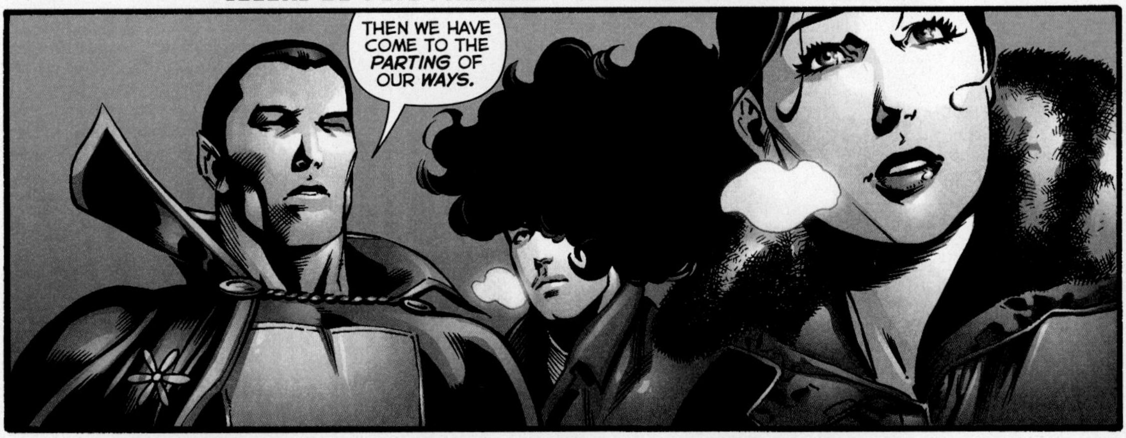

THEN WE HAVE COME TO THE PARTING OF OUR WAYS.

ASSISTANT EDITORS HARVEY RICHARDS & JEANINE SCHAEFER
EDITED BY STEPHEN WACKER COVER BY J.G. JONES & ALEX SINCLAIR

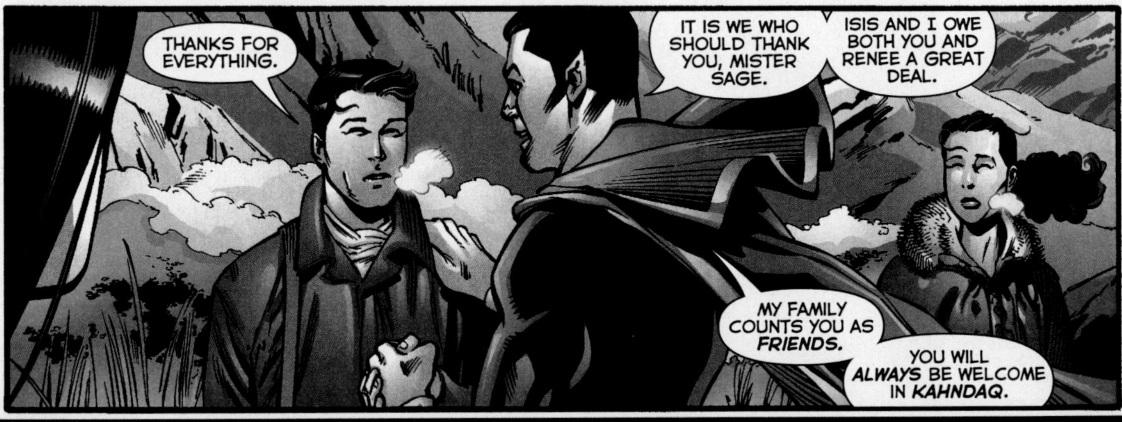

THANKS FOR EVERYTHING.
IT IS WE WHO SHOULD THANK YOU, MISTER SAGE.
ISIS AND I OWE BOTH YOU AND RENEE A GREAT DEAL.
MY FAMILY COUNTS YOU AS FRIENDS.
YOU WILL ALWAYS BE WELCOME IN KAHNDAQ.

Week 26

HALFWAY HOUSE

DC COMICS 52

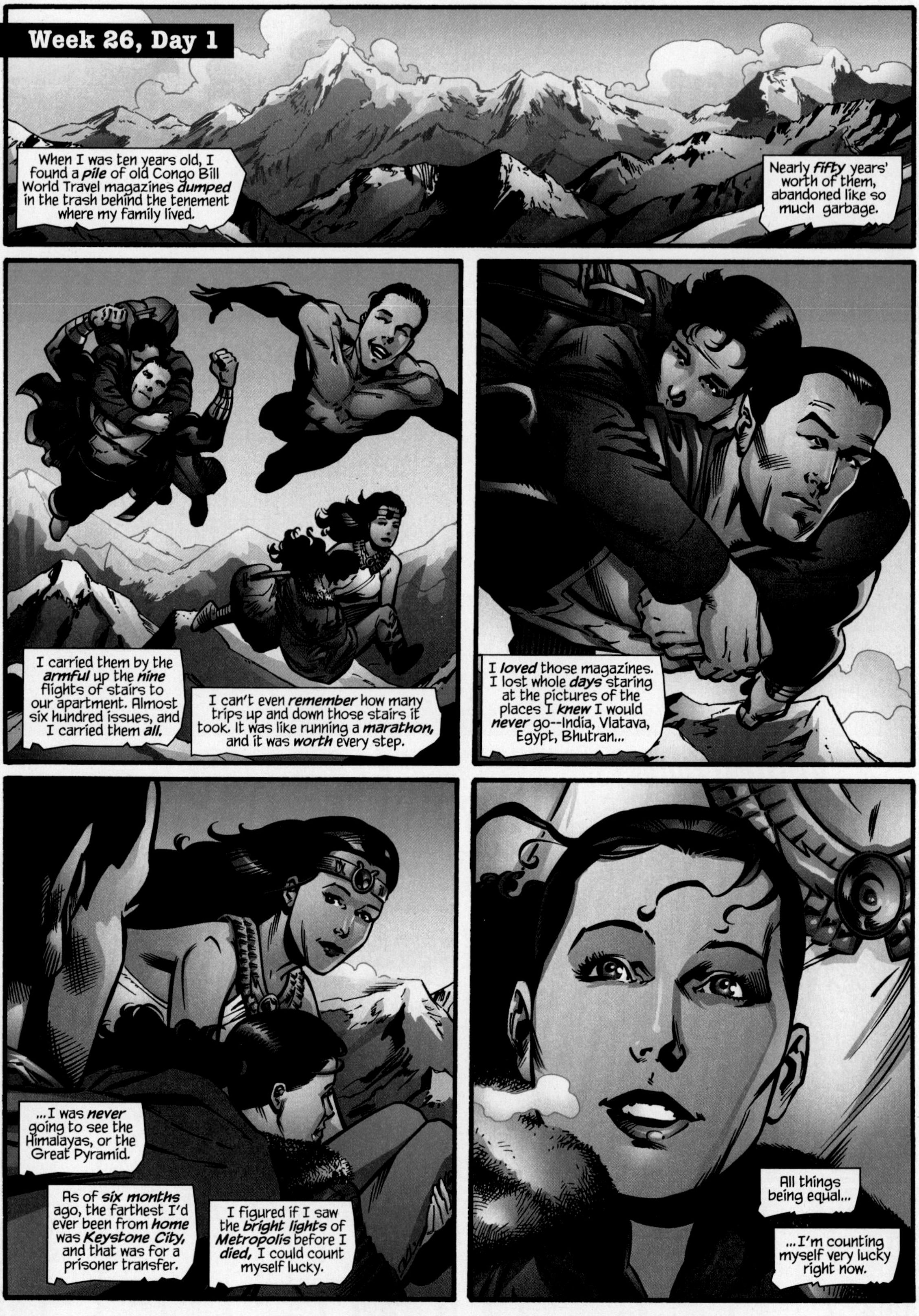

Week 26, Day 1
When I was ten years old, I found a *pile* of old Congo Bill World Travel magazines *dumped* in the trash behind the tenement where my family lived.
Nearly *fifty* years' worth of them, abandoned like so much garbage.
I carried them by the *armful* up the *nine* flights of stairs to our apartment. Almost six hundred issues, and I carried them *all.*
I can't even *remember* how many trips up and down those stairs it took. It was like running a *marathon,* and it was *worth* every step.
I *loved* those magazines. I lost whole *days* staring at the pictures of the places I *knew* I would *never* go--India, Vlatava, Egypt, Bhutran...
...I was *never* going to see the Himalayas, or the Great Pyramid.
As of *six months* ago, the farthest I'd ever been from *home* was *Keystone City,* and that was for a prisoner transfer.
I figured if I saw the *bright lights* of *Metropolis* before I *died,* I could count myself lucky.
All things being equal...
...I'm counting myself very lucky right now.

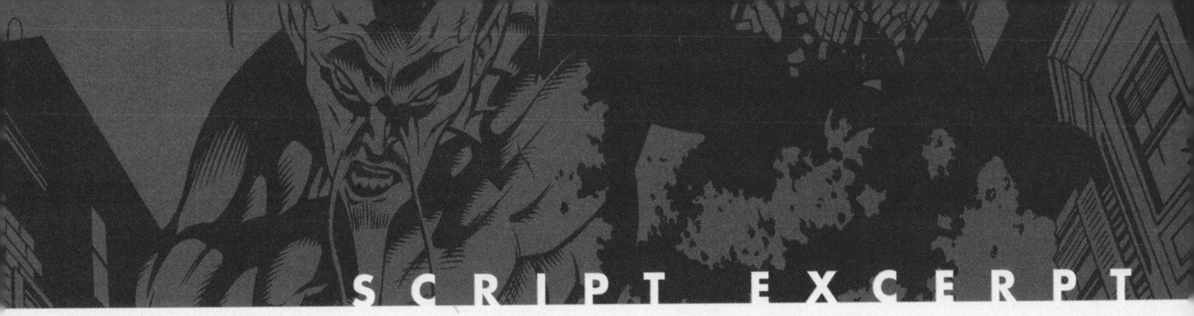

SCRIPT EXCERPT

(COMPARE WITH PAGE 274 OF THIS COLLECTION)

WEEK TWENTY-FIVE — PAGE TWENTY

PANEL ONE
Ground level shot. Looking towards hangar doors which open from the helipad into the complex. The doors slide upwards and something big moves beyond, attended by his soldiers.

EGG FU: Boss Mannheim.

PANEL TWO
Same POV. The doors slide up further, casting their shadow upon the huge ovoid shape which we can begin to see emerging from the darkness into the bright Pacific sunshine.

EGG FU: The pleasure is all mine.

EGG FU: How kind of you to visit us here.

PANEL THREE
Head and shoulders shot of Bruno Mannheim. His craggy, expressionless face.

BRUNO: This ain't a social call, Chang Tzu. We're mobilizing.

BRUNO: And they tell me you have a solution to my problems in Kahndaq...

PANEL FOUR
Big pic. Egg Fu emerges into the light and dominates this panel but instead of being funny or camp, we're making him SCARY. His gross egg-like body sits in a spider-legged throne-like contraption so that he can walk around. He looks like some awful mutation — a human being swollen beyond normal limits so that barely anything remains except for the stretched twisted face. His skin is hard like an eggshell except around his eyes and mouth where the hard material cracks and merges into softer tissue so that he can form rudimentary expressions. His eyes are narrow, dark, shadowed, filled with repressed rage and hate and corruption. His mouth is a long, cruel, downward-turning gash. A deformed monster of resentment and perverse appetites, Egg Fu is a true grotesque and should inspire a shudder of fear as well as a chuckle of derision.

His walking frame also comes equipped with multiple articulated robotic arms which beat and paddle at the air like intricately jointed insect limbs. His soldiers walk at his side, with rifles at the ready.

EGG FU: Oh, indeed I do: Weapons so terrible, only one name seemed suitable...

EGG FU: We call them the Four Horsemen.

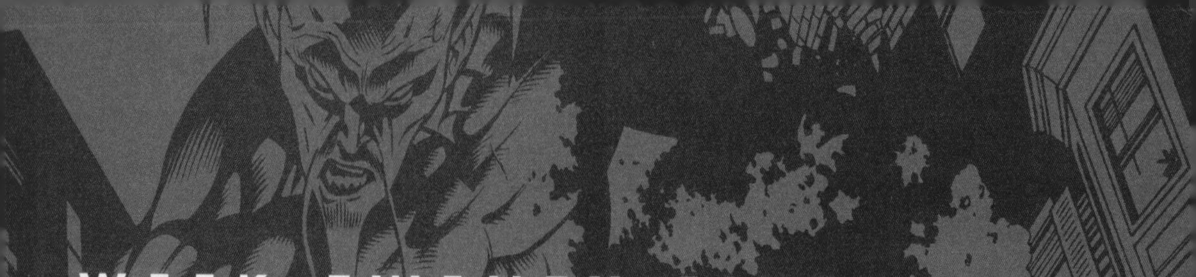

WEEK TWENTY-FIVE NOTES

KEITH GIFFEN

My all-time favorite "52" cover graced this issue, this in spite of the fact that I absolutely loathe cats. The little girl in the Question costume, alone, is worth the price of admission (and a pretty nifty piece of foreshadowing to boot). Twenty-five issues in and J.G. continued to amaze. I mean, c'mon, Dr. Fate's helmet as a trick-or-treat bag? Brilliant!

I could be wrong, and more often than not am, but I believe this issue was one of the first multiple artist issues, and before you start in, it was done deliberately. Bennett (still our anchor artist and thank God for that), Eaglesham (who came up available just when we needed him most), Jimenez (another talent I couldn't believe was open to us) and Pat Olliffe (comicdom's best-kept secret and a welcome addition to the "52" team) were each assigned specific vignettes and, to my way of thinking, it worked.

The Crime Bible took a bigger role in the scheme of things, the Black Adam family moved that much closer to the tragedy to come, Ralph got his first good look at the villain of his piece, and Alan Scott took his first tentative step up to major player. All in all, not too shabby.

And then there was Egg-Fu revealed in all of his questionable glory.

I can still remember the first time Egg-Fu was brought up at a "52" summit as a potential key player. No one even blinked. It was just assumed that the character could be modified to fit, even though no one, at the time, was exactly sure how. I know my first thought was about how much fun it would be to play around with his giant prehensile moustache (minds out of the gutter, I'm looking at you, Waid). Little did I know.

No moustache, no "Clazy Amelican" jargon... I was heartbroken. You see, I have a soft spot for the more... absurd characters that populate the fringes of the DCU. Ace the Bathound (who wore a mask so no one would know he was Bruce Wayne's dog), The Green Team (Paris Hilton times five), The Glop from outer space (ate rock and roll records, don'cha know); the list goes on and on and Egg-Fu always topped that list.

That this, this...*pretender* worked out so well is, to me, nothing short of astonishing and a tribute to the Big Four's ability to confound my expectations at every turn. That, in case you were wondering, was a good thing. It kept me intrigued, kept me guessing and, most of all, kept me excited about the stories being told.

By now we were almost halfway home and things were humming along nicely and all I could keep thinking was "calm before the storm."

I guess every project as ambitious as "52" needs a howling paranoid (and, for the record, Wacker was out to get me so back off), someone whose finger is never that far from the panic button, someone *way* too beholden to Murphy's Law for his own good. It was a dirty job, but someone had to do it.

At least that's what I keep telling myself.

When I'm not blaming Rucka, that is...

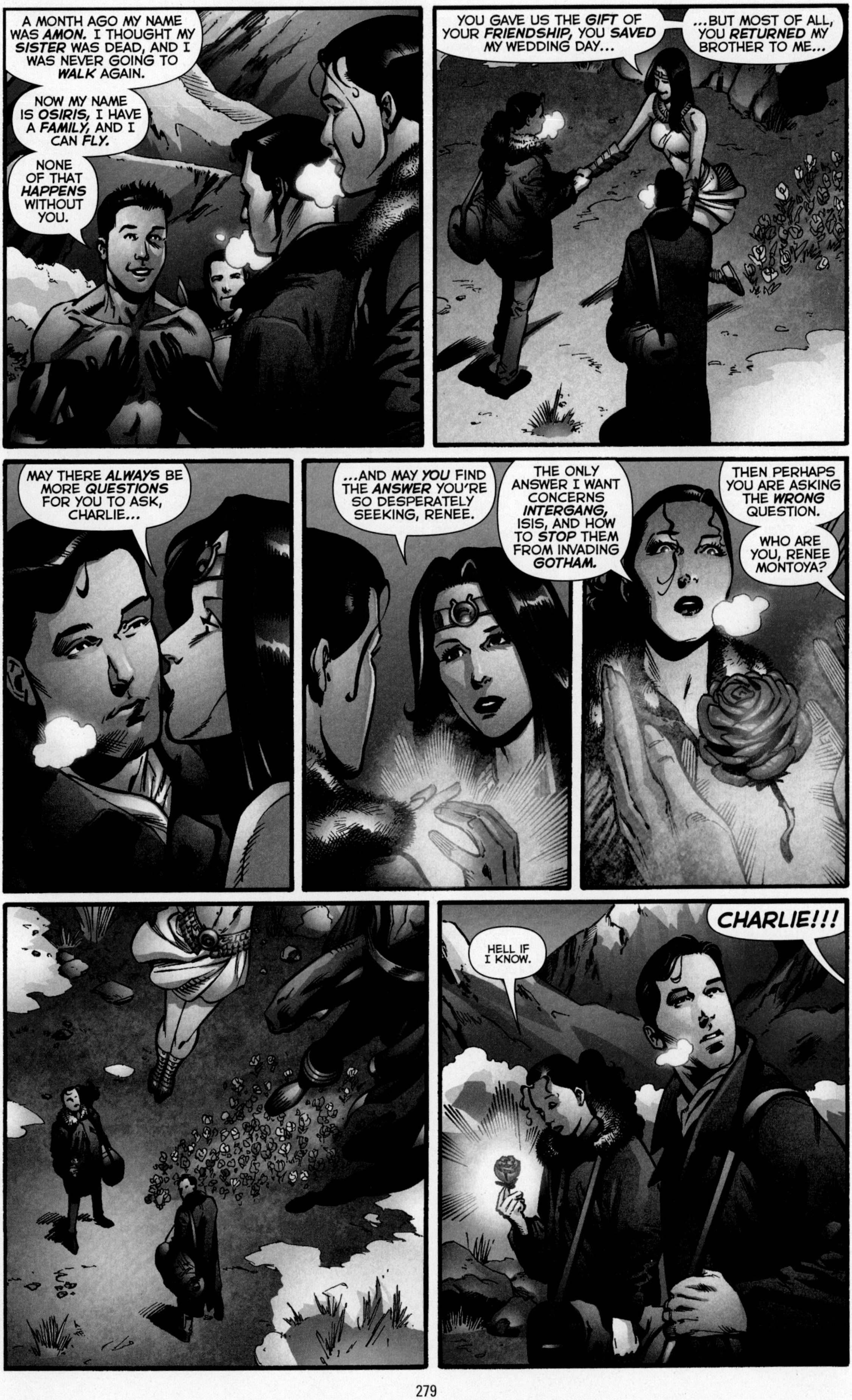
A MONTH AGO MY NAME WAS AMON. I THOUGHT MY SISTER WAS DEAD, AND I WAS NEVER GOING TO WALK AGAIN.
NOW MY NAME IS OSIRIS, I HAVE A FAMILY, AND I CAN FLY.
NONE OF THAT HAPPENS WITHOUT YOU.
YOU GAVE US THE GIFT OF YOUR FRIENDSHIP, YOU SAVED MY WEDDING DAY...
...BUT MOST OF ALL, YOU RETURNED MY BROTHER TO ME...
MAY THERE ALWAYS BE MORE QUESTIONS FOR YOU TO ASK, CHARLIE...
...AND MAY YOU FIND THE ANSWER YOU'RE SO DESPERATELY SEEKING, RENEE.
THE ONLY ANSWER I WANT CONCERNS INTERGANG, ISIS, AND HOW TO STOP THEM FROM INVADING GOTHAM.
THEN PERHAPS YOU ARE ASKING THE WRONG QUESTION.
WHO ARE YOU, RENEE MONTOYA?
CHARLIE!!!
HELL IF I KNOW.

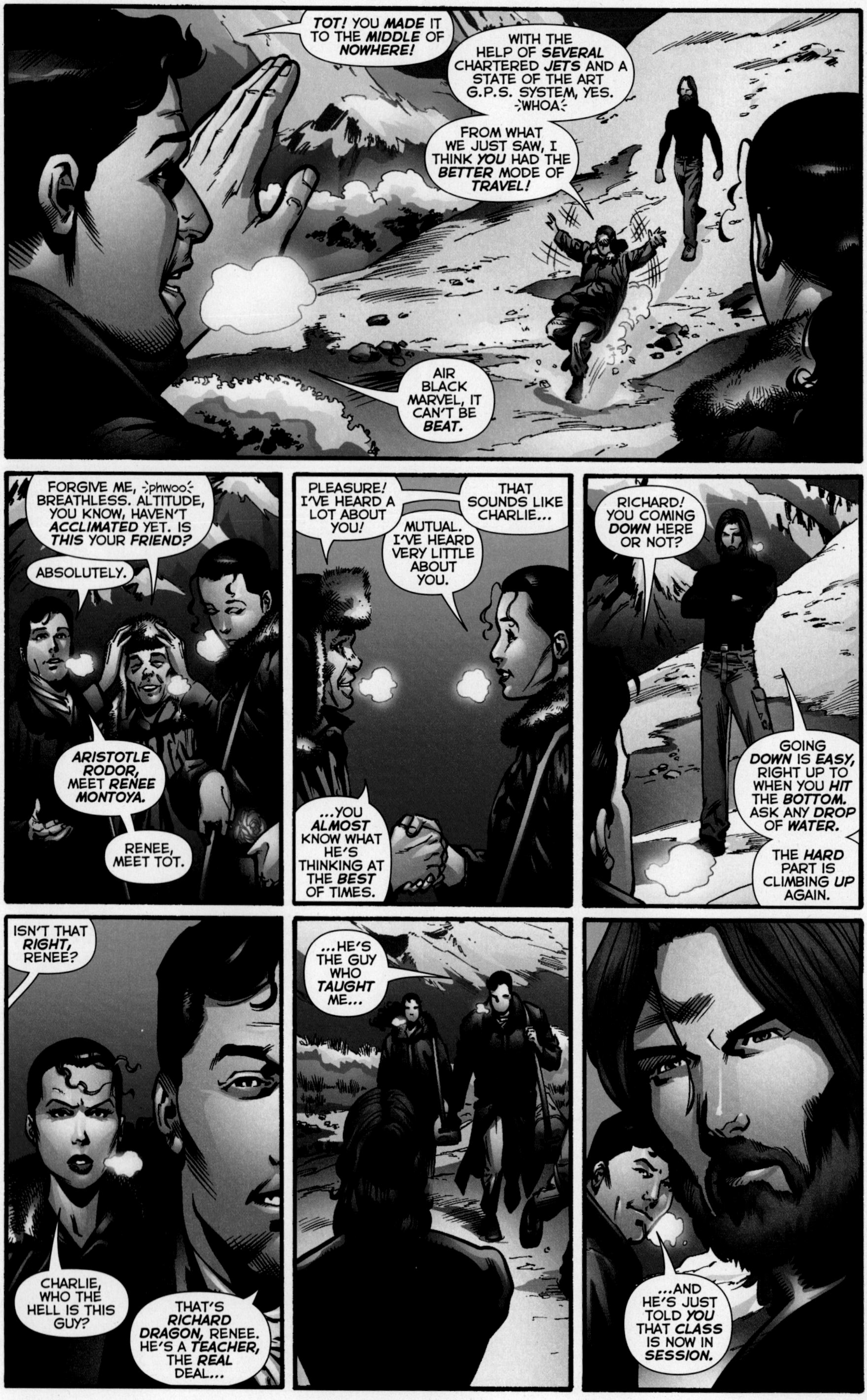
TOT! YOU MADE IT TO THE MIDDLE OF NOWHERE!
WITH THE HELP OF SEVERAL CHARTERED JETS AND A STATE OF THE ART G.P.S. SYSTEM, YES. WHOA
FROM WHAT WE JUST SAW, I THINK YOU HAD THE BETTER MODE OF TRAVEL!
AIR BLACK MARVEL, IT CAN'T BE BEAT.
FORGIVE ME, phwoo BREATHLESS. ALTITUDE, YOU KNOW, HAVEN'T ACCLIMATED YET. IS THIS YOUR FRIEND?
ABSOLUTELY.
ARISTOTLE RODOR, MEET RENEE MONTOYA.
RENEE, MEET TOT.
PLEASURE! I'VE HEARD A LOT ABOUT YOU!
THAT SOUNDS LIKE CHARLIE...
MUTUAL. I'VE HEARD VERY LITTLE ABOUT YOU.
...YOU ALMOST KNOW WHAT HE'S THINKING AT THE BEST OF TIMES.
RICHARD! YOU COMING DOWN HERE OR NOT?
GOING DOWN IS EASY, RIGHT UP TO WHEN YOU HIT THE BOTTOM. ASK ANY DROP OF WATER.
THE HARD PART IS CLIMBING UP AGAIN.
ISN'T THAT RIGHT, RENEE?
CHARLIE, WHO THE HELL IS THIS GUY?
THAT'S RICHARD DRAGON, RENEE. HE'S A TEACHER, THE REAL DEAL...
...HE'S THE GUY WHO TAUGHT ME...
...AND HE'S JUST TOLD YOU THAT CLASS IS NOW IN SESSION.

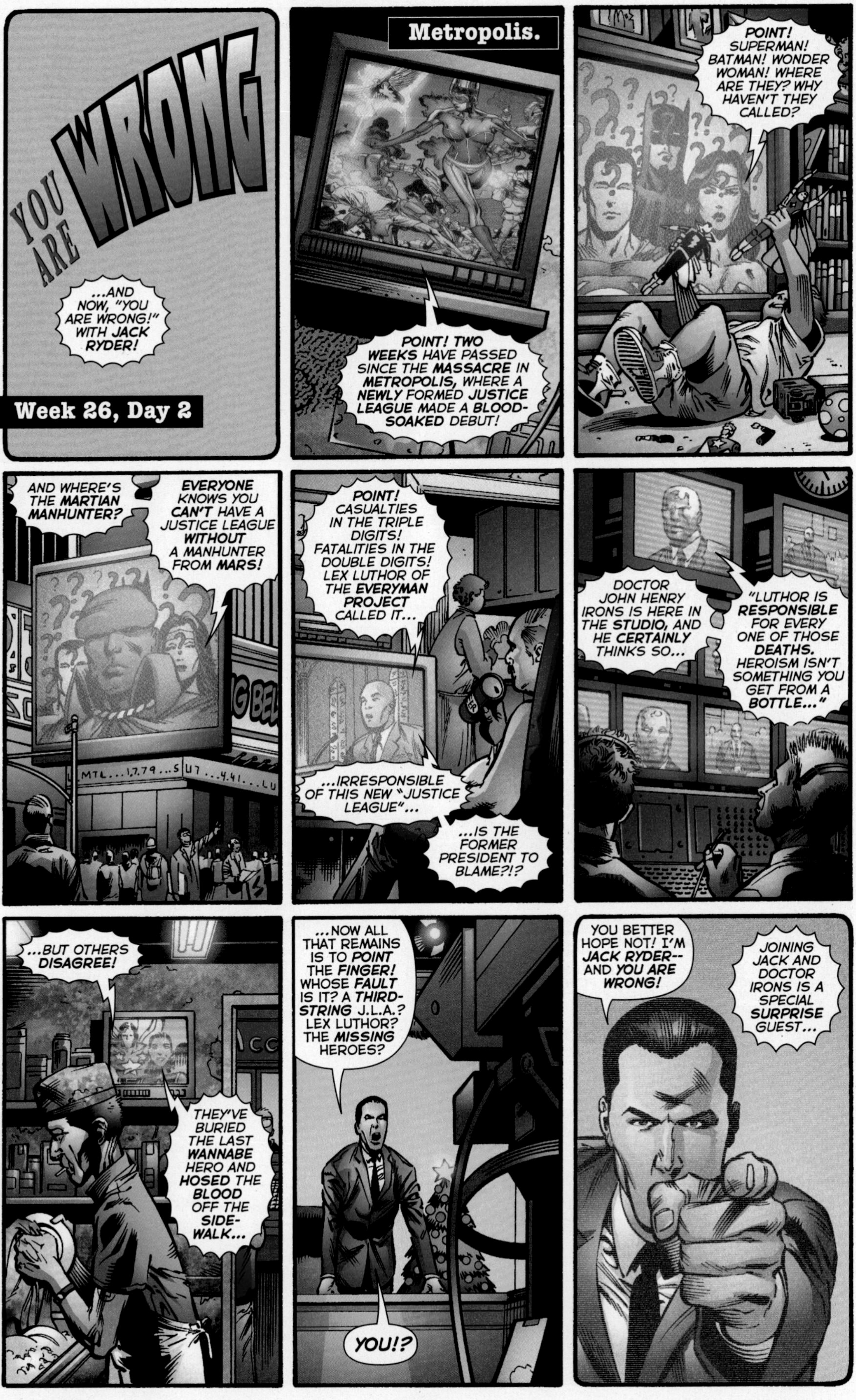
YOU ARE WRONG
...AND NOW, "YOU ARE WRONG!" WITH JACK RYDER!
Week 26, Day 2
Metropolis.
POINT! TWO WEEKS HAVE PASSED SINCE THE MASSACRE IN METROPOLIS, WHERE A NEWLY FORMED JUSTICE LEAGUE MADE A BLOOD-SOAKED DEBUT!
POINT! SUPERMAN! BATMAN! WONDER WOMAN! WHERE ARE THEY? WHY HAVEN'T THEY CALLED?
AND WHERE'S THE MARTIAN MANHUNTER?
EVERYONE KNOWS YOU CAN'T HAVE A JUSTICE LEAGUE WITHOUT A MANHUNTER FROM MARS!
POINT! CASUALTIES IN THE TRIPLE DIGITS! FATALITIES IN THE DOUBLE DIGITS! LEX LUTHOR OF THE EVERYMAN PROJECT CALLED IT...
...IRRESPONSIBLE OF THIS NEW "JUSTICE LEAGUE"...
...IS THE FORMER PRESIDENT TO BLAME?!?
DOCTOR JOHN HENRY IRONS IS HERE IN THE STUDIO, AND HE CERTAINLY THINKS SO...
"LUTHOR IS RESPONSIBLE FOR EVERY ONE OF THOSE DEATHS. HEROISM ISN'T SOMETHING YOU GET FROM A BOTTLE..."
...BUT OTHERS DISAGREE!
THEY'VE BURIED THE LAST WANNABE HERO AND HOSED THE BLOOD OFF THE SIDE-WALK...
...NOW ALL THAT REMAINS IS TO POINT THE FINGER! WHOSE FAULT IS IT? A THIRD-STRING J.L.A.? LEX LUTHOR? THE MISSING HEROES?
YOU!?
YOU BETTER HOPE NOT! I'M JACK RYDER-- AND YOU ARE WRONG!
JOINING JACK AND DOCTOR IRONS IS A SPECIAL SURPRISE GUEST...

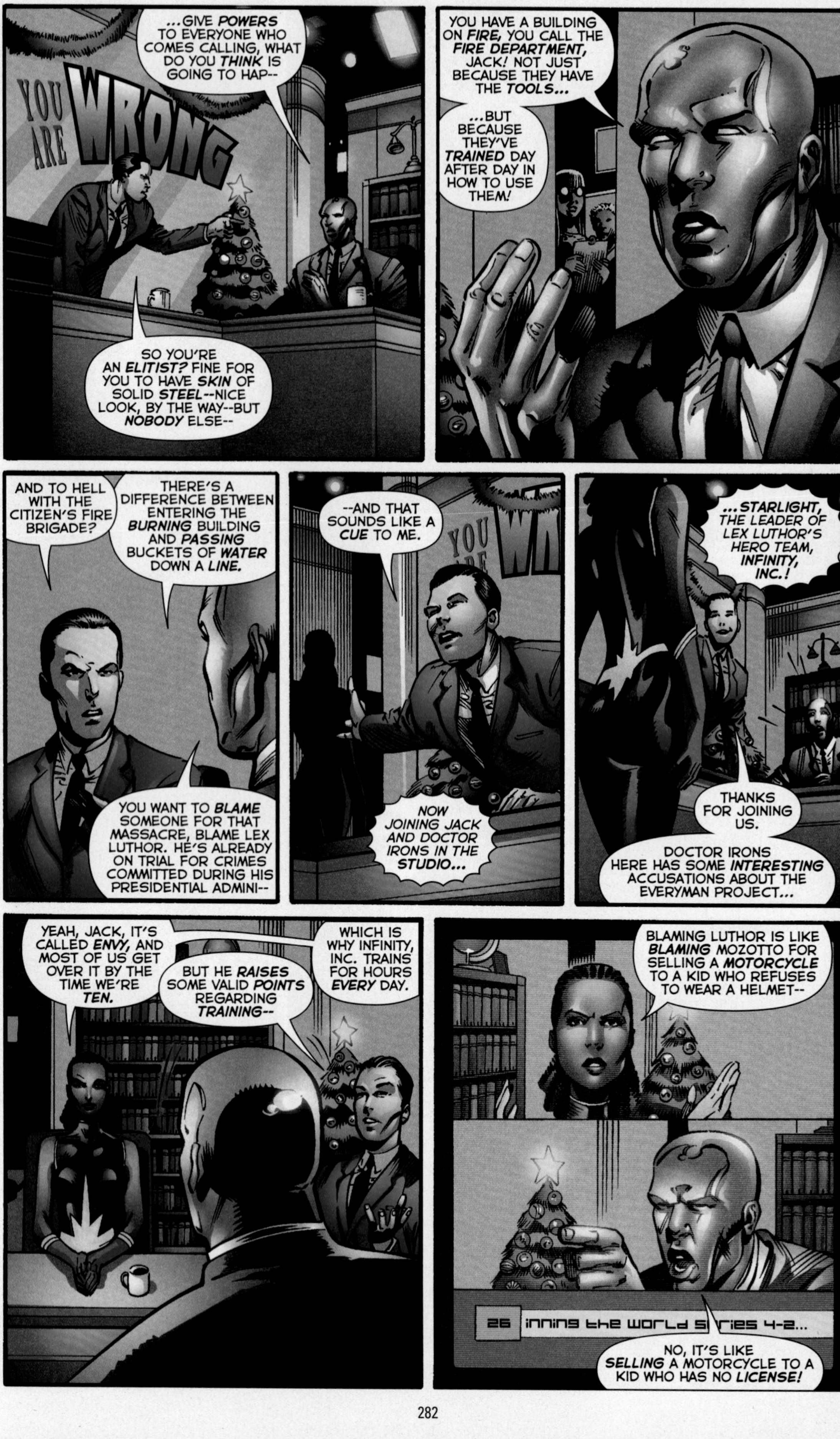

...GIVE POWERS TO EVERYONE WHO COMES CALLING, WHAT DO YOU THINK IS GOING TO HAP--
YOU ARE WRONG
SO YOU'RE AN ELITIST? FINE FOR YOU TO HAVE SKIN OF SOLID STEEL--NICE LOOK, BY THE WAY--BUT NOBODY ELSE--
YOU HAVE A BUILDING ON FIRE, YOU CALL THE FIRE DEPARTMENT, JACK! NOT JUST BECAUSE THEY HAVE THE TOOLS...
...BUT BECAUSE THEY'VE TRAINED DAY AFTER DAY IN HOW TO USE THEM!
AND TO HELL WITH THE CITIZEN'S FIRE BRIGADE?
THERE'S A DIFFERENCE BETWEEN ENTERING THE BURNING BUILDING AND PASSING BUCKETS OF WATER DOWN A LINE.
YOU WANT TO BLAME SOMEONE FOR THAT MASSACRE, BLAME LEX LUTHOR. HE'S ALREADY ON TRIAL FOR CRIMES COMMITTED DURING HIS PRESIDENTIAL ADMINI--
--AND THAT SOUNDS LIKE A CUE TO ME.
NOW JOINING JACK AND DOCTOR IRONS IN THE STUDIO...
...STARLIGHT, THE LEADER OF LEX LUTHOR'S HERO TEAM, INFINITY, INC.!
THANKS FOR JOINING US.
DOCTOR IRONS HERE HAS SOME INTERESTING ACCUSATIONS ABOUT THE EVERYMAN PROJECT...
YEAH, JACK, IT'S CALLED ENVY, AND MOST OF US GET OVER IT BY THE TIME WE'RE TEN.
BUT HE RAISES SOME VALID POINTS REGARDING TRAINING--
WHICH IS WHY INFINITY, INC. TRAINS FOR HOURS EVERY DAY.
BLAMING LUTHOR IS LIKE BLAMING MOZOTTO FOR SELLING A MOTORCYCLE TO A KID WHO REFUSES TO WEAR A HELMET--
26 inning the world s ries 4-2...
NO, IT'S LIKE SELLING A MOTORCYCLE TO A KID WHO HAS NO LICENSE!

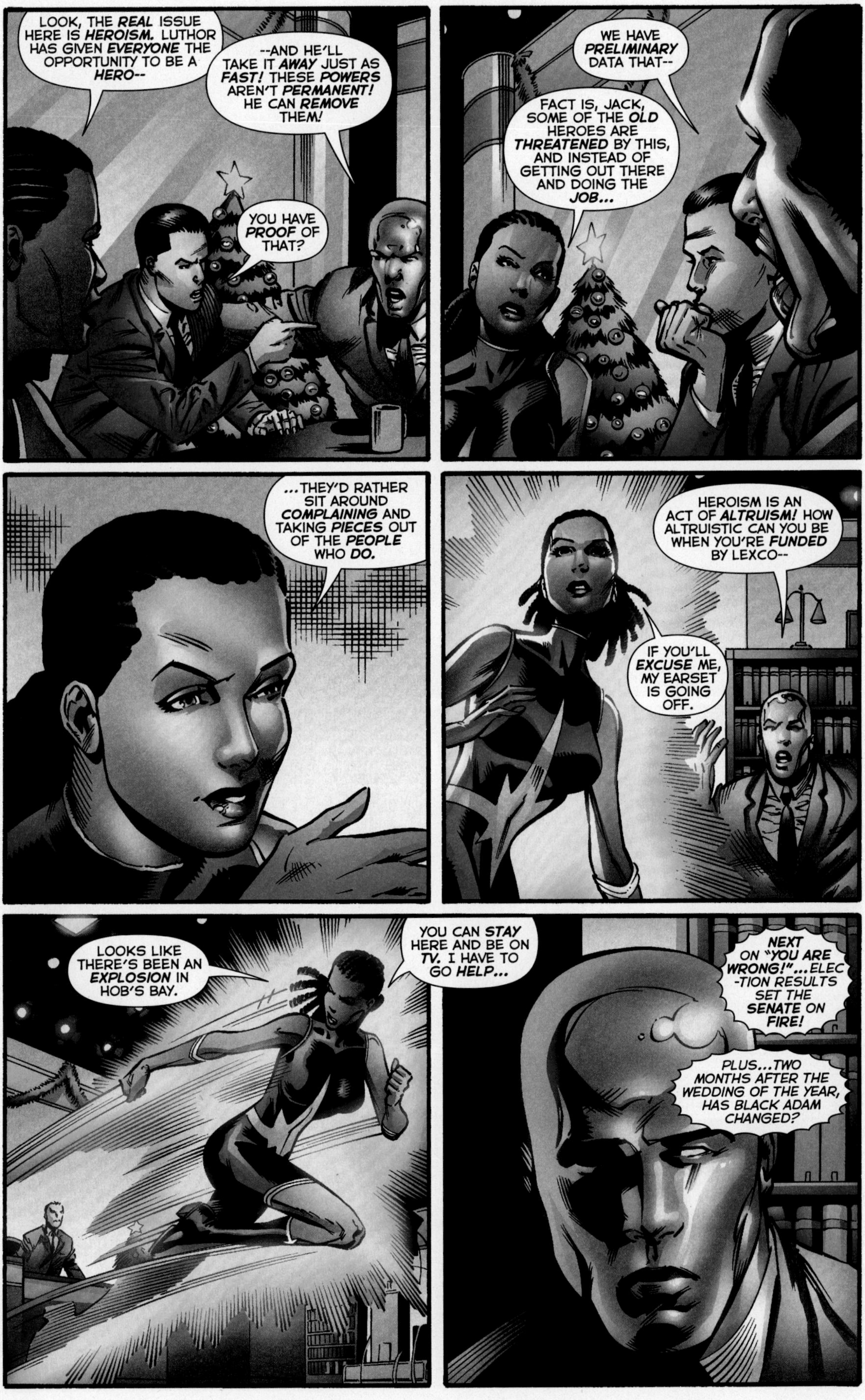
LOOK, THE REAL ISSUE HERE IS HEROISM. LUTHOR HAS GIVEN EVERYONE THE OPPORTUNITY TO BE A HERO--
--AND HE'LL TAKE IT AWAY JUST AS FAST! THESE POWERS AREN'T PERMANENT! HE CAN REMOVE THEM!
YOU HAVE PROOF OF THAT?
WE HAVE PRELIMINARY DATA THAT--
FACT IS, JACK, SOME OF THE OLD HEROES ARE THREATENED BY THIS, AND INSTEAD OF GETTING OUT THERE AND DOING THE JOB...
...THEY'D RATHER SIT AROUND COMPLAINING AND TAKING PIECES OUT OF THE PEOPLE WHO DO.
HEROISM IS AN ACT OF ALTRUISM! HOW ALTRUISTIC CAN YOU BE WHEN YOU'RE FUNDED BY LEXCO--
IF YOU'LL EXCUSE ME, MY EARSET IS GOING OFF.
LOOKS LIKE THERE'S BEEN AN EXPLOSION IN HOB'S BAY.
YOU CAN STAY HERE AND BE ON TV. I HAVE TO GO HELP...
NEXT ON "YOU ARE WRONG!"...ELEC-TION RESULTS SET THE SENATE ON FIRE!
PLUS...TWO MONTHS AFTER THE WEDDING OF THE YEAR, HAS BLACK ADAM CHANGED?

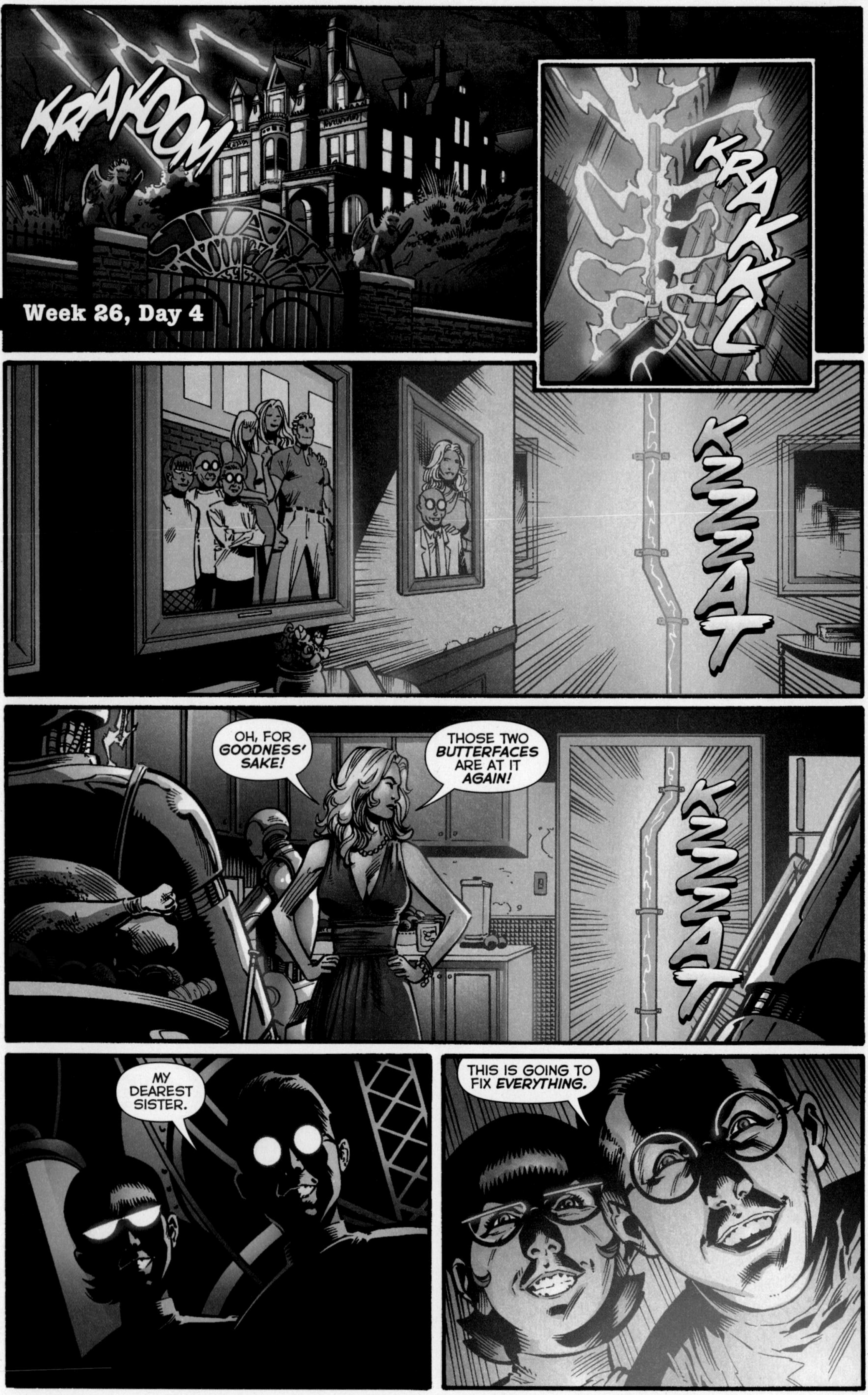
KRAKOOM
Week 26, Day 4
KRAKKL
KZZZAT
OH, FOR GOODNESS' SAKE!
THOSE TWO BUTTERFACES ARE AT IT AGAIN!
KZZZAT
MY DEAREST SISTER.
THIS IS GOING TO FIX EVERYTHING.

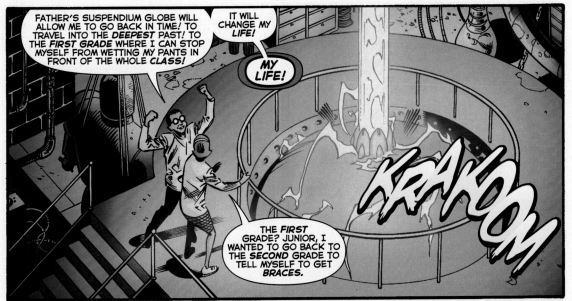

FATHER'S SUSPENDIUM GLOBE WILL ALLOW ME TO GO BACK IN TIME! TO TRAVEL INTO THE *DEEPEST* PAST! TO THE *FIRST GRADE* WHERE I CAN STOP MYSELF FROM WETTING MY PANTS IN FRONT OF THE WHOLE *CLASS*!

IT WILL CHANGE MY *LIFE*!

MY *LIFE*!

THE *FIRST* GRADE? JUNIOR, I WANTED TO GO BACK TO THE *SECOND* GRADE TO TELL MYSELF TO GET *BRACES*.

KRAKOOM

THEN-- =poof=--I'LL BE *PRETTY* LIKE BEAUTIA!

NOW LET ME RESET THE TIME COORDINATES.

NO, GEORGIA! WE'RE FIXING *MY* PAST FIRST.

NO! MINE!

KRAKKLL

I KNOW *WHY*.

WHO'S *THAT*? ONE OF DAD'S *ENEMIES*?

HOW WOULD *I* KNOW?

BOOOM

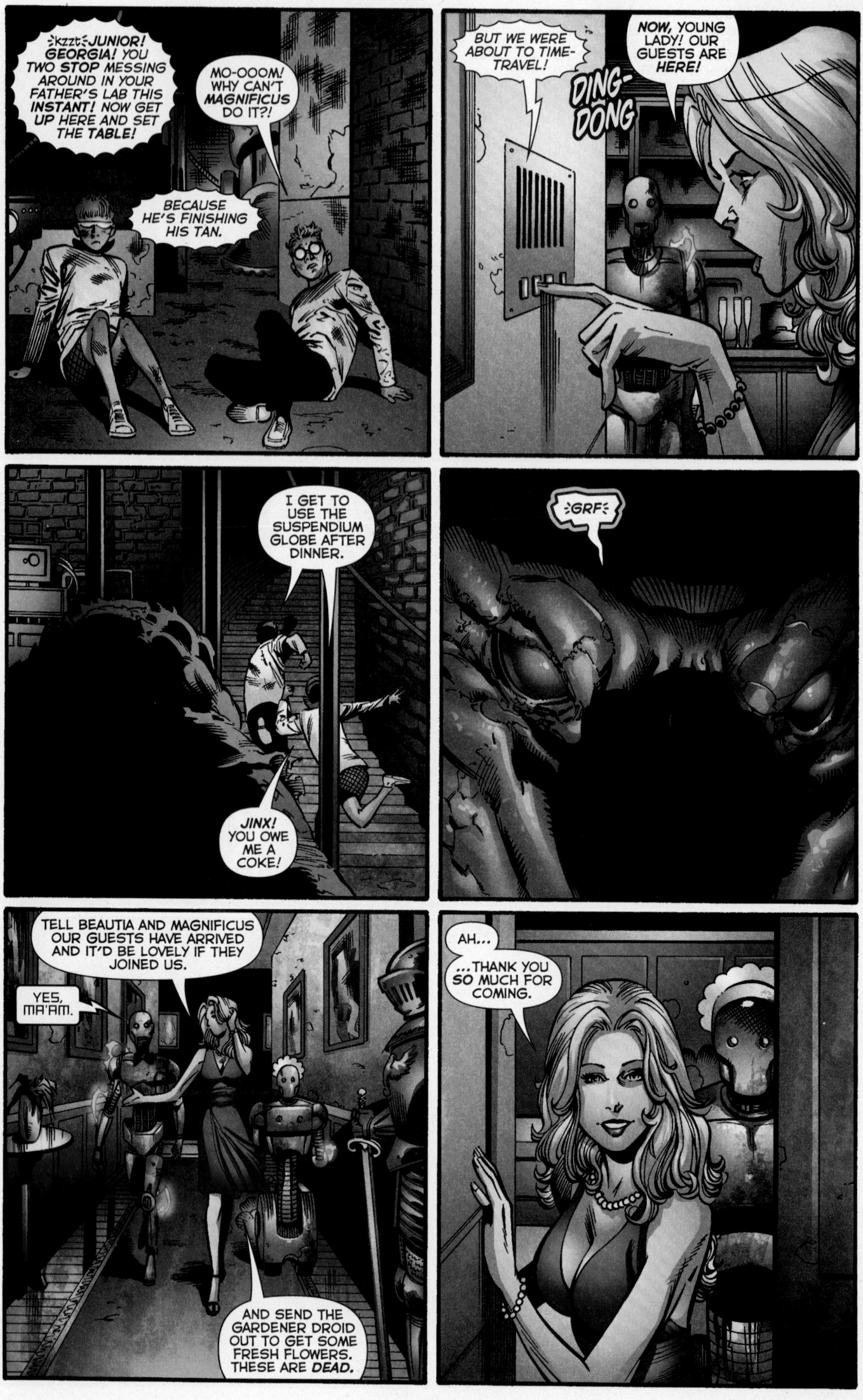
kzzt JUNIOR! GEORGIA! YOU TWO STOP MESSING AROUND IN YOUR FATHER'S LAB THIS INSTANT! NOW GET UP HERE AND SET THE TABLE!
MO-OOOM! WHY CAN'T MAGNIFICUS DO IT?!
BECAUSE HE'S FINISHING HIS TAN.
BUT WE WERE ABOUT TO TIME-TRAVEL!
DING-DONG
NOW, YOUNG LADY! OUR GUESTS ARE HERE!
I GET TO USE THE SUSPENDIUM GLOBE AFTER DINNER.
JINX! YOU OWE ME A COKE!
GRF
TELL BEAUTIA AND MAGNIFICUS OUR GUESTS HAVE ARRIVED AND IT'D BE LOVELY IF THEY JOINED US.
YES, MA'AM.
AND SEND THE GARDENER DROID OUT TO GET SOME FRESH FLOWERS. THESE ARE DEAD.
AH...
...THANK YOU SO MUCH FOR COMING.

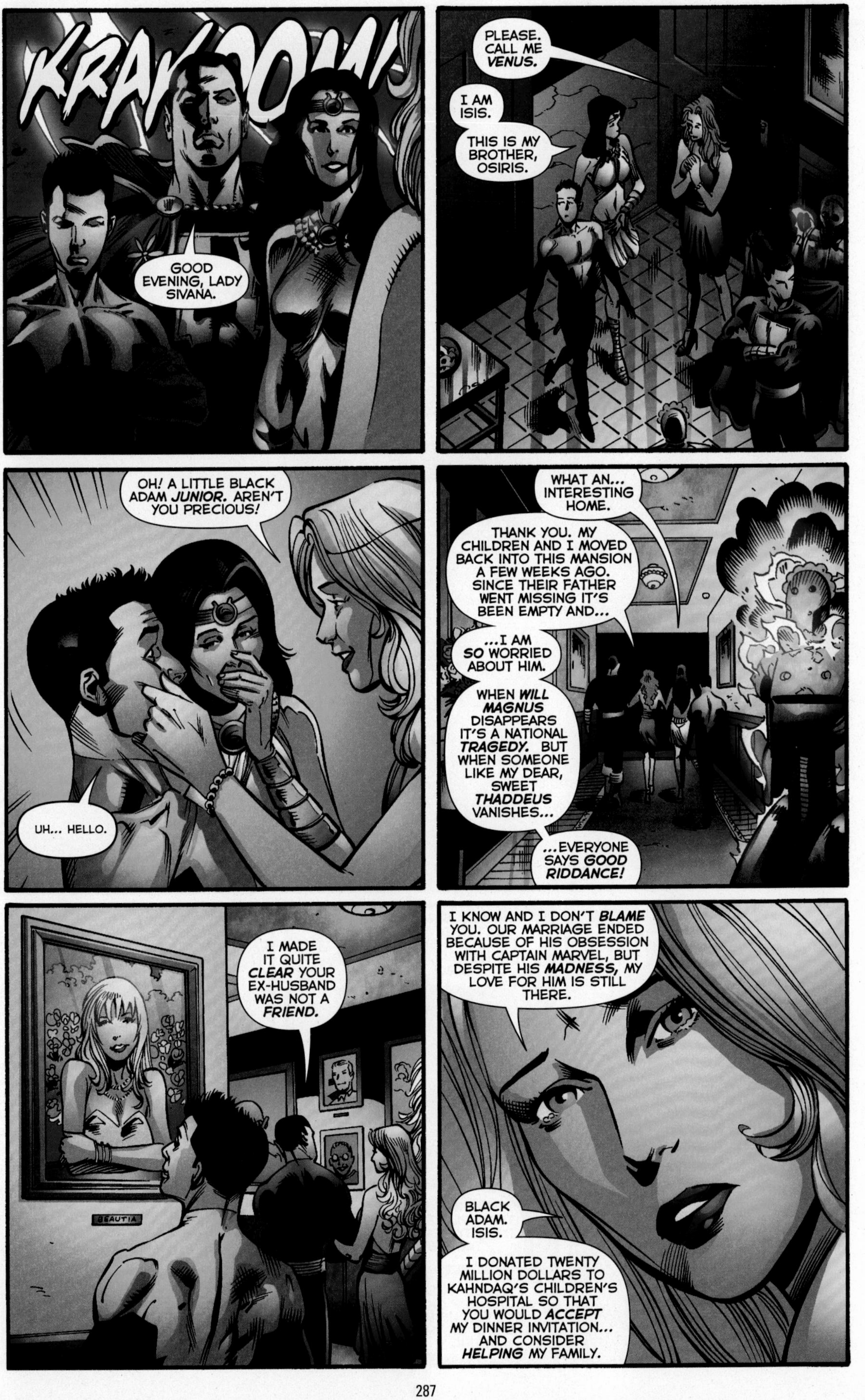
KRAKOOM!
GOOD EVENING, LADY SIVANA.
PLEASE. CALL ME VENUS.
I AM ISIS.
THIS IS MY BROTHER, OSIRIS.
OH! A LITTLE BLACK ADAM JUNIOR. AREN'T YOU PRECIOUS!
UH... HELLO.
WHAT AN... INTERESTING HOME.
THANK YOU. MY CHILDREN AND I MOVED BACK INTO THIS MANSION A FEW WEEKS AGO. SINCE THEIR FATHER WENT MISSING IT'S BEEN EMPTY AND...
...I AM SO WORRIED ABOUT HIM.
WHEN WILL MAGNUS DISAPPEARS IT'S A NATIONAL TRAGEDY. BUT WHEN SOMEONE LIKE MY DEAR, SWEET THADDEUS VANISHES...
...EVERYONE SAYS GOOD RIDDANCE!
BEAUTIA
I MADE IT QUITE CLEAR YOUR EX-HUSBAND WAS NOT A FRIEND.
I KNOW AND I DON'T BLAME YOU. OUR MARRIAGE ENDED BECAUSE OF HIS OBSESSION WITH CAPTAIN MARVEL, BUT DESPITE HIS MADNESS, MY LOVE FOR HIM IS STILL THERE.
BLACK ADAM. ISIS.
I DONATED TWENTY MILLION DOLLARS TO KAHNDAQ'S CHILDREN'S HOSPITAL SO THAT YOU WOULD ACCEPT MY DINNER INVITATION... AND CONSIDER HELPING MY FAMILY.

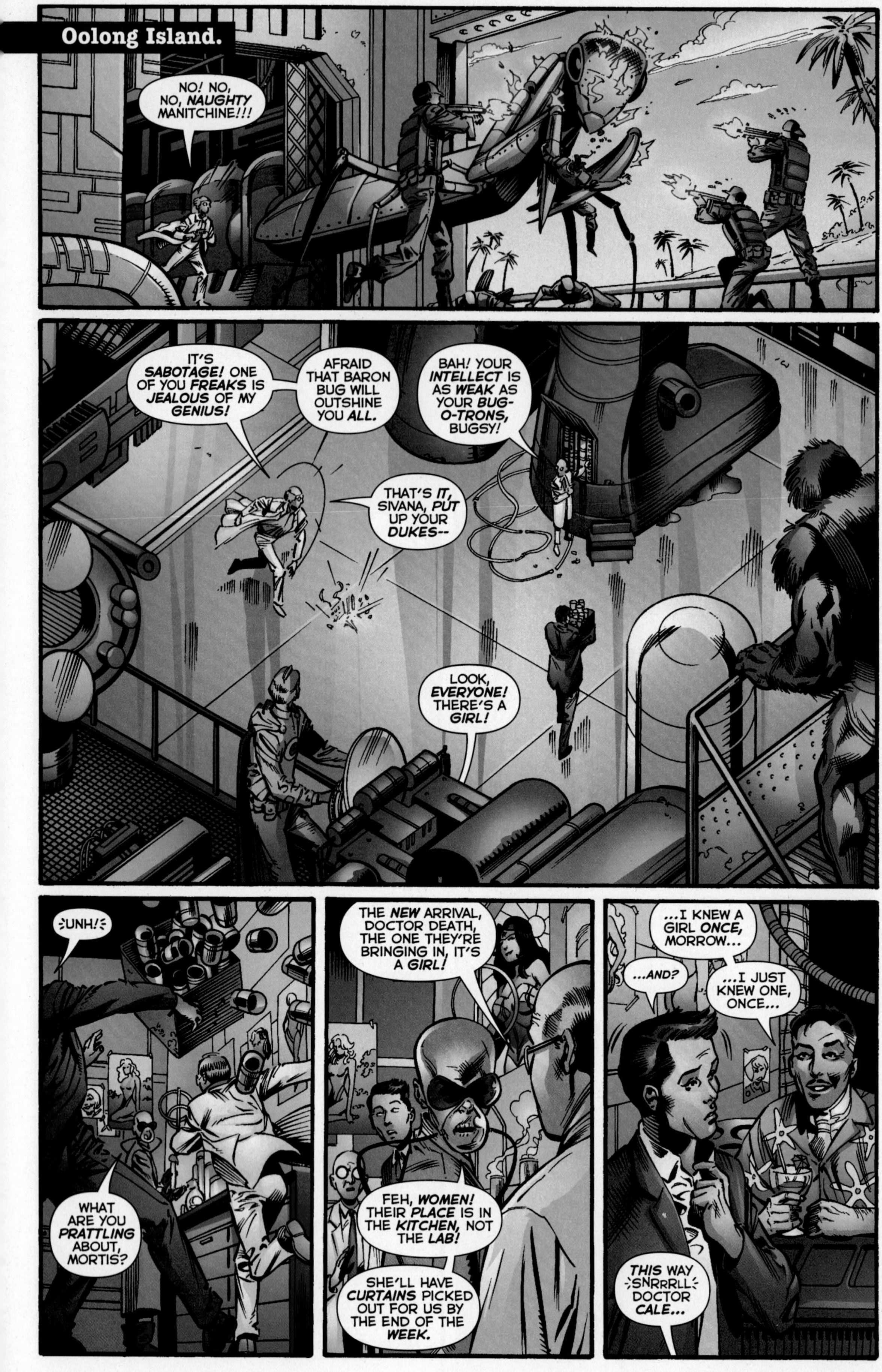
Oolong Island.
NO! NO, NO, NAUGHTY MANITCHINE!!!
IT'S SABOTAGE! ONE OF YOU FREAKS IS JEALOUS OF MY GENIUS!
AFRAID THAT BARON BUG WILL OUTSHINE YOU ALL.
BAH! YOUR INTELLECT IS AS WEAK AS YOUR BUG-O-TRONS, BUGSY!
THAT'S IT, SIVANA, PUT UP YOUR DUKES--
LOOK, EVERYONE! THERE'S A GIRL!
UNH!
WHAT ARE YOU PRATTLING ABOUT, MORTIS?
THE NEW ARRIVAL, DOCTOR DEATH, THE ONE THEY'RE BRINGING IN, IT'S A GIRL!
FEH, WOMEN! THEIR PLACE IS IN THE KITCHEN, NOT THE LAB!
SHE'LL HAVE CURTAINS PICKED OUT FOR US BY THE END OF THE WEEK.
...I KNEW A GIRL ONCE, MORROW...
...AND?
...I JUST KNEW ONE, ONCE...
THIS WAY SNRRRLL DOCTOR CALE...

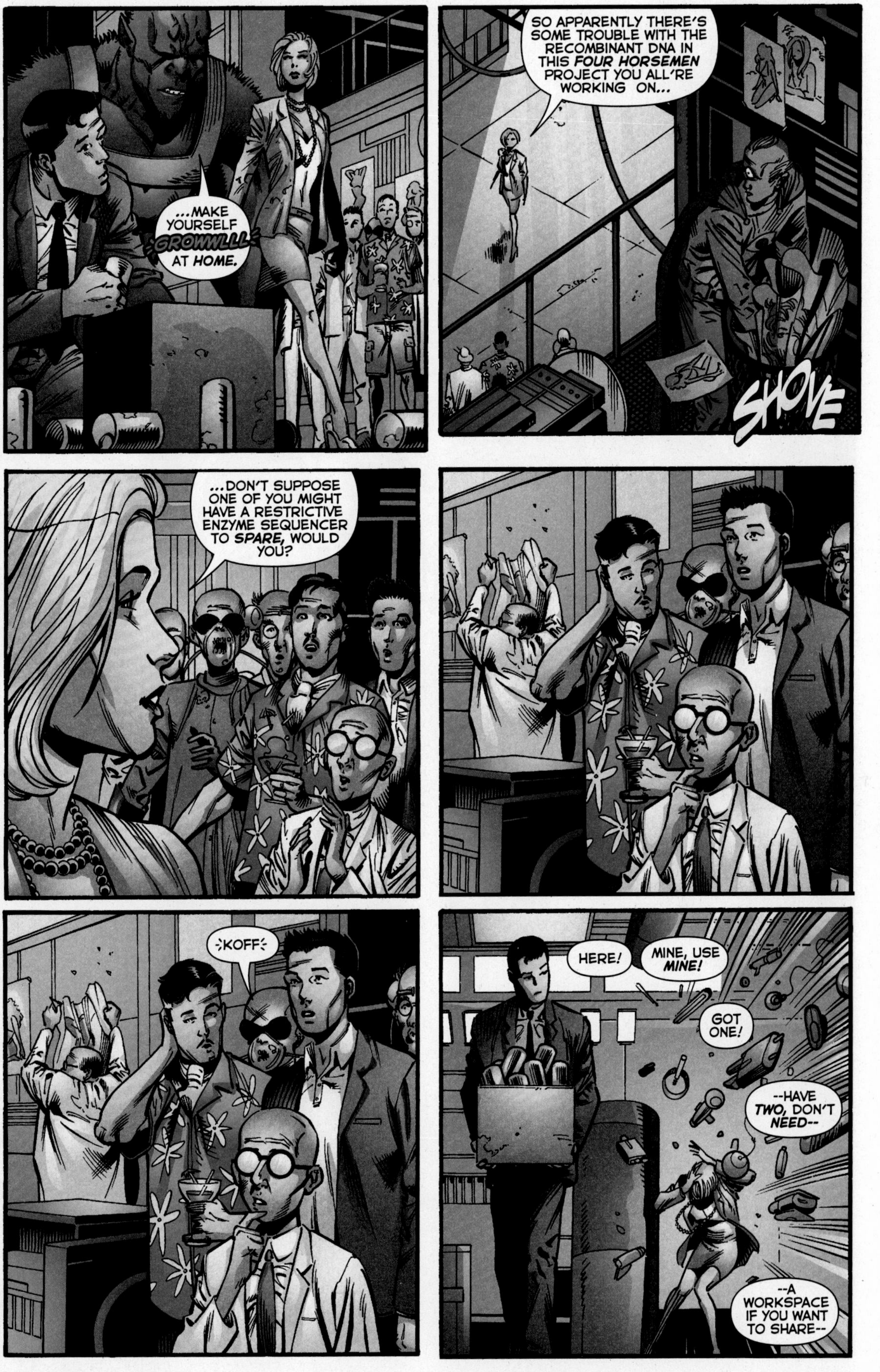

...MAKE YOURSELF GROWLLLL AT HOME.
SO APPARENTLY THERE'S SOME TROUBLE WITH THE RECOMBINANT DNA IN THIS FOUR HORSEMEN PROJECT YOU ALL'RE WORKING ON...
SHOVE
...DON'T SUPPOSE ONE OF YOU MIGHT HAVE A RESTRICTIVE ENZYME SEQUENCER TO SPARE, WOULD YOU?
KOFF
HERE!
MINE, USE MINE!
GOT ONE!
--HAVE TWO, DON'T NEED--
--A WORKSPACE IF YOU WANT TO SHARE--

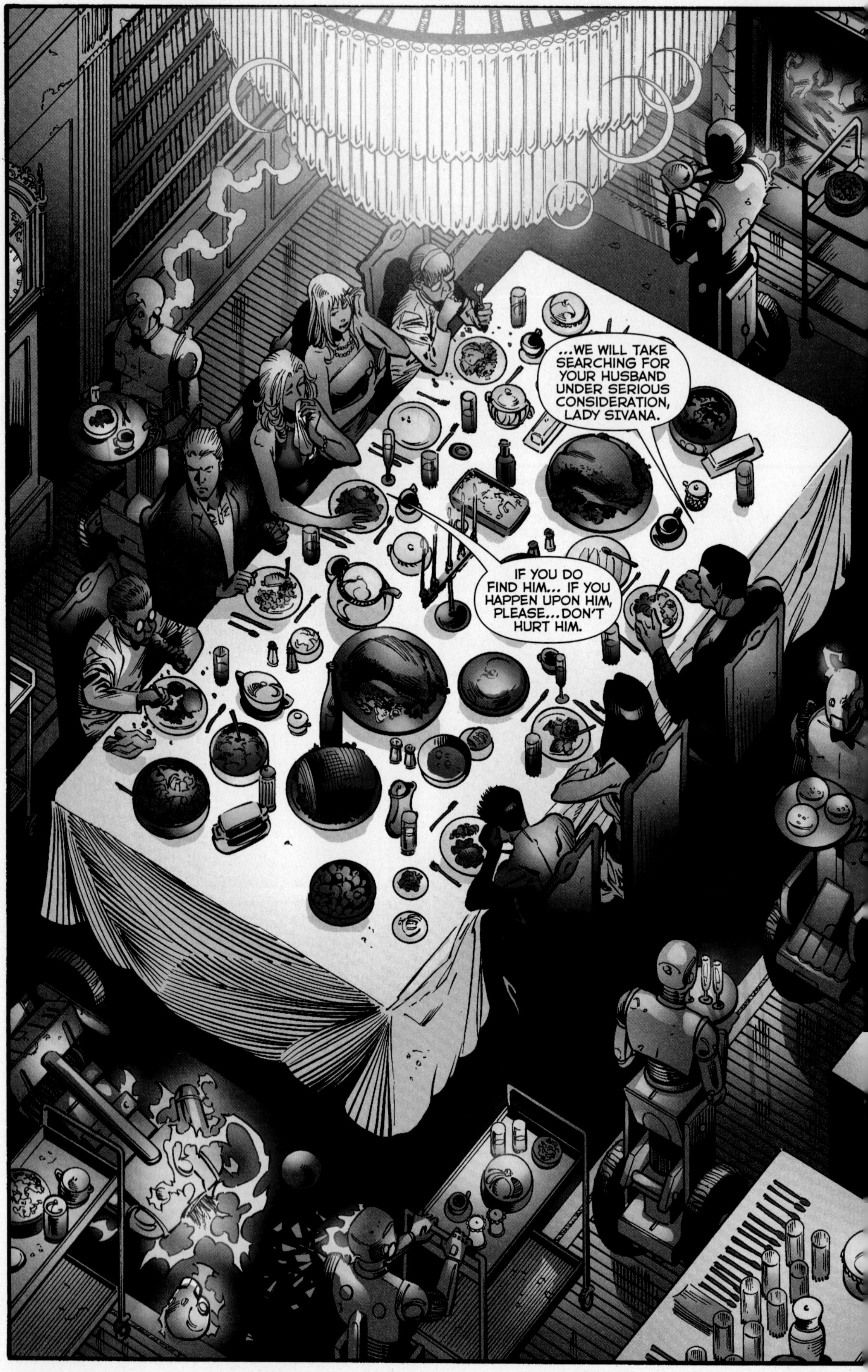
...WE WILL TAKE SEARCHING FOR YOUR HUSBAND UNDER SERIOUS CONSIDERATION, LADY SIVANA.
IF YOU DO FIND HIM... IF YOU HAPPEN UPON HIM, PLEASE...DON'T HURT HIM.

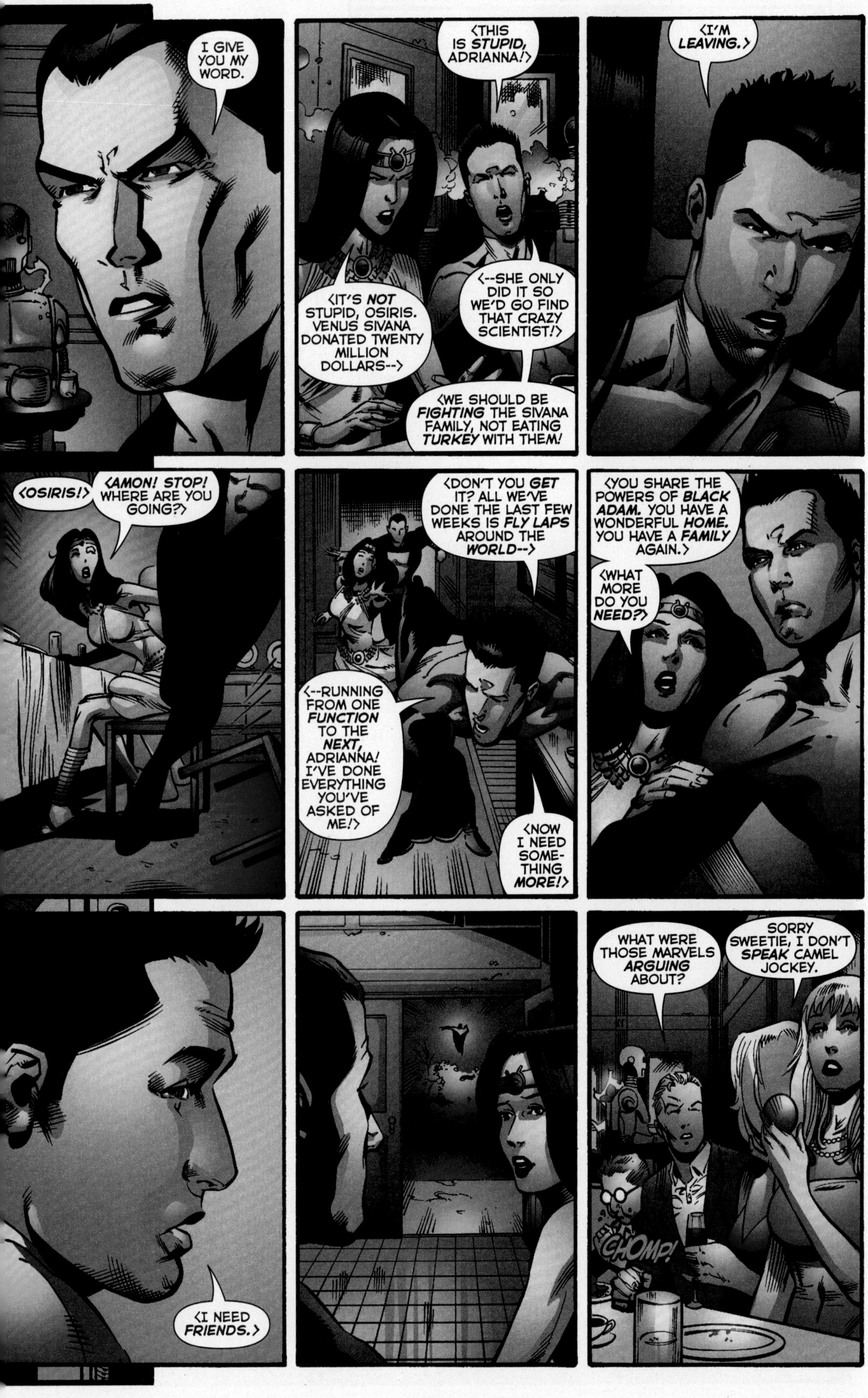
I GIVE YOU MY WORD.
<THIS IS *STUPID*, ADRIANNA!>
<IT'S *NOT* STUPID, OSIRIS. VENUS SIVANA DONATED TWENTY MILLION DOLLARS-->
<--SHE ONLY DID IT SO WE'D GO FIND THAT CRAZY SCIENTIST!>
<WE SHOULD BE *FIGHTING* THE SIVANA FAMILY, NOT EATING *TURKEY* WITH THEM!
<I'M *LEAVING*.>
<OSIRIS!>
<AMON! STOP! WHERE ARE YOU GOING?>
<DON'T YOU *GET* IT? ALL WE'VE DONE THE LAST FEW WEEKS IS *FLY LAPS* AROUND THE *WORLD*-->
<--RUNNING FROM ONE *FUNCTION* TO THE *NEXT*, ADRIANNA! I'VE DONE EVERYTHING YOU'VE ASKED OF ME!>
<NOW I NEED SOME-THING *MORE!*>
<YOU SHARE THE POWERS OF *BLACK ADAM*. YOU HAVE A WONDERFUL *HOME*. YOU HAVE A *FAMILY* AGAIN.>
<WHAT MORE DO YOU *NEED?*>
<I NEED *FRIENDS*.>
WHAT WERE THOSE *MARVELS* *ARGUING* ABOUT?
SORRY SWEETIE, I DON'T *SPEAK* CAMEL JOCKEY.
CHOMP!

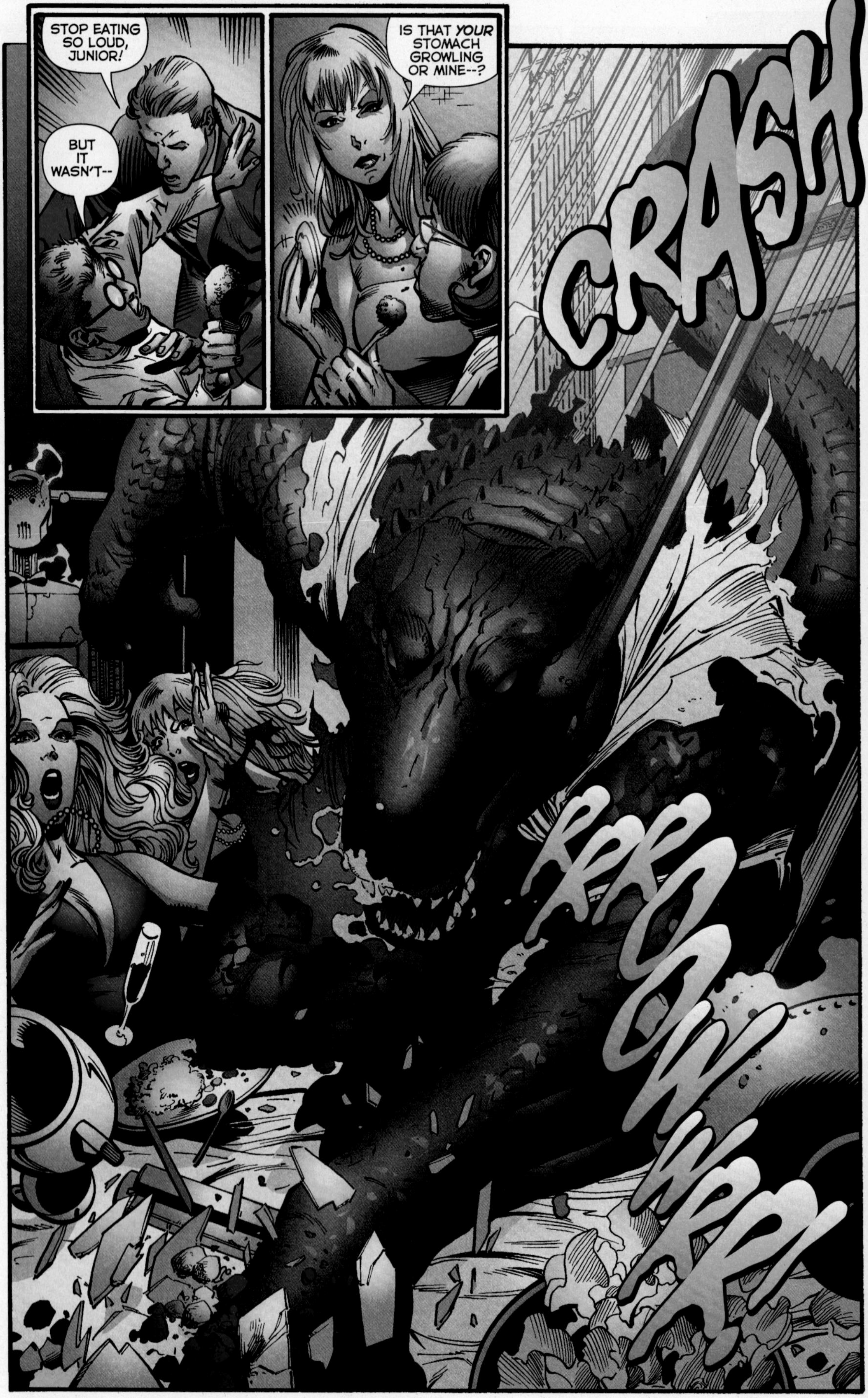
STOP EATING SO LOUD, JUNIOR!
BUT IT WASN'T--
IS THAT *YOUR* STOMACH GROWLING OR MINE--?
CRASH
RRROOWWRR!

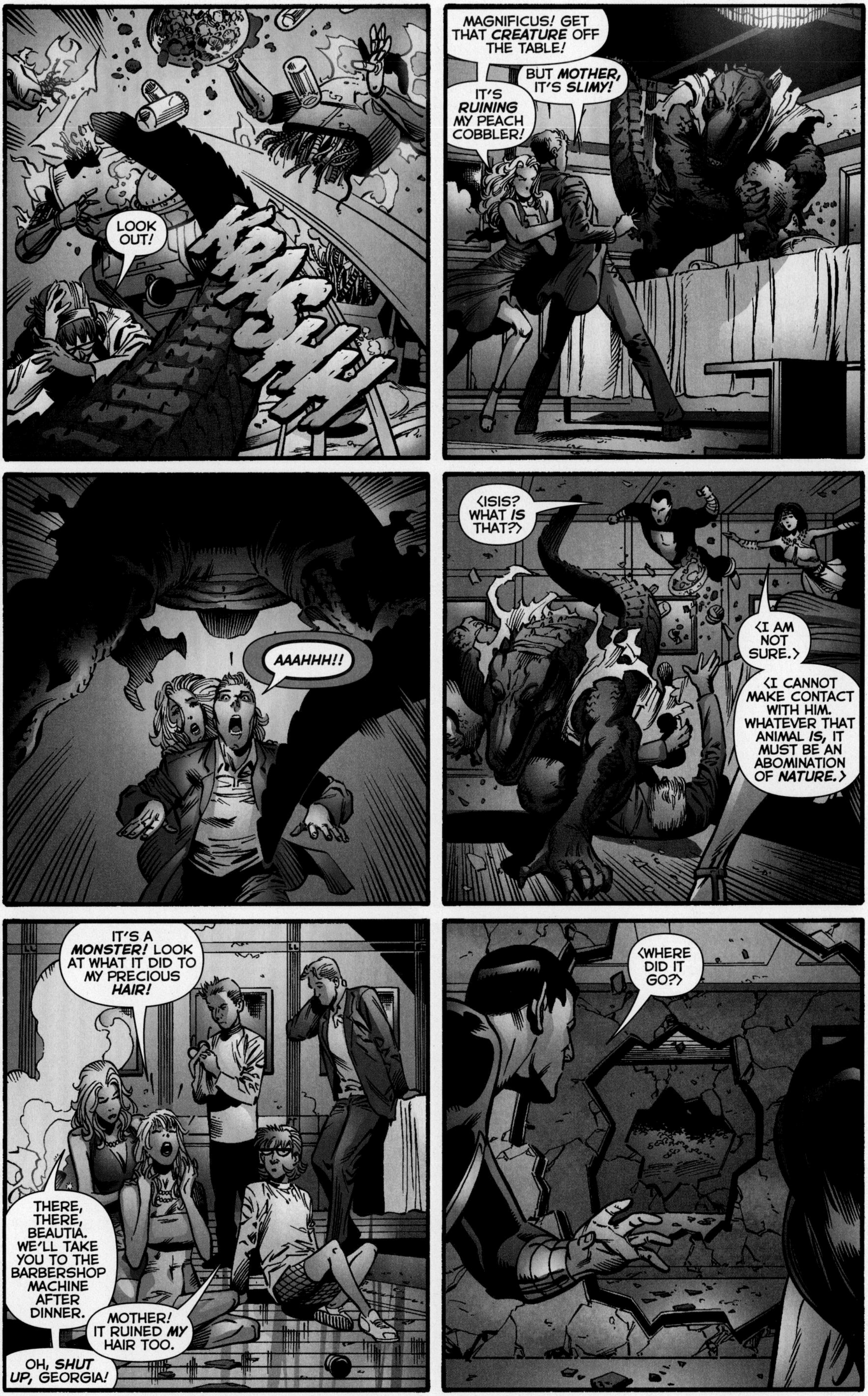
LOOK OUT!
MAGNIFICUS! GET THAT CREATURE OFF THE TABLE!
IT'S RUINING MY PEACH COBBLER!
BUT MOTHER, IT'S SLIMY!
AAAHHH!!
<ISIS? WHAT IS THAT?>
<I AM NOT SURE.>
<I CANNOT MAKE CONTACT WITH HIM. WHATEVER THAT ANIMAL IS, IT MUST BE AN ABOMINATION OF NATURE.>
IT'S A MONSTER! LOOK AT WHAT IT DID TO MY PRECIOUS HAIR!
THERE, THERE, BEAUTIA. WE'LL TAKE YOU TO THE BARBERSHOP MACHINE AFTER DINNER.
MOTHER! IT RUINED MY HAIR TOO.
OH, SHUT UP, GEORGIA!
<WHERE DID IT GO?>

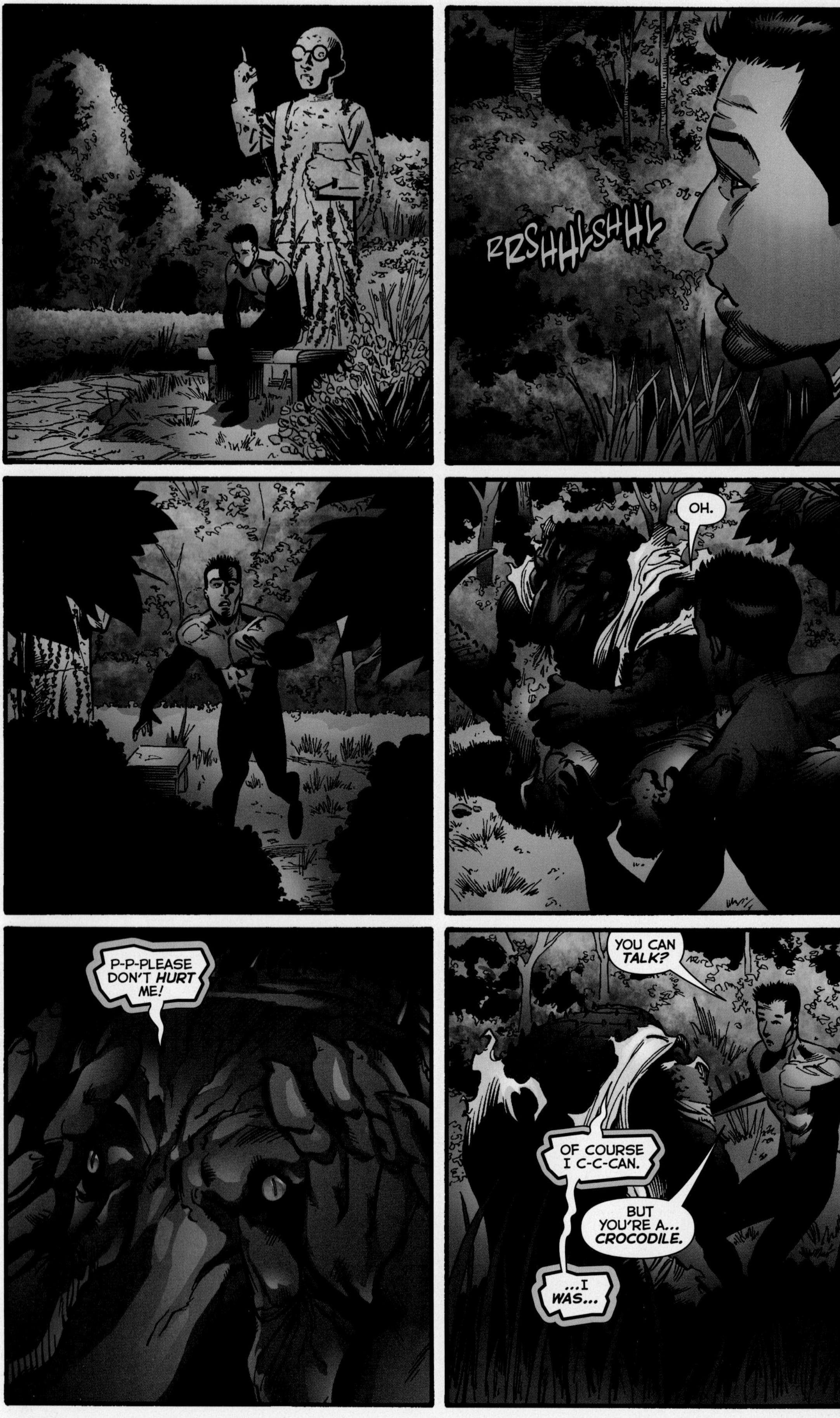
RRSHHLSHHL
OH.
P-P-PLEASE DON'T HURT ME!
YOU CAN TALK?
OF COURSE I C-C-CAN.
BUT YOU'RE A... CROCODILE.
...I WAS...

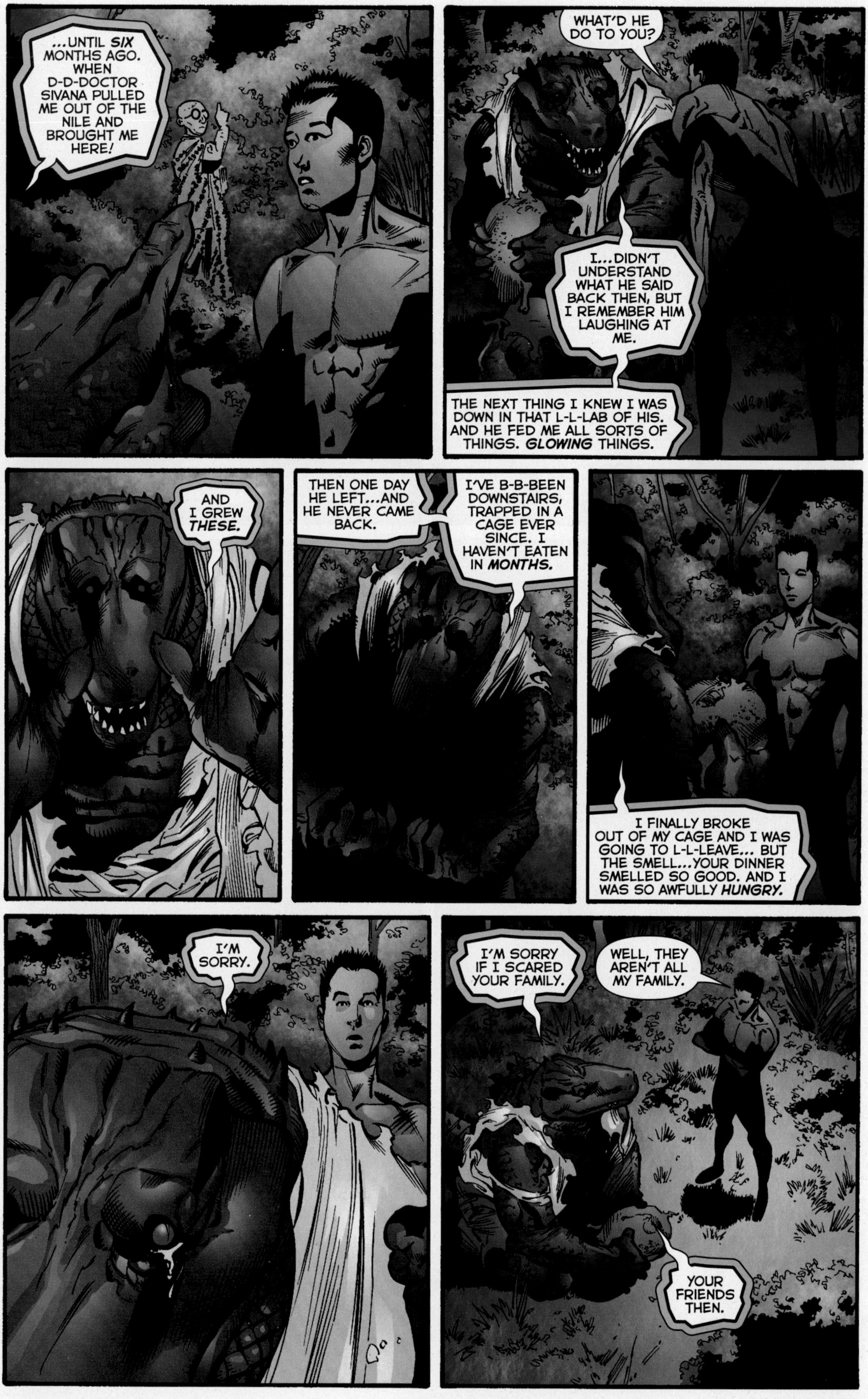
...UNTIL SIX MONTHS AGO. WHEN D-D-DOCTOR SIVANA PULLED ME OUT OF THE NILE AND BROUGHT ME HERE!
WHAT'D HE DO TO YOU?
I...DIDN'T UNDERSTAND WHAT HE SAID BACK THEN, BUT I REMEMBER HIM LAUGHING AT ME.
THE NEXT THING I KNEW I WAS DOWN IN THAT L-L-LAB OF HIS. AND HE FED ME ALL SORTS OF THINGS. GLOWING THINGS.
AND I GREW THESE.
THEN ONE DAY HE LEFT...AND HE NEVER CAME BACK.
I'VE B-B-BEEN DOWNSTAIRS, TRAPPED IN A CAGE EVER SINCE. I HAVEN'T EATEN IN MONTHS.
I FINALLY BROKE OUT OF MY CAGE AND I WAS GOING TO L-L-LEAVE... BUT THE SMELL...YOUR DINNER SMELLED SO GOOD. AND I WAS SO AWFULLY HUNGRY.
I'M SORRY.
I'M SORRY IF I SCARED YOUR FAMILY.
WELL, THEY AREN'T ALL MY FAMILY.
YOUR FRIENDS THEN.

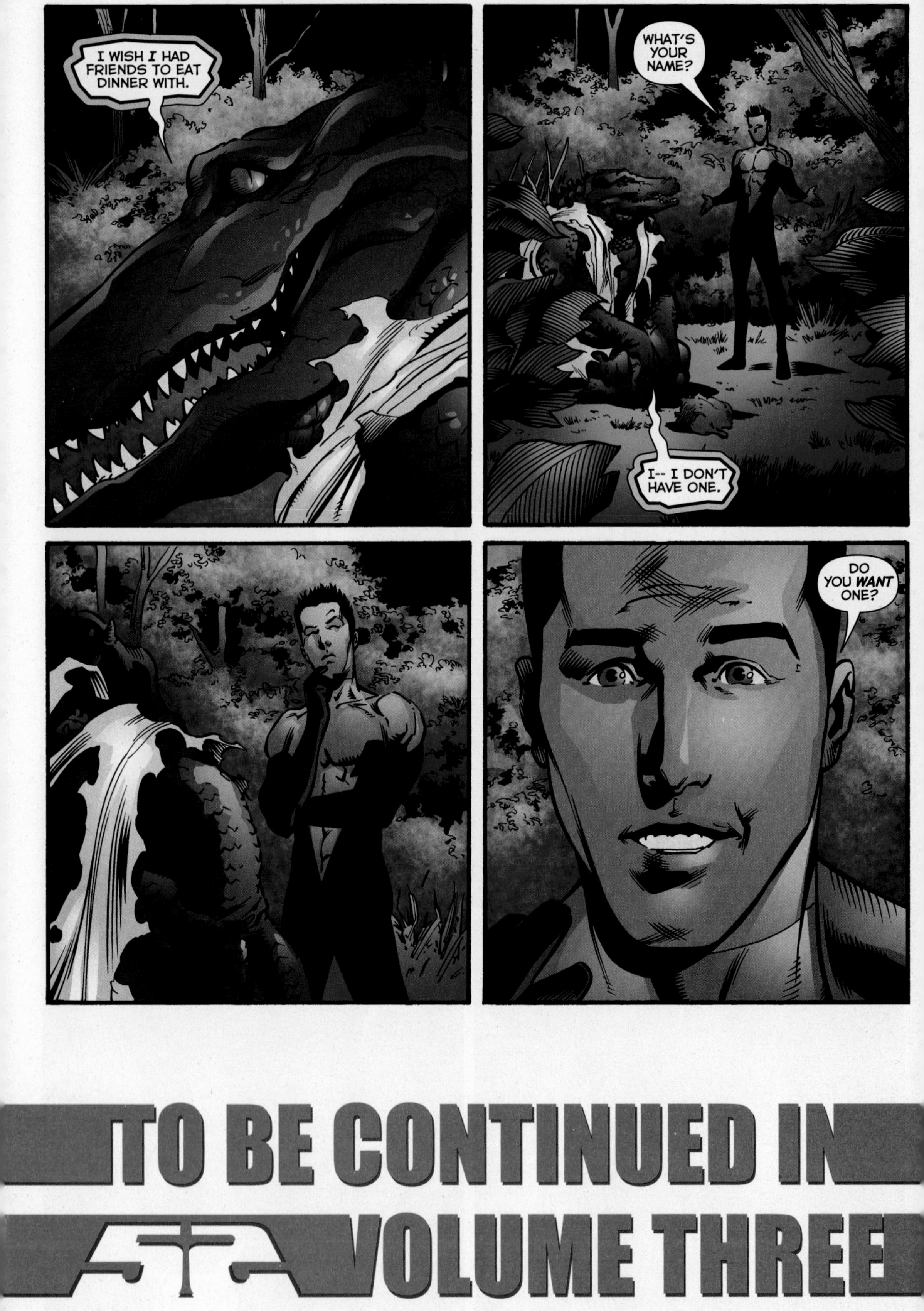
I WISH *I* HAD FRIENDS TO EAT DINNER WITH.
WHAT'S YOUR NAME?
I-- I DON'T HAVE ONE.
DO YOU *WANT* ONE?

TO BE CONTINUED IN
52 VOLUME THREE

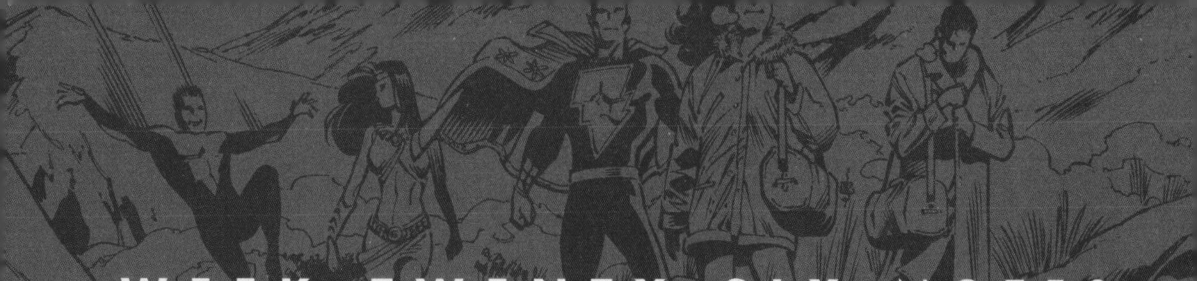

WEEK TWENTY-SIX NOTES

GEOFF JOHNS

52 Week Twenty-Six was a favorite of mine for several reasons, the first being all of us realizing, "Hey! We're halfway through!" The title, "HALFWAY HOUSE," even tells you that. (I have no idea where the title came from and in all honesty, I didn't even remember it until I reread this issue!) By this issue, it'd sunk in exactly how much time and energy doing a weekly comic book, and writing every issue together, took. That's not to say we weren't having fun.

By this issue, we were also getting comfortable enough to step outside of our safety zones. What I mean by that is, going into this, everyone had characters they'd written before or were very familiar with. For me, I'd spent a lot of time with Black Adam, some with Booster Gold, and almost none with the rest of the cast. The same could be said for Greg, Mark and Grant and the various characters we were playing with. I'd stepped into the waters of actually putting dialogue in Renee's and Question's mouths weeks earlier. Although that was intimidating, especially in the case of Renee since Greg had such an amazing grasp on her, it was exciting. Greg had written a large portion of the two inside Kahndaq with Black Adam and the Black Marvels. In the opening scene here, Greg once again tackled the Black Marvel Family and I think with great success. By this time, Greg had no questions about them. He knew. In many ways, this happened with all of us.

Now the other reason this was a favorite issue of mine: not only did I get tackle the ridiculously bizarre Sivana Family, who I could write a miniseries about, but it was the introduction of my favorite stuttering talking crocodile: Sobek. As the Marvel Family developed, and Osiris' character came into focus, it was clear he needed someone to befriend. But we didn't want to create any more Marvels like a Black Adam version of Uncle Dudley. And I didn't want to bring in a Teen Titan or another young hero. I'd always been a fan of the whimsical Tawky Tawny, the talking tiger, from Captain Marvel's Family. Upon thinking of the Black Marvel equivalent, the animal that sprung to mind immediately for the Black Marvels was a crocodile for various reasons — from locale to Egyptian gods and symbols. And I'd always been fascinated by the birds that rested inside a crocodile's mouth. How many hundreds or thousands of years did it take for that trust to develop? That's the analogy I took here between Osiris and Sobek. These two were destined to form an extremely tight bond of trust in 52.

MARK WAID

Mannheim literally murdering someone WITH the Crime Bible is Greg at his creepy finest.

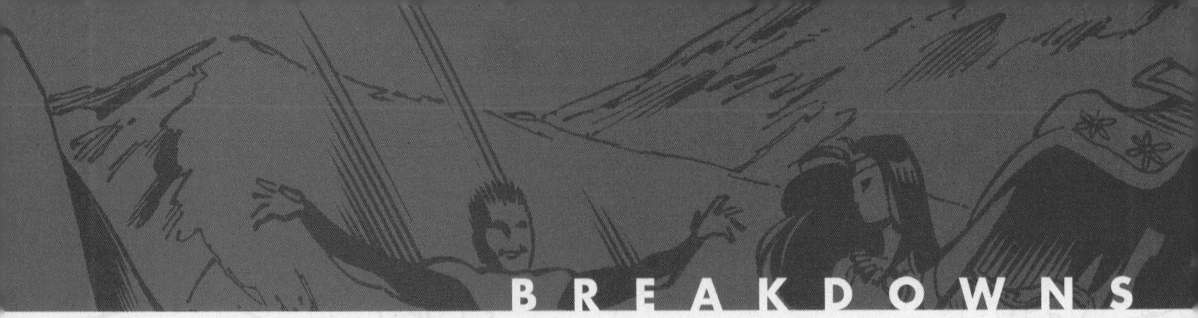

B R E A K D O W N S

BY **KEITH GIFFEN**

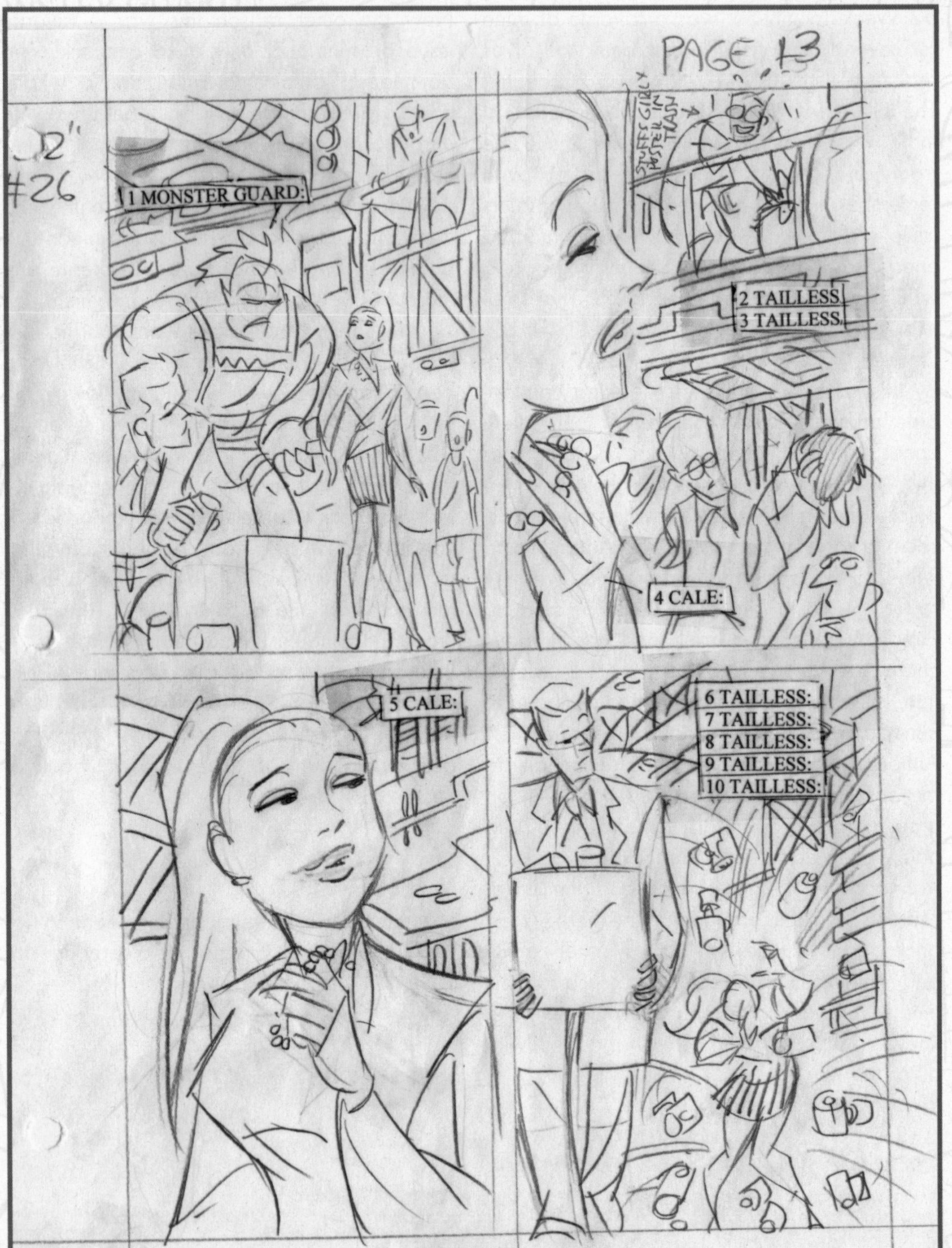

PAGE 13
#26
1 MONSTER GUARD:
2 TAILLESS:
3 TAILLESS:
4 CALE:
5 CALE:
6 TAILLESS:
7 TAILLESS:
8 TAILLESS:
9 TAILLESS:
10 TAILLESS:

Sometimes a scene simply needs a few more beats. Keith Giffen revised his original 4-panel layout for page 289 and changed it to 6 panels.

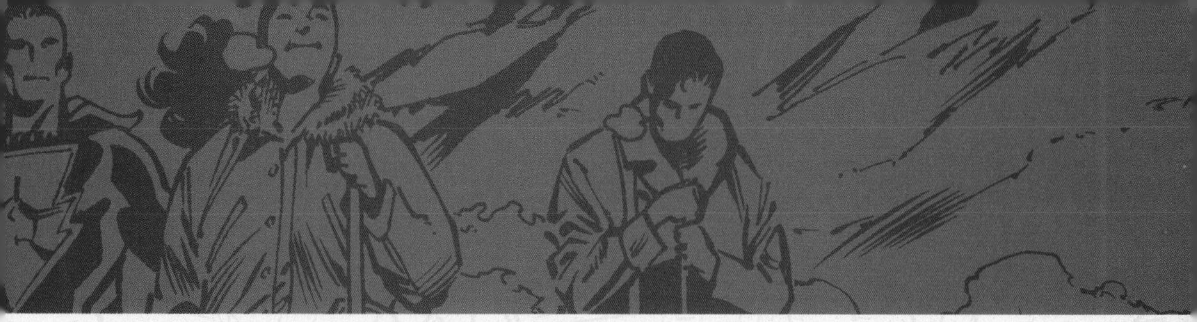

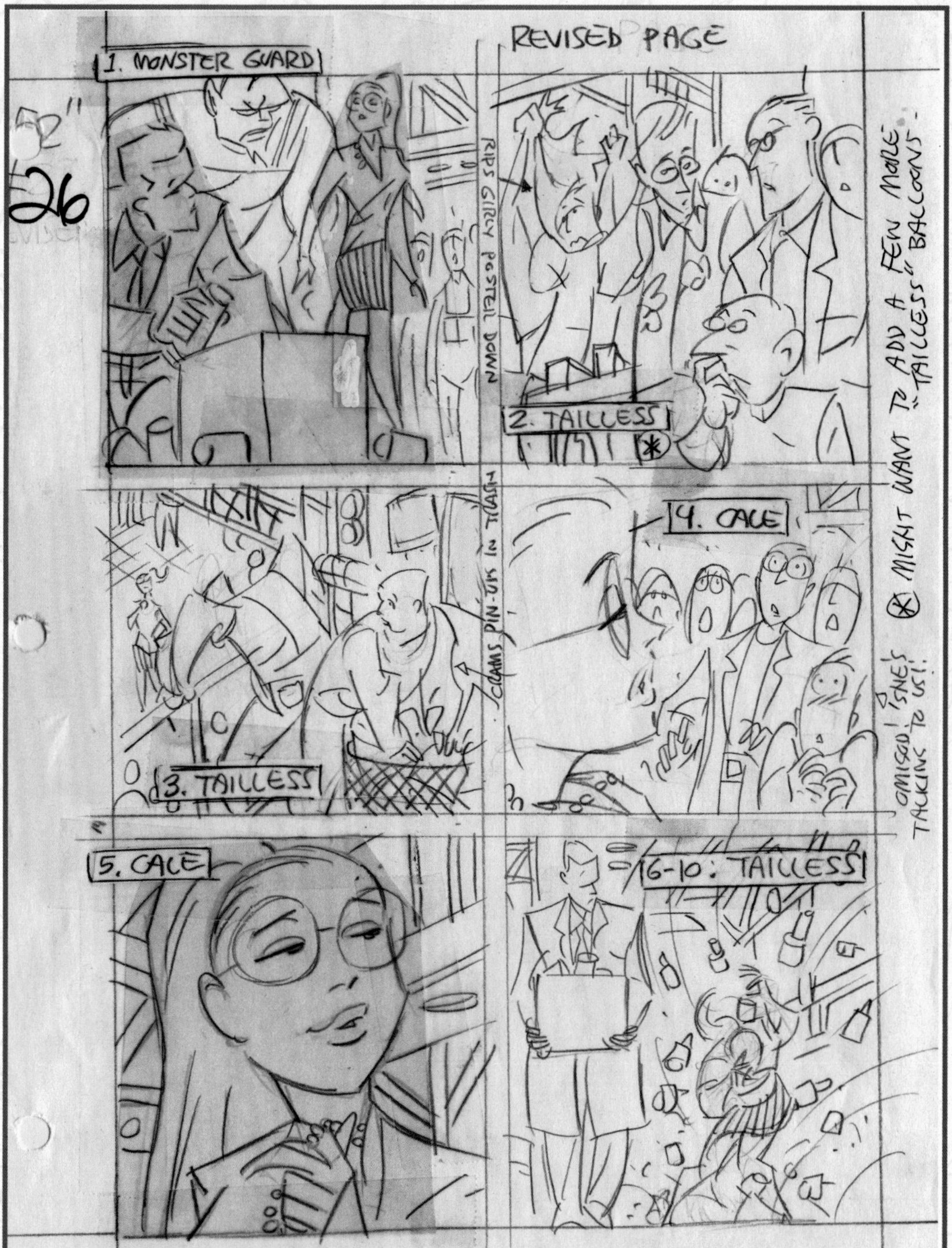
#26
REVISED PAGE
1. MONSTER GUARD
RIPS GIRLY POSTER DOWN
2. TAILLESS *
* MIGHT WANT TO ADD A FEW MORE "TAILLESS" BALLOONS.
3. TAILLESS
CRAMS PIN-UP IN TRASH
4. CACE
OMIGOD! SHE'S TALKING TO US!
5. CACE
6-10: TAILLESS

COVER GALLERY

ART BY **J.G. JONES** WITH **ALEX SINCLAIR**

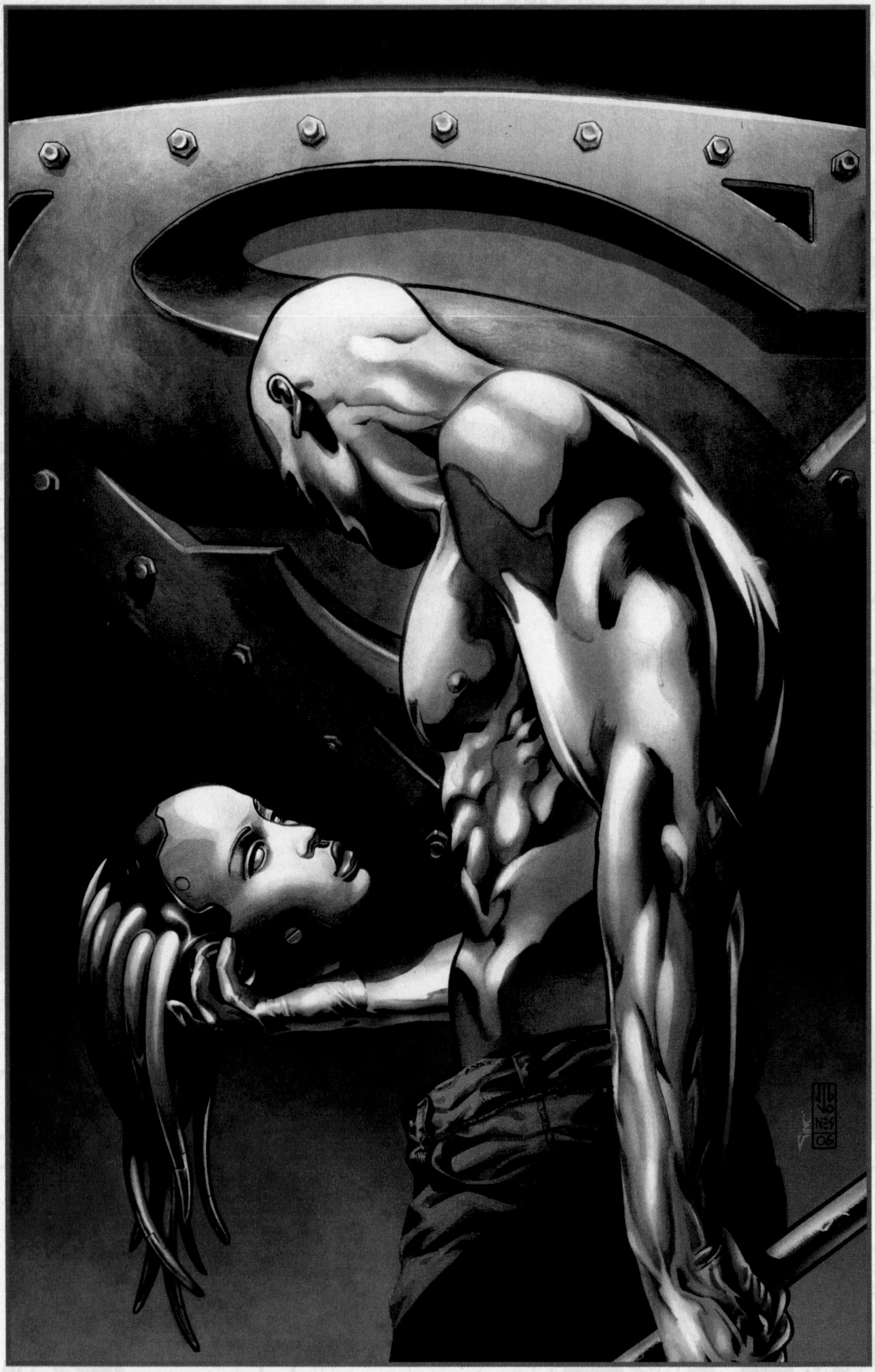

WEEK **FOURTEEN**

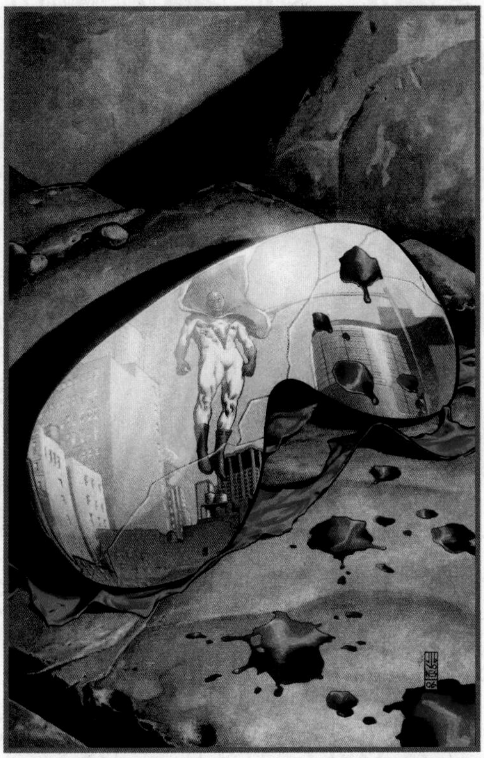

WEEK **FIFTEEN**

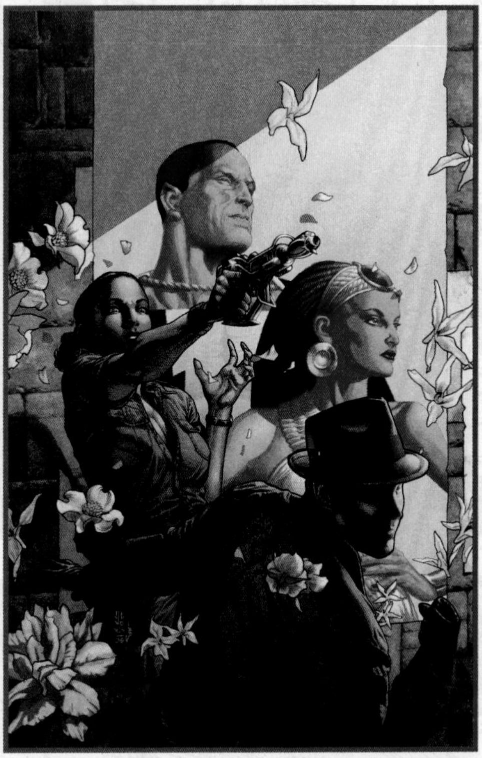

WEEK **SIXTEEN**

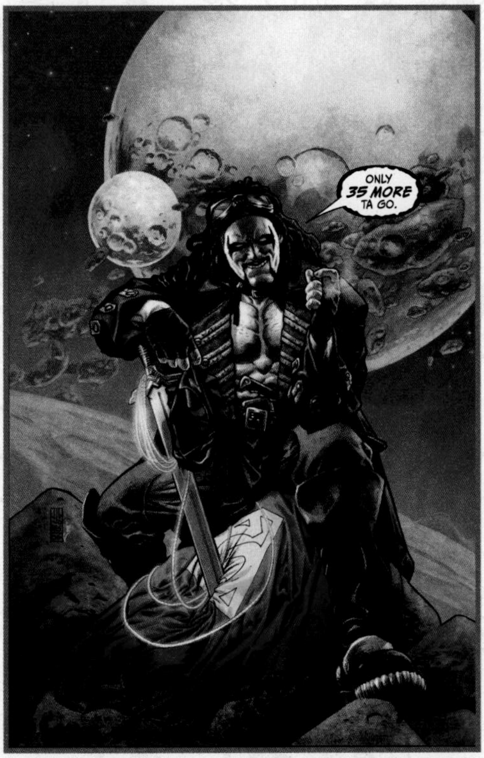
ONLY 35 MORE TA GO.

WEEK **SEVENTEEN**

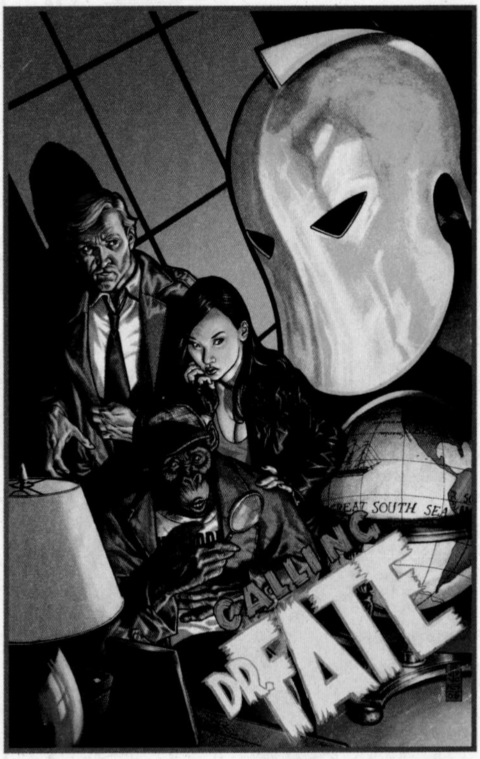
CALLING
DR. FATE

WEEK **EIGHTEEN**

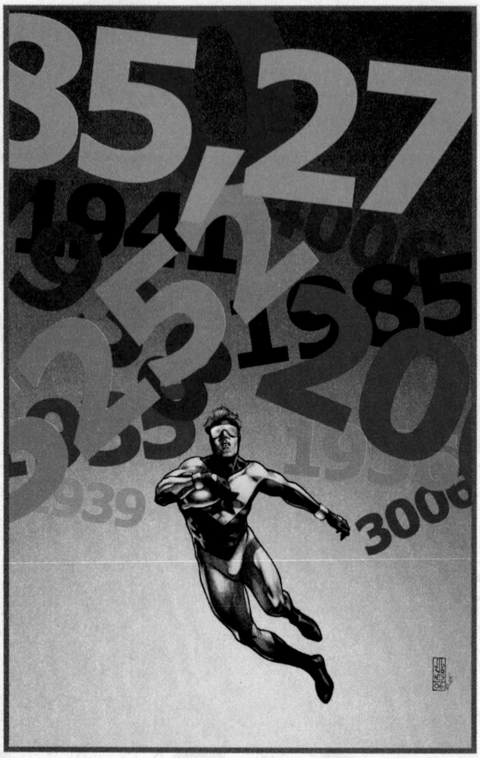

WEEK **NINETEEN**

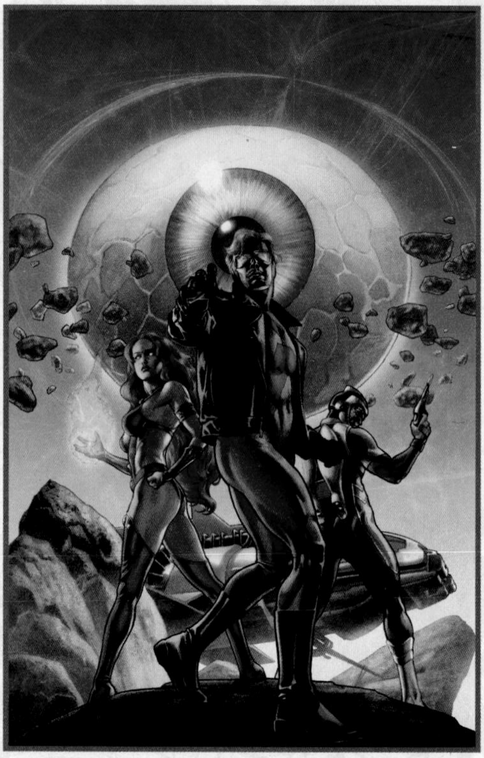

WEEK **TWENTY**

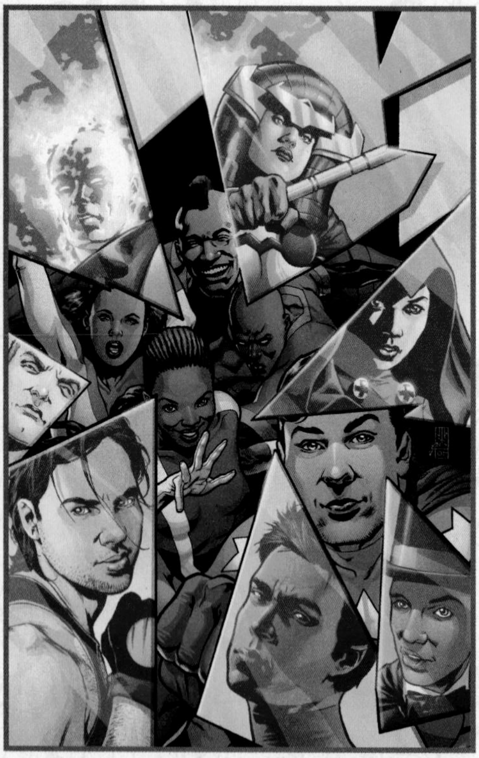

WEEK **TWENTY-ONE**

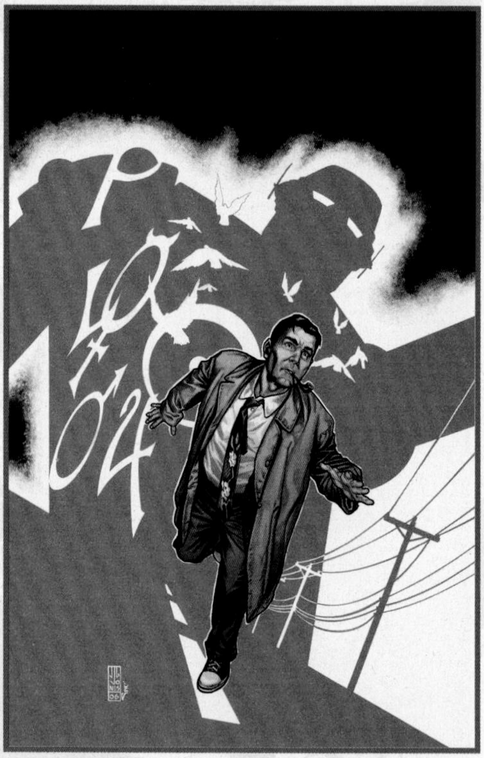

WEEK **TWENTY-TWO**